Sex, Schools, & Society

SEX, SCHOOLS, & SOCIETY
International Perspectives

Edited By
STEWART E. FRASER

With An Introduction By
ROBERT M. BJORK

Peabody International Center
GEORGE PEABODY COLLEGE FOR TEACHERS
and
AURORA PUBLISHERS, INCORPORATED
Nashville • London
1972

CONTENTS

Contents

PART III
PROBLEMS, CONFLICTS, AND SEX EDUCATION

PART IV
FOREIGN MISCELLANY ON SEX EDUCATION

PART V
BIBLIOGRAPHY

PREFACE

The increasing permissiveness of American adult society, with the concomitant changing nature of teen-age sexual mores, has forced the schools in recent years to re-evaluate, often reluctantly, their role in the sexual upbringing of young people. Parents, teachers, and pupils, as well as community organizations, churches, and political pressure groups, have become often vigorous protagonists in the conflict over sex education. The controversy continues to erupt as schools throughout the country attempt to fulfill the increasingly difficult task of assisting the young to understand their sexual-social responsibilities to one another.

The inordinate demands on the schools to provide adequately both family life education and sex counseling, and often to substitute for, rather than complement, the family's role in the physical and moral upbringing of children, have resulted at times in confusion, controversy, and cacophony. This provides diverse opportunities for a variety of social activists, religious bigots, and political opportunists, who enthusiastically capitalize on the schools' sometimes maladroit handling of sex education programs.

In the United States the curriculum problems of educators and the slow recognition by many parents of the imperative necessity for adequate family and sex education programs should be seen in world, as well as domestic, perspectives. The dilemmas which parents, students, and teachers face in America are those which confront their counterparts in many other nations, especially countries like Australia, Britain, and Sweden, which have similar democratic, social, and political institutions. But the Communist world is not immune from the pressures generated by youth demanding assistance with their sexual responsibilities and questioning the pious, ideologically bound moral precepts of their elders. Soviet youth exhibit many of the same anxieties and increasing inquisitiveness that characterize American youngsters. The Chinese, likewise, have been forced to give consideration to the pleas for guidance and information voiced by Communist youth uncertain as to the correct ideological and biological nature of their sexual yearnings.

Several of the articles which comprise this anthology deal with the themes of adolescent disquiet, the complexity of mistrust between the generations, and the opportunism of political perverts quick to exploit a sensitive social concern. They touch on topics ranging from college students' sexual problems to those of primary- and high-school

xi

students. Fortunately the essays, which do not all claim to be of recent vintage, for the most part have a certain timelessness, in that many of them touch on the perennially raised question of whether or not to provide formal sex education.

The question of institutional versus parental responsibility takes on new guises as the involved protagonists continually attempt to confront each other on moral issues. The nature of the controversy and the concern of educators and parents, as well as laymen and interested spectators, is amply illustrated in many of the articles, which have been grouped, for the reader's convenience, into three major divisions. The first, "Pedagogy and Sex Education," reflects the dilemmas of American educators as they face the professional problems and attempt to cater to their primary constituency of pupils and parents. The second major division, "Problems, Conflicts, and Sex Education," covers the heated and vocal arguments of those who find that on the subject of sex education they can easily, albeit crudely, demonstrate that conflict and education make an interesting combination. The third collection of articles is composed mostly of a miscellany on the sexual problems of young people in selected countries such as Australia, Britain, China, Singapore, Sweden, and the U.S.S.R. These range from college students' need for adequate prophylactic information (Australia) to the postponement of marriage plans after graduation for both ideological and physical reasons (China).

The collection is introduced by an overview illustrating the worldwide concern about the interrelated topics of sex education and population control. An extensive bibliography of English-language sources presents further material on this subject, which is attracting increasing attention. The bibliography does not claim to be comprehensive, but it illustrates clearly the range and type of material available for both the general reader and the serious student.

The compilation of an anthology is often the prerogative of an individual sometimes assisted, or hampered, in his selection by the oft-misplaced advice and/or criticism of colleagues, students, and friends, as well as interested spectators! This anthology bears the imprint of many hands and incorporates the work of writers with a wide range of social, political, religious, and educational beliefs. Included are pieces which cheerfully incorporate the skillful facetiousness of a professional humorist reacting against the solemn pronouncements of conservative fundamentalists who foresee yet another Communist plot to contribute to America's moral downfall by the licentious introduction of raw sex into the "little red schoolhouse."

The strictly religious American of either the Catholic or Protestant persuasion is profoundly disturbed by what he believes is the maladroit imposition of a new, swinging sexual morality in the classrooms of the public schools, where children are prematurely taught by sexually illiterate teachers not only "why to" but also "when to," "where to," and, sometimes anomalously, "how to." On the other hand, the concerned teacher, perturbed at his pupils' abysmal ignorance of the basic facts of reproduction, venereal disease, and teen-age promiscuity, addresses himself eagerly to the task of remolding a new sexual school order. Unfortunately, the new "sex education" has proven to be more complicated than the "new mathematics," and more susceptible to community irritation, anguish, and intervention. For those who enjoy the dialectics of an ideological conflict, and those who favor more sophisticated forms of conflict renewal, the unending ramifications of sex education will continue to present opportunities for brash involvement and intellectual exploitation.

No amount of prohibition, nor the careful apportioning of the subject between other academic disciplines, will diminish the importance of sex education as successive generations of schoolchildren pass through the wondering stage into the doing stage. Possibly it is due to the innate cleverness and good sense of the majority of children that neither their teachers, parents, nor friends are able to prevent them from obtaining a sexual upbringing which often incorporates, quite naturally and spontaneously, an understanding of the nature of sexual response and the quality of human happiness, obtained in a responsible and intelligent manner.

Unfortunately, for many children the problem is much more complicated, and those concerned with the continually changing quality of life in both developed and backward countries (the United States, of course, comes under both classifications) are aware that in the matter of sex education less reliance can be placed on the old-fashioned agents of moral persuasion, namely, the family and the church in Western society. American society, while slowly breaking down, transforming and, even more slowly, reintegrating itself, is subject to such pressures that instant morality and situational ethics become young people's philosophical datum point. While they may confuse a take-off point and a moral bench mark as their starting place for sexual encountering, this does not prevent them from happily attacking religious fundamentalists, whom they label intellectual perverts hampered with Freudian doubts and sexual repression. And fundamentalists, in their turn, rightly call foul upon the imposition of imperfect and often unsanitary sexual education "plumbing courses" in the public schools.

The net result is a continuation of the polemic and the further utilization of the school as a battleground for the social, sexual, and political viewpoints of diverse groups, all claiming to know not only what is morally good for children but also what is sexually permissible for all to see and read in the classroom.

The situation brings to mind the salutary reminder of an English writer who noted that "the saddest thing about so much of the writing of educationists on sex is that it compares so badly with Anna Karenina. . . ." This will continue to be so until writers address themselves more felicitously to the task, and to a topic which needs a balanced sense of humor, considerable human sympathy for young people, and a sense of purpose and dedication. This anthology exhibits what most of the authors would firmly and clearly believe to be an awareness of the problems involved in the sensitive trinity of "sex, schools, and society." The reader, on the other hand, can judge for himself whether the authors epitomize the highest canons of scholarly or journalistic research; he can determine whether they have taken sufficient editorial care with the facts at their disposal as they write persuasively to influence a reading public including both concerned laymen and professionals. The articles in this anthology cover only a few of the many controversial facets of the problem, but they are those of particular concern to the three groups most deeply involved, namely, the pupils, the parents, and the teachers.

Generally, spelling, punctuation, and format have, as far as possible, been standardized. In the foreign section unidiomatic translations have occasionally been rephrased, but the original spelling and punctuation have been retained.

Stewart E. Fraser   Peabody International Center
May, 1972   Nashville, Tennessee

Part I
THE PROBLEM

Soda Fountain Guru: Sex Education—A Must!

Art Buchwald

Washington—There is a big flap going on in the United States right now over the question of teaching sex education in our schools. The educators are mostly for it, and the ultraconservatives, including the John Birchers and the DAR, are mostly against it. I usually like to stay out of controversial matters as I hate to answer my mail, but in this case I have to come out for teaching sex education in the schools.

This is a very personal matter with me. I had no formal sex education when I was a student, and everyone knows the mess I'm in. If there had been a Head Start program in sex education when I was going to public school, I might have been a different man today.

When I was going to Public School 35 in Hollis, New York, we got all our sex education at the local candy store after three o'clock! The information was dispensed by thirteen-year-olds who seemed to know everything there was to know on the subject, and we eleven- and twelve-year-olds believed every word they told us.

Some of it, I discovered later on, did not necessarily happen to be true. For example, I was told as an absolute fact that if a girl necked with you in the rumble seat of a car, she would automatically have a baby.

This kept me out of the rumble seat of an automobile until I was twenty-three years old.

There were some other canards of the day, including that the method of kissing a girl on the mouth decided whether she would become pregnant or not. Every time I kissed a girl after that, I sweated for the next nine months.

The sex experts of Sam's Candy Store had an answer for every problem that was raised at the soda fountain. These included warnings that if you did certain things you would go insane. Most of us were prepared to be taken off to the booby hatch at any moment.

There was obviously no talk about birds, bees, flowers or animals. We couldn't care less what happened when they were doing it. Our only concern was what happened to human beings, and from what our thirteen-year-old instructors could tell us, it was all bad.

Now the worst part of my sex indoctrination was that when I turned

3

thirteen I became an instructor myself and passed on my knowledge to eleven- and twelve-year-olds at the same candy store. They listened in awe as I repeated word for word what I had been told by my "teachers."

So, on the basis of my own experience, I don't think we have much choice in this country when it comes to sex education. In order to avoid the agony and pain my fellow classmates and I went through, we either have to teach sex in the schools, or close down every soda fountain in the United States.

* * *

Surprise for Youngsters: Sex Education on TV

There has been a great deal of discussion concerning sex education in the schools. Actually children are getting more sex education in one week's viewing of television commercials than they'll get in four years in the classroom, and most of this TV-type sex education can become very distorted.

For example, the other evening I was watching a commercial for a 1970 automobile. The girl announcer challenged the virility of the TV viewer and wanted to know if he was man enough to drive it. If he wasn't, she said, then he obviously wasn't man enough to get her.

Well, I frankly didn't care that much about the girl, because her legs were too skinny. But I could see the effect it was having on several subteen-agers in my living room.

It's tough enough getting through puberty, but when you have to prove your manhood by first purchasing a $4,000 sports model, you might as well throw in the towel before you start.

The next commercial showed a couple walking through high grass hand in hand. They obviously were up to no good and were looking for a clear area to spread out their blanket. But before they got down to business, the man lit a cigarette and then handed it to the girl, who took a puff and looked at the guy as if the deal had been made.

Now once again I wasn't moved by this, mainly because I have a fear of snakes. But I could see the kids watching this scene and believing that an act of love had to be preceded by both parties first smoking a cigarette.

I tried to explain to the subteen-agers that this was not true and in many cases could cause unnecessary fires in bed.

A little later we hit a mouthwash commercial. The girl was stunning, but when boys took her home they just left her at the door without kissing her good-night. A girl friend finally produced a bottle of the mouthwash, and on the very next outing her date refused to let her leave him.

Later on, a blonde beauty was throwing herself all over a man who had been wearing a certain kind of after-shave lotion. The man had it made in the commercial. I tried to warn the young men in the room that wearing after-shave lotion was no guarantee of success when it came to blonde beauties.

But I couldn't seem to get the message across. In less than two hours the subteen-agers had been educated to believe that if you drove a sports car, smoked cigarettes, used mouthwash and after-shave lotion, not to mention shampoo, you would achieve the final act of bliss. Are these kids in for a surprise.

INTRODUCTION

Misconceptions and Conceptions on Sex Education: An International Overview

Robert M. Bjork

The world of 1970 is strikingly different from the world of 1950 in many ways, but perhaps no area of people's lives and attitudes has been so altered in this period as those relating to sex. There has been an extraordinary popularization of the term *population explosion,* and an increasing frankness in the way people now react toward such questions as size of family, contraception, abortion, and other aspects of the population problem. In both high and popular culture there has been a rapid acceleration in public acceptance of the candid use of sexual terms and descriptions. Social problems relating to sex, such as illegitimacy, venereal disease, divorce, sexual deviance, and sexual crime, are all much discussed; it is also clear that many of these problems, once thought to be almost automatically on the way to complete solution, have stubbornly persisted or become worse.

Thus, the current social climate in many countries is one in which human fertility is causing concern, and methods of limiting it are a major topic for discussion. Sexual description and symbolism in literature, popular media, and music have become more frank and more prevalent, and old sex-related problems once thought to be on the way to solution remain persistent. Given this ethos, people in a number of countries have become much more friendly to the idea of including rational programs of sex instruction in the school curriculum.

This paper presents an overview of sex instruction in the schools of Sweden, certain Communist nations, and the United States. There are considerable differences between these countries in the degree to which sex instruction has been instituted throughout the school system, in the relative emphasis given to various types of sexual learnings, and the degree of openness allowed in discussion and description. Much of the material in this paper, however, will concern Sweden, which has the most developed pattern of formal sex instruction in the schools.

In Sweden, sex education began to be introduced in the 1930s in a few enterprising urban schools. Government Population Commissions in 1935 and again in 1941 recommended sex instruction in the schools. These recommendations were not based at all on a concern for lowering the birth rate, since Sweden had then and has now one of the lowest

9

rates of natural increase in the world. Rather, it was felt that family stability and population quality demanded a rational attitude toward sex.

Swedish educational circles became convinced in the mid-1950s that voluntary programs of sex education were so widespread and generally approved that a mandatory program to spread sex instruction to all Swedish schoolchildren was the next logical step. Since only 1 percent of the students in Sweden attend private schools, and since even these schools are under the authority of the National Board of Education, the compulsory sex education program instituted by the National Board of Education in 1956 immediately affected each and every child in Sweden.

The National Board had published teachers' manuals on sex education during the 1940s. When sex education became compulsory in 1956, a new, authoritative edition entitled *Handbook on Sex Instruction in the Schools** was issued for the use of teachers. This handbook presented a general rationale for the inclusion of sex instruction in the schools, a list of topics thought to be appropriate to four different age groups (seven to ten years old, eleven to thirteen, fourteen to sixteen, and seventeen to twenty), subject matter commentaries and lesson-examples. Within three or four years, opposition to various parts of this official handbook became significant. Mainly this opposition came from the so-called cultural radicals, who were insistent on complete equality between the sexes, a single standard, tolerance of sexual deviance, a tentative and instrumental view of premarital and extramarital relations, and increased attention to and support of contraceptives and voluntary abortion. Since the handbook explicitly condemns premarital sexual relations, has little to say about contraception or sexual deviance, and does not grapple with the question of the "double morality standard," it was subject to increasing criticism. Lars Gustafson, a relatively moderate critic of the sex education program, had this to say in 1964:

> Instead of trying to adjust young people to a sound sex and family life, the schools are spreading terrifying pictures of the perils of relations before marriage. Instead of teaching about contraceptives and helping to make them an obvious measure of protection in such relations, the schools are warning pupils about their unreliability and contributing in that way to the social affliction of both children and parents involved in extramarital pregnancies at an altogether too early age. There is, it has been said, no rational argument against the fact that young people adjust to a normal sex life through premarital relations except the one about the perils of having a child. In this situation, it is more suitable to get rid of this argument by spreading the use of contraceptives and better sex education than to try to retain a prohibition which is proving to be ideologically empty.[1]

*See pp. 319-330 of *Sex, Schools, and Society*.

Not only articulate writers such as Gustafson protested. Complaining parents wrote letters to various newspapers; one father of a fourteen-year-old daughter wrote the following to a Stockholm paper in 1961:

> To teach our own prejudices, our own doubts, our own bewilderments, leads nowhere. We need an entirely new point of view, one which accepts teen-age sexual activity simply because it exists and there is nothing we can do about it. Therefore, we also need a thorough instruction in contraceptive techniques. Those who have no idea of how emotionally involved normal teen-agers are in their sexual relationships often claim that safe contraceptives would lead to increased promiscuity. This is probably untrue. But even if it should lead to twice as much intercourse, but only half as many unwelcome children, it would still be a step in the right direction.[2]

By 1964 dissatisfaction had mounted to the point that a government commission was appointed to revise the handbook and generally to improve sex education. The commission is in process of completing its revision, although, in 1965, a change was effected in the handbook material to be taught seventeen- to twenty-year-olds. It deleted some passages insisting on continence during adolescence and substituted a rather vague passage proposing that sexual norms are necessary, but they may vary from place to place and from time to time.[3]

There is little question that the issue surrounded by the greatest acrimony in the revision of the handbook concerns the question of premarital sex and premarital use of contraceptives. Passages in the original handbook such as the following from a lesson-example for ages fourteen to sixteen are those drawing the greatest criticism from people desiring liberalization:

> At your age, and in general while you are still growing up, you should not engage in sexual relations. . . . Don't imagine that you can rely on contraceptives to prevent pregnancy and children being born. Boys are very ready to assure girls that nothing of that sort can happen. But it happens sometimes all the same. . . . By abstaining from sexual relations during the years when you are still growing up, you are giving yourself the best prospects for one day building your own home with the one you love, and living happily together.[4]

This passage and others like it are the major targets for those who wish to break the hold of what they consider to be an outdated morality. For a time, it appeared that their strategy was to make the sex education programs in the schools wholly physiological, with all material relating to morality deleted. This change was, and is still, strongly opposed by various sections of Swedish public opinion. Many "free church" elements and also activists in the "established" Lutheran church are not at all willing to see the moral aspects dropped. At present in the upper grades, the medical and biological aspects of sex are covered in biology, the moral and ethical ones in religion classes (all Swedish schools have such classes), and the social aspects in history classes.

A 1963 article in *Dagen,* a "free church" Pentecostal paper, illustrates the reaction of certain conservative and church-oriented individuals to the drive to completely biologicalize the sex education program. In this article, strong opposition is expressed toward any modification of the ethical and moral aspects of sex education. Authorities should not change, it states, because "if we always let the majority lead us then morality will be thrown out." [5] Even a reform which would allow various moral positions to be presented to the students and then ask them to make up their own minds is opposed. The article contends that if the school doesn't hold to its duty to discourage premarital sexual experimentation, it would be the same as giving in to teen-age drunkenness just because such teen-age drinking is increasing.[6] Actually, some conservative-minded persons oppose any truly candid physiological treatment of sex for the young because they think such frankness degrades sex. A 1962 editorial in *Dagen* argued that the moral condition of Sweden had deteriorated, and that this was related to "premature sex education, which serves to make our population into sexual idiots." [7] The editor contended that people become sexual idiots if they fail to elevate sex to the level of poetry and thus give it a meaning far removed from its gross physiological aspects.

Even some leaders in the sex education movement, who are not in sympathy with some of the moral positions in the official handbook, are nevertheless wary of going to a sex education program which is wholly biological in nature. Mrs. Maj-Brigt Bergström-Walan, one of the major figures in Swedish sex education, wrote an article in 1962 in which she warned that "in the rush to get out of the ditch of convention and outdated moralisms, there is a risk that we may fall in another ditch where all inhibitions are lost and mere cold technique is foremost." [8] She was concerned that the biological facts were not being taught as well as they should be, but even worse was the situation with regard to the psychological and ethical point of view. Mrs. Bergström-Walan considers it essential to keep a moral and ethical dimension in sex education, but she feels that specially gifted and sensitive people should be sought out to discuss these matters with the children. Rigid preachments against premarital sex are not particularly useful. Within the last few years, it appears that those who would keep moral, ethical, and psychological aspects of sex in the curriculum are likely to prevail. However, the moral problems will probably be dealt with on a much more tentative basis than was intended in the original handbook. There has been much discussion about a new book used presently in many schools to present sex education to fourteen- to sixteen-year-olds. One professor of education, a very religious Free Lutheran, in an interview with the author, indicated he was sadly aware of the spreading use of this book, and was quite appalled by the trend. He insisted that the book clearly contradicts the official handbook's position on premarital sex, and he seemed to have some hope that something could be done to discourage the use of the book. The book, *Vägen till Mognad* ("Way to Maturity"), by Lis Asklund and Torsten Wickbom, makes an effort to be neutral, yet thorough, in its treatment of sexual morality. It states, without comment, those things which are prohibited in formal law, and then lists norms not legally codified, but upon which nearly everyone could agree. Then it presents the matter of premarital sex as an issue on which there is no clear agreement:

> Certain paragraphs in Swedish law deal with people's sexual life. Rape, for example, is punished by law. It is also prohibited by law to have intercourse with someone under fifteen years old. Also it is punishable by law to have intercourse with close relatives, sisters and brothers for instance. Neither can anyone have homosexual relations with anyone under eighteen years of age.
>
> Furthermore, there are quite a few norms and rules about sex life which are not printed in the law. Most often these rules are aspects of rules which apply to all human relations. Most people agree on the rule that one's actions should not harm a fellow being. Therefore, it is also immoral to have intercourse without contraceptives if one is not prepared to take care of the child which can be the result. Most people also agree that one should not lie to others. Therefore, it is also immoral to try to have intercourse with someone by untruthfully telling that person that one is in love with him or her.
>
> However, what makes the question about sexual morality so difficult is that in many cases people cannot agree about what one ought and ought not to do. Especially, many people consider the question, When may two people have sexual intercourse? as the main point at issue in sexual morality. The following viewpoints are rather common:
>
> 1. Sexual life belongs only within marriage.
> 2. Sexual intercourse is allowed with one with whom one is planning to marry. Many feel, for example, that if a couple are betrothed by rings (both the woman and man) and put an engagement notice in the newspaper, then intimate relations are allowed.
> 3. If a couple are going steady and are in love, then intimate relations are allowed, even if the couple are not engaged.
> 4. Sex relations between people who are only acquaintances have most generally been considered wrong. However, in our time, there are some people who think that such relations should be accepted.[9]

The book discusses at some length each of these four positions, and then asks the student to make up his own mind after serious and thoughtful consideration of the various arguments. The authors point out:

> . . . what we consider to be the most important thing is that each and every young person think through these problems. We know that many will come to agree with the traditional church point of view that sex life belongs in marriage only. Others may decide that it is defensible to start sexual life before marriage. We believe that a person is worthy of respect when he himself has worked to arrive at an opinion and resolves to live in accordance with it. The main thing is that he or she is prepared to take the consequences of his or her actions, and that full consideration is given the partner. A person should act according to his convictions and not in accordance with the feelings of the moment.[10]

Opposition to the Asklund-Wickbom approach tends to run along age or geographical lines. Many people over forty may have doubts about this approach, although the majority of people are probably willing to let the activists on both sides argue the issue to a conclusion. Active opposition tends also to be more prevalent in certain rural areas, particularly in Småland and the northwest coastal area near Norway.

Until very recently, there has been no tendency in school classes to discuss or describe actual sexual intercourse, but student groups in the last year or so have been active in efforts to include such material in the curriculum. A letter to the author from the chief medical officer of the National Board of Education describes this new aspect of debate over sex education in Sweden:

> . . . at the present time there is a vivid discussion about a pamphlet from the RFSU [National Association for Sex Education]. The pamphlet is regarded as rather advanced because of its detailed descriptions of intercourse and petting techniques. It is intended for the sixteen-year-old, and it is up to the local school board to decide if it should be used in the school. The pupils' organization (S.E.C.O.) is very angry at the school leaders who have decided not to use it. Nevertheless, many do use it in their schools.[11]

It appears that in this debate, as in the more longstanding debate over the morality of premarital intercourse, the young are quite willing to see a liberalizing of sex education.

Two other areas of the curriculum should be mentioned where the Asklund-Wickbom approach is sharply at variance with the treatment given in the original handbook. These are masturbation and contraception. The original handbook in its lesson-example for ages eleven to thirteen says:

Masturbation (self-abuse) is the name for producing sensations of pleasure by conscious irritation of the sexual organs. Masturbation occurs frequently among both boys and girls. It was once believed that masturbation produced illness of various kinds, but this is no longer held to be the case.[12]

In the Asklund-Wickbom book, a much more positive and accepting attitude is evinced:

In puberty, young people often stimulate the sexual organs with their hands, or in other ways, to achieve gratification and release. . . . Both boys and girls engage in this practice, but it seems more common among boys. Self-gratification is natural and completely harmless. . . . Adults also practice self-gratification. This is especially so among adults who have been accustomed to regular sexual relations, but who are in situations where these are curtailed. . . . Self-gratification can, therefore, be a way of dealing with problems arising from the sex drive.

Self-gratification is harmless, natural, and nothing to feel guilty about.[13]

On contraception, the original handbook in its lesson-example for ages fourteen to sixteen limited its discussion to the following:

. . . conception may quite well occur even if intercourse is broken off.

There are other ways of preventing conception. Perhaps you know that there are certain means called *contraceptives*. . . . The most widely used contraceptive is the *condom* (French letter), which is used by the man. Since the condom may burst, it is not a reliable protection against conception. The only other preventive which will be mentioned for the present is called the *pessary*, and is designed for use by the woman. The pessary is a bowl-shaped rubber membrane for covering the mouth of the uterus. . . . It is a good protection, but it must be pointed out that there is no contraceptive which gives complete protection. . . . Since you know that boys and girls who are still growing up should not have sexual relations, you will understand that contraceptives should not be used by them.[14]

In the Asklund-Wickbom approach and other recent books used by teachers mainly for fourteen- to sixteen-year-olds, the various contraceptive devices are thoroughly described—the condom, intrauterine devices, the diaphragm, vaginal jellies and foam, and contraceptive oral pills. The rather high reliability of these procedures is pointed out, and there is no effort to discourage their use as a means of frightening young people into refraining from sexual intercourse.[15]

In spite of the lively debates and the sometimes rather acrimonious arguments about various aspects of sex education in Sweden, there is no doubt that Sweden is in the forefront in attempting to bring sex into the light for young people. Sex education in Sweden proceeds in a general social environment where rational attitudes toward sex have become much more prevalent than elsewhere. A much respected Swedish writer, Lars Gyllensten, probably expressed the attitude of a surprising portion of the Swedish population when he posited his own "Ten Commandments" for the modern age. His "Sixth Commandment" is:

> Thou shalt not spread venereal diseases, or bring unwanted children into the world, or expose other people to sexual violence. Also, you should play your part in keeping the birth rate as low as possible because altogether too many children are born. For the rest, you may devote yourself freely to sexual intercourse, masturbation, pornography, and such other good things of this kind as your animal nature, in its grace, may cause you to desire.[16]

Most parents and teachers with whom Gyllensten talked considered it only natural that sex should be included in the school curriculum. They generally felt that the school could do a better job than the home. The commonsense attitude toward sex is perhaps illustrated by the fact that people in Sweden accept the idea of advertising contraceptives such as the condom in the newspapers and on billboards, and show no concern when these items are sold openly in the stores or from vending machines on most busy street corners.

Not very much data is available on how much students in Sweden know concerning sexual matters, or whether the instruction in the schools is effectively transmitted. Mrs. Bergström-Walan, director of the Swedish sex education program, indicates that in spite of some years of sex education in the schools in Sweden, the young people are still more naïve, ignorant, and unsophisticated than the educated Swedish public might believe. The following quotation is from a paper she gave in 1965 at a conference in Brussels:

> In the course of my lessons in Sweden on sexual matters, I asked my students for written and oral questions. . . . The age groups which I instructed for the most part were between fourteen and sixteen years of age. . . . The questions reveal ignorance and anguish as well as sincerity and interest:
>
> How does one discover if one is pregnant? If a girl has intercourse, and menstruates four days later accompanied by a fever and nausea, is she perhaps pregnant? What do they do to the part of the umbilical cord which does not remain attached to the child after being born? If one has intercourse while under the influence of alcohol, will there be effects on the child? How long must intercourse last for one to become pregnant? When, after having intercourse with a boy, one begins to bleed, what is the

cause? What age must one be in order to have intercourse for the first time? Is it natural to have intercourse at fifteen years of age? If one loves a boy and he asks to go to bed with you, what should you do? Why are boys always wanting to touch and pinch girls? Why do boys always neglect girls after having intercourse with them? What are contraceptives—is it necessary for parents to buy them if one is to procure them? If a boy and girl are always together, can the girl become pregnant? If one becomes pregnant before fifteen years of age, is one sent to the reformatory? How does one get a legal abortion? Can one give oneself a legal abortion?—I have heard that one takes a heat lamp and heats the womb; then one takes a hot bath. What becomes of a child after an abortion—is it buried? Is it dangerous to masturbate? What is gonorrhea? Is homosexuality a disease? [17]

Such questions from children, most of whom must have had some classroom instruction prior to their contact with Mrs. Bergström-Walan, indicate that only a limited amount of information on such things as abortion, conception, contraception, and venereal disease had been assimilated. This is in line with the findings of a recently released official study, "Sexual Life in Sweden," which shows that those children who had had sexual instruction knew only a little more than those who had not.[18] As for general trends in Swedish illegitimacy, venereal disease, divorce, and sexual crime, the direction shows a mixed picture. Venereal disease in 1965 was at its highest incidence since 1919.[19] This upward trend is not unique to Sweden and has occurred in most countries. The proportion of "illegitimate" (the term *out-of-wedlock* is used in Sweden) births to "legitimate" births was 9 percent in the 1940s while in 1964 it had risen to about 13 percent.[20] Again, many other countries have seen a sharp rise in illegitimacy over the past two decades. The Swedes are far more concerned about the venereal disease rate than illegitimacy, which has far less disturbing effects in Sweden than it has in the United States. Divorce rates in Sweden have not changed much since 1951, and at the rate of one divorce to six marriages are a good deal lower than the American rate of one to four. Of course, many Swedes enter into a trial marriage when they become formally engaged, and a breakup of such a union doesn't count as divorce.

It is probably too early to assess truly the Swedish efforts at sex education. Much opposition and ineffectiveness has had to be overcome, and it is the next ten years that may show more clearly what effect sex education has had on certain objective measures. To gauge its effect on human happiness is more difficult.

Sex education in various Communist countries has had to adjust to the shifting and twisting of the Party line. On the whole, the attitude of school officials and political leaders in these countries has been to de-emphasize sexual knowledge and discussion on the grounds that student energy and school time should be devoted to making good socialist citizens who are technologically competent and who are devoted whole-heartedly to socialist reconstruction. Also it is clear that changing attitudes on the part of top Party leaders toward the demographic situation in their particular country have affected policies toward sexual matters, including marriage, divorce, birth control, abortion, sexual morality, and sex education.

North Korea during the past fifteen years is a good example of a Communist country where the regime has been uncompromisingly anti-Neo-Malthusian, extremely puritanical toward youthful sexual interests, and consistently opposed to any direct inclusion of sex education in the school curriculum.

Part of the explanation for the North Korean attitude is, of course, the desire of the leaders to sustain the revolutionary impulse which they see threatened by any diversion of the people's interest toward such personal questions as love and marriage, sexual activity, and family size. Such diversion of interests to these questions is equated with Western "bourgeois" degradation and contamination. Youths are warned not to be drawn to personal pleasures, but to devote their passions to the construction of socialism and communism.

Along with the general desire of the North Korean regime to prevent any diversion from single-minded dedication to socialist construction is a very strong awareness on the part of North Korean leaders of the great inequality between the populations of North and South Korea. The population of North Korea is about eleven million while that of South Korea is nearly thirty million. This discrepancy has prevented any thaw in North Korea's denunciation of Neo-Malthusianism. This is in contrast to China and the Soviet Union, where some rather tortured efforts have been made to back off from the extreme anti-Neo-Malthusianism of the 1950s. In North Korea, birth control is still equated with cannibalism, and there is no place in the school curriculum for direct discussion of the facts or the morality of human sex. Even in biology classes for thirteen-year-olds, no mention of human sex is countenanced; teachers are told to teach about the planting and growth of trees, rice, cotton, corn, cabbage, and potatoes.[21] In home economics classes girls are taught only to be polite, wear traditional garb, cook food, handle a budget, bow to elders, and maintain a respectful silence.[22] This is in sharp contrast to South Korean home economics classes, where, in addition to traditional topics, family planning, pregnancy, child development and other sexual matters are discussed. Until North Korea's population is closer in numbers to that of the South the extreme puritanical avoidance of direct discussion of human sexual life and problems is likely to continue.

The ideological situation in Communist China has been somewhat similar to that of North Korea, except that the possibility that there are too many Chinese is a factor that has brought the birth control issue to the fore during various periods, such as the middle 1950s and the early and mid-1960s. Just as in North Korea, great concern has been shown in China toward directing all of the energy of youth toward socialist reconstruction. In speaking of the Chinese student's need to combine labor with study, a 1959 article in the Peking *People's Daily* stated that "because of their participation in the practice of labor . . . the students first experience a great change in the spiritual aspect and are taught the class viewpoint of the working class, the labor viewpoint, the mass viewpoint, the collective viewpoint, and the dialectical materialist viewpoint." [23]

It does not appear that any special effort has been made to introduce sex instruction into the school even during the periods when birth control campaigns have had official sanction. During the period of the early 1960s, the regime was strongly supporting the idea of late marriage as a major weapon to reduce births. Articles appeared in periodicals directed to youth which may have had some influence on school instruction. An article in 1962, directed to youth, developed at length the idea of late marriage and family planning:

. . . if they [young people] get married too early, their energy will be dispersed on account of family life, and if they give birth to children and thus burden themselves with a family, their studies will be affected to an even greater extent. . . . Because early marriage is such an impediment to studies, many people in history who were determined to become learned refused to get married too early. . . . In the rural areas and factories, many young women . . . have had to keep house and nurse children at an early age. . . . Some youths say, "Provided we practice contraception and have a planned family, early marriage will not produce great adverse effects on us." We say that in the case of youths who have already gotten married, it is of course better to have children late than early, thus reducing somewhat the adverse effects of early marriage. Planned birth is also good and is something which we advocate. However, this applies after all only to youths who have already gotten married, and besides, things do not always turn out as one has planned.[24] *

Articles appeared in various periodicals in 1962 extolling late marriage and contraception. Negative comments were made about women with four or five children, and detailed descriptions of condoms, diaphragms, and jellies were included.[25] †

---

*See pp. 283-289 of *Sex, Schools, and Society*.
†See pp. 271-282 of *Sex, Schools, and Society*.

Chinese Communist leadership is obviously not particularly averse to the "facts of life," but if concern over such matters seems to endanger single-minded ideological commitment to collectivist goals, then such interests must be foresworn. It seems likely, however, that the fact of overpopulation in China will force the regime reluctantly from time to time in coming decades to deal with sex, contraception, abortion, love, and marriage on a much more frank basis than the leadership, with its rather puritanical ideology, would prefer.

In the Soviet Union, during the early years after the Revolution, it was thought that legal and political emancipation of women, and a generally permissive attitude toward sexual behavior, would speed the demise of the old Czarist patriarchal "bourgeois" family structure. All legal disabilities of women were abolished. Incest, bigamy, and adultery were no longer statutory crimes. De facto marriage was accorded equal status with those registered through civil ceremony. After abortion was legalized in 1920, hospitals called Abortariums were established in Moscow and Leningrad. Abortion, in the cities at least, became more common; for example, in 1935, there were 150,000 abortions in Moscow as compared with 70,000 live births.[26] Contraceptives were in short supply and seemed to be associated with Neo-Malthusianism, which was thought to be "a bourgeois panacea for social ills."

After 1936, much of the early laxity toward marriage, sex, and family was modified. Abortion was made illegal unless pregnancy was a threat to the health or life of the woman. Divorce was made more difficult. Contraceptives were still in short supply. Family allowances were introduced, and taxation was introduced to penalize people with fewer than three children.[27] This drastic shift of policy was obviously related to the fact that the new regime had in 1936 had nearly twenty years of power, and the old patriarchal traditional family ways no longer posed a threat. Also, great losses of people in wars, famines, and epidemics occurring periodically from 1914 to 1934 indicated a change to a strong pronatalist policy for reasons of state.

Since 1955, there has been a partial return to the liberality which existed in the 1920s. Abortion is again legal, some Neo-Malthusian ideas have been allowed to be aired, and it seems contraceptives are quite widely available.

The school situation in the Soviet Union during the 1920s was extraordinarily experimentalist and behaviorist. Rostow points out that "it was not accidental that, in the course of his visit to the Soviet Union in the 1920s, John Dewey found the atmosphere congenial. Progressive education was practiced almost to the point of the 'withering away of the school.' "[28] By the mid-thirties all this had changed, and the school was moved sharply toward "strict, conservative training in useful techniques and methods."[29] Coeducation in secondary schools was generally abolished in 1943, although this never became universal. This shift in school policies and philosophy roughly paralleled the changes which sex and family life traversed in the same period.

The treatment of sex and family in the Soviet schools during the 1920s was in accordance with the experimental, environmentalist, non-traditional educational ethos of the time. It treated all problems as completely amenable to environmental influences. If the difference between the sexes, the so-called sexual drive, and the fascination of the young with matters related to sex were in many ways detrimental to the building of a new, socially conscious Communist citizen,[30] then it was necessary to act to overcome these survivals through social learning and by essentially ignoring any biological basis for these things. V. N. Kolbanovskii, writing in a 1964 Soviet education journal,* criticized the attitude of the educators of the 1920s for ignoring the reality of sex. He pointed out that, in the 1920s, "the process of the sexual development of children was ignored since, as it primarily involved natural laws, there again arose the [supposed] danger of being accused of overemphasizing the biological." [31]

When the schools returned to traditional ways after 1936 and a stable family life became a major focus of Soviet concern, the attitude toward sex education merely changed from a general vagueness due to a wish to avoid biologicalizing or diverting energies to a vagueness based on the belief that explicit treatment might weaken the family and sexual morality, and reduce the number of births. Many of the attitudes toward sex once condemned as "Czarist" now became prevalent. This almost "Victorian" stance has lasted more or less unchanged for the last three decades. A survey of the Soviet curriculum indicated that, in the late 1950s, in the ten-year school, only in grade eight is human biology touched, and even there human reproductive processes are left unmentioned unless the two hours devoted to the topic "Development of Organisms" devotes a little time to the subject. [32]

Even recent critics of the rather complete shunning of sex education in Soviet schools only wish to bring the subject to conscious treatment to combat what they feel is a spreading looseness in sexual morality. Kolbanovskii felt that teachers should bring up sexual topics in order to courageously combat immoral viewpoints:

> Some morally depraved people spread views among the youth to the effect that "maidenly honor" or a "woman's virtue" are narrow-minded prejudices which should have been overcome long ago, that love was given to man for his pleasure, and that if there is a "slip-up"—pregnancy—it is easy to get rid of it.[33]

In a 1963 article meant for Western consumption, the role of the Soviet teacher is idealized and one of the vignettes concerns a teacher's

---

*See pp. 253-269 of *Sex, Schools, and Society.*

treatment of teen-age love. The gingerly treatment of the issues, the emphasis finally given to chastity and romantic love, would satisfy the most ardent Victorian:

> I checked Alyosha's notebook. There was a note in it that he must have forgotten. It lay there unfolded. "Natasha, why do you go to the movies with another man?" And under it were the words "What business is it of yours?"
>
> I had to organize a debate among the seniors on the question of friendship and love. That started an argument in the teachers' room. "Should we have a debate on this subject?" The principal, Anna Zakharovna, supported the idea.
>
> "Who said that the school should teach children to solve only the problems in the textbooks? What about the problems with which life confronts them? When problems like these come up, you can't go running over to the neighbor's girl for help, or check your answer with the book."
>
> The ideas expressed at the debate were as bright and disturbing as flames. . . . The teacher also took the floor.
>
> "It seems to me that what is important in life is to wait for the beloved person, not to confuse him with anyone else, not to give your feelings, your tender, big words to anyone else."[84]

Attitudes expressed toward such topics as masturbation in Kolbanovskii's article remind one of the usual stance people approved in the West during the nineteenth century and are in sharp contrast with the Swedish positions mentioned earlier:

> And because adolescents are uninformed and unprepared as regards questions of sex life, they frequently go through the stage of pubescence with great harm to themselves. . . . the habit of onanism can have a grave effect upon the development of the personality.[85]

In general, there remains a very strong official aversion in the U.S.S.R. to any real liberalization of the treatment of sex. The Young Communist League, as late as October, 1966, has protested vigorously against lectures having to do with reproduction and sex presented before mixed audiences.[36] The alien and enemy "bourgeois" world today is not so much the world of false and rigid morals, patriarchy, and exploitation of women; rather, it is now envisaged as the world of sexual looseness, unchastity, preoccupation with sex, suggestive dances and literature; a cynical disregard for high-thinking, romantic monogamous love.

There are pressures to liberalize the sexual climate in the Communist countries. In China, the obvious difficulties overpopulation presents to economic development press the regime to come to grips with sexual matters. In the U.S.S.R. the increasing influence of public opinion and the example of Western trends are slowly moving the regime to a more candid discussion of sexual issues.

The United States, with the exception of occasional "avant garde" groups, generally has treated sex with a mixture of repression and uneasy fascination. Only in the past decade or so does there seem to be developing a truly widespread alteration in the stance most people take toward sex. Some people have argued that the main shift in American sexual behavior occurred in the 1920s, while the changes of the 1960s involve primarily a shift in attitude.[37] There were a number of personalities in the 1920s and 1930s who pleaded for a more rational attitude toward sex and programs of instruction in the schools. Judge Ben Lindsay was much maligned in Denver during the 1920s for advocating "companionate" or "trial" marriages. Harry Elmer Barnes complained steadily during the 1920s and 1930s about the lack of rational sex education. Writing in 1939, he argued:

> Today the sociologist hesitates to mention birth control and venereal prophylaxis, unless to condemn them, and he rarely describes these processes and methods in concrete detail. In a sane social and educational order such problems would be freely discussed and fully described.[38]

It is only in the last decade that any beginnings of a widely spread and fully discussed pattern of sex education in American schools have made much headway. The Sex Information and Education Council of the United States (SIECUS) was formed a few years ago by thirty-eight specialists in education, sociology, medicine, religion, and law to help existing sex education programs and to promote new ones. Dr. Mary Calderone, executive director of SIECUS, argued for a continuing program of sex instruction in the schools for all ages:

> By the age of ten or eleven a child should have full knowledge of the process of reproduction, given both at home and at school. In junior high school, students should consider the relational aspects of human and animal sex behavior. High schools should offer discussions of studies on venereal disease and unmarried parents.[39]

A pioneering program was instituted in 1957 in Evanston, Illinois, covering kindergarten children through those in the eighth grade, and it has received extensive coverage. The program includes a very graphic discussion of where babies come from, sexual development of the young, venereal disease, differences between the sexes, and so on. Much of the emphasis is on the family, the responsibility of fathers and mothers, and comparisons between human families and reproduction units in the animal world. The main responsibility for presentation lies with the classroom teacher, as it is felt that an overuse of outside experts, such as doctors or nurses, would lend an aura of specialness and abnormality to the subject.[40] Although questions on contraception arise and are answered, there is no effort to instruct children on this topic specifically. Also, girls and boys are sometimes separated for filmstrip instruction on menstruation, masturbation, homosexuality, and sex organ development. Freedom is allowed the teacher to ignore or disagree with some of the moral precepts which often accompany these audio-visual aids. For example, one filmstrip audio section condemns masturbation in this way:

> When you are tempted to do it, get busy doing something else. Play hard. Read an interesting book. Or if it occurs at night, think of something good to do tomorrow or recite some prayers. Boys with religious beliefs about these things may find they help to resist the temptation.[41]

Teachers may delete this section or have an open discussion on the topic so that the children are not left with the view that this sentiment is the last word on the morality of masturbation.

Programs were introduced in New York City, Anaheim, California, Jefferson County, Colorado (suburban Denver), and many other places. Most of the programs are more or less similar to the pattern in Evanston. They emphasize reproductive biology, a certain treatment of the etiquette of sex, and an emphasis on the need for solid family life and responsibility. Simon and Gagnon* of the Institute for Sex Research at Indiana University criticized the typical new sex education programs on the following grounds, among others. They argue that the schools present sex as something that merely happens, not something that is deeply experienced and subjective; there is a bland "sex is fun" orientation; many students knew it all before; teachers do not really present the moral alternatives, and leave the student to struggle to come to grips with his own concrete situations; and finally, they argue, we know less about sex than we think and schools may try to teach more than there is to be taught.[42]

The argument that American students know most of what is presented is perhaps partly true in some of the most emancipated areas and perhaps also in some ways among the urban lower classes. However, there is no thoroughgoing national study to indicate the degree of naïveté or sophistication among students on sexual questions. The author asked a capable sociology teacher in a Nashville high school, who had initiated some discussion of sexual issues, to ask two classes to hand in anonymous questions on sex which they wanted either discussed or answered in the classroom situation. In these two classes there

---

*See pp. 39-46 of *Sex, Schools, and Society.*

were fifty students (about half girls and half boys) all of whom were eighteen-year-old high-school seniors. The teacher had excellent rapport with her students, and the average ability of the students was generally in the top half of the senior class. The high school was in a somewhat better than average white neighborhood. The questions indicated a rather surprising degree of naïveté and bewilderment over many sex-related problems. A few of the questions which illustrate some recurring themes are included below:

In your opinion, is premarital sex recommended for mature engaged couples?

Do older married couples (late forties or fifties) still engage in sexual intercourse?

How many years can you take birth control pills?

What happens if a woman is so innocent that on her wedding night she becomes scared to death?

Is the government doing anything constructive about birth control?

Do you think that every marriage *has* to have sex all the time to survive?

After married people reach the age (such as our parents, generally) do they still continue their sexual relations?

How soon do you grow tired of sex after marriage?

When two eggs are fertilized is it from two different times of intercourse or the same one?

Does a strong douche often prevent pregnancy if a woman douches soon after sexual relations?

Does a male have to be all the way inside the female before she can get pregnant?

Is it easier to get a virgin pregnant than a girl who isn't a virgin?

If during intercourse the male gets out before releasing his sperm and ejects at the opening, is there still danger of pregnancy?

How safe are rubbers?

If you cannot get pregnant in one position, why can you get pregnant in another?

Can a person have intercourse with a Negro and have a black and white spotted baby?

Do you think the United States should stop having an abortion law?

Are there dangerous outcomes from interracial marriages?

Is it possible for a man or woman in their late sixties to have a baby?

Would you recommend more casual relationships with prostitutes or a meaningful (but not necessarily marriage-oriented) relationship with an equal?

What are the stages of a woman in marriage that makes it seem so painful and drab?

Do you condone animal love (free love) amongst groups of married couples (exchange of mates)?

What is your exact opinion on premarital sex?

How can a person get another person, if the other person this certain persons wants, wants this person for sex only, and the other person loves him mentally?

Are some positions in intercourse immoral?

Can a woman get infection from abortion?

How do drugs such as "Spanish fly" affect the body?

Do you think it's right for a husband to have affairs? I heard statistics that say about 90 percent of 100 percent have an affair.

Does the man have to be fully penetrated before the woman can become pregnant?

Should a couple either have premarital sex or wait until after the wedding night before having intercourse; because of all the excitement of the wedding?

How can one tell if he or she is oversexed?

Is there danger to the body in using contraceptives during intercourse?

The sensitivity of American public schools to small but vocal publics, much more than is the case in Sweden, seems to make it imperative for school people to make concessions to head off serious difficulties. A discussion of the San Diego, California, public schools by their director of school health services, G. G. Wetherill, contains this statement:

> A few areas of information that have controversial religious implications . . . are purposely omitted from the lessons, and if they come up as questions are given only very cursory answers and referred to parents for further discussion. The avoidance of just a few of these areas protects the program from criticism and makes it acceptable to all religious faiths.[43]

In general, sex education programs in America mirror the extreme heterogeneity of school quality, curriculum, clientele, and leadership which characterizes the educational system of the United States. In recent years, the fervor of dedicated private groups, teachers, and individuals has brought surprising change in the United States in bringing about some openness about sex in many schools.

The programs that have been started are mainly in urban or suburban settings, and the majority of these formal sex education programs do not start until grade six.[44] A good description of the present situation in the United States is presented by Malfetti and Rubin, who obtained outlines of a very high percentage of American school-based sex education programs which were underway by 1967:

At the few elementary schools giving it, sex education is usually taught by a generalist (classroom) teacher and consists primarily of a brief description of male and female reproductive systems (perhaps human, perhaps not), some indication of how they unite for conception, and a vague description of the development and the delivery of the child (rabbit or chicken). At the junior and senior high school levels sex education is reproduction education (human) with an emphasis on menstruation (for girls) and venereal disease. This teaching may be fragmented or integrated into different subjects covered in different courses. . . . or in isolated lectures by a physician or school nurse. . . . It is unusual for a high school syllabus to provide for discussions of sexual outlets like masturbation, homosexuality, premarital relations, or of standards of sexual conduct.[45]

In early 1969, right-wing groups in the United States launched a campaign against sex education in the schools and against SIECUS. The John Birch Society, acting in concert with Billy James Hargis's Christian Crusade, spent heavily to create public opposition to the spreading movement for sex education in the schools. The literature which they disseminated attacked school programs already in operation as creating more illegitimacy, sexual neurosis, promiscuity, irreligion, and so on. A passage from the most widely used booklet* in the campaign illustrates the kind of attack which was launched:

It should be evident that the sex educators are in league with sexologists, who represent every shade of muddy gray morality, ministers colored atheistic pink, and camp followers of every persuasion—offbeat psychiatrists to ruthless publishers of pornography. The enemy is formidable at first glance, but becomes awesomely powerful when we discover the interlocking directorates and working relationship of national organizations which provide havens for these degenerates.[46]

This campaign has created a furor in many areas. Established programs, such as the one in Anaheim, California, have been effectively attacked. In Nashville, Tennessee, the major evening newspaper ran front-page editorials condemning a proposed program there. Much of the material in the editorials was taken directly from the booklets disseminated from John Birch American Opinion bookshops. The furor was so intense in Nashville that the city council met in special session to consider the possibility of a city-wide referendum to see if the citizens wanted sex education in the schools. The proposed pilot program was dropped.

The wish to placate important pressure groups, particularly religious

*See pp. 171-200 of *Sex, Schools, and Society.*

groups, has caused and will continue to cause those wishing to open the classroom to sex to be wary of such obviously crucial topics as birth control, premarital sexual relations, and homosexuality. The universal and increasingly liberalized sex instruction of Sweden which reaches all children is perhaps far in the future for the United States. On the other hand, since the individualistic yet imitative spirit of American education does not, in our time, have to be shackled to the kind of secular puritanism which permeates efforts to grope with the sexual problem in the Soviet Union, much can and will be done.

NOTES

[1] Lars Gustafson, *The Public Dialogue in Sweden* (Stockholm: P. A. Norstedt and Sons, 1964), pp. 99-100.
[2] Sven Wernstrom, *Aftenbladet* (Stockholm), October 26, 1961. Cited in Birgitta Linnér, *Sex and Society in Sweden* (New York: Pantheon, 1967), pp. 123-24.
[3] Linnér, *op. cit.*, pp. 125-26.
[4] *Handbook on Sex Instruction in the Schools* (Stockholm: National Board of Education, 1956), pp. 50-51. [See pp. 319-330 of *Sex, Schools, and Society*.]
[5] J. Strömmer, *Dagen* (Stockholm), November 5, 1963.
[6] *Ibid.*
[7] Lewi Petrus, *Dagen* (Stockholm), April 1, 1962.
[8] Maj-Brigt Bergström-Walan, *Dagens Nyheter* (Stockholm), June 6, 1962.
[9] Lis Asklund and Torsten Wickbom, *Vagen till Mognad* (Stockholm: Radio Sweden, 1967), pp. 80-81.
[10] *Ibid.*, p. 84
[11] Letter from G. Rodhe, Chief Medical Officer, National Board of Education, to R. M. Bjork, December 21, 1967.
[12] *Handbook, op. cit.*, p. 40.
[13] Asklund and Wickbom., *op. cit.*, pp. 97-98.
[14] *Handbook, op. cit.*, pp. 51-52.
[15] Asklund and Wickbom, *op. cit.*, pp. 38-47.
[16] Lars Gyllensten, "Ten Commandments" in Lars Bäckström and Göran Palm, eds., *Sweden Writes* (Stockholm: The Swedish Institute, 1965), p. 227.
[17] Belgian Ministry of National Education and Culture, Maj-Brigt Bergström-Walan, "Nous parlons aux enfants de la vie sexuelle," International Conference of Schools, Parents and Educators, Brussels, May 24-27, 1965, pp. 7-9 (Mimeo).
[18] Findings of the study are summarized in J. Robert Moskin, "The Contraceptive Society," *Look*, February 4, 1969, pp. 50-53.
[19] Birgitta Linnér, *Society and Sex in Sweden* (Stockholm: The Swedish Institute, 1966), p. 32. [See pp. 331-370 of *Sex, Schools, and Society*.]
[20] Linnér, *Sex and Society in Sweden, op. cit.*, p. 34.
[21] *People's Education* (Pyongyang: Ministry of Elementary Education, February, 1966) pp. 7-8.
[22] *Technical Education* (Pyongyang: Ministry of Elementary Education, August, 1966), pp. 38-39.
[23] Yang-Hsiu-feng, "China's Educational Enterprise Goes through the Process of Great Revolution and Great Evolution," *People's Daily* (Peking), October 8,

1959, in Stewart Fraser, ed., *Chinese Communist Education* (Nashville: Vanderbilt University Press, 1965), p. 33.

[24] Yang Hsiu, "For Late Marriage," *China Youth* (Peking), No. 11, June 1, 1962, *passim*. [See pp. 283-289 of *Sex, Schools, and Society*.]

[25] Cheng Lin, "Editor's reply to a reader's letter 'What's to Be Done If One Has Married Young?' by K'ai Ko," *Chung-kuo Ch'ing-nien Pao* (Peking), July 7, 1962 [See pp. 271-273 of *Sex, Schools, and Society*]; Yeh Kung-shao, "My Views on the Problem of Young People's Marriage, Love and Children, *Chung-kuo Ch'ing-nien Pao* (Peking), July 21, 1962 [See pp. 275-278 of *Sex, Schools, and Society*]; Shu Ming-yen, "Several Contraceptives Recommended for General Use," *Kung-jen Jih-Bao* (Peking), July 24, 1962.

[26] Ralph Thomlinson, *Population Dynamics* (New York: Random House, 1965), p. 412.

[27] *Ibid.*

[28] W. W. Rostow, *The Dynamics of Soviet Society* (New York: New American Library, 1954), p. 108.

[29] *Ibid.*

[30] The Komsomol, young Communists mainly in their late teens, had had a strong influence on the school climate in the 1920's. They emphasized their own solidarity by fostering a "proletarian" morality which frowned on alcohol, tobacco and sexual looseness. See Ralph T. Fisher, Jr., *Pattern for Soviet Youth* (New York: Columbia University Press, 1959), p. 109.

[31] V. N. Kolbanovskii, "The Sex Upbringing of the Rising Generation," *Sovietskaya Pedagogika*, November 3, 1964. Translated in *The Soviet Review*, Vol. 5, No. 3, Fall, 1964, p. 57. [See pp. 253-269 of *Sex, Schools, and Society*.]

[32] William K. Medlin, Clarence B. Lindquist, Marshall Schmitt, *Soviet Education Programs* (Washington: U.S. Government Printing Office, 1960), pp. 57-60.

[33] Kolbanovskii, *op. cit.*, p. 55.

[34] Margarita Zatsepina, "A Teacher's Diary," *U.S.S.R.*, No. 10, October, 1963, p. 43.

[35] Kolbanovskii, *op. cit.*, p. 51.

[36] *New York Times*, October 8, 1966, p. 37.

[37] *New York Times*, July 11, 1966, p. 31.

[38] Harry Elmer Barnes, *Society in Transition*, 8th edition (New York: Prentice-Hall, 1946), p. 418.

[39] Mary S. Calderone, "Teenagers and Sex," *PTA Magazine*, October, 1965, p. 6.

[40] William Barry Furlong, "It's a Long Way from the Birds and Bees," *New York Times*, July 11, 1967, Section 6, p. 48. [See pp. 47-57 of *Sex, Schools, and Society*.]

[41] *Ibid.*, p. 55.

[42] William Simon and John H. Gagnon, "The Pedagogy of Sex," *Saturday Review*, November 18, 1967, pp. 74-76, 91-92. [See pp. 39-46 of *Sex, Schools, and Society*.]

[43] G. G. Wetherill, M.D., *The San Diego Sex Education Program*, (San Diego: San Diego City Schools Health Services Department, undated), p. 3. (Mimeo).

[44] "Sex Education: Who Wants It? A Grade Teacher Survey," *Grade Teacher*, (November, 1968), p. 63.

[45] James L. Malfetti and Arlene Rubin, "Sex Education: Who is Teaching the Teachers?" *Teachers College Record*, (December, 1967), p. 215.

[46] Gordon V. Drake, "Is the Schoolhouse the Proper Place to Teach Raw Sex?" (Tulsa, Oklahoma: Christian Crusade Publications, 1968) p. 31. [See pp. 171-200 of *Sex, Schools, and Society*.] For the John Birch Society contention that sex education is a Communist conspiracy against the West see Gary Allen, *Sex Education Problems*, (Belmont, Massachusetts, *American Opinion*, 1969). [See also pp. 201-224 of *Sex, Schools, and Society*.]

Part II
PEDAGOGY AND SEX EDUCATION

INTRODUCTION

The growing belief among the general public that school curriculum reform should lead to the inclusion of sex (or family life) education programs comes as little surprise to those educators who have watched the proliferation of diverse courses, the introduction of controversial materials, and the experimentation with novel teaching concepts in American schools during the past decade. However, what does surprise one is not the criticism—often justifiable—regarding the competency of sex education instructors, but the fact that some school administrators, together with their school boards and local parent-teacher associations, still seem to be largely unaware of the difficulties which may have to be overcome in the introduction of sex education programs in the schools.

The American educational penchant for attempting, in theory at least, to involve the many interested groups in a community prior to final decision making on controversial matters has provided regular exercises in democratic participation. However, it has also facilitated an open invitation to pressure groups to manipulate a sensitive situation for purely political and social ends rather than those which pertain more directly to the pedagogic processes and valid educational goals of the schools.

The essays in this section afford a thoughtful look at the problem from a variety of philosophical and practical viewpoints. They focus on the concerns of educators investigating the needs of children in a society characterized by changing moral codes, and suggest that biological knowledge, reproductive information, and sexual facts, while important, are insufficient for today's young people unless carefully linked with opportunities for understanding better how to manage their social relationships. The importance of the peer group in spreading informal sex instruction appears to be dominant, and sexual information available formally in a school setting may prove inadequate and boring, especially if ineptly taught. It is apparent, however, that an exploration of the multitude of social relationships, with sex as one among various components, can be stimulating, especially if students are helped to understand the physical consequences of their social acts, considered within the parameters of clearly understood ethical boundaries. The teacher is likewise constantly forced to reappraise the nature of his own philosophical and ethical involvement. The pedagogic disparity and cultural lag between what a teachers' college offers and the actual experience of classroom teaching ensure that teachers will often unhappily replicate what, if any, modest formal sex instruction they have themselves received in training. And teachers unsure of themselves may attempt to bypass the moral and ethical arguments which young people wish to raise in connection with sex education. The introduction and opening up of a biological topic will lead, often quite naturally, to questions of social interpersonal relationships, which teachers are sometimes ill prepared to handle.

The pedagogic aspects of sex education can perhaps be reduced to three avenues of philosophical inquiry: What should be taught? How and when should it be taught? Who should do the teaching?

Many of the contributors to this section of the anthology are actively engaged in the research, teaching, and applied social aspects of sex education. Other contributors include journalists, social scientists, and philosophers, writing on various societal themes, and discussing the interrelationship between the school, the community, and the implementation of sex education programs.

William Simon and John H. Gagnon in their article, "The Pedagogy of Sex," believe that there are three basic sources of sex information which affect the child, namely, peer groups, schools, and certain of the mass media. While the schools appear to be the main vehicle for formal programmed instruction, they are more amenable to direct social pressure or political manipulation than the other two and, accordingly, will obviously continue in the future to receive the most attention from specific interest groups, including, of course, parents and educators. But the authors suggest, disquietingly, that there are few direct correlations and little to indicate that "schools, parents, physicians, or religious institutions [play] a significant role in sex education except for a small minority of cases." The pessimistic and carefully worded tone of their analysis suggests that really very little is known about sex and that many of the sex education programs in schools are based on inadequate or minimal information.

The contribution by Michael Scriven, "Putting the Sex Back into Sex Education," a philosophical analysis, implies that the goals and aims of many sex education programs have escaped searching scrutiny. The author insists that such programs be recognized for what they are—merely courses in the "destruction of ill-based preconceptions." Pedagogically, he argues, the present state of sex education programs is somewhat akin to the teaching of science solely by disproving superstitions and is, of course, an equally unsatisfactory method of instruction. In "The Pill, the Sexual Revolution, and the Schools," the strictures of Ashley Montagu provide corroboration for some of the opinions expressed by Scriven, and their analyses and viewpoints are generally complementary. Montagu, an anthropologist and social biologist, discusses some of the social, rather than the moral, consequences of the Pill, and the implications for the schools and colleges as young people bypass age-old beliefs, practices, and institutions in their experimentation with sex. Among various controversial recommendations, Montagu advocates state tests before marriage to assess potential parents' ability to deal responsibly with children. This would impose additional responsibilities and new burdens on the schools, for they are expected to be the principal vehicle for teaching young people "love" and they appropriately emphasize the teaching of special courses on sexual responsibility. The barest suggestion that the schools should provide the beehive for "sexual appreciation" and "trial love alliances," brought forth the retort of a teen-ager, Gregory Spencer Hill, who vehemently answered Montagu in a cogent essay, "Premarital Sex—Never!" He found Montagu eloquent and articulate, but not convincing, and as a practicing Christian (Mormon) felt compelled to offer a religious rebuttal of Montagu's humanistic proposals. Hill suggests that the powerful sexual energies of youth should be directed into constructive channels. He lists, for example, those avenues available to him through church programs, which include athletics, music training, speech and drama club participation, and "wholesome recreation . . . and preparation for adulthood." He argues that the energies and sexual tensions of youth can be thoroughly dissipated through church-organized activities. Interestingly enough, without, naturally, the recognition of a church or religious influences, authors in the Soviet Union and China put forward somewhat analogous arguments and suggest similar practices to sidetrack youthful interest from love and sexual pursuits. A Chinese writer (see page 276) discussing the question whether students should marry if in love suggests that "they had better not" and quickly explains: "The reason is very simple: students should fully utilize their time to develop themselves mentally, morally, and physically. Love, which demands much time and energy, will affect the quality of their studies."

The Chinese, faced with a population explosion almost unequalled in the world today, are willing, for ideological, moralistic, and demographic reasons, to sublimate and deflect the sexual interest young people have in one another. Through Communist Party Youth Organizations, Chinese government officials, health specialists, and educators encourage young people to expend their sexual energies in activities similar to those which many Christian churches believe are important, namely, athletics, music, speech, drama activities, and the preparation for adulthood. At first glance, there would appear to be few major differences in program and goal emphasis between, for example, the Mormon program for youthful sexual sublimation (which features the above activities) and that enforced in China for Communist youth. Both are strongly moralistic and believe that the sexual interests and drives of young people can be successfully deflected through social persuasion and ideological encouragement.

The problems facing the American public school in the realm of sex and family education cannot, of course, be so facilely handled as is the case in China, where the ideological apparatus of a ubiquitous Party structure generally offers the firmest, if not the most persuasive, of guidelines. But the American public school is unable, for both political and institutional reasons, to call upon the resources of, for example, the churches for full-scale intervention and the application of sublimation programs of "good, healthy nonsexual exercises and fellowship circles." However, the schools wisely recognize that the introduction of sex education programs is often dependent on the community's acceptance of and involvement in, where feasible, a variety of community agencies, including those of a religious nature.

Accordingly, influential groups, such as parent-teacher associations and medical and social agencies, as well as religious bodies, are often consulted and involved to the extent that school administrators deem necessary. A thoughtful analysis of this community involvement is discussed in A. Gray Thompson and Edward P. DeRoche's study, "Sex Education: Parent Involvement in Decision Making." The current popular emphasis on sex education in the schools has induced many educators to consider it a necessary addition to the curriculum. Reluctance to do so in the past has often been based on uncertainty about the impact this would have on the community. The authors present an interesting description of an experiment which placed major responsibility for a new program on parents, thus defusing the potential explosion which could result from the ill-advised and noncoordinated introduction of programs without the direct involvement and consent of parents. The actual degree of parental involvement in establishing sex education programs is no guarantee either that the programs will be permanently accepted or that they will lead to increased sexual understanding on the part of children. Parental involvement in decision making should be a continual process, and the role of the family increasingly stressed ·and complemented. It has been parents' failure to recognize the need for family involvement and ongoing self-education which has often contributed to the difficulty children have accepting the schools' programs for what they are, namely, only one aspect of the many sources of formal and informal instruction available to them.

James Elias and Paul Gebhard in their analysis, "Sexuality and Sexual Learning in Childhood," present a longitudinal study of interviews with children aged four to fourteen, based on data originally gathered by the late Alfred Kinsey. The authors, from the Institute for Sex Research at Indiana University, suggest that the influence of the peer group in sexual learning is the prime factor among lower-class children. They do stress, however, that in providing sex information the educator has a singular opportunity to provide adequate and truly helpful programs to meet the requirements of children who are discriminated against because of their social class. Their conclusions suggest that "education should continue to initiate programs which will help fill this void created either by peer misinformation or by similar misunderstanding and reluctance on the part of parents."

William Barry Furlong's survey of school programs, "It's a Long Way from the Birds and Bees," affords a descriptive account of what some schools provide in their programs on sex education. His reportage stresses what can be accomplished by teachers who are both academically competent and socially interested in their tasks.

It might be presumed that one of the logical results of the introduction of sex education programs in schools would be the reduction of teen-age pregnancies and a more mature understanding of sexual responsibilities. This is not necessarily so, and the authors represented in this portion of the anthology are unable to arrive uniformly at specific conclusions on the effectiveness of school sex education programs. Some authors are clearer as to what has *not* been accomplished, while others can only agree on what they would *like* to see implemented. But the authors are not school administrators who would be ultimately responsible for the introduction and implementation of school board policy regarding sex education programs. Generally speaking, it is clear that the American public school is unable openly to advocate or give instruction in premarital contraception techniques—obviously for many young people a pertinent aspect of any sex education program. Edward Pohlman, a counseling psychologist, in his article, "Premarital Contraception and the School," explores some of the problems and, after a shrewd and blunt assessment of the difficulties involved, offers some practical suggestions. He recognizes that school administrators' involvement in seriously promoting "premarital contraception techniques" would be politically and professionally ruinous. But there are steps that thoughtful administrators may implement if they believe that their local situation warrants direct involvement. Ultimately, the decision to become involved in such action is often an administrative one that requires judgment and personal values which do not radically differ from those that already characterize the school community.

The Pedagogy of Sex

William Simon and John H. Gagnon

The problems associated with talking about, teaching about, or coping with sexuality are not new to American society, although the extent and intensity of the discussion about them are a relatively recent development. If anything, in terms of the actual cost to individuals, families, communities, and the society at large, we probably manage more adequately today than at any time since the processes of urbanization began to relax the overvalued and overrated controls of small-town morality. We are really closer to controlling VD than we are prepared to admit; knowledge about effective forms of birth control is considerably more widespread than ever before; and, while abortion remains an important problem, we can now begin to see its problematic nature as a result of collective stupidity rather than as the expression of a tragic individual decision. And, perhaps more important than anything else, the belief that sex is a potentially positive, joyous, and enriching experience is no longer the sole possession of an alienated and radical minority.

As part of this wider acceptance of sex as at least a potential good, there exists a demand that some programmatic form of sex education be developed in order to facilitate sexual careers that fulfill this potential. This is an important transition, for much of the earlier concern for sex education focused on the necessary, if unfortunate, aspects of sexuality, treating them as dangerous forces requiring careful control. One often had the sense in sex education classes that the teacher was dealing with the safety precautions normally advanced for handling highly explosive materials.

Some elements of this style remain part of the motivation for the growing interest in sex education, but few people take seriously the assumptions that sex education will lower rates of illegitimacy, venereal disease, or promiscuity (whatever that might be). Indeed, the disadvantaged and disorganized populations most vulnerable to these problems are precisely those populations in which education as a whole has failed. There is no reason to assume that systems which have virtually failed at every other level will suddenly succeed on that level where there is the smallest accumulation of skill and experience. The more viable assumption behind an interest in sex education is that it should work to make sex a more rewarding part of people's lives—to make sex education serve competence and not necessarily constraint.

Much of the rhetoric aiding and abetting this public and quasi-public interest in sex education is organized around the central image of a current or impending sexual revolution among the young. Since we are unable to assess with accuracy current sexual patterns, making us as a society victim to both anxiety and fantasy, the recent increased capacity for public talk about sex has been quickly translated into intuitions of impending social disaster. This illusion of revolution may be a necessary element in generating progress in this direction; before the conservative resistance to new and expanded programs of sex education can be overcome, we may actually require the effects of a sexual equivalent to Sputnik. The problem is that the usual response to the imagery of crisis tends to produce the most muddled and defensive kinds of thinking. And, as during the Sputnik-provoked crisis in American education, it becomes easy to slip into thinking that increased amounts of education of any kind represents progress. In that defensive posture, we fail to realize that, in the case of sexual behavior, more than not knowing *how* to teach (which was the essential problem in encouraging teaching of the hard sciences), we may not know *what* to teach.

Complicating this picture is the further fact that, unlike many content areas, if the schools do not provide sex education it does not follow that there will be no sex education. On the contrary, sex has special salience particularly from adolescence on, and there has been and there will continue to be sex education among the youthful recruits (*enlistees* may be a more proper term) on the pleasures and risks of sexual experience. In no survey do we currently find schools, parents, physicians, or religious institutions playing a significant role in sex education except for a small minority of cases. Moreover, there is little evidence to suggest that this privileged group make better sexual adjustments as adults, and there is some small evidence that they may actually make poorer adjustments.

In this society, the modal sources of sex information are age-mates who manage to put together odd pieces of information, legend, and first-, second-, and third-hand experience, frequently adding novel or innovative features that are purely consequences of distortions in the rumor process. For a long time to come, no matter what programing innovations are introduced on the school level, it is difficult to conceive of any school program that will be essentially supplemental to this basic source. The continued advantage of peer groups as sources of sex education is that they can do what very few schools can even begin to do—relate sexual learning to sexual experience.

Clearly, the peer group, the school program, and, to a lesser extent, the inadvertencies of mass culture will remain the major sources of learning about sex in our society. The other candidates for this role—

parents and the medical and religious professions—have not only been ineffective in the past but might properly remain so in the future.

The medical profession, fortunately, does not have the time to cope with this kind of program—fortunately, because there is some indication that the medical profession as a whole does not process the necessary information, and often its members are likely to have inappropriate attitudes. The religious organizations that command the affiliation of most of the young have, in one form or other, opted for this role and have been almost universally ineffective. We are tempted again to say "fortunately," because so many of our major religious organizations maintain positions of condemnation of what we know the young have done and will continue to do regardless of what the churches say.

Lastly, there are the parents, whose very concern and anxiety about having some societal agency take over this activity suggest good reason why they, as parents, should not be charged with the responsibility. For parents to take serious responsibility for the sex education of their children—beyond a concern for technical minutiae or behavioral imperatives—would immediately involve having to present a sense of their own sexuality to their children and, at the same time, admit to themselves the sexual nature of their children. We now can conceive of no way in which this can be done without provoking the most profound ambivalences on the part of the child and equally profound anxieties on the part of the parent.

Of the three effective sources—peer groups, schools, and forms of mass culture—the schools, to judge from available data, are the least effective. But they do have the virtue of being the only one of the three that in the immediate future might become the object of self-conscious programing. This is why recent trends toward increasing sex education in the school systems of the nation ought to be encouraged. However, while receiving as much encouragement as possible, it is equally important that such programs be subjected to the most critical scrutiny. This is clearly an area where good intentions are not enough. Too quickly, programs can become the empty rituals that serve to lessen the anxieties of parents and educators (i.e., "something is being done") and, at the same time, only reinforce the adolescents' already well-developed belief in the unhealthy and hypocritical posture of adults toward sex. Sex education as ritual becomes submerged in that rigidified structure known as "school system programing"—a structure that is nearly totally resistant to innovation or even the incorporation of new experience.

This demonstrated rigidity of the schools has provoked radical critics of the current educational process to resist the integration of sex education in the school curriculum. Their resistance derives from issues that transcend the question of sex education itself. With some cause, they suggest that, as a group, our public-school educators tend to be unintelligent and cowardly. The failure of the schools with so many children in so many areas of learning that require far less sensitivity and imagination, these critics contend, raises the question of why we should assume that they will make a meaningful contribution with a topic of this complexity and delicacy. Perhaps to this radical stance one can say no more than that the abandonment of any faith in our collective educational enterprise also implies the abandonment of hope for rationally planning the future.

The important questions in sex education that few have approached directly are: What should be taught? How and when should it be taught? Who should do the teaching? The answers to these substantive questions often reveal a fundamental retreat from many of the more important goals of a meaningful program of sex education. The first major commitment to what should be taught tends to make sex education a study of reproductive biology. The rationale in this focus, not totally unjustifiable, is that the understanding of the biology involved lessens the tendency for the child to become estranged from his or her own body. Too often, however, the desexualization of the experience through the use of a biological imagery, which helps the teacher control his or her own anxieties and also makes the program less politically vulnerable, produces a costly sense of estrangement between the biological events (particularly as they are never experienced) and the emotional and psychological events (which are experienced).

Sex education, as reproductive biology, characteristically centers around a naturalistic but strongly nonhuman imagery. Sex is represented as something so natural that it can barely be linked to the human experience, which is almost by definition unnatural in the sense that it derives its real meaning from an emotional content that is not located in, nor produced by, the biological functions. The most typical imagery is that of the noble sperm heroically swimming upstream to fulfill its destiny by meeting and fertilizing the egg. The sexual act is described in ways that either misrepresent or totally obscure the sources of pleasure and meaning in sex. The end result of this substitution of reproductive biology for sex education was summed up perfectly in the experience of a friend of the authors', a mother of two children. She responded to the question of how babies were made with what sounded like a reasonably accurate description of the internal biological events involved. At the conclusion, her child responded by saying, "Then you've done it twice."

The evidence is quite clear. An amazing number of youngsters and adults in our society have either extremely vague or totally inaccurate ideas of the biological processes salient to the sexual component in their lives. In the name of the ultimate good that should follow from increasing knowledge, it might be well to insure greater access to accurate knowledge of these processes. It is equally clear, however, that few of the problems young people have with managing sexuality (and they may be both numerous and difficult) derive directly from a lack of knowledge about the biological processes involved. The fact that entire societies have survived in ignorance of the technical biological facts is no reason ours should. The fact of their survival, however, suggests a different order of priorities in defining the content of sex education.

The other major content component of standard sex education programs attempts to respond to the undeniable fact that a considerable part of managing sexuality also involves managing social relationships. But, following from our own inability to cope with the fact of the sexual nature of our own children, this component is often transformed into the more desexualized forms of social etiquette. When should boys and girls go steady? When is it proper to engage in petting? Even the masturbatory prohibition tends to appear, not in the moral or physical or mental-health context, but in one of nonsexual social relations: In excess it leads to or encourages social isolation. The language of this approach to sex education eliminates any sense of a phenomenological feeling; the student is once again made aware of the fact that he is alone —or almost alone—in a series of important and dramatic experiences.

It would be naïve to think it possible, or even desirable, given the nature of the schools, to create situations where students can openly talk about their own sexual experiences or feelings. This, for better or worse, is something we may have to leave to the peer group. Between these two extremes, however, we should be able to find some way of programing content in sex education that allows the adult world to appear not as if it were determined to remain oblivious to or ignorant of what is being experienced by the young. We should not, for example, go on pretending an adolescent boy of fourteen is Andy Hardy with *all* sexual discoveries still ahead of him, when we can safely assume he is engaging in masturbatory behavior accompanied by a fairly rich fantasy life with considerable frequency. Of course, we can continue the pretense, but our discussions will have little relevance to the reality of his sexual experiences.

In essence, then, the content of sex education too often represents sex as something that merely is or something that merely happens. It is almost never presented as something that is experienced, as something that is thought about. We leave to the mass media, whose representation of the sexual experience is least trustworthy, the task of providing the young with an imagery not at all correlated with how they will experience their own sexual selves—that is, in terms of fear, passion, pleasure, and pain. The possible correlation between mass-media representations of sexual activity and what sexual activity turns out to be is, of course, not accidental; much of the training in how to be sexual derives from this very source.

Perhaps all we are trying to argue for is that between the exaggerated and frequently self-frustrating training provided by the mass media, and the overly bland "sex is fun (in its time and place) because it is the healthy way" that marks school sex education programs in the few places they can be found, there must be other, realistic alternatives. There ought to be some way of allowing young people (and perhaps adults) a meaningful exposure to a realistic objectification of the range of behavior into which their own experiences and those of their peers, as well as those of the larger world around them, will fall.

This indication of the need for sex education content that substantively allows for the approximately honest representation of the sexual experience clearly takes us into the realm of the utopian. After all, we rarely offer students an approximately honest representation of how we run our political or economic affairs, which on the surface, at least, appear less emotionally charged. It must also be remembered, however, that the young are more likely to experience an earlier confrontation with our collective dishonesty on the sexual level than they are on the more remote levels of politics and economics. But, once again, the guiding principle on this question might be: To be overly realistic is to leave the future to chance.

The "who," "how," and "when" questions of sex education are in one sense not as important as the content question. That is, settling for something less than a substantively honest program linked to what young people are experiencing makes of these questions interesting political problems, but they lose meaning as educational problems. This is simply because, without the content related to experience, sex education really will not make any significant difference.

To be sure, with a competent, sensitive teacher, student levels of anxiety about sex may decrease a measurable amount; an untalented teacher may needlessly increase fears. But there is little indication that either will have a powerful effect on ultimate sexual adjustments. Almost all males grew up with the gym teacher's standard anti-masturbatory plea, made in the name of sanity and good health. Few were seriously deterred for more than a week by those remarks. Positive or enlightened teachers of sex education (of the reproductive-biology and social-etiquette variety) are likely to be even less effective merely because they will be less salient to actual experience. One reason, however, that even inadequate improvement in the character of sex education programs ought universally to be encouraged is that, while the programs may continue to fail to help most young people to manage their own sexuality and move toward some kind of sexual maturity, they may encourage those who have eluded difficulty to be less punishing to that minority of the young who fall into serious sexual troubles.

Once we have a commitment of a broad and honest content in these programs, the "who," "how," and "when" questions become of major importance. Lecturing, as the authors do, to fairly wide ranges of audiences, we have become very much aware that a great deal of the positive effect that follows an exposure to information about sex has a great deal to do with the style in which it is presented. That sex can be talked about, not clinically, but casually and nonjudgmentally, appears to be the significant factor. Nonjudgmental talk about sex does not mean that widely held negative social attitudes about sexual behavior are ignored, nor that the legal proscriptions against certain forms of sexual activity are played down. What other people have done, how they have felt about their own sexual activities, and the disjuncture between what people do and what people will say they do, are all appropriate topics of discussion. The obvious connection between sex and what is considered to be moral behavior must come up as well; however, as part of the "how" there should be no attempt to convert the situation into one of character-building. The information has to be presented in a situation where the recipient does not feel that it is being provided for a predetermined "good" purpose, but rather, as an attempt to spell out the options that are available to him and the risks and joys that are the likely consequences of his choice.

The "who" answer is derived from the "how" answer; that is, the person will be someone, regardless of professional status, who feels comfortable with young people and whose own burden of guilt about his sexual feelings is sufficiently low that he can talk in the service of the children's needs rather than in the service of his own. What one does not need is the aimless masochism that produces an attitude that the kids are all really right in their criticism of adult hypocrisy, or the directive sadism that seeks to create a copy of the adults' image of the sexually free or the sexually moral.

The "when" question has this simple and impossible answer: When life, either through patterned process or sheer accident, compels the boy or girl to ask the question. The school should be able to do what the peer group can do: talk about something when there is need to talk about it. If the information comes too soon, the content is either meaningless or anxiety-provoking. When it comes too late, it can be of only limited significance. One of the real marks of the failure of many currently operating programs of sex education is that students more often than not report that they didn't learn anything they didn't already know and, moreover, that it was less than what they already knew.

Such answers as these to the "how," "who," and "when" questions may be more utopian than our answers to the content question. Unless there is a change in American school systems more radical than anyone is predicting, the chances of finding a system with a capacity for flexibility and a climate of genuine mutual trust are far less than the chances of finding a school system with a capacity for telling its students the truth about sex. If we become capable of telling the truth, no matter when or how, we are ahead of the game; if we become able to tell the truth without judging, when the child needs the information and in a way that ties to his daily experience, then there is the opportunity for changing human sensibility.

Finally, real progress on any of these levels will continue to suffer, simply because we really don't know a great deal about sex, particularly about sex as it falls into the normal or modal ranges. We talk a great deal, but our talk is based on very little information. We understand little of how a commitment to sexuality develops and the role it plays in general personality development. We may know more than any previous society about who does what to whom and how often. But we know little of the role it plays in organizing a life where, even under the best of circumstances, sex tends to play a minor role. In many ways, the resistance to systematic research in the sexual area is greater than the resistance to sex education, which is possibly defined as less threatening or less subversive. Indeed, what may produce the bankruptcy of the sex education movement is that, even among the advance guard, there is a tendency to believe that education without knowledge is possible.

It's a Long Way from the Birds and Bees

William Barry Furlong

If men and women are to understand each other, to enter into each other's nature with mutual sympathy, and to become capable of genuine comradeship, the foundation must be laid in youth.
—HAVELOCK ELLIS, "The Task of Social Hygiene."

Just how they are to build that foundation, particularly as it applies to sex, is the question now being raised in New York City, which this fall [1967] is to embark on a pioneer program of sex education in fourteen schools covering grades five through eight. Like many other cities across the nation which are now starting similar programs, New York must confront the problems of when to introduce the courses, how, what they are to contain, and how they are to be taught.

One model for the New York experiment is the system of School District 65 in Cook County, Illinois, which has perhaps the most prominent sex education program in the nation. The district has had a formal program in all its grade schools for ten years and an informal program in certain grade schools for fifteen years. The district embraces sixteen grade schools and four junior high schools, most of them in Evanston, Illinois, the suburb that borders Chicago on the north. Evanston is a large town—its population in the 1960 census was 79,283—with a full spectrum of ethnic and economic groups. Today there are 10,892 children enrolled in the schools of District 65, who, along with an estimated 93,000 previous children, have been exposed to the "family living" courses—i.e., sex education—of the district.

The program embraces all grades from kindergarten through eighth grade. But the first explicit exploration of sex in humans takes place in the fifth grade. At this age, around their tenth birthday, children regard factually many details which adults and adolescents regard emotionally. Their view is indomitably—and delightfully—that of children. Consider, for example, the give-and-take in a fifth-grade classroom at College Hill School in Skokie, just west of Evanston, during a review of the unit on "reproduction" early in May.

The class was made up of thirteen girls and nine boys. On the walls were charts showing the female reproductive system, with the vagina,

47

the ovaries, the Fallopian tubes, and all other parts labeled. In the back of the room was a glass cage containing infant grasshoppers, so small as all but to escape detection. "We caught some adult grasshoppers out on the lawn last fall and watched them mate and lay their eggs," said the boy running the project. "Then we watched the nymphs born and we watched them grow, and pretty soon they got old enough so we could watch *them* mate and lay their eggs." He paused and considered a tiny grasshopper crawling around the sides of the cage. "We're in our third generation now," he said.

On top of each desk was a mimeographed sheet of paper marked "Reproduction." It contained six drawings showing the movement of the ovum into the womb, being joined along the way by the sperm, becoming attached to the womb as the fertilized egg, and finally growing into a fetus four months old. ("Remember," says the teacher, "it's an embryo until it's two months old and then it becomes what we call a 'fetus.' ") Below the drawings were "Facts to Remember": "Life begins when a sperm cell and an ovum (egg cell) unite. . . ."

At the blackboard, two youngsters were discussing what happens when a female egg is fertilized and when it isn't. Jane was beginning to explain menstruation: "Every month the egg comes up the Fallopian tubes and passes into the uterus and the body sends out a chemical signal that fertilization can take place." Jeffrey indicated the chart with a pointer and commented, "Now if any sperm meets the ovum and enters the egg, fertilization takes place." If it doesn't, he went on, eventually "some blood passes out of the vagina and this is called menstruation."

One youngster named Ronnie had a question—a question that bothers many young people studying reproduction: "If there are hundreds and hundreds of sperm cells flowing up the vagina, how come only one combines with the ovum? What happens to the rest of them?" (Later a teacher explained to me that "somehow boys are bothered that the sperm might die in the female body. And the girls are concerned that the sperm stays alive and may fertilize the ovum weeks or months or even a year later.") In its groping way, the class discussed the probabilities of more than one fertilization by more than one sperm.

Ronnie was not easily convinced about what happened to the rest of the sperm. "They come up there pretty fast and one goes one way and another goes another way"—he was waving his arms to show the direction and velocity of the sperm—"and then ba*loom!* They hit something! Why doesn't more than one of them get into an egg?" He sat back, as if exhausted by his dissertation. The class fell into a discussion of what happens when there is a combination of more than one sperm cell with a female cell or cells—"What's the difference between identical and fraternal twins, class?"—but this didn't satisfy Ronnie. He envisioned a situation where "hundreds and hundreds" of sperm cells go roaring up the vagina—perhaps a little like thoroughbreds breaking for the first turn—and encounter several ova all at one time and then—ba*loom!* Instant pandemonium. Babies all over the place. Terrible overpopulation! Schools too crowded for fifth-graders! It was a delicious concept and he pondered it with great solemnity.

The class moved into a discussion of why the fetus rests in a bag of water within the uterus. "Many mothers enjoy sports—they like to bowl or play tennis or play golf—and if the fetus didn't have the bag of water to cushion him, it'd get pretty banged around," said the teacher. This stimulated the imagination of a boy named Barry, who immediately wondered out loud: "What if the bag of water breaks and the mother doesn't know it and she does something strenuous like falling down the stairs or something?" The teacher refrained from insisting that the mother-to-be would certainly know if the bag of water broke accidentally. Instead, he said, "All right, Barry is bringing up an unusual situation. We've got to help bring this baby safely into the world." Gradually, the discussion came to a point of agreement, perhaps only a little overoptimistic: it would be very unlikely for the bag of water to break much before the time of birth was near.

"But what if it breaks when she's on her way to the pediatrician?" asked Barry.

Jane: "Why, then she'd probably have a natural birth right there in the car."

Teacher: "That's right. Next time you ride in a cab, why not ask the cabdriver if he's ever helped deliver a baby?"

Barry: "But what if she isn't taking a cab? What if she's driving alone?"

Donna: "She'd never start out alone. She'd call her husband for help."

Barry: "What if he isn't at home? What if she can't reach him?"

At this point it was clear that Barry was less interested in sex than in the situation. He was going to make his point no matter what the explanation. One of the girls, Paula, was a little exasperated. "I don't know why the boys are worried about this," she said. "Nothing's going to happen to *them*. It's all going to happen to us."

This was the signal for the teacher to make one of the enduring points of the family living program: that both parents are deeply involved in the process and the result of reproduction—that the father is as deeply concerned over the welfare of the baby as the mother. The whole tone of the course, over all eight grades and kindergarten, is that reproduction involves the whole family and that it takes place ideally within the context of the family.

The program in District 65 got its start on an informal basis in 1950, when the nurse at the Willard and the Lincolnwood schools, Mrs. Margaret Rognstad, asked the Association for Family Living to aid her in finding a way to help the children in her jurisdiction cope with their awareness of sex. The association sent a pioneer in the field of sex education, Mrs. Sara Barth Loeb, to discuss the matter with the parents of children in the two schools and to set up a series of possible lectures. Gradually there evolved a pilot program in sex education, which was then brought to the attention of parents of children in other schools, and soon they were clamoring for committees to be set up and discussions to be held with the clergy, with medical groups, with the teachers. It was five years before a cohesive program was introduced formally into the curriculum, and in those five years every aspect of the problem was examined and re-examined. Here, for instance, are just some of the problems that must be faced in any such program.

The moral fears of some parents. To many people, the mere suggestion that sex be taught in the schools is a reflection of the declining morality of the nation. They see the proposal as being destructive of "our nation's youth" and are loath to allow their children to be exposed.

A poor understanding of what is taught. To many people, "sex education" means only demonstrations and illustrations of the reproductive act—or as one fifth-grader in District 65 described it, "sexual intercords." In Evanston, however, it involves a broad spectrum of sex-oriented matters, from the structure of family life to care of an infant to menstruation, masturbation, venereal disease, and homosexuality.

A conviction that the family has primary responsibility for sex education. Even the most ardent advocates of sex education in the schools agree. "We are only partners with the family in bringing an understanding of sex to the children," one Evanston schoolteacher told me. But few families are equipped to bring all the details of sex to their children. "What makes people think that parents are better equipped to teach the reproductive system than any other system of the body?" asks one teacher. "Doesn't it make as much sense to say that the muscular and skeletal systems should be taught in the home?" Moreover, relatively few parents appear to carry through on their responsibility. Surveys have shown that 82 percent of the nation's children get their knowledge of sex outside of the home.

Many educators see sex education as a profound and historical family function; if it is transferred to the school system, then it seems inevitable that other, lesser responsibilities will eventually be transferred to the schools—along with complaints over the cost of providing increased services in them. On the other hand, some educators can see a clear benefit to society in developing in the young a thorough and wholesome understanding of sex. For though children may never grow up to be historians or mathematicians or scientists—even if they are taught history and math and science—they will most certainly grow up to be sexual beings, even if they are taught nothing about sex.

Parents belong to a generation that by and large regards public discussion of sex with a certain puritanism. Even Loy Landers, principal of the Miller School in Evanston, was "dead-set against" the family living program when it was first introduced into the curriculum: "I come from a background where you just didn't talk about sex in public, much less with children. It was considered very undignified for a pregnant woman even to be out in public." The depth of the Puritan ethic suggested caution.

Ultimately it was decided in Evanston that all films and material on sex education would be previewed annually by the parents of the children in those grades where instruction became most explicit—the fifth, seventh and eighth grades, as it developed. Some principals went a step farther and provided lectures for parents by experts from the Association for Family Living, and some even drew up vocabulary lists for parents, just to make communication with the youngsters a little easier—or to ease the shock if a ten-year-old girl happened to remark at dinner, "Well, we had a good time discussing the penis in school today." In any case, any parent who wanted to withdraw his child from these classes could do so by writing a note to the principal. Astonishingly few have done so in the last ten years. "They accept it as part of the curriculum," says Landers—and, now, so does he.

Another decision District 65 made at the start was not to rely on outside experts, such as doctors, to provide the instruction. "Why bring in a specialist to discuss the reproductive system, as if normal people don't understand it?" asks one teacher. The whole classroom emphasis was to be on the normality of reproduction. "By bringing in an outsider, we'd be making it look like a 'big deal,' " says the teacher.

That still left the problem of finding teachers who could handle the subject. A decision was made not to bar anyone because of sex or marital status; the basic qualification would be the teacher's ability to communicate with the younger generation, to stimulate an honest dialogue. "You have to inspire them with a willingness to ask you questions they wouldn't ask their parents," says Robert Biddick, an Evanston teacher who has taught the subject to fifth-, seventh-, and eighth-graders. He points out that the teacher must be able to use the vocabulary of sex as unselfconsciously as a fifth-grader. "If she can't say words like *penis* and *vagina* as easily as *chalk* and *blackboard,* then she's going to be in trouble talking to our fifth-graders," he says. He also considers it imperative that the teacher think as the child thinks, not as a parent thinks. "If a girl asks, 'How can you tell if you're pregnant?' the parent immediately asks, 'Why do you want to know?' " says Biddick. "But the teacher must answer the question factually and clearly—that there is a change in the menstrual period, that there may be a change in the breasts, perhaps a change in the feeling in the uterus."

Even teachers who can handle all this may find the prospect unnerving. "I was scared stiff at the thought of teaching this unit," says Jerry Abern of the Miller School, who switched from teaching sixth grade to teaching fifth grade last September. "I thought that the kids would react all wrong, that we'd have chaos in the classroom." Instead, he found it astonishingly easy to handle the course. "The only people who really worry about this are the parents and the teachers," he says. "The kids take it all in stride."

The curriculum of the Evanston program focuses on family living, not on sex, through all the grades, not just one. It moves deliberately from the individual to his expanding world: in kindergarten and first grade, the child learns about his own body and how to care for it, and how his family helps him care for it. As he grows older, he is taught about the growing things all around him and learns how they all must satisfy certain basic needs to survive—food, rest, protection from danger, reproduction. He learns how and why animals and birds gather in families in response to those needs, each with a father to hunt for food and a mother to care for the children; thus he is made aware of the importance of his own family. Bit by bit, his scope is enlarged to embrace people outside his family, how they relate to each other, how they are alike in their basic needs and rights.

Throughout, the children are encouraged to talk about new babies in their homes, and the birth and care of family pets. They are also encouraged to become absorbed in classroom projects. In kindergarten, the girls sometimes build dollhouses in the back of the classroom, by way of expressing their own familial needs. In second grade one year, a teacher soaked lima beans to illustrate the embryo stage of the birth of a plant, then her students planted the beans and watched them grow and flower. In a third-grade class, chicken eggs were used to demonstrate the growth of the embryo, with the youngsters caring for the eggs themselves until the eggs were ready to hatch in a small incubator.

In all discussions, the vocabulary of reproduction is precise, not coy. The male cell that fertilizes the female cell is *sperm*, the fetus is carried by the human mother in the *uterus* or *womb*, not in the "tummy." The idea is to have the children learn the correct words as part of the tools of living—and in the classroom, before they learn the obscenity or vulgarism in the streets and alleys. There is never any hushed, embarrassed sidestepping of the biological aspects of sex. The hope is to give the child a "wholesome sense of the wonder of it all," says Miss Irma

Fricke, chief nurse for the district—to endow the subject with "a sense of dignity," to invest the child with a sense of security, "a knowledge that he can come to a wholesome and reliable source for his information."

The result in the lower grades—long before the instruction gets explicit—is sometimes startling. At a forum of the National Congress of Parents and Teachers in Chicago early in May, second-graders from a school in Evanston discussed candidly their awareness of the facts of reproduction. What a hen needs to have an egg, said one child, is a rooster. It takes nine months, said another child, for a new baby to arrive at her home. Still others explained that babies grow in their mother's womb "until they come through a special tube that stretches." One reported that inside his mother he breathed with his belly button. ("Yes," said the teacher. "We call that the navel.")

In the fourth grade, a child in District 65 embarks on the study of the various systems of the human body—the eyes and ears, the muscular system and the skeletal system; in the fifth grade, he studies the circulatory system, the digestive system, and the reproductive system. Thus the reproductive system comes up as a natural progression in the study of the body. "I really think we get more of an emotional reaction to the unit on the digestive system than we do to that on the reproductive system," says Catherine Mantonya, a fifth-grade teacher at Dawes School. "You can understand that talking about bowel movements and urination may arouse some reaction in the children."

The choice of fifth grade for tackling the more detailed aspects of reproduction was not a casual one. "In fifth grade," says Miss Fricke, "the child is about to enter puberty, but he does not yet have any emotional involvement with his body or with this subject." Besides, "the fifth-grader is a factualist, a realist," says Dr. William T. Nichols, principle of Dawes School. Not only is he highly objective in his approach to this subject, he instinctively filters out whatever he really isn't ready for. "Every one of these kids has a different receiving set," said one teacher. "When they're not ready to absorb something, they just tune it out altogether." But rarely is there a lack of interest in reproduction. "The only trouble we really have is bringing the classroom discussions to a close."

As a general policy, District 65 wants to keep open the lines of communication between parent and child, so it insists that all schools hold at least a one-night seminar for parents of fifth-graders. "We want to draw the parents into the dialogue," says Miss Fricke. "If a child goes home and says, 'We saw a film on menstruation today,' we want the parents to be in a position to say, 'Yes, we saw that film, too. What did you think of the way they showed how the body grows and develops?' " If the parent hasn't seen the film, then he doesn't have much common ground for a conversation. And if the child senses this is something the parents aren't going to talk about, then he "isn't going to stick his neck out asking questions."

The involvement of the fifth-grade children in the unit on reproduction is done with great ease. In the class on science, they are typically involved in a study of cells and how cells divide and reproduce.

The different types of cells and their makeup are studied. ("Cells are made up of a jelly-like substance called protoplasm," the curriculum guide says.) From here, it is only a short step to a discussion of how cells contribute to the reproduction of human life. ("Two special kinds of cells are needed to start the life of a human being." One is "an egg cell from the mother" that is "round like a ball and has a very thin wall," is "very small, no bigger than a pinpoint," and "contains twenty-three chromosomes, only half the usual number." The other is "a sperm cell from the father" that is "long and slender, somewhat larger at one end," is "smaller than the female egg cell" and "also contains only twenty-three chromosomes.") Thus the wonder of logic: "When an egg cell from the female and a sperm cell unite into a single cell, it is complete with forty-six chromosomes and life begins." It's a long way from the birds and bees.

At about this stage, the children are shown a series of films and filmstrips on human growth, sometimes in separate groups (a film on menstruation is usually shown only to girls). They are immensely helpful but they sometimes create problems.

In a film shown to boys only, for example, the narrator on a synchronized record goes through a fluent discussion of everything from growth to glands, from acne to whiskers to the male reproductive organ. Then the voice says, "Now the projector will be turned off while I talk to you a few minutes about the way to take care of yourselves." The voice goes on—in the darkened room—to talk about masturbation. The voice also talks about homosexuals: "They are not behaving in a normal and decent way and you must avoid them."

This segment has provoked objections based on everything from the "emphasis" on religion to the "emphasis" on guilt to the psychological effect of discussing these matters in the dark. Some teachers respond to the objections by lifting the needle from the record and going on to the next section on the filmstrip. Others wait till the end and then turn on the lights and immediately return to masturbation and homosexuality so that they can be discussed in a lighted room.

In any case, the filmstrips are quickly supplemented by classroom discussions of great candor. The techniques vary from teacher to teacher and sometimes from year to year. "It depends on the maturity of the class—their potential interest in the subject matter," says one teacher.

The classroom discussions, unlike some of the film shows, are always coeducational; to separate the children at this stage would make the subject seem like too much of a "big deal." The children rarely snicker or giggle over the subject matter; only an outsider would do that. "We don't have giggling or snickering when discussing the eyes and ears," says Miss Fricke. "There's no reason to snicker or giggle over another system of the body just because it involves reproduction."

Despite the emphasis on reproduction within the family, the question of birth outside of marriage comes up regularly. "And you must answer it truthfully," says teacher Bob Biddick. But he tends to temper his answer with an observation along the lines of: "All these years you've been learning how the family provides the basic needs of the baby for life, and what a great responsibility it is. Think how much more difficult it would be if you had to raise the baby alone." Even as fifth-graders, the children are aware of severe adult disapproval of birth or intercourse outside of marriage—but they are aware of it with the perspective of a child. Consider the question of one boy that invariably mystifies some adults: "If our parents do it, and the police do it, then why do they get mad if we do it?" What, asks the adult, do the police have to do with it? To the child, the inclusion is natural; from his perspective, the police and his parents are the mightiest symbols of discipline and disapproval.

Where adults instinctively focus their greatest interest on "sexual intercords," fifth-graders rarely do. Their questions concern other urgencies: "How does the baby go to the bathroom when he is in the mother?" "If the sperm cells die, does the man die?" "Do girls have wet dreams?" Children are peculiarly interested in fertility, in multiple births, and in the grotesque accidents of reproduction ("Why are some children born without hands and feet?" is a common question). In a sense, these interests are natural. "They are all interests stimulated by mass media—by what they see on TV and in the newspapers," says Ernest Roehrborn, a fifth-grade teacher at College Hill School. " 'The Pill,' contraception, the birth of quadruplets or quintuplets, even how measles affects the fetus now that they're talking about a vaccine—all this information is in the hands of children long before the parents realize it."

When questions about the details of intercourse come up, most teachers handle them smoothly enough by explaining: "You studied a lot of mathematics before you studied long division. That was because you couldn't understand all about long division when you were younger. It's the same way with reproduction—you'll learn some of it now, but there's always something that you won't really understand until you're older. And that's when you'll study it."

The handling had better be smooth and free of adult cant. "These kids'll spot a phony easily and they're pretty rough on a phony at that age," says Biddick. If they sense that the teacher is being a phony in her approach to the subject, they'll keep boring in until they nail her with a question that they know will infuriate or humiliate her. He cites this as the type of boring-in they'll engage in:

Q. How are the eggs fertilized?
A. By uniting with the sperm.
Q. But how did the sperm get there?
A. It moved up the vagina until it united with the female egg.
Q. But how did the sperm get into the vagina in the first place?
A. It was deposited there by the penis.
Q. But how did the penis get there?

"And now," says Biddick with a smile, "he's got you right where he wants you. If you were embarrassed or holding back at the start, there's no way you can go on answering his questions without getting more and more embarrassed."

Nobody knows how effective the family living course of District 65 is. "We have no objective data that say what the program has accomplished," says Ernest Roehrborn. Many parents, particularly in areas which don't have a sex education program, insist that the standard is in how much unwanted pregnancies are reduced among high-school girls. But this insistence reflects the fears, the tones, the attitudes, of the parents toward sex, not what a sex education program can accomplish. At best the school can only fill the child with the facts of reproduction, give him the perspective of the need for a family in reproduction, and inspire him with a sense of wonder at the miracle of his own sexuality. (In any case, using the test of unwanted pregnancies would reflect largely what has been learned about contraception, not about reproduction.)

The ultimate measure is intangible. How many of the children of District 65 can adjust more serenely to the difficulties of adolescence? How many will enjoy a more satisfying and fulfilling sex life as adults? How many will be able to discuss the facts of reproduction with *their* children? Even now, there may be a benefit to the parents of today's youngsters, who are made more secure in the knowledge that their children are gathering their sex information from a wholesome, reliable source—the school, instead of the streets.

For their part, the teachers of District 65 harbor few doubts about the program. One teacher has described it as the most important subject taught anywhere in the school system. Others accept it with a sense of humor and delight. "Every once in a while," one teacher told me, "somebody likes to needle you, to make you feel a little odd because you talk about sex to children. They always ask me when I'm going to give up this sex bit.

"I always tell them that I'll give it up when it isn't fun any more."

Putting the Sex Back into Sex Education

Michael Scriven

Sex education so far has usually been a half-hearted venture into the physiology of reproduction, with some vague remarks about dating behavior. It is perfectly clear that this is better than nothing; indeed, the first part of it is absolutely essential: but it's pathetically inadequate.

In the army and in very enlightened school systems they toss in something about contraceptives and venereal disease; in college something about Freud; and at home something about homemaking. Attempts have been made to develop courses which go beyond this, but they have not so far had a significant effect. For general ineffectiveness I'd say they were on a par with most citizenship training programs. I think we can do better than this, and I have some suggestions about what we can do.

PHILOSOPHY AND PRACTICE

To begin with, a point emerged at the [1967] Notre Dame conference on "The Role of Women Today" that impressed me as particularly important for this topic. This was that most of the apparent solutions to the problem of a life style (or role, or identity) for women are very insubstantial upon examination or trial. I think Edgar Berman (among others) was right to stress that contraceptive emancipation is not a magic wand that breaks the iron bonds on women. The contraceptive provides the *opportunity* for women to liberate themselves from *one* kind of restraint that impedes the development of *one* kind of life for them. On the other hand, having children is not a restraint, but rather the *goal* of another life style for women; and indeed within one woman's life it can change from being a goal to being an impediment as her family size becomes adequate to her needs. There's no way of escaping the basic problem of discovering or creating individual roles in life, which involves thinking about our own talents and preferences as well as the aims of man, the extent of his responsibility for his fate, and the foundations for his moral imperatives. In short, philosophy. (There's nothing quite so necessary as the discovery that one's profession is indispensable to the salvation of mankind, or even womankind.) The search for the female role or identity is not separable from the search for our place in the universe. But we can be more helpful than that: we can exhibit, in three

59

dimensions and not just in abstract terms, a full range of alternative actual life styles for women and for men. We can present, not just in those profusely illustrated guidance manuals, but on video tapes, film, and sound tape, the torments and stresses of the sexes' roles and relationships, and the many ways these can—by some people—be handled.

It seems a little unfortunate that *Peyton Place* should be the most realistic education vehicle of this kind in the adolescent life space. The resources of drama and film, especially in the form of novels and television designed and discussed from this point of view, are almost totally unexploited in the service of serious education about sex roles, and it is not too surprising to find that marriage counselors identify role conflicts as one of the significant causes of marital failure. We would do well to extend this attempt at serious role analysis and the creation of role possibilities to other careers besides marriage, but to avoid it in that instance, or to rely on the sloganized folk wisdom of schoolteachers rationalizing their own spinsterhood *or* motherhood, is to encourage disaster. As well discard what we know of medicine in favor of herbal remedies.

It might be countered that we are still very ignorant about the "right" role relations in marriage. In my view that is no sign of ignorance, since there probably is no such thing as the right role relations. But even if we believe there may be, it is disgusting to conceal a decent, well-founded ignorance when this is to allow conflicting dogmas to take over. An appropriate skepticism is one of the most valuable products of education, and it has the particular merit of permissiveness about idiosyncratic variations in this rigidity-ridden area. Enough has been written about the guilt of husband-cooks in this society, or about "the missionary position," to provide a host of fascinating illustrations.

This aspect of sex education should not, however, be confined to the profession of ignorance where ignorance is bliss. There is less cheering news to impart than that. We know a great deal about the range of disasters that can occur in the sexual life of the citizenry, whether marriage-connected or not, and an introduction to the calm discussion of these would be a valuable educational contribution. (Analogously, it would do a great deal for the basic course in school biology if it were oriented toward serious practical medicine, to say nothing of what it could do for national health.)

There's an ideology of the bland that stands opposed to this on the ground that one shouldn't burden the young mind with such horrors. Talking about sexual impotence and frigidity, it is argued, may not only take the bloom off the youthful dream, but induce the very phenomena discussed. This ideology would have us avoid discussion of the real problems of democracy on the grounds that it is unhealthy to have children concern themselves with "bad things." As a result, many "problems of democracy" courses become bland civics or international relations or introductory economics. The ideal of citizenship education deteriorates into education for a fantasy world. Reality arrives and the student is traumatized or retreats to the infantile level of projecting his crudest emotional reaction. Listening to the bourgeois reactions to the hippies or to the use of marijuana or to the death penalty or to "socialized medicine" is listening to tribesmen, not educated people. The same is particularly true in the area of sex, despite the impact of Kinsey and Hefner. That an entomologist and a magazine publisher should have been the major *beneficial* educative influences in this field is as incontrovertible as it is despicable. The realistic approach to sexual behavior needs only the defense of being realistic. Idealism is excellent icing on the cake but ridiculous without the cake. Those that think the implicit Hefner ideal is wrong should say why, produce a better one, and argue for that; but few, if any, of those who sneer or snort are equal to the task. Meanwhile a generation is acquiring the vote that just might get the forty-nine states besides Illinois to adopt a penal code that approximates sanity about sex. But without something more sensible inside the schools that outcome is uncertain. Certainly many millions of marriages and monastic lives will be founded on ignorance or misplaced guilt and will founder for that reason.

One often hears the argument that the best form of education about marriage is a good example of it. What an absurdity! Children do not learn to swim by living with those who can but don't have to, or those who have never had the need. Seeing a trained mathematician solve a problem at sight gives you no inkling how you can acquire this capacity. The analysis of case studies of marriage failure and techniques for handling its problems is the realistic approach. We may certainly supplement it with shining examples of successful marriage, for inspirational purposes at least. But the only child of the only totally unblemished marriage I know personally is in psychotherapy because of inability to handle other sex relationships.

So far I have been stressing two points: that the philosophy of life behind various conceptions of sex roles is very poorly worked out and usually crumbles with a probing question or trying situation, and that the practical side of sex education in the more usual sense has hardly been scratched. I would like to expand on each of these points briefly.

THE PHILOSOPHICAL SIDE

One of the oldest slogans in the sex role discussion is "Equality between the sexes." In this domain, as in discussions of democracy, the philosophical confusions smother the sparks of common sense. At the Notre Dame conference Charles Lecht was condemning any talk about the equality of woman—just as one frequently hears uneducated capitalists with degrees from our best universities, or political columnists with their usual ignorance of political thought, trumpeting their discovery that men are not really equal.

I venture to assert that no one who has ever advocated equality of the sexes was unaware of the basis for the other battle cry, *"Vive la différence!"* Equality in these contexts means equality of *rights,* not of size, skills, or sexual anatomy, and it is a sign of gross ignorance about the basic nature of democracy and morality to suppose the contrary. Equality of rights means equality in the courts of justice and equality of opportunity, in the sense of *the absence of unjustifiable discrimination,* whether racial, religious, or sexual. There are good grounds for sexual discrimination in hiring fashion models, washroom attendants, and topless waitresses, whether or not there are good grounds for the existence of all such occupations. When we come to discrimination based on probability considerations, the justification usually collapses. While it is true that men are usually stronger than women, it won't do to exclude women from applying for jobs where strength is of some importance, unless you can *also* show that the degree of strength required exceeds that of *all* women. A good example of illegitimate discrimination of this kind is the case of airline pilots. Conversely, the general prejudice against men as secretaries and nurses is in the category of those against women as doctors, lawyers, and architects. There is an intermediate area where a preference exists and no great harm results from accepting it; for example, some restaurants and customers prefer waiters to waitresses, and the same applies to receptionists and airline hostesses. (But the preference for *white* airline hostesses is neither universal nor non-punitive nor compensated by correlative openings.) The courts are currently involved in this area, and the matter has been complicated since the executive branch has muddleheadedly interpreted equality as implying that, for example, "Jobs Available" advertisements may not be divided into "Male" and "Female" sections. From the above argument it should be clear that such a subdivision can be justified both absolutely and for convenience.

The role of the woman as mother has consequences which usefully illustrate and amplify the above distinctions. It is still common for university departments to discriminate against the admission of female graduate students and the employment of female faculty, on the grounds that they will probably get married and terminate their professional training or career thereafter. In the first place, it may well be that this probability is overcome by an increased probability of academic success and stability amongst the females, a distinction known to exist with undergraduates and accentuated by the possibility of the draft later. Until such a case is established there is no way of justifying the discrimination. In the second place, however, it is not clear that a significant difference of this kind is adequate justification unless it can be shown that the department consistently employs all other discriminating characteristics of equal significance that are available to it; for example, it should possibly discriminate against younger candidates and those with strong outside interests or qualifications, as they are more likely to move before completion or substantial contribution.

It might be argued that no probability discrimination is defensible, since the individual is not a mere statistic. Again, if such distinctions *are* allowed, how can one argue, as I did earlier, that it is illegitimate to restrict the selection of cabdrivers or airline pilots to males? The alternative to probability is a virtually random choice amongst all applicants for graduate school admissions, apart from some minimal necessary qualifications such as some coverage of the relevant major field. But the selection of the best-qualified candidates can employ any relevant criterion, probabilistic or not, as long as nothing more reliable is available. It's just crude prejudice to exclude a woman candidate, or downrate her, even if women are usually less competent master chefs than men, when her name is Julia Child or she has other impressive qualifications. The result of this analysis is contrary to liberal intuitions. It may be that in some occupations where a woman meets all absolute requirements for a job and is as good as a male applicant on all the standard skills required, she is weaker on a peripheral skill. In a situation like this, which occurs in the case of cabdriving in many communities, the woman is an inferior candidate. The liberal intuition suggests that, because her sex makes her physically weaker, and because this is only marginally relevant to cabdriving (i.e., it's handy for fighting or deterring a thug), it's unfair discrimination to bypass her. The fallacy in that should be clear: sex differences that actually affect job performance can be considered relevant unless the reason they are relevant is an indefensible and harmful prejudice.

In other circumstances, a principal argument against women is that they may well become mothers and be unable or unwilling to work before or perhaps after that event. This is very like the phenomenon of "overqualification": applicants are frequently refused jobs on the grounds that their qualifications are so good that they will not find the job satisfying and hence either do it poorly in some sense (e.g., by questioning orders that seem pointless) or move on to another quickly. The "discrimination" against the college student who probably only wants short-term employment, until fall classes or until graduation, is a clearer example. In each case, the problem is largely one of intent, and similar problems have been solved in training teachers and paying the passage of European hired staff, by a contract arrangement. A contract to remain in a job, subject to some penalty, and under some supervision from union representatives to exclude discriminatory pressure, is not unworkable. The size of the penalty should be the hidden cost of replacement and retraining, and the company cannot simply apply such contracts to women, since it is a fact that men also leave. A company that made its offers of jobs subject to such a restriction would have a strong incentive to keep the estimates low, since the net wage would otherwise look too small in a competitive market. But it can handle the matter in an actuarially equivalent way by using a sharply graded wage scale or calling it an executive training program—and many do this. So there is little justification for discrimination here. It arises because employers would like to have the best of both worlds and offer large starting wages to those they think are the best bets, in order to get them; but, to compensate, they turn down others who may be really better bets. Not to allow the others the chance to prove this, e.g., by a contractual commitment, is then discriminatory. The matter is thus complex but resolvable.

THE PRACTICAL SIDE

Thus the philosophical theory of equality has some practical consequences, and indeed the practical issues are undecidable to a satisfactory treatment of the philosophical one. The theory of equality is not the only philosophical problem relevent to sex education—I have mentioned others, such as the question whether man has a goal or a maker—but it is, I think, a good example of one kind of omission from what is often thought of as progressive sex education. We now turn to another kind of omission.

Trying to make sex education three-dimensional involves trying to explore the life space of the people who are in conflict with our standard norms. You cannot cover *this* subject without looking at the evidence for our present norms and taboos, and you cannot do that without looking at the forms of behavior which the norms suggest we reject. There are many ways in which this can be done; one of the most remarkable documentary films now available is an interview with a black male prostitute. The thought of the effect of this on ten-year-olds is enough to prostrate most parents, interest some researchers, and bore most ten-year-olds. But the film itself would be most unlikely to bore anyone and rather likely to benefit them. For the destruction of ill-based preconceptions is unfortunately still the main task of sex education. It is to be hoped we can soon proceed beyond this level, which corresponds to teaching science by disproving superstitions. Until the superstitions cease to dominate our thinking, however, little can be done without first undermining them.

I shall take up a rather different example in detail, namely, the discussion of the institution of marriage. This topic can be treated as a sociological or anthropological problem area, a psychological one, a "contemporary social history" one, and in many other serious and trivial ways. I am primarily interested in treating it as a serious intellectual and practical problem for the students themselves. I think it should be obvious that getting across the capacity to think about this area will be facilitated by a teaching methodology which involves a good deal of discussion and background material from literature and social sciences as well as audio-visual resources. My concern is mainly with content, with the ideas that should be presented, identified, and discussed.

The general level of approach in most schools, and for that matter colleges, is simply chickenhearted. It totally fails to prepare the students for precisely those situations which can be handled well only if one is prepared for them. What will the married teen-ager do if her first-born is deformed or mongoloid? What are the arguments for and against abortion as part of a family-limiting procedure, or—on the other hand— as a device for avoiding social stigma? What is it like to have and keep (or not keep) an illegitimate child in various subcultures of this society? Exactly what is known about the effects of premarital continence on the long-run success of a marriage? The answers to these questions should not be restricted to a scientific assessment of the evidence, but should include exciting illustrations of the alternative ways of life involved; enthusiastic advocates of the unwed mother (or father) approach to parenthood should be seen, as well as those who regret their decision. Most of us know personally some representatives from each category, but not many teen-agers do and most of them marry before they do. This is simply bad education. The various mystiques about marriage associated with the approach of certain religions or cultures have quite clearly failed in their own terms, in this society. The usual explanation they provide for this points the finger at the corrupting influence of secular society. A simpler explanation would be that the students are getting too smart for fairy stories, and it's time to replace them. Cultures may need some myths to sustain them, but it has never been demonstrated that ignorance is always an advantage—and ignorance of the alternatives to the present paradoxical institution of marriage is the worst form of premarital ignorance.

Marriage, as it is commonly conceived in the "straight" culture of the Establishment, is an anachronism by not less than half a century and possibly as much as two millenia. One of its main functions is to provide a social device for protecting and educating the young; and as soon as public police and schools became moderately effective, alternatives became feasible. The actual effect of institutionalized marriage on children today is impossible to assess, but it is certainly arguable that it does more harm than good. For every home that lifts a child up there seems to be one that screws him up, and for every child born to good living there are two who are born to starve. The *actual* functions of marriage, e.g., as a device for providing legal sexual gratification, cheap labor, ownership of a desirable piece of property, or improved public relations, not surprisingly interfere with the child-rearing function.

The simplest approach must lay bare the fact that we try to make one institution achieve three aims which all too often lie in perpendicular dimensions. The aims are sexual satisfaction, social security, and sensible spawning. The simplest solution would be to create three types of marriage, arranged so that any combination is possible. We might call these preliminary, personal, and parental marriage. The first would be simply legitimized cohabitation, contractually insulated against escalation into de facto commitment. It would be a prerequisite for other kinds and would impose a period of, say, a year's trial relationship before the possibility of conversion to personal marriage. In the latter arrangement, mutual legal undertakings to support each other *sine die* would be involved. Only in such a case would it be appropriate for one partner to expect the other to abandon education or a career in order to take on partnership-oriented responsibilities like running a house. Divorce would be by consent or suit, and settlements simply aimed at recovering whatever was jointly earned and whatever it takes to establish an individual's independent life. The third possible phase of marriage, parental marriage, would require additional covenants for the support of children, as well as certain prerequisite periods of preliminary and/or personal marriage. Having children prior to parental marriage would be non-binding on either parent for support; in addition, civil penalties might be added, including tax penalty, e.g., by loss of exemptions, wage-garnisheeing to create a trust fund for the child, graded penalties, etc.

The absurdity of a system which provides special tax and draft advantages for parents when this society has no need to increase the population is surely overdue for legal recognition. It might also be appropriate to introduce some penalty-supported limits on family size and tests of parental capacity; e.g., the prospective parents might have to show they can housebreak and obedience-train a puppy without excessive intimidation. The skills involved are mainly those of consistency and self-control, a combination strikingly absent from, and especially needed by, most parents and probably by most people.

Tripartite marriage, with or without the trimmings mentioned, has the simple virtue of enabling people with at least three different needs from heterosexual relationships to see these needs as legitimate in themselves. But there are other needs which call for more flexibility in the institution of marriage, and discussion of them is a good way to get oneself and one's students thinking about the rationale of the whole business.

Why not preliminary and personal marriage between homosexuals? They often have the same needs in these dimensions. What present or possible evidence could show that the society ought to discourage this?

Why not polyandrous and polygamous marriage? How about incestuous marriages? A number of interesting possibilities open up as soon as one begins to question the traditional structure.

The "straight" reaction to such suggestions is the simplest proof of the pathetic failure of education to cover this area. The first three "arguments" produced are usually tawdry rationalizations, or failed attempts at *reductio ad absurdum*. For example: (1) What if *everyone* became homosexual? (2) How could a woman ever feel secure if she knew her husband might ask to bring his secretary home to join the family? (3) If you advocate equality between the sexes, how can you possibly suggest legitimatizing polygamous marriages? These are interesting questions, but no serious threat to the present proposals, which is not to say that Modified Marriage with *all* the trimmings hasn't some difficulties, especially with respect to incest.

But the absurdity of "straight" reactions is chiefly due to the ignorance they display of *reality*, rather than reason. In this culture there already exist (and have for fifty years or more) preliminary and personal and homosexual and polyspouse and incestuous marriage, explicitly recognized as such and frequently with quasi-legal status, e.g., de facto marriage and "mistress-trusts." What is need not be right, but it has to be workable; and polyspouse households, for example, appear from Dr. Bernard's research to have increased seven times faster than the stock model in 1960–66. Now, if it's workable and its practitioners enjoy it, and you don't want your children or your legislators to recognize this, you're going to have to give a good, sound *moral* argument against it. That challenge was picked up by a dozen editorial writers and columnists last winter after the wire-services reported the preceding modest proposals in covering the Notre Dame conference. Their performances will serve as useful material for my logic course this year, but will hardly persuade an undecided but moderately intelligent bystander.

CONCLUSION

I've only picked up two points in any detail at all and I haven't even discussed their relationship. Let me mention some other questions that might be interesting topics in a seminar or classroom or forum devoted to sex education. Is there a *Playboy* attitude, and if so, what's right/ wrong about it? What educational preparation is appropriate for evaluating vasectomy and other quasi-permanent birth control procedures? What shift in responsibility, if any, will occur with the development of (1) retroactive contraceptives, (2) the male pill, (3) Japanese-style abortion? Is there a female "need to be pregnant" that is separable from a need for kids? What is the political consequence of contraceptive- and abortion-supportive legislation on the correlation between family size and voting preferences? Can a call girl find happiness? What is the strength of the complaint that the teacher is, or would be, usurping the parental role as sex educator? What are the root causes of the failure of propaganda to get contraceptives more widely used?

So far this paper has been advocating and putting a rather *philosophical* kind of sex into sex education. This shouldn't be taken to imply that I'm against the participant kind or even that I'm against it in sex education. Nervous "straights" sometimes react to suggestions for beefing up sex education by saying, "The next thing, they'll be bringing prostitutes into the classroom for live demonstrations of sex play." Well, I do think there are some problems with that kind of approach, like establishing professional credentials in order to provide payment under an innovative techniques grant.

Sexuality and Sexual Learning in Childhood

James Elias and Paul Gebhard

The turn of the century saw an awakening interest in sexuality and sexual learning among children. The most significant work of this period was Freud's theory of infantile sexuality, which directed the attention of the world to sexuality in early childhood and its importance for the future adult role. A somewhat neglected work by Moll (1909) was overshadowed by the Freudian wave; but Moll's observations on the sexual life of the child were the first comprehensive writings done in this field. In an earlier study, Bell (1902) examined childhood sexuality through the study of the activities of children.

RESEARCH SINCE 1917

Numerous studies resulted from this increased interest in childhood sexuality. Among them were Blanton (1917), looking at the behavior of the human infant during the first thirty days of life; Hattendorf (1932), dealing with the questions most frequently asked by preschool children; Isaacs (1933), studying the social development of young children; Dudycha (1933), examining recall of preschool experiences; and Campbell (1939), writing on the social-sexual development of children. Conn (1940a, 1940b, 1947, 1948) has done a series of studies dealing with various phases of sexual awareness and sexual curiosity in children. Other important studies were made by Halverson (1940), on penile erection in male infants; Conn and Kanner (1947), on children's awareness of physical sex differences; Katcher (1955), on the discrimination of sex differences by young children; and Ramsey (1950), on preadolescent and adolescent boys. Sears, Maccoby, and Levin (1957) present a discussion of labeling and parental sanctioning of sex behavior, and Bandura and Walters (1959) examine parental response to sex information questions.[1]

Current research has tended to move away from direct studies of infant and childhood sexual behavior. Sexuality has its roots in man's biological makeup, and the development of gender role or sex differences has become one of the main focuses of present research.[2] Since the molding forces, or socializing agents, are the family and the peer group (among others), sexuality is being pursued as a form of social develop-

69

ment. Receiving special emphasis is the development of the male and female roles—for example, the part aggression plays in developing an aggressive adult male sexual role, and the concomitant emphasis on nonaggressiveness in the development of an adequate female role. Other areas of current research are found in the work of John Money and Joan and John Hampson, on the ontogeny of human sexual behavior.[3]

THE KINSEY DATA

This discussion utilizes previously unpublished data from the Institute for Sex Research, taken from case histories of prepubescents interviewed by Alfred Kinsey and his co-workers. These histories are somewhat outdated (before 1955), but the information contained in them provides one of the few sources of actual interview information on prepubescent children. Questions were asked regarding sources of sexual knowledge, extent of knowledge, homosexual and heterosexual prepubertal play, and masturbatory activity, all of crucial importance for any educator, counselor, doctor, or other professional who deals with children. Some of the critical problems encountered in preschool counseling find their source in the sexual area. Educators recognize that differences between males and females, ethnic groups, and socioeconomic status groups are essential for an understanding of the attitudinal and behavioral patterns that children exhibit. Adequate sexual adjustment in early childhood is a prime factor in later adult sexual adjustment, as healthy attitudes toward self and sexuality are the foundations of adult adjustment.

Partly through necessity, many school systems are presently moving into education programs with a maximum of speed and often a minimum of preparation regarding the specific needs of the population the particular program is to serve. Sex research can offer some aid to the educational community by providing information about critical factors in the lives of children and how these factors affect later adjustment.

THE SAMPLE

The sample consists of 432 prepubescent white boys and girls ranging in age from four to fourteen.[4] There are 305 boys and 127 girls in the study, and they are grouped by occupational class (social class) and age.[5] The occupational classifications originally used in the work at the Institute for Sex Research have been combined in order to increase the number of cases and to provide social-class categories. The occupational classifications consist of: (1) unskilled workers, who are labeled as lower blue-collar; (2) semi-skilled and skilled workers, who comprise the upper blue-collar; (3) lower white-collar workers; and (4) business and professional men, here termed upper white-collar. A mean age is given for the children in each social class to make explicit the unequal age distribution.

The sexual behavior of younger children often lacks the erotic intent attributed to similar adult activities, raising the question, in some cases, of the validity of labeling some childhood activities as sexual. This research does not label childhood behavior as sexual unless it includes one of the following: the self-manipulation of genitalia, the exhibition of genitalia, or the manual or oral exploration of the genitalia of or by other children. Of course, many of these activities could be motivated by mere curiosity concerning a playmate's anatomy.

The term *sex play* as used here includes those heterosexual and homosexual activities involving more than one person which occur before the onset of puberty. Among the males, 52 percent report homosexual prepubertal activity and 34 percent report heterosexual prepubertal activity. These percentages seem accurate when we compare them with the self-reports of adults in the earlier Kinsey volumes. Adult males recalled homosexual experience in their preadolescent period in 48 percent of the cases, just 4 percent less than is reported by these children in their preadolescence.[6] The adult males also indicated that heterosexual preadolescent activity occurred in approximately 40 percent of the cases, but the reports of the children indicate only about 34 percent of prepubescent males engage in heterosexual experiences.[7] However, many of the children in this study have not reached the average age at which these experiences first occur. The average age among males for homosexual play is 9.2 years, and for heterosexual play 8.8 years.

Among female children, 35 percent report homosexual prepubertal sexual activity and 37 percent report heterosexual prepubertal experiences. The incidence of homosexual activity in the females is much less than that reported by males, but is very close to the percentage recalled by adult females in the 1953 Kinsey volume (33 percent). The adult females recalled heterosexual preadolescent activities in 30 percent of the cases, and the reports of the children show 37 percent with such experience.

One of the noteworthy findings coming from this analysis of the case histories of preadolescents is the surprising agreement between prepubertal report and adult recall. Another important finding is the lack of any consistent correlation between sociosexual activity and parental occupational class. The percentages do vary, but in no meaningful way.

MASTURBATION

Masturbation is most often described as self-stimulation leading to sexual arousal and usually to climax or orgasm, accompanied (after puberty) by ejaculation on the part of the male. Some writers prefer to believe that prepubertal children do not masturbate but simply fondle their genitals. These present data concerning prepubertal masturbation are not derived from reported "fondling of the genitals" but rather from deliberate activity done for pleasure and often accompanied by pelvic thrusts against an object (e.g., a bed) or manual manipulation. Sometimes a state of relaxation or satisfaction comparable to the postorgasmic state is achieved; in other instances indisputable orgasm occurs.

More males than females masturbate in childhood, as is the case later in adolescence and adulthood. Among prepubescent males, 56 percent report masturbatory activity, while only 30 percent of the females do so. In comparison, information received from adults in self-reports indicates preadolescent masturbation in 57 percent of the cases. These actual childhood reports are within one percentage point of the recall data from adults as reported in the earlier works.

Looking at age groupings and social class, one finds that the blue-collar classes contain the highest percentages of boys who have masturbated— 60 to 70 percent. The majority of those in the blue-collar and lower white-collar classes who masturbate are in the eight- to ten-year age group. The upper white-collar class has the lowest percentage of those who have masturbated (38 percent), with more beginning in the three- to seven-year age group than at any subsequent time. The mean age for first masturbation is as follows: lower blue-collar, 8.6; upper blue-collar, 8.8; lower white-collar 7.8; and upper white-collar, 6.0. The probable explanation for the lower mean age, lower percentage of those who have masturbated, and lower average age at first masturbation for upper white-collar boys is the fact that their average age at interview is 7.2 years, while the average ages for the boys of other social classes are two to four years older.

Fewer girls tend to masturbate than boys, and only 30 percent of the girls report that they have masturbated. The highest percentage is among the lower blue-collar females (48 percent); the other three classes have lower and quite similar figures (between 25 and 29 percent). The average age of masturbation for girls is lower than that of the boys. By class, it is: lower blue-collar, 7.5; upper blue-collar, 7.4; lower white-collar, 5.7; and upper white-collar, 6.7.

Masturbation has been designated in the past as the prime cause of mental illness, low morals, and stunted growth, among other things. These stigmas are for the most part behind us, but tradition dies slowly and many children are still being told "old wives' tales" concerning the alleged effects of masturbation. This is unfortunate, for in early childhood masturbation might influence the child to accept his body as pleasureful rather than reject it as a source of anxiety. Society has progressed to a point where few parents punish their offspring for masturbating, but it is noteworthy that fewer still encourage it.

SEXUAL KNOWLEDGE

In this study, additional measures are taken of current knowledge while controlling for child's age and occupation of father. The occupational level is dichotomized into lower (blue-collar) and upper (white-collar) classes for purposes of analysis. Presence or absence of knowledge about the following topics is examined: intercourse, pregnancy, fertilization, menstruation, venereal disease, abortion, condoms, and female prostitution. In general, the white-collar class surpasses the blue-collar class in all sex knowledge categories. Of special interest to the educator are some of the differences in learning which occur on the part of the children in these two groups. For example, while 96 percent of the blue-collar boys have an understanding of sexual intercourse by ages thirteen to fourteen, only 4 percent have any knowledge concerning the "coming together of the sperm and the egg"—fertilization. Twenty-seven percent of the upper white-collar group in the same age range understand the concept of fertilization, and this nearly sevenfold difference is indicative of the language level and sources (hence quality) of information for the two groups. Blue-collar boys learn about intercourse, abortion, condoms, and prostitution earlier than do other males, especially by ages eight to ten. These words and activities become a part of the sex education of lower-class boys much earlier than of boys whose fathers are employed in higher-status occupations, as a result of most sex information being provided by peers on the street.

This earlier and more extensive knowledge of coitus is reflected in prepubescent heterosexual activity, wherein nearly three times as many blue-collar boys have, or attempt, coitus than do white-collar boys. Interestingly enough, more blue-collar males know of intercourse than know of pregnancy (except in the four- to seven-year-old group) and just the reverse is true for the white-collar males. The white-collar male surpasses the blue-collar male in sexual knowledge in later age groupings, perhaps indicating that many of the more formal aspects of his sex education come from his mother, with peers "filling in the gaps" concerning some of the more sensitive areas, such as methods of birth control and prostitution.

The pattern for girls stands in marked contrast to that for boys. Prepubescent girls, unlike boys, are not inclined to discuss or joke about sexual matters. Also, the girl eavesdropping on conversation by adult females is less apt to hear of such matters than is the boy listening to adult males. Lastly, there is reason to believe that the lower-class mother is more inhibited about, and less capable of, imparting sex education to her daughter. Consequently, the lower-class girl generally lags behind her upper-class counterpart in sexual information. Thus, for example, in age group eight to ten, not quite half of the lower-class girls know of coitus, whereas close to three-quarters of the upper-class females have this knowledge. The gap is found even with regard to menstruation, a thing sufficiently removed from overt sexual behavior that one would expect it to escape from taboo. On the contrary, at lower social levels, menstruation is often regarded as dirty and somehow shameful. The result is that among the eight- to ten-year-olds roughly a quarter of the lower-class and nearly three-quarters of the upper-class girls possess this inevitable knowledge.

On more technical matters the lower-class girls are equally or even more disadvantaged. For example, none of them grasp the concept of fertilization: the idea that pregnancy is the result of the fusion of an egg and a sperm.

Among upper-class girls from age group eight to ten on, the knowledge of pregnancy is universal, whereas many of their lower-class counterparts are unaware of where babies come from. Indeed, in age groups eight to ten and eleven to twelve, more lower-class girls know of coitus than of pregnancy. This situation, so incongruous to an upper-class reader, is explicable. Thanks to their contact, both physical and verbal, with lower-class boys (a substantial number of whom have attempted coitus), more lower-class girls hear of or experience coitus than hear of pregnancy. Note that while a boy may attempt to persuade a girl to have coitus, it is most improbable that he will defeat his aim by informing her of the consequence.

Lastly, the differences in knowledge between upper- and lower-class girls hinge to some considerable extent on literacy and on communication with parents. The upper-class girl, more prone to reading, and in a milieu where books and magazines with sexual content are available in the home, will educate herself or ask her parents to explain what she has read. The upper-class parent, having been told by innumerable magazine articles and books on child-rearing of the desirability of sex education, is far more likely to impart information than is the less knowledgeable and more inhibited lower-class parent. This statement will be substantiated in the following section on sources of sexual knowledge.

SOURCES OF SEXUAL KNOWLEDGE

By looking at the sources of sexual learning for children, one can see the origin of sexual "slang" terms and sexual misinformation frequently unacceptable to the middle-class teacher. Though a large portion of this mislabeled and often incorrect information is the product of children's "pooled ignorance," the problem is only confounded by adult noncommunication.

The main source of sex education for most boys is the peer group—friends and classmates. Nevertheless there are important differences, depending on the child's social class (measured here as father's occupation). The peer group is overwhelmingly important as a source of information for all the boys from blue-collar homes: from 75 percent to 88 percent of them report other boys as their major source. The boys of lower white-collar homes seem a transitional group, with 70 percent so reporting, while the boys whose fathers are lower white-collar men find their mothers as important as their peers with respect to information. The boys from upper white-collar homes derive little from their peers, most from their mothers, and a relatively large amount from combined educational efforts by both parents. These figures are in striking contrast to those of the blue-collar boys: only 8 percent cite peers as the main source, 48 percent report the mother, and 24 percent both parents. This inverse relationship between parental occupation and the importance of peers as an informational source is one of the major, though anticipated, findings of this study. As the occupational level of the home increases, the child's mother plays a growing role in the sex education of her son, rising to nearly half of the cases for males whose fathers are upper white-collar men. For all occupational levels, the father seems to play a marginal role as a source of sex information for boys, and when he does play a role in his boy's sex education, it is mainly when both parents act as a team. While we can only speculate on the basis of our data, the mother is probably the "prime mover" of the parental educating team. Other sources as major channels of information (e.g., siblings, other relatives, simple observation, etc.) are statistically unimportant, never exceeding 4 percent.

Some children report that their sources of information are so evenly balanced that they cannot name one as the major source. Boys reporting this situation are more common (20 percent) in homes of lower blue-collar fathers. The percentages tend to decrease progressively as parental occupational status increases, but this trend is unexpectedly reversed by the boys from upper white-collar homes. This reversal is probably not the result of small sample vagary, since the same phenomenon is to be seen among girls. No explanation is presently known.

TEACHER UNIMPORTANT AS SOURCE

It is interesting to note that the teacher is not mentioned by any of the children as the main source of sex education. In fact, throughout the study the contribution of the teacher and the school system to the child's information about sex is too low to be statistically significant.

However, with the current proliferation of formal sex education programs in some of our nation's school systems, the role of the teacher and the school has no doubt increased in importance since the time these interviews were conducted, before 1955.

When looking at the main source of sex knowledge for girls, we see similar trends. Peers provide the main source of sex information for 35 percent of the girls whose fathers are lower blue-collar men and for 25 percent of the girls whose fathers are upper blue-collar workers. By contrast, only 9 percent and 4 percent, respectively, of the girls whose fathers are white-collar men report the peer group as their main source of sex education. The mother's importance as a source of sex education increases with increased occupational status, being the major source for 10 percent of the daughters of lower blue-collar workers and for up to 75 percent of those whose fathers are upper white-collar men.

For girls, fathers provide very little sex education, and then only as a member of a father-mother combination. It is interesting to observe that significantly more girls than boys report no main source of sex education, especially those girls from homes in which the father has a lower-status occupation. For example, 45 percent of the daughters of lower blue-collar workers report no main source of sex education, as compared to 20 percent of the boys whose fathers are at this occupational level. Other possible informational sources, such as siblings and printed material, are inconsequential.

NUDITY

The general level of permissiveness regarding nudity in the home, a sex-related phenomenon, also varies in relation to the occupational level of the family. As a rule, boys are allowed more nudity than girls, except in homes where nudity is a common practice—in which case the girls report a higher incidence of nudity. Differences between occupational groups are great, with 87 percent of the lower blue-collar workers never allowing nudity among their sons, as compared to only 28 percent of upper white-collar men. Again for boys, 40 percent who come from upper white-collar families report nudity as very common, compared to only 3 percent whose fathers are lower blue-collar workers. Among girls, we find the same patterns emerging, with 44 percent of the girls from upper white-collar families reporting nudity as very common, and none of the girls from lower blue-collar families reporting nudity as usual in the home. Thus nudity in the lower-class home is more the exception than the rule for both girls and boys; in the upper-class home almost the reverse is true. The upper-class permissiveness regarding a sex-related behavior, nudity, fits nicely with our finding that upper-class parents communicate more freely on sexual matters with their offspring.

IMPLICATIONS FOR EDUCATION

The main implication of the reported data for those in the field of education is the need for educators to be aware of the differences in information and experience which exist between boys and girls, between different occupational and socioeconomic groups and (though not treated in this article) the differences which may occur between ethnic groups. An apparent problem regarding these differences, still evident in much of our educational system today, is an often inflexible adherence to the "middle-class yardstick."

The sexual experiences and the sexual vocabulary of the heterogeneous student population, especially the pupil who has not come from the same socioeconomic, occupational, or ethnic background as his teacher, create definite problems in expectations, understanding, and communication between teacher and pupil. An adequate knowledge of the sources of sex education, types of experiences, and the vocabulary and attitudes of these students will enable the teacher to gain a wider understanding of some of the problems of pupils regarding sexual matters and to modify his or her teaching accordingly.

Counseling the child in the school system raises some of the same problems encountered by the classroom teacher in an even more intense, personal situation. The counselor should have some idea of differences in preadolescent sexual activities and knowledge, enabling him to aid the child and his parents more intelligently as they deal with questions and problems of sexuality. If the average age for preadolescent homosexual experiences, for instance, is around nine years, this activity should be recognized as possibly a part of normal sexual development rather than as a sexual aberration. There is great danger of confusing activities accompanying normal sexual development with pathological behavior.

It is also apparent from the data presented here that many lower-class children will probably experience problems in learning and adjustment because of the lack of accurate information from informed sources. Neither the teacher nor the parent will completely replace peer-group influence in the process of providing sexual information, especially in the lower class, but the educator has the opportunity to provide programs to meet the needs of children otherwise inadequately prepared to cope with sexuality because of restraints imposed by social-class position. Therefore education should continue to initiate programs which will help fill this void created either by peer misinformation or by similar misunderstanding and reluctance on the part of parents.

NOTES

[1] Sigmund Freud, "Three Essays on Sexuality," *Standard Edition of the Complete Psychological Works*. London: Hogarth, 1953, pp. 135-245; Albert Moll, *The Sexual Life of the Child*. New York: Macmillan, 1923 (originally published in German in 1909); S. Bell, "A Preliminary Study of the Emotion of Love between the Sexes," *American Journal of Psychology*, 1902, pp. 325-54; M. G. Blanton, "The Behavior of the Human Infant during the First Thirty Days of Life," *Psychological Review*, 1917, pp. 956-83; K. W. Hattendorf, "A Study of the Questions of Young Children Concerning Sex: A Phase of an Experimental Approach to Parent Education," *Journal of Social Psychology*, 1932, pp. 37-65; S. Isaacs, *Social Development of Young Children: A Study of Beginnings*. London: George Routledge and Sons, 1933; G. J. and M. M. Dudycha, "Adolescent Memories of Preschool Experiences," *Pedagogical Seminar and Journal of Genetic Psychology*, 1933, pp. 468-80; E. H. Campbell, "The Social-Sex Development of Children," *Genetic Psychology Monographs*, 1939, p. 4; J. H. Conn, "Children's Awareness of the Origin of Babies," *Journal of Child Psychiatry*, 1948, p. 140-76; "Children's Reactions to the Discovery of Genital Differences," *American Journal of Orthopsychiatry*, 1940a, pp. 747-54; "Sexual Curiosity of Children," *American Journal of Diseases of Children*, 1940b, pp. 1110-19; J. H. Conn and Leo Kanner, "Children's Awareness of Sex Differences," *Journal of Child Psychiatry*, 1947, pp. 3-57; H. M. Halverson, "Genital and Sphincter Behavior of the Male Infant," *Journal of Genetic Psychology*, 1940, pp. 95-136; A. Katcher, "The Discrimination of Sex Differences by Young Children," *Journal of Genetic Psychology*, 1955, pp. 131-43; C. V. Ramsey, *Factors in the Sex Life of 291 Boys*. Madison, N. J.: Published by the author, 1950; R. Sears, E. Maccoby, and H. Levin, *Patterns of Child Rearing*. Evanston, Ill.: Row, Peterson, 1957; A. Bandura and R. Walters, *Adolescent Aggression*. New York: Ronald Press, 1959.

[2] R. Sears, "Development of Gender Role," in Beach (ed.), *Sex and Behavior*. New York: John Wiley and Son, 1965; E. Maccoby (ed.), *The Development of Sex Differences*. Stanford, Calif.: Stanford University Press, 1966.

[3] J. Money, J. Hampson, and J. L. Hampson, "Hermaphroditism: Recommendations Concerning Assignment of Sex, Change of Sex, and Psychologic Management," *Bulletin of Johns Hopkins Hospital*, 1955a, pp. 284-300; "An Examination of Some Basic Sexual Concepts: The Evidence of Human Hermaphroditism," *Bulletin of Johns Hopkins Hospital*, 1955b, p. 301-19.

[4] The following table presents the number of boys or girls in each category (N) and the mean age of that category:

| | | Males | | Females | |
		N	Mean Age	N	Mean Age
Blue-Collar	Lower	59	11.2	21	9.5
	Upper	79	11.5	17	10.1
White-Collar	Lower	115	9.9	53	6.9
	Upper	37	7.2	35	6.6

[5] The blue-collar—white-collar distinction provides an excellent indication of social level vis-à-vis the occupational level. The association between occupation and education (used in the original Kinsey publications) is very close. See p. 328, *Sexual Behavior in the Human Male*. Philadelphia, Pa.: Sanders, 1948.

[6] A. Kinsey, W. Pomeroy, and C. Martin, *Sexual Behavior in the Human Male*. Philadelphia, Pa.: Sanders, 1948, p. 168.

Sex Education: Parent Involvement in Decision Making

A. Gray Thompson and Edward P. DeRoche

Although it is axiomatic in curriculum theory that those affected by a decision should be involved in its formulation, the pragmatic administrator often tends to regard the axiom as impractical.

When it comes to including sex education in the curriculum, however, there are compelling practical reasons for involving parents in decisions to be made. After all, the area is so charged with emotional dynamite that if the parental community is not consulted, the administrator can be dynamited right out of his job. In this article we report an involvement experiment; it includes some suggestions for administrators contemplating change in the sex education curriculum of their schools.

Many elementary schools have a "Fathers' Night" at which presentations are made about the new math, the reading program, discipline, federal aid, and perhaps sex education. Frequently these meetings end with a question-and-answer period, and all go home until the next Fathers' Night. In the situation described here (Henry Ford Elementary School, Redwood, California) the desire on the part of the school for community involvement and sharing in decision making is evident.

Although other curriculum areas at Ford's Fathers' Night sparked questions and discussion, it appeared that the fathers felt a more direct involvement and concern with what the school was doing about sex education. They queried and probed about existing programs and available materials. Fathers wanted to know about the program and material used. The principal explained that traditionally the school provided films on menstruation for girls, and the classroom teachers provided some "sex instruction" via science and health units. The principal pointed out, in response to a father's question about the contents of this material, that "the human body as far as the textbook is concerned ends just below the navel."

Some fathers asked why. Others wondered if this might not be an extension of the "dirty and secret" syndrome characteristic of sex discussions in Victorian days. Other questions were asked: What should the school do in this area? How can we help teachers and mothers? What materials are available for boys as well as for girls? What do they talk about in films on menstruation? Do the films discuss masturbation?

It was evident from the questions that fathers wanted something more than what the school was providing. They wanted to see the films their daughters see. They wanted to see the few films available for boys. Finally, they wanted the staff to select such materials to be presented at a follow-up meeting. The principal clearly pointed out that he wanted them to help make decisions with respect to curriculum material. The fathers agreed.

An overcrowded library provided a theater in which the fathers viewed the films and other materials selected by the staff. After intensive discussion five major decisions were developed:

1. *The Story of Menstruation* and *Human Growth* became a part of fifth- and sixth-grade curriculum.

Fathers decided that the school principal should lead the discussion, rather than nurses or doctors, in order to avoid, in the words of one father, an "antiseptic atmosphere."

2. The film *Boy to Man* would be shown at an evening meeting at which fathers would bring their sons.

The major reason this film was selected for a father-son showing was the attitude it takes toward masturbation. Although there were differences of opinion of an ethical nature, most fathers agreed that this problem could be overcome. One father wondered whether the program might encourage "bad behavior." Others reacted by saying that the presentation of facts alone would not assure proper behavior. This discussion led to agreement that there should be communication and dialogue between fathers and their preadolescents based upon the facts of the film.

3. Boys and girls would see and discuss the films together.

The fathers decided that the opportunity to view the films and ask questions in a mixed group could help develop a mutual respect for physical differences and perhaps initiate an openness to communication about sex. The fathers were determined *not to extend the "dirty-secret" notions* if at all possible. It was also decided that the principal would guide the question-answer period for the mixed group.

4. Boys would have an opportunity to ask questions of the principal, girls of the school nurse.

Fathers felt that certain questions might not be asked in the mixed groups. Working to develop openness in relation to sex, these "special questions" might be best answered in segregated groups.

5. The mothers would have an opportunity to see and discuss the films.

The films and materials were viewed and discussed. The fathers' decisions were enthusiastically supported by the mothers. They expressed pleasure in having their husbands become involved both in school matters and the children's welfare.

It is important to note here that these decisions were made by consensus. Parents did not feel threatened or pressured, because *they* were involved in the decision-making process. They admitted the need, wanted to do something, and had trust in the school. Given the opportunity for honest involvement in matters which have an impact on the family, parents will, we discovered, come to school and make important decisions.

The principal prepared himself for the programs by viewing the films several times, jotting down ideas, vocabulary, and potential questions. He consulted with teachers and reviewed questions and comments resulting from the various meetings with parents. He studied several articles and pamphlets on sex education. He reviewed material in textbooks at various grade levels, noting what was provided and what gaps, misunderstandings, or omissions existed. Actually, through self-education, the principal became something of a specialist.

Each meeting (one with fifth-graders, the other with sixth-graders) lasted almost two hours. The principal showed both films *(The Story of Menstruation* and *Human Growth)* and spent about one and one-half hours in discussion. Following this two-hour session, the principal took the boys out on the lawn area of the school and spent another hour answering questions in a free and open discussion. The principal had prepared for this by informing the parents that if they wanted their youngsters to venture into the area of sex education, every question was to be answered honestly and intelligently. He also indicated to parents that they should be prepared to follow up on the questions asked.

The school nurse and female teachers reported that the girls were equally open in their discussion. Both the principal and school nurse found that fifth- and sixth-graders asked the same kinds of questions. There was little difference in the quality and depth of these questions, although it appeared that the fifth-graders were more open, willing to explore every area of the subject in the mixed group.

The following five questions serve as an example of what was asked. Do people mate just once? If you masturbate, do you get diphtheria and go crazy? How do sperm cells know which way to go? Why do people have to learn about mating when other animals don't? My aunt takes pills to get pregnant. Why?

A fathers-sons meeting followed by one week the students' meeting with the principal, school nurse, and teachers. At this meeting fathers and sons (some of junior-college and high-school ages) viewed the film *Boy to Man.* Few questions followed, but this may be the result of the incident which occurred at the beginning of the discussion period. One boy raised his hand shortly after the discussion began and asked, "What is masturbation?" Before the principal could answer the question, the boy's father indicated that he would appreciate the opportunity to discuss this question with his son alone. This seemed to set the tone.

Most fathers wanted to take their boys out of the meeting and talk "man to man."

It is difficult to provide conclusive evidence of the worth of such a program. Evidence of increase in knowledge gained was not statistically evaluated. Yet the experience seemed worthwhile on other grounds.

First, the climate and relationship between the principal and fifth- and sixth-grade boys seemed to change in a positive direction. The school nurse and teachers also felt a change in attitude, something conveyed in the phrase "Oh, you know too; thanks."

Both the principal and nurse felt extreme pressure from the provocative questions asked by pupils and the push for meaningful answers. But, because of the involvement of parents and the careful preliminary planning, they did not hesitate to answer these questions to the best of their ability.

It was exhilarating for the staff to see how fathers involved themselves in school planning and curriculum decision making.

Teachers indicated to the principal that they had to go back to old biology notes and read college textbooks to continue to answer questions on cell division, twins, heredity, and the like.

Parents were quite enthusiastic about the program. They enjoyed becoming involved with school personnel in designing and implementing the program. About 75 percent of the families were represented. We believe that acceptance of the program is directly related to the fact that *parents were involved in the decision-making process from the beginning in this curriculum area.* Parents did not feel that outside "do-gooders" were going to set things straight. Nor did they feel that their privacy was being invaded in the very private matter of sex.

Parent attitude towards the program is perhaps best illustrated by the following incident. Two days after the formal presentation had been completed, the principal received an anonymous phone call at school. The mother calling indicated how appreciative she and other parents were that the program had been inaugurated. She concluded by saying, "What you did caused my husband and me to sit up until two o'clock in the morning talking about sex as it relates to us and the kids. This is the first time in sixteen years of our marriage that this had ever happened."

Premarital Contraception and the School

Edward Pohlman

Without giving numerical data, we can simply assert that pre-marital intercourse, conception, abortion, birth, and contraception are occurring on a significant scale among students in America's high schools and junior high schools. Many school leaders can provide painful examples to illustrate these generalizations. One facet of this inter-related constellation, contraception, is the focus of this paper. The average public school cannot advocate, or give instruction in, premarital contraception. But if contraception is discussed in the classroom—ostensibly "for marriage only"—there may be an impact on premarital contraception. In counseling individuals, especially students known to be engaging in intercourse, contraception may be quietly suggested. Is it desirable to encourage premarital contraception?

THE SOCIAL CONTEXT FOR STUDENTS

The American student lives in a society where premarital intercourse is made logistically convenient by the absence of parents and servants from the home, automobiles, motels, anonymity, free time, the no-chaperone system, and a host of other factors. Internal controls are often equally lax; organized religion plays a largely ornamental role; values are heterogeneous, relative, and unclear. There is a duplicity in sex standards, so that parents who condemn high-school intercourse are often involved in extramarital affairs. For Phi Delta Kappa or any other professional organization, it would be interesting to tabulate the proportion of members whose sex relations had been confined to the marriage bed. Popular media frequently glamorize sex out of wedlock. Many youths experience positive social pressure to have intercourse, added to biological pressures which are relatively forceful at their age. Prolonged education and other factors postpone marriage age.

But there is a horror of premarital conception and birth, at least in the middle class. The same two-faced society that snickered at premarital sex looks cold, pious, accusing, or the other way if pregnancy occurs. In the lower classes condemnation is less likely to be wholehearted, and sometimes is mere lip service to norms of higher-status groups. Some unmarried students want pregnancy—to hurt parents, shame the sexual

83

companion, force marriage, gain status with peers, and the like. But for most Americans premarital conception is perceived as extremely undesirable.

Granted permissiveness toward premarital sex intimacies joined with strong penalties for pregnancy, couples seek some adjustment, especially in the middle class. One avenue is through semi-intercourse: petting to climax, sleeping together nude without intercourse, "technical virginity" based on hairline definitions. Another avenue is contraception. This fits with a technical society where gadgets abound and taking drugs for innumerable reasons is common. Contraceptives, especially those of the newest style, have status in some groups. Like cigarettes, automobiles, and marijuana, birth control pills or loops can symbolize adulthood. Condoms need never be used, but only carried around, to create awe.

Some publicly supported universities give oral contraceptives to certain girls. The intended quietness of such policies is often broken by shouts of angry protest, but the fact that the policies are even considered is a barometer. Our society does not consider it totally unthinkable for a public educational institution to take a hand in premarital contraception. Public high schools and universities are not totally distinct, despite differences; similarities in parents, students, and taxpayer support do exist.

ENCOURAGING PREMARITAL SEX?

A recurrent question is whether knowledge and/or availability of contraception merely keeps down pregnancy among those who would be having intercourse anyway, or whether it encourages an increase in premarital sex relations. This question was discussed in several articles in the April, 1966, *Journal of Sex Research,* but with little data. Schofield's [1] research is distinctive in that the interviews were with random samples of British youth from different social-class and age groups. Half of the "sexually experienced" boys and 70 percent of the girls had felt real fears of pregnancy at some times (p. 108). Nevertheless, the majority of the experienced girls reported that they "neither took precautions themselves, nor insisted upon their partners using any contraceptive method" (p. 107). Schofield's "experienced" sample did not know more about contraception than the others. Although this one study does not prove that an increase in contraceptive availability will not produce some increase in premarital sex, it does document squarely that *lack* of contraceptive information and supplies, and fear of pregnancy, will not necessarily prevent premarital intercourse.

Studies showing a correlation, over time, between contraceptive availability and volume of premarital sex would simply demonstrate the old truism that correlation does not prove causation. What is needed is an experimental study in which one group or community is given a concentrated program of premarital contraceptive information and/or supplies, and compared with controls. Dependent variables should include measures of volume not only of premarital sex but of premarital conceptions. Some would regard this as a highly dangerous experiment which "used our impressionable youth as human guinea pigs." But the idea is not so far-fetched, especially if it concentrated on pregnancy-prone groups. The March 8, 1967, newsletter of Planned Parenthood–World Population described a program in Baltimore involving 2,000 teen-agers from slum neighborhoods shown to be prone to out-of-wedlock conceptions. "In some instances, if parents agree, contraception will be begun at a very early age. Teen-age programs are afoot in Washington, Syracuse, New York, San Francisco, and other cities." It would appear that these projects need only control groups and some attention to experimental design to constitute research such as we have suggested above.

RESEARCH ON PENALTIES

The penalties of pregnancy, especially to middle-class girls, are well known to "common sense." In the white non-prison sample of the Kinsey studies, 89 percent of the pregnancies to single women reportedly ended in induced abortion, in contrast to 17 percent for married women.[2] Although this sample is open to much criticism, abortion is a major "way out" among pregnant single girls. Even those who argue that abortion is often preferable to continuing the pregnancy will readily agree that it is only the "lesser of two evils" and still poses many problems in our culture. When done under haphazard conditions and/or by a nonskilled abortionist, it can be medically dangerous. Even when properly done, it is extremely expensive. And some women carry a load of guilt for years.

When an abortion does not occur and the pregnancy continues, a degree of social ostracism often results. Whether the child is kept or given for adoption, guilt often remains for years. If the child is kept, anger and guilt felt toward him may wreck the mother-child relationship. Forced marriages are not desirable ones.[3] Even when income and social class are controlled as carefully as possible, studies show that divorce is more likely,[4] and the economic well-being of the couple is less,[5] when the first pregnancy was premarital.

PREMARITAL CONTRACEPTION MORAL?

Questions of morality can be phrased into three questions, asking (1) whether it is immoral to have premarital conceptions; (2) whether it is immoral to have premarital sex; and (3) whether avoiding premarital pregnancy would "offset" a certain increase in volume of premarital sex, if it occurred. On the first question, we have just mentioned some of the personal and social consequences of premarital conception. Although it is *not* written, "Thou shalt not conceive premaritally. . . ," premarital conception does involve "sin" against oneself and one's sexual partner, the child, and society. A broad conception of morality must include society-wide responsibilities and not only personalistic and pietistic ones. At least by such broader standards, premarital pregnancy is immoral and the individual sex partner or the community leader who helps reduce it is acting morally. In the aforementioned newsletter of Planned Parenthood, the organization's president, Alan Guttmacher, opined that when sex relations do occur out of wedlock they "must be protected by effective contraception," and failure to use such protection "is the grossest form of sexual immorality and irresponsibility. . . ."

Discussions of the possible increase in premarital sex following availability of premarital contraception start with the assumption that an increase in premarital sex would be bad. This point should not be taken for granted. There are those who adopt a relativistic view—a "situational morality" view—concerning premarital sex, arguing that for some individuals with some partners under some circumstances premarital sex is moral and desirable. Some claim that taboos on premarital and extramarital sex might logically disappear—eventually. Society, it is claimed, may be moving in this direction.

In all such discussions the adult discussants may be influenced by their own not-too-conscious problems. Advocacy of premarital sex may be a vicarious way to achieve the liberty one would currently like, or wishes one had had as a youth. Crusades against premarital sex may involve overreaction against one's own desires. Youths are sometimes very perceptive when they accuse adults of being jealous, and it is not only celibate priests who may be open to such a charge.

Let us scramble out of this marsh of relativity and head for some firmer ground. From the practical viewpoint of school administration, one must agree with the official public consensus that an increase in premarital sex would be undesirable. From a more speculative viewpoint, one may argue that, even though for *some* individuals premarital sex may be acceptable or desirable, for the group as a whole an increase in premarital sex is undesirable. In any event, for purposes of this article we shall assume that an increase in premarital sex is undesirable.

The dilemmas we have been posing above do not exist in the case of persons known to be having intercourse—for example, students who confide during counseling that this is occurring. Advising them to practice contraception does not run the risk of encouraging them to intercourse, for this they are already doing.

This brings us to the third of three questions listed at the start of this section. We have argued that both premarital sex and premarital conception are undesirable, and that decreasing them is moral and increasing them immoral. Now let us assume a condition which has *not* been demonstrated by research: that making contraceptive information and/or supplies available may lead to some increase in premarital sex, but will result in a net decrease in premarital conceptions. Would one then be justified in advocating premarital contraception? For most of us the answer would depend on how much increase was expected in intercourse, and how much decrease in pregnancy. Research does not quantify these variables. The answer would also depend on judgment about the relative morality of premarital intercourse and pregnancy, and these are matters rooted in values and religious beliefs. The writer has been working with two research instruments related to these issues. One lists nine sins—including premarital sex with contraception (no pregnancy) and without contraception (pregnancy results)—and asks respondents to rank their relative sinfulness. The other instrument asks respondents the number of "extra" net premarital unions, if any, which might be "justified," in respondents' thinking, by the prevention of one unwanted conception.

There is often a respect for the status quo, and the latter is confused with "nature" or even the "will of God." As a result it may seem that acting, doing, and changing involve responsibility—because they interfere with the "natural" status quo—whereas doing nothing involves no responsibility. Encouraging premarital contraception interferes with the status quo, but *not* encouraging it may also be a decision which should be responsibly made.

In 1965, a modified probability sample of the United States population—over 3,000 respondents—was asked, "Do you believe that information about birth control ought to be easily available to any single adult person who wants it?" [6] Half the respondents said yes, and 7 percent were not sure. "Yes" answers were given by 39, 51, and 63 percent of those with grade-school, high-school, and more education, respectively; and 43 percent of Catholic and 52 percent of non-Catholic respondents. It appears that a considerable proportion of Americans do not regard it as necessarily immoral to encourage premarital contraception. Of course, the question not only specified "adult" but spoke of those "who want it," with the possible implication that they were already engaged in sex relations.

THE INFLUENCE OF RELIGION

Religious teachings take shape as the individual conscience and its expression, and also as the collective influence of groups holding a common faith. In the United States the Roman Catholic Church has traditionally regarded as immoral all methods of contraception except the "rhythm" method. Currently the unofficial voice of the church is not united on this point; some Catholic couples have received clerical approval for "unnatural" methods, and over half the Catholic couples in America married ten or more years and without evidence of reproductive problems use methods not approved by the church.[7] Nevertheless, Catholic influence on the particular contraceptive methods which are or are not proper is still a major consideration. Most Protestant groups join Catholicism in opposing abortion (equated with murder) and premarital intercourse.

Whether or not premarital contraception can be encouraged, in the face of objections from religious groups, is a question that can be debated from either a theoretical or a practical standpoint. Invoking the concept of church-state separation, religious groups can claim that giving contraceptive information in the schools is an invasion of the domain of religion, since it encourages beliefs and actions that are contrary to church teachings. (Religious groups that do not accept the theory of evolution can make the same claim concerning the teaching of evolution in the schools, incidentally, but their numbers are not practically important.) Invoking church-state separation, one might also claim that *not* to give contraceptive information in the schools is bringing religion into state concerns, since it is because of religious objections that contraception for the unmarried is excluded from discussion. The Catholic precept that "evil has no rights" implies that certain topics cannot be decided by the majority; if a great majority favors the legalization of contraception among the married, for example, this does not make it "right," since unnatural contraception is still wrong. It is wrong for non-Catholics, too, and Catholics should work to prevent others from doing wrong. But as we have suggested, Catholic thinking is in flux.

From a practical as well as a theoretical standpoint, the school must respond to its community and society. In the United States there is a general concern over premarital conception, but a general opposition to advocating contraception as a means of doing something about it. There is a general perception that "all moral people" are opposed to premarital sex, abortion, and the encouragement of premarital contraception. Religious and other groups refer to these generalized perceptions, and the school cannot be unresponsive.

PREMARITAL CONTRACEPTION BLOCKS

Students of birth planning find that contraception is often difficult for married couples. The unmarried face additional difficulties. Because intercourse probably tends to occur less frequently and expectedly, advance planning for the routines of contraception—securing and storing or carrying materials—may be especially difficult. For an unmarried youth to be found with contraceptive supplies is incriminating evidence of intent to have intercourse. Purchasing equipment and/or arranging for it with a physician or pharmacist involves facing others, who may be perceived as condemning the contemplated intercourse. Vending machines for condoms owe their success largely to this factor.

Some youths claim they would not wish to use contraceptives even if they were readily available at the appropriate times. Contraception may diminish physical or psychological gratification or interrupt the spontaneity of sex relations. Premarital sex sometimes constitutes an exultant defiance of the authority of parents and school personnel, of advice to be generally prudent and planning and cautious, of warnings against illegitimate pregnancy and venereal disease. Breaking all the barriers, in wild abandon, may be prized in itself. To live without contraception—not even pills—may be viewed as more spontaneous and natural. Precisely because it involves a risk, it may have some of the wild attraction of danger shared by a game of Russian roulette.

Among more conservative youth, to make contraceptive plans is to admit to oneself an intention that may seem sinful. To be "swept off one's feet" when the moon is full requires but a weak moment and can be explained as sudden passion. But planning may mean living with a knowledge of premeditation to sin. The same individual may experience repeated cycles of uncontracepted sex relations, repentance, resolutions never to "sin" again, and backsliding. Hence it would seem that, among those having premarital sex, the individuals feeling most guilty would be *least* likely to use contraception! We have some unpublished data consistent with this hypothesis, although the sample is not adequate to test it properly.

PREMARITAL CONTRACEPTION METHODS

Some methods are particularly suited, and others particularly unsuited, to the premarital situation. Thus the relative merits of various contraceptive methods are not the same for the premarital as for the marital situation. If our reasoning in the preceding section is correct, the ideal contraceptive method for the unmarried should be one that can be decided upon and used *after* a woman has, perhaps with no premeditation, had intercourse. Two or three methods satisfy this requirement, but are objectionable or imperfect on other grounds. It is obvious that the ideal contraceptive for the unmarried has not yet been developed.

In the public mythology it is oral contraception which is supposed to have opened up premarital contraception to the multitudes. But some physicians are warning against the use of oral contraception by women whose skeletal development is not complete, and this seems to make "pills" inadvisable for many teen-agers, married or not. Also, it may seem illogical and expensive to a woman to take the Pill daily if she anticipates only occasional and sporadic unions. Taking pills requires advance planning, with all the psychological difficulties noted above. Pills may work for some mature women who are having intercourse fairly predictably and often, perhaps with fiancés. But for the sporadically and infrequently promiscuous girl, or the one who intends to be chaste but unexpectedly slips, pills are not highly suitable.

Intrauterine devices are more difficult to insert in never-pregnant women than in those who have had babies. Whereas other women can usually have IUDs installed in a physician's office, a hospital setting is sometimes deemed advisable for never-pregnant women because of the greater likelihood of complications. The IUD has the advantage over the Pill of not requiring that the girl remember to do something each day. Both these highly effective methods usually involve some side effects, but these are serious in only a tiny minority of cases, and physicians can take this minority off the method.

A diaphragm may be a particularly inconvenient contraceptive for unmarried girls to carry about with them to the assorted places where intercourse is likely to occur—in contrast to the wife's predictable location in the marriage bed. Diaphragms, IUDs, and pills are all "medical" methods, requiring a physician's cooperation. In almost every sizable community there are physicians willing to prescribe contraceptives to the unmarried under some circumstances. Many require parental permission, but others do not. The whole business of facing a physician, often perceived as the stern representative of father, society, and God, is an impossible barrier to many girls. The result is often a turning to nonmedical methods.

The "rhythm" method and *coitus interruptus* ("withdrawal") are found to be relatively ineffective methods in virtually all field studies among married couples. But they may have value for the unmarried, since even an ineffective method works better than none at all. These methods do not require the user to purchase or secure anything in advance, to plan ahead of time to "sin," or to store and carry anything to have handy at the appropriate time. But both "rhythm" and "withdrawal" require self-control, especially of the male—a characteristic for which he is not noted in this context. The unmarried male may be even less concerned about avoiding a conception than is a husband. Fear of the proverbial shotgun wedding, or a sense of responsibility, may make him take appropriate precautions. But the research of Schofield,[8] noted earlier, suggests that reliance on the male for contraception may be somewhat unsatisfactory. The same conclusion is implied in the report of research by Kirkendall.[9] His tabulations show that in general college couples who had more sustained friendships and attachments to one another were more liable to use contraception. One disconcerting implication: there was greater risk of pregnancy, apparently, to those women who had less basis for expecting the fathers of any resulting children to marry them.

The condom shares with the methods just discussed the characteristic of relying on the male, although some women carry condoms and insist that males use them if intercourse is to be permitted. The condom is the one method that provides some protection against venereal disease—albeit imperfect protection—and this is an especially important consideration among the unmarried. Indeed, as American men know, vending machine sales of condoms are advertised as disease prevention and not as contraception. The fact that they can be purchased from vending machines without embarrassing personal contacts with authority figures gives them a key role in premarital contraception. If used, condoms are highly effective in preventing conception.

There has been some research on a possible "morning-after pill." Any method that does not have to be used until *after* the event has advantages. Douching meets this criterion, but is relatively ineffective even as used by married couples. Also, unmarried couples often lack the equipment and the motivation to douche immediately after intercourse, although the "coke" is backed by some folklore as a method among high-school students. Hence the "retrocontraception" of a pill taken after intercourse would have advantages. If a woman could wait until she discovered pregnancy before taking retrocontraceptives, she might be more strongly motivated, and physicians and parents and society more willing, to do what was necessary to get the pills into the woman. But as presently envisioned, retrocontraceptives would need to be taken within a few days of coitus, before it was known whether pregnancy had occurred. To secure and take medication "just in case" might seem less imperative and justifiable to all involved. Whether or not retrocontraceptives—if perfected—would be classified as abortion and hence condemned is not clear.

ABORTION

Abortion is not contraception, but is the one possibility when pregnancy occurs; as such it is probably contemplated by most premaritally pregnant girls. A careful study in Europe by eminent American physicians found that abortion during the first three months of pregnancy, induced by an experienced doctor in a hospital, involved "far" less risk to the mother than those medical risks accompanying full-term pregnancy and delivery.[10] The operation is not inherently dangerous; but it is dangerous when performed by the incompetent and/or under unfavorable circumstances. Abortion is often followed by long-lasting guilt feelings; the act may be perceived as murder, and the whole complex of feelings may be related to guilt over sex. In cultures such as Japan, where the whole pattern of thinking supports abortion, guilt is not notable. If the culture gives legal approval to abortion, this itself probably reduces the feeling of having done something wrong.

The writer believes that abortion should be categorically available to any woman who wants it during the first three months of pregnancy. Those who do not wish to have or perform abortions should not be forced by others, but neither should those who wish to have or perform them be denied this alternative. Of course, the writer can understand the deep objections of those who feel otherwise. If abortion is equated with murder, then the fact that a woman and her physician want to "take life" does not mean that society should permit it. The view that life is an either/or matter, something which does not exist in sperm and ovum but exists full-fledged once the two join, cannot be supported from contemporary science. And the early church fathers can be cited as holding that life did not begin until several months after conception.

Whatever our personal beliefs, we live in a society where abortion is condemned. After rape or incest a hospital abortion board will often approve abortion. Some states are moving toward slightly more lenient laws. But in general poor girls run high medical risks with cheap abortion. Others pay fantastic fees, and still may often have second-rate medical help and many other difficulties. Guilt remains a severe reality. In many states, school leaders who refer a girl to an abortionist run the risk of legal prosecution as well as public condemnation.

THE ROLE OF THE SCHOOL

From the above discussion we must conclude that the average public high school cannot and should not encourage premarital contraception in any open way. (Some adventurous schools in high-risk areas might try out a program.) But the school has a number of ways of promoting premarital contraception, if it chooses to do so. Whether a given administrator or other educational leader believes that he should do so in his sphere of influence is a value judgment. Some considerations underlying this judgment have been reviewed. If a leader favors premarital contraception, he can encourage it without making the open display which would be politically and professionally ruinous in many areas. Here are some ways this can be done.

The very fact of including discussions of contraception in classes gives some encouragement to premarital contraception. For even though students are told that "of course this is for marriage only," they may apply what they learn premaritally. In the guidance and administrative and other phases of the school program, when individual students discuss their problems and decisions, premarital contraception can be encouraged or discouraged. This is especially possible when students indicate, by their actions or words, that they are already engaging in intercourse. School leaders can refer students to physicians and other agencies where contraceptive information and supplies can be skillfully dispensed.

Schools can be cooperators or initiators in research on premarital contraception. There is almost no research in this area. Despite the great stakes which schools have in avoiding pregnancies among students, schools are often reluctant to get involved in research in this area, because of fears of public pressures. We are not thinking primarily of frightening experiments with programs of contraceptive emphasis, but of more simple surveys of student pregnancy, contraception, abortion, forced marriages, and the like.

School leaders are also influential community leaders, and even though they cannot or do not wish to promote premarital contraception in the schools, they can influence decisions in sectors of the community agency structure which are less sensitive. The federal anti-poverty program in the United States includes provisions for family planning. Unmarried women were originally excluded from receiving contraceptive devices or pills at government expense. But in late 1966 this exclusion was "repealed," so that the matter is now up to local discretion; funds are available if the local area wants to use them in this way. One of the ironies of family planning generally, and premarital contraception specifically, is that the lower classes are, in essence, discriminated against. Other groups know about contraception, and can afford private physicians to prescribe their methods and do their abortions; but poorer people must depend on public facilities, where religious group pressures have heretofore meant that nothing is said about family planning. This situation seems to be changing now.

Whether or not school leaders choose to take some quiet steps encouraging premarital contraception is largely an individual decision, based on personal values and judgments and on considerations of the type we have reviewed. Perhaps no decision can be made that will avoid all evils; it may be a question of choosing a path that involves the least amount of evil, as evil is perceived by the individual making the judgment.

Although we have just stressed individual decisions, it is possible that Phi Delta Kappa, collectively, could make some assessment and recommendations concerning the role of the school in premarital sex, pregnancy, abortion, and contraception. Individual courage and initiative and judgment go only so far; there are points where wide-angle, large-scale, collective decisions and action are needed.

NOTES

[1] M. Schofield, *The Sexual Behaviour of Young People.* London: Longmans, Green, 1965, especially pp. 13-16, 105-13.

[2] P. H. Gebhard, W. B. Pomeroy, C. E. Martin, and C. V. Christenson, *Pregnancy, Birth, and Abortion.* New York: Harper and Hoeber, 1958, pp. 29, 57.

[3] E. Pohlman, *The Psychology of Birth Planning.* Cambridge, Mass.: Schenkman, 1967, Chap. 17.

[4] H. T. Christensen and H. H. Meissner, "Studies in Child Spacing: III. Premarital Pregnancy as a Factor in Divorce," *American Sociological Revolution,* 1953, pp. 641-44; G. Rowntree, "Some Aspects of Marriage Breakdown in Britain during the Last Thirty Years," *Population Studies,* 1964, pp. 147-63.

[5] R. Freedman and L. Coombs, "Childspacing and Family Economic Position," *American Sociological Revolution,* 1966, pp. 631-48.

[6] Population Council, "American Attitudes on Population Policy," *Studies in Family Planning,* 1966, No. 9, pp. 5-8.

[7] R. Freedman, P. K. Whelpton, and A. A. Campbell, *Family Planning, Sterility, and Population Growth.* New York: McGraw-Hill, 1959.

[8] M. Schofield, *op. cit.*

[9] L. A. Kirkendall, *Premarital Intercourse and Interpersonal Relationships.* New York: Julian Press, 1961, pp. 284-86.

[10] C. Tietze and H. Lehfeldt, "Legal Abortion in Eastern Europe," *Journal of the American Medical Association,* 1961, pp. 1149-54.

The Pill, the Sexual Revolution, and the Schools

Ashley Montagu

The Pill! The fact that it is referred to so magisterially represents something of the measure of importance that is generally attached to this genuinely revolutionary development. For it *is* a revolutionary development, probably to be ranked among the half-dozen or so major innovations in man's two or more million years of history. In its effects I believe that the Pill ranks in importance with the discovery of fire, the development of the ability to make and employ tools, the evolution of hunting, the invention of agriculture, the development of urbanism, of scientific medicine, and the release and control of nuclear energy.

This is rather a large claim to make, but I do not think that it is in the least exaggerated, and I should like to underscore this statement in the best way possible: by setting out the facts and the consequences that are likely to flow from the changes they imply. Since the consequences of the Pill are likely to be manifold and profoundly alterative of age-old beliefs, practices, and institutions, it will be helpful to deal with the most significant of these in a systematic manner.

BIRTH CONTROL AND ITS ROLE IN THE HUMANIZATION OF MAN

For the first time in the history of man, the Pill provides a dependable means of controlling conception. For the first time, the Pill makes it possible to make every individual of reproductive age completely responsible for both his sexual and his reproductive behavior. It is necessary to be unequivocally clear concerning the distinction between sexual and reproductive behavior. Sexual behavior may have no other purpose than pleasure—pure hedonism or impure hedonism, without the slightest intention of reproducing—or it may be indulged in for both pleasure and reproduction. Sexual behavior is much more rarely indulged in for the purposes of reproduction than it is for the purposes of pleasure. Hedonistic sex is to be regarded as purely sexual behavior. Sex that is indulged in with a view to the generation of children constitutes reproductive behavior. In these senses the female tends to be the reproductive creature, and man more often the sexual creature.

No society can long tolerate any form of anarchic behavior in its

95

midst, and therefore sexual promiscuity especially has been prohibited in all human societies. In all societies every individual is made responsible (1) for his sexual behavior, and (2) for his reproductive behavior. In nonliterate societies this has been regulated in the following manner: sex for the sheer pleasure of it has been allowed everyone, but reproductive behavior has been permitted only to those persons who are married to one another. Since in almost all such societies girls marry at or shortly after the attainment of the first menstruation (menarche), premarital sexual relations practically never result in children,[1] so there are no problems. In marriage the number of children, especially at the food-gathering hunting level of economic development, is planned. For example, in order to control the size of their families the Bushmen of the Kalahari Desert simply abstain from sexual intercourse as the most effective means of birth control. The same is true of many other nonliterate peoples. The love and respect these peoples have for their children and for each other, and the vital necessity of controlling the size of their families and total population, are things that the so-called more developed peoples, who have gone so far in the opposite direction, must learn if they are again to be able to love their children and each other—indeed, if they are to survive at all.

With the gift of the Pill we now have the power placed comfortably in our hands for accomplishing all these ends, and more. And unless we begin immediately, the debasement of humanity which has proceeded at such an alarming rate in the recent period will continue in its destructive effects at an accelerating pace, for we are not far now from the very edge of doom. With the Pill, not to mention the improved versions which are already in process of development, we have it in our power to begin the rehumanization of man at the very foundations. The task of making human beings out of people literally becomes impossible when their numbers exceed the limits consonant with a successful issue to such an undertaking. That, then, is the first of the contributions made by the Pill: it provides the basis for the humanization of man.

THE SEXUAL EMANCIPATION OF THE SEXES

In civilized societies the fear of conception has produced anxieties about sex in the female which have had a variety of effects upon the sexual relationship. Among these has been the strong resistance which females have traditionally offered to the male's sexual advances. Largely because of this resistance the male has been forced into a predatory exploitative attitude toward the female. With the freedom to enjoy sex for its own sake which the Pill affords, women's attitudes towards sex will change, becoming less anxiety-ridden, more relaxed— and the attitudes of men towards women will undergo a complementary change. The double standard, which has had so damaging an effect upon both sexes and upon our society, will make way for a healthier view of sex and of the relations between the sexes.

It will become possible for the first time for the sexes genuinely to complement each other, and to live and love together on a basis of full equality. The shortsighted "viewers with alarm" will be relegated to their proper places when what they so wrongheadedly deplore, namely, the alleged feminization of men and the alleged masculinization of women, are discovered to be advances in the right, rather than in the wrong, direction.

It is only in recent years that we have learned that what we have always taken for granted as biologically determined, namely, masculinity and femininity, are in fact genders which are virtually wholly culturally determined. We now know, beyond dispute, that whatever the sex of the child may be, its gender role is what it *learns*. One learns to be either male or female according to the manner in which one is socialized, or, to put it more accurately, *genderized*.[2] Hence, when one sex assumes some of the behaviors traditionally associated with the other, no violence is done to any supposed biological functions. Males have long stood in need of such feminine qualities as tenderness, sensitivity, compassion, gentleness, and the like. Women, for their part, will benefit from the adoption of traits hitherto considered purely masculine, such as courage, adventuresomeness, enterprise, intrepidity, and the like. Men need to be humanized; women to be energized. Men need to become more secure, compassionate, and less violent. Women, to achieve their full status as human beings, need men to go with them who have also acquired, or are on the way to acquiring, that status.

THE SOCIAL EMANCIPATION OF WOMEN

Possibly the greatest revolution resulting from the advent of the Pill is the social emancipation of women that this will bring about. Menstruation, for example, for virtually all women has been to some extent socially handicapping. Because of it, in a male-dominated world, the female has everywhere been relegated to "the menstrual hut," discriminated against, and permanently demoted in the status hierarchy. Furthermore, many women during the menstrual cycle have been the captives of their hormones, often moody, characterized by premenstrual tensions, and not infrequently "ill." All these things have in the past combined to make menstruation a "curse" for women physiologically and psychologically. The Pill, by inhibiting the processes that lead to menstruation, suppresses that function, and frees women for the first time from the discomforting and often disabling effects of menstruation and the possibility of unwanted pregnancy. With all these psychologically handicapping conditions which were formerly incident to her physiology removed, the last of the grounds for discrimination against women is gone, and women may at long last enter into that full social equality which, until the development of the Pill, had been so long denied them.

The Pill in its present form, effective as it is, is but the precursor of more sophisticated forms of hormone regulators, as they may be called. Pills are already in process of development which are designed to produce long-term inhibition of ovulation, conception, and menstruation. A single pill will produce immunity for years, its inhibitory effects being cancelable at will by taking another pill that restores the normal physiological functions.

Foresight is the last of the gifts granted by the gods to man. All the more reason, therefore, to reflect upon and prepare for the developments which these revolutionary changes, in the very beginnings of which we are now living, will bring about. This is nowhere more important than in its effects upon the young.

PREMARITAL SEX

The prohibition against sex in civilized societies, in which societies the age of marriage is delayed well into reproductive age, has a long and interesting history behind it. In the Western world, the attitudes, customs, practices, and beliefs concerning the relations of the sexes to one another in all age-grades and statuses has largely been transmitted through the teachings of the Judaeo-Christian tradition. Since in such societies children born out of wedlock had no legal father, nor for that matter a legal mother, and since society was so structured as to offer no means of incorporating the child, and often the mother, into the society, and since sexual intercourse outside of wedlock was itself stigmatized as a sin, the negative sanctions against such immoral and illicit sex were severely enforced. Thus premarital sex came to be held as both morally and legally and socially abhorrent. Virtually all the reasons created to justify the prohibitions against premarital sex were little more than rationalizations. These concealed the real reasons why premarital sex could not be tolerated in such societies, namely, the havoc caused by such disallowed conduct to the social and religious organization of such societies. The ostracism and punishments that were often inflicted upon the offenders served as sufficient deterrents to keep premarital intercourse from growing to unmanageable proportions. But with the advent of two world wars, and the breakdown in moral, religious, and social values that followed upon them, there was a notable increase in all forms of forbidden sex.

The Kinsey Report, in part, constitutes a monumental record of the status of sexual mores in mid-twentieth century. Kinsey found that there was a great deal more covert sexual activity of every forbidden kind than was overtly admitted, or even suspected. In the sixties the pregnancy rate of girls of school age has risen spectacularly. These are facts which must be squarely faced.

It is not, for many reasons, desirable for girls of school age to bear children. In the first place, they are physiologically unprepared in most cases for such a function, with the result that a large proportion of children born to such immature mothers suffer from all sorts of deficiencies. This would be reason enough to discourage early pregnancy, but in fact this first is the last of the reasons why early pregnancy should be discouraged. The primary reason for such a discouragement is that adolescent girls are themselves in process of development, of maturation as persons, and are in every way socially and psychologically unready for the responsibilities of motherhood. The optimum age for childbearing from every point of view, physiological, psychological, and social, is between twenty-one plus or minus two years and twenty-seven plus or minus two years. Childbearing before the age of twenty-one plus or minus two years should therefore be discouraged.[3]

With the Pill, premarital sex without any fear of sex or the birth of children becomes for the first time possible, and hence the principal barrier against it is removed. But with the removal of this barrier the responsibilities involved in this particular relationship are maximized beyond anything that has hitherto been anticipated or required. For, once the barrier has been lowered, the danger of the debasement of this delicate, this tender, this most sensitive of all human relationships, is greatly increased. Hence no one should ever consider entering into such a relationship who is incapable of behaving responsibly in it. Responsibility to others is something one must learn. It is not something one is born with. It is here that the schools must assume *their* responsibility, for it is in the schools that the parents of future generations must be prepared in the meaning of sex and responsibility. What, then, is sexual responsibility, and how can it be taught in the schools?

SEXUAL RESPONSIBILITY

By "responsibility" I mean essentially involvement in the welfare of the other. It seems to me that involvement in the welfare of others should be the basis of all human relationships. If one cares about others, it is difficult, possessed of the requisite knowledge and responsibility, to behave in such a manner as to harm one's fellowman. It is necessary, however, to underscore the fact that involvement is not enough, because, without the requisite knowledge and sensitivity, it is possible, with the best of intentions, to wreak havoc upon others. The evil that well-intentioned people have done adds up to a sizable quantity. It is not enough to be good; it is necessary also to be knowledgeable and understanding. All these qualities can be and should be taught in the schools.[4] They should, of course, also be taught in the home. But unless we can satisfactorily establish the criteria by which the good, the true, and the beautiful can be measured, we shall not get very far in the discussion of sexual responsibility. I mention the "true" and the "beautiful" because these are fundamentally the same as "knowledge" and "understanding." Let us further define our terms. "Goodness" or "love" is behavior calculated to confer survival benefits in a creatively enlarging manner upon others. It is conduct which enables others not only to live, but to develop and live more fully realized than they would have done had you not communicated to them your involvement in their welfare.

By "knowledge" is to be understood verifiable information, and by "understanding" is to be understood the ability to appreciate what that knowledge is capable of doing—not merely what knowledge *is,* but what it is *for.*

Sexual responsibility, like every other kind of responsibility, implies moral involvement, the moral strength to be responsible to others for oneself and for them. This implies the goodness, the knowledge. and the understanding of what, in the special case of sexual behavior, are the indispensable qualifications before one may enter into any sexual relationship. Spelled out in practical terms, what this means is that our schools must become institutes for the teaching of human responsibility, with this as the primary purpose of education, and instruction in the three "Rs" as purely secondary to this main purpose. To understand the nature of human nature is not beyond the capacity of a child. Nor is. it beyond the child's capacities to understand the vulnerabilities of human beings, to respond with sensitivity to the needs of others with thoughtfulness and consideration, to learn to understand the facts about sex (including its philosophy, psychology, and ethics). These are matters that can be taught at every school age. Courses in these subjects can, of course, be graduated to meet the requirements of the young at every age.

What will be required will be skillfully organized teaching materials and well-trained, congenially sophisticated teachers. Our teachers' colleges are at the present time, for the most part, wholly unequipped to prepare such teachers. Hence a tremendous amount of work must be done, and most of it, it is to be feared, will be done by trial and error—

which is better than not being done at all. However it will be done, it were well that it were done as soon as possible, for the hour is late and human beings much in need of that goodness, knowledge, and understanding for lack of which so many avoidable tragedies have blighted the lives of countless individuals and families. Never was there a period more favorable than the present in which to introduce into our schools the teaching of sexual responsibility. The sexual revolution should precipitate the educational revolution, which should in turn swiftly lead to the human revolution.

Let me explain. The teaching of sexual responsibility can be a fascinating experience for both teacher and pupil. It is not only an extremely interesting subject in itself, but, since it gets down to the fundamentals of human relationships, it constitutes a uniquely sensitive introduction to the whole world of human relations. This is how, I believe, the course on sexual responsibility (or whatever other name it may be called by) should be taught—not as a course on sex, but as a part of the course on human relations. Thus one would begin with the exciting evolutionary history of the manner in which human beings got to be the way they now are. What it means to be human from the evolutionary point of view, the nature of human nature, the facts about the physiology and psychology of reproduction, birth, the needs of the newborn and the means of its humanization.[5] By such a route we might for the first time genuinely realize the purposes of education: the making of fulfilled humane beings, the making of humane beings out of people.

It will take time. How long will depend on how widespread this kind of teaching becomes throughout the land. Toward the furtherance of that end it would a great boon if we could drop the euphemistic phrase "the facts of life." "The facts of life" are strictly for the birds, the bees, and the bats, especially the bats that are addicted to belfries. What growing young human beings need is the understanding of their own growth and development, how they came into being, and what their presence in fact means upon this earth for the great and continuing enterprise of human relations. And that is the point, I believe, that should be the main theme of education in sexual responsibility—what one owes to others and what one has a right to expect from others as humanely accomplished human beings. As I have already remarked, education in sexual responsibility becomes essentially education in human sensitivity, in knowledge, understanding, and loving-kindness. I *know* the teacher can do this. I know because I had such teachers.

Young unmarried individuals who are sufficiently responsible will be able, in the new dispensation, to enter into responsible sexual relationships in a perfectly healthy and morally acceptable and reciprocally beneficial manner, which will help the participants to become more fully developed human beings than they would otherwise have stood a chance of becoming. The dead hand of ugly traditional beliefs (such as the nastiness and sinfulness of sex, the wickedness of premarital sex), which has been responsible for untold human tragedies, will be replaced by a new flowering of human love. This is a critical point.

LOVE

Love, for far too many males in the Western world, has been identified with sex. Females for such men have amounted to little more than sexual objects. Such attitudes on the part of men have resulted in the debasement of the most important of all human relatednesses—the ability to love.

Love is by far the most consequential of all the needs which must be satisfied if the growing creature is to be humanized. It stands at the center of all the other needs, like the sun in our solar system around which the other planets move in their orbits. It is the one and only need which must be adequately satisfied if we are to become healthy human beings. By health I mean the ability to love and the ability to work. Spelled out, love means the communication of one's deep involvement in the welfare of the other: the communication of one's profound interest in the realization of the other's potentialities for being the kind of human being you are being to him: the communication of the feeling that you will always be standing by; that you will never commit the supreme treason that human beings so frequently commit against their fellowman, of letting him down when he most stands in need of you, but that you will be standing by giving him all the supports and sustenances and stimulations that he requires for becoming what it is in him to be; and, knowing that to be human is to be in danger, to be terribly vulnerable to the damage that people are capable of inflicting upon one another, that you will be particularly careful in caring for the other not to commit such errors against him. If one can communicate these messages to the other, then I believe one can be said to love him. And this is the sort of thing that we should be teaching in our schools. As I have said, this should be the primary purpose of the schools. Within the matrix of such teaching, a special course on sexual responsibility would hardly be necessary, except insofar as details were concerned.

As a corollary of this discussion on love, it should follow that those who are unable to love in this manner should refrain from entering into human relationships involving the deepest sensibilities of others. Such persons should be rehabilitated as human beings before they are permitted to enter into such relationships.

MARRIAGE

From the above discussion it should also follow that no one who is unprepared for it as a person aware of all that is required of one in the marital relationship should be permitted to marry. Certainly everyone should always remain free to choose whom he desires to marry, but fitness for marriage should be determined by the state until such time as human beings have attained the maturity and responsibility to make such decisions for themselves. At the present time most persons are certainly not able to do so, hence the enormous separation, divorce, and broken-home rates. The state requires us to go to school, to be vaccinated, and to prove our ability to drive a car before we can get a license to do so. Surely, evidence of ability to marry and bring up a child is not less important.

Furthermore, those who are able to pass the tests of marriageability are not thereby to be construed as giving evidence that they are necessarily prepared to deal responsibly with children. Hence I would not permit persons to bring children into the world who failed to give adequate evidence of their ability to minister responsibly to the needs of children. Nor, of course, should anyone be permitted to adopt children who is unfit for the task of responsible parenthood.

Those who do pass the tests for responsible parenthood will understand the importance of spacing the births of their children. They will plan the spacing and the number of children they propose to have, and in this connection there are unlikely to be the slightest problems. However, these are matters which will require careful teaching long before the principals involved reach the stage of seriously contemplating parenthood. Hence as part of the teaching of sexual responsibility I would make the teaching of birth control and the spacing of births an integral part of the course taught at progressively sophisticated levels as the levels of maturity of the students increase.

Since nothing can concern the individual or the state more than the quality of the citizenry, the state must assume the regulation of that quality. This is dangerous doctrine, for, obviously, in the hands of the wrong people great havoc could by this means be wrought. But I am not thinking in terms of the wrong people or of dictators. I am thinking of a democracy. Democracy is, however, a form of government which can only work as well as its citizens want it to. It demands a great deal of work on the part of its citizens. The citizens of a democracy must be taught to be worthy of it, otherwise they will get exactly the kind of government they deserve. Democracy is a privilege, and privileges entail obligations. Our job as teachers should be to make democracy work by teaching the young what obligations a citizen worthy of a democratic government should know and discharge. The first thing I would teach our developing citizen is that the most important quality of a human being is the ability to relate himself to others in a warm, loving manner, and as one who is capable of using his mind as the finely analytical instrument it is capable of becoming, joining knowledge, understanding, sensitivity, and responsibility to loving-kindness.

And where does one begin making the required changes? The answer is clear and unequivocal: In oneself. A teacher cannot mean any more to his pupils than he means to himself. A school is an institution, and an institution is an agreement among people to behave in certain ways. How teachers agree to behave about sex education or anything else is what their schools will be, and what their products will be.

NOTES

[1] For a discussion of the physiology of this see Ashley Montagu, *The Reproductive Development of the Female* (New York: Julian Press, 1957).

[2] See John Money (ed.), *Sex Research: New Developments* (New York: Holt, Rinehart & Winston, 1965).

[3] See Ashley Montagu, *op. cit.*

[4] See my three books *The Direction of Human Development* (New York: Harper, 1955); *On Being Human,* Second Edition (New York: Hawthorne Books, 1967); *Education and Human Relations* (New York: Grove Press, 1957).

[5] In these connections see Ashley Montagu, *The Human Revolution* (New York: Bantam Books, 1967); Ashley Montagu, *The Direction of Human Development* (New York: Harper, 1955); Ashley Montagu, *The Humanization of Man* (New York: Grove Press, 1963).

Premarital Sex—Never!
A Teen-ager's Point of View

Gregory Spencer Hill

The subject to which Mr. Montagu* addressed himself holds special interest for me. You see, I am a seventeen-year-old boy, and my generation is the first to directly confront "The Pill" and "The Sexual Revolution." I found Mr. Montagu very eloquent and articulate, but not convincing. Mr. Montagu claims: "Young unmarried individuals . . . will be able . . . to enter into responsible sexual relationships in a . . . morally acceptable and reciprocally beneficial manner, which will help the participants to become more fully developed human beings than they would otherwise have stood a chance of becoming. The dead hand of ugly traditional beliefs . . . will be replaced by a new flowering of human love. This is a critical point." This is indeed a critical point, Mr. Montagu, and one which pits you opposed—diametrically—to my way of life and the one which I intend to pass on to my children.

I suspect that Mr. Montagu means to educate society into a utopia in which virtue and loving-kindness have demolished every vice and all hatred, making controls over sexual behavior (indeed over *any* facet of human behavior) unnecessary. I wish him luck. It is without bitterness that I reject Mr. Montagu's theory, but as a matter of necessity due to my religious convictions: I am a Mormon. I believe that should every teacher in every school system become a moral replica of the Saviour and be 100 percent effective in molding his charges, each resultant angel would adopt the strictest standard of sexual morality: sexual continence outside of marriage and absolute faithfulness to marital partners. For a Mormon, marriage is a sacred and eternal covenant, and sex outside of marriage ranks next to murder as a serious sin. Our eventual goal dictates such an attitude: we seek not that Protestant haven of peace and tranquility and eternal rest (which prompted that most irreverent remark from Tom Sawyer!) but to become as God is with our Heavenly Mother—in a literal sense father of spirit children.

But let us shunt Mormon philosophy aside here and return to a most urgent question: Is it wise for unmarried young people, with our mortal strengths and weaknesses, to experiment with sexual intercourse, seeking a "new flowering of human love"? The question seems to me to divide itself into the following subquestions: (1) Why and how have

*See pp. 95-104 of *Sex, Schools, and Society.*

our ancestors formulated and perpetuated our moral code forbidding premarital and extramarital relationships? (2) What would be the actual effect of social acceptance of premarital sex as a behavioral norm? (3) Is there an alternative to "ugly traditional beliefs" or wholesale indulgence in premarital sex which is more attractive than either one?

In answering the first question Mr. Montagu takes an essentially negative approach: Society has heretofore banned premarital relations because of the havoc to social and religious institutions caused by illegitimate children, enforcing its ban by social ostracism of mother, child, and occasionally father.

There is a positive approach more palatable to us prudes. Its basic premise is that our traditional moral code evolved from many years of experimentation with all sorts of man-woman relationships as the most practicable way to minimize the strife of jealous men fighting over their women, and simultaneously to allow tenderness, possessiveness, and exclusiveness in love relationships. Thus marriage became society's most important institution, and the family became its building block. Through the institution of marriage, society could effectively channel the priceless energies of its members away from never-ending sexual feuds, anxieties, and frustrations and into productive and creative endeavors. Conformity to the moral code became comfortable. To defy it the rebel had to defy conscience, effectively and thoroughly instilled in him by the family, a defiance which could only mean rejection of parents, teachers, and friends and estrangement from society. Rebellion in one form or another, with the consequent turmoil, has always held its attractiveness for the adolescent group, but conscience has heretofore triumphed, social harmony becoming much more important to the mature individual. The mature individual found that temporary affairs were "almost all risk and little promise," that the most satisfying relationship was the one prescribed by the code, and that conformity to the code allowed him to use the energies he possessed to more effectively work in concert with others, thereby growing as an individual personality.[1]

Let us now examine the second question: What would be the actual effect of social acceptance of premarital sex as a behavioral norm?

Answering this question becomes easy if we totally embrace the negative approach to the previous question and totally reject the positive one. If we can (1) prevent unwanted children, and (2) rid ourselves completely of guilt complexes instilled in us by two-faced Puritan ethics ("relax and learn to enjoy each other's bodies"), premarital relationships can be hedonistically, harmlessly, and almost *casually* enjoyed.

I do not accuse Mr. Montagu of totally embracing this argument. He realizes (eloquently!) that "with the removal of this barrier [unwanted pregnancy], the responsibilities involved in . . . . this delicate, this tender, this most sensitive of human relationships, is greatly increased.

Hence no one should ever consider entering into such a relationship who is incapable of behaving responsibly in it." I wish Mr. Montagu had explained further the "dangers of debasement," his prose and expertise being so far above my own.

But he did not, so I must hazard a guess as to what he could have meant. The most obvious danger in removing all barriers from pre-marital relationships is the danger that the sex relationship could become (as in Huxley's nightmare) so banal that it differs little from any biological function in its meaningfulness to the participants, equating it with the blowing of one's nose or urination or excretion. We might well become as well adjusted and comfortable in our sexual relationships with others as the cow—and have all the personality of the cow. Such debased relationships would not even be acceptable to the true hedonist. He often postpones his pleasure—forcibly deprives himself of it for a time—in order to more fully enjoy it at a later time.

Mr. Montagu avoids such a catastrophe for sex by insisting upon "sex-ual responsibility" as a prerequisite to sexual relations. It seems that he sees our society adopting some of the practices of the Bushmen of the Kalahari Desert. Since premarital sex does no apparent damage to the Bushman family structure, due to the fact that illegitimate children as results of the premarital union are extremely improbable, "respon-sible" premarital sex in America would do no damage to the American family structure, "the Pill" preventing premarital conception. Or so the analogy seems to go.

I find two faults with the analogy. First, premarital relationships among the Bushmen are limited to the extremely immature sexually. Thus it is difficult to visualize any real satisfaction resulting from such relationships which would emotionally involve one partner in the welfare of the other, and it is exceptionally easy to feel that such relation-ships would debase sex by making it too banal, too impersonal, some-thing entered into with little of the reverence "this delicate, this tender, this most sensitive of human relationships" deserves. Secondly, I doubt seriously that the Bushmen demand nearly so much of their sexual and family relationships as we do in our society. The terrific tensions built up in our technologically-oriented society are carried into the family and must there be released. The significance of the sexual union in releasing much of that tension has been widely acclaimed by sociologists and poets alike. Thus we cannot forego sex entirely in order to limit the size of our families as the Bushmen do, for the sexual union means too much to us psychologically once we have actually entered into a stable, socially accepted sexual relationship.

A logical question at this point is, Young people, unready during adolescence for marriage, suffer from extremely complex tensions, so why not make the sexual union available to them to release some of this tension? Some of the inherent dangers of such action have already been pointed out. Assuming that they could be overcome by Mr. Montagu's "sexual responsibility," I still feel that such an arrangement would entail more risk than promise and would in all likelihood create more tension than it would relieve.

What is the greatest threat to successful, long-range sexual adjustment, after all? Sallie Clinton, a fellow Mormon teen-ager and a poetess, puts it this way:

> Free Love?
>
> Yes—Isn't that what
>   has always made
>   love . . . love?
>
> But unrestrained
> gratification of
> one's lusts—
>   Isn't it self-
>   control that
>   separates man
>   from animals?
>
> Yes. Love is free.
>   Lust has an
>   ugly price.[2]

I have seen *no* evidence, *absolutely none, not one shred* of evidence, to indicate that premarital "practice" improves one's chances of being sexually well adjusted. Yet my liberal, "scientific" friends assume that such is the case, ignoring the fact that many of the best-adjusted, apparently most happy, prosperous, and creative members of our society do adhere and have always adhered strictly to the moral code. On the other hand, if the hippie subculture (which indulges frequently and without apparent guilt hang-ups) is an example of the "new flowering of human love" awaiting us, of the creative, well-adjusted social order of the future these liberals foresee, then I will shortly become a reactionary of the first order.

I agree with Mr. Montagu: irresponsibility is the greatest threat to healthful sexual adjustment. But such irresponsibility is not fostered by the alleged deprivations of the "dead hand of ugly traditional beliefs." Generations have coped successfully with such restrictions, and this one is just as capable of doing so as were its predecessors. Irresponsibility is fostered now, as always, by lack of self-control and self-discipline. Too many people, steeped in the delusions of the *"Playboy* philosophy"— that self-indulgence and maximization of physical enjoyment are the soul and purpose of life—have but one reaction to the bumps and bruises inevitable in marital conflict: they go to the divorce courts and call it quits. These people are not "bad people," but they are people who had better learn that nothing beautiful or worthwhile comes quickly, easily—or without self-restraint.

My generation has a crying need for such a lesson, and premarital sex—abject surrender to powerful urges, yes, but urges that can be controlled—is not likely to expedite the teaching. Should we surrender to our powerful instinctive urges, we might well placate those urges. At the same time, the level of rejection felt by a girl friend or boy friend found less attractive than another might be raised so high that a good day's cry might be replaced too often by a bullet in the brain. With very little prospect for improved marital relationships, we would be traveling the "blind alley," full of dangerous imponderables. Experimentation might well give rise to unprecedented feelings of insufficiency, insecurity, rejection, cheapness, and guilt, creating unimaginable mental havoc. Sex is powerful but neutral; it deserves our respect and caution as we use it. It deserves the total commitment we now demand of couples seeking to use it. We toy with fire in demanding anything less; I fear we would start a forest fire.

Now for the third question: Is there an alternative to "ugly traditional beliefs" or wholesale indulgence in premarital sex which is more attractive than either one?

Mr. Montagu's touching discussion of love, and his obviously genuine desire to help us Americans out of the moral jungle we have created for ourselves, impress this American deeply. Certainly the unbending, letter-of-the-law Puritan ethic of Victorian America was responsible for a great deal of human tragedy. Certainly a "predatory exploitative" male attitude toward sex is unhealthful. Although I retain my belief that premarital sex is wicked and unwise, I realize that sex is not nasty or sinful in and of itself. Certainly, youthful sexual energies must be expressed, not repressed. But is it necessary to gamble with something as dangerous—potentially devastating—as premarital sex, as total abandonment of traditional moral values, in order to escape the jungle, in order to achieve healthful, wholesome sexual adjustment?

I think not. The alternative I seek to the Puritan ethic of America's past, and the equally unrealistic *Playboy* attitude urged on us now, involves a change of emphasis, nationwide. It is all well and good to be able to accept one's sexuality. To say that the sexual process is a mere fact or part of life is to insult it. It is the very means by which human beings may become co-creators with God. It is the law upon which all human life is predicated; for us there is no life without obedience to this law. It is not because we moralists hold the sexual process unclean, undesirable, or ugly that we seek to protect it from wholesale publicity, but because we consider it somewhat sacred. Is the beauty of the sexual process enhanced by commercializing it, by forcing it to permeate every phase of our existence, by joking about it in connection with every subject, by cheapening it to the level of fun or "kicks" or thrills? It is unequivocal blasphemy! Cheap, commercialized, subtle and not-so-subtle goads toward sexual arousal must be played down: our youthful urges need little of this perverted stimulation.

It amazes me that modern intellectuals seem to see no release from sexual tensions or channel for sexual energies outside of the bedroom. We need desperately to recapture the pioneer American's capacity for good, clean fun. I do not appreciate the sneering condescension with which some "intellectual" movie critics greeted the wholesome simplicity of Walt Disney and *The Sound of Music*. I was exhilarated and inspired by most Disney shows, and that masterpiece of movie-making moved me to tears three times over. The ideals Disney and the von Trapps represented—personal dignity and courage, self-restraint, harmony with nature, unspoiled innocence—need not be apologized for; they have a place in modern society. Youth must be provided with and guided toward wholesome activity through which our powerful sexual energies can be channeled into constructive accomplishment.

Again I must turn to the way of life which has meant so much to me in order to provide specific examples of what activity I mean. Our church has a program for young people that we call the Mutual Improvement Association. A partial listing of MIA activities (in which I have participated at one time or another) includes the following: (1) athletics—basketball, softball, volleyball, and swimming; (2) music training—talent contests and shows, ample solo opportunities, choral and instrumental ensemble groupings, and just recreational group singing; (3) speech and drama activities—road shows, plays, skits, extemporaneous speaking, public speaking, and debate; (4) wholesome recreation—dancing, picnics, barbecues, swimming parties, outings, hikes, etc.; and (5) preparation for adulthood, which for boys includes scouting and exploring, career investigations, discussion of contemporary problems (including the frank discussion of sexual matters), and myriad opportunities for leadership; and which for girls includes studies of nutrition, cooking, sewing, housekeeping, child care, literature, and art. The program can create well-rounded individuals!

Of course, the program cannot work perfectly without the whole-hearted participation of young people, or without dedicated, patient, talented adult leadership—and often neither prerequisite is completely met. Nevertheless we try, and we have been rewarded with one of the lowest divorce rates (especially for temple marriages) and highest percentages of really happy marriage and family relationships in Christendom. The lasting friendships, social skills, and individual talents developed in MIA bless a teen-ager far more than could a life of mere "fun" or self-indulgence. The energies and tensions of youth are as thoroughly dissipated through MIA activities and respectful, companionable dating relationships as through premarital sexual relationships. MIA tends to place sex in perspective by providing a forum for, and encouraging less-than-flippant discussion of, issues such as religious standards, personal etiquette, political leanings, family problems and awkward situations, personal finance—issues vital to marital life, which are too often clouded by the bedroom. So why should teen-agers voluntarily take the risks inherent in premarital sex, standing to gain so little and lose so much? Perhaps the world could consider our way before it plunges down the proverbial "blind alley." I certainly prefer it.

NOTES

[1] I rely heavily on Reuben Hill's chapter, "Morality Makes Sense," from Evelyn Duvall and Reuben Hill, *When You Marry*. Boston: D. C. Heath, 1945.
[2] Sallie Clinton, "Free Love?" *Improvement Era,* June, 1968, p. 143.

Part III

PROBLEMS, CONFLICTS, AND SEX EDUCATION

INTRODUCTION

The articles in this section of the anthology are those which best portray the delicate but abrasive nature of the domestic controversy aroused in the United States by the topic "schools and sex education." The protagonists include religious and fundamentalistic groups ranging from those who wish schools to handle the subject on a purely religious and moral basis to those who demand that the matter be left entirely to the family or church. In addition, there are those who work professionally in the field of sex education and family counseling. They too have their divisions and are often unable to agree about whether the emphasis in sex education programs should be on purely factual information or on ethically oriented instruction geared to the relativistic needs of students.

Some religious organizations maintain a critical interest in the activities of certain controversial institutions devoted to sex research. One of these religious groups, the Christian Crusade organization, based in Tulsa, Oklahoma, under the leadership of the Reverend William Hargis, has taken a strong stand against what it regards as the "indiscriminate introduction of sex education programs into the public schools." A secular and politically partisan viewpoint against unwarranted sex education programs is espoused by the John Birch Society of Belmont, Massachusetts. The society views the introduction of so-called programs in educational sexuality as a debilitating force and further proof of the extension of communistic and subversive influences in American public education. One of the principal targets of the Christian Crusade and the John Birch Society is SIECUS—the Sex Information and Education Council of the United States—a privately financed and nonprofit organization based in New York which conducts research and hands out information and materials for use in school sex education programs. Its stated goal is the "establishment of man's sexuality as a health entity," to assist individuals "towards responsible use of the sexual faculty and towards assimilation of sex into their individual life patterns as a creative and re-creative force." SIECUS frequently provides extensive bibliographical guides of graded reading material for children from the preschool to the high-school level. The activities of the SIECUS staff, especially its controversial and outspoken executive director, Dr. Mary Steichen Calderone, are described extensively in John Kobler's article, "Sex Invades the Schoolhouse," and in Marjorie F. Iseman's "Sex Education."

Some of the school programs developed by SIECUS have come under severe attack from community groups. Criticism of SIECUS is widespread, but it is probably nowhere as virulent or as critically documented as in the extensive analyses by Gordon V. Drake ("Is the Schoolhouse the Proper Place to Teach Raw Sex?") and Gary Allen ("Sex Study: Problems, Propaganda, and Pornography"). In school districts where sex education programs are in operation or soon to become established, concerned citizens' groups have been organized to provide resistance and opposition. Drake gives details on how sex education programs can be most effectively blocked and notes some of the organizations which have sprung up for this purpose—for example, MOMS (Mothers Organized for Moral Stability), POPE (Parents for Orthodoxy in Parochial Education), and POSE (Parents Opposed to Sex Education). He advocates that parent groups should be formed "before your community has been invaded by sexologists," and warns the MOMS, POSES, and POPES throughout the United States of the unhealthy alliance between sex educators and sexologists who "represent every shade of muddy gray morality, ministers colored atheistic pink, and camp followers of every persuasion."

Dr. Drake is a particularly active opponent and is in wide demand as a lecturer. He has toured the United States fulminating against the introduction of sex education programs, singling out for attack SIECUS, the National Education Association, and the U.S. Office of Education, because of their involvement either in supporting and developing or in financing sex education programs in the schools. The sex educators' goal of extending their programs with the utmost frankness and without moral inhibitions and religious taboos is, according to critics like Dr. Drake, driving a diabolical, Communist-inspired wedge between the school, the family, and the church. Drake believes that if the New Morality is accepted, American children will become "easy targets for Marxism and other amoral, nihilistic philosophies— as well as VD!" (Attention should be drawn to Mary Breasted's book, *Oh! Sex Education!* [1970], a carefully documented and highly readable history of the sex education controversy which caused considerable disquiet in America during the years 1968 and 1969. The involvement of the "pros" and "antis" is treated in the manner of a historical novel and includes an analysis of the activities of Gordon V. Drake, Mary S. Calderone, and many of the other leading figures.)

Gary Allen takes a similar stance to that of Gordon Drake, focusing on the aims of SIECUS and the private lives of its board of directors, and suggests that the activities of SIECUS and those associated with it, the "Leftist sex educationists," are often blatantly Communist-inspired. Allen presents an extensive survey of the nationwide sex education programs and warns "against putting the sexual morality of all children at the mercy of the atheists and pornographers and Communists who are supporting and directing SIECUS." His critical analysis, like that of Gordon Drake, is diametrically opposed to those of John Kobler and of Marjorie Iseman, who provide non-polemical observations which are both constructive and entertaining.

The discussion by Ira L. Reiss, a university sociologist and former associate of SIECUS, on the topic "Sex Education in the Public Schools: Problem or Solution?" shows the kinds of difficulties which may be encountered in establishing programs and gives recommendations for alleviating problems. He believes that the schools should provide sex instruction but that the families and parents are ultimately responsible for teaching the moral aspects of sexuality, for "we cannot control sexuality directly, nor can we stop the flow of information. . . ." Parents can provide "an element of enlightenment" if they are prepared to support "an unbiased approach" to sex education "throughout the educational system." His position is one with which other contributors to this section of the anthology, such as Gordon Drake, Gary Allen, and Max Rafferty, would be prepared to disagree.

Likewise, they would be averse to many of the views expressed in the interview with William H. Masters and Virginia E. Johnson in *Playboy,* which provides further underpinning for the view that sex education "should begin as soon as youngsters are old enough to observe their parents relating to each other." Masters and Johnson stress the constructive and positive role of the family and church as major agents for enhancing the sexual understanding of young people. Perhaps the most telling point to emerge from the *Playboy* interview comes in answer to the question, How well is sex education being handled in America today? The reply tersely provides ammunition for both opponents and proponents of school sex education programs when Masters and Johnson state: "We have no scientific knowledge as to whether it is worth a damn. . . . there is absolutely no objective study that has been done in this area to determine its real value."

The blame for much of today's teen-age confusion and sexual immaturity should be laid on the parents, believes Max Rafferty, the highly controversial former superintendent of education for California. Rafferty, in his pungent essay, "The Dropout Parents: How America Got on a Sex Binge," blames not the children but their parents for encouraging "instant sex education" through pornographic movies and lurid descriptive material on drugs and sexual perversions which is freely available at newsstands. He chastises parents: "You let the schools take over your own immemorial job of telling your children the facts of life, and you didn't care that the resulting school sex education programs were as devoid of morality and personal dignity as a third-generation computer." Not only does Rafferty castigate parents for neglecting their children's sexual upbringing, but he attacks "the jelly-spined college presidents" who "pontificated solemnly about their institutions not being 'custodial' in relation to their inmates. . . ."

The blame for inadequate sex education Rafferty attributes to parents; but the irrelevance and inadequacy of school sex education programs Masters and Johnson, not to mention Reiss, lay on inadequate teachers; while the ill-advised programs and immoral sexuality classes Drake and Allen attribute to the overly active and enthusiastic entrance on the scene of groups such as SIECUS.

Whatever one's ideological, social, religious, or moral persuasion, there are sufficient viewpoints represented in this section of the anthology to interest, if not irritate, all but the most phlegmatic readers. The material in the preceding section ("Pedagogy and Sex Education") dealt more specifically with institutional problems concerning the nature of school-imposed sex education. This section illustrates the nature of the community antagonisms which are aroused when the school curriculum includes controversial courses on "practical sexuality" and "situational morality" within the scope of formal sex education programs.

Sex Education in the Public Schools:
Problem or Solution?

Ira L. Reiss

Within the next decade the majority of our public schools will in all likelihood have some form of sex education program. Whether this change in our public-school curriculum will be the solution to existing problems in the area of sex or whether it will create more problems is a vital question that we ought to face up to now. We still have time to assess the way sex education is being integrated today and arrive at a judgment on the wisdom of continuing or changing the present trends.

I have had the opportunity to become familiar with much of the material utilized in the public-school sex education programs and with the way the courses are taught and integrated into existing school programs. I don't pretend to have taken a representative sample, but I have become familiar with a great many sex education programs. The chief impressions that I have been left with are that the key characteristics of the sex education programs that exist in most of our public schools today are: (1) the courses have strong moralistic and propagandistic elements; (2) the courses stress physiological aspects of sexuality; (3) the courses are isolated, and sexual materials are not integrated into other relevant courses in the school system; (4) the teachers of these courses are inadequately trained for an inadequately defined task. It should be clear that much of what is said critically about sex education could be said critically about many other aspects of the educational system, but I will leave that broader task to someone else.

The moral aspect of sex education courses is probably their most easily detectable quality. One has only to glance at course descriptions to find frequent references to teaching the students the "value" of chastity, or the "dangers" of going steady, or a list of reasons why one should avoid heavy petting, "excessive" masturbation, or premarital intercourse. On the positive value side one finds the emphasis on married life so strong that the clear implication is that those from broken homes are in a very "bad" situation. The specific values that are stressed vary somewhat, although they are almost invariably the status quo type. What is crucial is not the specific values but the fact that teachers are morally indoctrinating children in the name of education.

This raises the question that many public schools do not seem to have faced. That is, the basic philosophy of education under which

119

they operate. As an academician I can answer this question in a broad way quite easily. There is a general philosophy of education that is most accepted in the colleges among those who are in the education departments as well as among most others. The position is that education is aimed at teaching people *how* to think and not *what* to think. Education is not propaganda or indoctrination. If one teaches about politics, one does not teach that the Republican or Democratic party is the best party. Rather, one teaches people how the political processes work, so that the students may be able to handle their own life in this area more intelligently. Similarly, if one teaches about American religions, one does not teach that Catholicism or Protestantism is the best religion. Rather, one teaches how the religious institution is organized and how it operates in our society, so that if the individual has questions regarding religion this educational background may aid in his handling of them. The same should be true for teaching about sex. According to this generally accepted philosophy of education, we would not tell the student that abstinence or permissiveness before marriage is the best form of behavior. We would teach how sexual relationships occur and analyze this so as to increase the student's ability to think calmly and rationally in this area and thereby better handle whatever problems may arise.

Of course, no social institution such as the public schools is free of moral judgments. Judgments of value must be made to decide what is an important enough part of our cultural heritage and our current and future life to be included in the school curriculum. It is also a moral judgment that good education is education that is objective and impartial in its treatment of subjects. But such judgments do not bias the way a particular topic is treated; they do not allow us to preach in favor of one political party, one religion, or one sexual standard. The moral judgments that schools allow are operational judgments concerning how the school system should function in our society—and that is quite different from moral judgments favoring a particular moral position on the substance covered in a course.

Granted, it is a difficult thing to be impartial and to maintain an interesting presentation and to avoid mere memorization of facts. In the area of sex, when an objective stance is not taken, when we resort to moralizing, the student's typical reaction is to tune out the teacher. Such indoctrination courses often bore the students, who have heard the same thing year after year from other adult sources. Students may take such courses because they are easy and because they take little preparation, but they hardly take them for educational reasons. The goal of teaching people how to think without indoctrination is difficult and achieved at best in part only. But if we do not at least try for this goal, the likelihood of failure to be objective and the likelihood of our educational system becoming more propagandistic would increase greatly.

The ideal serves to maintain approximation to standards. Such limitation on moralizing would naturally not apply to religious institutions. Sex education within a church would be expected to contain some moral commitment to the church's position.

The question arises here as to precisely how sex should be taught in order to fit into the public schools. At the present time, the heavy emphasis on physiology and the lack of an integrated curriculum regarding sex are in part a result of the fact that the physiology of sex is an area where teachers find it easier to avoid facing their own hang-ups on sex, i.e., their own emotional feelings. But the stress on physiology overlooks the crucial areas of attitudes and social pressures that mean so much in the full explanation of human sexuality. Also, the educational aids, such as the charts showing the fetus during all nine months of pregnancy and the internal and external organs of the male and female, are readily available. Similar educational materials on the psychological, sociological, and anthropological aspects of sex are not so easily available. However, this is being remedied by publications issued by SIECUS and other groups. In addition, the National Science Foundation has given grants that will soon lead to revisions in our social studies offerings in the public schools. Some of these changes will include more materials on the entire area of family life.

Part of the question of content is the question of the level of sex education and the specific courses utilized. An isolated course on sex education at the seventh-grade level is hardly an effective way to handle the needs for sex education. If we have decided, as most Americans have, according to recent polls, that sex is an important enough aspect of our life that it should be handled in the public schools, then we have to do more than simply insert one course and feel that we have solved the problem. We must realize that the reason there is a felt need for sex education in the public-school curriculum is that the curriculum has been denuded of its sexual content over the generations. Almost all disciplines have had the sexual aspects of their fields removed.

This "sex-ectomy" can be corrected. For example, in economics one of the most fascinating areas to study would be the economics of prostitution. To what extent do the classical laws of supply and demand apply here? In history one would gain much by studying the ways in which the sexual codes of society affected the political life of presidents and kings. The question of the illegitimate child of Grover Cleveland, the sexual interests of Catherine the Great, are but two examples of prime relevance. Social problems courses could discuss the relative effectiveness of various birth control methods in controlling population growth in countries like India. English literature is one of the very few areas where sex hasn't been removed as thoroughly as in other fields.

This is predominantly so because to remove it would eliminate much, if not most, of the valuable literature that forms the subject matter of this field. This is one reason why it is in literature courses that some parents find books to which they object. Such parents lack the philosophy of education we have been speaking about and have more of a moral indoctrination philosophy of education.

My point is that the sex-ectomy should be remedied by putting sex back into all fields. In this way it can be viewed in its social and cultural context and will not be given undue importance. After all, sex is not an academic discipline; one cannot major in sex. Thus it has no place as a separate course in a public-school system unless one wants to take a kind of "driver's education" approach to it. If we want sex education to have the respect of the teachers and the students, then it would seem that the best path to follow would be to integrate it into the legitimate existing disciplines. To do otherwise will make it likely to be taught in moralistic fashion. Of course, such total integration into various courses cannot occur without proper teaching materials and properly trained teachers. It is not something that can occur overnight. However, if we lack integration as a goal, we may feel that the one seventh-grade course in sex education really is transmitting all the sexual awareness that is needed, and thereby we would fail to achieve an adequate sex education program. In the public schools, as in other institutions, it is having well-thought-out, long-range goals that leads to progress.

This brings us to the last characteristic of present-day sex education— the poor quality of many of the teachers involved. Partly, this is due to the fact that what is supposed to be done is poorly defined and often is defined in ways that are nontraditional in American education. By this I mean that the course is defined as a kind of moral indoctrination which parents hope will cut down on VD, premarital pregnancy, and premarital intercourse. Note that such a demand for "practical" con- sequences would eliminate most of the courses in our current public- school system, particularly those in the humanities area.

Why is it that when we add the "new math" to the public-school sys- tem we use arguments regarding the ease with which the new math can be learned, its better integration with more advanced forms of mathe- matics, and so forth? We don't find many arguments that ask, Why bother to get so involved with mathematics, since most of us won't need to do more than count our change at the movie theater? We don't find such arguments, because we have accepted the intrinsic value of mathe- matics as an area of knowledge that is important enough to our civiliza- tion for us to preserve a high level of awareness about it. Why don't we use the same reasoning about sex and justify the "new sex" by contend- ing that such knowledge is an important enough aspect of our way of life that we should have a sound understanding of it? Such an approach would lead to better-prepared students in our colleges. The answer is, I think, that in sex we allow our emotions to blind us to the educational philosophy that guides us in the case of mathematics. By doing this we take sex out of the usual academic structure; then it becomes a question of who is qualified to teach this unusual type of course. Often the coach or a friendly housewife is given the task. For a moralistic, applied approach to sex such people may well be relevant, but for an educational approach they clearly are not adequate.

From the point of view of educational philosophy, our basic mistake is to think that when we deal with sex in the public schools we must somehow treat it differently than we do all our other subjects. Different subjects may well require somewhat different pedagogical techniques, but the pedagogical requirement of sex is well within the limits of existing methods. Many classes handle emotionally charged subjects (often more emotional to the teacher than the student) when discussing social problems, novels, and cross-cultural differences. Is sex really so different?

The qualifications for teaching sex in the public schools should be the same as the qualifications for teaching in most other fields. A good teacher needs to be able to establish rapport with the class and needs to be sensitive to ways of clearly communicating with that class. A good teacher must know the subject matter thoroughly and must strive to communicate it at a level that can be understood. A good teacher must be able to handle all aspects of the field, and not be emotionally blocked from covering a particular part of it.

Ideally, sex education would be taught in an integrated fashion; materials could be added to the social science units at all levels. I stress all levels, K–12, because it seems best to start before emotional blocks are too strong and to treat sex as a natural part of all instructional levels. It would seem to be psychologically advantageous to discuss common events like menstruation, masturbation, and marriage before they occur. Children of all ages have a sexual quality to their lives, and the discussion of sex is something they are "ready for." They are "mature" enough to handle it if it is presented in accordance with sound educational principles.

A teacher whose substantive training is in psychology, sociology, and anthropology would be best equipped to see the obvious places where sex could be incorporated into the social science units. A few of the many ways in which sex could be brought easily and naturally into the elementary classroom are: in discussions of the family, in comparisons of courtship in animals and man, in comparisons of different societies, in discussions of different customs regarding marriage, and in discussions of how our self-image affects our sex life. I stress here the social studies units, for the physiological aspects of sex can more easily and clearly be added to the biological science areas without as much difficulty. Home economics and health courses can incorporate the more applied aspects of sex—the problem-centered and direct role-preparation aspects. Naturally, the knowledge of sex gained in a variety of other courses has implications for role preparation and should give greatly increased insight to the students, but home economics and health courses can focus more directly on this applied area. Nevertheless, sex education should not be conceived of as predominantly present in these applied fields, but rather as predominantly centered as one integrated part of many fields. This approach puts sex into a broad human context rather than singling it out as an isolated problem area.

The question of the practical strategy necessary to get a sex education program adopted makes it likely that a school system may want to start with one course at a certain grade level. However, unless the person running that course plans to get educational materials and to help coordinate the integration of sex throughout the existing curriculum, the course will not really become part of the educational life of the students. One can, of course, have an interdisciplinary applied-type course on sex; but if that is all one gets into the school system, then sex has not been put back into our schools, but rather has simply been fused onto the academic educational system. As long as that state of affairs remains, the course will have low prestige. It will thus be poorly staffed, and students will take it for "laughs" and easy grades rather than for educational purposes. The faculty in college education departments will also not look favorably upon an applied course and will do little to further the preparation of competent teachers. The same holds true for "family life education" courses; they, too, most often have no disciplinary "home" and are no more readily accepted. Such family life education also needs to be integrated into existing disciplines.

The real danger in America today is that almost all of our schools will add a type of moralistic, unintegrated, and poorly staffed applied course in sex education and then feel that they have taken care of the needs for sex education. This is exactly what I see happening today in our country, and unless we take a longer and more careful look at the matter we may have a sex education program on a national scale that really is an anti–sex education program.

Now let us briefly look at some of the key factors which seem to be pressuring sex education toward becoming an educational failure. One very crucial area affecting the popularity and the success of sex education programs today is the attitude of parents toward sex in their own families. An observer from another culture would be immediately struck by the fact that, although parents will readily admit the great importance of sex to their youngsters' future lives, they have a noticeable tendency to avoid discussing sex with their children. It would be difficult to find a comparable situation in any other pattern of American socialization. For example, parents who feel that religion is an important part of their child's present and future life do not hesitate to talk about religion. They do not wait to be asked and then just answer a direct question and go no further. The modern parent seems to do just this on sex. He may rationalize this position by statements about the "readiness" of his child. He may feel that he will give the child "ideas" about sex if he raises the topic. The practical consequences of such an approach are to lessen the influence of the parents and increase the influence of one's peers on one's sex life. By minimizing talk about sex, one does not end the sexual interests of one's child. The child still plays the usual sex games of curiosity and exploration with other children. Sexual information, accurate or not, and sexual attitudes of various sorts inevitably filter down from the older boys and girls to the younger boys and girls. There is no way for parents to stop this; there is only the possibility of extending the parental influences by a more concerted effort to deal with the topic of sex even if the child doesn't initiate it.

Obviously, one key reason for the hushed approach to sex is that the parents haven't yet come to terms with their own attitudes. Also, the parent may feel he doesn't have the needed information. He may feel inadequate to cope with the possible consequences of initiating conversation about sex. Given such parents, it is clear that the consequences of talking about sex might be different if one had parents without such informational and attitudinal hang-ups. In fact, I believe it is the partial realization of this situation that has made sex education in the public schools popular and that has made it of the poor quality that it is at present. Let me briefly explain what I mean.

Many parents may have decided that, since they cannot handle sex discussions comfortably with their children, maybe the public-school system can help them. It is difficult to say why this didn't happen a few generations ago, but I think one reason is the fact that there has been a shift in the premarital sex partners of middle- and upper-class males from prostitutes to the "girl next door," and so the parents of the girl next door are concerned. Also, many more children are in school now during their most sexually active years. There is increased awareness of the widespread nature of VD and premarital pregnancy even among middle- and upper-class groups. Although the changes are too gradual to be called revolutionary, there has been a noticeable removal of adult heads from the sand. The difficulties of hiding sex become greater when it is occurring nearby and when historical and cross-cultural studies point out further its pervasiveness. All our evidence suggests that no culture anywhere at any time on this planet has brought up even the majority of one generation of males to physical maturity as virgins. The major historical shifts have been predominantly in terms of the partners of men—are they prostitutes or are they the girl next door? Such a factual situation needn't affect one's moral values. One can favor for oneself or others goals that cannot be achieved by all, but even so, one must realize that the universality of premarital sex of some kind in a child's life experiences makes it an important area to include in a child's education.

Most parents are, naturally, not very conversant with educational philosophies. Thus they haven't generally internalized the idea that teachers should not be moralistic in presenting their subject matter. When social changes make parents think of accepting sex education in the schools, they tend to project their own parental roles on the teacher and feel that she should be moralistic. By this they mean, of course, moralistic in their own way; for they would object violently if the teacher's moralism were in accord with that of some other group of parents and not with their own.

Public-school teachers do not have as highly developed a sense of academic freedom as do college teachers; thus they are more easily intimidated by these parental pressures. In fact, many of them have become so accustomed to pressures from parents, school boards, and principals that they have only retained a very watered-down version of the educational philosophy they were taught in college. Therefore, if one wants to obtain an academically respectable approach to sex in the public schools, it is essential to educate the parents and to strengthen the academic freedom of our public-school teachers. They may then abide more closely with their original educational philosophy.

Such a closer adherence to accepted educational philosophy would force some parents into an uncomfortable situation. For if they accept the fact that the school is not going to teach their personal morals to all its children, then they cannot thereby escape from teaching sexual morals themselves. That means they will still have to transmit, directly or indirectly, their own moral values regarding sex to their children. Perhaps an adult-education program on sex can help. It can aid the parents to understand their own values and the place of sex in their lives, to think through what they want to teach their youngsters and how.

Many practical problems are associated with any attempt to instigate a sound educational approach to sexuality in the public schools. As a sociologist, I realize that the social and cultural setting of the school cannot be fully excluded. It is obvious, for example, that Christmas and Easter and many other religious holidays permeate the school program and very often in obviously religious ways. Perhaps the best one can hope for is that at least films asserting the divinity of Christ will not be used in the schools. But if one does not aim at some objectivity, then such films and similar religious elements would surely permeate our school systems. Accordingly, perhaps certain widely shared values such as the vague notions of the value of love, respect, and responsibility will be endorsed in almost all sex education classes. But this is still closer to our ideal of impartiality than would be the teaching of abstinence or permissiveness as the only moral way to behave. Sometimes we overestimate the public opposition to various educational endeavors. For example, I have seen reports that Catholic schools in some cities include more birth control information than do public schools in the same cities. While we cannot totally ignore social pressures, we can avoid exaggerating their potency.

It is also clear that different school settings will affect the emphasis on many school subjects, including sex. In a lower-class neighborhood with high VD and illegitimacy rates one can expect these factors to loom larger in the program. In an upper-class setting the psychological subtleties may well gain more attention. In both cases the approach could be objective. The question of whether to require sex education for all students becomes irrelevant in any school system that incorporates sex into its natural context in a wide variety of fields. Requirement is only an issue when one has but a single isolated course on sex education. The U. S. Office of Education announced in August, 1966, that funds were available to assist communities in the integration of sex into their public-school programs and in the training of teachers. The specifics of the program are left up to the judgment of the communities.

One major point to bear in mind is that at least in recent American history the attempt to keep children ignorant of sex has rarely succeeded except in correlating highly with premarital pregnancy rates. The attempt to moralize about sex in public institutions has also not succeeded in changing major patterns of behavior. If we feel that sex is an important aspect of life, then it is important to enable people to think clearly about it. This the public-school systems can do if the parents of America will let them. Sex education will not necessarily reduce to nothing our VD and premarital pregnancy rates, but it can, if taught in accordance with accepted educational principles, make the sexual choices of our children less psychologically costly. A sound sex education can aid the individual student to choose his or her sex ethic in a more calm and less compulsive fashion. The choice of sex ethics is already an accepted part of youth culture. Young people feel that they have just as much right to choose their sex ethic as to choose their political party or their religion. They feel there are different ways suited best for different people. This is what is often called the "New Morality." Parents may well favor one type of choice, but ignorance or public moralizing will not achieve that goal. The parents have their chance to influence their child's choices by the values and attitudes they pass on. If they miss out there, they are not likely to change things by preventing a public discussion in a reasonably impartial manner of this area in the public schools. At least by having a sound sex education system parents can assure a less compulsive basis for choice. Given the free courtship system we have, we cannot control sexuality directly, nor can we stop the flow of information and attitudes about sex. But we can add an element of enlightenment and control to our youngsters' sexual life by supporting an unbiased approach to it throughout the educational system.

As an educator I feel that we should adopt sound educational approaches to sex in the public schools. As a sociologist I feel that we should not distort by our moralizing the research findings that are available. As a father, I feel that I, and not the public schools, should do the moral teaching of my children in my own way. If we do not realize the distinct qualities of these various roles we play, we will have sex education in our public schools in a form that will not prepare our children for the sexual aspects of the lives they lead. We will have missed the opportunity to make the best case for our private moral positions.

Sex Invades the Schoolhouse

John Kobler

The fastest-spreading new fad in American education is sex instruction, but its critics still ask: Should boys and girls be taught together? What ought the teachers to say about premarital intercourse? Contraception? Wouldn't it be better simply to scare the youngsters away from the whole subject?

In San Diego, California, they are called "social-health teacher-counselors." Five of them—two men, three women—circulate among the city's thirty-one secondary schools, trying to promote "wholesome attitudes toward boy-girl relationships and respect for family life," in the words of Dr. G. Gage Wetherill, director of health services, who initiated the effort. The counselors carry from school to school big canvas bags containing classroom materials which, not so very long ago, would have scandalized the community and even invited prosecution. The materials include literature, charts, models, tapes, and films, dealing in explicit terms with such formerly taboo subjects as sexual anatomy, masturbation, homosexuality, and premarital intercourse. The counselors, however, shock hardly anybody. They go their rounds with the majority approval not only of school administrators but also of local physicians, clergymen, civic leaders, and the Parent-Teacher Association. "Though the program is optional," Dr. Wetherill reports, "we have ninety-nine percent parental consent."

As she threads a film entitled *The Game* into a projector, a young counselor named Mrs. Persida Drakulich matter-of-factly announces to the forty girls in one ninth-grade class at Pershing Junior High, "You're going to see how a boy feels after intercourse with a virgin."

Her listeners are predominantly from white middle-income families. There are four Negro and two Mexican girls. (Boys get the film too, usually under the guidance of a male counselor, but at a different time, it being San Diego school policy to segregate the sexes for sex education.)

"Pay lots of attention to the game they're playing," Mrs. Drakulich continued. "Do you know why they're playing it? And listen carefully to the words they use. 'Cherry' means what we call the 'hymen.' That's what the boys in the film are referring to. You'll also hear one of them say, 'Did you bounce her high?' Not all boys talk or feel that way. Often the boy who talks big is insecure about his masculinity."

129

Lights out. Music. Peter, a high-school senior, who brags about his prowess as a seducer, is challenged by his companions to prove it. Let him try his wiles on his virginal classmate Nicky. At first Nicky resists. But gradually she succumbs to flattery. Her downfall occurs in the back of a car borrowed from Peter's father. Afterward Peter, conscience-stricken and ashamed, avoids Nicky. She grows resentful and angry at herself for having ignored her girl friends' advice. Hadn't they warned her that Peter would drop her once he "scored"? The film ends with Peter's cronies vicariously enjoying his adventure.

During the remaining twenty minutes of class Mrs. Drakulich leads a "buzz session" about the moral implications of *The Game*. "Now, what was really going on? Yes, Judy."

A blue-jeaned fourteen-year-old, her blond hair tumbling to her waist, ventures, "He didn't really want to go through with it."

Counselor beams. "Precisely. I've talked to boys who told me, 'I was hoping she'd say no.' "

Second girl: "I don't think that Nicky was really so innocent."

Mrs. Drakulich: "How many think she was enjoying the game? *(Up go some thirty hands.)* You remember when Peter phones and asks, "What are you doing?' and Nicky tells him, 'I just got out of the tub.' She wanted him to picture her in the nude, didn't she? 'I'll be right over,' he says. Then she plays coy. 'Is that nice?' When he does arrive, why should she receive him in her bedroom, with her parents absent? Eventually she falls for the oldest line. 'You're laughing at me,' Peter says. So she has to show him she takes him seriously. . . . You have a question?"

Third girl: "Why does Peter always wear dark glasses, even when he's taking a bath?"

Mrs. Drakulich: "Can anybody answer that?"

Blue Jeans: "He's sort of hiding behind them."

Mrs. Drakulich: "Now consider the cultural influences on Peter and Nicky. The rock-'n'-roll music at the beach. Dancing in their swimsuits. The car—a car can be a mobile bed, you know. Weren't they both losers? The guilt, the shame? Why is Peter so dejected?"

A Mexican girl: "He's afraid she won't accept him any more."

Mrs. Drakulich: "How many think he'd like to have intercourse with her again?"

Chorus *(minus three or four dissenters)*: "NO!"

Mrs. Drakulich: "What will happen to them?"

Mixed reaction: "They'll drift apart" . . . "He's going back to her and I'm so happy" . . . "She'll never speak to him again" . . . "They'll come back together, only relations will be like they should have been in the first place. . . ."

Mrs. Drakulich: "Remember, all boys don't behave and think the way they do in *The Game*. Some boys don't like the film at all. They're

afraid you girls will get the wrong idea and suspect everything they
say. . . ."

The bell interrupts. Class dismissed. One little girl lingers, shyly approaches the counselor. "I got a problem, ma'am, a real problem."

"Tell me about it, dear."

"There's this boy. He's seventeen. He wants to come see me alone at
my house when my folks is workin'. I tell him no. So he says for me to
come to his house. But his folks are away all day too."

"Do you know what he has in mind?"

"I know."

"Well, what's the problem?"

"I want to."

They talk for an hour. Mrs. Drakulich concludes, "You want to play
the game of love; he wants to play the game of sex. But you're not
ready for sex, and he's not ready for love. It's a trap."

Later the child sadly reports that she has stopped dating her pursuer.
"I told him maybe we'd meet again when we was both ready."

"And what did he say?"

"He say, 'Quit talkin' to teachers.' "

San Diego's sex education program comprises seventeen lessons. They
begin in the sixth grade at elementary school, where special teachers
devote an hour a day for five days chiefly to the mechanics of reproduction. Among their audio-visual aids are colored slides depicting male
and female genitalia, drawings tracing fetal growth, and a Walt Disney
animated cartoon, *The Story of Menstruation,* in which a maiden re-
sembling Snow White symbolizes pubescent girlhood. The teachers also
give chalkboard talks, mincing no words, about the formation of sperm,
wet dreams, copulation. During the ensuing discussions they undertake
to answer all questions, however disconcerting, with total candor.

The youngsters hear no more about sex from the faculty until they
reach ninth grade. Then the roving teacher-counselors conduct a series
of six meetings (review of early lessons plus new material on sex
deviations, sex outside marriage, illegitimacy, venereal diseases, and the
psychological dangers of promiscuity, on social attitudes toward sex,
and on selecting a mate, on courtship and marriage and family responsibilities). Another three-year hiatus follows, then, in senior year,
the counselors cover much the same topics again, but in slightly greater
detail and depth.

This curriculum exemplifies what has recently become a major fad
in American education. Though the San Diego program got under way
twenty-six years ago [in 1942], most of the others mushrooming all over
the country are newer than the new math, having been introduced within
the last two or three years. America seems to have suddenly discovered
an urgent need for universal sex education—from kindergarten through

high school, some enthusiasts insist—and is galloping off in all directions at once to meet it.

Only a few years back the idea of teaching schoolchildren about sex would have aroused consternation among the public. "Not long ago they'd have hanged me from the nearest telephone pole for what I'm doing," says Superintendent Paul W. Cook of the Anaheim, California, Union High School District, which maintains one of the country's most publicized sex education programs.

In Chicago, up to 1965, school biology students might scarcely have imagined, for all the teachers ever told them, that humans had a reproductive system. Plants and animals, yes, but when it came to people—awkward silence. The Board of Education prohibited any teaching about sex. Then, three years ago [in 1965], the Illinois General Assembly, yielding to various pressures—especially that of the Parent-Teacher Association—passed an act sanctioning a less squeamish policy. The next fall a pilot program was incorporated into the fifth-grade science units at twenty-seven Chicago schools. When 3,200 students' parents were queried about having their children take the course, only sixteen children's parents, most of them fundamentalists from the Appalachian hills, withheld their consent. The following year the program was extended to 114 more elementary schools and all the high schools. By 1970, according to present plans, sex education will have become routine for all grades in all 600 city schools.

For a time before 1955, several schools in the Miami area gave a course called "family living." It had nothing to do with sex. The mere title, nevertheless, suggested to parents an encroachment upon their domain, and they angrily opposed the course. The animal pets which some schools collected, not for biology instruction, but simply to make the classroom seem friendlier, fell under suspicion. One principal recalls, "We couldn't even keep a pregnant rabbit around." Every copy of one biology textbook was withdrawn when the School Board decided that a drawing of the female body revealed the internal reproductive organs in needless detail. The art instructor given the task of "purifying" this illustration complained to the principal, "I'm exhausted. I've just performed three hundred hysterectomies."

Nowadays, however, Miami parents by the thousands enthusiastically subscribe to the new doctrine. At suburban Coral Gables's Ponce de Leon Junior High, for example, seventh-, eighth- and ninth-graders anonymously submit in writing the questions about sex that they most want answered. Using the commonest questions, a surgeon, Dr. Beverly Jones, then delivers to the boys three earthy physiological talks peppered with cautionary advice ("Don't you and a girl go pairing off in a corner. It'll only lead to frustration. You're not prepared for sex except as animals. Don't start a relationship you're not ready for"). Dr. Lynn Bartlett, a youth counselor, gives the girls three lectures based on *their* questions ("Should a girl kiss a boy on their first date? Certainly not. A kiss should be a token of affection, not a favor freely distributed. Going steady? It's too easy to slip into an overly close relationship").

The trend toward sex education in the schools is nationwide. Nearly 50 percent of all schools, including both public and private, parochial and nonsectarian, are already providing it, and at the present rate the figure will pass 70 percent within a year. Clergymen, including many Catholic priests, not only do not oppose sex education, they are often members of the local planning committees. The federal government has pledged financial aid: last year the Department of Health, Education and Welfare awarded grants totaling $1.5 million to support programs in thirteen school districts.

As a result of all this pedagogical exuberance, a lusty new commercial market has come into being. From publishing firms big and small there pours forth a deluge of sex education textbooks, teachers' manuals, laboratory kits, and the like. The publishing house of Harcourt, Brace & World, Incorporated has committed itself to a multimillion-dollar investment for the development of a kindergarten-through-twelfth-grade curriculum. Business machine manufacturers, notably IBM, plan to produce elaborate audio-visual equipment. Television and motion-picture studios are grinding out footage for classroom use with about the same range of quality as that in the films intended for movie theaters or TV. Medical supply companies offer plastic models illustrating human sex characteristics and the cycle of gestation. One polychrome number, costing $500, comes with interchangeable male and female sex organs. And at the center of the whole vast and growing sex education movement, advising school administrators, evaluating programs— praising some and condemning others—stands a new breed of specialist, the sex education consultant.

As a general concept, sex education is hardly novel. From 1900 on, agencies like the YWCA, the Child Study Association, and the American Purity Alliance were pressing for it. But with the exception of a few cautious ventures confined mainly to imparting the bare biological facts of life ("plumbing courses," in academic vernacular), their appeals failed. Most parents recoiled in horror. Today, on the contrary, it is the parents who speak out most strongly to urge the schools to provide sex education.

Parental panic, in fact, has given the revolution its main impetus. National statistics tell part of the story. Venereal diseases among teen-agers: over 80,000 cases reported in 1966, an increase of almost 70 percent since 1956—and unreported cases doubtless dwarf that figure. Unwed teen-age mothers: about 90,000 a year, an increase of 100 percent in two decades. One out of every three brides under twenty goes to the altar pregnant. Estimates of the number of illegal abortions performed on adolescents run into the hundreds of thousands. One of the findings that decided New York City's New Lincoln School to adopt sex education was a poll of its eleventh-graders on their attitudes toward premarital intercourse: the majority saw nothing wrong with it. Teen-age marriages have risen 500 percent since World War II, and the divorce rate for such marriages is three times higher than the rate for marriages contracted after twenty-one. Newspaper reports of drop-outs and runaways, of drug-taking, sexual precocity, and general delinquency intensify the worries of parents.

But these evils are only the grosser symptoms of a widespread social upheaval. Communication between the generations has stalled ("Don't trust anyone over thirty"), and moral values once accepted by children because Mom and Dad said so have given way to a morality of the relative ("What's right or wrong? It all depends on the particular situation, on the individual"). In addition, parents' own emotional conflicts, and their reluctance to recognize in their children the same drives they experienced during childhood, make it all but impossible for them to talk honestly to their children about sex.

In desperation parents turn to the schools, which often lack the competence to assume this responsibility. As one harassed school superintendent puts it, "We've inherited the job by default."

Among the organizations shaping the structure of American sex education, by far the most influential is SIECUS (pronounced "seek us"). The acronym stands for Sex Information and Education Council of the United States. Set up four years ago in New York City, privately financed and nonprofit, SIECUS defines as its goal—in the lofty, if somewhat fuzzy, language of its charter—"To establish man's sexuality as a health entity: to identify the special characteristics that distinguish it from, yet relate it to, human reproduction; to dignify it by openness of approach, study and scientific research designed to lead towards its understanding and its freedom from exploitation; to give leadership to professionals and to society, to the end that human beings may be aided towards responsible use of the sexual faculty and towards assimilation of sex into their individual life patterns as a creative and re-creative force."

Fifty-two officers and directors pool their expertise as physicians, psychiatrists, sociologists, jurists, clergymen, and editors. The council publishes a quarterly newsletter expounding its philosophy and recommending films, books, and articles in the sexology field; it reprints articles that it judges particularly valuable; and issues a reading list and a series of forthright "study guides" such as *Characteristics of Male and Female Sexual Responses* and *Sexual Relations during Pregnancy and the Post-delivery Period*. In addition staff members tirelessly range the country, offering their expertise to communities and schools that want to start sex education programs.

When SIECUS responds to an appeal for help, its first representative on the scene is usually Miss Frances Breed, a professional administrator previously attached to the Planned Parenthood Federation of America. She serves as a kind of advance agent, grappling with some of the preliminary organizational problems. Later comes Dr. Esther Schulz, a Ph.D. in education, who gets down to the specifics of what textbooks and audio-visual aids to acquire. At some point in between, the council's executive director, Dr. Mary Steichen Calderone, M.D., Quaker, Vassar alumna, and for eleven years Planned Parenthood's medical director, may appear, with considerable fanfare, to preach the SIECUS gospel to representatives of the local power structure.

It is largely to Dr. Calderone's charm and dynamism that SIECUS owes its formidable influence. A sweet-faced, silvery-haired grandmother, with the evangelical fervor of Joan of Arc, she is a great persuader. Frequently, listeners who start by being hostile to the idea of public sex education end up as her confirmed disciples. To encourage candor, she avoids sexual euphemisms and has even been known, in all her matriarchal dignity, to use four-letter words.

According to the dicta enunciated by the forceful doctor: "Everything that science knows about sex and sexuality, our children must have access to. . . . We must give full information. . . . The willingness to answer, to discuss any question no matter how distasteful, should be the emphasis." Contrary to the views of most child psychoanalysts, Dr. Calderone holds that sex education should start in the nursery. Around the age of three the child should assimilate such knowledge, along with the correct terminology, as "The penis of the father is made to carry the sperm into the mother through the vagina." Kindergarten teachers should then impart additional clinical details. "If you tell five-year-olds that this [intercourse] is the way fathers and mothers reaffirm their love for each other, and that science and religion have made it possible for parents to choose when they will have a baby, you are teaching responsible parenthood, responsible sexuality, right in the kindergarten." By age ten *"at the latest"* both boys and girls should have mastered "the factual aspects of reproduction. . . ."

With such a foundation built during their elementary-school years, Dr. Calderone claims, students will be ready to explore the total male-female relationship. "Sex is not just something you do in marriage, in bed, in the dark, in one position. . . . Sex is what it means to be a man or a woman." For children between ten and thirteen she prescribes required courses covering the family, interpersonal responsibilities, marriage, the disparate feelings of boys and girls and how to understand them; from thirteen to fifteen, the family within society, the individual within marriage, birth control (regarding contraception, Dr. Calderone reiterates, "This is responsible parenthood, and even very young children can grasp it"). Due attention should be given to alcoholism, drug addiction, promiscuity, venereal diseases, broken homes, homosexuality ("Every boy in an urban environment is going to have a homosexual advance made to him, and therefore he should understand what it is and what his attitude about it and about himself should be, and how to handle it"); from fifteen on, all social issues relating to sex, the techniques of dating and courtship, "the whole panorama of marriage."

As to sexual morality, Dr. Calderone is no absolutist. "Do's" and "don'ts," she believes, cannot be imposed on the young by fiat. They simply won't accept them. In her own moral code the key words are "exploitation" and "responsibility." Sex with no object except transient physical pleasure she scorns as the crassest exploitation of one's partner. A moral person considers the welfare not only of the opposite sex but also of family and society. Though Dr. Calderone feels that the odds against a responsible, meaningful sexual relationship outside marriage are overwhelming, she concedes the possibility. "But [before making any decision on the subject] young people should be given all information and help *to make a good decision.*"

Discussing different sex education programs, Dr. Calderone observes pragmatically: "You cannot go faster in the community than the community itself is willing to go. If the community will accept something at the fifth-grade level only, then that is the level at which to start. . . . We shall probably get farther if we allow any child whose parents seriously disapprove to be excused from those classes." Such accommodation, however, distresses her. "For too long," she complains, "we have listened to the vociferous minority."

Between the ideals professed by sex educators and the practical realities of the schoolroom lies a wide gap. The Anaheim Union High School District, with its highly touted "family life and sex education course," involving about 32,000 teen-agers, is a SIECUS show window. Here, SIECUS representatives collaborated with local planners. The registered nurse who supervises "family life," Mrs. Sally R. Williams, also serves as a SIECUS director. Many other schools have modeled their programs on Anaheim's.

In line with SIECUS philosophy, Nurse Williams and Superintendent Cook agree that sex education can scarcely begin too soon. But on this point they are thwarted by the fact that their authority extends only to the high schools, whereas Anaheim's elementary schools have not seen fit to develop a preparatory program. Consequently, sex education in school doesn't begin until seventh grade, or about age thirteen.

The course calls for at least 132 classroom periods during the six remaining years. It's all spelled out for the teacher's guidance in a 290-page manual. One wonders, however, how many ninth-graders are likely to swallow such "facts" as these presented to them under the headings Fact One, Fact Two, Fact Three, etc.: "One of the chief reasons for having extramarital relationships is to impress friends. . . .

In premarital sex relations there is usually little, if any, concern for the other. There is considerable evidence to prove that premarital sex relationships among young people—except where [they are] honestly engaged—are often dog-eat-dog propositions. . . ."

The manual also includes a number of warnings addressed to the teacher—for example, "It is not considered appropriate to have the class label the parts of the male and female anatomy on a diagram." Asked why not, when the illustrations in every biology textbook are labeled, Mrs. Williams replied, "It would upset the parents."

Deference to parental attitudes also explains why the Anaheim program, like many another, violates principles it claims to honor. "We won't try to impose moral standards," runs a common resolution. "We'll give our students the whole, true picture as a basis on which they can make their own decisions." Actually, the teachers' guidebook bristles with moralisms. They are implied or explicit in suggested tragic case histories to feed the youngsters, in recommended films and tests, in loaded questionnaires, true/false tests, and self-evaluation charts. A great deal of the verbiage can be boiled down to the same commandment parents have always handed their children, the one word they really want the schools to pass on—"Abstain." To reinforce it, the same old scare techniques are resorted to—"*One* act of intercourse (even if it's your first mistake) can lead to an unwanted pregnancy."

Student reactions to Anaheim's program vary from "The best and most helpful course I've had" to "Some of the movies you have to sit through look so ancient they just make you laugh. How can you take the moral lesson seriously when the girls are wearing skirts down to their ankles?"

In Evanston, Illinois, which also boasts a famous sex education program, a junior-high-school teacher responds to the frequent question "Why is premarital sex wrong?" by handing around a list of horrifying statistics on venereal disease, illegitimacy, abortion, and divorce.

One of the most forthright sex education courses is offered by the school system of Palo Alto, California. This is a comparatively sophisticated, high-income community, in which Stanford University faculty members and electronics engineers predominate.

To introduce sex education in the Palo Alto kindergartens, teachers occasionally borrow babies from their mothers and bathe them in class. One small boy, who knew the right word but was seeing a naked male infant for the first time, shouted in a sunburst of happy comprehension, "Look, look, another penis!"

Recently, a visitor to Palo Alto watched an eleven-year-old girl unselfconsciously drawing on a blackboard a detailed sectional view of the male sex organs. On the wall of a senior classroom hung a montage, the homework assigned to a seventeen-year-old student, composed of the main contraceptive devices, each with a neatly typed card beneath, explaining how it worked. A boy the same age read the class a paper he had written which summarized the psychological, legal, and moral aspects of homosexuality. Questions to the teacher were sometimes couched in the language of the streets, for which the teacher, when responding, would casually substitute the polite terms.

Boys and girls study together, and much of the instruction comes in the form of general discussion such as the following, in which a senior class took up one of the great sexual dilemmas of youth. As the teacher, Robert Shreve, framed it: "The male's sex drive at sixteen or seventeen is much stronger than the female's. She wants to have her hand held, not necessarily to go to bed. Is this a valid observation?"

"I'm not so sure," said a boy. "Plenty of girls enjoy sex. It depends on the individual."

Another boy: "If I like a girl, holding hands isn't enough."

"But if you like her," said a third boy, "you don't want to hurt her, do you?"

Shreve put in, "When a boy and girl are unaware of their psychological differences, it can make serious trouble for them, can't it?"

"Yes. He might go after her just for sex."

It is when questions about birth control arise that many schools suffer their worst lapses from honesty. They do not tell the whole truth. Chicago, for example, is a city where petty crooks, counting on the ignorance of youngsters, hang around high schools, peddling contraceptive pills at a dollar each, with the promise that one swallowed before intercourse guarantees protection. Yet the new Chicago sex education program excludes the subject of contraception altogether. "Ask your minister or family doctor," is the customary formula. At Evanston's Nichols Junior High, the former director of physical education, Ronald Thompson, says he never ducked the subject of birth control pills. "The main thing I did," he admits, "was to stress their unreliability." Gynecologists insist, however, that the Pill, when correctly used, has proved to be just about 100 percent effective.

A good many independent, or private, schools also accept sex education as their proper concern; indeed, some of the more progressive private schools were quietly taking it up long before the present frenzy swept the nation. North Shore Country Day in Winnetka, Illinois, for example, originated a program thirty-two years ago [in 1936], which it recently broadened in scope because, as Headmaster Nathaniel S. French explains: "It seemed to us that the experience of our students in college must reflect their secondary-school experience; the stories of male-female relationships in the most prestigious institutions disturbed us. Then we found that in our own community there were similar tales to be told. Lastly, we began to discover relationships between boys and girls in our own school which demanded that the problem be reviewed.

Sadly, we had to admit that some individuals had suffered hurt which might have been prevented."

Because, in the main, they have small, relatively homogeneous enrollments and freedom from official constraints, and can offer the kind of salaries and working conditions that attract superior teachers, private schools can do things in sex education that are impossible in the overcrowded, understaffed, community-controlled public schools. On the whole, private-school programs are so low-keyed and gradual that they scarcely qualify as programs at all, in the SIECUS sense. They are inclined to avoid using the sort of minutely structured, one-two-three teaching manuals put together by the planners, and they set aside no special classroom period when teacher tells Johnny, in effect, "Now we're going to talk about sex." They prefer to treat the subject as it may arise naturally within the context of other courses. For example, Mrs. Allan J. Sanker, who heads the English department at Cincinnati's Hillsdale School, notes that *The Scarlet Letter* affords an opportunity "to give consideration to adultery in the novel, in various times of history, and in the present day."

Some of the private-school teachers come up with highly individualistic, often impromptu techniques. When a young married teacher at Shady Hill, a Cambridge, Massachusetts, day school (400 boys and girls, ages four to fourteen), reached the visible stage of pregnancy—to the fascination of her five-year-old pupils— she began to use her own unfolding experience to explain human reproduction to them in very personal terms.

The countrywide clamor for sex education has not completely drowned out the protests of a dissenting minority; their vehemence compensates for their numerical weakness. One group of dissenters is composed of the sort of die-hard conservatives who oppose any liberalizing trend. They variously protest that sex education consumes taxpayers' dollars that would be better spent improving conventional teaching facilities; that it encroaches on areas where the state should never tread; that it misleads immature minds. A second group is made up of educators and psychologists who, while not opposing sex education in principle, object to the methods employed.

The Anaheim program, for example, is under constant attack from local conservatives. In this community, where 92 percent of the parents are said to stand solidly behind Superintendent Cook's family life program, the arch-conservative local newspaper, the *Bulletin,* keeps up a relentless drumfire of criticism. According to its editor, Sam Campbell, the premise "that sex information is the pathway to morality . . . if pursued to its rational extremity, would elevate Sodom to the Puritan capital of the universe and substitute Paris for Jerusalem as the Holy City."

Ironically, in California, where public-school sex education has moved farther and faster than in any other state, one of the most caustic critics is the state's superintendent of public instruction, Max Rafferty.* A syndicated columnist on the side (and now a candidate for the United States Senate), Rafferty headed a recent column, WHO NEEDS MORE SEX EDUCATION? "How can the schools unilaterally solve a problem which originates outside the schools and which permeates society as a whole?" he wrote. "And the answer is: They cannot. Only when we adults . . . set a decent example and demand decent behavior from the young will children start growing up to become the kind of people we want them to be, and should have been ourselves."

Some of the sharpest criticism comes from psychologists and psychoanalysts. Dr. Rhoda L. Lorand, a noted New York child analyst, author of *Love, Sex and the Teenager,* deplores organized, insistent sex education for the very young. "How far is this folly going to go?" she demands. "They're repeating the same mistake the Freudians made years ago. The rationale then was that since repressions may cause neuroses, get rid of all repressions. So parents made a point of calling their children's attention to sexual matters, and they condoned primitive sexual behavior. Yet children so reared often developed severe anxieties. When psychoanalyzed, they revealed the damage this system caused. We know now that the sublimation of sexual curiosity and behavior is necessary if children are to acquire intellectual training. Otherwise they might play sex games all day long. Sublimation, in fact, is the price we must pay to live in a civilized society. Cramming sex knowledge down kids' throats does not promote healthy growth. The likely effect is more anxiety, not less."

A child's spontaneous questions about sex, Dr. Lorand agrees, should receive straightforward, honest answers, but neither teachers nor parents should anticipate curiosity. A cardinal Victorian blunder was scaring children, telling them they were evil little monsters for inquiring into such dirty things. Many sex education programs, in Dr. Lorand's view, commit the opposite excess by force-feeding children this once-forbidden knowledge.

She further challenges the propriety of throwing teen-age boys and girls together in sex education classes, asking, "Why not let girlish shyness develop into womanly modesty?" Not long ago a sex education zealot, arguing that co-ed classes made for naturalness between the sexes, spoke approvingly of a fifteen-year-old boy who remarked to the girl beside him, "You look depressed today. Are you menstruating? Are you having cramps?" "Now wasn't that nice?" commented the enthusiast. "Didn't that show understanding?" "Nice?" retorted Dr. Lorand. "I think it was an atrocious invasion of privacy."

She also found appalling the slides used in a Westchester County ele-

---

*See pp. 225-227 of *Sex, Schools, and Society.*

mentary school, which show dogs copulating, followed by a human couple under bed sheets, as a recorded voice explains, "Mummy and Daddy are doing the same thing the dogs do."

As Dr. Lorand and a lot of her colleagues see it, such explicit public displays inflict harm by creating an emotional split—by arousing sexual excitement while requiring its immediate suppression.

Intense sexual curiosity begins at about the age of three, psychologists say; children start to explore their own bodies and also try to discover how other people are made. They want to watch each other being undressed and bathed—a natural, healthy urge, the psychiatrists say. Let them touch themselves; let them watch. It does not follow, however, that they should be allowed to see adults in the nude, because this overstimulates their sexual curiosity. When a child attempts to do so, the parents should declare their preference for privacy, but at the same time offer to explain whatever the child wishes to know. Around the fifth year, sexual curiosity, if not overstimulated, will normally shift to other areas, and the child can then proceed to academic learning. For children around ten—no younger—the school can usefully provide a limited amount of uncomplicated, direct teaching in preparation for puberty. During the teens advanced sex education can be valuable.

"If parents can't talk about sex comfortably to their children," Dr. Lorand concludes, "even embarrassed silence may be less injurious than exposing them to an ill-conceived school program. The trouble with parents today is that they're so petrified of doing the wrong thing they tend to retreat from involvement with their children."

Among the experts who concur, in general, is Dr. E. James Lieberman, a psychiatrist at the National Institute of Mental Health. "Don't overwhelm the child," says Dr. Lieberman, chief of the Institute's Center for Studies of Child and Family Mental Health. "Even perfectly accurate information can . . . be disturbing . . . if the child is not ready intellectually or emotionally."

If the present frantic scurry to set up new programs subsides without falling back into apathy, a calm, sane, generally applicable model program may well emerge. But formidable obstacles intervene. One of these is the shortage of teachers. There are scarcely enough teachers available to handle the ordinary "safe" subjects, let alone to cope with one that requires the sensitivity and balance needed for sex education.

A more formidable obstacle is the rampant controversy over the meaning and purpose of sex education. The schools are still unsure about what moral values, if any, they should try to instill, with the result that they tend to put off children with evasions, half-truths, and downright falsehoods. In this uncertainty lies the basic problem: What do we really consider is the purpose of sex education? What do we really want our children to be taught? The straight facts? Well, yes. But above all we want them to avoid premarital sexual relations, don't we? And isn't classroom frankness apt to overstimulate them, tempt them to experiment? So we expect the teacher to mingle fact with propaganda, maybe throw an occasional scare into the kids by stressing the traditional dangers of sexual misconduct—i.e., infection, conception, and detection.

A beleaguered West Coast high-school principal summed up the resulting dilemma: "You can't sustain any kind of sex education program without the community's support—which is to say, the parents' support. Unhappily, what we hope to accomplish as educators, and what the parents demand as parents, are often miles apart. We're really in a bind."

Sex Education

Marjorie F. Iseman

It's too late to debate whether or not there should be sex education in schools. It's here. Schools have not merely accepted sex; they have embraced it and in so doing have changed its aura from that of a shady mistress to that of a prim matron who can be taken everywhere in broad daylight.

Hardly a day passes without a press report heralding some new sex education program somewhere in the United States, one state after another dutifully joining the parade. Television has given prime hours with full network coverage. Professional pollsters are scurrying around sampling the attitudes of parents, while other pulse takers are doggedly questionnairing students before and after their new courses, to discover exactly what they learned. Meantime, source material for the teachers of these courses is being pumped out by the ton: textbooks, manuals, recordings, graphs, charts, illustrations, plastic models of the human anatomy, movies, filmstrips, slides. Pet shops are being drained of any species guaranteed to reproduce efficiently in a classroom, so that city youngsters can get a sense of what mating is all about. There must even be a big run these days on lima beans, or any other quick-sprouting seed, for those teachers who wish to make the point with plants.

Classroom sex has fired a whole new industry of such vast and blue-chip possibilities that the *Wall Street Journal* was prompted recently to issue a full report on it. Leading publishing houses and companies such as International Business Machines (IBM) are pouring literally millions of dollars into texts and teaching aids for the sexual enlightenment of the young.

Along with this, there is emerging a new constellation of advisers on sexual matters. They are the consultants to the commercial firms that are supplying all the new sex instruction paraphernalia. They also advise schools and, most importantly, advise those who are organizing training programs for teachers. Since the field of sex education is so new, it is without established standards, and its many spokesmen vary greatly in their backgrounds, the extent of their expertise, their roles on the educational scene, and their attitudes toward sex instruction. They also differ widely in their views of acceptable sexual behavior, which range from premarital abstinence to extremist anything-goes.

143

The result is somewhat chaotic, leaving teachers and school admin- istrators on their own to choose which advice they wish to heed. The debates can involve parents and religious and civic leaders in an entire community while educators try to figure out when students are to be taught what, how, and by whom. This seems hardly a simple matter, yet several of the leading organizers of sex education keep repeating that it is "no harder than introducing the new math." Is it? I set out on a tour of the schools to find out.

SIECUS

Today's atmosphere in sex education cannot be described without mention of a high-voltage, nonprofit organization called SIECUS, which is without doubt the single most important force in sparking sex educa- tion in schools. SIECUS (pronounced seek-us) stands for Sex Informa- tion and Education Council of the United States. It is based in New York City and has the distinction of being the only listing under "Sex" in the Manhattan Telephone Directory, where the alphabetic lottery has placed it between "Sewtime, fabrics" and "J. A. Sexauer Manufac- turing Co., Inc., plumbing supplies."

The council's dedicated staff members range out tirelessly by jet to any institution seeking help in founding a sex education program, and it is not unusual for SIECUS representatives to crisscross the United States many times a month. Common practice is for a member of the SIECUS team to address a conference, often lasting several days, which has been organized by a given school community well in advance. Usually there are separate or overlapping sessions for students, teachers, administrators; representatives of the Parent-Teacher Association, church, public health, or other civic groups; and, often, representatives of television, radio, and the press.

To the uninitiated—perhaps a visitor from Rome—it might seem remarkable to see a well-tailored, grandmotherly SIECUS speaker get up before an audience of hundreds of educators in some huge hall and hear her, with the most elegant diction, say words like *coitus* and *orgasm* into a microphone, say, with television broadcasting the per- formance. But the visitor would soon learn that this approach serves as an ice-breaker. In turn, it allows the educators, and finally the students, to talk with equal candor, so long as the words used are multisyllabic ones of Greek or Latin origin, not one-syllable Anglo-Saxon slang. The visitor might also be surprised to find that in America, if one wishes to change attitudes toward sex, one begins with vocabulary. As a teacher from Evanston, Illinois, commented recently, reflecting the SIECUS philosophy, "If a teacher can't say words like *penis* or *vagina* as easily as *chalk* and *blackboard,* then she's going to be in trouble with our fifth-graders."* A European still cherishing the difference would seem very, very square.

If these conferences appear at times to be a step toward the de-sexing of sex, or to suggest the atmosphere of rallies, it should be said that they also accomplish a good deal. SIECUS barnstorming has coincided with nationwide concern over the mores of youth, and these conferences in city after city, often drawing in a whole regional network of schools, have met one important need. They have given voice and a cool vocabulary to these worries and have given educators and community leaders a welcome chance to exchange views.

SIECUS has also served as a valuable clearing house for information. Even more important, some of the experts connected with SIECUS have written study guides on such topics as homosexuality, masturbation, the characteristics of male and female sexual responses, and premarital sexual standards. These are scholarly yet simply written booklets of some ten pages each. They do not take a position on any issues, but instead have the stated aim of replacing "condemnation based on ignorance and fear" with "understanding based on the best scientific knowledge available." They have made an admirable start in this direction and might well be read by anyone (even a parent) who deals with children.

But while in some ways SIECUS is caringly building sex instruction into a new discipline combining many branches of learning, in other ways it seems to be undoing its own work. Its pronouncements at conferences and in some of its newsletters often reduce sex instruction to something very simple, aseptic, and businesslike. In addition, its representatives frequently fall into an alarmist approach. They *say* programs must be developed slowly, that schools should not "hop on the sex education bandwagon," but they convey a sense of urgency which often leaves an audience of educators visibly shaken and with the clear impression that the only road to salvation is a sex education program—now.

The problem is that this spirited agitation for sex education comes before there are sufficient numbers of people prepared to teach. The SIECUS advice to schools is that any sex education is better than none and that any interested teacher can teach it—both rather self-defeating views *if the goal is to improve on what now passes for sex instruction in homes.*

Quite a different stand is taken by Birgitta Linnér,† who has done pioneering work in sex education in Sweden for some fifteen years. To quote from her book *Sex and Society in Sweden:* "When lack of teacher

---

*See p. 51 of *Sex, Schools, and Society.*
†See pp. 331-370 of *Sex, Schools, and Society.*

training is combined with entrenched inhibitions that make teachers un-comfortable even in talking about sex to young people, the resulting in-struction often has a worse effect than no instruction at all."

A number of experts on this side of the Atlantic seem to agree with Mrs. Linnér on this point. They feel that the biggest problem here is the great rush, the need to get any old show on the road.

THE GREAT BAFFLER: WHAT IS SEX EDUCATION?

On its simplest level, the term *sex education* means instruction in the basic biology of the male and female reproductive systems taught in elementary school, as a rule by the classroom teacher. When it is taught in the fifth and sixth grades, the trend now is to deal directly with the facts of menstruation, seminal emissions, and related physiology. A more extensive course in reproduction may be scheduled at the junior- or senior-high-school level, usually as part of a course in general science, biology, health education, or home economics, or in isolated lectures by a visiting doctor or the school nurse.

There is nothing revolutionary about teaching primary reproductive physiology. To a greater or lesser degree, this has been taught for years. The tendency today is to introduce more and more earlier and earlier, and controversies arise over such questions as what is appropriate sub-ject matter for a certain grade and whether boys and girls should be taught together or separately. But at least in reproduction education there is general agreement on what the facts are (an ovum is an ovum) and that it is an advantage for children to learn these facts correctly, along with the proper scientific terms—hopefully from a teacher who is cordially disposed toward sex.

The headache for school administrators is that the expectations for sex education have now gone way beyond teaching the facts of repro-duction. High schools are being pressured to have their teachers lead discussions on such topics as masturbation, homosexuality, premarital relations, standards of sexual conduct, venereal disease, birth control, divorce, abortion, adoption, child rearing, and even what constitutes love. Some of these subjects have a scientific, factual core a teacher can latch onto; but others involve facts that are open to wide swings of personal interpretation—or are not matters of fact at all. With a teach-ing agenda like this, the possibilities for disagreement on what sex edu-cation should be are staggering. Many a beleaguered school principal must long secretly for his boyhood, when open mention of sex in school was limited to scribblings on the locker-room wall.

Yet there is a demand for ever more comprehensive school coverage of sex. Today, classes limited to the simple anatomy of reproduction are often regarded as quaint and are known in professional lingo as "plumbing courses." The big new element that is causing so much confusion, and the new term that has entered the language, is *sexuality*. As little as one or two years ago, this meant, by dictionary definition, "the state or quality of being sexual; interest in or concern with sex." Not now. It is a tribute to the zeal of the sex education organizers and the receptivity of the press that, in no time at all, the reading public has accepted a new meaning of the word.

According to a SIECUS newsletter, *sexuality* now "connotes the totality of being and the expressing of maleness and femaleness." And another explanation, given by a leading sex education spokesman at an educators' conference, is as follows:

> What interests me is maleness and femaleness, what it is to be a man or a woman. Unfortunately, the difficulty young people have today is that adults have not given them a clear picture of what maleness and femaleness mean. Adults have often downgraded or limited the concept of sexuality to the genital act.
>
> Now what about this business of males and females? I have asked many adults, "What does it mean being a woman? What does it mean being a man?" In the end what we are talking about is how people relate to each other; this is the essence of sexuality, the relationships a person forms in all his comings and goings, not just the strictly sexual ones.

All right, how *about* this business of maleness and femaleness? What *does* it mean, being a woman? a man? In the shifting ground of modern society, *who knows?* And how about this totality of being? Shakespeare could deal with such questions; Rembrandt could, as could a twentieth-century artist such as the late James Thurber, who, with real totality, even included dogs. But how about asking the school nurse to cope with all this, on the basis of a summer cram course? The answer is that she, and thousands of men and women like her all over the country, at this moment are dealing with this immense, philosophic question of cradle-to-grave "sexuality"—or "family life," as it is also called—*from teaching manuals*. These manuals make sexuality education easy, even simpler than the new math.

As a sample of how such enormous questions are reduced to bite size in teachers' manuals, one might skim through the manual of the 30,000-student Union High School District of Anaheim, California. This manual runs to some three hundred pages, can be bought for ten dollars a copy, and, because the Anaheim program has become a model for school systems all over the United States, is widely imitated. The following selections are topic headings for instruction of the tenth and eleventh

grades and reveal a ledgered neatness any accountant would be proud
of:

APPENDIX IV: WHAT IS MORAL AND IMMORAL?

Moral Behavior Leads to: [seven good results]
Immoral Behavior Leads to: [seven matching bad results]

APPENDIX VI: GUIDE TO DISCUSSION OF PREMARITAL SEX RELATIONS

   I. Casual-Transitory Relationship
  II. Relationship with Person with Whom There Is Some Communication
 III. Relationship with Person to Whom Engaged or with Whom There Is a Deep Emotional Involvement

[These are arranged as parallel headings, with a related, though
different, column of text under all three. The basic content of all
is: Don't do it.]

APPENDIX VII: WHEN AN ENGAGEMENT SHOULD BE RE-EVALUATED

Check Yourself
Which of the following engagements should be re-evaluated with
the possibility of a definite break?
1. . . . .
2. . . . .
3. . . . .
4. . . . .
5. . . . .
6. John swears he will commit suicide if Dorothy breaks their
    engagement; he waves a revolver to prove it.

Number 6 impressed me as a situation in which there was little
room for doubt, and I wondered why it was included for instructive
classroom debate. Were this my class, I would tell Dorothy not to stop
to make a check mark. I would say, "Don't even walk, Dorothy—run!"
I would advise her always to run away from boys like John, from
loaded revolvers, and, above all, from family-life and sex education
courses that depend on such manuals.

When I haven't been toying with the soap opera possibilities in
manuals, I have been trying to find clarification of another popular new
term in sex education: *responsible sexuality*. This idea is the spine of the
whole movement. Actually, it is as admirable a set of goals as has been
presented to the human race since the Ten Commandments, and no one

but Satan himself would question these as concepts. The only problem, again, is how these are to be taught by the average schoolteacher.

Responsible sexuality is defined variously by educators in different communities and covers a wide range. The following are some fairly common examples:

Self-respect: not to use sex as a means of feeling popular or loved; not to "prove" one's masculinity or femininity by engaging in precocious sexual relations; to understand that being a truly mature male or female rests on other (often vaguely defined) manifestations.

Responsibility toward one's partner: not to cause pregnancy by irresponsible accident (sometimes with, sometimes without, mention of birth control); not to "use" sex or pregnancy as a marriage trap; not to "use" a member of the opposite sex as an object.

Responsibility toward one's family: the need for affectionate and supportive behavior toward husband, wife, children, parents, and a positive redefinition of all these roles.

Responsibility toward society: not to burden it with unwanted babies; or inflict on it the problems of abortion, adoption, desertion, divorce.

Control of venereal disease fits into any image of responsible sexuality, but most family life courses take it up separately, as they generally do with tobacco, alcohol, and drug habituation. It is felt, quite rightly, that these are negative aspects of life and should not be confused with sex as a positive entity.

Teaching responsible sexuality, or any aspect of sex, is obviously a complicated and sensitive assignment. But the present campaign to get this teaching started, immediately, is so forceful that many schools—to conform and not be left behind—are resorting to drastic shortcuts and oversimplification in the preparation of teachers. Often, teachers, school guidance counselors, or other members of a school staff are "trained" by attending ten or twenty sessions with experts and then being handed a detailed teaching manual. After this, the instructor is supposed somehow, magically, to be able to lead a class. This is the basis of many big-city public-school programs, including New York City's initial efforts in sex education, which this year [1968], as a starter, will affect 166 schools, with a total enrollment of 55,000 pupils.

Frequently, the teachers who take their obligations to students most seriously are the ones most concerned about these shortcuts. One such teacher was a man who took part in a three-week sex education institute last summer in New Jersey. "I'd like to ask you all a question," he said to the class. "The state and school administrators are all oriented toward sex instruction. Now I tell you, I'm scared. I see myself being bombarded with kids' questions, and I'll be in some fix if I don't have some answers. I'm a phys.-ed. instructor. I'm not a psychologist. I haven't had any experience teaching this stuff. And I ask you, how in three weeks can I make myself an expert?"

I, too, had been looking for answers to such questions, and I visited many schools to get a sense of how some of the new programs were working out in classrooms. The visits were limited to mainstream, middle-class, urban junior and senior high schools and did not include parochial schools, schools in substandard ghetto areas, or colleges and universities. A number of private schools were included, even though they are not mainstream institutions, because some of them seemed to be pacesetters in meaningful sex education.

Throughout, the attempt was to find out what good sex education might be.

THE PERSONAL FACTOR = X

There is an adage holding that a teacher essentially teaches himself, and nowhere is this more true than in the field of sex education. Whether dealing with the geography of the male and female reproductive systems, or the twilight zones of personal morality, a teacher conveys not only facts but his own attitudes. It is absolutely impossible to discuss any aspect of sex without revealing some flicker of emotion, however subliminally; by rhythm of speech, choice of words, facial expression or even the lack of it—or any of the many other subtle ways in which adults transmit their inner views of sex to children. As a nineteen-year-old Swedish girl wrote in her evaluation of classes, "Can anyone refrain from laughing at a teacher who, instead of using the word *copulate,* says that two rabbits 'got married'?"

Another example of poor casting for the role of sex educator concerns a teacher from New Jersey. She confided to other instructors in a training course that the first year she taught the subject, she blushed so uncontrollably that she took to wearing a red dress on the days her sex class was to meet, hoping this would camouflage her blushes. I doubted that any students were fooled. A year later, the subject still made her tense and fidgety, and I wondered what positive associations her class could possibly have made about sex as it emanated from her presence.

There is no guarantee, either, that being intellectually trained, say as a psychologist, qualifies someone to teach. At one suburban junior high school in New York State, I observed a class of seventh-grade girls in the last of four one-hour cram courses in reproduction biology. The teacher was a visiting psychologist, a woman who entered the room carrying a heavy briefcase. She meant business. The children looked cowed. Her voice was shrill, her delivery rapid-fire, and she kept using unfortunate phrases, such as "Girls, I want to help you *struggle* with all this"—by which she meant sex.

It was a grim hour, in which facts were rained on the class like shrapnel. At the end of it, she explained to me in a professional aside that "any program, of course, is as good or as poor as the teacher."

TASTE

The rarest of rare ingredients in today's sex instruction is good taste. (What seminar can teach this?) There is a very thin borderline, which has to be *felt*, between answering a student's question correctly and honestly and, on the other hand, alluding to private experience.

For example—and I choose from many—one day last spring, I attended a class of some sixty high-school seniors, boys and girls, at a big public high school on the northeastern seaboard. (The instructor had said to me by telephone: "Try to get here in the early afternoon. Abortion meets at 12:56. Birth Control at 1:48.") When one of the girls in the class asked a question about spontaneous abortions, it could easily have been answered with textbook examples. Instead, the teacher replied by detailing, in personal terms, the difficulties that had caused the miscarriage of her first three pregnancies. She might still be talking had all of us not been saved by the bell.

The problem is that no screening process for emotional fitness, or even for good living-room manners, has yet been devised to keep verbal exhibitionists out of sex education programs. And such people are constantly volunteering to teach.

A similar question, this time about a sordid aspect of illegal abortion, was handled quite differently at another class I visited. This was at New York City's Hunter College High School, a leading and rather special public school, which, being independent of the city's Board of Education, has been free to create its own sex education program. This is a six-year, full-coverage course, developed over some fifteen years by Jean Binnie, chairman of the Physical Education Department. The teacher in this case, a young woman trained by Miss Binnie, believed that students do not always have to be told everything and that a rigid policy of total candor can at times be more harmful than helpful. She knew intuitively that an honest answer to this particular query would not benefit all the pupils. "That's an interesting question," she said, "but we're running late. You can ask me about it after class."

It seems always that if the person conducting a program has innate good taste, an entire program will have it. This works equally, of course, in reverse.

Should anyone think I am exaggerating the outer limits of poor taste that are being explored today in classrooms, let me quote from the teaching manual of a large public high school. It is, as usual, neatly outlined.

2. Methods of illegal abortion
   a. ....
      (1) ....
      (2) "Instruments" used by amateur abortionists include
          the following:
          (*a*) crochet hooks
          (*b*) nail files
          (*c*) knitting needles
          (*d*) wires
          (*e*) wire coat hangers
          (*f*) combs
          (*g*) plastic bottles
          (*h*) hair pins
          (*i*) turkey quills
          (*j*) nut picks
3. These instruments often puncture the uterus or its surrounding
   tissues, causing serious damage that may lead to tragedy.
   (*a*) ....
   (*b*) ....

And so on. Are all these examples necessary? Wouldn't a simple
warning be enough?

Yet I heard an entire class structured on this outline. Fortunately,
the eleventh-grade girl entrusted with reading this "report" went from
(*a*) through (*j*) in a monotonous singsong, as if reciting the multipli-
cation table, which robbed it of its impact. It seemed to be her way of
preserving some last remaining shred of good taste.

THE UNINTENDED MESSAGE

The intent of school sex education is usually some combination of the
following: to give correct biological information, to reduce fear of sex,
to put sex in a positive light, and to try to upgrade moral standards.
What has struck me continually, however, is that sometimes all these
goals are defeated by something else that keeps slipping in—the unintended message, which can often influence behavior in a far more
powerful way than the intended lesson.

Again, I am hard put to choose from a score of examples which kept
floating into my notes as I visited around. One, the movie *Phoebe*,
should make my point. I saw it at no fewer than three sex education
tutorials for teachers; apparently it is highly regarded as an educational
film and is making the rounds of junior and senior high schools.

Phoebe, The Story of Premarital Pregnancy shows the emotional torments of an unmarried teen-age girl who becomes pregnant and the
bafflement of the teen-age boy who is the prospective father. It was

designed as a spur to discussion and as a deterrent to premarital sex, and is a marvelously well-acted film. Teachers who have shown it in their classrooms have told me that girls tend to identify very closely with Phoebe and that the talk which follows is inevitably heated. These teachers liked the movie and thought it very "useful." As one of them said, "It showed my girls the consequences of fooling around."

A few teachers, however, felt that the scene showing the pregnant Phoebe retching violently in a locked bathroom was unduly harsh, because it tended to confirm the fears many young girls have about pregnancy. As one teacher pointed out, this scene placed untrue emphasis on morning sickness, since nausea does not necessarily accompany early pregnancy and, when it does, is rarely experienced in the frightening context so vividly suffered by Phoebe. "My eleventh- and twelfth-graders thought it was a powerful and very scary movie," this teacher explained. "Some girls said it didn't only scare them about unmarried pregnancy, but made them scared of ever getting pregnant at all."

This last message certainly is not the one anyone planned to convey. It is unintended, but nonetheless there—even if, say, "only" one out of forty girls who see the movie gets this harmful negative view of pregnancy. Again, this is one of the dangers of making sex education too simple.

CHEATING ON THE STUDENTS

With all the emphasis on information, it is startling to find that where information really counts, the schools often cheat. To take the subject of birth control as an example, important facts are commonly withheld or are presented in a dishonest light.

This is not to blame individuals. In dealing with birth control, many schools feel trapped. Though numerous experts have said that giving students such information does *not* encourage precocious or promiscuous sexual relations, schools still worry that it will. Schools also worry that if they refuse to answer questions about something as basic as birth control, they make a mockery of their frank new sex education programs.

Another trap for schools, as it is for parents, is that for countless generations the main control of premarital sex has been the threat of pregnancy, and modern birth control makes this threat obsolete. There are other, more contemporary considerations teachers can offer to students in the interest of restraint. But these are of a more subtle emotional nature and are harder to convey than simple threats.

As a result, many teachers compromise. They answer questions on birth control and cling to the old pregnancy threat at the same time. This may sound like—and is—double-talk, but it is one of the prevailing dishonesties in schools today. This is how it's done: A teacher will describe the various contraceptive devices and then crisply remind students that no method is a hundred percent safe. As a teacher of high-school seniors at a girls' school explained at one training seminar for teachers: "I don't think premarital sex is right. So when the girls ask about birth control, I tell them that nothing is foolproof." While this is technically true, it is basically untrue, because it gives the impression that all birth control is useless.

This is an outmoded, dishonest way to preach abstinence, and it often boomerangs. To quote again from Mrs. Linnér's book, which discusses this same problem as it exists today in Sweden: "Small wonder that so many people neglect to use contraceptives when they are fed this negative information in school." It is Mrs. Linnér's view that such teaching can only add to the number of out-of-wedlock pregnancies.

In this country, not only do we have the problem of confused teachers giving out wrong birth control information; we have the added problem in many public-school systems of being unable to give out any such information at all—because of church or parental objections. Whether educators agree with them or not, these objections must be respected. But this means, as in New York City, that a school must go through the pretense of giving a complete modern course in sex and family life without any mention of birth control. The Anaheim, California, program, recently criticized for this failure, has had the courage this year [1968] to add birth control to its official curriculum, under the heading of family planning.

There is doubtless some bootleg instruction in birth control in schools where the topic is censored. But this is hardly a general solution. What happens in the schools of many states is that in some of its most important aspects—and birth control is only one of them—sex education is being tossed right back to the home or church or even the street corner, as the case may be.

THE CURE CAN BE TOO MUCH LIKE THE DISEASE

One of the main reasons advanced for moving sex instruction into the classroom is that children are not getting enough positive, correct information from their parents. Another is that they are getting too much wrong information and erotic stimulation from commercial sources. My concern is that the poorer forms of school sex education, which are widespread, combine all these failings—and sometimes even intensify them.

The sex educators generally explain that teen-agers are too involved emotionally with their parents to make good communication possible in sexual matters; also that parents are likely to lack the right attitude or information needed to answer the questions a modern adolescent might ask.

As a result, the argument goes, teen-agers will get their information, or misinformation, from one another, swapping stories on street corners. In sex education circles, what is considered even worse is that today's adolescents can easily get more elaborate misinformation than ever before by buying pornography at drugstore counters, seeing titillating movies at the neighborhood theater, or reading *Playboy*. (One story going around is that so many boys are now looking at *Playboy* that an entire generation of males is growing up thinking that the ideal female nude has a staple just above the navel.)

While the lacks of the home and the oversupplies of the marketplace are both unfortunate, the scene does have its brighter side. That is, if a teen-ager gets mumbling, bumbling half answers or wrong answers at home, he is at least likely to pursue his quest for information elsewhere, on the ground that his old-fogy parents aren't experts anyway. This is also true, I think, of all the erotic literature, films, news-magazine coverage, song lyrics, and perfume ads, which are part of the modern child's environment. Young people can't help but see it, read it, hear it. Yet it all flows in as commercial stuff in a circus of contradictions, one image canceling the next, and it has been my limited observation, as the mother of three children who are now in their teens, that after a while teen-agers tend to question any of it as gospel and to look for their own "real" answers elsewhere.

Sex information given out in schools, however, is another matter. Anything conveyed under the school roof is presumed to be correct. Students think that, at last, they are hearing the truth. And this is why dishonest information or straight ignorance, as dispensed by teachers, can be ten times more harmful than anything absorbed from the various gutters.

What's more, the dominant philosophy in sex education today seems to encourage repetitive erotic displays, both visual and verbal, which seem as harmful as any "hard core" pornography—and for the same reasons. They lack the leavening of high art forms and are totally lacking in feeling. In the classroom, as in low pornography, the strip-bare repetition can numb the audience to the more feeling and human nuances of sex.

This does not apply to the pictures, charts, models, and other scientific abstractions needed to teach a biology course. I am speaking instead of all the frills that can now be introduced because of the new information-happy atmosphere. For example, to quote one line from an article on sex education in *Time* magazine: "Teachers try to make the subject matter as specific as possible—especially in the elementary grades where they assign children to model the male and female genitals in clay." Or: At a private school I visited, I learned of a group of some fifty high-school juniors and seniors, boy and girls, who, in a sex education class watched a visiting lecturer apply a contraceptive to a life-size plastic phallus. There is no need to list further examples.

Such displays are provocative. Dr. Rhoda Lorand, a highly respected psychologist and the author of *Love, Sex and the Teenager,* has warned that these displays can be much more threatening to adolescents than any pornography read in private—because they occur in a classroom, which is not an appropriate place for sexual arousal. To defend themselves against this, she explained, students are forced to detach themselves from the erotic content. They are obliged to suppress all feeling. In other words, the only way teacher and students can calmly participate in such happenings is to behave like robots and pretend that the material they are dealing with is, after all, no different from the new math. One needn't be a psychologist to understand that such a repressive process is not "liberating." It is emotionally and spiritually confining.

This is not to suggest that exhibitionists have run amok in classrooms. They haven't. It is only to question the climate of much of today's teaching, which in one way or another tends to take all human feeling out of sex. Either it dehumanizes relationships between men and women by reducing them to cut-and-dried lists in a manual or, at the other extreme, presents erotic material in a way that requires students to blank out their feelings. It is one thing to give students correct facts and terms in a physiology course, because it is helpful for them to know reproductive anatomy. It is something else, as reported in the *New York Times,* to transport a busload of twenty-six second-graders to the stage of a public forum in Chicago, attended by 300 parents and teachers, to show off how "typically uninhibited" the children had become about sex. When, as the headline announced, "Parents and Teachers Laud . . . Demonstration," something has gone wrong. Apparently it had. The article mentioned that one of the "duties" the class assigned to a father was "to love his family."

Is this the way to promote affectionate, "responsible," "adult" sexuality? It would appear more likely to promote the sexuality of hamsters or guppies. If some of the current trends in sex education continue, they may well make Aldous Huxley's prophetic vision of test-tube infant-seeding laboratories seem like a romantic's dream.

THE BETTER NONPROGRAMS

It comes as no surprise that the better the school, the better its sex education—or its freedom to have no such program until it's good and ready. As the superintendent of a junior high school in Vermont explained: "We've needed this for a hundred years. Another couple of years or so to set up a really good program isn't going to make any difference."

It is also not surprising that the better schools rely on their selection of teachers, not on lengthy, naïvely well-ordered manuals.

I found that a number of leading schools, while they felt a need to expand and update their teaching, have had sex education going for many years before this was a fashionable thing to do. In such instances, these schools took the idea so much for granted that, when asked, a principal might reply that the school had no program—when, I would discover, there was indeed a program. But it would run so subtly through an entire curriculum that, except for the biology courses and some informal talk sessions for high-school students, the sex program was difficult to isolate. At any rate, it would not exist in the currently popular sense of a rigid progression from kindergarten through twelfth grade, or, as it is known, "K-through-12 sex education," designed to reach the "primary target group"—the boys and girls. Such phrases always suggest to me the roll of drums and the orderly plans of a military campaign.

My problem as a reporter was that the best teaching, because it was casual and crisscrossed many departments of a school, was often the hardest to find.

For example, the report on sex education at the Georgetown Day School in Washington, D.C. (written by the school's director, Edith Nash), reads like a fresh breeze. It ties sexual attitudes into an entire curriculum, into a philosophy of "teacher-hiring." It is also a rare document because it is written, not in percentages, or in IA(1)(a) outlinese, but in a personal and readable style, without any ongoing jargon, by someone who apparently is more involved with the humanities than with the detailed mapping of the Fallopian tubes. It is the product of a first-class school, which appears not to be frightened by sex or change; which centers sex education in a school's total emotional environment rather than in "pouring all available information about sex into children" before it is "too late."

The Ethical Culture Schools in New York City reflect a similar attitude. Here again, sex education is integrated naturally into the entire curriculum, not only with the help of the school guidance and medical departments and other experts, but in the teaching of elementary science, literature—or, for many years, in ethics classes, where discussion of sexual topics, when they happen to arise, can be absolutely frank and basic. Typically, the school does not refer to this as a formal sex education program.

When this open atmosphere exists throughout a school, it makes sex education less of a special problem. It reduces the risk of having one or another teacher, "assigned" to sex instruction, fill students with a torrent of information and one man's or woman's views. It allows a student to hear a number of views and to hear them in many contexts: physiology, art, history, anywhere. In this way, students can explore the subject of sex in a framework that approximates life.

It also takes some of the highly charged, personal context out of sexual topics if teen-agers can cloak some of their own hot questions and feelings in some slightly abstracted form; for example, discussing the sexual behavior of characters in a novel in English class or debating birth control in a history class while studying the problems of over-population. Dr. Mary S. Calderone, executive director of SIECUS, has often suggested such methods as the ideal way to air matters of sex and morality. The problem is that there are too few teachers equipped to do this.

The casual approach also capitalizes on what is known as the "teach-able moment," which arrives in a classroom when students seek the knowledge an instructor has to offer. For sheer learning, exchanges at these moments are worth a dozen canned lectures, even if the lec-tures are festooned with impressive reading lists and a whole kit of audio-visual aids.

Unfortunately, the "teachable moment" cannot always be counted on, which is why there is a need for organized classes. Past the level of straight physiology, the good classes, in both schools and training semi-nars for teachers, appear to be few and far between, but they do exist. The teachers of these reveal knowledge, well-placed humor, and reserve. They also bring to sex education the same intangible, educated sensibility that goes into good teaching of literature or music or the workings of democracy or even high cuisine—or any of the other valued products of civilized life that distinguish people from animals and machines and that resist instant definition.

While not always, I frequently found the best sex education among the independent, or private, schools. I'm not sure why. One guess is that being, literally, independent of any city or state administration, these schools feel less need to respond to community and other pressures for crash programs. For the same reason, they are also freer, if they wish, to give honest answers when questions arise on such matters as birth control.

The National Association of Independent Schools (NAIS) also has the benefit of having as a consultant on sex education programs a former headmaster, John Chandler, Jr., who is a reassuring presence on the scene these days because of his thorough but low-keyed approach. His aim is not to blitz the schools with packaged programs but to expose entire faculties to new attitudes and new knowledge about sex.

The NAIS has sponsored some unusually excellent seminars for teachers, directed by Dr. Warren Johnson at the University of Maryland, where invited experts from many disciplines—medicine, psychiatry, psychology, sociology, anthropology, public health—offer teachers a prism of views. In New York, Dr. James Malfetti, a professor of education at Columbia University's Teachers College, gives another fine course, in partnership with Dr. Lawrence Crawley of the same college. The course is for NAIS teachers and for others from public schools.

It is worth noting that at these NAIS seminars one finds a high proportion of headmasters, and teachers of English, history, and other matters of the mind—not the customary preponderance of school nurses and gym teachers, who, I suppose because they deal with the body, are generally given the task of sex education in schools. Certainly, many nurses and physical-education instructors are capable of—and are—doing an excellent job, especially with some training and in cooperation with other departments of a school. What's wrong is the Victorian notion, widely held, that sex education rightfully belongs in these body-only, extracurricular areas of school life. In essence, it puts sex on the level of sprained ankles and basketball, and I think this is the message, again unintended, that teen-agers will get, no matter how much information and uplift talk is ladled out in the classroom.

It may be that some of the independent schools, with their greater freedom to experiment, may lead the way. Some interesting experimentation is also going on in public schools throughout the country, often in cooperation with private foundations or with various branches of the United States government, which has pledged its first million dollars toward sex education.

But this will all take time. Meanwhile, the hastily concocted programs are doomed to ineffectiveness. To have sex education continue on its present generally low level is to show a disrespect for students which they don't deserve.

THE SCHOOLS AS MORALIZERS

This disrespect is often apparent in a school's treatment of moral values. Sometimes it all sounds like a big selling campaign, full of phrases that seem more suitable to merchandise than to human beings. "Our sampling of parents showed that 92 percent approved our sex education package," I was told by the superintendent of one populous public-school district. "Now we're going at it wholesale. We don't lecture or give sermons. The truth is, though, we *are* selling middle-class morality."

It is puzzling to find educators working so hard to "sell" something that adolescents are literally asking schools to offer: discussion of sexual values. These students want not only facts, but guidance from respected adults in their search for a satisfactory and workable code of behavior.

The troubling aspect of this scene is that there appears, often, to be a wide gap between the serious gropings of students for meaningful values and the cheap, warmed-over answers they get from many schools. These come either as prepackaged manual-morals or, worse, morals that are not labeled as morals at all but are presented as facts. Vague, threatening "research" and scraps of statistics are brought in to support a teacher's or school's *opinion*—a use of facts that parallels the old use of hell's-fire warnings, to keep young people in line.

The key question is why anyone should expect the schools to be good moralizers. Whose morals are they presenting? The principal's? The science teacher's? Those of the football coach? The parents? And if the parents, which parents? If a church, which church? It may be that schools by their nature are equipped only to give factual information about sex and should try to limit themselves to this, a hard task in itself.

For better or for worse, moral values seem to emerge primarily from the home. When they emerge positively from a high school—as they sometimes do—it is because of certain admired teachers whom the students try to imitate. This is why schools that focus on teacher selection generally accomplish more with moral values than the schools which embalm these values in rigid texts and positions.

The problem for high schools is that more and more students want honest discussion of *relative* sexual values. This may reflect a spirited inquiry which is going on elsewhere at the moment—the objective, nonmoralizing, sweeping re-examination of sexual behavior by scholars in such fields as medicine, the behavioral sciences, and theology. But it takes expertise to interpret this material to adolescents, an expertise that high schools generally do not have. Until they do, they might keep better faith with their students by resisting the temptation to dabble awkwardly in this field—and just maintain an honest silence.

THE TIMID PARENTS

It might help to realize that an untrained schoolteacher is only some other child's parent, and expecting some magic mantle of wisdom and clarity to descend on him as he enters the classroom is wishful thinking. To put such teachers in charge of sex education does not meet the needs of students, but only meets the needs of parents to have somebody, anybody, take them off the hook.

It is the view of Dr. Elisabeth Geleerd, a leading psychiatrist in New York who works with adolescents, that parents of this generation have been made to feel so generally guilty that they are constantly "afraid they'll make some psychological mistake" in raising their children. She feels this is one reason parents are so ready to hand sex instruction over to the schools. Then, at least, if "mistakes" are made, it will be "the school's fault, not theirs."

Until some really meaningful sex education—past the biology courses—evolves on a wide scale, it may be that parents will have to try to re-establish communication with their children. The churches are trying to, and if some of the school-affiliated ministers I have listened to at conferences represent any trend, some very honest and feeling sex education could develop from advance-guard members of the church.

One of the big achievements of school sex education so far is that it has made sex a respectable topic of conversation between generations. It has given children of all ages a dignified vocabulary with which to ask questions at home. Another of the schools' known successes, at Anaheim and elsewhere, has been in the offering of separate sex education classes to parents, originally just to bring them up to date on what their children were learning. Apparently parents throughout the country have welcomed this. They seem to want information and discussion of values as much as their children do. Why not make parents an equal focus of the entire sex education program?

Dr. Geleerd feels that schools and parents should work together as much as possible. She also thinks parents should feel less timid than they do about expressing their own views to adolescents. As she explained: " In their struggle for independence, teen-agers tend to reject what parents have to say. But that's no reason for parents to give up. A teen-ager is in too much turmoil to be reached, but what he does not seem to hear now, he'll remember in his twenties." Dr. Geleerd's point is reminiscent of the passage in *The Autobiography of Lincoln Steffens* in which Steffens describes how surprised he was, on returning home from college, to discover how much his parents had learned while he was away.

As with most of the real experts, Dr. Geleerd's "answers" are questions: "Don't parents make their views clear to children anyway, whether or not they put them into words? And aren't most teachers just as confused as parents?"

WHO WILL TEACH?

A distinction should be made between the many organizers of sex education and a small but growing nucleus of experts worthy of the term *expert*. To hear people of this caliber lecture or lead discussions at teacher-training seminars can be an enlightening experience, very different from the nonsense often doled out as sex instruction in classrooms. I don't see why the honesty and range of information of these experts could not be adjusted to a high-school level, say in a series of closed-network television programs, which might also be available to parents, church groups, settlement houses, or any other groups wishing to tune in. This might be one way of meeting the demand for sex education while qualified teachers are still in short supply.

For example, when Dr. Warren Johnson describes male and female roles in many cultures covering a wide span of history, or outlines conflicting patterns of sexual mores that exist side by side today in our own society, it has meaning because it is specific and informed. It is not vague talk about "maleness" and "femaleness." It is educational in the biggest sense of the word. It makes the listener stop in his tracks and try to redefine his own ideas. This is teaching geared to the relativistic values of the 1960s and is a far cry from listing the seven matching good and bad results of "moral" and "immoral" behavior, an approach that seems right out of the Middle Ages.

Those I refer to as experts are generally people whose knowledge crosses many areas and who have acquired it over a period of some twenty or thirty years. Many of them teach at various universities, teachers' colleges, or medical schools.

As elsewhere, the people with the greatest experience in this field seem to have the greatest humility. They have no ready answers, but regard confusion today on sexual mores as a legitimate state of mind. They try to help teachers and students discover what their personal views are and then to see these views against some larger framework. They don't twist facts to suit moralizing purposes. They don't pretend that sex isn't sexy and therefore treat the subject with scholarly reserve. What's more, they are familiar with a substantial bank of theory and research on sexual behavior, which has been contributed by Freud, Kinsey, and many others—material that cannot be mastered in a three-week, or even a six-week, summer course.

Sex education is a demanding new field, and hopefully schools will stop handing it over to the first staff member who volunteers to teach.

After all, it's taken thousands of years for sexual behavior to become an approved subject of academic investigation. Why do schools now think they must rush every aspect of it into every classroom overnight?

Playboy: Interview with Masters and Johnson

W. H. Masters and V. E. Johnson

PLAYBOY: How about sex education for laymen? At what age do you believe it should begin?

MASTERS: It should begin as soon as youngsters are old enough to observe their parents relating to each other.

PLAYBOY: What can you teach children about sex at such an early age?

MASTERS: I don't think you have to "teach" them anything. If there is real warmth and interpersonal exchange in the marital relationship, the kids absorb it.

PLAYBOY: Do you think sex education should be restricted to the home?

MASTERS: No. It should be taught in the church and in the school as well. I don't think you can teach it any one place and do it well. Most homes can't teach reproductive biology—apart from unsophisticated "where babies come from" answers. At the other extreme, some homes teach all the biology in the world, but the kids never see Mom and Dad holding hands. The point is that parents can and should demonstrate to children the importance of an effective and outgoing sexual relationship.

JOHNSON: There's a kind of pseudo-avant-garde parent who wants so much to be "in" that he or she will overtalk the subject of sex. There will be great freedom with terminology, and a studied, self-conscious atmosphere will be created; but no values will be imparted.

MASTERS: Religious authorities should present their views of course; and as for the schools, sex education should be a part of the curriculum, but I don't have any definitive opinions about how that should be done.

JOHNSON: One of the problems that haven't been solved yet is who should do the teaching. A good teacher of sex education has to impart some of his personality. He has to teach that sexuality is good and that there is a place for it. He has to teach values that are realistic, that make sense in the context of how things really are. It seems sad to me that we feel it necessary to design sex education "curricula" and put formidable barriers around the subject. We have not yet learned how to treat the subject naturally.

163

PLAYBOY: A. S. Neill makes a similar point in *Summerhill*—that once we are faced with a concept of sex education, we have already failed at it. In other words, sexuality should be learned naturally, from life experience.

MASTERS: Yes; but, of course, Neill was dealing with a controlled environment in his progressive school. As American society is constituted today, we have to make the best of a sorry bargain, which means some sex education on a formal basis, at least for the foreseeable future.

JOHNSON: You know, there is a kind of natural sex education in the communication of children with one another.

MASTERS: The kids spread a lot of fallacies and misconceptions, but they have one thing going for them: they learn to talk about sex. Even if it's hush-hush or snicker-snicker, there's value in communication.

JOHNSON: The pitfall in this is that knowledge picked up from the peer group frequently works as a barrier to sex education from adults. Often a good job can't really be done at home, because one has to contend with misinformation conveyed by other people's children, not to mention teachers who insist on making judgments.

PLAYBOY: What qualifications do you think are desirable for teachers of sex education?

MASTERS: A sense of confidence and a nonjudgmental approach to the concerns of sexual response. A certain amount of academic orientation is in order, but all the academic orientation in the world won't amount to a row of beans if the teacher isn't comfortable with the subject.

JOHNSON: Besides being well informed, he or she should have *lived* the subject—in other words, should have had the experience of a stabilized sexual relationship.

PLAYBOY: When you say that teachers should be nonjudgmental, do you mean in terms of teaching when it's right and when it's wrong to engage in sex?

MASTERS: No, we don't mean that. Everyone has a right to teach his own basic concepts; but sexual activity must be taught as a perfectly natural, normal phenomenon of human expression, and not one that should be hidden, avoided, or discussed in whispers.

JOHNSON: If you're really going to guide and direct young people, you have to be willing to listen to and accept their experiences as they express them in a classroom situation. If you express any condemnation there, you can turn off a young person, as far as communicating his or her sexual experiences is concerned, and thereby lose a vital opportunity to provide guidance.

PLAYBOY: Do you think sex education should include contraceptive information?

MASTERS: Depending on the age group, certainly. To my mind, the greatest tragedy in the dissemination of contraceptive information is that it's usually disseminated after the young person has started having intercourse. Rarely is there pregnancy protection at the first opportunity.

PLAYBOY: What do you think of Wilhelm Reich's claim that society's taboos on infant, child, and adolescent sexuality are responsible for impotence and frigidity in adults?

MASTERS: I think in some instances he is quite correct. This is a contributing cause in many of the cases we have seen.

JOHNSON: And the effect of these taboos is frequently a factor that has had to be *overcome* even by those who don't develop problems because of them.

PLAYBOY: Do you think masturbation plays an important role in an adolescent's sexual development?

MASTERS: That depends on the individual. There are a large number of people who have never masturbated and yet have developed into sexually responsive adults. So you can't say it's a requirement. But, obviously, it has played a major role in the sexual development of most individuals.

JOHNSON: I wonder if the negative side isn't more important. The fact of masturbation is nowhere near as dramatic a concern as the misconception that it's dirty, objectionable, or what have you. Of course, this starts the individual out with a concept of guilt. A permissiveness about early genital expression is not nearly so important as the *absence* of a negative approach.

PLAYBOY: On the whole, how well do you think sex education is being handled in America today?

MASTERS: We have no scientific knowledge as to whether it's worth a damn. There are a lot of people who climb on the sex education bandwagon and say it's great. But somebody is going to have to take the time and effort to find out whether there is any real value in the entire concept of formally disseminating sexual information to youngsters. I don't mean to say that I think sex education is valueless; I just want to emphasize that there is absolutely no objective study that has been done in this area to determine its real value.

JOHNSON: Yes, but the fact that sex education is being done at all has greater value—at least at this point—than the actual material being disseminated. Wouldn't you agree?

MASTERS: Of course. The mere fact that one can talk about the subject and consider it with some degree of objectivity—all this shows incredible progress.

PLAYBOY: The kind of progress you're talking about is part of what's been called the Sexual Revolution—a revolution that is defined in many ways by many people. Can you give us your own definition?

JOHNSON: To begin with, we don't call it a revolution; we call it a renaissance. People tend to forget that the greatest deterrent to female freedom of sexual expression in this country was the invention of the steamboat—in other words, the Industrial Revolution.

MASTERS: It was this that pulled the men off the farms and into the city. In an agricultural community, female sexual equality never became an issue. Time and time again, Mom—in order to avoid the kids—would take Pop's lunch out into the back field. They had lunch—and something more—by the creek under a shade tree. Fulfillment was thus taken for granted. Sex in this culture was presumed, valued, enjoyed— and lived. Then, as we became an industrial culture, puritanism spread and eventually Victorianism took over. With it came the repression of female sexuality that has existed until very recent years—the "Thou shalt nots," the double standard, and so on.

JOHNSON: So you see, we're talking about a *rebirth* of natural sexuality. We're beginning to hark back to a time when there was an earthy acceptance of oneself as a sexual being, when sex was taken for granted as a healthy part of life. If I may inject a personal note, our work is very much a reflection of this renaissance. Even though people have been somewhat shaken by it, society has still *permitted* it.

MASTERS: Precisely. We have not existed in spite of our time; we have existed *because* of it.

JOHNSON: Actually, Kinsey was a pioneer—and so were R. L. Dickenson and Havelock Ellis before him. But they reflected a deep cultural need. We have emerged as a reflection of society's changing attitudes. For example, Bill [Masters] started as a gynecologist—a physician— and I know that his early interest in the basic science of sex research developed almost parallel with the maturation of society's attitudes toward the subject. Kinsey, on the other hand, pioneered this renaissance; he helped lead it and make it what it is.

PLAYBOY: Many critics of this sexual renaissance, as you know, think that the pendulum has swung too far in the direction of permissiveness, that the new emphasis on sex has inflated its importance out of proper proportion. Are we correct in assuming that you disagree?

MASTERS: If the importance of sex was ever overemphasized—by its obsessive and moralistic negation—it was in the Victorian period, not now. It was then, not now, that sex could not be accepted and that sexuality was denied as a dimension of the total personality. If the pendulum has swung too far, I'm sure it will swing back. Let's put it this way: A certain amount of healthy objectivity needs to be injected into the field. We hope that something like this interview—appearing in the magazine I regard as the best available medium for sex education in America today—will help do it.

PLAYBOY: You are obviously pleased to see the double standard disappear. But many clergymen fear that the vanishing "Thou shalt nots" are being replaced by libertarian "Thou shalts" that may deprive young women, by virtue of a kind of reverse puritanism, of their freedom of choice. Do you see this happening?

MASTERS: Absolutely not. What has developed with the use of contraception is a new sense of selectivity for young women. They now have more freedom to say no than they ever had before. It may have something to do with the fact that the female no longer makes her decisions on the basis of fear—fear of pregnancy, fear of disease, fear of social ostracism. In no sense does this imply a rejection of elective chastity, but chastity based on the innumerable fears is entirely a false premise; an objective decision cannot be made on this basis. Today the young woman is free to make her choice, pick her time, her place, her circumstance, without the old fears. With all the druthers now available to her, we have a hunch that the intelligent girl tends to be more sophisticated in her selection—simply because it is *her* selection.

JOHNSON: If effective contraception is being used, then a woman must be honest with herself and realize that she is engaging in sexual activity as an expression of herself within a relationship. She is not, consciously or unconsciously, playing the old game of sex for marriage entrapment, nor is she using sex to represent her femaleness by "willful exposure to unwanted pregnancy"—to quote Dr. Hans Lehfeldt's tongue-in-cheek but accurate comment.

PLAYBOY: Do you think it's possible, as some clergymen predict, that the elimination of fear will break down all the barriers?

MASTERS: Is it possible? Yes. But there is no reason to believe that removal of fear inevitably results in the destruction of value systems. In fact, there is some evidence that modern young men and women are much more concerned with the quality of interpersonal relationships than with sex per se.

JOHNSON: What I'm about to say may not go over well with some *Playboy* readers, but the fact is that, for the first time in many decades, the girl is running the sexual show. She is not a victim; she doesn't have to put up or shut up. Although this issue is still in limbo, we're on the right road toward placing value on sexual activity within a human relationship as opposed to simple emphasis on natural drives—you know, "Let's do it, even though the timing is wrong, the people are wrong, and the place is wrong; we have to satisfy a natural human need." The young woman now has many things to contemplate in making her choice. She can decide, after proper self-evaluation, whether her goal is reproduction and homemaking or whether she wants to express herself in some other fashion while deferring—or even rejecting—marriage. There are so many options to consider, and the concerns of venereal disease, pregnancy, or social ostracism need no longer be the foremost factors in influencing her decision.

PLAYBOY: Then you don't think that the Pill culture necessarily leads to promiscuity?

MASTERS: It depends on what you mean by promiscuity.

PLAYBOY: What do *you* mean by it?

JOHNSON: In our concept of the term, someone who exploits another person sexually is promiscuous, regardless of the circumstances.

MASTERS: Sexual expression, to me, is either mutual orientation, satisfaction, enhancement, and stimulation, or it's promiscuous—inside or outside marriage. The old concept of sexual promiscuity, meaning excessive interest outside of socially approved channels, leaves me cold. A woman who adequately serves three different men sexually and enjoys all of them, and gives each as good as she gets, is more honest than the "faithful" wife in her own bedroom who serves one man but thinks of another. I think there is both mental and physical promiscuity—the latter being the old concept. The more dishonest concept, and the one that offers the least hope of effective development of mature sexuality, is mental promiscuity. Let me give you another example. Take the young male who makes seven chalk marks on the wall in one night. As far as I'm concerned, he may be promiscuous—mentally rather than physically—if he is interested in his partner only as a proving ground for his sexual athleticism.

PLAYBOY: There have been predictions that another by-product of increasing sexual freedom will be the proliferation of homosexuality. What do you think?

MASTERS: If the majority of reasons given by scientists and by homosexuals themselves for turning to homosexuality are true, a liberalization of sexual attitudes would remove some of these reasons; it would help lessen the homosexual's self-rejection. This is, of course, only theorizing. We have no evidence to support it.

PLAYBOY: Marshall McLuhan predicts that the gradual blurring of stereotyped psychosexual roles for men and women will soon make the differences between the sexes less significant than the similarities. Add to this the influence of the Pill, he says, and it will become "possible for sexual woman to act like sexual man." Do you think we're heading toward a kind of unisexual society?

JOHNSON: "Unisex" is a rather unappealing term, but McLuhan is obviously correct in predicting that the old stereotypes of male and female will disappear; to an extent, they already have. We no longer require a stronger sex to go out and kill the tigers and to defend the home. Most of us know that the football hero and the physically well-endowed woman are not necessarily more effective sexually than the rest of us. So why don't we turn to the important things—like real communication and re-enforcement of one another's reason for being? Why concentrate on wearing ruffles to prove we're women and un-adorned clothing to prove we're men? It hardly seems important to have a program to tell the players apart; the players know very well who they are—or if they don't, clothing will hardly solve the problem.

PLAYBOY: One more prediction related to the sexual renaissance is that it will weaken and perhaps even obsolesce the institution of marriage. What are your views?

JOHNSON: Society has not yet come up with any social grouping more functional than marriage and the family. Quite obviously, we think the renaissance of sexuality will strengthen it, not weaken it.

PLAYBOY: How so?

JOHNSON: One of the most threatening things to the marital relationship is the separation of sex and sexuality—sex being the physical expression of sexual activity, and sexuality being a dimension or expression of the total personality. The Victorians negated sexuality and thereby made sex a behind-the-stairs, in-the-dark sort of thing. Communication regarding sexual matters most likely did not exist. There may have been people who worked this out in the privacy of their own one-to-one relationship, but all the evidence tells us that this was the exception, not the rule. The point is that sexuality can hardly flourish in a forbidden atmosphere. If two people enter into a sexual relationship, they have to let it live on a twenty-four-hour basis. Sexual response can be sparked by the fact of its being forbidden, just as it can be triggered by hostility—but that's hardly a lovely way to live, and it certainly doesn't create an aura of love, of affection, of warmth, to be conveyed to children. So I think that marriage has endured in *spite* of the Victorian attitudes, not because of them. I should add that, in my opinion, marriage is not a static institution; in the future, it may be constituted differently. It's undergoing change today, but I don't think it will be altered in a noticeable way during our lifetime.

PLAYBOY: What can you tell us about the future of sex research—specifically, your own?

MASTERS: At the moment, we're working on the biochemistry of reproductive fluids—that is, such things as vaginal lubrication, Bartholin's and Cowper's glands secretions. No work has ever been done in these areas. We're also doing a great deal of work in homosexuality and have been since early 1963. We're studying the female homosexual in particular, as we feel she has never been examined in depth. We want to learn as much as we can from the sociological, physiological, biochemical, endocrinological—and, ultimately, the therapeutic—points of view. But any concept of therapy is far beyond our current concern, and we won't have anything to report for perhaps a decade or more. At the moment we're merely learning about the subject.

PLAYBOY: What is your goal in the homosexual research?

MASTERS: We hope eventually to move into some concept of sexual reversal for those who wish it. From what we know now—which is very little—we can't conceive of homosexuality of itself as an inversion or abnormality. It seems to be a basic form of sexual expression— a minority form but a very definitive one.

We also want to continue working in sexual physiology, but hopefully we're well past the nose-counting stage of experimentation reflected in *Human Sexual Response*. Our future projects in this area are quite specific and include investigation of sexual response as it relates to the damaged heart—that is, the coronary, the hypertensive and rheumatic hearts. We're also particularly interested in studying the sexuality of the aging population, in terms of understanding metabolic, endocrinological, and physiological changes involved, with the ultimate goal of enhancing the effectiveness of sexual response among the aged. And we certainly hope to do some work on the massive problem related to the sexuality of the physically handicapped.

PLAYBOY: What do you think the future holds for sex research in general?

MASTERS: Sufficient maturity and controlled expansion, we hope, so that research may be done in the *total* area of sexual behavior—not just from the psychological and physiological points of view, the "why" and the "what," but also, for example, from the sociological and theological perspectives.

Human sexual behavior is of vital concern to every single individual throughout his or her life. Aside from the instinct for self-preservation, it is the most forceful response we know. Yet it is the response about which we know least. Look at the massive amount of time and effort that has been spent on the control of poliomyelitis, for instance—an effort that was worthy, since it brought the disease under control—but compare the occasional individual who contracts polio with the daily concern of *every* individual about his or her sexuality. Although we are obviously in favor of any medical approach that helps eliminate the major pathologies, it must also be realized that the one physiological activity, after eating and sleeping, that occupies the greatest part of human life is no less worthy of definitive and objective research. We intend to devote the greatest part of *our* lives to that research.

Is the Schoolhouse the Proper Place to Teach Raw Sex?

Gordon V. Drake

I. SIECUS — THE UNCERTAIN TRUMPET

Dr. Mary Calderone, executive director of the Sex Information and Education Council of the United States (SIECUS), has a burning mission: to alert and convert the youth of America to a new sexuality. She pursues children and youth for her cause as ardently as the missionary of old pursued souls.

"I have a covenant with the young people of these times," Dr. Calderone confides, "a personal covenant by which I will settle for nothing less than total honesty with them." [1] The "honesty" she refers to is in telling young people about their right to enjoy premarital intercourse—if they so desire. As she jets across America from school to community hall to college campus, she preaches her revolutionary gospel.

For example, speaking to 320 boys at Blair Academy in New Jersey, Dr. Calderone declared, "What is sex for? It's for fun . . . for wonderful sensation. . . . Sex is not something you turn off like a faucet. If you do, it's unhealthy."

She continued: "We need new values to establish when and how we should have sexual experiences. Nobody's standing on a platform giving answers. You are moving beyond your parents. But you can't just move economically or educationally. You must move sexually, as well."

When a Blair student asked her, "What is your opinion of premarital sex relations among teen-agers?" she snapped back, "What's yours? Nobody from up on high [referring to God] determines this. You determine it . . . I don't believe . . . the old 'Thou shalt nots' apply anymore." [2]

This is a remarkable admission coming from a person who claims to be a religious person, a Quaker with "concerns." Dr. Calderone's concern—after tossing God aside—is to teach American youth a new sex morality independent of church and state.

As executive director of SIECUS, Dr. Calderone heads the most influential organization promoting sex education programs in the schools today. She holds degrees in both medicine and public health.

171

Established in 1964, SIECUS has now reached full bloom in its goal to create "something new in the world: knowledge in depth, *and attitudes in breadth,* about that part of the human individual that is central to his total well-being, his sexuality." [3] For the uninitiated, sexuality as defined by SIECUS and its constellation of sexologists includes the entire span of activities of men and women.

Dr. Calderone's Curious Contradictions

Dr. Calderone readily admits that in the early 1900s "parents lived their sex education before their children, and the peaceful, happy relationship of a well-matched husband and wife was good sex education. The simple facts of reproduction . . . could be acquired later in good time." [4] The child's rate of sexual development has not measurably changed in the last fifty or sixty years. Therefore, what Dr. Calderone terms an appropriate time for sexual facts to be learned in the early 1900s could, and should, be the appropriate time today. However, the thrust of SIECUS is to get the most sex information to the child as early as possible, ostensibly to counteract what Dr. Calderone describes as misinformation children learn from parents and the mass media— misinformation that is "smeared in their faces from the time they can see and hear." [5]

In the matter of birth control, however, Dr. Calderone is quite willing for young people to learn from the "mass media" despite its distortions and delusions. In fact, she says, "I must confess that I have to warn communities not to teach anything about birth control that the children haven't already learned from the mass media." [6] What curious reasoning is this? Her enigma further mystifies us when she says that sex education does not really include the simple facts of reproduction.[7] In reference to teaching youth the facts about venereal diseases, she astounds us by saying, "I don't think they are a part of sex education." [8]

Further evidence of Dr. Calderone's confusion is her suggestion that teachers of sex education do not need special training—that "any teacher can teach a course on human sexual behavior." [9] Her answer to the question "How can I judge if our sex education courses are good?" is an amazing "I'm afraid that parents cannot exercise judgments as to quality in terms of content, because most parents are not qualified." "Even many doctors are not qualified," she declares, "except to judge the accuracy of the biological and physiological content. But the emotional and behavior content requires a different kind of judgment," which she then identifies as "good" if young people can talk with their parents about sex "without the feeling that this is something to be ashamed of." [10] Despite her apparent confusion, Dr. Calderone is popularly acclaimed the most authoritative sex educator in America today.

Dr. Mary Calderone, who previously served as medical director of the Planned Parenthood Association, formed SIECUS in 1964 with a group of like-minded professionals from such diverse fields as sociology, psychiatry, education, religion, and law. In a matter of four years, SIECUS has attained the position of undisputed leader and consultant in organizing school sex education programs. It enjoys a tax-free status as a nonprofit organization and is financed by private contributions and well-known foundations such as the Ford Foundation.

SIECUS helps promote and organize seminars and special training courses for teachers in sex education. During 1967 at least sixteen summer institutes for teachers were held across the country. In 1968 this number more than doubled. In SIECUS's own words, this is a "dramatic change." Its immediate goal is to provide teachers with specific sex knowledge, but the "ultimate purpose is the development of teachers who . . . can meet youngsters where they are with frankness and honesty, and can discuss their concerns objectively and *nonjudgmentally* with them." [11] Nonjudgmentally simply means that SIECUS does not want teachers to inject into their discussions with children the restraints of old-fashioned morality.

Teacher training courses offered during the summer of 1968 were varied. Teachers College, Columbia University, offered "Human Reproduction and Sexual Development," which could be bypassed by "students already knowledgeable." A sensitivity training course called "Group Processes in Sex Education" might be substituted. The University of West Virginia devised a broadening course for sex educators, administrators, clergymen, and social workers entitled "Family Insights through Literature." This remarkable learning experience delved into premarital, marital, and postmarital relationships in modern society as reflected in novels, stories, and plays. It might just as well have been subtitled "A Short Course in Current Pornography."

Exhibit A: Dr. Isadore Rubin

SIECUS board members staunchly support Dr. Calderone's philosophy. One of the most influential men on the board is Dr. Isadore Rubin, a founding member and the organization's treasurer since 1964. He wears another hat as editor of *Sexology* magazine. The sworn testimony of an undercover operative for the New York Police Department identified Isadore Rubin in 1955 as a member of the Communist party. After his dismissal as a teacher by the New York City Board of Education in 1951 for refusing to declare whether he was a Communist, he became active in the New York City Teachers' Union—which was expelled from the AFL-CIO because it was found to be Communist controlled.[12]

One of Dr. Rubin's favorite concerns is homosexuality. He concurs that since antihomosexuality laws encourage "police corruption" and "repressive enforcement procedures," and, furthermore, do not "significantly control the behavior," the community should free itself of "punitive attitudes" toward this form of sexuality.[13] Dr. Rubin's Marxist slip is showing.

Rubin's *Sexology* magazine wallows in sex-sationalism. Joining him in the mire are his associates on the SIECUS board of directors: Dr. Lester A. Kirkendall, the Reverend William H. Genné, Dr. John Money, and Dr. Wardell B. Pomeroy. All hold dual positions on the SIECUS board and the board of consultants to *Sexology*. In addition, Dr. Kirkendall is an editor of the magazine. Other members of the SIECUS board, such as past president Dr. David Mace, are frequent contributors to *Sexology*. In turn, SIECUS frequently recommends reprints of *Sexology* articles, such as those written by rabid atheist, psychiatrist Dr. Albert Ellis.

Sexology is little moie than a slick smut magazine which contains pictured and written erotica. It is replete with "informative" discussions such as "The Prostitutes of Ancient Greece," which revealed that the early Greek prostitutes achieved enviable positions of honor, wealth, and fame, [14] "Alcohol Can Solve Sex Problems," "Group Sex Orgies," "My Wife Knows I'm Homosexual," "Gangs That Hunt Down 'Queers,'" and "Do Sex-Change Men Want to Be Mothers?"

Exhibit B: Dr. Lester Kirkendall

One of the most outspoken and prolific SIECUS sexecutives is Dr. Lester Kirkendall, who believes that any absolute moral standard is utterly unthinkable—aside from the absolutism of nonrestraint. He brands patriotism and defense of one's country as immoral. He says:

> A tremendous feeling of national unity, a sense of closeness, good will, and harmony, may result from fearing another nation or from the effort of trying to destroy another nation. Such unity . . . is immoral.[15]

As a past director of the American Humanist Association and writer for *The Humanist* magazine, we can expect Kirkendall to elevate man and declare God expendable. Morality, he writes, cannot be found in the context of "supernaturalism or a supernatural deity." Rather, he defines his religion as a "respect for and a *belief in people,* and a concern for true brotherhood among men." This is "genuinely religious." [16]

Like Isadore Rubin, Dr. Kirkendall is a founder and board member of SIECUS and serves as an editor of *Sexology* magazine. He employs a simon-pure humanistic frame of reference for his morality of situation ethics:

The essence of morality lies in the quality of interpersonal relationships which can be established among people. . . . Immoral behavior . . . dehumanizes.

Kirkendall feels that this concept should be "central to both our personal and corporate lives, and we need to study it, pursue its ramifications, and put it into practice." [17] This indeed he does as one of the leading spokesmen for sexual emancipation.

Kirkendall's writings are voluminous. He has published eight full-length books, and eighteen chapters in books of special studies. Over two hundred articles have appeared in learned publications, and he lectures incessantly throughout the United States. He sees humanizing sex education as reaching far beyond the public schools to preschool, higher education, and adult education. All programs are essential in developing man's sexuality. Therefore, "the purpose of sex education is not primarily to control and suppress sex expression, as in the past, but to indicate the immense possibilities for human fulfillment that human sexuality offers. . . ." It must be thought of as being education, "not moral indoctrination." [18] Kirkendall is referring, of course, to traditional Christian morality.

He campaigns for individual choice and decision in the existential context of today as he reclassifies forbidden fruits of the past into juicy sexual plums for today. He joyously announces that "the significance of such sexual expressions as youthful erotic play, masturbation, homosexuality between consenting adults, mouth-genital contacts, and other variations from genital heterosexuality is being re-examined [today] in the light of new knowledge. The enhanced capacity among educated people to look at sexuality with objectivity suggests that some things formerly considered to be of social concern might now be reclassified as private, personal concerns, or, if having social concern, for different reasons than formerly." [19]

"Forty or fifty years ago," Kirkendall reminisces, "sex education scarcely recognized the possibility of choosing among alternative patterns of sexual behavior. There was only one 'right' way. Only one course of action was considered acceptable: renunciation of all sexual expression in nonmarital situations. . . . *Quite a different situation now exists. There is now a very real freedom for adolescent couples*" [emphasis added]. The humanistic orientation of Dr. Kirkendall is clearly expressed by this final statement: The sexually adjusted person "will not be driven by guilt, anxiety, or compulsion to engage in sex with little regard for what this means to other persons or to his total situation. . . . He is in a position to direct and manage his sexuality." [20]

Exhibit C: Dr. William Masters

Another member of the SIECUS board is Dr. William H. Masters, co-author with Virginia E. Johnson of the bestseller *Human Sexual Response*. This book relates an investigation by the authors of the sexual responses of 382 females and 312 males in the acts of intercourse and automanipulation. The researchers used a unique invention to assist them in the study of female responses—an artificial plastic phallus which recorded vaginal responses. Dr. Masters describes it as follows: "The equipment can be adjusted for physical variations in size, weight and vaginal development. The rate and depth of penile thrust is initiated and controlled completely by the responding individual." [21]

The investigators had no qualms about employing unmarried subjects to perform before cameras in their study of intercourse. The rationale offered by Dr. Masters was that the subjects had had a "history of similar experience in nonexperimental situations." [22] In other words, fornication was not new to them. Dr. Masters' moral approach is cogently evident in his statement that "a woman who serves three different men . . . and enjoys all of them . . . is more honest than the 'faithful' wife . . . who serves one man . . . but thinks of another." [23]

Exhibit D: Dr. Albert Ellis

Albert Ellis, Ph.D. has been lauded by Isadore Rubin as "one of America's leading sexologists." Though not a SIECUS board member, Ellis is one of its "status" resource persons whose writings are recommended. Let us look at the facts. Dr. Ellis, fifty-two years old, twice divorced, is a practicing psychoanalyst in New York City who peddles his Freudian analyses at twenty-five dollars an hour. His favorite adjective in private conversation is "S——," which he cites "incessantly in tones of contempt." [24] He objects violently to any and all of the sexual taboos of a saner age and insists, "If I were stuck on a desert island with my sister, I would almost certainly copulate with her and let the chips fall where they may." [25]

During the 1930s Ellis was a leader in one of the dozens of left-wing political groups in New York City, and he put *Das Kapital* into simple English for the lay reader. Oxford University Press, after indicating interest in the manuscript, reversed its decision to publish it. Another of his books, started under the title *The Case for Promiscuity,* years later was published under the banner *The Case for Sexual Liberty.* [26]

Today, Dr. Ellis authors such books as *If This Be Sexual Heresy, Sex without Guilt,* and a vitriolic pamphlet entitled *The Case against Religion.* SIECUS, which recommends and sells many tape recordings, offers a taped discussion between Dr. David Mace and Dr. Albert Ellis. The tape is described in a SIECUS publications list as "a provocative and stimulating dialogue. . . . The discussion contrasts a liberal and permissive approach to sexual expression with an approach that em-

phasizes responsibility and sensitivity toward the partner." [27] This semantic manipulation simply means that the taped discussion contrasts
Ellis's "sexual anarchy" with Mace's "situation ethics."

In his SIECUS-recommended book *The American Sexual Tragedy*,
Ellis with warped logic denounces "men who cannot be sexually satisfied
with any form of sex activity but coitus" as "probably fetishistically
attached to this idea." He recommends psychotherapy to alleviate the
problem.[28] Employing a bizarre example, Ellis declares that "a man
who has no penis whatever could be an excellent lover," for women and
men alike have "hands, lips, and other organs which are in many ways
capable of giving exquisite pleasure." [29]

We certainly question whether this sexologist's philosophy can contribute anything but sheer degeneracy to the education of our youth. It
should be obvious to any decent human being that the perverted sexual
filth that Ellis peddles adds to the massive stench which arises from the
SIECUS SEXPOT. Even with its deceptive excuse that such material is
justified in presenting all sides of the question, SIECUS conveniently
omits the legitimate Biblical position, and tends to define depravity as
new-found sexuality.

THE CASE AGAINST RELIGION

The sick sexology of Ellis stems from his hatred of religion and is
clearly stated in his treatise *The Case against Religion*. He and SIECUS
spokesmen agree that traditional sex standards must be replaced because they are based "on premises that are now totally unsupportable—
on the folklore of the ancient Hebrew and the musings of medieval
monks, concepts that are simply obsolete." [30]

Ellis finds "exceptionally pernicious" religion which has a supernatural system. The following excerpts seethe with these feelings. Religion is "faith unfounded on fact, or dependent on some supernatural
deity." This, according to Ellis, "seriously sabotages mental health." He
believes that the religious person has no real views of his own, and that
in sex matters and love affairs he must "discover what his God and his
clergy would like him to do." [31]

Ellis contends that "masochistic self-sacrifice is an integral part of
almost all organized religions. . . . [It] stems from an individual's deliberately inflicting pain on himself in order that he may guiltlessly . . .
experience some kind of sexual or other pleasure." In fact, Ellis sees
religiosity as masochism, and "both are forms of mental sickness." The
"absolutistic, perfectionistic thinking" of religion as it must essentially
be by God-given standards "corrodes human emotions," and "develops
anxiety and hostility" in the individual. Of necessity, then, "religious

people hold neurotic beliefs," for the "religious commitment . . . is often motivated by guilt or hostility, and may serve as a frenzied covering-up mechanism which masks . . . these underlying disturbed feelings." [32] Religion, to a large degree, is fanaticism: "The religious person sells his soul, surrenders his own basic urges and pleasures, so that he may feel comfortable with the heavenly helper that he himself has invented. Religion, then, is needless inhibition." [33]

Dr. Ellis's conclusion is inescapable: "Religion is . . . directly opposed to the goals of mental health . . . it encourages a fanatic, obsessive-compulsive kind of commitment that is, in its own right, a form of mental illness. . . . This close connection between mental illness and religion is inevitable and invariant. . . . In the final analysis, then, religion is neurosis." [34]

His solution is simply this: "The therapist, if he himself is not too sick or gutless, [will] attack his patient's religiosity. Not only will he show his patient that he is . . . fanatic, but he will also quite vigorously and forcefully question, challenge, and attack the patient's irrational beliefs. . . . This is what is done in my own system of psychotherapy, which is called rational-emotive psychotherapy." Ellis says he keeps "depropagandizing" his patients so that the beliefs "acquired from his parents and his culture can be thoroughly combatted until they are truly non-existent." [35]

Dr. Ellis's case against religion is clear, and, whether sexologists, psychologists, and school counselors admit it to parents or not, mental health and sex education programs are frequently determined to crush religious belief. We are reminded of Karl Marx, who declared that "religion is the opiate of the people." He knew that religion had to be destroyed before Communism could hope to maintain control of a nation by reducing it to slavery and dumb obedience to the Communist masters.

The Reverend William Genné

The Reverend Mr. Genné, a founder, board member, and present secretary, of SIECUS, is also the director of the National Council of Churches' Commission on Marriage and Family Life. (Dr. Calderone is a member of the same NCC Commission.) In a SIECUS newsletter, the Reverend Mr. Genné points out that the theological new moralist believes "the ultimate sanction for a system of values or morality rests above any person or group of persons." Only God can judge each individual's morality, and therefore we should first love God, and, second, love our neighbor as ourself. Genné then concludes that "when any church regulation, civil law, or personal act contravenes that criterion, it becomes an immoral act." [36] By this logic, the Reverend Mr.

Genné and his compatriots can accept premarital sex—with love—as well as a reasonable amount of homosexual activity.

To support his view Genné quotes an English theologian who observed that nonmarital intercourse had helped some men gain confidence in their manhood: "Wherever healing takes place, Christ is present, no matter what the church says about fornication." [37]*

Dr. Joseph F. Fletcher

Dr. Fletcher, religious author of *Situation Ethics—The New Morality,* which is recommended by SIECUS, shares the "Newsex" point of view. Professor of Ethics at Cambridge Episcopal Theological School, Fletcher suggests that the Ten Commandments be amended as follows:

> Thou shalt not covet, ordinarily
> Thou shalt not kill, ordinarily
> Thou shalt not commit adultery, ordinarily[38]

Fletcher says: "For me there are no rules at all . . . anything and everything is right or wrong according to the situation—what is wrong in some cases is right in others. . . . A situationist would discard all absolutes except the one absolute; always act with loving concern." [39]

Dr. Fletcher has strong Communist sympathies. The House Committee on Un-American Activities released a report entitled *Review of the Scientific and Cultural Conference for World Peace.* Fletcher is listed as one of the conference sponsors. The report has this to say regarding the conference:

> Parading under the imposing title of Scientific and Cultural Conference of World Peace the gathering at the Waldorf-Astoria Hotel in New York City . . . was actually a supermobilization of the inveterate wheelhorses and supporters of the Communist party and its auxiliary organizations.

The report lists the Communist fronts with which the sponsors were affiliated, and the name of Joseph Fletcher appears in connection with thirteen such fronts.[40]

A later report of the House Committee on Un-American Activities presented the sworn testimony of Herbert Philbrick, undercover agent for the FBI for nine years. Philbrick described how the Communist party used the facilities of churches for their purposes over long periods of time and declared that it was "impossible that the minister in charge

---

*A report dated May 22, 1968, of Information from the Files of the Committee on Un-American Activities, U. S. House of Representatives, shows that the Rev. William H. Genné was affiliated with Communist-front organizations such as the 1950 World Peace Appeal and the repeal of the anti-Communist Internal Security Act of 1950 by the National Committee to Repeal the McCarran Act, and others. [Author's note.]

did not know . . . what was going on." He identified the Reverend
Joseph Fletcher of the Episcopal Theological Seminary in Cambridge,
Massachusetts, as one of the ministers involved. Philbrick testified: "Joe
Fletcher worked with us on Communist party projects and an enormous
number of tasks." [41]

The Reverend Messrs. Fletcher and Genné, and Drs. Kirkendall,
Calderone, Rubin, and Ellis, leave little to the imagination in their stand
against Biblical morality, and in their purpose for promoting free sex
in the schools of America. This sampling of sex philosophies should
suffice to warn parents not to be deceived through the treacherous use
of semantics, nor to adopt a sex education program in their schools
using SIECUS counselors or materials. Only tragedy can result, as
demonstrated in Sweden, where a program of compulsory sex education
has been in effect for ten years. It has resulted in sexual hysteria and
disease among the youth of that country.

THE BIBLICAL TEACHING OF MORALITY AND SEX

After surveying the garbage theology of situation ethics and the rantings
of atheists, it is refreshing at this juncture to present a few summary
statements of the Biblical teaching on sex and morality:

Sex in the Old Testament is clearly regarded as a precious gift from
God, not only for bringing children into the world but also for the
satisfaction of one of mankind's deepest needs and for sheer enjoyment.
The one basic restriction placed on the satisfaction of sexual desire is
that it should occur only within the framework of God's holy institution
of marriage.

God speaks out plainly and repeatedly against all adultery, fornication, prostitution, and such perversions as homosexuality. [42]

The attitude toward sex expressed in the New Testament reinforces
Old Testament conclusions. . . . This is expected by those who acknowledge the same Lord as the Author of both divisions of Scripture. The
New Testament knows no double standard of morality. It emphasizes
that the purpose of sex and its proper use occur only within the marriage relationship. . . . The New Testament condemns all immorality,
adultery, fornication, harlotry, not only in acts but also in words and
thoughts. Those who persist in such sins cannot inherit the kingdom of
heaven. . . . Various sexual perversions are severely condemned, especially homosexuality. Like the Old Testament, the New emphasizes that
sex is a wonderful gift of God. Like all other blessings, it is to be
received with thanksgiving and sanctified by the Word of God and
prayer. [43]

II. THE PEDAGOGY OF SEX

The public school is intruding into a private family and church responsibility as it frightens and coerces parents into accepting the teaching of sex in their schools. Sexologists and educators charge the home and church with having failed to educate youth to fulfill their sexuality. It is now the school's duty to come to the rescue. To this end, sexologists analyze the American scene.

Dr. Ben Ard is a prominent writer recommended by SIECUS. His humanistic evaluation is as follows: "The American sexual tragedy is that our puritanical sex views create untold havoc in our love, marriage and family relations." He concludes that the United States is "one of the world's sickest cultures as far as sex is concerned," and calls for new value judgments based on *"scientific evidence,* reality, and the nature of man, rather than supernatural moralistic considerations." [44]

Newly appointed SIECUS board member John H. Gagnon assures us that "we are really closer to controlling VD [venereal disease] than we are prepared to admit." [45]* Dr. Gagnon prevaricates!

The National Communicable Disease Center of the Public Health Service reported in 1966 that "venereal disease has reached epidemic proportions in nearly all metropolitan areas. . . . Alarmingly, teenagers account for most of the rise." In addition, there is a rise in abortions and homosexuality as well as an out-of-wedlock pregnancy rate of from 10 to 22 per 100 unmarried women over a fifteen-year period. [46]

Gagnon demands that some "programmatic form of sex education be developed in order to facilitate sexual careers that fulfill this potential." He contends that this is long overdue to counteract the prevalent prurient puritanical treatment of sex. In teaching sex education, he dismisses the parents and the medical and religious professions for their ineffectiveness in the past, and suggests that they "might properly remain so in the future." [47]

He believes the school is the only place where sex can be discussed freely and "nonjudgmentally" in a casual rather than clinical manner. There should be no attempt to build character; merely spell out the options available in the sensual grab bag of sexual delights.

The teacher should be someone "whose burden of guilt about his sexual feelings is sufficiently low that he can talk in the service of the children's needs. . . ." [48] If we implement Mr. Gagnon's advice, we would precipitate a complete moral collapse of our society.

Clever sex semanticist Don Cannady, assistant director of the Family Health Association in Cleveland, Ohio, conjures the primary goal of sex education as being the "celebration of sexuality." He defines "celebration" as a "continuing positive and joyful acceptance of being

---

*See pp. 39-46 of *Sex, Schools, and Society.*

sexual . . . in ways that will be most beneficial for the individual and the community." "Sexuality" is "the whole gamut of being males and females in any kind of relationship. This includes, of course, the whole puzzling richness of masculine-feminine dimensions." [49]

It would seem that Mr. Cannady and other sexsearchers have recently discovered that boys and girls are *different!* With this tremendous emphasis on the uniqueness of the male and female, we wonder where fashion designer Rudy (topless swimsuit) Gernreich fits in with his campaign to converge and blur the differences through his "Unisex" styled clothing. And for that matter, what shall we do with Dr. Ellis's non-penile males?

WHAT, WHEN, HOW MUCH?

Our main concerns at this point are: What should be taught, at what ages, and with what educational materials? The sex educators have ready answers, and they begin with dramatic visual aids such as the Little Brother Doll (anatomically correct) at seventeen dollars each, and a lovely set of slides called *How Babies Are Made.*[50]

This set of colored slides, largely designed by Dr. Mary S. Calderone, executive director of SIECUS, presents an animalistic viewpoint of sex which is shocking and completely inappropriate for children three to eight years of age—the age group for which they were designed.

The slides, which are cleverly and realistically executed in paper sculpture, depict animals and human beings in the act of sexual intercourse. While the children watch the slides, the teacher reads the narrative which describes the "action" in adult, medically accurate terms.

The brochure describes this series as a "delightful and effective educational" program which teaches your children the origins of life, and gives them "a thorough knowledge of basic reproduction," [51] but it does not develop a moral attitude toward sex. In fact there is no mention that marriage is part of the process, since the story of reproduction moves from dogs to the higher animals—people.

Schools desiring to launch into full-scale sex programs are able to secure immediate assistance from "the professionals" of SIECUS, the U. S. Office of Education, and from the multimillion-dollar publishing world, which has prepared a fantastic array of sex models and materials. These entrepreneurs of Newsex programs glibly mouth such foul phrases as *"Children must discover their sexuality no later than kindergarten,"* and *"We must give them the whole story as quickly as possible."* WE MUST ask WHY.

Sexologists admit that there have been no studies made which scientifically confirm the effectiveness of sex education programs to reach their stated goals. In fact, Dr. William H. Masters, a director of SIECUS, committed near heresy when he emphatically declared that "we have no scientific knowledge as to whether it's [sex education] worth a d———. There are a lot of people who climb on the sex education bandwagon and say it's great. But somebody is going to have to . . . find out whether there is any real value in the entire concept of formally disseminating sexual information to youngsters." [52]

Despite this lack of certainty, sex education, as a symbol of curricular innovation, is in the classroom with all of its rawness, its tactlessness, its erotic stimulation. The flood of materials for classroom use includes books, charts, and unbelievably clever models which even include multicolored plastic human figures with interchangeable male and female sex organs—instant transvestism. The sexologists, who we cannot help but feel are Johnny-come-lately pornographers, are devoting their full creative powers to inventing sexual gimmickry (such as the previously mentioned bisexual anatomical model).

In the competition and passion to enliven the sex education programs, and also to make the subject matter as specific as possible, teachers integrate sex education with art class in the elementary grades. For example some "gold star" schools have gained "innovation" notoriety by conducting clay modeling sessions where the male and female sex organs are fashioned by little children.[53]

Another super-realistic classroom demonstration is the application of a condom on a life-size plastic phallus. And, the young high-school student who made a collage of contraceptive devices should at least be awarded a booby prize.

The latest school tactic in desensitizing children and freeing them of their inhibitions is to install joint boy-girl toilet facilities without partitions. This is a triumph for the sexologists, who despise "false modesty" and "inhibitions" about sex and private matters. Everyone, they say, must learn to live in a group.

Sexologists no doubt dream of the day when adult public bathrooms will likewise be integrated and void of privacy so that everyone will be able to enjoy their sexuality without "guilt."

"Everything that science knows about sex and sexuality, our children must have access to . . . . no matter how distasteful." [54] Dr. Calderone would bring sex education into the nursery at age three. And she feels that statements such as this should be used:

> "The penis of the father is made to carry the sperm into the mother through the vagina." Kindergarten teachers should then impart additional clinical details. "If you tell five-year-olds that this [intercourse] is the way fathers and mothers reaffirm their love for each other, and that science and religion have made it possible for parents to choose when they will have a baby, you are teaching

responsible parenthood, responsible sexuality, right in the kindergarten." By age ten *"at the latest"* both boys and girls should have
mastered "the factual aspects of reproduction. . . ." [55]

It has not occurred to Dr. Calderone that kindergarteners are not
physically, emotionally, or intellectually mature enough to learn "responsible parenthood." The three- to five-year-old is not interested in
accepting such an awesome responsibility. He may want to know—in
general and accurate terms—where babies come from, but does not
require a detailed account of the sex act, which he would naturally
relate to his mother and father.

The dangers of the program are many. For example, near-satiated,
casual use of sex terminology is encouraged by the sexologists to the
point where the teacher should be able to discuss the penis and clitoral
excitation as unemotionally as she would chalk and an eraser. In fact,
one sex educator proudly stated that now young children could speak to
their parents at the breakfast table about seminal emissions and menstruation as easily as they did of baseball and bicycles.

The embarrassing frankness of many sex education programs forces
the sensitive child to suppress his normal, emotion-charged feelings in
listening to class discussion. This may develop into serious anxieties. On
the other hand, he may either become coarsely uninhibited in his involvement in sex or develop a premature secret obsession with sex. The
kindergartener and primary-grade child may very well resort to sex
play and involved experimentation.

Most sex education programs suffer from a lack of knowledgeable
instructors because of the urgency to implement them. The teacher may
be a warmed-over biology or physical-education instructor, in which
case the course generally becomes one of the identification and geography of human sex anatomy—commonly called a "plumbing course."

At the other extreme is the sensitivity-trained amateur psychoanalyst
ex-guidance counselor turned sex educator, who revels in the intricacies
of the sexual athleticism and gymnastics of his young students. He
indulges in class discussions which, though given the supposed dignity
of the classroom, are still just plain dirty talk.

What the sex educators have in mind is simply this: Sex should be as
easily discussed as any other subject in the curriculum, and any inhibitions or moral and religious taboos should be eliminated. This, obviously,
drives a wedge between the family, church, and school—bolstering the
authority of the school while casting cynical doubts on the traditional
moral teachings of the home and church. If this is accomplished and
the new morality is affirmed, our children will become easy targets
for Marxism and other amoral, nihilistic philosophies—as well as VD!

III. THE GAME OF LOVE

Sex education programs offered in the schools today vary greatly. Even where the curriculum is similar, the level at which the information is presented may range from kindergarten to the junior high school. The question of morality is usually avoided. Guidelines are sometimes provided to warn the students of the dangers involved in certain sexual activities—without, however, giving him the moral reasons. The most common technique is to present a variety of answers so the student may have his choice!

In San Diego, California, traveling sexologists carry their wares in large canvas bags from school to school. They display their formerly taboo materials in unemotional succesion to the sex-liberated students. Masturbation, homosexuality, abortion, and premarital intercourse in films such as *The Game* (which depicts a boy's feelings after coitus with a virgin) are but a sampling of what students are exposed to. *The Game* purports to warn thirteen- and fourteen-year-old girls of *the game of love* and its many traps. They also learn about sex deviation, illegitimacy, and venereal diseases. In the senior year, students will plunge deeper into more of the same.[56]

A high-school teacher in Van Nuys, California, asked his students (ages fifteen to eighteen) about their participation in the following activities: kissing, masturbation, light petting, fondling breasts or genitals (for boys), fondling male genitals (for girls), sexual intercourse, sexual activities to near intercourse, homosexual activities, and *sexual activity with an animal*.[57] The next step? We shudder!

If your child should be a kindergartener in Palo Alto, California, he may very well have the opportunity of bathing a little boy. If she is in kindergarten in Evanston, Illinois, she will be exposed to the full details of the human birth process, and perhaps listen to the heart beat of the baby inside a visiting pregnant woman.[58]

Parents in some schools can withdraw their children from these classes—or at least excuse them from the films. However, we find that in the Chicago area, for example, parents of only 16 out of 3,200 children refused to consent. They were identified as "fundamentalists from the Appalachian hills" [59] by the *Saturday Evening Post* writer.*

TIME OF YOUR LIFE FILM SERIES

The *Time of Your Life* series is a filmed sex education program used by schools in California's San Francisco Bay region. Though lessons 10 through 15 are designated for nine- to eleven-year-old children, the

---

* See pp. 129-142 of *Sex, Schools, and Society.*

teachers' manual recommends the lessons for lower elementary grades as well. The series was prepared for KQED Instructional Television Service to be used in the public schools. The advertisement flyer of KQED describes the moral position of the program: "This series is based upon a philosophy of humanism." [60]

The series has been shown in both public and Catholic schools in San Francisco and San Mateo. The teachers' guide which accompanies the film suggests how to put down a "critical parent," and how to answer "difficult" questions. The manual explains:

> Differences in moral and religious views of sexuality can be handled by pointing out that different people have different ideas, all worthy of respect . . . [thus] if a child asked if reading *Playboy* or telling dirty jokes or sex play was all right, the teacher should not feel obliged to give answers, but rather comment on the variety of standards and refer them to their parents and religious counselors. [61]

Excerpts from the script for *Time of Your Life* follow. Lesson 10, *The Male,* presents a Dr. Ayres, Mrs. McCurdy, and a child, who exchange questions and answers. Photographs, diagrams and "sparkling" dialogue are used in discussing the look, feel, and work of the male sex organs. Dr. Ayres explains circumcision by comparing the foreskin to the sleeve of a baggy sweater hanging down over his hand. He comments that "the left testicle hangs just a little lower than the right." But he cannot answer Mrs. McCurdy or the child as to why. [62]

Lesson 12 reviews the "man's body and the parts of the woman's body that have to do with reproduction. Through animation the penis is shown having an erection and the sperm . . . traveling from the testicles, through the tubes, and out the end of the penis. This is an ejaculation." [63]

After the female organs and reproductive process are reviewed, Mrs. McCurdy explains that "men and women marry each other for a great many reasons. *Some* reasons are that they love each other. . . ." At this point, the ten-year-old students are given a detailed description of human sexual intercourse. This is followed with the step-by-step filmed growth of a baby inside the mother, the woman in labor, and the baby's birth: "We can see that the head is out. The doctor is now able to see the child's head. Very quickly now you will see that he is able to help to get the arms free and then the waist and finally the hips. There he is holding the baby." [64]

In lesson 13, the "child" asks:

> CHILD: Why do parents get embarrassed in discussing sex with their children?

DR. AYRES: Well, I think it is difficult to understand unless you think about how things were fifty years ago. Fifty years ago the kind of things that are now written about in the newspapers and magazines and seen on television and in movies would not have occurred. People were much more strict about sex. They worried about it and felt that to talk about sex was a shameful thing. Since this was the atmosphere, the kind of attitudes that your parents may well have gotten as they were growing up, that they should not talk about sex and should not know about it, it was quite different.[65]

Obviously, the majority of today's ten-year-olds do not have parents who are fifty years of age or older. In addition, the reluctance to explain in detail and visually how a baby is born and what Mom and Dad do behind the closed bedroom door is not due to shameful notions of sex—it is just common decency and concern for their ten-year-old's emotional and spiritual growth at this tender age. Forcing a ten-year-old to visualize his mother and father doing the things pictured in this film could easily cause great emotional anxiety and embarrassment.

The teachers' guide for *Time of Your Life* admits that "in most instances teachers *are* going to be anxious and so are the children. . . . It was discovered that no preparation [for the film] at all created the best atmosphere for listening and learning." [66]

Lesson 14 is a masterpiece of contradictions which can only result in totally confusing the child.

In speaking to the young child about growing up, he is told:

Sex . . . is easily controllable. A child in adolescence should venture forth, in terms of getting involved in holding hands, kissing and necking according to his amount of self-control. . . . After a relationship with mutual trust has been established . . . sexual display of affection . . . can then be naturally added within the perspective of the relationship and does not lead to exploitation. . . .

Early adolescents who become involved with sexual intercourse experiences tend to get focused on sex. . . . Children should be made aware of the danger of sexual experimentation and promiscuity in terms of their development. Using physical sexual closeness for personal warmth and caring does not work.[67]

THE SWEDISH WAY

The Swedish philosophy of sex education has a familiar ring: "Sexual intercourse must always take place with a feeling of responsibility and with regard to the consequences." Sex education teaches children how to make responsible choices—to make up their own minds.[68]

It is the same philosophical tune now being crooned by American educators, liberal ministers, sexologists, and particularily SIECUS crusaders. After ten years of mandatory public-school sex education in Sweden the results can now be measured:

> Most high-school-aged Swedes regard premarital sexual relations as natural and acceptable. This radical change in attitudes is engulfing young people in other Western cultures, including our own. Swedish conservatives . . . charge that sex education stimulated the new attitudes. . . . If there is disagreement about this, at least there *is agreement* that Sweden's sex education program has not done anything to improve the young people's sexual morality. "Premarital abstinence [is] a religious idea that most youngsters no longer believe."[69]

Starting with first grade, Swedish children are given the entire story of sex: human anatomy, how egg and sperm meet, how the fetus develops, how the baby emerges from the mother's body—similar to many American sex education programs. In the upper grades, through imaginative audio-visual aids, all remaining phases of sex are covered in depth—discussed and dissected!

Contraceptives are easily obtained from automats along Swedish streets. "It is now accepted by Swedish society (90 percent, a recent survey indicates) that engagement includes bed privileges, and in more and more social groups this privilege applies also to couples going steady—apparently on the theory that *the couple that sleeps together keeps together*." [70] Unmarried mothers are encouraged to keep their children and they are entitled to be called Mrs.

In spite of all the talk of sexual responsibility and meaningful human relations, the VD picture "is what some Swedes describe as a 'catastrophic' increase in venereal disease among youngsters, especially since 1959. . . . Physicians say that gonorrhea and syphilis are more widespread in Sweden today than in any other civilized country in the world. A recent inquiry revealed the startling fact that about half of all boys who had become infected with venereal disease admitted having sexual relations with at least forty different girls—and 10 percent said that they had had relations with as many as two hundred." Reported rapes went up 55 percent in the two-year period.[71]

Drug-taking among Swedish schoolchildren has "risen wildly over the past few years" and students operate as narcotics agents in the schools. Swedish pornography is flourishing, clubs for homosexuals advertise for new members in newspapers and magazines, and movies frequently display a couple having intercourse.[72]

Again returning to the sex education program in Sweden's schools, the present trend is indicated by the recent suggestion of a Stockholm teacher that

What every good high school needs is a "sex room" where teen-age lovers can seek respite from the rigors of reading, writing and arithmetic. . . . . *The idea was turned down but the teacher noted that* many taboos have disappeared and [he] recalled . . . that smoking was not to be thought of in Swedish schools just fifteen years ago *and today it is perfectly acceptable.*[78]

The sexual crisis in Sweden was evident in 1964, when the king's physician, Dr. Ull Nordwall, and 140 other eminent Swedish doctors and teachers petitioned the Swedish government with their "concern over sexual hysteria in the young." They asserted that "since it appears to be a product of modern education, it is now the business of the schools to correct it." The Swedish Board of Health sent a warning to the government as well.

The petitioners charged that

The advanced pedagogues who now rule Swedish education have bombarded schoolchildren with sexual instruction for which their immaturity ill fits them . . . and the result has been an unnatural oversexualization of the rising generation . . . the young have confused instruction in method with encouragement to practice. . . . The crux of the report, however, is that the whole matter of sexual education has been unnaturally inflated, producing an obsession among adolescents. . . .

As expected, the doctors' petition and charges "incurred the ire of a powerful coterie which dominates Swedish cultural and intellectual life." These cultural radicals—composed of critics, writers, editors, college intellectuals, and *prominent educationists*—charge that "medical men should confine themselves to their own subject." [74]

America take note—we are well on *the Swedish Way!*

IV. THE PLAN

Dr. Mary S. Calderone, executive director of SIECUS, has outlined the basic steps necessary to get a sex education program started in your community. She warned eager sex educationists to "make haste slowly" because "we don't yet know what it should be, or how to do it, and lots of people are bound to be against it" unless the community is carefully prepared to accept such a program. She suggested that the key to success was the establishment of a leadership group, which would include school administrators, teachers, clergy, medical and other "family-helping professions," parents, and the communications media.[75]

The leadership group should, according to Dr. Calderone, broaden its reading base—using SIECUS literature—and then share with the community its findings and recommendations for a sex education program. Included in the list of five basic readings for leadership groups were Dr. Lester A. Kirkendall's SIECUS Pamphlet No. 1 (extolling the New Morality approach), a pamphlet by the NEA, and a reprint of an article by Dr. Calderone.

Where such leadership groups have been organized and "indoctrinated," they have enjoyed stunning success. Well-known community figures are invariably tapped, and the group is usually so well organized that the unorganized resistance is usually caught off balance, at which time the program "is voted in."

SAN LUIS OBISPO

In San Luis Obispo, California, two such groups were influential in getting a K–12 sex education program adopted in their large, unified school district.

The initial leadership group was the San Luis Obispo School Health Council, composed of representatives from the County Health Department, County Mental Clinic, the Police Department, Ministerial Association, and from the San Luis School District and others. During its proceedings, the council "turned its attention to health education, including sex education in the School District." [76] After a few months, it met with the new School District administration and recommended that a sex education program be developed.

A kind of "shirt-sleeve" committee was appointed in 1965. Composed only of teachers and school administrators, it was called the Health and Family Living Committee. It studied "the works of various authorities in the field of family life education," using SIECUS-recommended material among others, and finally developed a K–12 sex education curriculum for the schools, which included such areas as personality development and group sensitivity.

The next step was the appointment by the Board of Education of a thirty-member Citizens' Advisory Committee. Its first order of business concerned a draft of the K–12 sex curriculum which it was to study and approve. This group was controlled by a subcommittee which was chaired by the assistant superintendent of schools. The larger body was advised that the startling increase of juvenile delinquency, illegitimate births, and VD made the K–12 sex program a necessity. In addition, they were told that such a program was inevitable since California state law would soon make sex education mandatory in schools (this has been defeated as of September, 1968).

Statistics were also quoted which indicated that a majority of local organizations and service clubs had given their approval of the program. Actually, however, only three groups had officially endorsed it in principle—not in content—and one of these, the Lions Club, later withdrew its support by letter.

In any event, the thirty-member Citizens' Committee recommended that the Board of Education establish a sex education program and adopt the curriculum outline developed by the teacher-administration group.

The board unanimously approved these recommendations at their June, 1967, meeting. The program was in!

Parents and the public in general did not know what the new program would include except in a general way. After it was adopted, parents began to view specific audio-visual materials. Under board regulations, "all materials used were to be made available for parental inspection and parents were to be given an opportunity to preview certain audio-visual material before it was shown to their children." [77]

As the details of the curriculum become known, opposition to it is growing. Irate parents have organized to remove the program from the schools. The most recent development is a court hearing which challenges the school's program on the basis of its interference with the parents' right to teach this *private* subject, as well as declaring that the public-school sex program is potentially harmful to the child.

JEFFERSON COUNTY

The same procedure with only slight variations was successfully used to install a K–12 sex education program in Jefferson County schools of suburban Denver. In this instance, the County School Health Advisory Council recommended that a sex education program be developed. A leadership group was formed, comprising a central corps of teachers, school principals, and counselors. They worked under the supervision of the county's special services director in writing the *Curriculum Guide for Family Living Education*. This base was broadened by calling upon community leaders, such as doctors, clergymen, nurses, and parents including the local winner of the civic-minded Woman of the Year award, for suggestions and discussion of the program. This committee suggested that the parents of the community need *not be advised* of the step-by-step program and that sex education classes would be mandatory.

The program was presented to the Board of Education in public session without objections or criticism. But before approving it the board voted to initiate a series of community meetings to outline the proposed guide in detail and educate parents on objectives of the course.[78]

The first public meeting two weeks later brought out a record crowd of angry parents who violently objected to the proposed "family living" course both in principle and on the basis of materials to be used. The parents had not had enough time to effectively organize, but the majority of parents were opposed to the program. The School Board was surprised and chagrined.

Other meetings were then held throughout the district, and the opposition gradually divided between factions which opposed the entire program on any grounds and those who felt a program would be acceptable if major changes were made. In fact, the hassle grew so intense, and debate so passionate, that Huntley and Brinkley of NBC televised one of the frenetic School Board meetings.[79]

Parents and ministers earnestly question whether the program should be initiated at all.

The Jefferson County Ministerial Association was a key opposition group which was won over in this manner. Its concern was, *Whose morality will be taught?* An agreement was made that the school would not give any specific reference to religious moral teaching (to avoid misrepresentation), but would tell the students to ask their parents or ministers for their opinion where a question of moral view was involved.

The ministers did not appear to understand that this was exactly the danger. In order to uproot in the child's mind the notion that religion has anything important to say about sexual morality in today's world, modern sexologists recommend that the moral view *must not be used, or given a hearing.* Thus, rather than gaining a concession, the ministers relinquished their only opportunity to influence the school's program in teaching family living education.

As a result, children are told, in the words of one principal: "This is the way I think about it, but perhaps your mother, father or minister don't agree, and they are entitled to that. But you are entitled to know how *all* of us think." [80] Obviously the teacher, by virtue of his position, has a tremendous psychological advantage in giving his "learned opinion."

Despite the many angry confrontations, 3,000 signatures on a petition, and an official school survey which clearly stated that less than half the community wished to have the program placed in the schools, it was approved as a pilot program by the School Board in 1967.

Owing to the unexpected resistance, however, the board chose to institute the pilot project only "where faculty members feel it is desirable" and where a canvass of parents and Parent-Teacher Association members would permit the pilot program in their school. This was done in several schools in Jefferson County.[81]

After the pilot study had been approved in a school, parents were invited for the first time to meet with the school officials, who explained the program in detail and showed the textbooks to be used. If a parent objected to the curriculum, he could request that his child be excused from the class.

On May 21, 1968, following a superficial evaluation of the several pilot programs, the Board of Education officially approved the program for all K–12 in all schools of the 50,000-student district.

In speaking to the resource teacher who had helped plan the sex education curriculum, I was told that there had been only "negligible" resistance to the program. The newspaper accounts and the testimony I personally heard belie the official school version. This is merely one facet of the defense used by school administrations to belittle honest opposition.

SEX IS EVERYBODY'S BUSINESS

It should be evident that the sex educators are in league with sexologists, who represent every shade of muddy gray morality, ministers colored atheistic pink, and camp followers of every persuasion—offbeat psychiatrists to ruthless publishers of pornography. The enemy is formidable at first glance, but becomes awesomely powerful when we discover the interlocking directorates and working relationship of national organizations which provide havens for these degenerates.

However, be not faint of heart, for to know your enemy is half the battle. The sex educators have been successful in instituting their programs through no more than a token garnering of public opinion. Though, according to some authorities, even this is hardly necessary. Head torchbearer for this viewpoint is the National Education Association, which has long held the view that only the teachers—the professionals—are qualified to decide how, when, and what is to be taught to your children.

The NEA, of course, is not only committed to sex education in the schools, but to SIECUS as well. Dr. Calderone has contributed articles on the subject in the *NEA Journal*, while NEA president Mrs. Elizabeth D. Koontz serves on the board of directors of SIECUS.

Commissioner Harold Howe II says the U. S. Office of Education will support

> family life education and sex education as an integral part of the curriculum from preschool to college and adult levels; it will support training for teachers and health and guidance personnel at all levels of instruction; it will aid programs designed to help parents carry out their roles in family life education and sex education;

and it will support research and development in all aspects of family life education and sex education. Schools, communities, and State agencies which want to establish or improve sex and family life education programs may apply for grants authorized under Titles I, II, III, and V of the Elementary and Secondary Education Act; Titles II, V, and XI of the National Defense Education Act; the Cooperative Research Program; and various vocational and library services acts. Teacher and counselor institutes, graduate fellowships, State leadership training, adult education, library improvement, curriculum development, and research and demonstration are among the projects that may qualify for funds.[82]

The United States government awarded grants in 1967 to the tune of one and one-half million dollars to support sex education programs in thirteen school districts. This was an increase of half a million dollars over the previous year.[83]

In addition, officers of the U.S. Office of Education have served or are serving on the board of directors of SIECUS. Currently on the board is Dr. Catherine S. Chillman, chief of the Research Utilization and Development Branch of the U.S. Department of Health, Education and Welfare.[84]

The National Congress of Parent and Teacher Associations passed a resolution recommending that sex education be taught in schools, for "only through the development of sound value systems will children achieve personal responsibility in the areas involved in morality and appropriate conduct." The National PTA statement is quickly seconded by SIECUS and the NEA. However, it is clear that the leading sex educators have no such goal in mind, at least in the traditional definition of morality and appropriate conduct.

The National Council of Churches is officially represented on the SIECUS board by the Reverend William H. Genné, director of the Commission on Marriage and Family Life of the National Council of Churches of Christ in the U.S.A. The Catholics are represented by Father John L. Thomas, S.J., of the Cambridge Center for Social Studies, Cambridge, Massachusetts (1967), and Father George Hagmaier, associate director of the Paulist Institute for Religious Research, New York, who serves as secretary of SIECUS (1968). To complete the religious cluster of SIECUS sexologists, the Jews have offered the services of Rabbi Jeshaia Schnitzer of Montclair, New Jersey.

As discussed earlier, professors of sociology, psychology, and numerous medical areas abound on the SIECUS board of directors. And the American Medical Association has a joint committee with the National Education Association which produces pamphlets and supports the SIECUS programs and materials.

The worlds of business and communications have been attracted to the sexologists' attack on "puritanical America," like flies to honey.

The television industry contributes Earl Ubell, science editor for WCBS-TV News, to the SIECUS board, and the publishing field offers Vivian Cadden, senior editor of *McCall's* magazine, and Dr. Isadore Rubin, editor of *Sexology* magazine. A founder and treasurer of SIECUS since its beginning, he is joined by four other SIECUS board members who serve as editors or are on the board of consultants: Dr. Lester Kirkendall, the Reverend William H. Genné, Dr. John Money, and Dr. Wardell B. Pomeroy.

Perhaps benefiting most by the surge of sex education programs are the producers of educational materials. For example, Harcourt Brace and World Corporation have plunged into a multimillion-dollar publishing project to create a sex education curriculum for K–12. Executive Jack Goodman says that they "are prepared to throw everything out and start over again in a new area." As expected, SIECUS board members will provide consultant services for them.

Other companies which are eagerly expanding their sex education materials are such giants as Minnesota Mining and Manufacturing Company (3M), International Business Machines Corporation (IBM)—through its educational arm, Science Research Associates—and McGraw-Hill, Incorporated, which is producing textbooks, audio-visual aids, and laboratory models for all ages.[85]

In the headlong competitive rush to feed sex-starved kindergarteners, film producers and television and motion-picture studios are producing films on every possible aspect of sex.

Since business is frequently amoral, literally anything is made available that will sell. Advertising has proven its zest for sales, irrespective of moral standards and social consequences.

This impressive array of institutions and resources is converging on classrooms throughout America, and if the experts are right, by 1970 at least 70 percent of the schools in America will offer sex education—unless the parents of America recapture their traditional right to control their own schools.

V. IT TAKES YOU!

The public schools had better begin teaching the virtues of Hebraic-Christian morality—which is traditional to America. The mass media's exploitation of sex serves ostensibly as the reason why schools must teach all the facts of life as early as the nursery. Rather, the schools should spearhead a campaign to rid radio, television, movies, books, and magazines of raw sex. If teachers are the powerful lobby they claim to be (Dr. Sam Lambert, executive secretary of the NEA, says it has the power to *change society*), we suggest this is a good place to begin!

In addition, rather than incriminate and slight the parents and church for their *lack of effectiveness,* the school should make every effort to upgrade the sex knowledge of parents and ministers so that they can do a better job of teaching their own young people about sex.

School sex programs are generally based on situation ethics which accept all points of view. There is a precipitous balance between sexual plumbing information and that dealing with the larger aspects of character building and interpersonal relationships. All of this is now marshalled in the term *sexuality.*

The word *sex* has been expanded to *sexuality,* which includes all the activities of man. The child is led by the schools and the mass communications media to a situational interpretation of every act. Children are made aware of their *maleness* and *femaleness* in everything they do. The approach of some sexologists is reminiscent of Madison Avenue's motivational research in sex symbolism, which identifies retractable ballpoint pens and church steeples as evidence of our emerging phallic society.

Before a Sex Education Program Has Come into Your Schools You Can

1. Alert your community to the problems of sex education programs in other schools, with particular reference to SIECUS materials and the philosophy behind them.
2. Organize parent groups now—before your community has been invaded by sexologists; before the public-school sex education curriculum is presented to the board of education.
3. Parent groups should engage in an active education program of their own, enlisting the understanding and support of service organizations, ministers, educators, school board members, elected officials, and the news media.
4. Parent groups should TAKE THE POSITIVE APPROACH:
   (a) Promote interest in parents to TEACH THEIR OWN CHILDREN about matters of sex. Offer a list of recommended books, films, etc.
   (b) Contact legislators to help clean up pornography on newsstands, in advertising, and in movies and TV. Perhaps a few more old-fashioned Blue Laws (ordinances) on a community-by-community basis would help. Start at the mayor level of government—and work up—and down!
   (c) Contact advertising companies and advertisers about your objections to sex-symbol advertising and tell them why. This includes the newspapers' advertising of vulgar movies.

(d) Study your public school's program and make positive suggestions for improving vital sex information within the framework of science and health courses already there. Or perhaps
other courses might be added under careful advisement of the
content.

Communities in which a sex education program is well entrenched
will have an extremely difficult task in undoing the harm already done.
Furthermore, most programs are continually enlarging in depth and
scope. In some areas there is the impending threat that state law will
obligate the schools to teach sex education from kindergarten through
high school. This threat may, however, serve to rally the responsible
forces in the community.

In those areas where sex education is being taught or is being considered, citizens' groups invariably spring up. Resistance groups form,
such as an organization of Catholics in San Francisco, POPE (Parents
for Orthodoxy in Parochial Education); POSE (Parents Opposed to
Sex Education); and MOMS (Mothers Organized for Moral Stability).
A Committee for Better Schools was formed in Jefferson County,
Colorado.

These organizations can be instrumental in forcing the role of the
school to be re-examined. Parents must make it crystal clear to the
school board (which is their duly elected body) that it is the board's
responsibility to reflect the educational programs desired by the parents.
This is the historical position, and the only position which is morally
defensible.

In too many instances the school superintendent has a rubber-stamp
school board which he dazzles and then leads into grandiose new
schemes. Rather, the administrator should implement the policy which
the school board makes—as it reflects the needs of the school community.

The basic problem here is that the public generally has a feeble voice.
It follows uncertain trumpets because it has not been forced to crystallize
its convictions and put them into action. Our society has been so taken
over by professional guideline writers and "great society" expeditors that
the average citizen has had little more to do than receive its benefit.

Parents, therefore, are easily quashed when they are unequivocally
told by the teachers: "You are not qualified. We are the professionals.
We are qualified. We will make policy concerning the education of your
child. We have the answers because of our training and advantageous
position—and, therefore, we must lead the way." Recognizing the
parents' vulnerability to this argument, the liberals never fail to use
this line of reasoning against parental resistance. After such a con-

frontation, parents often respond by saying, "I feel so inadequate and inferior."

Changes have always been made by a small corps of highly organized or disciplined people who are dedicated to their cause. In a local parent-teacher association it takes only one person who is fearless and sure of his stand, and who commands respect, to crystallize the views of the majority of silent—but thinking—members. It takes one person with intelligent and persuasive gifts as a speaker, or a letter writer, to enunciate the unspoken feelings of the majority of well-meaning Americans.

IT TAKES YOU!

NOTES

[1] Dr. Mary Calderone's "Letter to the Editor," *Saturday Evening Post,* August 10, 1968, p. 4.
[2] "Education Comes of Age," *Look,* March 8, 1966.
[3] SIECUS Newsletter, Spring, 1968.
[4] Dr. Mary Calderone, "Parents' Questions about Sex Education in the Classroom," *Family Weekly,* March 3, 1968.
[5] *Ibid.*
[6] *Ibid.*
[7] *Ibid.*
[8] *Ibid.*
[9] *Ibid.*
[10] *Ibid.*
[11] SIECUS Newsletter, Winter, 1968.
[12] "Investigation of Communist Activities, New York Area—Part III," HCUA May 3-4, 1955, pp. 819-855; "Subversive Influence in the Educational Process," Committee on the Judiciary, U.S. Senate, 82nd Congress, September–October 1952, pp. 143-166.
[13] Isadore Rubin, "Homosexuality," SIECUS Study Guide No. 2, 1967.
[14] *Tustin News,* Tustin, California, April 25, 1968.
[15] Lester A. Kirkendall, "Searching for the Roots of Moral Decisions," *The Humanist,* January–February, 1967.
[16] *Ibid.*
[17] *Ibid.*
[18] Lester Kirkendall, "Sex Education," SIECUS Discussion Guide No. 1, October 1965.
[19] *Ibid.*
[20] *Ibid.*
[21] William H. Masters and Virginia E. Johnson, *Human Sexual Response.*
[22] *Ibid.*
[23] "Masters and Johnson," *Playboy,* May, 1968. [See pp. 163-170 of *Sex, Schools, and Society.*]
[24] "Albert Ellis: Brave New World's First Citizen," *Cavalier,* October, 1967.
[25] *Ibid.*

[26] *Ibid.*
[27] SIECUS Newsletter, Spring, 1967.
[28] *Cavalier, op. cit.,* p. 26.
[29] Albert Ellis, *Sexual Intercourse: Psychological Foundations,* Institute for Rational Living Incorporated (pamphlet).
[30] Albert Ellis, *The Case against Religion,* Institute for Rational Living Incorporated (pamphlet).
[31] *Ibid.*
[32] *Ibid.*
[33] *Ibid.*
[34] *Ibid.*
[35] *Ibid.*
[36] SIECUS Newsletter, Fall, 1966.
[[37, 38] missing in original. Ed.]
[39] *The Leader,* Corning, New York, November 14, 1967.
[40] "Investigation of Communist Activities, New York Area,—Part V," HCUA July 6, 1953, p. 2017.
[41] *Ibid.*
[42] *Sex and the Church,* (O.E. Feucht, Ed.) Concordia Publishing House, St. Louis, Missouri, pp. 25, and 39.
[43] *Ibid.*
[44] "Teen-agers Told Adults' Sex Ideas Wrong, Expert Says," *Denver Post,* April 13, 1965.
[45] John H. Gagnon, "The Pedagogy of Sex," *Saturday Review,* November 8, 1967. [See pp. 39-46 of *Sex, Schools, and Society.*]
[46] *Almanac and Yearbook, 1968,* Readers Digest, p. 725.
[47] John H. Gagnon, *op. cit.*
[48] *Ibid.*
[49] *PTA Magazine,* April, 1968.
[50] *The Instructor Magazine,* August, 1967.
[51] "How Babies Are Made" (brochure), Creative Scope, Inc., 1 East 42 Street, N. Y.
[52] "Masters and Johnson," *Playboy,* May, 1968, p. 67.
[53] *McCall's* magazine, January 1968; *Sex in the 60's,* Joe D. Brown (editor), Time Life Books, 1968.
[54] *Saturday Evening Post,* June 29, 1968, p. 27. [See pp. 129-142 of *Sex, Schools, and Society.*]
[55] *Ibid.,* p. 64.
[56] *Ibid.,* p. 24.
[57] "Know Your Enemy," by Hurst B. Amyx, Radio Broadcast Script 472-95A; questions asked by Cecil M. Cook, teacher in the Van Nuys, California, High School.
[58] *Saturday Evening Post,* June 29, 1968.
[59] *Ibid.*
[60] Advertisement flyer for KQED Instructional Television Service on "Time of Your Life" filmed sex education series.
[61] "Time of Your Life," Family Life and Health Education for Intermediate Grades, Preliminary Teachers' Guide, Programs 10-15, by William H. Ayers, M.D., and Mrs. Marilyn McCurdy, p. vi.
[62] *Ibid.* Narrative in script, p. 4.
[63] *Ibid.,* p. 19.
[64] *Ibid.,* p. 24.
[65] *Ibid.,* p. 32.
[66] *Ibid.,* p. ix.

[67] *Ibid.*, Lesson 14, p. 34.
[68] *Look,* November 15, 1966, p. 36.
[69] *Ibid.*
[70] *Christian Century,* September 21, 1966, p. 1144.
[71] *U.S. News and World Report,* February 7, 1966, pp. 59-60.
[72] *Ibid.*
[73] *Tulsa Daily World,* April 5, 1967.
[74] *Los Angeles Times,* March 1, 1964.
[75] SIECUS Newsletter, Winter, 1966.
[76] San Luis Coastal Unified School District Regular Board Meeting Agenda, April 2, 1968.
[77] *Ibid.*
[78] *Jefferson County Sentinel,* (Lakewood, Colo.) November 17, 1966.
[79] *Ibid.*, December 8, 1966.
[80] Tape Recorded "Report to the Jefferson County School Board," Spring, 1968.
[81] *Jefferson County Sentinel,* December 8, 1966.
[82] "What's Happening," *Education,* November, 1966, p. 22.
[83] "The Facts of Life," by Neil Ulman, *Wall Street Journal,* Spring, 1968.
[84] SIECUS Newsletter, Winter, 1968, p. 11.
[85] "The Facts of Life," *op. cit.*

Sex Study: Problems, Propaganda, and Pornography

Gary Allen

Sex education in the schools is not new. Most high schools have for years conducted courses which teach the biological facts of life. What is new is that these are now sneered at by sex educationists as "plumbing courses," inadequate for "modern social needs." What is needed, we are told, is a jet age "sex education" which really gets down to the nitty-gritty.

And that is just what we are getting.

As the *Saturday Evening Post** related before its recent demise, the "sex education" programs which are now "mushrooming all over the country are newer than the new math. . . . America seems to have suddenly discovered an urgent need for universal sex education—from kindergarten through high school, some enthusiasts insist—and is galloping off in all directions at once to meet it." The *Post* trumpeted that 50 percent of public and parochial schools are now [1968] providing the glories of academic sexuality, and that at the present rate the figure will pass 70 percent within a year.

Nothing happens in a vacuum, and the educationists' sex explosion would not be taking place unless a great deal of influence, organization, and money were being poured into its promotion from somewhere. It is. The organization behind the new "sex education" now sweeping the nation is SIECUS, Sex Information and Education Council of the United States. (Pronounced, seek us.) As the *Post* noted, "Among the organizations shaping the structure of American sex education, by far the most influential is SIECUS." *McCall's†* puts it this way: "Today's atmosphere in sex education cannot be described without mention of a high-voltage, nonprofit organization called SIECUS, which is without doubt the single most important force in sparking sex education in our schools." The *Wall Street Journal* records that "SIECUS reports fifty to seventy inquiries a week from schools, churches, and other organizations seeking guidance on sex education."

A leaflet distributed by the National Education Association describes SIECUS as a voluntary health agency founded in New York City in 1964 to provide "assistance to communities and schools wishing to em-

---

* See pp. 129-142 of *Sex, Schools, and Society.*
† See pp. 143-162 of *Sex, Schools, and Society.*

201

bark on sex education programs. SIECUS will act as a clearinghouse for research and education in sex, as a source of information about sex education in the schools, and as a public forum where consideration of various aspects of man's sexuality can be carried out in dignified and objective fashion."

The tax-free SIECUS organization operates largely from foundation grants—which means that American taxpayers are ultimately footing the bill. Those who write to the Department of Health, Education and Welfare concerning "sex education" are now advised to contact SIECUS. The Department of Health, Education and Welfare is also putting your money where its commitment is, and in 1967 granted $1.5 million to support the new "sex education" programs in thirteen school districts. In addition, officers of the U.S. Office of Education have served, or are serving, on the board of directors of SIECUS.

Chief torchbearer for SIECUS is Dr. Mary Calderone, the organization's executive director—referred to by *McCall's* as the commander in chief of "sex education" forces. Since the commander in chief's attitudes must of necessity be reflected in the choice of materials for the SIECUS program we are all required to subsidize, her views have undergone close scrutiny by concerned parents. Dr. Calderone has, for example, often made clear her commitment to the "New Morality"—as old as Sodom and Gomorrah. In speaking to 320 boys at Blair Academy in New Jersey, SIECUS director Calderone commented: "What is sex for? It's for fun . . . for wonderful sensation. . . . Sex is not something you turn off like a faucet. If you do, it's unhealthy." And, she continued: "We need new values to establish when and how we should have sexual experiences."

What sort of "new values"?

According to *Look* magazine, when a student asked, "What is your opinion of premarital sex relations among teen-agers?" Mrs. Calderone snapped back, "What's yours? Nobody from on high [God] determines this. You determine it. . . . I don't believe . . . the old 'Thou shalt nots' apply anymore."

She certainly doesn't.

In *Seventeen* magazine, the SIECUS executive director claimed that "sex is not the prerogative of Christianity," and the *Saturday Evening Post* quotes her as declaring that sexual "do's and don'ts" cannot be imposed on the young. After telling her youthful audiences that "there doesn't seem to be any correlation between premarital sex and success in marriage," she regularly leaves the decision of premarital intercourse up to the glands of her young listeners. The *Boston Globe* of December 5, 1968, quotes her as telling a blushing audience of 500 high-school boys and girls:

The question goes far beyond "Will I go to bed?" and it's one you must answer for yourselves. You boys may know a girl is physically ready, but you have to ask yourselves, "Am I ready to take the responsibility to say, yes, she is ready emotionally and psychologically?"

Though described by the *Post* as a Joan of Arc for "sex education," Dr. Calderone is more often referred to as "a sweet-faced, silvery-haired grandmother" who shocks audiences by using four-letter words to make her point. Her motto is "Tell them everything and tell them early." According to the *Saturday Evening Post:*

> Contrary to the views of most child psychoanalysts, Dr. Calderone holds that sex education should start in the nursery. Around the age of three the child should assimilate such knowledge, along with the correct terminology, as "The penis of the father is made to carry the sperm into the mother through the vagina." Kindergarten teachers should then impart additional clinical details.

That's right, *kindergarten teachers!*

As you might expect, the SIECUS executive director also has very progressive ideas concerning homosexuality. As she is fond of telling youngsters: "Almost everybody has some attraction to people of the same sex. . . . I cannot condemn it." Every boy in an urban environment, she says, "is going to have a homosexual advance made to him, and therefore he should understand what it is and what his attitude about it and about himself should be."

And what *should* that attitude be? Concerning homosexuals, the SIECUS commander in chief smirks to boys in her lectures: ". . . you owe that person your responsibility and understanding, even if you don't share his conviction." Dr. Calderone adds, sadly, that "it will be some time before homosexuality receives general acceptance." Unless, of course, her "educational" efforts on behalf of SIECUS are successful.

If Dr. Mary Calderone is the Joan of Arc of the school-sex revolution, Dr. Lester Kirkendall, professor of family life at Oregon State University, and a member of the SIECUS board of directors, is its Pied Piper. Dr. Kirkendall, a prolific author of sex books and magazine articles about every conceivable sexual foible, will never be accused of being an old fuddy-duddy by even the hippest of the pornopoliticians. Still, Kirkendall is referred to by *Reader's Digest* as "without question, one of the most respected authorities in the whole field of sex education and family life." He has, according to the *Digest,* "helped to create today's new generation of sex educators."

Lester Kirkendall says he believes that "if present trends continue, premarital intercourse will almost certainly increase." But, the professor adds, he doesn't feel this is necessarily bad. He writes in *Sex and Our Society* that if couples "do experiment with sex only to have their relationship flounder, their honest efforts to understand and be responsible to one another may well have been more gain than loss."

Like Mrs. Calderone, SIECUS director Kirkendall is not "hung-up" with the religious and moral foundations of sex. He is, in fact, a past director of the antireligious American Humanist Association, and has written in its magazine that morality cannot be found in the context of "supernaturalism or a supernatural deity." Instead, he defines his religion as a "respect for and a belief in people, and a concern for true brotherhood among men." Just as Kirkendall rejects God for "people," he also rejects patriotism, actually going so far as to brand defense of one's country as immoral. In "Searching for the Roots of Moral Decisions," he writes:

> A tremendous feeling of national unity, a sense of closeness, good will, and harmony may result from fearing another nation or from the effort of trying to destroy another nation. Such unity . . . is immoral.

Another founder of SIECUS—and its long-time treasurer—is Isadore Rubin. He too shares Dr. Kirkendall's rejection of patriotism. Rubin was on May 3, 1955, identified in sworn testimony before the House Committee on Un-American Activities as a member of the Communist party by Mrs. Mildred Blauvelt, an undercover operative within the Communist party for the New York Police Department. Rubin was subsequently editor of the *New York Teacher News,* published by the New York Teachers' Union—which was expelled from the AFL-CIO when it was found to be controlled by the Communists. So total was his commitment to the Reds that he even had to be dismissed from his job as a teacher in New York City because of his refusal to deny his membership in the Communist party.

In addition to his subversive work for SIECUS, Comrade Rubin now edits the notorious *Sexology* magazine. Although SIECUS proclaims that one of its purposes is to counter exploitation of sex, its own officers are involved in the wildest sort of sex exploitation. Rubin's pulpy *Sexology* magazine dwells on sex sensationalism, with lurid pictures of men and women in the most intimate positions, presenting crass articles dealing with the worst sort of perversion. Examples of features in recent issues include "Can Humans Breed with Animals?" and "Witchcraft and Sex— 1968," and "The First Sadists," and "Wife Swapping in Naples," and "My Double Sex Life" (the story of a bisexual), and "Gangs That Hunt Down Queers," and "Why I Like Homosexual Men," and "Unusual Sex Demands," ad nauseam. In addition, *Sexology* also features film reviews of the latest "adult movies," carries advertisements for rank sex books, and has published its own titillating work on Transvestism.

Mr. Rubin's *Sexology* periodical has for years been available at certain seedy stores around the country (often from behind the counter, with the pages stapled together), but bigger and better things are in store for the magazine. Speaking in December of 1968 to a group of educators at an institute on "sex education" sponsored by the International Business Machines Corporation, SIECUS's Lester Kirkendall revealed that *Sexology* is currently being revised with a different cover and titles so it can be used in the schools.[1]

Now, get this: Dr. Lester Kirkendall serves with Communist Isadore Rubin as an editor of *Sexology* magazine. Also on the staff of this pornographic sheet are SIECUS directors William Genné, John Money, and Wardell Pomeroy.

Another of those laboring with Communist Isadore Rubin and his fellow pornographers on the board of directors of SIECUS is Mrs. Elizabeth Koontz, the newly elected president of the million-member National Education Association.[2] The radically Leftist Mrs. Koontz urges teachers to "organize, agitate, and strike." In paraphrasing the Communist Black Panthers to call for "Teacher Power," she explains, "We cannot teach democracy and ignore what is wrong. . . ." It is thus not surprising that NEA has been in the forefront of promoting SIECUS throughout the nation, and that Mary Calderone has been a contributor to the *NEA Journal*.

Earlier we mentioned *Sexology* staffer William Genné—a director, founder, and officer of SIECUS who calls himself "Reverend" and is director of the Commission [3] on Marriage and Family Life of the National Council of Churches. The "Reverend" Mr. Genné, who offers the view that those who think, "Whenever healing takes place, Christ is present, no matter what the church says about fornication," has quite a background himself. In addition to his consultation in pornography at *Sexology*, the files of the House Committee on Un-American Activities record that Genné has affiliated himself with such Communist fronts as the Stockholm Peace Petition, the World Peace Appeal, the National Committee to Repeal the McCarran Act, the Committee for Peaceful Alternatives to the Atlantic Pact, etc.

Then there is SIECUS director William Masters, who published with Virginia E. Johnson the best-selling *Human Sexual Response*. That incredible volume records Dr. Masters' studies in intercourse and auto-manipulation of 694 persons. Masters had no qualms about employing *unmarried* subjects to perform before the cameras for this subsequently popularized study of intercourse, and used an artificial plastic phallus which recorded female responses. The SIECUS director was quoted in *Playboy* [4] (May, 1968) describing the tortuous device as follows:

The equipment can be adjusted for physical variations in size, weight and vaginal development. The rate and depth of penile thrust is initiated and controlled completely by the responding individual.*

The immediate past-president of SIECUS is the sociologist David Mace, who stated his case for the "New Morality" in the April, 1968, issue of *Sexology* as follows:

> The simple fact is that through most of our history in Western Christendom we have based our standards of sexual behavior on premises that are now totally insupportable—on the folklore of the ancient Hebrews and on the musings of medieval monks, concepts that are simply obsolete.

The current president of SIECUS is Lester Doniger, said to be the former publisher of *Pulpit Digest,* director of the Pulpit Book Club, and president of the Pulpit Press. Curiously, Doniger's autobiographical note in *Who's Who in World Jewry* does not mention his Protestant publishing business, and he has variously listed his birthplace as Raczki, Poland, and Vienna, Austria. We do know that the *Great Neck* [New York] *News* of February 14, 1947, carried an article entitled "U.S.-U.S.S.R. Committee Announces Meeting," which reported that a forum would be held under the auspices of the Great Neck Committee of the Communist National Council of American-Soviet Friendship, Incorporated. Among those scheduled to appear was Jessica Smith, wife of Communist party attorney John Abt and widow of Communist Hal Ware of the notorious Soviet spy ring called the Ware Cell. Mrs. Abt was editor of *Russia Today.* The article stated that tickets for the council [5] affair were obtainable from Mrs. Rita Doniger, wife of SIECUS president Lester Doniger.

TRAINING FOR ILLICIT SEX

The philosophy, attitudes, and beliefs of the above officials of SIECUS have been projected into the curriculum it recommends for our schools. The SIECUS program is more than just education. After all, it isn't any good to know what, if you don't know how. And how requires training in the required "sex skills." As SIECUS Study Guide Number 1 states, ". . . the time-tested principles accepted in other areas of education must be supplied; to equip youngsters with the skills, knowledge

---

* See pp. 163-170 of *Sex, Schools, and Society.*
(Note that the passage cited does not occur in this article. Ed.)

and attitudes that will enable them to make intelligent choices and decisions."

To burden a "sex education" program with folderol about morality would, in the opinion of SIECUS, simply muddy the water in teaching children to express their "sexuality." According to the SIECUS Study Guide: "Sex education must be thought of as being education—not moral indoctrination. Attempting to indoctrinate young people with a set of rigid rules and ready-made formulas is doomed to failure in a period of transition and conflict." More specifically, when Esther Schulz of SIECUS listed in *Redbook* the qualifications for "sex education" teachers, she emphatically noted, "He must not be a moralist."

Not tolerating moralists, SIECUS naturally makes no judgments on perversion. And from the point of view of the Leftist SIECUS propagandists, why should it? As one of the SIECUS informational brochures states: "It is not the job of any voluntary health organization, which SIECUS is, to make moral judgments; SIECUS can be neither for nor against illegitimacy, homosexuality, premarital sex—nor any other manifestation of human sexual phenomena." When little George asks about homosexuality, or little Betty inquires about having children out of wedlock, you just know that you want their teacher to follow SIECUS procedures and remain neutral. We wouldn't want any "moral" judgments, after all. Such judgments might warp the little psyches of our children!

A guiding theme throughout SIECUS material seems to be to release students from any inhibitions, or feelings of guilt or conscience, about illicit sexual activity. The SIECUS Study Guide Number 5 begins: "The best way to gain insight into premarital sexual standards today is to start with the realization that among young people abstinence is not the only nor in some cases the dominant standard." This pamphlet draws attention to the fact that there are four premarital standards in use today: total abstinence; the double standard; affection-centered relations; and, permissiveness without affection. Naturally, SIECUS doesn't take sides. Instead, the guide tells your children: "The choice of a premarital sexual standard is a personal moral choice, and no amount of facts or trends can 'prove' scientifically that one ought to choose a particular standard. Thus, the individual is in a sense 'free,' "—to make up his own morality on the spot.

In discussing such consequences of permissiveness as venereal disease, promiscuity, and illegitimacy, Study Guide Number 5 drags out the old shell game and assigns the blame to parents:

> The difficulties of doing anything about the consequences of greater permissiveness become apparent when one realizes that our type of courtship inevitably involves a certain amount of such consequences. The same parents who decry the consequences favor

a free courtship system—a system that encourages permissiveness. Even more paradoxical is the stress parents place on love as the basis for marriage and happiness. The research findings on female permissiveness indicate that love is a key factor promoting sexual intercourse. Thus, the more parents stress love the more their daughters will engage in coitus.

Got that, parents? Stress permissiveness and your children will find themselves in trouble, or stress an abiding love and things will be even worse. Either way, you are to simply surrender your children to the indoctrination and "skill" provided in the schools by Comrade Rubin and the Leftist pornographers of SIECUS.

Many parents have concluded that the SIECUS stand on masturbation verges on advocacy of it as a salutary pastime. Dr. Warren Johnson, of *Sexology* fame, informs seventh-graders in the SIECUS Study Guide Number 3:

> Most students have some experience with this activity [masturbation], sometimes before puberty, although many of them are unfamiliar with the word: masturbation. They hear it called ———. It is an almost universal practice among healthy boys and is also a common, but not so frequent habit in girls. . . . From the medical point of view it is necessary to emphasize the fact that the commonly quoted medical consequences of masturbation are almost entirely fictitious. . . . Any harm resulting from masturbation, according to the best medical authorities, is likely to be caused by worry or a sense of guilt due to misinformation.

Dr. Johnson even tells us who the bad guys are in our society causing all of these feelings of guilt. Ready? It is the churches.

Who says so?

Why, the authorities at SIECUS say so. The study guide relates: "Moreover, it should be recognized that in our society most religious groups are strongly opposed to this practice [masturbation], and it is quite difficult for boys and girls to practice it and not feel some sense of guilt or fear."

Got that? "Guilt and fear" are a product of the churches, and masturbation is "universal" and "healthy."

In the past, young people were encouraged to work off their nervous energy through athletics, study, dancing, and other wholesome activities. Now we have the Leftists of SIECUS working in the schools to tell our teachers that masturbation is a healthier outlet. Page 18 of Study Guide Number 3 maintains:

> As a general rule, parents and adults concerned with youth are best advised to disregard evidence of private masturbation in juveniles, not to look for it nor to try to prevent it directly or even

indirectly by attempting to divert the youngster's attention to other activities. In adulthood, as well as in childhood, masturbation by individuals in private is coming more and more to be regarded as an acceptable means of releasing sexual tension.

According to SIECUS, not only is this practice not harmful, it actually performs a positive function of building manly self-confidence. The study guide remarks: "During adolescence, masturbation and its attendant fantasies may not only be a means of releasing sex tensions, but often serve as part of the adolescent struggle to achieve a sense of identity and a sexual self-image."

In addition to preparing study guides, SIECUS publishes a quarterly newsletter expounding its philosophy and recommending films, books, and articles in the field of sexology; it reprints articles that it judges particularly valuable; and it issues new reading lists of sex books. Included in the reprints are articles from Communist Isadore Rubin's grisly *Sexology* magazine. And, among the books recommended are such erotica as *Prostitution in Europe and the Americas, Unmarried Love, Women's Prisons,* and *Sex and the Social Structure.*

One of the most controversial educational tools being used in "sex education" courses is a slide-film called *How Babies Are Made,* prepared with the aid of SIECUS. This film, which is recommended for grades kindergarten through six, uses papier-mâché models to teach sexual reproduction. While the children watch the film the teacher reads the narrative which describes what is happening in adult, medically accurate terms.

One slide, which shows two dogs copulating, carries this dialogue: "When a father dog wants to send his sperm into a mother dog, he climbs on her back. . . ." The film then shows human male and female anatomy, indicates how a baby is produced, and ends with an optional slide showing a man and woman in bed with the narrative: "You have already learned how a father's sperm meets and fertilizes a mother's egg to create a new baby. To do this, they lie down facing each other. . . ."

One such film set used in a Westchester County elementary school shows dogs copulating—followed by a human couple under bed sheets—as a recorded voice explains, "Mummy and Daddy are doing the same things the dogs do."

As part of its educational program SIECUS cooperates with a number of other Leftist efforts in the sexology field. For example, SIECUS lists Barney Rosset of the notorious Grove Press as a source of information. Rosset has been in court many times over his publication of pornography and was the subject of an article in the January 25, 1969, issue of the *Saturday Evening Post* entitled "How to Publish 'Dirty' Books for Fun and Profit." The *Post* revealed that Mr. Rosset relinquished his "fiery pacifism" when Hitler broke his pact with Stalin and attacked Russia. With Mother Russia in trouble, Barney joined the army. (Yes, ours.)

Besides pornography, Rosset also specializes in books glorifying Communism—such as *Reminiscences* by Ernesto "Che" Guevara, Edgar Snow's *Red Star over China,* and Communist Kim Philby's *My Silent War.* Not surprisingly, SIECUS has even run advertisements in Rosset's lewd *Evergreen Review.*

The SIECUS organization has also run its ads in the disgusting *Nude Living* magazine, published by the Elysium Institute. Although SIECUS proclaims itself to be against "sexual exploitation" and claims it wishes to "dignify human sexuality," it has picked another strange bedfellow in the Elysium Institute—whose specialty is perversion and pornography dressed up as "health" faddism and "scientific inquiry." Elysium's magazines are composed mostly of photographs of nude men and women in sickening sexual positions, photographed from angles clearly designed to attract the pervert. They promote everything from necrophilia to nude Satanism and are frankly beyond description by a normal human being.

Of course, those magazines published by Elysium contain a page which lists the Institute's connection with SIECUS and others of the "growing number of organizations in this country which are concerned, as is the Institute, with seeking means to man's physical, emotional, and intellectual development in an environment of openness, understanding and tolerance." [6]

Among the books recommended by SIECUS as source material is *Situation Ethics—The New Morality* by Dr. Joseph Fletcher. Fletcher has been a member of thirty organizations cited by the federal government as Communist fronts. Herbert Philbrick, former undercover operative for the FBI, testified that "Joe Fletcher worked with us on Communist party projects and on an enormous number of tasks." Needless to say, Dr. Fletcher thinks the "New Morality" is simply glorious.

The recordings and books of Dr. Albert Ellis are also recommended by SIECUS. Ellis, a much-married former used-car salesman who obtained his Ph.D. late in life, is another "New Moralist." He is quoted in *Life* magazine as observing: "I certainly agree that if we are ever to become at all rational about our system of dating and marriage, the double standard will have to go. However, it seems to me that *one of the main ways of getting rid of the standard is to encourage premarital sex relations today.*" During the 1930s Ellis translated *Das Kapital* for the lay reader. In his book *The Case against Religion* he writes: "The religious person sells his soul, surrenders his own basic urges and pleasure so that he may feel comfortable with this heavenly helper that he himself has invented. Religion, then, is needless inhibition."

In a SIECUS-recommended book, *The American Sexual Tragedy,* Ellis castigates "men who cannot be satisfied with any form of sex

activity but coitus" as "probably fetishistically attached to this idea."
The effect of the efforts of Dr. Ellis on our children can only be called
calculated and sick.

Anthropologist Ashley Montagu, a member of the SIECUS board of
consultants, is another whose materials are recommended to schools by
SIECUS. Writing in the *Phi Delta Kappan*,* Montagu visualizes a
future in which

> Young unmarried individuals who are sufficiently responsible
> will be able, in the new dispensation, to enter into responsible
> sexual relationships in a perfectly healthy and morally acceptable
> and reciprocally beneficial manner, which will help the partici-
> pants to become more fully developed human beings than they
> would otherwise have stood a chance of becoming.

As a SIECUS authority, Montagu even views the de-masculinization
of American men with forthright approval: "The shortsighted 'viewers
with alarm' will be relegated to their proper places when what they so
wrongheadedly deplore, namely, the alleged feminization of men and
the alleged masculinization of women, are discovered to be advances in
the right, rather than in the wrong, direction."

HERE IT COMES

The SIECUS program which has been described by the national press
as the model effort in community "sex education" is being committed
in the schools of Anaheim, California. The *Saturday Evening Post*
called it "a SIECUS show window." In Anaheim, 32,000 students from
seventh through twelfth grade get six weeks of coeducational "sex education" yearly.[7]

Sally Williams, who supervises the family life and sex education
program at Anaheim, is on the SIECUS board of directors, and Dr.
Esther Schulz of SIECUS helped to develop the Anaheim program,
which relies heavily on SIECUS materials. Yet, strangely, both SIECUS
and the School District, headed by Superintendent Paul W. Cook, stead-
fastly maintain that Anaheim has nothing to do with SIECUS. Apparently it is felt that the Leftists and pornographers of SIECUS are
vulnerable to criticism and that it is best to provide the program while
doing everything possible to avoid the label. Certainly the *Saturday
Evening Post* wasn't fooled about who is running the show—nor is anyone else.

The Anaheim scheme has stimulated opposition in the form of a
Citizens' Committee formed by Mrs. Janet Townsend. Mrs. Eleanor

---

* See pp. 95-104 of *Sex, Schools, and Society.*

Howe, now a committed activist, is typical of the committee members. She became upset at what was going on in her son's eleventh-grade "sex education" class when she learned that the teacher asked young Howe what he would do if he discovered his son masturbating. That was a little too much for this courageous youngster, and he walked out of the class. Mrs. Howe told me:

> You wouldn't believe some of the reports we get from parents about these classes. One young man became so upset at the thought that he might be a homosexual, after the way the subject was treated in his eighth-grade class, that his parents had to send him to a psychiatrist to calm his fears. He was simply a normal adolescent, but the sex program proved too much for him.

In addition to the Citizens' Committee, the Anaheim program has also provoked opposition from the local newspaper, the *Anaheim Bulletin*, which has an old-fashioned editor by the name of Sam Campbell, who, along with the reporter John Steinbacher, has not been afraid to challenge the educational power structure. The *Bulletin* has published literally scores of letters from distraught parents. Such parental objection is mushrooming, and far from confined to Anaheim. Here, for example, is a letter of November 27, 1968, from a Mrs. Erwin Handel to the *Phoenix American:*

> We just received our November 6 . . . issue of "The American." I noted the article on the front page about sex education—which might better and more accurately be termed "obscenity education" in the Phoenix schools.
> We just moved from Phoenix—and for that reason. We have a twelve-year-old son who was taught this smut last spring, and about nine weeks thereafter we had a near disaster in our home.
> I walked in and caught him sexually molesting our four-year-old daughter. He had been taught all about intercourse at school and wanted to "try it out" on his sister. (I caught him before he actually committed the act.)
> Now, teaching young kids this in school is nonsense. . . . It's like giving someone a recipe to discourage cooking. It won't discourage, but rather encourage, experimentation.
> We hope that you might publish this—so some other parents might realize just what this "education" is doing to our children before they actually suffer a disaster—just as we nearly did.

You think it can't be that bad? Tell it to Mrs. Handel. Or, take a look at some of the supplementary books used in the $375,000 per year program to push sex at the children of Anaheim. A typical example is Kenneth Barnes's *He and She*. The theme that "America is a repressed puritanical society," constantly proclaimed by the Leftists and "New Moralists," is emphasized by Barnes on page 80:

> The sad result of the way the world upsets the attitudes of young people is that it encourages a divided feeling about sex and about people. It ought to be possible for a young man to see a girl naked and to enjoy her nakedness without any sense of guilt, accepting it not just as the nakedness of a female body, but as something that is part of her personality and that arouses respect for her as a whole person. There are countries in which the taboo on nakedness is not so strong as here.

Barnes also informs the students of Anaheim that God-centered religion is passé. In advocating a new-style religion, he writes:

> This religion must have a person at its centre; nothing less will do, no dogmas or rules or pseudoscientific notions will suffice, for these are all thoughts produced by persons and therefore less than persons. Nothing less than a living person can give us the complete truth about humanity.

Since the Anaheim program has been part of the curriculum for over three years, many residents have been trying to get the School Board to assess the results. Unfortunately, the School District absolutely refuses to release any statistics concerning the subsequent increase in venereal disease and illegitimate births. However, the Orange County Health Department says that venereal disease in the area is "out of control." And Richard Taylor, vice-president of the Orange County branch of the Florence Crittenton Society, which operates homes for unwed mothers, reports of this matter in the area, "The 'New Morality' is leaving a broad trail of heartbreak in Orange County."

There can be no doubt about it. When newspaper reporter John Steinbacher asked a young marine why so many servicemen congregated in Anaheim every weekend, the reply was "Man, everybody knows that the high-school girls here are 'available.' " The comment, Steinbacher found, was typical.

Although the retardation of venereal disease and illegitimacy is promoted as the reason why local school districts must adopt sexuality training, even SIECUS officials confess that the program will not ease these problems. Lester Kirkendall of SIECUS and *Sexology* magazine admitted in the June, 1968, *Reader's Digest:*

> Most people have the vague hope that it [sex education] will somehow cure half of the world's ills—reduce casual sex experi-

ence, cut down on illegitimate births, and eliminate venereal disease. To be perfectly blunt about it, we have no way of knowing
that sex education will solve any such problems.

Identified Communist and treasurer of SIECUS Isadore Rubin stated
at a symposium on "Sex and the Teen-ager": "For the community to
ask the sex educator to take on the responsibility of cutting down on
illegitimacy or on venereal disease is to ask him to undertake a task that
is foredoomed to failure." With SIECUS in charge, there can be no
doubt of that! What else could be expected with morality thrown out
the window?

The fact that many parents are aware of the efforts of the sex educationists to divorce the teaching of sex from morality has created growing resistance to the SIECUS-style programs. It seems that every
"expert" and sexologist associated with the SIECUS program rejects
traditional Judeo-Christian concepts of sexual morality. Again and again
we hear from its proponents that SIECUS maintains that sex education
"must not be moral indoctrination," and that "it is not the job of
SIECUS to make moral judgments; SIECUS can be neither for nor
against premarital sex." Many of us find it ironic that our youngsters
can be given instruction in our schools on various positions for sexual
intercourse—or, as McCall's noted, shown how to apply "a contraceptive
to a life-sized plastic phallus"—but a student saying a prayer in that
same school would be violating the law.

Even so, Anaheim School Superintendent Cook advocates presenting
a sexual smorgasbord and letting the teen-ager take his choice. Cook told
an audience at Chapman College recently:

> We give the kids the whole picture—we lay all the facts out on
> the table for them and we tell them they are going to hear dif-
> ferent ideas and attitudes than in their churches. We tell them that
> after all they do have to make up their own minds, and they're
> the only ones that can choose their own level of morality.

No prayers, you understand. No firm moral code. None of those
"different" ideas from home and church! Listen to Comrade Rubin.
Listen to the pornographers of Sexology.

The advocates of SIECUS go farther. They attempt to picture all
opposition as that of ignorant reactionaries and religious fanatics. Not
only do the concerned taxpayer-parents resent this characterization as
grossly unfair, but they point to the fact that their objection to sex instruction for the "New Morality" is supported by many medical authorities. Dr. Max Levin, in strenuously objecting to the amorality of the
SIECUS position on "sex education," writes:

I speak not as a clergyman but as a psychiatrist. There cannot be emotional health in the absence of high moral standards and a sense of human and social responsibility. I know that today morality is a "dirty word," but we must help our youth to see that moral codes have meaning beyond theology: they have psychological and sociological meaning. Even the atheist, who rejects religion, should be able to understand this.

You don't have to be a psychiatrist like Dr. Levin to realize that today's teen-agers already have more sophistication about the mechanics of sex than they have the maturity to handle. Telling teen-agers to choose their own level of morality, while emphasizing that premarital intercourse might be desirable, can only lead to tragic consequences. Teach biology and physiology, yes. But let's get the antimoral, Leftist sex-pushers out of our schools! They are an embarrassment to the professions which they trumpet and an out-and-out danger to our children.

Look at the truth. The preponderance of both scientific and practical support for traditional morality is simply ignored by the permissive SIECUS programs and the frantic school sexologists. As psychiatrist Graham Blaine writes: "The steps necessary to take in following unplanned pregnancy—adoption of the child, abortion, or premature marriage—are clearly unfortunate ones, and their increasingly frequency would seem to be a cogent argument for holding the line against permissiveness. . . ."

Indeed!

Dr. Paul Gebhard has recently conducted surveys of twelve hundred college students which also support traditional views of sexual morality. He found that the first step was likely to be decisive in the case of a girl. If she once crossed the "Rubicon," it was not easy for her to subsequently avoid such sexual activity thereafter. In such a case, he noted, she was jeopardizing her own prospects of a good marriage in the future, as well as running other risks. As the sociologist Robert Blood, Jr. points out:

> Premarital intercourse is associated more closely with broken relationships than with strengthened ones; twice as many engagements are broken among couples who have intercourse as among those who did not; the more frequent the intercourse, the greater the number of rings returned; both divorce and adultery are more common among those couples who indulge in premarital intercourse, and . . . even among those who do not separate, the incidence of marital unhappiness is greater.

New York psychiatrist Max Levin comments on SIECUS activist Warren Johnson's contention that "an increasingly safe and potentially wholesome sex life is said to be becoming available to the married and the unmarried who desire it; and there seems to be a growing feeling that this is a decision to be made by individual women and is not the business of society at all." Dr. Levin writes: "The young unmarried woman who has a sexual affair is harming herself emotionally. She cheapens herself when she yields to a seducer. There can be no mental health without a measure of self-respect."

With teen-agers being steeped in boggling sexual stimuli from the mass media, our schools should be bolstering those who are moral, and promoting self-control rather than providing rationalization for promiscuity. According to Dr. Melvin Anchell, the only justification for the SIECUS-style program is "the misconceived notion that if you can't beat them, join 'em." Many sex education courses turn out to be only an exercise in destroying the conscience. Is it surprising that, after hearing sexual intercourse discussed in class and shown in classroom movies, the reserves of young people are broken down and they are stimulated to experiment? As Dr. Anchell observes:

> The sexuality instinct is one of the strongest that we human beings have, and if we have a conscience associated with that sexuality then we cannot express it like amoebas. But the desensitization program is taking away the conscience and making the sex act a raw instinct.

The way homosexuality is treated in SIECUS sex education is also destructive. According to psychiatrist Anchell: "I'll be frank with you. I haven't had a pervert yet that I have cured, but I don't know anyone else who has either. The answer is in the prevention. And [this sort of] sex education, paradoxically, doesn't prevent it, but is causing it."

Today's teen-agers have been sold by the Left on the idea that they discovered sex and that sex is "in." When has it ever been out? It's been "in" since Adam and Eve. But, teen-agers are not the only target of the Leftist SIECUS operators. As I have noted, they want to start by selling their amoral sexuality to kindergarteners. The fact is that most reputable psychiatrists believe that presenting such information to young children can cause drastic psychological problems. Psychiatrist William McGrath explains in this way:

> There is a phase of personality development, called the latency period, during which the healthy child is not interested in sex. In this interval, from about age five until adolescence, a boy learns how to get along with other boys. And he can dream of becoming a man among men, a hero.
> This latency period is not just a cultural or moral intervention. It serves a very important biological purpose. It affords the child an opportunity to develop his own resources, his beginning physical and mental strength. Later, when he is ready, he can take on other responsibilities. . . .

Sophomoric and supercilious persons who are without learning in philosophy or in science fail to realize the significance of the latency period. When we plead that it should remain inviolate, they scoff and accuse us of narrow-minded prudishness. . . .

Premature interest in sex is unnatural and will arrest or distort the development of the personality. Sex education should not be foisted on children; should not begin in the grade schools.

Anyone who would deliberately arouse the child's curiosity or stimulate his unready mind to troubled sexual preoccupations ought to have a millstone tied around his neck and be cast into the sea.

A letter asks: Isn't sex the source of most psychological problems? No; not in a man who has been allowed to develop character before his introduction to sex. Sexual problems are almost always secondary, or symptomatic of a deeper immaturity.

To be first and above all a man among men is what one begins to learn in the latency period. This is sacred territory. A plague on those who trespass.

Psychiatrist Rhoda Lorand, after viewing the type of sex material now being used in the elementary schools, puts it this way: "It is overwhelming, disturbing and embarrassing, upsetting and exciting and very likely to lead to sex difficulties later in life." Author of *Love, Sex and the Teenager,* she is a long way from being a blue-nose on this subject. Psychiatrist Anchell agrees, noting:

The one thing [this sort of] sex education is supposed to do for us—that is, help our children become mature adults—it actually destroys. It does it by interfering with the normal instinctual growth of the child. It catapults the child into advanced sexual information; it perverts the child. . . . If you turn into an obstetrician at eight years of age, you have developed a fixation. . . . I think it is creating more perverts than were ever created before, and more-diversified perverts.

Indicative of the fact that elementary-school children do not have the maturity to handle the material being thrown at them is that many children, after having seen the SIECUS-prepared *How Babies Are Made,* have come home and asked to watch Mommy and Daddy plant the seed. This has already prompted a lawsuit against the school system by a local committee in San Luis Obispo, California. No doubt further legal action is on the way.

Frankly, the program is proving downright dangerous. Even SIECUS's Dr. Kirkendall admits: "There's no way that you can proceed without some risk (to the students). You have to admit that there are people teaching in schools who have sexual problems of their own they haven't worked through." The subject would obviously have an overwhelming attraction for instructors with voyeur tendencies. Dr. Anchell, himself the author of a fine book on sexual adjustment, warns:

> Many of the so-called sex experts are no more qualified to be involved with this problem than a used-car salesman would be. Many are misguided disciples of Freud who call themselves psychiatrists. Many are social workers. Many are teachers who don't know anything about the subject. These people have set themselves up as experts. What they have been attempting to do is promulgate the sexuality instinct into that of an instinct related to a bodily function such as eating, breathing or going to the bathroom. But it really isn't . . . you could do all these other things alone, but sexuality takes two.

Danger or no danger, however, Anaheim Superintendent Cook has admitted that what he is involved in is "changing attitudes." That, alas, is precisely the problem.

THE SCANDINAVIAN MODEL

The SIECUS style of "education" is too new in this country to draw any statistically based conclusions as to what its cumulative effects will be. We do, however, have a model at which we can look for a glimpse of the future. The Scandinavians have had compulsory "sex education" of the type SIECUS is promoting for two decades. In fact, Professor Ira Reiss of SIECUS maintains: "Where Sweden is today is where we're going to be in ten years. Sweden has a culture that accepts 'permissiveness with affection' standards." [8]

The SIECUS Study Guide Number 5 says: "The Scandinavian countries have developed even further than we a type of affection-centered premarital sexual permissiveness. We seem to be heading toward a Scandinavian type of sexuality." Promoting this "trend," SIECUS recommends the book *Sex and Society in Sweden* as part of its curriculum, explaining: "Because it is a book that is open, honest, and reliable regarding the real situation in Sweden, it should prove of unusual value and interest to parents and educators everywhere." Dr. Kirkendall, in praising Denmark's "sex education" program, states: "The consequences for young Danes seem to be far less damaging than here. . . . Hence guilt and conflict over premarital sex are minimal. . . . They may even let the child be born before they marry, since there is little stigma on illegitimacy."

Perhaps local citizens will want to look at the "real situation" and the "minimal" negative consequences of "sex education" in Scandinavia before embarking on a SIECUS-type program. A third of the brides in Denmark kneel at the altar pregnant. In twenty years the number of brides aged fifteen to seventeen has swelled by 400 percent. One legal, and four to five illegal, abortions are now performed for every twenty births. In Sweden the increase in venereal disease is described by officials as "catastrophic." According to *U.S. News & World Report* of February 7, 1966:

> Physicians say that gonorrhea and syphilis are more widespread in Sweden today than in any other civilized country in the world. A recent inquiry revealed the startling fact that about half of all boys who had become infected with venereal disease admitted having sexual relations with at least forty different girls—and 10 percent said that they had had relations with as many as two hundred.

The Swedish education system has been accused by a highly respected group of 140 eminent Swedish doctors and teachers, including the king's physician, Dr. Ull Nordwall, of producing sex obsession among adolescents because, as they put it:

> It has bombarded schoolchildren with sexual instruction for which their immaturity ill fits them and the result has been an unnatural oversexualization of the rising generation [in which] . . . the young have confused instruction in method with encouragement to practice.

As for the SIECUS contention that while sex education will not lower venereal disease or illegitimacy, it will produce healthy, happy, well-adjusted young men and women, the results in Sweden prove the contrary. An article in the issue of *Reader's Digest* for August, 1966, relates:

> There is a significant report from Sweden, which for so long prided itself on the removal of moral restraints and what amounts to the encouragement of sexual freedom, even in the schools.° Yet the human toll has been so great that we now read of a growing movement, headed by the country's leading doctors, to put an end to sexual laxity. But note: The doctors . . . observe that, for all their sexual freedom, "young people in Sweden are not happy today," and urge the schools to spend more time on moral and religious leadership and instruction which will help the children know "what is right and wrong" in terms of their own ultimate well-being.

What has been the effect of the efforts of the sex educationists on the family in Sweden? Psychiatrist Graham Blaine writes:

In Scandinavian countries extra-marital affairs have increased. It would seem logical to assume that a family environment which includes a philandering father or a promiscuous mother, or both, would be less healthy for children than one in which fidelity prevailed.

The inevitable results of adopting the Scandinavian attitudes pushed by SIECUS? As Professor Russell Kirk notes: "In another generation or so, American church communicants may be as scarce as they are in Denmark or Sweden today—that is, 1 to 5 percent of the population, or even fewer."

LEFTIST HARASSMENT

Still, parents who rebel at having the public school lead their children into the pit which proved so disastrous for the Scandinavians are astonished to find that they have run into a veritable Leftist buzz saw. The SIECUS proponents even hold seminars in how to deal with their conservative opponents. At one of these seminars, Dr. Lester Kirkendall characterized all such opponents as "a fringe group of dissidents who don't think rationally." He maintains that those who oppose the program to "change America's sexual attitudes have hangups about sex." To skirt these "sick" people, Kirkendall recommends:

> Just sneak it [the sex program] in as an experimental course. . . . Go to your PTA and get support. That's where the power lies. . . . Don't say that you are going to start a sex education course. Always move forward. Say that you are going to enrich, expand, and make it better. The opposition can't stop something that you have already started.

This strategy puts the opponents in a position of being "aginners" who are "out to destroy our modern, progressive family life course."

Another strategy used by the Leftist sex educationists is to form a committee of civic leaders, including doctors, clergymen, and businessmen, to endorse the introduction of the program into the local school. Many, if not most, of these men are not aware of just what they are endorsing, but feel that sex education is generally a good idea. Once having committed themselves, pride and ego require them to defend their stand even as the educationists turn a presumed course in physiology into out-and-out indoctrination for premarital sex and amorality.

The educationists, as usual, want complete autonomy—free from the "interference" of those who pay the bills. Citizens' groups have found that once the program is begun their letters are not answered and that it is almost impossible to get school boards to give specific answers to questions about these sex programs. Complaints are met with educationese and mumbo jumbo.

SO WHAT IS TO BE DONE?

Is the alternative to a SIECUS-type program to keep teen-agers in total ignorance about sex, as has been charged by some? The question is not whether "sex education" should be provided, but what kind, where, and by whom. There is a significant minority, if not a majority, of parents who believe that sex cannot be divorced from morality—and who are convinced that sex education is the province of the home and not of the state. Are their civil rights to be trampled by arrogant behavioral scientists, social anthropologists, and educationists? It is argued that some homes will abrogate their responsibility in this field. And, this is true. But, critics ask, does this justify putting the sexual morality of all children at the mercy of the atheists and pornographers and Communists who are supporting and directing SIECUS?

Many concerned parents believe that just as all that glitters is not buried in Fort Knox, all that is called "sex education" is not really education. They know that the SIECUS effort has turned out to be indoctrination in promiscuity.

WHAT'S REALLY HAPPENING

As terrible as are the personal tragedies produced by the SIECUS programs, let us pause here in conclusion to note the broader effect on our national life which may well be the real object of these programs aimed at our sons and daughters—and, through them, at the health of our nation.

We have already noted the ties of SIECUS directors to the Communists. We note now in passing that the motivation of the SIECUS-style efforts directly parallels the various "mental health" programs promoted by the World Health Organization. Instrumental in the founding of WHO was Soviet spy Alger Hiss, who declared that "health is a state of complete physical, mental, and social well-being, and not merely the absence of disease or infirmity." Selected to lead the creation of this "social well-being" was the notorious pro-Communist Canadian Brock Chisholm, who spelled out the foundations for the "New

Morality" when he wrote in the February, 1946, issue of *Psychiatry* (with an introduction by Abe Fortas):

> The re-interpretation and eventual eradication of the concept of right and wrong which has been the basis of child training, the substitution of intelligent and rational thinking for faith in the certainties of the old people, these are the belated objectives of practically all effective psychotherapy. Would they not be legitimate objectives of original education. . . ? Freedom from morality means freedom to observe, to think and behave sensibly . . . free from outmoded types of loyalties. . . . This is a new kind of world and there is no ethical or moral system that is intended for anyone in this world.

Chisholm's chief administrator at WHO was Dr. Frank Calderone, husband of the SIECUS commander in chief, Mary Calderone.

Everywhere one turns with these people the reins lead back to the Far Left. Why? Clearly because it is in the interest of the Communists to promote programs like SIECUS for destroying American sexual morality and enervating the moral fiber of our nation's youth.

Nationally syndicated columnist Henry J. Taylor, playing Devil's Advocate, delineated a sixteen-point program for the destruction of the United States. One of these points reads: "Preach 'permissiveness.' If 'anything goes' then, of course, everything goes. Every internal and external enemy knows the advantages of destroying a nation's standards. The rewards are as old as the Trojan horse."

As far back as May of 1919, Allied forces in Dusseldorf, Germany, first captured a Communist document entitled "Rules for Revolution." Number One on that list of objectives was: "Corrupt the young, get them away from religion. Get them interested in sex. Make them superficial, destroy their ruggedness." Again, in the early 1950s, Florida State Attorney George A. Brautigam confirmed that "the above 'Rules for Revolution' were secured by the State Attorney's Office from a known member of the Communist party, who acknowledged it to be still a part of the Communist program for overthrowing our Government."

The *Sacramento Union* has recently editorialized:

> Diabolical as it may seem, it has been a common tool of Communism for many years to undermine values and substitute their opposites. The Communist Conspiracy has always used the weak to infect the strong. In fact history shows that often the strong have been betrayed into surrendering to the weak. It would not be too difficult . . . to gain control of the minds of the young and the weak. It can be done by systematically denigrating all that a person has been taught to be worthy of respect. It would be done

very cleverly with an appeal to the reasonableness of each argument, the use of half-truth. . . . It would be necessary to attack belief in Americanism, morality, and personal integrity. These will be replaced by un-Americanism, immorality and personal anonymity. Perhaps this begins to sound shockingly familiar. If what we presently see and hear on the American scene is any indication, the process is well under way. . . .

It would test our credulity to propose that our schools and other influential institutions are deliberately aiding this hideous process. It is possible, however, to believe that such institutions are being used by conspirators to accomplish the aims of the world-wide Communist movement.

It might also be pointed out that fanatical Marxist Stuart Chase noted in his book *The Proper Study of Mankind:* "Theoretically, a society could be completely made over in something like fifteen years, the time it takes to inculcate a new culture into a rising group of youngsters."

Do you doubt that it can happen?

Historically, the destruction of morality has often been used as a technique to ready a country for Communist revolution. Nowhere was this more evident than in Spain, where 5 percent of the nation's inhabitants were slaughtered in a bloody civil war. Before the revolution, kiosks sprung up on nearly every corner of the major cities, peddling the most lurid pornography, and the cry "Long live free love" was a regular part of student demonstrations. *The Red Domination in Spain,* an official report of the Spanish government, states with regard to this degeneracy: "The moral corruption and disintegration of family and social ties reigning throughout the Marxist zone of Spain during the civil war were a direct consequence of communism . . . . Degradation amongst children during pre-revolutionary days [led to] . . . degradation of spiritual life and morals."

The same was true in Russia with the Nihilists, in Greece when the Communists sought to take power, in post-Kuhn Hungary, and in a dozen other places where the Communists have moved. Surely the vast majority of those promoting SIECUS-style "sex education" are perfectly loyal, if misguided, Americans. However, it is impossible to deny that there is Communist influence within any parent organization which contains an identified Communist as its treasurer and has such a number of its directors who have been active in officially cited Communist fronts. It would seem only logical that their motives and/or judgment should be subjected to the closest scrutiny. Their target, after all, is our own children—and America's future.

One remembers a recent comment by my colleague George S. Schuyler, which seems to provide the only proper conclusion here. Writing in the January [1969] *American Opinion,* Mr. Schuyler noted:

When General William F. Dean was released from a Korean Communist prison camp, the young Chinese psychologists who had been trying to break him said: "General, don't feel bad about leaving us. You know, we will soon be with you. We are going to capture your country." Asked how, they replied: "We are going to destroy the moral character of a generation of your young Americans, and when we have finished you will have nothing with which to really defend yourselves against us."

Those are powerful words to remember. And they provide, beyond doubt, the single best explanation of What's Really Happening.

NOTES

[1] Kirkendall, according to the *Anaheim Bulletin* of December 19, 1968, ridiculed those at the IBM-sponsored sex institute who noted that Isadore Rubin was identified as a Communist before the House Committee on Un-American Activities. "Rubin," said Kirkendall, "only wrote a paper for the *Daily Worker.*" The sworn testimony of the New York detective who was in the same Red cell as Comrade Rubin contradicts Dr. Kirkendall's claim.

[2] Mrs. Koontz has just [1969] been named by President Nixon to head the Women's Bureau of the Department of Labor.

[3] SIECUS director Calderone is also a member of that NCC Commission.

[4] Listed as sponsors of SIECUS's second annual dinner were the notorious Hugh Hefner of *Playboy,* John Cowles of *Look,* Secretary of State and Mrs. Robert Strange McNamara, Leftist Stewart Mott (heir to a GM fortune), best-selling author Vance Packard, Steven Rockefeller, and James Warburg of the international banking family.

[5] This organization is described by the federal government's *Guide to Subversive Organizations* as being "created by the Communist party in 1943." It is cited on the U.S. Attorney General's list of subversive organizations as "subversive and Communist."

[6] Some of those wildly Leftist efforts with which Elysium exchanges information (in addition to SIECUS) are the University of Humanism, Institute of Rational Living, Institute for Sex Research, Pacifica Foundation, Joan Baez' Institute for the Study of Non-violence, Sexual Freedom League, and the Underground Press Syndicate.

[7] Because the elementary school is a separate system and has not yet adopted the program, children in the kindergarten through sixth grade have thus far been deprived of SIECUS sex in Anaheim.

[8] What is happening in America, according to Professor Reiss, is "not a sexual revolution but the evolvement of a system which has replaced the prostitute with the girl next door." [See pp. 119-128 of *Sex, Schools, and Society.*]

[9] The trend is indicated by the recent recommendation of a Stockholm teacher that "what every good high school needs is a sex room where teen-age lovers can seek respite from the rigors of reading, writing, and arithmetic. . . ."

The Dropout Parents:
How America Got on a Sex Binge

Max Rafferty

Let's face it. Americans today are sexually pathological, no matter how you look at it. The evidence:

—A massive rise in the increase of brutish and revolting sex crimes. Everything from the Boston Strangler to the Chicago nurse butchery.

—The puffing of pornography into big, big business.

—The rotting away of our once proud motion pictures to the sordid status of stag movies. Every vile nuance from lebianism to fetishism is now deemed acceptable for what has always been a family entertainment medium.

—The decline of the American novel to a mere vehicle for four-letter words and dreary sexual perversions.

—The nauseating material on our neighborhood magazine and pocketbook stands, which more resembles the private collection of the late King Farouk.

Regardless of how broad-minded you may be, or how healthy and beautiful you may think sex is, you'll have to agree that this kind of leering and lip-smacking preoccupation with a single bodily function is at best bizarre and at worst maniacal.

WHO'S TO BLAME?

—Some of our ministers, such as those who organize well-financed and slickly publicized associations like the one in San Francisco which exists to promote the cause of homosexuality.

—Too darn many judges, who call hard-core pornography "avant-garde literature."

—Quite a few psychologists and psychiatrists, who seem dedicated to the uplifting proposition that everybody ought to be able to do his own thing any way he wants to, the nastier the better.

—And of course those news media which grant goggle-eyed, respectful attention to some pitiful apologist for pederasty.

But the folks most to blame for our present sex syndrome are you, Mom and Pop.

225

You let your children grow up thinking that premarital sex is OK so long as nobody gets pregnant, diseased, or jailed. It isn't, you know.

You let your neighborhood movie houses and newsstands get away with their gradual switchover from family entertainment to filth for profit. You didn't picket them or boycott them or even keep your own kids away from them, did you?

You let the schools take over your own immemorial job of telling your children the facts of life, and you didn't care that the resulting school sex education programs were as devoid of morality and personal dignity as a third-generation computer.

You let the tax-supported colleges abrogate all standards of simple decency. You didn't raise hell, cancel your endowments, or yank your kids out of school. So now we have mixed dormitories, obscene school newspapers, free-love assemblies, and dirty movies and drama projects on campus.

YOU DROPPED OUT, didn't you, Mom and Pop? And now you're blaming everybody you can find for the mess we're in—teachers, legislators, Supreme Court justices, movie producers, and magazine publishers.

Stop blaming them. They'll do whatever you let them get away with, and they'll stop in a hurry anything you show them you won't stand for. So far, they've been able to find darned little you won't put up with.

Why did you drop out of this sex push? Why did you consent to exposing your own kids to the sexual Typhoid Marys of the Sick Sixties? Because you allowed yourselves to be sold a bill of badly damaged goods.

The dirty novelists bellowed, "Freedom of expression," and you bought it.

The bawdy-movie-makers raised their eyebrows, pointed enviously to some odorous films turned out overseas by a few degenerate Swedes and Frenchmen, and brayed, "Adult entertainment."

The jelly-spined college presidents pontificated solemnly about their institutions not being "custodial" in relation to their inmates, and you bought that, too. With it, you also bought the convenient contraceptives, the four-letter chants from student activists, the psychedelic orgies, and all the rest of the sorry sex parade which promenades interminably across too many college campuses these days.

You got put down, Mom and Pop. You were so hung up over being thought square and Victorian and unmod that you ended up an uneasy vegetable, doing nothing at all. Except once in a while viewing with alarm, of course, and even then worrying that someone would think you were guilty of widening the generation gap.

IT'S NOT TOO LATE to get back in the ball game. Here are the things you ought to start doing right now about this sex binge we seem to be on:

—Stay away from the morbid movies and the purulent plays, and urge everybody you know to do the same—especially your children.

—Organize neighborhood patrols to inspect, boycott, and picket the obscene magazine stands.

—Elect local judges and civic officials who hate pornography for profit, and who guarantee in advance of election to harry the youth corrupters relentlessly and ingeniously every day they're in office.

—Tell your state legislators in no uncertain terms to cut off all money to tax-supported colleges which refuse to police their own facilities and student bodies, and which decline to adopt definite, hard-boiled standards of sex conduct on their respective campuses.

—*Above all, see that your own children know what's right and what's wrong about sex before they blow themselves up with its age-old dynamite.*

And don't let anybody box you into that old semantic trap about what's "right" and what's "wrong." The rightness and the wrongness of sex are as old as our Judeo-Christian heritage—as old as the Ten Commandments—almost as old as Adam.

So stop trying to justify yourself. Stop dropping out. Adopt a code of behavior you really believe in and stick to it. Eventually, you'll get something from the kids you are certainly not getting now: respect.

Tell them the human body is supposed to be a temple, not a brothel.

Part IV
FOREIGN MISCELLANY ON SEX EDUCATION

INTRODUCTION

It may be little consolation to American parents that the difficulty children have understanding their sexuality naturally is a problem which parents have had to face all over the world. Some societies try to ignore the problem for as long as possible; others exhibit a group of ideological fetishes at each discernible period in the growth of a child through adolescence into adulthood.

The problems concerning sex education which confront American parents, schools, and community groups have their counterparts in Australia and New Zealand, as well as in Britain and Canada, though these do not always arouse quite such heated political passions as do those in the United States. But there is still a virtual prohibition or restriction on specific sex education programs per se throughout most of the world. In many countries—for example, Spain, Italy, and Portugal in Western Europe; Thailand, Malaysia, and Indonesia in Asia; Bolivia, Brazil, and Mexico in Latin America; and Syria, the Sudan, and Egypt in the Arab world—children are without benefit of substantive nationwide school programs offering a modicum of sex and family life education. Apparently sex education is regarded as entirely a family matter and a very personal responsibility in over 80 percent of the world's national school systems.

But of those countries which do provide formal sex education programs in the schools, perhaps Denmark and Sweden, particularly the latter, best illustrate the extent to which a nationwide program can be incorporated throughout all levels of education and can secure the general acquiescence, if not acceptance and involvement, of much of the population. However, this is not to suggest that all Swedes complacently accept the National Board of Education's program which was introduced over fifteen years ago. The Swedish program has been closely watched by visitors from many countries, and the evaluative research on the results of Sweden's extensive curriculum has provided material for a range of spectators, especially the pro and con factions from the United States. They readily cite Sweden's experience in order to bolster or destroy their opponents' arguments on the merits or otherwise of introducing sex education programs modeled on the Swedish formula in America.

In the previous two sections of the anthology the Swedish program has been discussed or referred to by various contributors. Sweden's role as a pioneer of a nationwide, comprehensive sex education program in the schools has been featured with some regularity in various American popular journals, such as *McCall's, Redbook, Look,* and the *Saturday Evening Post,* and has also furnished an inexhaustible

source of copy for both muckrakers and serious social-science researchers.

This section of the anthology includes two articles pertaining to the
sex instruction program in Swedish schools, one of which represents
the earliest official statement of government policy from the Board of
Education, and the other, by Birgitta Linnér, a recent comprehensive
overview of the various educational and societal forces at play in
Sweden. The presentation by Mrs. Linnér affords a useful summary
on the topic by one of the best-known of Sweden's spokesmen. Her
writings have been widely translated and carefully studied in many
countries, including the United States.

The development of programs in Britain presents Americans with
a further point of view and a profile of the attempts to meet the sex
and family life education needs of British children. The analysis by
Alan Little offers the reader a concise picture of the scope of programs
and developments currently in force in Britain. He illustrates the nature
of the involvement of both Central Government agencies and Local
Education Authorities, and their responsibility for program implementation vis-à-vis other interested groups in the community in recent years.
Dr. Little, in his report to the 1969 International Planned Parenthood
Federation Conference on "Responsible Parenthood and Sex Education," suggests that "in Britain, there is evidence of a noticeable increase
in interest and activity in the field of sex education during the last decade
and particularly during the past five years."

This is not to say that concerned groups in Britain, particularly
religious organizations, were previously remiss in fulfilling their responsibilities. On the contrary; for example, the Church of England, through
both its Board of Social Responsibility and its Board of Education, is
committed to educational propaganda and to producing sex education
material for parents. The Catholic Marriage Advisory Council, with
over seventy counseling centers throughout Britain, provides various
educational services. Likewise, the Catholic Truth Society has long
been concerned with providing information on a wide range of topics
"to assist all Catholics to better knowledge of their religion . . . and to
spread amongst non-Catholics information about the Faith."

The society is responsible for the publication and widespread dissemination of a pamphlet, *Sex Instruction in the Home,* by the Reverend
Aidan Pickering. The pamphlet, first published in 1949 (177 thousand
copies in distribution by 1965) is intended primarily for the use of
clergy, parents, and teachers. It presents a concise but classic exposition
of the Catholic view on the role of Christian parents in the proper family
upbringing of children and their sexual understanding. The pamphlet,
though intended mainly for Catholics in Britain, appeals to people
everywhere with similar religious and philosophical beliefs. The more
recent, widespread, and important public declaration on the same

topic, that by Pope Paul VI in his 1968 encyclical letter, *On the Regulation of Birth,* provides a universal statement on family sex education and practice to be followed by faithful Catholics. Pope Paul's encyclical was intended "to render the life of parents and of children within their families not only tolerable, but easier and more joyous, to render the living together in human society more fraternal and peaceful, in faithfulness to God's design for the world."

These two documents representing Catholic orthodoxy in sex and family life education are included because they are important for an understanding of the subject as it is seen by a large and influential religious body which is especially important, among English-speaking nations, in the United States, Canada, Ireland, Britain, Australia, and New Zealand. The fact that these orthodox viewpoints have come under severe and strident attack in recent years, both within and without the Roman Catholic Church, in the countries noted above, as well as in many developing nations where Catholicism is important, does not diminish the continuing importance and influence of such a pronouncement as Pope Paul's encyclical *On the Regulation of Birth.*

The orthodox Catholic norms regarding sex education bear some similarity to those of Communist ideology and the pedagogical application of the subject in both the Soviet Union and China. Professor V. N. Kolbanovskii of the Soviet Academy of Pedagogical Sciences in his article, "The Sex Upbringing of the Rising Generation," discusses the increasing awareness of the nature of teen-age anxieties, and the role of Soviet educators in the responsible sexual instruction of children. The author suggests that "children constitute the natural goal and the loftiest meaning of human love." It is obvious from the gradually increasing body of literature available on the topic that Soviet society continues to be confronted with the need to adapt to new demands and the changing life styles of young people. The younger generation in the U.S.S.R. sometimes react against their elders for the usual reasons of youth everywhere. They resent what they see as the at times perhaps unsympathetic and firm strictures of a Party ideology imbued with puritanical and moralistic overtones. Critics would suggest that these strictures have a strong parallel in the fundamentalist religious zeal to be found in Western society, particularly in the United States and Canada. Kolbanovskii believes that the principal role of teachers and cultural leaders in Soviet society is to encourage the development of a "highly moral character" regarding the "relations between men and women in socialist society." It is important for readers to understand that "Soviet writers and artists are faced with the responsible task of satisfying the spiritual needs of our youth, in particular the task of reflecting the essence and dialectic of love in the spirit of the lofty principles and norms of communist morality." Soviet society's need to maintain and increase cultural standards is reflected in the moralistic and ideological foundation of sex education programs, and is echoed, as a Soviet credo, in Maxim Gorky's dictum "Culture must triumph over what is base in man, inasmuch as culture is the organized rule of reason over the animal instincts of people."

The sex education problems of China are not entirely similar to those of the Soviet Union, its geographical neighbor and one-time close ideological partner, but there are some parallels between the two. There is a strong practical base to the Chinese approach of viewing the interrelated topics of sex education, family life education, and population control. There may be legitimate, though compulsive, reasons in China for the strict attempt to enforce family size limitations throughout the country and for the persuasive arguments encouraging young persons to refrain from sexual activity until well past their mid-twenties.

The series of articles from China included in this section illustrate clearly both the human problems and the ideological approaches of health, education, and Party authorities to the topic. The reasons for postponing marriage are summed up by one author, who reflects the official line when noting: "By getting married late, young people can in the meantime spend more energy in caring about State affairs and group life, in studying political theories, and taking part in political struggles, and in this way continuously raise their political and ideological levels and become qualified for [Young Communist] League and Party membership."

Not only are there sound ideological reasons for directing the full physical energies of young people toward the service of the State, but there is, especially in China, the urgent necessity of reducing the birth rate through the encouragement of late marriages and a nationwide Draconian sex and family education program.

The articles from China on sex education and its practical application to population control, while not necessarily of immediate currency, are still pertinent and relevant to China's present situation. The 850 million people who constitute the People's Republic of China are faced with the continuing and imperative need to put into effect the most drastic of birth control programs. One of the major attempts to undertake such a program is carefully described by Professor Pi-chao Chen, a political scientist at Wayne State University, in his article, "China's Birth Control Action Programme." Though focused on the period 1956–1964, it still has relevancy today in view of the lack of more recent studies on the interrelationship of sex education programs for youth and a national population control program.

Communist youth's need to develop a sound sexual understanding of themselves has obvious parallels in other societies which may not have such pervasively strong ideological structures. Two articles from vastly different countries—one Asian and the other Anglo-European—are included to represent the problems of college-age youth, through aspects of practical sexual education at the Universities of Singapore and Melbourne.

The former institution has a polyglot student population coming from greatly diverging subcultures with a wide range of moral codes and sexual values. The University of Singapore is faced with unusual problems in a multi-cultural society which has had varying success in attempting to bring together its different races. The nature of the problem is summed up by Dr. Z. N. Kadri of the University of Singapore Health Services, who notes: "Our students come from a wide variety of cultural backgrounds. . . . The only common sex denominator in the past between the Chinese, the Malays, and the Indians was the practice of polygamy in its different forms. . . . recent legislation, the influence of Western culture with its Christian values, and the emancipation of women through modern education, have given a new dimension to our sex attitudes." The solution to the sexual impulses of Singapore University students, it is suggested, lies in suppression and sublimation. Dr. Kadri believes that the drives of love can be expressed through more socially acceptable channels—for instance, through better academic studies, extracurricular activities, and participation in sports and athletics—and he suggests hopefully to the students that historically "a large amount of sublimated sex energy" has resulted in "famous paintings, pieces of music, literary works and medical and engineering discoveries." The author concludes by saying that Asian students, particularly those with whom he is most familiar at the University of Singapore, "talk a lot about sex, but, generally speaking, they are much more conservative in action."

Leaving Singapore and moving to the University of Melbourne, one finds a different ethos prevailing, and students who are apparently less inclined to be conservative in their collegiate publications, especially where matters of sexual activity and public discussion are concerned. The University of Melbourne student newspaper, *Farrago,* has been cheerfully prepared to offer its readers a buyer's guide to prophylactics and a student's rating sheet to advise freshmen on the relative effectiveness and aesthetic factors of various birth control devices. Unlike the careful, moralistic, and directive advice given to Asian university students at Singapore University, that handed out to students at Melbourne is refreshingly frank and nondirective.

Farrago reminds student readers that "a great conspiracy of silence still reigns on the serious discussion of practical problems associated with sex," and the article "Sex and the Single Student: How Not to Be a Mummy" presents factual information to remedy this situation, but points out that "decision about moral issues, if any, rests with the student." Freshman students coming up to Australian universities are presupposed not to possess "much knowledge of sex or training in making decisions about sexual behaviour"—sufficient rationalization for this buyer's guide to student contraception and abortion techniques. The direct approach in the *Farrago* article reflects Australia's permissive academic society and the self-educative role expected of those students who are able to meet the rigid admission quotas and gain entrance to Australian universities.

These two articles provide material for reflection upon the different intellectual conditions which would permit the publication of the *Farrago* article, on the one hand, and encourage the paternalistic views expressed by the Asian university's Health Service staff, on the other. But university students' need for information, instruction, and counseling in sexual matters at both Singapore and Melbourne is patently obvious. The necessity of catering to community mores and what is socially desirable is also a factor which might inhibit the public discussion and publication of sexual information of the type displayed by *Farrago* in, say, Singapore. The student health physician at the University of Malaya (Kuala Lumpur) recently conducted a "survey of knowledge of human reproduction among university students," and the results were somewhat depressing in a nation like Malaysia, where "successful application of methods of population control requires a community that is well instructed in the facts of reproduction." The University of Malaya attracts the most educated section of the nation, yet the study by Dr. E. Patrick of the University Health Services shows students' total unawareness of supposedly commonly known facts on reproduction. Out of a university population of 3,600 some 408 (325 men, 83 women) volunteered to answer a questionnaire based on H. Frederick Kilander's "Information Test on Human Reproduction." The results suggested that, with the exception of students who had included biological sciences in their course of studies, there was among the university students "considerable ignorance both in men and women about the anatomy and physiology of human reproduction." But the problem of student ignorance is compounded and the future of Malaysian population control severely retarded when the questionnaire reveals that "women are more ignorant than men pertaining to their own sex and even more ignorant of facts about the male sex." For example, two out of three women were ignorant of the process of fertilization of the ovum; one out of two did not know what ovulation means; three out of four were unable to suggest reasons for common sterility in women; one out of four did not know why menstruation occurs.

To sum up, it is apparent that if the most highly educated level of Malaysian society betrays such ignorance of the common factors involved in sexual education and human reproduction, there may be considerable difficulties ahead in implementing a nationwide program of population control! One conclusion which may be drawn from the difficulties encountered by the medical services of both the University of Singapore and the University of Malaya is the necessity of including, certainly at the university level and equally importantly at the secondary-school level, satisfactory sex and family life education programs. However, the availability of adequate sexual information for students is no guarantee that they can understand, appreciate, and use information of the type available in the *Farrago* article. Unfortunately, this can be said whether the students come from the University of Malaya, Singapore, or Melbourne.

Sex and the Single Student: How Not to Be a Mummy

Tranquilla Rathmines

A great conspiracy of silence still reigns on the serious discussion of practical problems associated with sex. This factual article attempts to remedy the situation. Decision about moral issues, if any, rests with the student.

Our Freshers, Freshettes will have reached a certain educational standard or they would not have made the Quota. They will have the foundation of knowledge, the rudimentary disciplines of thinking, evaluation, making choices. Unless they went to one of the few public schools with a responsible attitude to sex education, they will not have much knowledge of sex or training in making decisions about sexual behaviour.

Such sexual education as they have had will probably be pure, not applied. It will almost certainly be deficient in the basic but contentious areas of contraception, abortion and venereal disease. Here are some of the facts which may give a basis for discussion and decision-making.

This article assumes a knowledge of basic biology—"What the man does to the woman, what the woman does to the man, how the baby pops out", as Neil Singleton so engagingly puts it. If readers are unsure of themselves at even this level, they could begin by reading *Ideal Marriage,* T. H. van de Velde, (Heinemann)—NOW.

It also assumes that readers will want to make decisions about sex, not simply follow blind habits which are no more laudable than blind instincts. If you have never thought about thinking about sexual behaviour, read John Wilson's *Logic and Sexual Morality* (Penguin) and Frank Jackson's review of this book in *MUM,* Autumn, 1966.

I. CONTRACEPTION

Even where contraceptive information is readily available, it is often neglected because the possibility of pregnancy seems remote until one is actually involved with it. (Married couples are just as unrealistic in this as single ones.) Sometimes there is a feeling that taking precautions reduces a spontaneous and innocent encounter to a studied and somehow tarnished act; contrariwise, it may be suspected of giving unintended permanence to a relationship. To the strict moralist unmarried sex is fornication whether one takes precautions or not; a liberal one might consider such foresight evidence of responsibility and good faith between the couple.

Contraceptives can be divided into His and Hers. Only lower socioeconomic groups, the army, and casual civilian males still rely on His. While Hers are generally dearer and less easily available, they are more efficient and pleasant.

Methods vary in cost and reliability, but generally a cheap method consistently used is as successful as a more efficient method used carelessly. The human error is the most important factor influencing contraceptive reliability. Laboratory tests have so little to do with the real-life situation that statistical measures of reliability are misleading—only approximate ratings are given here.

Not all doctors will prescribe contraceptives for single girls; however, many feel that while withholding prescriptions will not prevent sexual encounters, giving them will minimise the risk of hurting the couple, their parents, and their possible children. Even the most scrupulous doctor rarely asks for an engagement notice if approached by a girl wearing a ring.

1. Between Ourselves, not worth worrying about

(*a*) *Safe-time:* not called Roman Roulette for nothing. The human cycle is not as accurate as a twenty-eight-day clock. Human emotions do not follow a calendar.

(*b*) *Withdrawal:* not as easy as it looks. Not reliable. Messy. Emotionally inadvisable.

(*c*) *Douches:* not reliable. Emotionally inadvisable.

2. (See table)

TYPE	RELIABILITY	COST	CONSIDERATIONS	COMMENTS
2. Over the Counter.				
(a) condoms	Fair	12/6 to 16/6 doz.	Interrupts love-making. Uncomfortable for Him.	Protection against VD if partner is unreliable, otherwise strictly for the army.
(b) spermicides:				
(i) foaming tablets	Poor	9/- doz.	Unobtrusive. Uncomfortable for Her— rarely dissolve completely, leave granules. Irritate sensitive skin.	Effectiveness depends on freshness—cannot always rely on this. Easily washed away by semen.
(ii) suppositories	Poor	16/- doz.	Sticky for both partners— worse for Her. Unobtrusive.	Melt at blood heat—difficult to store in Australian temperatures. Less easily washed away than foaming tablets.
(iii) creams and jellies	Fair	11/- tube (about 15 doses)	Sticky for both partners, worse for Her.	More effective spermicidal agents than tablets or suppositories. Less easily washed away by semen than tablets.
(iv) pressure pack cream	Fair	Not available in Aust. Less expensive than tubes.	Least sticky.	As for iii.
3. On Prescription Only.				
(a) diaphragm or cap—usually used with cream or jelly	Good	Initial fitting £4/4/-. Set: £2/2/-. Includes jelly and applicator, cap and inserter. Subsequent cost as for cream.	Need not interrupt love-making. Sticky for both partners — a chore for Her.	Cap or diaphragm must be carefully inserted—it can shift during intercourse. Probably best buy for single students. May cause bleeding.
(b) Intrauterine Devices	Good	Initial fitting: Gynaecologist £4/4/- Anaesthetist £4/4/- Theatre £4/4/- I.U.D. silver 10/- plastic 6d. Annual check £4/4-	Most satisfactory.	Least susceptible to human error but can be expelled or simply fail. Unlimited return for cost.
(c) Oral Contraceptive Tablets	Excellent	18/- per month appr. £3/10/- to £4 for bulk packets. G.P.'s fee, plus 5/- per prescription.	Does not affect love-making. May cause weight increase. A chore for Her.	Even allowing for human error this is the most reliable method. Not suitable for people with kidney, liver disorders. Varying side effects from brand to brand and person to person— at least 20 brands are available, so experimentation is essential before rejection. Slight delay in effect at beginning, and between brand changes. Must be taken under medical supervision. More suitable for going steady or engaged couples.

II. ABORTION

Sex is human, not mechanical, and mistakes happen even to conscientious people. Before you start discussing what to do about a pregnancy, make sure that it is not a false alarm; 40 percent of women applying for a legal termination of pregnancy in Sweden were found to be not pregnant. A urine test costs from two to three guineas and takes only two days. A hormone test costs less than a pound with a prescription and takes up to a week. DO THIS PROMPTLY. It is an investment in peace of mind and ensures that you have time to make a considered decision about what to do next.

1. Forced Marriage

This is the preferred solution to the problem of unwanted pregnancy among single couples. In 1963, 28.7 percent of all first children born in wedlock in Australia were born within eight months or less of marriage, and most of these were born within six months of marriage. The illegitimacy rate for 1963 was 5.7 percent of total births, but only three illegitimate births occurred for every fourteen pre-nuptial conceptions. There is evidence from the United Kingdom that forced marriages and youthful marriages are less stable than others, suggesting that it is a temporary solution which has its own problems, but no local evidence is available on this point.

2. Adoption [Left blank in original. Ed.]

3. Keeping the Child

Local evidence suggests that this is not a preferred solution in the socio-economic group from which most of our students come. It is also less favoured throughout the community than termination of pregnancy when marriage is impossible. There are probably three terminations for every live birth among single girls. *The Unmarried Mother and Her Child,* by Virginia Wimperis, is a helpful discussion for those who would prefer this way out.

4. Termination of Pregnancy

(a) *Your family chemist can't help:* Thinking about abortion is often dangerously naïve; girls who would hesitate for moral or pragmatic reasons to approach a doctor for termination are still prepared to try old-wife remedies, although motorcycle rides have probably replaced the traditional fall downstairs, and the something-from-the-chemist is less likely to be lethal. The moral issue is the same whether termination is professionally done or not, but the end result can be disastrous if unprofessional methods are used. About a third of fertilised ova do not implant, or, if they do, later abort spontaneously (miscarriage), usually because the foetus is defective. Many irritants can encourage this natural tendency to miscarriage, but these points should be considered:

1. Any abortifacient strong enough to kill a foetus would probably be lethal to the mother. Now that hormones are readily available, chemists are less likely to sell the old mixtures of quinine, ergot and strychnine which used to be a stand-by. However, hormones such as duogynon and amenerone are not abortifacients; they merely cause a withdrawal bleeding if a woman is not pregnant. They are relatively harmless, but useless, expensive if purchased illicitly, and time-consuming. So is the use of a month's prescription of oral contraceptive tablets in one dose.

2. Even if the foetus dies, the body is left to expel it. A miscarriage can be an extremely painful experience and is just as liable to the complications of haemorrhage and infection as mechanical interference.

(*b*) *Do-it-yourself is out:* The use of random instruments, particularly a syringe or catheter, and amateur interference generally, tends to be restricted to lower income groups. However, others are sometimes persuaded to accept syringing from an unqualified helper or to do it themselves. This can cause almost instantaneous death through air-embolism. A large number of the deaths from abortion result from this. The remainder are accounted for by haemorrhage and infection associated with unqualified interference, often when the pregnancy is too far advanced to be terminated outside of hospital, and occasionally on women with a tendency to anaemia or some other complicating factor. The death rate is a minor problem compared to the rate of chronic illness, sterility, etc., due to unqualified interference.

(*c*) *The qualified practitioner:* The most commonly practised method of terminating pregnancy is the curettage. Other techniques are available for more advanced pregnancies, but are only possible within hospital conditions. The curette is used for many minor feminine complaints, such as excessive menstruation, polyps, aftereffects of miscarriage, etc. The procedure is routine, quick, and safe. Even when the procedure is used on a pregnant uterus, it is five times as safe as childbirth, if carried out in optimum conditions. The qualified practitioner aims at these conditions of hygiene, skill, and efficiency; he has a genuine interest in his patient's welfare, for the unskilled or careless person represents a public menace and is more likely to be apprehended and heavily punished.

The psychological effects of termination are probably more significant than the physical ones. A single girl not only loses a possible child, but has failed to secure a husband and may feel that she herself has been rejected even when she did not particularly want a baby. The strain of an illicit operation is probably more intense for the single girl. Nevertheless, these effects are not great and would only cause significant, lasting distress to someone predisposed to mental disturbance. Even women with religious objections to abortion—and there are probably as many of these who undergo termination as others—do not suffer undue stress.

III. THE OLD QUESTION

The University is not a vast sexual playground.

It is, on the whole, very much like the rest of the world.

Your sexual desires will probably be thwarted at every step by lack of opportunity, or ignorance, or lack of confidence in your own discrimination, or sheer inability to master the mechanics of getting in, on, or under a bed with someone else, or fear, or timidity, or most likely a great porridge of all these.

Yet the University does differ from the rest of society in some sexually relevant respects. Many people are not at home for the first time in their lives and hence have a greater sense of independence. Attitudes are likely to be modified by the new environment. You are also likely to have deeper and more important contact with other people.

After all, sexual relations rarely exist in limbo, but are extensions of friendship and acquaintance, and your general outlook on the world. In its simplest terms what the University does offer is somewhat more opportunity. But one cannot even generalise about this, because it is a function of a host of variables both within yourself and without.

It is more likely to be these mundane little things, rather than decisions of principle, which will dominate your sex life. That is assuming that you have a general bias in favour of sexual intercourse. Unfortunately, this cannot be assumed at all.

Policy decisions made without regard for situations in which you actually find yourself are absurd, for they are a retreat into dogma from the facts of your existence. The rule 'Pre-marital sexual intercourse is always wrong' is an abnegation of individual judgement. Principles of living should emerge from your experience and not be planted on you from outside.

Handling sexual encounters, like all human relationships, tests your moral and social skill. A skill is something learned; it is not the invariable application of a hard and fast rule.

Religious objections are of a special sort because, no matter how well reasoned they may appear, they ultimately appeal to something beyond the reasons themselves, namely, the supernatural power of God and the emotional force of the concept of evil. Deciding whether you will sleep with someone is a practical, not a metaphysical, problem. Human situations must be handled in human terms.

The arguments that sexual intercourse is unnatural when it is not for the purpose of having children, and that it is degraded when it is not sanctified by marriage, appeal to concepts which can only be regarded as quaint when we pause to look at the facts with which we are all familiar. Indeed, this is the form of religious objections, that they subordinate facts that we know about particular human situations to rigid and contrary rules from beyond the realms of human experience.

As for the matter of degradation, like any human contact making love can be either trivial or very important, and it rests with your own discrimination whether you elevate or degrade your body. The dilemma remains: if you value your virginity too much you may never lose it.

Social objections are certainly less important at the University. The value of virginity slumps a little. People who sleep together are more likely to evoke a slight admiration than condemnation. But discreetness prevails here as elsewhere, and one does not become a slut or a rake overnight. On the whole, the fact that people do sleep together is taken much more for granted.

Sheer sexual ignorance, and hence fear and uncertainty, remains as the ogre hiding behind many elaborate arguments. There is just as serious a lack of sex education at the University as there is in the rest of our education system. Indeed, here it is much more serious because people are more likely to be going through a crucial period in their sexual lives. Knowing that you ought to use contraceptives is hardly enough to guarantee a successful night in bed.

The important thing about arguing the rights and wrongs of pre-marital sex is that the arguments should not become dissociated from the facts, petty as they may often seem to be. All that the decision in favour can be is a general bias. It is the decision against which is rigid because it rests on a prediction about individual cases which seems to be unjustified. It means that particular situations in which you find yourself are irrelevant. It is the claim that pre-marital sex is wrong no matter what: that it is intrinsically evil. This is no argument; it is at best an excuse.

The Student Health Service and Sex Education

Z. N. Kadri

INTRODUCTION

The function of our Student Health Service is threefold: to prevent and treat minor and major sicknesses, to administer medical counselling, and to impart health education whenever possible. It is in our role as medical counsellors and informal health educators that we come across the complex sex problems of our youth.

When the word *sex* is mentioned it arouses all sorts of mixed feelings in different individuals. It may produce feelings of curiosity, amusement, excitement, pleasure, or even disgust, depending upon one's background and upbringing. To some the subject of sex is taboo. But sex should not be equated with sexuality or promiscuity. There are many parents and seniors who feel that the imparting of sex education will lead to sexual experimentation by young people. In their view, the imparting of sex knowledge is tantamount to condoning and encouraging sexuality. But this fear is entirely unfounded. In my opinion, sex education given to the younger generation will not lead to sexuality; on the contrary, it will give them a better understanding of the physical and emotional aspects of love and sex, and help them in developing better inner controls and strengthening their sex personalities. Scientific knowledge of sex is meant to prepare and equip the young to face distressing psychological conflicts arising from various sex situations they may face from time to time.

The subject of sex and the problems arising from it in the Student Health Practice fall into four distinct categories:

1. To Provide Medical Information (Remedial Sex Education)

One may be surprised, but our youngsters can often be victims of old fairy tales and misconceptions regarding menstruation, nocturnal discharge, masturbation, masculinity, feminity, homosexuality, and menopause. Most of our young men and women need to be enlightened and given scientific information on these subjects.

2. To Help in Developing Healthy Sex Attitudes

In this category fall the actual prospects and problems of human sex relationships between a young boy and a girl. There may be the problem of uneven romance. Or, there may be the problem of dating and going steady and the consequences following upon the heavy investment of emotion by both partners in their relationship. Here the student may be in conflict as to whether the deep emotions which go with love should or should not be translated into physical relationship. This raises the question of pre-marital sex and all the consequences arising from it.

3. Pre-marital Medical Examination and Counselling

In the case of couples seriously contemplating marriage or who are already married, we are at times called upon to discuss methods of contraception, including the advantages and disadvantages of various methods.

4. Research

Lastly there is the research aspect of sex in our society, which, in so far as our Student Health Service is concerned, has unfortunately remained totally neglected because of lack of time and shortage of staff.

UNIVERSITY EDUCATION AND SEX VALUES

The function of university education is not only to acquire degrees and diplomas, to gather information and advance the frontiers of knowledge, but also to be critical of our traditional standards and values in an ever changing world. In this respect, I would like to emphasise that our student community, especially in a multi-cultural society like ours, should be in the forefront of cultural realignment.

Our students come from a wide variety of cultural backgrounds. These cultures in turn have many subcultures, with their own moral codes, standards, and values, even in regard to sex. The only common sex denominator in the past between the Chinese, the Malays, and the Indians was the practice of polygamy in its different forms. However, recent legislation, the influence of Western culture with its Christian values, and the emancipation of women through modern education, have given a new dimension to our sex attitudes.

However, in the immediate wake of these benevolent social influences which were in the process of preparing us to switch from polygamous to monogamous societies, we are now faced with an entirely new situation with its new attitudes towards sex, especially in our younger generation. This new sex atmosphere, as I will mention soon, is due directly or indirectly to the tremendous technological and medical advances that have taken place within the past twenty years; and to the economic affluence of Singapore and Malaysia.

CAUSES OF CHANGING SEXUAL ATTITUDES AND MORALITY

Let us examine the causes which have led, within the recent past, to changes in our attitudes towards sex and the relaxation of sexual moral controls.

1. We suddenly find ourselves living in an atmosphere which not only condones casual attitudes toward sex but appears to encourage sex. Take, for example, our popular movies, TV films, novels, magazines, and commercial advertisements. They seem to give the impression to young people that there is nothing wrong with these new sex attitudes. It is interesting to note that we, the so-called mature adults, put a seal of approval on the products of these mass media, but at the same time become critical and even resentful when young people indulge in the behaviour borrowed from these media.

2. The first social need of a young individual is to achieve economic security for himself and his family. In this complex and competitive age with its technological culture, better economic security requires an increasing specialisation in education and vocational skills. This entails longer years of study, during the age period when the biological sex impulses are not only new but very strong. Thus marriage and consummation of sex have to be delayed till one starts earning a living.

3. Since we started learning to conquer nature through modern science and technology, the influence of religion has gradually declined. Consequent upon this, the fear of divine wrath in matters of sex is diminishing fast.

4. In our highly authoritarian society, until recently, parents and guardians had all the say in the selection of marriage partners. But, they have now started relaxing these controls.

5. Before coming to the university most of our students were sheltered by the environment of family and friends, which meant living within a framework of traditional rules and customs. Entry to the university or any institution of higher learning generally speaking removes these controlling influences or supports.

6. Fear of catching venereal diseases from clandestine sex relations

has diminished considerably. And this is obviously due to modern medical advances in the field of treatment of these diseases.

7. Another impact of modern medicine on our sex attitudes is manifested through contraceptives. New knowledge of contraceptives and their easy availability have decreased the fear of unwanted pregnancies.

8. In an affluent society, better communication systems, (e.g., telephones) and better transportation (e.g., motor-cars) afford better opportunities to unmarried young couples to be alone and to resort to frequent wooings and courtings.

9. Knowledge of psychology and Sigmund Freud's influence on the young sophisticated youth have given intellectual respectability to sex. But this, as I will mention later, is a rather distorted view of the original theory propounded by Sigmund Freud.[2]

10. Lastly, it may be added that anthropologists believe that puberty, or biological maturity, occurs earlier nowadays, by about two years, than it used to at the turn of the century. In support of this argument it is pointed out that girls used to start menstruating at the age of about fifteen years then, whereas now the menarche starts when they reach the age of twelve to thirteen years. Early physical maturation also occurs in boys. Thus, it is obvious that physiological and biochemical maturity, with the resultant sex urges, are achieved much earlier than social maturity and economic independence and security.

HOW PARENTS CAN HELP IN THE DEVELOPMENT OF HEALTHY SEX ATTITUDES

In the light of what has been said, no amount of high-handedness and authoritarian moral codes imposed by parents and society will change the new perspective of sex among the young people of today. Since all the previously enumerated external controls which guided our past sex attitudes are gone or are in the process of tottering, we have to look for better inner controls. Let us examine how, as future teachers of our own children at home, or as teachers in schools, or as administrators and community leaders, we should go about helping better inner controls in the succeeding generations.

Parental responsibility in preparing sound sexual health and stability of their children can be summarised thus: [3]

(a) Love and affection to be shown and given freely and equally to all children.

(b) Discipline to be applied firmly and consistently. This should be exemplified by example and not precept.

(c) Parents should devote as much time, attention, and interest to their children as possible.

(*d*) Parents should discuss objectively with their teenage children the significance of all the past and present values, social codes, and customs. A free and democratic approach involving the pros and cons of various value systems will stimulate critical thinking.

These four parental attitudes will give inner strength and control to the young man's personality. This approach will give the young men and women in a university a better chance to confront moral challenges and extreme forms of undesirable influences, and to withstand adverse pressures from other friends and companions.

HOW TO DEAL WITH SEXUAL IMPULSES IN A UNIVERSITY

Suppression

Freud demonstrated that many psychological and psychosomatic disorders resulted from repressed sexual conflicts or problems. Repression is an involuntary and unconscious mechanism, and psychologically not a healthy phenomenon. But suppression of sex is an entirely different way of tackling our sexual desires and conflicts. It is a deliberate and conscious refusal of the mind to entertain a thought pertaining to sex; or, having entertained the idea, there is a conscious refusal to act upon it. Suppression is rarely considered harmful, psychologically speaking. Freud himself pointed out that restraint in sex is necessary for the survival and progress of civilisation.

Freud believed that refraining from sex for good reasons or necessity for certain lengths of time cannot be harmful. On the contrary, it can help build character, and this is applicable, for example, to unmarried couples deeply in love. It is in their own interest that emotional relationship, however intense it may become, should be stopped short of physical relationship.

Sublimation

Sex is a powerful force but at the same time it is a respectable force. One should not be afraid or ashamed of it. Sex, however, should be sublimated. This means that one should try to express basic drives of love through more socially acceptable channels, for instance, through better academic studies, extracurricular activities, and participation in sports and athletics. It must be remembered that many famous paintings, pieces of music, literary works, and medical and engineering discoveries are the products of a large amount of sublimated sex energy.

Boredom is one of the common causes which lead some young people to experiment with sex. They have no stimulus or inspiration to do anything, and therefore they find life boring and turn to exploits in the field of sex. Hence, it is desirable that all young men and women should, besides routine academic work, take an interest in and participate in various cultural activities. If they keep themselves occupied during their leisure hours by constructive social and cultural activities, the chances of being obsessed by ideas of sex will be reduced.

In conclusion, I would like to state that, in spite of all their sex problems, our students are a very sober lot in matters of sex and possess relatively high moral standards. I would also like to add that students may talk a lot about sex, but, generally speaking, they are much more conservative in action.

NOTES

[1] Text of a speech delivered to University of Singapore students at Raffles Hall on 30th August 1967.

[2] Dalrymple, W. "A Doctor Speaks of College Students & Sex", *Journal of American College Health Association*, February 1967, Vol. 15, No. 3, p. 280.

[3] *Ibid.*, p. 283.

The Sex Upbringing of the Rising Generation

V. N. Kolbanovskii

The sex life of man is a field that has received relatively little study. The natural laws of the sexual development of men and women have been studied more profoundly, but the role of social conditions and their influence on the sex life of people have been elucidated much less adequately. Yet it is in this very area that the contradictions between the natural and social laws of development of a person manifest themselves with particular force, and they are by no means always resolved normally and painlessly.

In spite of the high level of consciousness of our people, which has been attained on the basis of tremendous sociopolitical, economic, and cultural transformations, there is still much that is inappropriate in the sex relations between men and women. The attention of the public has frequently been drawn to facts of unbecoming behavior on the part of some young people. We also see it in the "moral freedom" that is displayed in licentiousness.

The sexual development of the rising generation proceeds in a completely spontaneous way. Parents, teachers, and doctors devote much attention to questions concerning the physical and mental development of children. They develop the aesthetic tastes and needs of their charges and instill positive moral qualities with great care. But where questions relating to the sexual development of children and adolescents are concerned, adults pay extremely little attention to them and even prefer to ignore them in order to avoid difficult situations. Young people are forced to seek an explanation of the phenomena that puzzle them on their own and to get their knowledge from sources that are not always pure. And because adolescents are uninformed and unprepared as regards questions of sex life, they frequently go through the stage of pubescence with great harm to themselves. Sometimes they gratify their sexual need artificially, and the habit of onanism can have a grave effect upon the development of the personality. In some cases young people begin their sex life prematurely or, under the influence of depraved adults, descend to sexual perversion.

When we ponder such phenomena, our attention first turns to an analysis of their causes. When there are crimes, of course, those who are directly guilty should be punished. But that is not enough. Parents and teachers also are responsible for the behavior of their charges, for their sex development and upbringing.

E. Rozanova, in an article entitled "While There Is Still Time" (*Molodoi kommunist* [Young Communist], 1963, No. 1), writes that, under the impression produced by the trial of a group of rapists in the city of Kuibyshev, she decided to find out what scientific institutions in our country are engaged in investigating questions concerning the sexual development of the rising generation. With this aim in view, this journalist visited the scientific institutes of the RSFSR Academy of Pedagogical Sciences and the U.S.S.R. Academy of Medicine, but did not find a single section or laboratory, or even a researcher, occupied with these questions.

Is it not time for those of us who work in the fields of pedagogy, psychology, and medicine to admit, in self-criticism, that such an attitude toward one of the important questions relating to the development and upbringing of the rising generation is absolutely intolerable? We well know that in our country all questions concerning economic and cultural development and the rearing of the new man are solved on a solid scientific basis. And it is only from such a standpoint that we must approach, in particular, questions having to do with the sex upbringing of the youth.

However, there are theoreticians in the fields of pedagogy and medicine who declare that we have no sex problem, that individual excesses and abnormalities still do not provide grounds for occupying ourselves with these questions. A large part of the youth are healthy in this respect, but there have always been, and perhaps there will continue to be, individual sexual psychopaths. Such arguments testify to the shortsightedness of their authors, and to their complete lack of understanding of the fact that if we do not combat evil, it can assume the dimensions of a great social danger.

There is another viewpoint of sex upbringing. According to this view, it cannot be isolated from the entire system of moral upbringing. If it is, an inevitable magnification of the sex question will begin, and that is nothing else than Freudianism with its inherent hypertrophy of the sex life of man, which the Freudians regard as the key not only to an explanation of the various neuroses and psychoses, but also to an understanding of the more complex phenomena of social life. This position is also profoundly incorrect. Soviet psychology and medicine have long outlived the period of noncritical enthusiasm for Freudianism and other associated concepts. It was partly as a reaction to this former enthusiasm that the position of "noninterference" in the sex life of young people originated, a position which the sciences of medicine and pedagogy have long occupied. But along with the soapy water of Freudianism, they also threw out the child—the problem of the sexual development of a person from his early years to maturity. As a result, Soviet pedagogy and medicine do not have at their disposal sufficient scientific material to enable them to elaborate substantiated scientific recommendations.

For many years Soviet pedagogy was reproached with being childless. And when the child finally occupied an appropriate place in the pedagogical literature, it turned out to be sexless—neither a boy nor a girl, but a creature of neuter gender. In reality, however, there are no children of this kind. From the very first days of the child's life, we must take sex differences into consideration, if only in the hygienic care provided. We must also bear in mind the sex differences in the maturing of the speech-locomotor system. Girls are usually half a year ahead of boys. Pubescence in girls also begins somewhat earlier.

There are no grounds for taking sex differences into consideration in mental and aesthetic upbringing. But as regards physical upbringing, we must, apart from general physical exercises and the hardening of the body, make distinctions in our choice of certain types of sports for girls and boys. The norms for boys with respect to running, jumping, swimming, skating, skiing, and bicycling differ from those for girls. Some gymnastic exercises—weight-lifting, pole-vaulting—and such types of sports as football, hockey, boxing, and wrestling, are contraindicated for girls, not only because of biological considerations, but also for aesthetic reasons.

Certain distinctions must be made between girls and boys in their moral upbringing. Without doubt, the general principles of the moral code of the builder of communism must be learned and applied in practice by both girls and boys. But there are certain norms of behavior that are specific for boys and for girls. Unfortunately, they have not become a subject of ethics and moral upbringing and do not regulate the mutual relations between boys and girls in the early age periods of their development. These moral standards and principles, along with hygienic recommendations, should constitute the specific character of sex upbringing.

The complete liberation of women from a twofold exploitation—that of the husband and of the boss—and their achievement of equality as regards all rights are among the great gains of the socialist revolution. For thousands of years the leaders of various religions, and also reactionary philosophers, scientists, and political leaders of the ruling classes, spread slanderous lies about the alleged biological and social inferiority of women. These concoctions became part of the traditions and customs of peoples, of their folklore and social psychology. The ideologists of the exploiters made a great effort to consolidate an attitude toward woman as a being of a lower order whose lot in life was the limited world of the family.

The experience of the socialist revolution has refuted, on a tremendous scale, this malicious propaganda of the reactionaries. Woman, having entered into the great work of building a new life, became a powerful creative force of socialist society. She received access to the summits of education and has been actively participating in all fields of sociopolitical, economic, and cultural work.

Thanks to this, the nature of the relations between men and women also changed in socialist society. The suppressed and desecrated feeling of love was freed from the oppression of private ownership relations. This most powerful and beautiful of human feelings developed and blossomed under the new social conditions. It became the chief and basic motive in marriage and the creation of a family.

Children constitute the natural goal and the loftiest meaning of human love. When born and reared in a family where the mutual love and respect of the parents are firmly established, the children grow and develop normally, experiencing the love of their parents and feeling filial love for them. Under the beneficial influence of the parents, they themselves begin to display feelings of brotherly and sisterly love, which becomes an expression of their humane feelings for their contemporaries.

A. S. Makarenko ascribed great significance to the experience of nonsexual love which children acquire in harmonious families. Through this experience they are prepared for their future love, when the time for it arrives. The foundations of the future individual, his physical and mental abilities, the aesthetic tastes, needs, and moral qualities of the future person and citizen, are laid and formed in a setting of firm family happiness. This constitutes the lofty goal and basic content of rearing children in the family. Makarenko said that in providing the child with a sex upbringing, we are not yet rearing the future citizen and person. But if we rear the child as a future person and citizen, we thereby rear him sexually as well.

Unfortunately, carried away by the idea of the social equality of men and women and by the propaganda on the achievements in this field, we completely ignored the question of the essential biological differences between them. Sexual differences are not limited to the specific features in the anatomical structure of the body of the man and woman, and the corresponding differences in physiological processes that are closely linked with psychological experiences. The chief difference is the dissimilarity in the fulfillment, by the man and the woman, of the main function of continuing the human species. The functions of the woman, the mother, in many respects surpass the duties of the man, the father, as regards their significance and complexity. It is the woman who, in the main, takes care of the child, feeds him, sees to it that he has the proper food, sleep, and hygienic care, develops his ability to understand the world, and molds his behavior. Even the widely developing system of children's educational institutions cannot fully relieve her of these functions. The attachment of a mother to the child whom she bore under her heart, her concern for every step in his development, her care for his health, her control over his deeds, her sharing of the child's first joys and griefs—all that is customarily called a mother's love, which has so frequently been extolled by poets of all times and all peoples, is a guarantee of the happiness of the child. We by no means want to belittle the role of the father in rearing the child, but in terms of its biological and, in part, its social significance it can in no way be compared with that of the mother. Our Party and state have placed a high value on the function of the mother, rendering her financial aid in rearing a third child and increasing this aid with the birth of every additional child. Our country has over seventy-five thousand heroine-mothers, and more than eight million mothers who have been awarded the order of "Maternal Glory" and the "Motherhood" medal.

However, in the rearing of the youth, attention is not always paid to the need to accord special respect to the woman who fulfills, or is getting ready to fulfill, the responsible function of a mother. Many fathers have also not become accustomed to doing that. They are indifferent to the fact that their wives are burdened with important, but petty and dulling, housework, and to how much energy the women expend in bringing up the children. Husbands do not always try to lighten this labor and to assume part of the care.

Sociological investigations conducted in Moscow, Sverdlovsk, Izhevsk, and Novosibirsk to ascertain how men and women who work under the same industrial conditions use their free time, showed that women spend three to four hours daily on housework and rearing the children, and nine to eleven hours on their free days. The men, however, use this time for self-education, participation in the rationalization of production, sports, and amateur art activities. Naturally, such an uneven distribution of duties in the family sooner or later leads to the woman lagging behind in her cultural development, to her becoming prematurely worn out physically, and to her wasting away. And this is often the cause of dramas and even tragedies in the family, which begins to crack and fall apart, the children remaining semiorphans while both parents are alive. If the family does remain intact, the children become the witnesses of tiffs, arguments, and even major quarrels. The parents do not hesitate to hurl serious, sometimes groundless, accusations at each other in the presence of their children. Every such situation is contrary to pedagogy. The husband's coarse treatment of his wife leaves a terrible imprint on the child's mind. On the one hand, the young son feels like protesting and defending his mother, but, on the other hand, the thought arises that women deserve such treatment. It is therefore not surprising that the boy who has received such an up-bringing in the family becomes a threat to girls of his own age and beats them every time he has an opportunity to do so. How important it is to explain to parents that the slightest violation of the principle of "mutual respect in the family" is fraught with pernicious conse-quences for the children, especially for boys, who inevitably develop traits of rudeness and caddishness and an inclination to resort to violence. Makarenko showed no mercy to those members of the colony who were even slightly rude to the girl members of the colony. Today a boy will pull a girl's braid, and if we close our eyes to this prank, when he becomes an adolescent he will insult the girl with coarse, foul language; later, when a young man, he will commit violence against her.

From the boy's early years, from the moment when he begins to speak, it is necessary to instill in him a feeling of respect and regard for girls. Inasmuch as boys are physically stronger than girls, it is impor-tant to explain to them that man has been given his strength in order to protect the weak. Kindergarten teachers are doing the right thing when they teach the boys to help the girls put on their coats, to give them something they have dropped or some toy, and to offer them their seats at some children's matinee. Politeness that is instilled in children from their early years and becomes a habit can have a favorable effect upon the entire manner of the future relations between children of the two sexes when they become older.

An attitude of respect toward women must be cultivated in school as well. All elements of hostility in the relations between boys and girls, especially elements of aggressiveness on the part of the boys, must be eliminated. Aggressiveness is not an innate trait, but it is frequently taken over from the ideology and morality of the old society. Coarse scenes sometimes take place in the presence of children, and the youths acquire bad experience in the treatment of women. That is why it is so important to develop in schoolchildren staunch resis-tance to bad examples which they may take over from life uncritically.

The dialectics and beauty of the relations between men and women must be revealed to boys, especially to adolescents and youths. By using the finest examples of their creative cooperation and the portraits of literary heroes of classic and modern works, we must show them the beauty of the physical and spiritual aspect of woman and explain the profound meaning of the happiness that sincere love brings to man. The poetic perception and cognition of love should be a prelude to the actual experience of this wonderful feeling.

On the other hand, we must also develop in girls pure, tender reciprocal feelings for their brothers or the boys who play and study with them. When pubescence begins, the girl must be gradually pre-pared to understand the future role of the woman and mother. This must not affect the main task, that of preparing girls for their future productive and socially useful work. But regardless of the type of work the woman will do in the future, it is important that she be prepared for the experience of pure and honest love, and for motherhood.

The frivolous behavior of some women is a serious obstacle in the way of such upbringing. Sometimes the mothers themselves behave in that way; more often it is others, whose behavior the adults describe in great detail, regardless of the presence of children. Bad examples are particularly infectious. Katia Ts., a fourth-grade pupil of a Moscow school, sent ten notes simultaneously to boys in her class, inviting them to her home on various days at different hours: "Misha, come to see me on Wednesday at seven o'clock in the evening. We'll kiss. Katia." When, besides Misha, other boys, such as Petia and Kolia, received similar invitations, they took them to their grade teacher. "How could you send notes to ten different boys? Anyway, it's too early for you to make appointments with boys. . . . I can understand that you might like one or another of them, but why did you send notes to all ten of them at once?" the teacher asked the girl. And Katia answered: "My mama always does that. As soon as Papa leaves for the institute, Mama first phones Iuri Andreyevich and invites him to the movies; then she phones Pavel Semenovich and arranges to meet him at the ballet; she wants to see Valerii Fedorovich at the exhibition, and she invites Mikhail Konstantinovich to the house for supper when Papa goes off on a business trip." It never even occurred to Katia's mother that she was crippling her daughter morally with her telephone conversations. And other adults hardly consider this when, in the presence of children, they relish the piquant details of the behavior of their acquaintances and relate scabrous anecdotes.

Some morally depraved people spread views among the youth to the effect that "maidenly honor" or "a woman's virtue" are narrow-minded prejudices which should have been overcome long ago, that love was given to man for his pleasure, and that if there is a "slip-up"—pregnancy—it is easy to get rid of it.

Such antisocial arguments must be combated by rearing adolescent girls and young women to be serious in their attitude toward love. They must be persuaded that any flippancy in love results in the inevitable squandering of this feeling, to the spiritual bankruptcy of the person, not to speak of more terrible consequences.

In firmly established, harmonious families, the young men and women are usually prepared for their first love. And when this radiant, joyous feeling comes to them, they are far from the thought of sexual intimacy. They are more attracted by the spiritual contact, the community of interests and plans, joint participation in sports, science, art, or cultural entertainment. And if the parents and teachers are suitably tactful in their attitude toward these experiences, the young man or woman will not suffer any unpleasant experiences. But it frequently happens that the adults, fearing possible excesses, interfere in the experience of the young lovers in a coarse and tactless way. The Kiev film studio produced a movie entitled "What If It Is Love?" We may differ about its artistic merits and defects, but there is one unquestionable conclusion that we can draw from it: The unreasonable, insensitive attitude of the parents and the sanctimonious behavior of the teachers inflicted a grievous wound on two loving hearts. This conflict almost ended tragically for the girl, and the young people lost hope that they would find happiness in the future.

Both parents and teachers should be very thoughtful, serious, and tactful in their attitude toward the first feelings of love. They must win the confidence of the lovers so that they will be frank and share their personal feelings and plans for the future with the older people. The tactful intervention and advice of people who have been made wise by experience will not cause the young people any suffering, whereas coarse mockery, vulgar insinuations or outright insults can result in a complete break in the relations between parents and children, between teachers and their charges.

We began our consideration of the problems of sex upbringing with an analysis of the relations between men and women in socialist society and in the family, inasmuch as the healthy, highly moral character of these relations is the chief condition for the correct sex upbringing of the rising generation.

When stressing the importance of positive examples of behavior on the part of parents and teachers, it is also necessary to call attention to the development in children of staunch resistance to the bad influence of men who still have a coarse and cynical attitude toward women, and of those women who have taken over aspects of wanton behavior from the old morality.

"To teach to love, to teach to recognize love, to teach to be happy means to teach for oneself, to teach human dignity," A. S. Makarenko wrote.[1] Parents and teachers must use all the means of ideology and culture in order to achieve this goal—fiction, films, the theater, painting, sculpture, music, and the dance. It must be pointed out that young people do not find works in present-day fiction about the beauty of great and real love, works that produce a deep impression. And so they have recourse to other sources, which, in this respect, are far from instructive. For instance, a study of readers' interests recently done in several Moscow libraries showed that the books in greatest demand by young readers are the works of Remarque, in particular his *L'Arc de Triomphe;* then come the works of Guy de Maupassant, and in third place, the works of Zola, especially his *Nana.* The youth, "children up to sixteen years of age," watch with equal interest, and with the obvious connivance of the adults, movies and TV broadcasts of Western films that treat sex life in the spirit of bourgeois amorality. A similar attitude is developed toward Western music, and especially dance music. It is a short step from this to imitating the sexual morality of a world that is alien to us.

Soviet writers and artists are faced with the responsible task of satisfying the spiritual needs of our youth, in particular the task of reflecting the essence and dialectics of love in the spirit of the lofty principles and norms of communist morality. And it must be done in an interesting, artistic form that instills purity and honesty in relations between men and women that are free of all vulgarity and abomination.

"Sexual life reveals not only what has been given by nature, but also what has been introduced by culture, whether lofty or low," said V. I. Lenin.[2]

The lofty in love contributes to the nobility, purity, and beauty of human relations and to the moral progress of society as a whole. That which is base in love leads to a coarsening of morals and a lack of restraint, to an arousing of the animal in man and to the moral degradation of the person. Culture must triumph over what is base in man, inasmuch as culture is the organized rule of reason over the animal instincts of people (M. Gorky).

In the 1920s the pedagogical and psychological literatures paid serious attention to the natural laws governing the development of the child. Then it was considered that this placed too much emphasis on the biological, and the chief stress was placed on social laws. Such avoidance of the issue could not help but harm the subject of study. In particular, the process of the sexual development of children was ignored since, as it primarily involved natural laws, there again arose the danger of being accused of overemphasizing the biological. There is a saying to the effect that "if you drive nature out through the door, it will fly in through the window." Life itself compels us to take up the question of the sexual development of the rising generation. The task consists only in considering the natural and social laws of this process from all aspects, and in giving each its due place.

The first question that arises is, When does the sex life of man begin, with the start of his pubescence or earlier?

Freud, other like-minded persons, and his followers declare that the sources of man's sexual life are latent in early childhood. In one of his essays, Freud describes an infant at the moment he is suckling. The infant greedily sucks his mother's breast, then, feeling satisfied, releases the breast, caresses it with his hand, and again begins suckling and plays with the breast once more. His little face has become flushed, his eyes shine, and he smiles. In other words, he experiences not only the gratification of satiation, but also real erotic pleasure. Although this description is rather colorful, it is, as regards its objective content, a slander of the innocent infant. Those systems which would enable him to experience erotic pleasure have not as yet developed in his body.

Even more muddled and just as speculative is the notorious "Oedipus complex," according to which a little boy is capable of feeling real jealousy with respect to his mother and a desire to kill his father. According to Freud, a little girl is capable of feeling similar emotions, although in not so sharp a form; she is jealous of her father and ready to get rid of her mother. The creator of psychoanalysis relates many of the neuroses and psychoses of adults with the "Oedipus complex," although such scenes of "jealousy" on the part of little children are, from beginning to end, artificially provoked by adults. Children are incapable of experiencing such feelings if adults, when playing with them, do not incite them in corresponding ways.

We are absolutely opposed to the assertions that child sexuality arises in early childhood. However, a number of studies (P. P. Blonskii's *Ocherki detskoi seksual'nosti* [Essays on Child Sexuality]) and observations made by doctors and teachers persuade us that if certain elementary rules regarding the hygienic care of children are violated, a premature development of sexuality may occur. That, however, is not the norm, but the exception, the deviation from the norm.

What violations do we have in mind? First of all, instances in which little children are kept in a slovenly state. Doctors and teachers, when instructing parents, do not always call their attention to the importance of hygienic care of the sex organs of children, and to the need for struggle against onanistic actions that arise unconsciously. Various kinds of helminths also incite early child sexuality. Boys and girls, beginning from the age of five or six, like to slide down the banisters of stairways. They receive pleasure not so much from the actual process of sliding as from the rubbing and warming of their genitals, which, at this age, is accompanied by erotic sensations. Sometimes early sexuality is stimulated by physical punishment, as when the child receives a blow on his buttocks from a parent's strong hand.

Irritation of the genitals can be eliminated if the causes for it are eradicated. If attention is not paid to these abnormal phenomena, onanistic actions become habitual. When children are washed at home, the nursery, or the kindergarten, boys and girls are together and they display curiosity regarding their genitals. Most of them are content with a simple statement of the fact of sex differences, but some show an abnormal interest in examining the genitals or in displaying their own peculiarities. If the curiosity of the children does not extend beyond contemplating and thinking about what they have seen (exhibitionism), there is no great harm in this. But some children proceed to handling their genitals, which results in obvious erotic excitation. In such cases it is better to separate even little children according to sex during bathing.

A lack of restraint on the part of parents and other adults in expressing their feelings is of great harm to the children. Children sometimes see the adults kiss each other passionately, and, what is much worse, they become involuntary witnesses of their intimate life. They begin to show curiosity and try to find out from their older and better-informed friends what it all means.

Those parents who take their little children into their beds are making a serious mistake. At first this action is prompted by the simple desire to play with the child or to quiet him. The child becomes accustomed to awakening in the morning in bed with Mama or Papa, and then begins to insist upon sleeping with them the whole night. If such sleep with the parents continues for a number of years and the vague erotic sensations of the child are not, naturally, completed, they often become transformed into a fear of space (agoraphobia). This is difficult to cure later, even among adults.

When analyzing the facts of child sexuality, we are not inclined to exaggerate their importance. They constitute a relatively rare exception to the general rule about the laws governing the development of young children. However, they do testify to the consequences that can arise in children before the beginning of pubescence if parents and teachers do not take timely measures. It goes without saying that it is necessary to train doctors, teachers, and parents for prophylactic measures against such phenomena.

Under conditions of a temperate climate, pubescence in boys and girls begins at the age of twelve and continues for two or three years. This age (adolescence) differs from the younger school age as regards the impetuous changes in the body, the intensive development of the personality, and the considerable changes in the system of the endocrine glands. The goiter, or thymus, gland ceases its activity, and the sex glands, which until this period were in a somnolent, inactive state, begin theirs. The entire endocrine system is connected with the complex interrelations of individual glands—antagonists and synergists. The sex glands are both endocrine and external secretion glands. When secreting hormones that enter the blood stream, the sex glands affect the activity of the thyroid gland, the adrenal glands, the pancreas, the hypophysis (the pituitary gland), and others. It is well known that insignificant quantities of hormones, expressed even in hundred-thousandths of a milligram, have a considerable effect upon growth and the functioning of the body tissues, and intensify or retard various forms of metabolism.

The beginning of pubescence is manifested in a number of ways, as in the intensive growth of the skeleton and the muscular system, with which the growth of the inner organs—the heart, lungs, gastrointestinal tract, etc.—cannot always keep up. This accounts for the fact that boys and girls often suffer from dizziness, and that their extremities turn blue and cold; the heart cannot cope with supplying blood for the entire body.

The most important sign of this age, which foreign educators and psychologists call the age of pubescence, is the beginning of sex processes—the periodic monthly cycles (menstruation) in girls, and the involuntary night discharge of semen (pollution) in boys, which is often accompanied by erotic dreams. If adolescents are not prepared for these phenomena, they arouse complete bewilderment in them. The periodic tension in the sexual sphere frequently prompts them to seek release in artificial self-gratification, i.e., in onanism. In some the actualization of onanistic manipulations which arose in early childhood takes place, while in others they appear for the first time. In the early period of pubescence, boys and girls concentrate much of their attention on their sexual experiences, ask their friends about them, read literature that is chiefly about love. Sometimes those who suffer from onanism exert all their efforts to get rid of this vice.

The whole intricate perturbation that takes place in the body and in the psychic make-up of the developing personality cannot help but be reflected in the activity of the central nervous system. The brain is not only a regulator of the entire vital activity of the body and an organ for the adaptation of man to his surroundings, an organ of psychic activity. It also feels the reverse action that proceeds from the internal medium of the organism. Under the influence of its intense activity during this period, the brain, too, becomes somewhat overstrained. The operation of the "force and effect" law, which was discovered by I. P. Pavlov, changes. Its essence consists of the following: the response reaction of the normal organism or organ to irritation is directly proportional to the force of the irritation. When the central nervous system is overstrained, its normal excitability passes into the so-called leveling phase: strong and weak stimuli evoke the same response. When the brain is further overstrained, its excitability passes into the paradoxical phase, when strong stimuli evoke a weak effect, and weak ones a strong effect. When, finally, the overstrain of the brain reaches almost the limit, the excitability passes into the ultraparadoxical phase, when the responses are contradictory not only to the irritation, but also to the source of irritation, and a negative reaction is established.

This brief excursion into the field of physiology was necessary in order to explain certain strange aspects of the behavior of adolescents in a period that is critical for them (apathy, an indifference to events taking place around them). Before this, the boy or girl who received good and excellent marks in school subjects sincerely rejoiced, and felt upset if the marks were bad. Now they begin to be equally indifferent to an excellent or bad mark for their studies. Some mothers complain to the children's teachers: "I don't know what's wrong with my Kolia. He used to be a person, but now he's like an unfeeling idol; nothing bothers him, nothing gives him pleasure." Such behavior is characteristic of the leveling phase of the excitability of the nervous system.

In other cases the adolescent reacts weakly to a failure in his work or, on the contrary, to praise for a good deed. But if he should fail to find a pencil in the place where he put it, he can go into a hysterical tantrum over what is essentially a trifle, and shout, stamp his feet, strike the table with his fist. This is a characteristic feature of behavior in the paradoxical phase of the excitability of the nervous system.

Finally, we find that negativism is a frequent manifestation in the adolescent age. Any request or suggestion from adults is frequently refused, and even rudely. The adolescent, without a moment's hesitation, can insult his mother or favorite teacher in defiance of their just demands. When he is alone he will bitterly regret his rudeness, but at the moment when it happens he is unable to act differently. This behavior is characteristic of the ultraparadoxical phase of the excitability of the nervous system.

In connecting certain instances of the not completely normal behavior of adolescents with various phases of the excitability of the nervous system, we are not relying on experimental material, inasmuch as such research has not as yet been conducted. But theoretical considerations support our suppositions. If parents and teachers knew the reasons for certain strange features of the behavior of an adolescent in the pubescent period, it would be easier to avoid many conflicts. Indeed, the adolescent is not always to blame for the fact that his character "has spoiled." Considering his state, one should not make a frontal attack, for roundabout ways are much more effective.

The phases of excitability of the nervous system are unstable. They change when the nervous system is less tense and when the adolescent himself attempts to regulate his own behavior. As the adolescent period nears its termination, all the processes of vital activity again become stabilized and the nervous system becomes perfectly normal. At the same time, the behavior of the boy or girl changes for the better, and relations with parents and teachers become adjusted.

The period of pubescence is also noted for a considerable upsurge in the mental activity of the person. A qualitative leap takes place in the development of his thinking. It is at this age that most adolescents develop the capacity for abstract thinking, elements of which are also manifested earlier. The pupil begins to apprehend reality and its laws much more profoundly. He develops a thirst for knowledge, and frequently, even to the detriment of his school studies, he reads books with a passion, thus broadening his educational outlook considerably. Frequently his thirst for reading is combined with the practical need to perform scientific experiments in physics and chemistry, to take part in a mathematics circle, to study machinery, and even to invent something; he may be carried away by an interest in local lore or by the desire to make observations of animate nature. Some adolescents reveal an inclination for writing poetry, painting, sculpture, playing musical instruments, and dramatics. At the same time they become more interested in social affairs. A diversity of interests that, in the beginning, are unstable, but which later assume a more stable character, absorb the attention of the adolescent.

This period sees the development of fantasy, which is chiefly of a creative nature: a desire for the outstanding, unusual activity of the future scientist, inventor, writer, or actor. In his daydreams, the adolescent frequently takes the wish for the possible, and the possible for the actual. Some dreams become dispersed because they are obviously groundless; others are realized in purposeful activity.

If we know about the specific psychic features of the adolescent, it is easy to get along with him and to influence him. Formerly this age was called the "difficult" age, but actually it was the parents and teachers who were "difficult," for they did not take into consideration the peculiarities of pubescence and the sharp changes that take place in the body and personality of the adolescent.

Freud's teachings devote a prominent place to the theory of sublimation, that is, the diversion of sex energy to various other forms of activity. We deny the existence of a specific sex energy. As regards diverting the adolescent to different, diverse forms of activity in order to distract his attention from his sex feelings, that was justified by pedagogical practice long before Freud. Indeed, observations of the activity of pupils in well-organized schools and other children's educational institutions show that the more adolescents are engaged in various types of creative activity, and the more intensively they are occupied with them, the easier is their passage through the pubescent period.

The opinion exists in the psychological literature that the adolescent is no longer a child, but not yet an adult. He is at an important turning point in his life, and parents and teachers must bear that in mind. This should be manifested, first of all, in a change in the manner of addressing him and of approaching him. A child is accustomed to obeying; he can be given orders. However, with the adolescent it is better to take counsel, giving him the right to make a decision independently or tactfully prompting that choice.

If the adolescent displays apathy, indifference to what is going on around him, if he tries to be alone, loses interest in his studies, if his movements become sluggish and he develops an irresistible drowsiness and laziness, it means that the process of pubescence is not proceeding in a completely normal way.

Adolescents, like adults, are not disposed to frankness in such matters. Even when they fully trust their fathers or mothers, their doctors or teachers, they do not realize what oppresses them physically, and especially morally. It is necessary to help them, in a tactful way, to mobilize their own willpower, to switch over to any form of activity that interests them, to develop their own self-control, their ability to refrain from what attracts if it is objectively harmful for their development. In this connection, *Dnevnik Kosti Riabtseva* [The Diary of Kotia Riabtsev] by the writer N. Ognev, a book that is not unknown but which has been pretty much forgotten, would be an excellent example of how an adolescent, by the force of his own willpower, surmounted his weaknesses.

The social content of moral upbringing helps to overcome certain physiological impulses and inclinations, and to subordinate them to control by the mind; it also teaches one to direct and control one's feelings.

In the early period of pubescence, boys begin to avoid girls, and the latter respond with the same estrangement. Sometimes we can observe a suppressed, at times even open, "hostility" between adolescents of the two sexes. They seem to be shy of one another. This shyness increases if a girl or a boy was the object of dreams with an erotic overtone. What takes place resembles an effort to protect oneself against these impressions.

With the advent of early youth, all this "estrangement" of adolescents gradually vanishes, giving way to increased mutual interest. Young men and women begin to seek each other's company, and they acquire common interests—scientific and technical studies, art work, sports. Mutual relations of sincere comradeship and friendship become established, feelings that, in many cases, grow into a first love.

These are pure, honest relations that are based on an unconscious attraction, but are far from any thought of sexual possession. As P. P. Blonskii convincingly shows in the material he has collected, such mutual relations serve as a sort of antidote to onanism if the boys or girls have not as yet succeeded in freeing themselves from this habit. In their desire to appear better and purer in the eyes of the beloved boy or girl, the sweethearts, by exerting their willpower, subdue the weakness which makes them think less of themselves. This is very important, for if boys or girls cannot rid themselves of onanism when they are young, the habit can establish itself permanently. In such cases, even marriage and sexual life in the family do not always free adults from this habit. It not only has a pernicious influence on the physical state of the body, but also has a negative effect on the psychic make-up of the person.

The profound and pure experience of first love in youth plays a tremendous role in achieving the moral health and perfection of the developing person. We need only see to it that vulgar gibes and insulting insinuations on the part of people around the lovers do not interfere with this feeling, and that the mutual relations of the boy and girl who love one another are absolutely free from cynical suspicions.

Of course, it is impossible to exclude fully such a development of relations as can lead to sexual intimacy. Sometimes this takes place as a result of the development of deep feelings. More often it happens when chastity and the ability to control their feelings have not been instilled in the young people. In these cases a considerate attitude on the part of the parents and teachers toward the feelings of the young lovers, and timely, tactful interference can prevent premature marriage at a time when the young people have not as yet acquired sufficient knowledge and strength and are still incapable of an independent family life.

The sex upbringing of the rising generation, which is a complex field of knowledge that has been little studied, requires the concentrated attention of teachers, psychologists, and doctors. The joint efforts of specialists are needed in order to make an all-round study of the specific features of the moral and physiological development of young men and women and to elaborate scientifically substantiated recommendations. We must put an end to the nihilistic attitude toward these problems, just as we must not exaggerate their significance. Sex upbringing will occupy its coordinative place in the solution of general tasks of moral upbringing only if we do not forget the biological specifics of the child's development. "Direct answers to the question" of the sex development and upbringing of the youth can be given on the basis of a paintaking scientific analysis of the specific features of the anatomic and physiological development of children and adolescents, of their endocrinal sphere and neuropsychic dynamics, on the basis of a profound study of the moral and aesthetic shaping of the developing person.

We must set up an interinstitute laboratory of the "psychophysiology of the sex development of children and adolescents" within the system of the RSFSR Academy of Pedagogical Sciences. Its staff should consist of specialists from the various branches of knowledge: physiologists, psychologists, doctors, and teachers. It would be desirable to draw into the work of the laboratory, on a voluntary basis, a group of philosophers concerned with problems of ethics and aesthetics, lawyers, criminologists, men of letters, and people in the arts. The work of the laboratory must be based on recourse to preschool and school institutions, nurseries, kindergartens, children's homes, and boarding schools. Special investigations should also be conducted in the family.

We will find the correct solution of this problem if, when studying the interaction of the natural and social laws of sexual development, the leading role of the social laws is revealed and sex upbringing becomes the "instilling of the culture of the social personality" (A. S. Makarenko).

NOTES

[1] A. S. Makarenko, *Soch.*, Vol. IV, Izd-vo APN RSFSR, Moscow, 1957, p. 220.
[2] K. Zetkin, *Vospominaniia o Lenine,* Gospolitizdat, Moscow, 1955, p. 49.

What's to Be Done If One Has Married Young?
A Reader's Letter and Editor's Answer

K'ai Ko and Cheng Lin

Dear Comrade Editor,
   The article "What Is the Most Suitable Age for Marriage?" by Comrade Yeh Kung-shao* in the April 12 issue of *Chung-kuo Ch'ing-nien Pao* is very enlightening. But there is a new problem baffling me. What's to be done for a girl married too early? The unpleasant consequences likely to ensue from my early marriage have haunted my mind and give me the jitters. I am now only twenty-one years old, married last year. My "lover" [spouse] and I are both engaged in work. We love each other and lead a happy life. But things can't be the same for long when children come along. There can be no getting away from an increasing weight of family responsibilities. Our work will inevitably suffer as we are beset with anxiety. I know there is no use crying over spilt milk. However, Comrade Editor, can you give me some hints as to how to maintain a happy husband-wife relationship, so as to cure the headache from early marriage?

REPLY TO THE ABOVE LETTER BY CHENG LIN,
THE EDITOR OF
CHUNG-KUO CH'ING-NIEN PAO

Dear Comrade K'ai Ko,
   Early marriage has many evils. I find many female comrades have, through early marriage and lack of birth control, become mothers of four or five children at the youthful age of twenty-four or twenty-five. Their health and progress suffer immensely. The physical growth of their children naturally leaves much to be desired, to say nothing of their education. Under the tremendous weight of family responsibilities, the young fathers are denied a well-earned rest after work. Things get out of their hands, as they are mentally and physically overtaxed. Considering your present age of twenty-one, you married rather too

* See pp. 279-282 of *Sex, Schools, and Society.*

271

early last year. But don't worry about it. To undo the evils of early marriage in a way, you need only pay attention to birth control and order your life well. In my opinion, you are still very young and are in the later stage of physical growth. Motherhood will not do you any good. I therefore suggest that you do something along the following lines.

First, you should carefully avoid conception. That means the adoption of scientific and artificial means of regulating conception and spacing out births so that the mother's health will not suffer under the great strain of unwanted pregnancies and births. A woman afflicted with certain diseases may suffer complications or even the loss of her life because of conception. She must try not to conceive until she has been cured. Therefore, the practice of contraception, while serving the goal of birth control, is also an important device for protecting the health of mothers and babies and guaranteeing family happiness. Then what are the best contraceptive methods? Artificial methods of contraception are many. At present, our clinical studies show that the combined use of devices with medication gives the most reliable results. The following methods may be recommended:

1. *The condom* (contraceptive sheath). This is used by the man, who places it in such a position that the penis is covered down to its root. The sheath's outside is smeared with contraceptive jelly or cream so that it can be inserted into the vagina without causing the female discomfort because of its dry surface. This is also necessary because of the possibility of a ruptured sheath. After the release of sperm, the man should pull his penis out prior to its complete contraction, pressing hard at the lower end of the sheath which is being taken out at the same time. Care should be exercised to prevent the sperm finding their way into the vagina or the sheath being left entrapped therein. The device after use should be wrapped up in a wet towel to be cleansed in warm water the next day. During the cleaning process, the gadget should be filled with water to see if there is any possible leak. The cleaned gadget should be wiped dry and sprinkled with powder and then aired in a clean place for further use.

2. *The diaphragm.* This is for women. It is recommended for its safety and reliability, harmlessness to health, and noninterference with the enjoyment of the sex act. Any woman using the diaphragm should consult a gynecologist to find out whether it is good for her and what's the correct size for her. She will be given the necessary instructions for using it. At first, the user will feel some inconvenience but she will soon get used to it after some practice. As things now stand, the diaphragm used together with contraceptive jelly produces the most effective results.

3. *The "safety period"* method of birth control. It is based on the physiological fact that the sperm and the egg cannot survive for very

long. Continence is practiced during the period of ovulation—the release of the egg cell—to prevent conception. In the case of a woman who has a regular cycle of menstruation (once every twenty-eight to thirty days), ovulation generally occurs about two weeks before the beginning of her next menstrual period. During the four or five days before and after ovulation, intercourse is liable to result in conception. The other days are called the "safety period." The effectiveness of this method depends on a regular menstrual cycle and a proper approach. But as one's living conditions, emotional state, and sex urge may cause irregular ovulation or extra-ovulation, it should be noted that the "safety period" method is not an ideal and reliable one.

To prevent conception, the couple must be firm in their determination. The man should especially take the initiative and doggedly seek mutual cooperation in the regular use of a device in every intercourse. Utmost care should be exercised, as the least negligence may lead to pregnancy. The above-mentioned methods just give you some information. You may refer to the book entitled "Contraceptive Knowledge" written by Sung Hung-chao and others, and other relevant publications. A doctor's advice is also very necessary.

When you are well prepared in every way for the arrival of a baby, you may give up the contraceptive effort. But after your first baby arrives, you must keep on with your efforts to regulate conception.

Second, proper continence should be exercised in sexual life. For a woman of your age, intercourse may take place once to thrice a week but not more than that. In this regard, you should overcome impulses with reason; indulgence will undermine your health.

Third, you should build up a nest egg through practicing industry and thrift. With both you and your husband making money, careful budgeting and planning will enable you to live comfortably with some money left to be banked away. With a nest egg you are not only helping the State in the development of industrial and agricultural production, but also promoting the well-being of the family and preparations for the arrival of your children.

In conclusion, I hope that you and your "lover" will work shoulder-to-shoulder for the proper arrangement of family life and concentrate more of your energies on work, study, and advancement, in order to give full play to the fervor and drive of youth.

My Views on the Problem of Young People's Marriage, Love and Children

Yeh Kung-shao

Editor's Note: We received many letters since our publication of Comrade Yao Lan's letter concerning the problem of marriage. A great majority of these letters oppose early marriage, hope that young men and women take their career into due consideration when they make decisions concerning their marriage, and suggest that they solve the marriage problem together on the basis of mutual respect and mutual understanding. These views are doubtlessly all correct. They reflect the spirit of mutual assistance and mutual love among the comrades of the revolutionary rank and file. Meanwhile some letters bring up some concrete problems. Here, with an aim to promoting young men's and women's understanding toward the problem of marriage, love, and children, we invited Comrade Yeh Kung-shao to write another article. We shall publish still another article to sum up this discussion. We shall not return letters which were sent to us in connection with this subject, but shall retain them for reference instead.

The *Chung-kuo Ch'ing-nien Pao* published Comrade Yao Lan's letter concerning the marriage problem in its "Physical Health Column." It is said that young people have been enthusiastically discussing this problem and have sent many letters to the editors presenting them with many views. I read some of the letters and found them very interesting. Marriage is a matter of great import in our lives; the happiness of the young men and women, as well as the healthy growth of the next generation, hinges on this matter. I feel it is good for the youths to discuss this problem because this can promote a serious attitude in them in connection with this matter and enable them to avoid suffering from undesirable consequences on account of insufficient consideration or imprudent handling of problems similar to those mentioned in the letters.

I do not want to present any concrete opinion about the question of whether Comrade Yao Lan should marry or not. I shall leave this for him and his girl friend to decide after mutual consultation. Here I only

275

want to present some of my views concerning other related problems.

On the age of marriage: About the ideal age of marriage for young men and women I have already presented my opinion from the angle of physiology and health in my last article (published in the "Physical Health Column" of the April 12 issue of this paper—Editors).* I suggested that the ideal age for women is from twenty-three to twenty-five, for men twenty-five to twenty-nine. But this is by no means rigid; individual concrete situations should be taken into consideration. For instance, some youths may have attained the marriageable age of twenty-four or twenty-five, but if they still do not have the ability to make a living independently it would be better for them not to hurry. In other words, I mean marriage cannot be viewed solely from the point of view of physiology and age, which are only part of the conditions, although an important part. We must also consider the matter from other angles to make our consideration complete.

On young men's and women's marriage and love: I am strongly opposed to marriage by young students and am especially opposed to female university students bearing children while still attending school. We must know that in our country it is not easy to have a chance to receive higher education! The State provides very favorable conditions for university students to study—annual expenditure for one university student is equivalent to the fruits of labor of six to seven peasants toiling throughout the entire year. But once a young student marries and has children, he or she will have to devote a part of his or her time and energy to the children and family life. In this way how can the student study properly? Therefore, I hope young men and women can suitably delay their marriage so as to make full use of their youthful days to study and train their brains in preparation for the fulfillment of more difficult tasks in the future.

Some people ask whether students can fall in love if they should not marry. Generally speaking they had better not. The reason is very simple: students should fully utilize their time to develop themselves mentally, morally, and physically. Love, which demands much time and energy, will affect the quality of their studies. It is regrettable to notice that some students who have been very good at their studies during the middle-school years suddenly fail in their studies after they enter the university because they fall in love. Meanwhile, it is a natural tendency that people who love each other want to get married. It is generally difficult for the young people to control their emotion. After a year or two (sometimes it takes even shorter time) the lovers would become too emotional not to want to get married; or they might be compelled to contemplate marriage because of pressure from the masses or their parents. Such cases happen very often; therefore I feel that to

---

*See pp. 279-282 of *Sex, Schools, and Society.*

oppose early marriage we must also oppose falling in love at too early an age.

On birth control: Some youths got married before they were mature and had the ability to make a living independently; then they regret it and become depressed when they discover that marrying too early is no good. There are also young women who have already had the requirements for marriage and want to get married but are afraid that marriage will bring too many children and therefore too much trouble to the family. Actually these problems can be solved so long as they practice birth control. Birth control, however, does not mean not to have children at all; instead it means to have children in a planned way (including planning as to when to have children and how many children to have). Medical advancement has long put the initiative of childbearing in our hands. Therefore we should adopt the same serious and careful attitude toward childbearing as the one we adopt toward work and study; we must work the problem out in a planned manner and must not let it take its own course. There must be mutual understanding between man and wife: the husband must especially respect his wife's opinion; he should never indulge in momentary sexual impulse and bring about a series of evil consequences.

But how often should we have children? We should consider the first child first. In addition to considerations as to the attainment of physical maturity and the possession of physical health on the part of the man and wife, it is best for them to have their first child after they have laid a preliminary foundation in their work and in their financial situation. This is especially true of the mothers. I suggest that women have their first child generally at the age of twenty-six or twenty-seven and then have the second one after three to five years. If the circumstances are especially good, they may have a third one after another three to five years. At this time the mother would still be about thirty-four or thirty-five.

The reason for keeping an interval of three to five years before having another child is mainly out of consideration for the health of the mother and child as well as for the work of the mother. We must know that during the nine months of pregnancy the mother has to supply the three kilograms of embryo with all the nourishment it needs. Meanwhile the development of her own mammary glands and the enlargement of the uterus also require a definite amount of material foundation. Furthermore, delivery, which is like a major operation, consumes much energy and nourishment. Then, to bring up the child healthily the mother must breast-feed the infant for another year, or at least for six months. As a result, the physical burden on the mother during the nine months of pregnancy and the twelve months of feeding is considerable. So we must allow one and a half to two years' time for recuperation. When the first child reaches the age of three, and when all other conditions permit, she can consider having a second one. Naturally education and upbringing of the child must also be taken into consideration here.

As for the problem of how many children we should have, I think if we consider from the viewpoint of protecting the mother's health and insuring the normal growth of the child, we should generally have only two. We should have fewer but better children. When conditions permit, we may consider a third one, but it is best not to have any more than three.

In this way the mother can complete her childbearing plan pleasantly with much in reserve before she is thirty-five. Furthermore, when the mother reaches fifty-five and the father sixty they can retire with the first child nearing thirty and the third at twenty. At this time the first child will be financially independent and the parents' financial obligations to the children will become light.

Therefore generally speaking, delaying the age of marriage and practicing planned parenthood have many advantages. Viewing from an immediate standpoint, this practice can safeguard the health of the parents and children and insure happiness in the family. From an indirect standpoint, it enables young people to contribute fully to socialist construction and to create good conditions for the growth, education, and upbringing of the next generation.

Finally I have one suggestion to make to parents with marriageable children. Please do not exercise pressure on your children to make them marry early so that you can enjoy the pleasure of becoming grandparents. Times have changed and some old practices are no longer continued. From your standpoint it may seem to be out of goodwill to let them marry early and have children early, but in reality this may ruin your children by forcing them into a situation in which they will injure their health and have a large number of children and a subsequent heavy burden before they have laid a foundation for their career. This you may not have anticipated. So I hope you will be prudent in matters concerning your children's marriage and leave it to themselves. There is no need for the parents to interfere.

For Students and Youths:
What Is the Most Suitable Age for Marriage?

Yeh Kung-shao

"When a man is old enough, he should get married; when a girl is old enough, she should be given away." This is a saying which has been handed down from generation to generation during the past several thousand years. However, as to what the term "old enough" implies as the most suitable age for marriage, views are quite divided. Some people marry as soon as they reach the full age of fifteen; in other places people marry even at the age of thirteen or fourteen. Is this "old enough" or not? In my view, age, of course, is a dominant factor as to when one may get married. For example, the Marriage Law of our country provides that the minimum legal age for marriage is eighteen for a girl and twenty for a boy. But, apart from that, one will have to take into consideration the physical condition and some practical conditions of the individuals concerned. Generally speaking, it is too early to get married at fifteen, for it is not only incompatible with the provision of the Marriage Law but, what is even more serious, will bring great harm to health after marriage because one has not yet reached the stage of maturity of physical development at fifteen. A letter from a reader to this newspaper provides an illustration. He said that he married at fifteen, and due to excesses after marriage he was now suffering from neurasthenia. Moreover, he had become impotent, and felt extremely painful both mentally and physically. In the case of some married young girls who have reached the minimum age (eighteen) laid down in the Marriage Law, successive childbirths, pregancies, and breast-feeding have adversely affected their health and progress. Neither is the development of their children satisfactory. Besides, some comrades who are still in university are preparing to find their wives before their graduation or become so anxious that they get married immediately. In their case, they fear that their youth will be wasted as they will be twenty-four or twenty-five years old when they leave university. But the result is that they are not able to solve many problems in livelihood. Both husband and wife are beset with hardships, cannot study with ease, and find it too late to regret. All the above cases show that the problem of marriage is indeed a practical,

279

personal problem for many young people at present. In order to help them recognize and solve this problem correctly so that more of them will not go astray, I feel that there is need to put it into clearer perspective. For the benefit of young people, I would here discuss some physiological aspects of the marriage problem.

First and foremost, I am going to make a few remarks concerning the problem of choosing the most suitable age for marriage. I feel that this problem should be considered from several aspects.

1. From the aspect of maturity of physical development and procreation

It is best for a human being to begin to produce children when he (or she) has really attained the stage of full maturity. At what age will maturity be attained? Generally, sexual secretive glands will begin to function at twelve to fourteen in the case of a girl, and fourteen to sixteen in the case of a boy. We call this the age of puberty. At this time, in the case of a girl the sign of puberty is menstruation, and in the case of a boy it is seminal emission. At this time, the human body will grow rapidly. At this time, however, the sexual function has just begun, and will not attain maturity until eighteen to twenty. But even then the development of the whole body is still not fully attained. For instance, the process of calcification of the bones will not be completed until twenty-three to twenty-five years of age, when the cerebrum will be undergoing a complex process of cerebral building. The complete formation of the epithelial cells of the cerebrum finds expression in the rapid development of the power of thinking, inference, abstraction, and generalization on the part of the youth. Generally it coincides with the period in which the youth is taking up comparatively advanced studies in an institution of higher education. For this final stage of growth and development to be attained, a youth is required to lead a more regular life. It is only after the various parts of the human body have developed and matured that marriage should be considered.

2. From the aspect of sexual life and physical health of young men and women

We know that the development of the inhibition process of the cerebrum is relatively late. In the period of puberty, sexual impulse is relatively strong, and the power of restraint is thus relatively weak. At this time, if one does not get married but instead devotes one's whole energy to study or work, one will still feel the sexual impulse, but it will soon pass without doing any harm. On the contrary, if one gets married at this time, it is bound to lead to excessive sexual impulse and sexual activity, thereby affecting one's physical health and at the same time affecting one's study and work. As one grows older and the cerebrum becomes more mature, the power of the cerebrum to restrain itself will correspondingly increase. And with the experience of real life further enriched, one will be able to consider problems more intelligently. By then, one's actions will not be controlled by reckless sexual impulse, and in this way one will be able to adjust and lead a happy sexual life. This will not only add to the happy life of the husband and wife, but will promote the physical health of both.

3. From the aspect of procreation and the health of children

This problem concerns young women more than it does young men. If a girl bears a child before she becomes fully mature physically, calcium will be extracted from her body to develop the bones of the embryo even before the process of calcification of her own bones is completed. This is apparently harmful to the health of the girl herself. Besides, if a girl under twenty becomes a mother, it would be unrealistic to expect her to be a very ideal one. From documents prepared by obstetricians the following statistics are available: The highest percentage of difficult labor for first childbirth is found among women between fifteen and twenty and between thirty-six and forty. This goes to show that the first childbirth will not be too ideal if the girl is too young or too old for that. In addition, the rate of survival of children and infant mortality can also reflect the danger of early marriage.

Judging from the above-mentioned three aspects, the harm that can be caused by early marriage is very obvious indeed. What, then, is the comparatively ideal age for marriage? I think that the best age for a girl to get married is between twenty-three and twenty-seven, and that for a boy is between twenty-five and twenty-nine. Naturally, concrete conditions should be concretely analyzed. There should be no rigid rule here.

Some people may perhaps ask, "Since you say that early marriage is harmful, why is it that the Marriage Law permits a boy to be married at twenty and a girl at eighteen?" Well, I should say a few words about how we should correctly understand the provision of the Marriage Law concerning the age of marriage. I believe that the marriage age limit provided for in the Law is a minimum requirement; that is, to get married under this age limit is illegal. This provision is put forward with a view to coping with the evil practice of early marriage caused by economic poverty and cultural backwardness among the broad masses of the people subjected to manifold pressures during the last several thousand years. Although it does not say that marriage will be better after physical development is fully attained, it implies that this is so. It does not encourage young people to get married at eighteen and twenty.

Finally, I earnestly hope that young comrades will first consider what the aim of life is. You are living in the happy era of Mao Tsetung, and it is you who are going to build up an affluent socialist society. This is an extremely glorious and formidable task. There will be many things for you to consider and to learn, and you must avail yourselves of the most precious period of youth in your life to lay a good foundation for study, work, and health. This is the Party's and people's expectation of you. As for the problems of choosing a wife or a husband and the problem of marriage, they will naturally be solved satisfactorily following further enrichment of experience of individual life and the improvement of material conditions.

For Late Marriage:
Advice for Students

Yang Hsiu

Marriage is a necessary step in life. Both boys and girls, upon attaining a certain age, will consider this matter and do something about it. This is quite natural. However, it is worth discussing what the best age is at which young people are to get married and whether it is better for them to get married a little early or a little late.

Youth is an important period for intellectual and physical growth, for political progress, and for active improvement in work. People should spend most energy on studies, political progress, and work during youth and thus lay a preliminary foundation for success in life. True, marriage can bring happiness, and a boy and a girl, when they get married, can help each other in studies and work. However, marriage, together with the resultant founding of a family and birth of children, is sure to take up some of the couple's time and energy and produce some adverse effects on their studies and rest. Such effects will be smaller if the couple handle their family affairs well and will be greater if otherwise. By getting married a little late, one can, in the first place, delay such effects, and secondly, because one will be older, one will be able to handle the problem of marriage more properly and thus reduce such effects. For this reason, we think that late marriage for youths has great advantages, so we approve and advocate it.

FROM THE POINT OF VIEW OF INTELLECTUAL GROWTH

Youth is the most suitable period for the acquisition of knowledge and skills. People in their youth are energetic and vigorous, their thoughts active, and their memory and imagination powerful. They are specially sensitive to new things, and they can accept new knowledge and increase their intelligence quickly. If young people make the best of their youth and concentrate on learning skills and techniques, reading books, and seeking truths, they will be able to raise their standard of knowledge and technical level rapidly and thus lay a foundation for studies and work throughout the rest of their lives. If they do not do so, if they get married too early, their energy will be dispersed on account of family life, and if they give birth to children and thus burden themselves with a family, their studies will be affected to an even greater extent. This applies especially to schoolgirls. If they get married before graduation, they usually will have their studies adversely affected by pregnancy and childbirth or even have to leave school. We often see examples of this. A general survey was once conducted in a certain normal institute. That institute had 2,425 students, of whom 325, accounting for 13 per cent of the total, were married. Of these, 98 were women. Forty of these women had their studies seriously affected by pregnancy and childbirth, and some of them took six years to complete the university course because they gave birth twice during their studies. Some of the married men there also had their studies adversely affected, because they had to take care of their wives, perform domestic labor, and handle domestic contradictions of various kinds. Because early marriage is such an impediment to studies, many people in history who were determined to become learned refused to get married too early. Lo-meng-no-so-fu [Lomonosov], a great Russian scientist, is an example. He was a scientist in the eighteenth century, famous not only in Russia but all over the world. When he was nineteen, his father decided to find a wife for him. He was at the time infatuated with arithmetic, astronomy, and several languages and literatures. Considering these branches of learning as the "second world" of life, he made up his mind to explore the secrets of this "second world." He knew that if he got married, he would have a family to look after, and this would adversely affect his exploration of the new "second world." Accordingly, he firmly turned down his father's plan concerning his marriage, and even left his parents on this account. After that, he was able to concentrate on studies and the exploration of the world of knowledge. He waited for ten whole years, till he was twenty-nine, before he got married.

Some young comrades may say, "Many learned people in history got married early. It is thus clear that early marriage will not necessarily produce adverse effects on one's studies." Indeed, we must not set marriage and studies against each other completely as if they were water and fire. We merely say that late marriage will be good for one's studies, while early marriage may produce adverse effects on them. Such adverse effects may be obvious in the case of some youths and not quite obvious in the case of other youths. If the matter is correctly handled, such effects may be minimized or eliminated. However, most young people are unable to handle the matter correctly.

FROM THE POINT OF VIEW OF POLITICAL AND IDEOLOGICAL PROGRESS

Youth is also a period when one can make very rapid political and ideological progress, or, in other words, when one sets a definite political direction for oneself and preliminarily forms a conception of the world and life. What purposes one chooses for one's life, what course one plans to take, and what kind of a conception of the world and life one will take—all these are decided in one's youth. To be sure, it will take one a long period of effort to set up a proletarian conception of the world and life thoroughly. However, if one lays a foundation in one's youth for a proletarian conception of the world and life, one may be said to have begun one's life well and to have chosen the correct road, by continuing to advance along which one will find it easy eventually to set up and consolidate a proletarian conception of the world and life and become a strong proletarian warrior. By getting married late, young people can in the meantime spend more energy in caring about State affairs and group life, in studying political theories, and in taking part in political struggles, and in this way continuously raise their political and ideological levels and become qualified for League and Party membership. Thus, late marriage provides an objective condition favorable for political progress. Though someone who has gotten married early can also make political improvement and ideological progress if he works hard enough, yet in fact some youths, if they get married too early, will have their progress adversely affected by the actual difficulties which marriage brings. The adverse effects of early marriage are specially clear in the case of women comrades. They will have, for instance, to keep house and nurse children, and these jobs will take up some time and energy and, because they are inexperienced in life and cannot plan family life well, will be very difficult indeed. Their chances of taking part in political studies and social activities and of receiving education and training will necessarily be affected, and their progress will probably not be so rapid as that of others who are not married. If they are not very ambitious, they will probably concentrate on family life and gradually lose all desire for progress. In the rural areas and factories, many young women have had their political progress affected because they got married too early and consequently have had to keep house and nurse children at an early age.

FROM THE POINT OF VIEW OF CONTRIBUTIONS TO THE MOTHERLAND

Youth is also a period when one should work hard and labor actively and play useful roles in socialist construction. Youth is characterized by vigor and vitality, by bravery and activeness, and by boldness to create and to struggle against all evil influences and difficulties. Youths should make use of these good points and struggle bravely at posts where the motherland requires them to work. Youth is a period when one can achieve a great deal. One will find it a great help to get married late and in the meantime to have no family to worry about and to be able to go wherever one likes. There were and are many people in China and abroad who, being dedicated to their work, did not get married early. Huo Ch'ü-ping, a general in China during the reign of Emperor Wu of the Han dynasty, was famous for his brave defense of the country against invaders from outside. Once, upon his return after winning a war against the Huns, the emperor advised him to get married and have a family. But he replied, "How can I have a family now, when the Huns have not yet been exterminated?" True, success in life requires life-long effort, and we do not mean that youths should wait till they have attained great accomplishments before getting married or that early marriage will necessarily affect one's success in life. However, advantages and disadvantages are only relative. As the saying goes, "Of two good things, choose the better; of two evils, choose the lesser." In comparison with early marriage, late marriage is more conducive to success in life.

FROM THE POINT OF VIEW OF PHYSICAL GROWTH AND THE HEALTH OF THE NEXT GENERATION

Youth is also a period when one grows physically. During this period, all parts of one's body are developing and are yet immature. Generally speaking, a man's physical development is not complete till he is twenty-three to about twenty-five. One whose body is still developing must observe a set of normal rules of life, for instance normal rising and sleeping times, normal working hours, normal rest, and normal physical exercise, so that all parts of one's body may develop healthily and normally. Late marriage can provide some objective conditions favorable to healthy physical development. By getting married late, people in the meantime do not have family affairs or children to worry about and consequently can get sufficient sleep and rest. Also, if people get married when they are older and their physical development is complete, then, at the time of marriage, their brains will have assumed greater control over their bodies, enabling them to handle problems more intelligently and to decrease their sex urge so that they will not have their health impaired because of excess.

From the point of view of the health of the next generation, late marriage also has great advantages. Generally speaking, if parents are physically mature and healthy, children will also be healthy. If a woman whose physical development is not yet complete has to supply various kinds of substance to a baby in her, her health will be adversely affected and the baby, when born, will be weak because it has not been able to obtain adequate nourishment. Besides, some young parents are still in school and financially not yet independent, and some have just begun to work and are as yet not well-off. Thus, because young parents have financial difficulties and do not know how to plan family life, they cannot properly look after and raise their children, whose physical and mental development will consequently be affected to a greater or lesser extent.

From the above, it is clear that, from whichever point of view, it would be better for youths to get married late (say between twenty-three and twenty-five or twenty-six years old in the case of women and between twenty-five and twenty-eight or twenty-nine in the case of men).

ABOUT SEVERAL VIEWS

In order to advocate late marriage, we also advocate that youths do not fall in love at too early an age. Though love and marriage are two different things, yet as love is the prelude to marriage, to make love too early may also produce adverse effects on youths and will often lead to early marriage. It will be best for young people, especially middle-school students, not to fall in love. If one is so impatient that one begins to do so while still studying in middle school, one will not only dissipate one's energy, but also, because one is young and ignorant, handle the matter improperly, with consequences for which one will feel sorry in the future. Even if one can handle the matter properly, one will have to spend a great deal of time and energy on them. So, in either case, for a middle-school student to fall in love with a girl will produce adverse effects on his studies.

Some youths say, "Since late marriage is so good, why does the Marriage Law allow young men to get married at the age of twenty and young women at the age of eighteen? Does the advocacy of late marriage not contradict this provision by the Marriage Law?" We say that there is no contradiction. The ages mentioned in the Marriage Law are the minimum ages which young men and women must respectively attain before they can get married. This provision takes account of the habit of the masses, especially the rural people. It does not mean that it is best, still less compulsory, for young men and women to get married at the ages specified [. . . .]

Some youths say, "Provided we practice contraception and have a planned family, early marriage will not produce great adverse effects on us." We say that in the case of youths who have already gotten married, it is of course better to have children late than early, thus reducing somewhat the adverse effects of early marriage. Planned birth is also good and is something which we advocate. However, this applies after all only to youths who have already gotten married, and besides, things do not always turn out as one has planned. We have many youths who had worked out sound plans for the future when they got married, but who nevertheless gave birth to children soon afterward and thus began to carry a family burden at an early age. Rather than take such chances, one should simply wait longer before getting married.

Some youths think that if one gets married early, one's mind will settle down early and one will then be able to concentrate on one's studies and work, and that man and wife can help each other and make improvement together. True, those who got married early do not have to worry about finding a spouse, and if man and wife get on well, they can help each other and make improvement together. However, if married people do not have to worry about finding spouses, they have to worry about family life and all kinds of problems consequent on marriage, and whether one will be able to handle such problems well does not depend completely on one's wish and, in fact, depends more on one's conception of life, knowledge, and experience. Generally speaking, young people do not firmly cherish the revolutionary conception of life, are deficient in knowledge and experience, and lack the ability of correctly handling problems consequent on marriage and family affairs, which, unless properly handled, may produce adverse effects. For instance, if man and wife are very young, they are liable to be impulsive and will not be able to survive big storms in life's voyage, and sometimes, simply because of some small contradictions, they may have a big quarrel which will impair their love for each other, or may even sever their relations. If one gets married at too young an age, one will probably place family life in an undue position and thus confine all one's considerations to the interests of one's small family. If youths wait for a few more years before getting married, they will at the time of marriage be more mature, more experienced, and fuller of social knowledge, and thus be able to consider problems more thoroughly and intelligently, and after they have gotten married they will be able to handle family affairs and make arrangements for family life more properly, and man and wife will be able to help each other and make improvement together.

Some youths think that getting married and setting up a small family early is a "blessing," and that if one gets married in one's youth "one's life will be rich," and if not, one's life will be void and meaningless. Indeed, youths should lead a richer and more meaningful life, and getting married and leading a family life is of course a blessing and something meaningful. However, this is only one side of the matter. In order that one's life may be rich and meaningful, a more important thing is for one to make contributions to the motherland and the people and to attain accomplishments in one's studies and work. Only youths who make use of their precious time in fully developing and training themselves, in securing proper physical and intellectual development, in increasing knowledge, in making improvement, and in rendering meritorious services to the motherland are not wasting their time or living in vain but are leading a life which is the most meaningful. For this reason, when we advocate getting married a few years later, we do not call upon youths to restrain themselves negatively or to be Trappist monks, but ask them to work hard and concentrate energy on work and studies. If youths understand this and act accordingly, they will not feel life to be empty because they are not married, and even should they feel so, will be able to overcome such a feeling easily.

SEVERAL POINTS TO ATTEND TO IN REAL LIFE

When we say that it is best for youths to be in love or get married late and that youths should not be in love or get married too early, we only mean that late marriage should be generally advocated among youths and in society. After all, it is up to each young person himself or herself whether or not he or she gets married or falls in love. Provided two people's love is moral, provided they are both willing to get married, and provided their marriage is in accordance with the provisions of the Marriage Law, nobody should normally interfere with or obstruct them. Nor should people discriminate against or jeer at young people who are already in love or have already gotten married. We only hope that those who are still very young and not yet in love will be patient; that those who have just begun to have boy friends or girl friends will try to be steady if both sides think that they do not sufficiently understand each other or if their love for each other is not yet steady; that those who have steady boy friends or girl friends will try to be sensible always, will not let their love adversely affect their studies or work, and will not impatiently seek to get married; and that those who have already gotten married will handle their family life properly, will practice planned birth or wait for one or two more years before having any children, and will not have mental burdens to carry because of improper arrangements for family life, still less spend too much energy on domestic trifles or become absorbed in thoughts about their small families, spouses, and children. It is our belief that, provided ideological education is conducted and concrete guidance and help are given, youths will be able to handle their love and marriage correctly.

China's Birth Control Action Programme, 1956–1964

Pi-chao Chen

Any organized effort to spread birth control must undertake two tasks: (1) to inform and persuade the people, and (2) to make birth control services easily accessible and widely available to them. It is difficult enough to reduce fertility in a relatively modernized country, where social and economic conditions are favourable to a spontaneous fertility decline. The problems are even more difficult, if not impossible, in a relatively unmodernized country with a large, rapidly growing population, where the need for lowering the fertility rate to manageable proportions in a relatively short time is great. The Chinese leaders have indicated that the target of their birth control campaign is to lower the natural growth rate to 2 per cent in the near future and to below 1 per cent before A.D. 2000.[1] This is a highly ambitious goal; to reach it will require not only the commitment of enormous human and financial resources but also organizational innovation and ingenuity.

The Chinese Communists have already proved to be highly resourceful in their attack on China's health problems. By maximizing the employment of their abundant human resources, and by applying well-tested public health techniques, the Communist regime has succeeded in reducing China's mortality to a level which it took the United States a century to accomplish.[2] However, while the mortality rate can be lowered by means of mass campaigns, the fertility rate cannot. Mortality can be reduced independently of individuals' decisions; the government can do it through appropriate public health measures. Fertility reduction depends on the aggregate decisions of individual couples to practise birth control; positive co-operation of individuals is imperative. The task of reducing fertility is therefore much more complicated and difficult.

What measures have the Chinese Communists taken to realize their stated goal? What action programmes have they undertaken? What organizational innovations have they adopted? We shall try to answer these questions by focussing on four aspects of the action programme: (1) organization, (2) modes of communications and persuasion, (3) products and services provided, and (4) strategy. Because we do not have access to much of the information we would like to have, we shall make no attempt to treat the 1956–58 and the post-1962 campaigns separately, but, instead, draw upon information from whichever period is available.

1. THE ORGANIZATIONAL SET-UP

The Ministry of Health, which had already assumed the major responsibility for planning the successful public health programme, was assigned the task of implementing birth control policy. During the 1956–58 period an Office of Birth Control was created, directly under the State Council, with representatives from the Ministries of Health, Propaganda, Culture, and Commerce, the All-China Women's Federation, the Young Communist League, the All-China Red Cross Association, the Chinese Medical Association, and others. The precise function of the Office of Birth Control was never revealed, but available evidence seems to indicate that it was an *ad hoc* internal unit of the State Council, responsible for co-ordinating activities of the related ministries and organizations and for drafting the basic policy guidelines related to birth control.[3]

At the national level, the Ministry of Health is responsible for the following functions: (1) formulating and promulgating birth control regulations and measures; (2) supervising the subordinate units in implementing them; (3) sponsoring the Chinese Medical Association's research on various contraceptive methods; (4) training high-level birth control personnel; and (5) compiling and distributing birth control materials, such as handbooks, booklets, slides, and movies; mobilizing the support of, and co-ordinating with, the pertinent ministries and mass organizations in the pursuit of the birth control campaign. It seems that most of these functions are performed by the Maternal and Child Health Section of the Ministry.

Birth Control Organization at the National Level

State Council
Office of
Birth Control

- Ministry of Health: Planning over-all action programme
- Ministry of Propaganda ⎫ Mass communications
- Ministry of Culture ⎭ and persuasion
- Ministry of Commerce: Supply of contraceptives
- Chinese Medical Association: Contraceptive research
- All-China Women's Federation ⎫
- Young Communist League ⎬ Informal communication, distribution of contraceptives
- All-China Red Cross Association ⎭

At the next level, each province (or autonomous region) has set up its own committee on birth control guidance, comprising representatives from the provincial Party committee, provincial health department, mass media and propaganda units, and the provincial branches of various mass organizations such as the Young Communist League, the Women's Federation, the Red Cross Association, the Trade Unions, the Society for the Popularization of Science, and so forth. Under the supervision of the provincial committee on birth control guidance, the provincial health department assumes the major responsibility for formulating the provincial action programmes. These consist in (1) setting up and operating a provincial centre to train birth control personnel; (2) supervising the lower units in implementing the central and provincial policy directives; and (3) organizing and dispatching roving medical teams (doctors, nurses, and propaganda cadres) to visit the countryside regularly.

Birth Control Set-Up in China

National level	State Council Office of Birth Control Ministry of Health
Provincial level	Provincial Committee on Birth Limitation Guidance Provincial Health Department
County level	County (or city) Committee on Birth Limitation Guidance County (or city) Health Bureau; hospitals
Village level	Health stations, infirmaries, or clinics attached to communes, production brigades or teams, maternal- and child-health workers, midwives, nurses, and part-time health workers.

At the *hsien* level, the *hsien* (or *chen* or *cheng*) health bureau is the unit responsible for implementing the action programme. Its function consists in (1) supervising the setting up of birth control clinics by the hospitals, infirmaries, clinics, and health stations under its jurisdiction; (2) training full-time and part-time health workers (nurses, midwives, maternal- and child-health workers) in the 'know-how' of birth control work; (3) mobilizing and collaborating with local units of trade unions, the Young Communist League, propaganda sections, neighbourbood committees, schools, and other mass organizations to operate local birth control exhibitions, group sessions, and home visits; (4) setting up or improving the local contraceptive supply network.

Finally, at the commune or production brigade level, the burden of actually bringing the birth control message to the peasants lies with the women pioneers and the part-time health workers. (The two categories are quite often the same people. They usually have had two weeks or so of training in the 'know-how' of birth control work—giving information and counselling about birth control methods and distributing contraceptives.)

At the grass-root level the government wisely assigns the tasks of delivery, maternal care, and birth control to the same group of medical personnel, the maternal- and child-health workers and midwives. Since they perform deliveries and provide maternal care, they have easy access to women who might otherwise be hard to reach. The mother's trust in these workers may greatly facilitate their attempts to persuade her to practise planned childbearing. This is particularly true in the post-partum period, when the mother is likely to be more receptive to the idea of birth control.

The building of this organizational network began in August 1956, when the Ministry of Health issued instructions to its subordinate organs at each level to collaborate with local mass organizations in publicizing birth control methods and providing technical services to those seeking assistance.[4] In December a national conference of maternal- and child-health workers was held in Peking to discuss the best of way of promoting birth control.[5]

Even before this conference some localities had already taken steps to implement the new policy. During the second half of 1956 many provinces, notably Manchuria,[6] began to set up their own training classes for health workers from lower levels. These were usually set up in the provincial capitals or the larger cities, where there were adequate medical personnel and facilities. For two weeks to one month the trainees studied basic reproductive physiology, birth control techniques, and ways of publicizing the idea of birth control and of approaching the target population. On completing their training they returned home to organize similar local training programmes, recruiting as trainees midwives, nurses, part-time health workers, traditional herbalist doctors, and drugstore saleswomen, and people from the co-operative production brigades or production teams.[7] In this way large numbers of birth control workers were trained in a relatively short period.

Simultaneously, the provincial health department also undertook various activities—organizing exhibitions, group sessions, and lectures in conjunction with a number of mass organizations. Each of these mass organizations directed its efforts to the target group most relevant to itself. The Women's Federation mobilized its members, especially those with three or more children, to visit local birth control exhibitions and to attend group sessions and lectures. The Young Communist League and the trade unions preached the virtues of late marriage and contraception to their members. The Association for the Popularization of Science and the Red Cross Association promoted various methods of contraception through lectures, films, or travelling exhibitions. Neighbourhood committees organized lectures and group sessions to which 'mothers with many children' were particularly invited. Hospitals and health stations set up clinics to provide technical guidance. The mass organizations also distributed contraceptives to their target population at nominal prices.

In the course of 1957 and early 1958 the campaign, which had begun in the major urban centres, was gradually extended to smaller cities and finally to rural villages. In most of the populous provinces the campaign had reportedly 'descended to the *hsien* level' by the end of 1957. In Honan, Kangsu, Shangtung, Hopei, Fukien, and elsewhere, the campaign 'had generally reached the overwhelming majority of lesser cities and villages'.[8]

For example, by December 1957, every one of Hunan's ninety-five *hsien* and cities (except for the areas inhabited by minority groups and the mountainous regions) was reported to have set up a permanent organization to promote planned childbearing, and over 20,000 basic level cadres, mostly female, had been trained.[9] In Hopei, most *hsien* reportedly had by then set up their own guidance clinics; in twelve *hsien* alone 9,334 clinics had been established. Most cities and *hsien* had created local committees to co-ordinate the work. It was further reported that 'about two-thirds of the province has held exhibitions, and about 700,000 persons have received birth control education'.[10] In Fukien over two-thirds of the province had held planned childbearing exhibitions by the end of 1957.[11] Even in Inner Mongolia, where population density was comparatively low, the Inner Mongolian Maternity Hospital was reported to have trained over 100 maternal- and child-health workers in methods of birth control by March 1957.[12]

A survey of the local and national newspapers for the period 1956–58 suggests that the campaign was pushed more vigorously in the provinces along the coast and in the Yangtze valley, where the majority of China's population live. These provinces (especially Hunan, Kiangsu, Hopei, Fukien and Chekiang) were also the ones frequently praised in the national press for their vigorous implementation of the birth control policy.

In accordance with the basic policy guideline,[13] the campaign was not promoted in the areas inhabited by minority nationalities in the period 1956–58. It is not clear whether this policy was still in effect after 1962. Since these minorities constitute only about 6 per cent of the population, it does not make much difference to the overall national fertility level whether birth control is promoted or not in the areas settled by them.

As a rule, the composition of a region's planned childbearing committee was a good indication of the priority given to the campaign. In general, in provinces where planned childbearing was regarded as a priority policy, the First Party Secretary headed the committee; otherwise, the head of the local public health department served as the chairman. In provinces where the provincial First Party Secretary assumed the chairmanship of the committee, with the heads of the provincial public health department and the Women's Federation as vice-chairmen, the representatives or heads of the various administrative departments and mass organizations would serve as members of the provincial committee. The same organizational pattern applied to the *hsien* and *hsiang* levels, with some variation.[14]

II. COMMUNICATION AND PERSUASION

A campaign aimed at persuading people to change their childbearing practice, like any attempt to change beliefs and attitudes that involve important goals and values, is likely to meet strong resistance. The values have deep roots in ancient norms, and sexual matters are not a subject of free discussion in Chinese society. According to the accounts of Communist newspapers, some peasants said that 'childbearing is a personal matter of the parents. Why should the Communist Party concern itself with such matters? The earlier we plant, the earlier we will harvest. The earlier we give birth to children, the earlier we will enjoy the blessings. Why practise contraception?' Others said, 'The number of children one gets is predetermined by fate.' Still others felt that contraception caused 'too much trouble and nuisance'. Some, reportedly influenced by 'vestigial feudal thought', and limited by their 'scientific and cultural standards', regarded contraception as an ugly thing and dared not listen to propaganda or attend planned childbirth exhibitions. The refusal of the husband to co-operate and objections by the parents were also listed as obstacles.[15]

Accordingly the government mobilized the mass media to overcome popular resistance. Thousands of articles were published in the press; pamphlets were distributed in large quantities.[16] Radio stations frequently broadcast programmes on planned childbearing. In the cinemas, films or slides illustrating methods of contraception were shown before or after the main feature.[17] Thousands of exhibitions were organized. These activities were aimed both at persuading people to practise late marriage and contraception and at instructing them in how to do it.

Various techniques of persuasion were employed, either separately or in combination. For instance, locally prestigious persons, Party leaders and others, contributed articles to the local newspapers preaching the virtues of contraception and late marriage.[18] This was an attempt at influencing through prestige suggestion and legitimization by the leadership. Doctors expressed personal and expert opinions on the harmful effects of early marriage and the virtues of planned childbearing and late marriage.[19] This was an attempt at influencing through professional authority. These arguments invariably appealed to the individual's self-interest.[20]

1. Early marriage interferes with one's study and work. Youth should devote their entire energy and time to study and work so as to make a greater contribution to the 'socialist construction of the fatherland'. While one is young one should not allow oneself to be distracted by such personal affairs as 'talking about love' or marriage.

2. 'Giving birth to too many children at too early an age, or at too short an interval', adversely affects the health of both mother and children, impedes the appropriate upbringing and education of the children, lowers the living standards of the family, and interferes with the mother's study and work.

3. Conversely, planned childbearing, that is, not giving birth to the first child too early and spacing births at an interval of every four or five years, protects the health of mother and children alike, facilitates better upbringing and education of the children, raises the living standards of the family, and is of help to the mother's study and work.

Furthermore, the government presented both 'positive' models to emulate and 'negative' models to avoid. Many people, mostly cadres, wrote articles relating their personal experiences. They described what a happy life they led after having decided to postpone marriage or of leading happier lives after using birth control—the wife was healthier and did well in study and work, the children received better care and education, the family was not pressed financially, and the husband and wife did not quarrel as often as they used to.[21] (Positive models were rewarded.) Others described what a miserable life they led because they got married too early, or told about the miserable life the Li's next door had because they did not practise planned childbearing—the wife suffered from poor health, the children did not receive proper care and education, the husband and wife quarrelled all the time.[22] (Negative models were punished.) Some reported that they had continued to lead a full sexual life after a vasectomy.[23] (The doctor's opinion that vasectomy would not interfere with sexual life was confirmed.) Still others said that it was not too inconvenient to use contraceptives. These articles always brought home the relevance of planned childbearing to the welfare of individuals and families.

Since 1962 the government has attached more importance to postponement of marriage as an approach to population control. Since then a number of articles have appeared in the press praising model young men and women who either had shown more concern with their job than with love or marriage or, heeding the Party's advice, had voluntarily postponed their wedding dates.[24] These young people are re-garded as 'positive' models whose 'socialist' and selfless behaviour was to be emulated by all. They are praised not because they help the government solve population problems by postponing marriage, but because they provide positive socialist models more concerned with socialist construction than with satisfying sexual impulses and desires.

A significant proportion of China's population cannot be reached by the written mass media, because they either cannot afford them or are illiterate. Furthermore, there is the problem of self-selective exposure; people tend to read information and ideas congruent with their existing attitudes more readily than incongruent ones. These factors limit the usefulness of mass media, except radio and television, as a channel for disseminating information and effecting attitudinal change. To overcome this limitation the government adopted the face-to-face approach, home visits, small group discussions, and cultural entertainment.[25]

Maternal- and child-health workers, women pioneers, female activists (or cadres), and others were mobilized to visit homes and to hold small-group discussions with married women who had several children and who were regarded as the high-priority target population. Jan Myrdal, who spent a month in a backward, remote village in the interior in 1962, gave a vivid account of how the Chinese combined the birth control programme with maternity and child care services and how the face-to-face approach was carried out at the basic level. Li Kui-ying, the village woman pioneer and part-time health worker, told Myrdal:

> We go to see the women who are pregnant and talk with them about what to do and tell them how to look after their infants. Before, a woman had to be sitting straight up and down on her *kang* three days after having her baby. And you can understand how that must have felt. Now we say to them: 'That is all just stupidity and superstition. Lie down with the child beside you and rest. You're not to sit up at all.' We tell the women to let themselves be examined regularly and follow the doctor's advice. We instruct them in birth control and contraceptive methods. The women follow our advice because they have found that with the old methods many children died, but with our new scientific methods both mother and child survive.[26]

Since this kind of activity was carried out in such a remote village, one may expect more vigorous programmes in the more populous and advanced provinces.

When persuasion fails, the Communist government does not hesitate to apply pressure whenever feasible. Li Kui-ying told Myrdal how she managed to persuade the peasant husbands to practise contraception:

Birth control is primarily a matter of propaganda. Firstly, many say: 'We want to have more children.' Secondly, after all, birth control is voluntary. We have discussed which contraceptives are best. Personally I find the condom to be the most reliable. They are rather inexpensive too: thirty-three pieces for one *yuan*. But there are other methods, too, and certain of the families don't use any contraceptives at all but only simple techniques . . . .

In certain families with lots of children, the women would like birth control, but the husbands say: 'There's not going to be any family planning here!' Then we women go to them and try to talk sense into them. We say: 'Look how many children you have. Your wife looks after the household and sees to all the children and she makes shoes and clothes for both you and the children, but you don't think of all she has to do or of her health, but just make her with child again and again. Wait now for three or four years. Then you can have more if you want.' Usually, they will eventually say: 'If it isn't going to go on all one's life, then all right. But if she's going to go on with birth control forever, then I'm not having any.' In those cases, all goes well and usually they do not decide to have any more afterwards. But in other cases the husband just says: 'No.' Then we women speak to him about every day, till he agrees to birth control. No husband has yet managed to stand out for any length of time, when we are talking to him. Actually, of course, they know that we are right. They know that they are responsible. It's only their pride that stands in the way, and we have to tell them that such pride is false and not at all right.[27]

What she describes is not persuasion but harassment, or 'struggle by reasoning', to use the Communist terminology. ('Struggle by reasoning' is an attempt to induce attitudinal and behavioural change by using group pressure to raise the individual's anxiety level.)

Another type of oral diffusion of the birth control message involves the use of the Cultural Workers Corps. They travel from village to village entertaining peasants with drama, comic dialogues, and other kinds of conventional entertainment. In this way the government attempts to overcome the obstacle posed by widespread illiteracy in rural areas by combining propaganda with entertainment. In 1962 the Cultural Workers Corps was entrusted with the responsibility of spreading the message on birth control. The following account was given by a former member:

In May or June the Chinese Communists were seriously trying to push forward this birth control campaign. All Cultural Workers Corps in the nation co-operated with the All-China Federation of Democratic Women and the All-China Federation of Trade Unions to get the movement started. . . .

Take our province (in Central China). Our Cultural Workers

Corps was given a large share of propaganda responsibility. It almost appeared as if we university students had started the programme on our own.

We managed to have a large number of speeches given, plays produced, and various kinds of propaganda activities organized by students. We had exhibitions, too. We even had a little song which went something like this: *Chia Chia lo pi yuen* (Every family is happy because of birth control drugs). I personally wrote a lot of *hsiang sheng* (comic dialogues). We even had exhibitions of birth control drugs on stage while such *hsiang sheng* were being performed. We also had girl students deliver fundamental, commonsense knowledge that the people should have. . . . Our audience for such shows was mobilized by different women's groups, government organizations, etc.

You can never be sure of the effectiveness of such campaigns. You can only be sure of one thing; we get the message across. Those people—especially the uneducated women—knew what birth control was all about. They laughed at the 'shameless' college girls who could talk about such things in public. But they got the message nevertheless. . . . And the important function of our propaganda activities was to get the message across.[28]

If the Cultural Workers Corps' attempt at getting the message across succeeded, as the informant insisted, this should be regarded as a major accomplishment. A study in Taiwan showed that women are more interested in the methods than the reasons for birth control. After an educational campaign teaching both methods and reasons was conducted in a township, samples of women were interviewed six months later. About 96 per cent were able to recall birth control methods as against 35 per cent who recalled the reasons for birth control.[29]

The public-school system is also used. In 1962 the schools in China reportedly began giving extremely frank sex education.[30] In colleges the girls are given information on various methods of contraception.[31] The potential of this approach is vast. With approximately 45 per cent of the total population under the age of nineteen, an effective diffusion programme that reaches all those attending school for any period of time cannot fail to contribute to stabilizing population growth in the long run. An education system is likely to be very effective in transmitting information and inculcating norms, since pupils are at an age when their attitudes are relatively susceptible to influence by an authoritative figure, the schoolteacher.

III. MEANS AND SERVICES PROVIDED

A careful study of the various types of contraceptives popularized by the government in mainland China has been undertaken by H. Y. Tien.[32] Our discussion of the subject will therefore be brief.

Contraceptive Devices

To judge from the press reports, condoms are by far the most popular contraceptive in mainland China. China has several rubber plants capable of manufacturing condoms. The production capacity was reportedly to have been greatly expanded during the 1956–58 period, but, although there were numerous scattered references to the quantities supplied, no total figures for that period were given.[33] Between 1958 and 1962 some of the plants were actually shut down for lack of demand.[34] The price of condoms has been cut repeatedly.[35] In 1962, according to Myrdal, thirty-three condoms were sold for one *yuan*.[36] According to an Indian diplomat who left China in April 1966, the price was further reduced in late 1965 or early 1966.

Foam tablets, diaphragms and jellies are manufactured. During the 1956–58 period, unknown quantities of them were imported from abroad. In March 1957 the government announced a plan to increase both manufacture and import of various contraceptives by 500 per cent over that of the previous year. However no actual figures were given. The sale price has also been cut repeatedly.

As early as January 1958, some Shanghai hospitals began to provide an IUD insertion service for their patients.[37] The type used was apparently the old-fashioned Ota ring, not the new, improved Lippes loop. According to a contemporary newspaper account, in addition to starting to manufacture IUDs locally, Shanghai had recently imported 20,000 from Japan. The Shanghai hospitals charged seven *chiao* for insertion and another seven *chiao* for registration.[38] A newspaper in Chengchou, Honan, reported that some hospitals had begun to provide an IUD (Ota ring) insertion service as early as 1955–56 and had found the results satisfactory.[39] When the active birth control campaign was resumed in 1962, some Peking and Shanghai newspapers again recommended IUDs to their readers.[40] To judge from a letter to the editor in *Chung Kuo Fu Nu* [Chinese Woman], the use of IUDs has apparently gained popularity. The author, reportedly a 'rural woman' living in Wu Ching hsien, Hupeh, wrote that she was thinking of having an IUD inserted but was not sure about its safety. The editor referred the letter to a doctor, who answered that the IUD is a very effective, safe, and trouble-free contraceptive device.[41] The doctor apparently was talking about the Ota ring, not the Lippes loop. Evidently the Chinese medical profession had not yet discovered the potential of the new, improved IUD and so has not pushed for its wide adoption.

A Shanghai newspaper reported in May 1957 that a new type of oral contraceptive pill had been preliminarily synthesized.[42] In August 1957 the *Ta Kung Pao* of Peking reported that a pharmaceutical plant in Tientsin had also succeeded in synthesizing a new type of oral contraceptive pill from inexpensive raw materials.[43] And according to Dr. Yen Jen-ying, who went on a medical mission to India led by Chou En-lai in December 1956, the mission brought back an Indian formula for oral contraceptive pills.[44]

Induced Abortion

In May 1957 the Ministry of Health issued new regulations, which permitted induced abortion without restrictions, provided that the woman had had no induced abortion in the preceding twelve months and that the operation was performed within three months of conception.[45] The new regulations immediately provoked a strong protest from the medical profession; a few days after they were promulgated, the Standing Committee of the Chinese Medical Association held an emergency meeting which passed unanimous resolutions protesting against the Ministry's decision and requesting a re-evaluation.[46] The medical profession's protest received wide coverage in the press. (This was in the Hundred Flower period.) Many doctors in other parts of the country voiced their support for the action of the Chinese Medical Association.[47] Ma Yin-ch'u, the staunch advocate of birth control, also agreed and bluntly called induced abortion 'outright murder'.[48]

On 4th June 1957 the Minister of Health released a statement in order to calm the protest. Madame Li Teh-chuan said that in liberalizing the law the Ministry had no intention of encouraging induced abortion as an appropriate way of practising planned childbirth. On the contrary, the Ministry stressed late marriage and contraception as the appropriate approaches. Induced abortion was to be resorted to only in the event of contraceptive failure.[49] In spite of this official explanation, the medical profession continued to raise the issue and to condemn induced abortion as a 'negative' approach to planned childbearing. Since 1962 the government has apparently pressed hard for induced abortion as a major component of its birth control programme. In Shanghai in 1962 legalized abortion clinics were reported to be doing a brisk business throughout the city.[50] A Japanese woman repatriated from Manchuria in 1963 reported that induced abortions were performed every Monday, Wednesday, and Friday at the hospital where she had worked as a nurse, and that on these days 'the hospital performed more induced abortions than deliveries'. She also said that the Chinese Red Cross Society had actively encouraged birth control, including induced abortion.[51] Accounts of refugees fleeing to Hong Kong also testified to official encouragement of induced abortion.[52]

In March 1964 Dr. Kan Majima paid a visit to China. In Peking he was shown the obstetrical and gynaecological hospital of a university, where he was surprised to see a billboard 'in praise of artificial termination of pregnancy'. He later remarked: 'Nowhere else in the world would such a poster be found in an obstetrical and gynaecological hospital.'[53]

In addition to the conventional methods, the Chinese have developed a vacuum method of induced abortion. Dr. Majima was shown an abortion, in which an electrical vacuum apparatus sucked out the contents of the uterus.[54] A Shanghai newspaper reported in 1963 that a Shanghai medical instrument plant had succeeded in developing a new type of electrical sucker for abortions, 'as big as a six-tube radio receiver'.[55]

Although the potential role of induced abortion in reducing fertility levels cannot be neglected, as the cases of Japan and Taiwan have demonstrated,[56] it is difficult to see why China should have opted for it, given the shortage of medical facilities and personnel. One plausible explanation is that the government, desperate to lower fertility, deems termination of pregnancy preferable to allowing the baby to be born, provided that the mother concerned agrees to induced abortion. Despite the fact that the regime has a strong ideological bias against material incentives, they are provided for those volunteering to undergo induced abortion. The practice of providing pecuniary incentives varies from place to place and from one category of patients to another. Thus, if the patient or her husband is an employee, the employer pays for the medical expenses. In cases where the patient has no employer, the hospital charges very little or nothing for performing the operation.[57] In contrast to the pre-1962 regulation, which required the consent of both the husband and wife, now the initiative of the woman alone will suffice.[58] The government uses 'persuasion' and semi-coercion to get pregnant women to agree to induced abortion.[59] Evidence seems to indicate that the incidence of induced abortion is fairly high, although not as high as in Japan or some East European countries.[60]

Vasectomy

Although in the period 1956–58 the government recommended vasectomy as an 'effective means of practising planned childbearing' to married men with two or more children,[61] it seems to have placed more emphasis on contraception by women. Since 1962, however, great stress has been laid on vasectomy.

Starting in April 1963, several major newspapers and periodicals launched a campaign to promote vasectomy. *Chung Kuo Fu Nu* carried a report of a medical study of vasectomy. According to the author, Dr. Sung Hung-chao, a vasectomy could be performed in the outpatient clinic, and the patient could go home immediately and be back at work after one or two days of rest; the operation would not affect the patient's virility. Statistics reportedly have shown that after the vasectomy operation, 72 per cent of the patients experienced no change in sexual urge, in 13 per cent the urge was stronger, while 10 per cent had a weaker urge. Compared with the tubectomy operation performed on women, a vasectomy takes less time and hospitalization, and hence is preferable.[62] To reassure readers further, the same issue also carried an article by a cadre who had undergone a vasectomy, giving his experience before and after the operation; he concluded that he had had a happier life since the operation.[63]

Peking Jih Pao [Peking Daily], *Kung Jen Jih Pao* [Daily Workers] and *Chung Kuo Chin Nien* [Chinese Youth] followed suit and printed articles urging vasectomy upon their male readers. They argued that the responsibility for planned childbearing does not fall upon the female exclusively; the male, too, has a responsibility. He should get rid of 'feudal' ideas of male supremacy and selfishness.

Although the principle of 'voluntarism' is stressed, the regime has not hesitated to apply administrative sanctions against non-compliants when 'persuasion' fails. According to one account,

> If a man had made two women pregnant, he was 'encouraged' to be sterilized. If he refused, there was no apparent punishment, but thereafter he was considered to be a 'rightist' and unworthy of holding a decent job.[64]

Presumably this kind of pressure can only be applied to those who depend on the government for their position, such as the Party cadres and the employees of state-operated enterprises. It is doubtful whether such pressure can be effectively applied to the ordinary peasants, who comprise the overwhelming majority of the population.

The government also resorts to pecuniary incentives. If an employee has a vasectomy, his employer will pay him 20 per cent of his monthly salary as expenses in addition to paying for all medical (operation as well as hospitalization) fees. Furthermore, the employee is entitled to receive his regular pay while hospitalized, plus one week of paid leave afterwards.[65]

Indigenous Contraceptives

In a country as backward and as large as China, making means of birth control available to the whole population poses formidable financial and distribution problems. With the possible exception of IUDs, modern contraceptives are costly in relation to average income, and there is also the problem of acceptance. Modern contraceptives may be reliable and trouble-free, but they have to be used to be effective. The majority of Chinese are illiterate peasants for whom the traditional folklore is still supreme. Recognizing this fact, the government quite early sponsored laboratory research to test and improve on traditional contraceptive methods. The practitioners of herbalist medicine were encouraged to publish their contraceptive formulae.[66] The Committee on Birth Limitation Technical Guidance of the Chinese Medical Association and other doctors then undertook clinical trials of each indigenous method. Research on contraception was listed as a high-priority item for the medical profession in 1957–58.[67]

During the 1956–58 period, many traditional contraceptive formulae were freely recommended in the mass media.[68] In the process some untested formulae were publicized. The most notorious instance was the publicity given to the use of live tadpoles as a contraceptive. Shao Li-tze first publicized this formula at the 1956 session of the National People's Political Consultative Conference,[69] and many newspapers later gave wide publicity to it. Subsequent experiments showed that swallowing live tadpoles was not only ineffective as a contraceptive method but also hazardous to health.[70]

Another traditional method which received some publicity was contraception by acupuncture and cauterization.[71] We do not know whether this method was still being promoted after 1962.

Apparently, prolonged lactation has been widely believed to be an effective way of preventing conception. Time and again the mass media have found it necessary to warn readers of the unreliability of prolonged lactation as a method of practising planned childbearing.[72] The safe period has also received some publicity.[73]

IV. DELAYED MARRIAGE [74]

One of the earliest reforms of civil law promulgated by the Communist government after its advent to power was the reform of the Marriage Law. Article 4 of the new Marriage Law states, 'A marriage may be contracted only after the man has reached twenty years of age and the woman eighteen years of age.' Shao Li-tze proposed at the National People's Consultative Conference in 1956 that the legal age of marriage be raised to twenty-three for men and twenty for women,[75] but his proposal was turned down by the Sub-Committee on Legal Affairs on the grounds that, although late marriage was desirable for both the individual and the State, the decision should be left to individuals. The question of raising the minimum *legal* age of marriage was thus dropped, but in March 1963 the Party quietly handed down a recommendation on the *optimal* age.[76] The Party recommended an optimal age at marriage of thirty for men and twenty-two for women. The government makes a careful distinction between the 'minimum legal age' and the 'optimal age' at marriage. According to the official explanation,[77] the age for marriage set forth in the law is the minimum age; the government has no intention of encouraging young people to marry at that age. On the contrary, such early marriage is regarded as detrimental to the health of the married couple, their children, and the whole population. Besides, young people should devote their entire energy and time to the 'socialist construction of the fatherland' and should not allow such trivial matters as 'talking about love' and marriage to interfere. In addition to helping slow down the population growth rate, delayed marriage also postpones the pressure on housing. Unmarried people can stay in dormitories, but the government has to provide married people with apartments or other separate quarters. However, for obvious political reasons, the government cannot frankly admit this without embarrassment.

While the government left the legal age for marriage unchanged, it does not hesitate to apply administrative sanctions, whenever possible, against those who fail to comply with its advice about the optimal age. Whatever the law says, the average college student heeds the government's advice and refrains from getting married while in college or right after graduation and before job assignment.[78] As students of contemporary China are well aware, what matters is not what the law provides for, but what the Party says. The government decides who gets what job and goes where after graduation. It can, and from time to time does, assign the non-compliants to unpromising jobs or to inhospitable frontier or rural areas.

The government condemns the practice of 'speculative marriage', in which college boys and girls marry after graduation and before job assignment time so that they will be sent to the same place.[79] If a couple is found guilty of speculative marriage, the chances are that they will be assigned to different places. If married couples are not guilty of speculative marriage an attempt will be made to place them together, though there is no guarantee of this.

Although the government can and does force its 'advice' about the optimal age at marriage on college students, it is not likely to be able to apply it on rural youths, because it does not have the same power over them. Given the state of economic development, the government cannot promise non-agricultural jobs to rural youths (or to many urban educated youths) as a reward for compliance. Nor, conversely, can it use the denial of non-agricultural job opportunities as a punishment for non-compliance. Neither does it seem likely that the government can resort to either economic deprivation or discrimination (e.g., lowering wages) as a punitive device. Rural peasants already live at a subsistence level; a reduction of economic rewards would most likely provoke resentment and resistance too strong for the government to contain, however totalitarian it may be. For these reasons the compliance rate is bound to be much lower among young people in rural areas than among the urban, educated youth.

V. STRATEGY OF IMPLEMENTING ACTION PROGRAMMES

In promoting birth control, the administrative organs at each level seem to have consistently followed a strategy which the Chinese call the *tien hsien man hou* working style (literally, 'start with a point and then extend outwards'). This strategy means that in implementing a policy or programme organized efforts are initially concentrated on a particular project, area, or section of the population, rather than spread among all areas and all parts of the population at once. For implementation of the birth control policy, this strategy had three specific implications:

1. Efforts were initially concentrated in metropolitan areas, then spread to smaller urban areas, and finally to rural areas.
2. First efforts were made with the educated section of the population, such as cadres, intellectuals, skilled industrial workers and professionals, and then extended to cover the uneducated people, such as peasants and unskilled workers.
3. Some pilot projects were carried out, and the experience gained from them was applied to larger areas.

At the provincial level, they concentrated first on big cities, then on smaller cities (*chen cheng*), and finally on the countryside. At the *hsien* level, they began with more densely populated areas such as the capital seat, *cheng,* and selected agricultural producers' co-operatives.

According to the Chinese Communist theoreticians, emphasizing a small point or operating a pilot project is the way to begin understanding and changing the world. Also, it guarantees adherence to the so-called 'mass line' working style, presumably because it ensures close association between the cadres and the masses. Third, it is a way of developing models as well as of training cadres. The theoretical basis for this strategy seems to be Mao's theory on the conduct of guerilla warfare,[80] which says that available forces should be concentrated to surround and eliminate individual units of the enemy forces one by one, instead of being scattered to confront the enemy forces at all points simultaneously.[81]

The strategy seems also to be consistent with the Japanese and Western patterns of demographic transition. Demographically, the practice of birth control usually begins with the upper socio-economic, well-educated classes of a population, then spreads to the middle and less educated classes, and finally to the rest of the population. Geographically, the practice of contraception first begins in urban areas and then spreads to the rural areas. In adopting this strategy the Chinese Communists might or might not have been aware that it is quite consistent with the usual patterns of fertility decline. (The *tien hsien man hou* strategy is not confined to the birth control campaign alone.) There are reasons for using such a strategy. First, the urban areas can provide better medical facilities and clinical services than the rural villages. Second, most of the cadres, industrial workers, and state employees are concentrated in urban areas; since the Party and government have 'fate control' over them, pressure for compliance can be more easily applied to them.

Progress reports published during 1956–58 showed how the strategy was applied. For example, in the second half of 1955 the province of Hopei began to propagate birth control among the cadres in government agencies and enterprises. A year later, the campaign was extended to employees in industrial and mining enterprises, as well as to urban dwellers. Beginning in 1957, the campaign began to descend into the rural areas; by the end of the year most of the *hsien* in the province reportedly had been touched by the campaign.[82]

In March 1957 the Party committee of Ning *hsien,* Hunan, announced the approach it would take to implement the birth control campaign. Initially, organized efforts would be concentrated on cities, *cheng,* industrial and extractive enterprises, and schools. The rural villages would be the last to be reached. The persuasion campaign would be directed first at the cadres and functionaries; the masses would be reached later. The Party committee chose Feng-ching-chou agricultural producers' co-operative as the pilot project, where a concentrated persuasion campaign would be launched. Experience gained from this project would then be applied to other areas of the *hsien.*[83] In operating pilot projects, the emphasis is placed on the experience and lessons that might be learned and generalized from such projects.[84]

The national leaders also described the employment of this approach. In an interview with Edgar Snow in February 1965, Premier Chou En-lai said: 'We are promoting family planning, especially in schools, factories, and government offices, and we have had pretty good results. Young people at these places know the advantages of late marriage, and after marriage they have the desire to plan their families. Thus, family planning can be spread, if we try, but since it does require proper propaganda and education, it will take time.'[85]

The uniform pattern of waging a birth control campaign leads one to suspect that either the Ministry of Health or the Second Office of the State Council had actually prepared a detailed manual instructing the lower units on how best to conduct the campaign.

The government also used a strategy of press coverage of selected 'models'. Those *hsiang* or agricultural co-operatives that had vigorously pursued the policy were singled out in the press for praise, and their experiences described in detail. Others were urged to 'emulate', to 'compare with', and to 'surpass' these models. From time to time the major newspapers or periodicals would give nation-wide publicity to some outstanding successes, and exhort the nation to emulate or surpass them.[86] According to the Chinese Communists, developing and singling out models is an important working style. Models provide criteria for comparison, experience to be gained and extended, targets to be reached, and objectives to be surpassed.[87]

It is interesting to note that the Chinese strategy coincides with an American demographer's advice on how best to conduct birth control campaigns in underdeveloped countries. At the First International Conference on Family Planning Programmes held in Geneva in August 1965, Ronald Freedman summarized the major themes and implications of the conference; one was that

> The power of indirect diffusion in spreading information about family planning is being demonstrated in one study after another in various countries. This suggests that serious consideration should be given to plans for systematically and deliberately spacing the maximum organized efforts to reach every second or third village or area rather than to try to blanket all areas more thinly. . . . There was apparently greatest success where group reassurance was possible. . . . Some have suggested that it is desirable to get at least one couple in each village practising family planning. Quite the contrary, I would argue that it is better to have ten couples each in ten villages. With nucleation and concentration of effort and practice the couples will reinforce each other, the limited programme personnel can provide services and further reassurance. The 'good word' will spread then by diffusion to the other places, as a basis for organized programmes there in the next phase.[88]

While the Chinese strategy entails more organizational control over both positive and negative reinforcement, Freedman's strategy stresses the role of social reinforcement (or group reassurance) and the power of indirect diffusion of information. Although the two schools have different theoretical foundations, they may converge in application.

Another striking feature of the Chinese birth control programme is that it was a mass campaign, rather than a mere routinized administrative procedure. This mode of operation has its roots in the techniques of mass mobilization developed and perfected by the Chinese Communists in the course of their long struggle for power. Since their advent to power in 1949, the Chinese Communist leaders have launched an endless series of mass campaigns as a way of implementing their policies.[89] A. Doak Barnett describes a mass campaign involving 'the setting of a few clearly defined immediate aims, the concentration of efforts and attention on these aims above all others, the mobilization and training of large numbers of cadres drawn from many segments of the political system to carry out a campaign, and finally the mass mobilization of the population as a whole to take action to achieve the defined goals'.[90]

The way in which a mass campaign proceeds is best characterized as a 'wave-like development', as the Chinese Communists call it. Each campaign has its fermentation, surging, high tide and recession. The birth control campaign also had its fermentation period (1956), surging period (mid-1956 to early 1957), high tide (mid-1957 to 1958), and recession (mid-1958 to 1961). A new cycle began in 1962, with fermentation in the early spring, surging period in mid-1962, high tide in late 1962 to 1963, and recession from 1964 on. The Chinese birth control campaign may therefore be regarded as a mass campaign.

Admitting that the 1958–61 recession could be attributed to the leadership's overconfidence, or more appropriately misestimate, of their ability to bring about fundamental socio-economic transformation in a short period of time so as to make their previous concern with the question of population growth ridiculous and superfluous, it is less clear why since 1964 the publicity campaign has again been reduced. This pattern of promoting birth control raises the question, whether the wave-like mass campaign approach can be effective in bringing about fertility decline.

As mentioned before, any organized effort to spread birth control aims at two things: (1) to change the attitude of the sceptics and non-acceptors, and (2) to accommodate the ready acceptors. As the nature of the two aims differs, so does the approach to their realization. The realization of the former involves communication and persuasion, while the realization of the latter requires the setting up of nation-wide information and supply networks to place the methods and means of birth control within easy reach of millions.

The communication and persuasion campaign aims at convincing the populace of the benefits of birth control, making the populace aware of the possibility of controlling fertility, and sensitizing them to the availability of means and service. There are, broadly speaking, two ways of achieving these aims: (1) a sustained, intensive and extensive campaign involving all·means of communication but lasting for a relatively long period of time; (2) a crash, intensive and extensive publicity campaign involving all means of communication but lasting for a relatively short period of time. In the case of China, the publicity campaign, as opposed to efforts to set up a supply and service network, took the second form. The 1957–58 and the 1962–63 publicity campaigns are cases in point.

During the first high tide in 1957–58, the government employed all means of communication at its disposal to spread and promote the idea of birth control among the populace as well as to inform them about the possibilities and availability of various contraceptive methods. The second high tide in 1962–63 was more or less the same, with the addition of the deployment of the Cultural Workers Corps. After the intensive, short publicity campaign was over, sometime in 1963 the government ceased to employ the mass media, although it has continued to rely upon personal contact. Further, it seems to have concentrated on setting up more accommodating facilities and improving the existing ones.

In Taiwan it was found that an intensive, short publicity campaign without involving the mass media proved to be successful in spreading birth control as measured by the following two criteria. First, it raised the rate of birth control acceptance by bringing many couples to their first use of contraception. Second, it sustained the rate of birth control practice by helping many couples who had already used birth control of one kind or another to adopt more effective and satisfactory methods.[91] If Taiwan's experience has any relevance for mainland China, it is that although a wave-like mass campaign approach to policy implementation may not be effective in other spheres,[92] it seems to be an economical way of publicizing the idea of birth control, provided that the other aspects of the campaign—provision of means and services for practising birth control—are also done properly. Even if there is an adequate network of supply and services existing, there is still no guarantee that a birth control campaign will succeed. For to an even larger extent and in the long run, the success of a birth control campaign depends on the existence of certain 'preconditions'—i.e., certain levels of social and economic development.

NOTES

[1] 'Edgar Snow's five-hour interview with Chou En-lai', *Washington Post*, 3rd February 1964; Edgar Snow, 'An interview with Premier Chou En-lai', *Asahi Januaru*, Tokyo, 7th March 1965, p. 16.
[2] J. Salaff, 'Mortality Decline in Mainland China and the United States' (unpublished manuscript), 1966.
[3] Huang Yu-chuan, *Birth Control in Communist China* (Hong Kong: Union Research Institute, 1967), pp. 77-78.
[4] 'Ministry of Health has issued directives concerning the work on contraception', *Kuang Ming Jih Pao*, Peking, 13th August 1956.
[5] 'National conference of women and children health workers discussed ways of expanding work on contraception', *Kuangsi Jih Pao*, Naning, Kuang Hsi, Peking, 27th November 1956.
[6] *Chung Kuo Ch'ing Nien Pao*, Peking, 20th July 1956; *Heilungkiang Jih Pao*, Harbin, 25th October 1956; *Harbin Jih Pao*, Harbin, 29th November 1956, 19th March 1957.
[7] *Hsin Hunan Jih Pao*, Changsha, 27th October 1956, 27th March 1957; *Yang Cheng Wang Pao*, Canton, 13th April 1962; *Hangchow Jih Pao*, Hangchow, 24th May 1957.

[8] 'Propaganda on contraception has penetrated deeply into rural villages', *Wen Hui Pao*, Shanghai, 29th November 1957.

[9] 'Further expand the work on birth limitation: Propaganda on contraception is descending from cities to rural villages in Hunan', *Jen Min Jih Pao*, Peking, 28th December 1957; also *Wen Hui Pao*, 12th August 1957.

[10] 'Guidance work on contraception has penetrated deeply into rural villages; Twelve *hsien* in Hopei have established more than 9,000 guidance stations'. *Kuang Ming Jih Pao*, Peking, 30th January 1958.

[11] 'Penetrate the propaganda on birth limitation deeply into families; Kiangsu, Honan and other provinces have universally expanded the birth limitation campaign', *Wen Hui Pao*, 8th January 1958.

[12] 'Principal cities and some rural villages in our region are gradually expanding the propaganda on contraception and guidance work', *Nei Mong Ku Jih Pao*, Kweisui, 14th March 1957.

[13] Editorial: 'Birth limitation must be practised appropriately', *Jen Min Jih Pao*, 5th March 1957.

[14] *Hsin Hunan Jih Pao*, 8th December 1957; *Hsin Hunan Jih Pao*, 21st March 1957, 3rd September 1957.

[15] For instance, *Hsin Hunan Jih Pao*, 1st December 1957; *Kung Jen Jih Pao*, Peking, 8th July 1957.

[16] *Kuang Ming Jih Pao*, 5th April 1957.

[17] *Peking Jih Pao*, Peking, 3rd April 1957; *Chien Kang Pao*, Peking, 2nd April 1957; *Hsin Min Chu Wan Pao*, 10th February 1957. At one point the movie on contraception was shown in all cinemas including children's. This indiscretion caused a delegate to express disapproval at the National People's Congress in July 1957. See *Jen Min Jih Pao*, 20th July 1957.

[18] Chen Pan-tien, 'Promoting birth limitation', *Anhui Jih Pao*, 11th May 1957; Yu Ta-fa, 'Birth limitation benefits individuals as well as the State', *Shensi Jih Pao*, Sian, 6th September 1957; Chen Yu-chieh, 'Run the household industrially and economically, practise birth limitation', *Changsha Jih Pao*, Changsha, 28th December 1957.

[19] 'Chairman Fu Leng-chang discussed the problem of delayed marriage', *Chiao Shih Pao*, Peking, 5th March 1957; Dr. Yeh Shao ch'iu, 'A formula for the young men and women who are to get married soon', *Chiao Shih Pao*, 5th March 1957; Dr. Yeh Kung-shao, 'My opinion concerning the questions of youth marriage, love and childbearing', *Chung Kuo Ch'ing Nien Pao*, 21st July 1962, and 'What is the most suitable age for marriage?', *Chung Kuo Ch'ing Nien Pao*, 12th April 1962. [For the last two articles, see pp. 275-278 and 279-282 respectively of *Sex, Schools, and Society*.]

[20] For example: 'The advantages of planned childbearing are countless', *Peking Jih Pao*, 8th June 1958; Dr. Shen Li-meng, 'On the question of marriage and planned childbearing', 25th April 1962; *Yang Cheng Wang Pao*, Canton, 25th April 1962; 'What results will too numerous childbearing bring about?', *Kung Jen Jih Pao*, 4th January 1958; Yu Feng-ying, 'Birth limitation is the demand of the broad masses', *Liaoning Jih Pao*, Shen Yang, 11th May 1957; 'Birth limitation is the demand of the masses', *Kiangsi Jih Pao*, Nanchang, 29th March 1957.

[21] Tsou Ming-chou, 'I gave up my plan for an early marriage', *Kung Jen Jih Pao*, 14th July 1962; Hsu Shang-chi, 'I do not want to get married too early', *Chung Kuo Ch'ing Nien Pao*, Peking, 10th May 1962; Ti T'ing-lun, 'Early marriage hinders my work', *Jen Min Jih Pao*, 4th April 1962; 'The happiness of one's family depends on birth limitation', *Kung Jen Jih Pao*, 7th July 1962; 'Absorb the lesson from (examples of) too early childbearing', *Yang Cheng Wan Pao*, 17th November 1963.

[22] Ch'un Hsian, 'The harm caused by my early marriage', *Kung Jen Jih Pao*; Chen

Pai-leng, 'A lesson gained from early marriage', *Kung Jen Jih Pao*, 18th September 1962; Liu Fa, 'The hardship brought about by early marriage', *Chung Kuo Ch'ing Nien Pao*, 10th May 1962; Yun La-Mei, 'I broke old custom and postponed the date of wedding six times', *Chung Kuo Fu Nu*, Peking, No. 11, 1st November 1965.

[23] 'My feeling after vasectomy', *Hsin Hsiang Jih Pao*, Honan, 13th August 1958; Liu Ta-chun, "My experience before and after vesectomy', *Chung Kuo Fu Nu*, 1st April 1963; Wang Chun, 'My experience with vasectomy', *Chingtao Jih Pao*, Chingtao Shangtung, 1st September 1957; Pao Shu-hao, 'Sixteen months after I have undergone a vasectomy', *Hsin Hua Jih Pao*, Nanking, 27th December 1957.

[24] *Peking Review*, 30th March 1962, p. 20; Wang An-ching, 'Wang San-san postponed her wedding date three times', *Chung Kuo Fu Nu*, May 1963; Yen Chih-jen, *Chung Kuo Fu Nu*, June 1963; Tu Cheng-hsiao, 'How the late marriage fad developed in Chung Yu ti', *Chung Kuo Fu Nu*, March 1964; The Propaganda Department of the Women's Federation of Kiangsi Province, 'Late marriage becomes a fad in Santung Brigade', *Chung Kuo Fu Nu*, November 1965; Yin La-Mei, 'I changed my wedding date six times', *Chung Kuo Fu Nu*, November 1965.

[25] The Communist reliance on personal contact as a way of inducing attitudinal and behavioural change has been often commented upon by students of mass communication in China. See, for example F. Y. T. Yu, 'Communications and politics in communist China', in L. W. Pye (ed.), *Communications and Political Development* (Princeton, 1963), pp. 259-297. For a brief discussion of how the Communists organize face-to-face, oral propaganda at the grass-root levels, see Alan P. L. Liu, *Communications and National Integration in Communist China* (Cambridge, Doctoral thesis for MIT, 1967). Backwardness of mass media aside, there are good reasons for resorting to this approach. As students of communication have often pointed out, when communication between the change agent and the people to be changed is of a personal face-to-face nature, the results are often better. Personal contact and face-to-face communication are often more effective in inducing attitudinal and behavioural change than communication via impersonal channels such as radio and newspapers. See Everett M. Rogers, *Diffusion of Innovations* (New York, 1962), Chap. VIII; Elihu Katz and Paul F. Lazarsfeld, *Personal Influence* (New York, 1965).

[26] Jan Myrdal, *Report from a Chinese Village* (New York, 1965), p. 226.

[27] Myrdal, *ibid.,* pp. 226-227.

[28] This information is derived from an interview conducted by Frederick T. C. Yu in Hong Kong in connection with a research project on international communication under the direction of Ithiel de Sola Pool of the Center for International Studies, MIT.

[29] Laura Lu, 'Group meeting as a method of community health education for the family planning health programme', *Proceedings of the Regional Conference—Western Pacific Region*, May 1965.

[30] *Far Eastern Economic Review* (7th March 1963), p. 517.

[31] Chi-ping Tung and H. Evans, *The Thought Revolution* (New York, 1966), p. 157.

[32] H. Yuan Tien, 'Sterilization, oral contraception, and population control in China,' *Population Studies*, 18, 3 (March 1965), pp. 215-235.

[33] 'Large quantities of inexpensive contraceptives will be supplied to rural villages', *Wen Hui Pao*, 16th March 1957; 'Extend the propaganda on birth limitation to families', *Wen Hui Pao*, 8th January 1958; 'Shantung will further expand the guidance work on birth limitation', *Kuang Ming Jih Pao*, 10th November 1957.

[34] S. Chandrasekhar, 'China's population problem', *Contemporary China*, 3,

1958-59 (Hong Kong, 1960), pp. 25-32; *Yang Cheng Wan Pao*, 17th and 21st August 1962.

[35] 'Large quantities of inexpensive contraceptives will be supplied to rural villages', *Wen Hui Pao*, 16th March 1957; 'Ministry of Commerce and Ministry of Health decide to augment supply and reduce prices of contraceptives', NCNA, 28th March 1957.

[36] Myrdal, *op. cit.*, p. 227; *Wen Hui Pao*, 5th and 28th January 1958; *Shanghai Hsin Wen Jih Pao*, 6th January 1958; Liu Wei-ya, 'T'ai-tien's contraceptive ring', *Chien Kang Pao*, 19th April 1957.

[37] *Wen Hui Pao*, 23rd January 1958.

[38] *Shanghai Hsin Wen Jih Pao*, 6th January 1958.

[39] *Cheng Chow Jih Pao*, Chengchow, Honan, 9th and 15th March 1958.

[40] *Peking Wan Pao*, 12th June 1962; *Hsin Min Wan Pao*, Shanghai, 29th April 1963; *Chung Kuo Fu Nu*, No. 5, 1st May 1963.

[41] 'Will insertion of IUD affect health?' Shu Feng, 'Questions and Answers on Contraceptive Rings', *Chung Kuo Fu Nu*, 1st November 1963.

[42] *Wen Hui Pao*, 28th May 1957.

[43] *Ta Kung Pao*, 2nd August 1957.

[44] Yen Jen-ying, 'Marriage and work on planned childbearing in India', *Kuang Ming Jih Pao*, 25th March 1957.

[45] *Wen Hui Pao*, 12th April 1957; *Jen Min Jih Pao*, 23rd May 1957.

[46] 'The Chinese Medical Association wrote a letter to the Ministry of Health protesting against the liberalization of the regulations on induced abortion', *Ta Kung Pao*, Peking, 30th May 1957.

[47] *Wen Hui Pao*, 20th April, 24th May, 29th November 1957; *Szechwan Jih Pao*, 3rd June 1957; *Lao Dung Jih Pao*, Tang Shan, Hopei, 28th May 1957; *Hsin Hunan Jih Pao*, 6th April 1957; *Chungking Jih Pao*, Chungking, 9th April, 15th September 1957; *Fukien Jih Pao*, 31st March 1957; *Chekiang Jih Pao*, 5th May 1957; *Kiangsi Jih Pao*, 23rd February 1957.

[48] 'Man Yin ch'u on the question of population', *Wen Hui Pao*, 27th April 1957.

[49] *Jen Min Jih Pao*, 5th June 1957.

[50] *Hong Kong Standard*, Hong Kong, 7th July 1962.

[51] *Hong Kong Shih Pao*, Hong Kong, 21st February 1963; *South China Morning Post*, Hong Kong, 21st February 1963.

[52] Yu-chuan Huang, *Birth Control in Communist China* (Hong Kong: Union Research Institute, 1967), pp. 119-120.

[53] Kan Majima, 'The birth control controversy in China; Induced abortion is coming to the foreground', *Bungei Shunju*, February 1965, p. 145.

[54] Majima, *ibid.;* also 'Superior points of electrically induced abortion', *Yangcheng Wan Pao*, 8th April 1964.

[55] *Hsin Min Wang Pao*, Shanghai, 26th October 1963.

[56] For the important role induced abortion played in lowering fertility in Japan, see Yoshio Koya, *Pioneering in Family Planning* (Tokyo, 1963); also Kingsley Davis, 'The theory of change and response in modern demographic history', *Population Index*, 29, 4 (October 1963), pp. 345-366. For the importance of induced abortion in averting births in Taiwan see 'Taiwan: Births averted by the IUD programme', in Population Council, *Studies in Family Planning*, No. 20 (June 1967); see also R. Freedman, J. Y. Takeshita and T. H. Sun, 'Fertility and family planning in Taiwan: A case study of the demographic transition', *American Journal of Sociology*, 70 (July 1964), p. 21.

[57] Union Research Institute, *Interview Data on Machine Industry* (Hong Kong, 1964), quoted in Yu-chuan Huang, *op. cit.*, p. 119.

[58] 'Fewer and better.' *Far Eastern Economic Review*, Hong Kong, 14th October 1965; Union Research Institute, 'The condition in a people's commune in Chun

Teh *hsien* of Kuangtung Province', *Interview Data on Agriculture*, Vol. 11, 1964, quoted in Yuan-chuan Huang, *op. cit.*, p. 102.

[59] Yuan-chuan Huang, *op. cit.*, p. 119.

[60] According to a refugee's account, at one point in 1963, when a roving Birth Limitation Propaganda Team (consisting of doctors, interns, nurses and so forth, dispatched by the Party to the countryside) visited the commune which the refugee came from, there were some twenty pregnant women. The team, with the help of local authority, managed to persuade seventeen to accept induced abortion; *op. cit.* According to an intra-party study document issued by the Canton Municipal Party Committee which a refugee doctor claimed to have seen, the annual number of induced abortions in Canton amounts to 15,000 to 20,000 cases. In 1956 Canton had a population of 1.8 million. Assuming that there were 2 million population in Canton in 1966, the ratio of induced abortion cases to population would be 7.5–10 per 1,000 population; *op. cit.*

[61] *Shanghai Hsin Wen Jih Pao*, Shanghai, 5th March 1957; *Yen Tai Lao Dong Pao*, Shantung, 28th May 1957; *Wu Hsi Kung Jen Shen Ho*, Kiangsu, 7th February 1957; *Wei Hai Pao*, Shantung, 26th May 1957; *Chien Kang Pao*, Peking, 27th April 1957.

[62] Dr. Sung Hung-chao, 'Will vasectomy affect health?', *Chung Kuo Fu Nu*, No. 4, 1st April 1963.

[63] Liu Ta-chun, 'My experience before and after vasectomy', *Chung Kuo Fu Nu*, No. 4, 1st April 1963.

[64] 'Red China', *Look*, 1st December 1964, p. 26.

[65] Yu-chuan Huang, *op. cit.*, p. 122.

[66] 'Famous practitioners of Chinese obstetric medicine exchanged medical experience', *Kuang Ming Jih Pao*, 4th July 1956; 'The practitioners of Chinese medicine of the city of Hangchow held a discussion session on prescription for contraceptives', *Chekiang Jih Pao*, 12th August 1956; *Nang Feng Jih Pao*, Canton, 14th May 1957; *Hangchow Jih Pao*, 18th October 1956.

[67] *Wen Hui Pao*, 17th April 1957.

[68] Dr. Chou Ngo-feng, 'Prescription for contraception—Contraceptive paste', *Kung Jen Jih Pao*, 18th March 1957; *Kung Jen Jih Pao*, 8th April 1957; 'Salt-starch contraceptive paste', *Wen Hui Pao*, 7th April 1957.

[69] Shao Li-tze, 'The problem of birth control', *Jen Min Jih Pao*, 26th June 1956.

[70] 'The use of tadpoles as contraceptive', *Hsin Shu Chou Pao*, Shuchou, Kinagsu, 19th August 1956; *Ta Kung Pao*, Tientsin, 2nd July 1956; *Chien Kang Pao*, 1st May 1957; *Kung Jen Jih Pao*, 2nd September 1956; *Shanghai Hsin Wen Jih Pao*, Shanghai, 9th September 1956.

[71] *Chung Kuo Ch'ing Nien Pao*, 19th August 1956.

[72] 'Will one get pregnant while in the breast-feeding period?', *Yang Cheng Wan Pao*, 9th March 1963; Sheng Tan Chin, 'Will prolonged breast feeding prevent pregnation?', *Chung Kuo Fu Nu*, No. 5, 1st May 1962; 'Prolonged breast feeding is an unreliable method of contraception', *Kung Jen Jih Pao*, 18th August 1963. It should be pointed out that lactation does delay pregnancy in many cases.

[73] 'The safe period contraceptive method designed by Japanese medical doctors', *Wen Hui Pao*, 7th April 1957; 'On safe period contraceptive method', *Hangchow Jih Pao*, 6th September 1957; *Chien Kan Pao*, February 1957; 'Safe period contraceptive method', *Kung Jen Jih Pao*, 4th March 1957; 'Bear child in accordance with need'—'Introducing the safe period contraceptive method', *Shensi Jih Pao*, 21st March 1957; also *Shensi Jih Pao*, 4th April 1957.

[74] A. J. Coale and C. Y. Tye, 'The significance of age patterns of fertility in high fertility populations', *The Milbank Memorial Fund Quarterly*, 39, 4 (October 1961), pp. 631-646; Norman B. Ryder, 'The conceptualization of the transition in fertility', *Cold Spring Harbor Symposia on Quantitative Biology*, 22 (1957).

Postponement of marriage can contribute substantially to reduction in birth rates and population growth even when completed size of family is not reduced. This contribution is potentially greatest in those countries which have high fertility and a low average age of marriage. To the extent that the average size of family is also more likely to fall than to remain unaffected by later marriage, this contribution is likely to be even greater.

[75] 'Shao Li-tze discussed several controversial questions concerning birth limitation', *Jen Min Jih Pao*, 20th March 1957.

[76] Chi-ping Tung and Humphrey Evans, *The Thought Revolution* (New York, 1966), p. 157.

[77] Chou Hsin-min, 'On the question of promoting delayed marriage', *Kung Jen Jih Pao*, 15th November 1962. Although delayed marriage has been officially urged upon the youth, there has, however, been no uniform recommendation as to the 'optimal' age for marriage. The variation ranges from 25 to 32 for men and 22 to 28 for women. See *Kung Jen Jih Pao*, 28th June and 15th November 1962; *Chung Kuo Ch'ing Nien Pao*, 12th April and 1st June 1962 [see pp. 279-282 and 283-289 respectively of *Sex, Schools, and Society*]; *Chung Kuo Fu Nu*, 1st April 1963; *Peking Review*, March 1962, p. 20.

[78] Tung Chi-ping, a Chinese diplomat who defected to the U.S.A. in 1964, said: 'During my last year at the Institute (of Foreign Languages in Shanghai), a new law forbade any girl under 25 or any man under 30 to marry.' See 'Red China', *Look*, 1st December 1964, p. 26. Another defected diplomat said: 'The law isn't too bad. It says men can marry at 20 and women at age 18. But the Party says men shouldn't marry until they are 27 and women until they are 25. You must understand that, in China, what the Party says is more important than the law. So, generally, in the cities, men can't marry until they are 27. In the countryside, however, more people get married earlier—following the law rather than the Party.' See 'A first-hand report on Red China to-day; Interview with a Chinese who grew up under Communism', *U.S. News and World Report*, 7th November 1966, pp. 58-61.

[79] Teng Ying-chao, 'Greeting to university graduates who are to graduate this year', *Chung Kuo Ch'ing Nien Pao*, 30th May 1963; also Chi-ping Tung and Humphrey Evans, *op. cit.*, p. 159.

[80] Chang Ping-fa, 'On operating pilot', *Jen Min Jih Pao*, 7th March 1966; see also Liu Tse-chiu, 'On operating the point', *Hsueh Hsi*, No. 10, 2nd October 1953.

[81] Mao Tse-tung, 'On the strategic questions of anti-Japanese guerilla warfare', *Selected Works of Mao Tse-tung* (Peking, 1964), Vol. II, pp. 395-428.

[82] 'The Health Department and other units of Hopei discussed the work on birth limitation', *Jen Min Jih Pao*, 4th March 1957. In August 1957, a responsible official of Hunan's provincial public health department gave the following instruction on how best to develop work on birth control: 'The work on birth control in our province will proceed in accordance with the following sequence—cities first, villages later; cadres first, masses later.' See 'Responding to the urgent demand of the broad masses, the provincial birth limitation work has scored outstanding achievement', *Hsin Hunan Jih Pao*, 12th August 1957.

[83] 'The Party Committee of Nin *hsien* pays great attention to the masses' demand for contraception. Deputy Secretary of the *hsien* Party committee heads the work on birth limitation'. *Hsin Hunan Jih Pao*, 21st March 1957.

[84] In November 1963, refugees from Kwangtung reported in Hong Kong that word was spreading throughout the countryside in south China that couples who had had three children would be denied a ration card if a fourth child was born after March of the next year. (See *Morning Post*, Hong Kong, 21st November 1957.) Since no official statements have been issued in China concerning the denial of ration cards to a family's fourth child born after March 1964, it appears

that the threatened action in some areas in south China was a pilot project to test the popular reaction. Apparently, after having tested popular resistance to this measure, the government simply withdrew it.

[85] Edgar Snow, 'An interview with Premier Chou En-lai', *Asahi*, Tokyo, 27th February 1965. Also in *Asahi Januaru*, 7, 10 (March 1965), p. 16. Also, *Chen Yi's* remarks to Portische, in *New York Times*, 7th August 1964.

[86] 'How does Ho Chien *hsien* popularize knowledge about contraception?', *Kuang Ming Jih Pao*, 20th May 1958; 'An agricultural producers' co-operative in Shuang Feng *hsien* (Hunan) pass a five-year plan for childbearing aimed at reducing the growth rate of population from 4 to 1.8 per cent', *Wen Hui Pao*, 9th January 1958; 'The young and adult women of Wang Chian Chuan practise contraception and thus unleash labour potential', *Chung Kuo Ch'ing Nien Pao*, 6th January 1958; 'The achievement and experience of birth limitation propaganda at Shanghai's textile plants', *Kuang Ming Jih Pao*, 31st December 1957; 'Kuang ming agricultural producers' co-operative debated on the question of contraception; more than 100 couples adopted childbearing plan', *Ta Kung Pao*, Peking, 8th December 1957.

[87] Chang Ping-fa, *op. cit.*

[88] Ronald Freedman, 'Family planning programs to-day: Major themes of the conference', in Bernard Berelson *et al.*, *Family Planning and Population Programs* (Chicago, 1966), pp. 811-821.

[89] Frederick T. C. Yu, 'Campaigns, communications and development in Communist China', in W. Schramm and D. Lerner, *Communication and Change in Developing Countries* (Honolulu, 1967), pp. 195-215.

[90] A. Doak Barnett, *Cadres, Bureaucracy, and Political Power in Communist China* (New York, 1967), p. 437.

[91] See Ronald Freedman's and John Takeshita's forthcoming study of birth control programmes in Taiwan.

[92] A. Doak Barnett, *op. cit.*, pp. 437-438.

Handbook on Sex Instruction in the Schools

National Board of Education

PREFACE

The purpose of sex instruction in Swedish schools is to give biological information and to impart knowledge in a manner that will help both in the moulding of ideals and in the building of character. Instruction on these lines is intended to have a pronounced ethical basis.

Sex instruction is compulsory in Swedish schools. This handbook on sex instruction has been published by the National Board of Education for the use of teachers. It contains, among other things, general views on sex education and instructions about what to give pupils in different age groups. Suitable ways in which this can be done are outlined in lesson-examples on the subject.

I. THE NEED FOR SEX INSTRUCTION IN SCHOOLS

There are several features of society today which clearly indicate that school instruction in sexual matters is essential for social training. The subject matter of such lessons is in itself of great educational significance. The importance which is attached to the subject is demonstrated by the fact that sex instruction is a compulsory subject in Swedish schools.

Many doubts have been raised about the value of sex instruction in schools. The subject is undeniably a delicate one, making great demands upon teachers. One objection has been that it ought to be taught individually by parents, preferably in answer to direct questions. Again, all children in a class may not be at the same level of development and security, so that collective instruction, even when it helps those for whom it is suitable, runs the risk of harming others at a different level of development. It has also been suggested that lessons on sex would impose on teachers greater demands than they could always fulfil, especially in mixed classes and in rural schools where several classes are taught together in the same room.

The happiest solution would undoubtedly be for children to be taught in their own homes. However, parents often lack adequate knowledge themselves, or do not recognize their children's need for education in these matters, or they may have marked inhibitions and be quite unable to establish any rapport with their children in this field. When the home is unable to provide the necessary guidance, responsibility passes to the school.

There is a greater need for sex instruction in the upbringing of children than has hitherto been realized. Society today confronts young people with great difficulties of adjustment, not least in the sphere of sex. Many tragedies have been the result of a deficient sense of responsibility on the one hand and, on the other, ignorance of sex life and the risks involved in improper sexual relationships. Proper school instruction at the right time could make a significant contribution to protecting young people. There is in these matters a lack of clear information and guiding norms, and it is the school's responsibility to impart them.

The view that children should be given information about sex only in the form of answers to direct, spontaneous questions on the subject does not stand up to critical examination. Children are for various reasons reluctant to ask questions on this subject. The fact that they have questions does not mean that they have not already suffered harm from not having them explained in a satisfactory manner—indeed, the harm may have occurred even before such questions were raised. Questions about sex require an answer whether they are asked or not, and the answer must come from those who are responsible for bringing up the rising generation.

Young people need protection both against the kind of teaching which produces shock and guilt-feelings and against teaching which reduces their resistance in a critical situation. It should provide some safeguard, too, against the influence of thoughtless, ill-disposed, or abnormal individuals.

Sexual instruction for older children can be a preparation for parenthood. The leaving class is often the last chance of obtaining factual information on marriage, on the setting up of a home, and on welfare facilities during pregnancy, childbirth, and nursing; it is also an opportunity to develop the ethical, social, economic, and hygienic viewpoints which should go with these matters. This side of sex instruction is important in training the individual for his role in society.

The purpose of teaching about sex is to help children so that sexual development may occur as naturally as possible. Forming a healthy outlook on this side of life will be a great help to them in mastering the various problems connected with sex. The instruction must recognize that love relationships of the right kind can ennoble a youth's character and raise his ideals, and, far from undermining personality, help to build it up and to endow it with dignity and stability. The school is also the means by which society acquaints its younger members with the measures, laws, and institutions which in various ways affect their lives, sometimes protecting, sometimes restricting.

It is the school's task to provide a unified course of instruction on sex which pays due attention both to society's demands on the way an individual lives and to the good of the young people themselves—an instruction which is also an upbringing completing that given in the individual home.

II. GENERAL CONSIDERATIONS ON SEX INSTRUCTION IN SCHOOLS

The guiding principles in teaching about sex are, firstly, to create respect for it, and secondly, to help young people. All the essential facts need to be supplied, correctly and clearly formulated, and presented in a way that is natural, unaffected, and free from sentimentality. The teaching can then achieve its basic purpose of developing character by giving fundamental factual information.

The obscurity and mystery with which these things have been shrouded in the past was harmful from many points of view. Many young people in our own and previous generations have learnt to their cost what sexual ignorance means; the purpose of giving sex instruction is to prevent the new generation from being handicapped in the same way.

One difficulty in drawing up the subject is to find a balance between its different parts. If only the biological, medical side is given, children can easily get a one-sided picture of sex, whatever the teacher's intention. Some pupils, especially the more mature and reflective ones, will probably feel that something is missing, even if they do not say so openly. On the other hand, teaching which lacks firm biological foundations will fail to convince and to produce its full educational effect. Teachers who have misgivings about giving thorough biological explanations and are inclined to treat that part of the subject briefly and superficially must try and overcome their difficulties. Otherwise without a foundation the moral and psychological consideration and discussion of the subject, which require a foundation of primary biological knowledge, will lack the impact necessary to achieve their educational purpose.

Many teachers, when they deal with the subject, confine themselves to the home, parents, and children—i.e., the sheltered area within the bounds of marriage. They intend in this way to follow a clear and simple line and avoid delicate questions. But sex has other, social aspects, which it is dangerous to ignore. If, before they finally leave school, children are told about situations in society which have gone wrong and what can be done about them, then they have a chance of developing attitudes to such situations which will help them resist their harmful possibilities.

Another problem in teaching about sex is to suit the teaching material to the pupil's level of development. The difficulty here is not so much at the junior level or at the top of the high school as with pupils between the ages of thirteen and seventeen, who are at extremely varied stages of development. Some have reached puberty early and possess an extensive preliminary knowledge of the subject, which needs correcting, completing, and deepening. Others have developed normally and need information of a more elementary kind. Others again are strikingly late in development, have not thought about sexual questions, and are not ready for detailed information. Teaching must aim at meeting the legitimate needs of all these groups. The "early developers" may have a coarse and perhaps defiant attitude to what the school has to tell them, and look down on its advice as fussy correction and amplification of what they already know. Highly sensitive pupils, and those with a twisted and guilt-loaded attitude to sex, may find descriptions of anatomical and physiological details disgusting and painful; it is specially important for these children that lessons should throughout be given with tact, judgement and sensitivity. Well-meant instruction unsuited for a particular pupil may produce a distaste for the teacher's presentation and even for sex in general. Some pupils cannot bear to be questioned on anatomical facts, so that a teacher must depart from the usual principles about questioning and rely on his knowledge of each pupil before asking him about the lesson.

Children in Special classes have a particular need of sex instruction, and so have those in schools for the blind and schools for the deaf. The teachers who tell these children about sex have a great responsibility. They should follow the directions given in this handbook as far as is possible, but adapt their teaching according to their pupils' defects and stage of development.

It may help towards understanding pupils if some attention is paid to the general psychological context of sex development in youth. Love at this age is usually experienced as two separate things—romantic love and sexual desire. The romantic kind of love usually belongs to the period before desire makes itself felt. Sometimes the relationship is reversed, or desire and romanticism alternate. The growth of romantic love and the development of an ideal under its influence are conducive to a healthy development of the personality. It should be stressed that sex only reaches its full development when conjoined with love—that it is a gift to mankind which can bestow great happiness, providing it is the expression of a deeper relationship between man and woman.

However, sex instruction is not intended for youth only at the romantic age; it must begin long before that. As early as the junior level, teaching needs to be carried out with this period in mind—always avoiding, however, material which would prejudice a slow awakening by anticipating it.

The natural shyness which marks youth's attitude to sex should be preserved as an asset. It is a mistake to be matter-of-fact and to try and free young people from this natural feeling by teaching them that it is an unnecessary inhibition, since it is in fact a protection against experiences for which they are not yet ripe. Shyness is not to be confused with prudery. The prude makes a point of showing ostentatiously what he feels about the improper—which includes anything to do with sex, a subject he considers dirty and shameful. It is this mistaken valuation of sex which the sexual enlightenment of our time has rightly cast aside.

There is no other field in which it is so important to emphasize that the school's task is not only to give information but also to train character. If there is one aspect of living which cannot be divorced from character and conscience, it is sex. Since an individual's experiences of sex can leave deep traces on his character, for good or evil, it is most important that an educator should continually bear in mind the intimate effect of sex on the formation of ideals and moral attitudes. The romantic period, with its characteristic view of sex and love, is a fertile nursery for the formation of the right kind of ideals. Sex and an inclination to aspire after high ideals go together in young people—just as a failure to aspire in this way is often associated with a vulgarized experience of sex and love.

The moral element in teaching about sex should stress the tension between opposing tendencies in the individual, but also show the necessity of controlling the sexual urge by willpower and self-discipline. In doing so the individual has to impose on himself restrictions that may feel oppressive and hard to bear, but it should be made clear that this is better in the long run than giving in to the desires of the moment.

It has already been stated that it is neither desirable nor permissible for the school to teach a way of living as morally and socially right which does not agree with what pupils know life actually is, for the disparity would seriously jeopardize the result of the school's educational effort. Instruction should not, on the other hand, be adapted to suit standards which are not worthy or desirable either for the individual or for society. No one should underestimate the school's ability to influence the development of young people into adults with healthy habits of living. Teaching should aim at showing which things are not morally desirable from a personal and social point of view and cannot, therefore, be accepted as norms of behaviour. Young people can thus be given a good start to forming attitudes which will help them in the healthy development of their personalities.

It is a requirement of society that children shall leave school with enough knowledge to understand what society demands of them as citizens. They should have learnt through the school the broad outlines of the norms which govern the way people live together in a civilized community, and the consequences of following or not following them. This is an important part of the school's educational activity: it enables young people to appreciate what is socially and morally involved in sexual life, and to understand what they should aim at. Most young people have certainly got to know in their own homes what their parents and society expect of them; it is the school's responsibility to see that it is made quite clear to all, without exception, what this is. Sex instruction must give them a clear understanding of the obligations which accompany sexual relations between man and woman. It is necessary to bring the understanding home that these are not just a personal matter between a man and a woman, but that they have consequences—especially for any children—and are in general a social matter of great importance. Young people must be shown that it is their parents, and often society too, that have to bear the economic and other consequences of their engaging in sexual relations while they are still growing up.

The danger of separating sexual desire from love should be stated, and the fact that sex can never give any real satisfaction without an emotional attachment towards the partner, whereas sex combined with communion of spirit bestows lasting happiness. Young people must be taught to understand that those who do not live in accordance with these precepts run great risks, which are all the more serious in that they find it difficult to see them. Attention should be drawn to the fact that free liaisons for the sake of satisfying instinctual desires can result in children being born without the parents having a home to offer them. Such free liaisons hold a serious consequence of another kind—quite apart from the risk of venereal diseases. This is the risk of impairing capacity for deeper communion when the attachment is also one of love. Since the first sexual experience can have such great significance for the whole course of sexual life, it is most important that it should have the right setting, and not be accompanied and followed by disillusionment and accusations of conscience.

The teacher must uphold the view that continence during adolescence is the only course the school can recommend with a good conscience. It gives the individual the best prospects for achieving personal happiness later on. The justification for this view can be given as the adolescent's lack of spiritual and physical maturity. The most important psychological consideration is probably that when sex life is started too early, it is likely to be detached from its objects—home, family, and children. Sex life should from the start be associated with these, and should accordingly develop with a sense of responsibility and consideration towards the partner and towards society; but during adolescence the prerequisites of such a relationship are nonexistent. Pupils must be taught to understand that the concepts of honour and of thought for one's neighbour which apply in everyday life are absolutely essential in everything man does in his sexual life.

With regard to continence, attention should be drawn to its positive virtues. It is advisable for the teacher to point out that it is in no way harmful for a young person.

It may be objected that much of what has been said above is not an immediate problem for pupils at school, except possibly those pupils in the top classes of the high school, and that to tell younger ones about it is neither necessary nor appropriate. The objection is not unjustified, especially as regards boys, who are not as mature for such instruction as girls. But it must not be forgotten that, for many of the pupils who leave school while they are still young, school is the last opportunity to get advice on these matters. This is a question of giving *preventive* advice and guidance for the whole of life.

There is no question of saying everything that has been said on these pages about the connection between sex and morality. The important thing is that a teacher should have in his mind the idea of love, with all the rich facets for moral upbringing which it embraces, and that this idea should underlie and inspire the picture of sexual life which he draws.

A teacher should not set up sexual norms for adolescence without thoroughly justifying them. He should not, for example, make a bald statement that continence is the only course that the school can recommend. This, which is quite right in itself, should be said clearly and without reservation, but it should not be said only in the context of the positive value of continence; the class should also be shown what can happen if restraint is not observed. Only then is the need for continence seen in its true light. Pupils should, in other words, be taught not only that they ought to restrain their desires while they are still growing up, but the *reason why* they ought to do so, for only then will the lesson achieve its real purpose. This is done in the lesson-example [. . .] so that the justification is as convincing as possible.

Marriage occurs at a relatively late age in modern society. Pupils should be made to understand that it is better to establish a home at an early stage, even if under modest circumstances, than to enter without any further scruples into an intimate liaison. The teacher must pay special attention to the loosening of morals involved in the not uncommon tendency to consider it normal and permissible conduct to live according to one's primitive desires within one's social group or circle of acquaintances. This is conducive to self-indulgence and, besides, reduces the sense of responsibility, thus inviting unpredictable personal and social consequences. There is no place here for advice that is hesitant. The difficult situation in which a great part of modern youth live is such that they gradually acquire a warped view of what normal life is at their age; and this should be borne in mind in teaching them. There is good reason for dealing with the effect of unsuitable books, films, and plays on young people. Many of these are directly calculated to undermine firmness of character and power of resistance, and contribute in a dangerous way to creating a false picture of the way to happiness.

Young people are usually eager to start a discussion, and they seldom hesitate to point out—either in class or in club groups—that what they pick up about sex from the world around them is not always in agreement with the school's view of what adolescent behaviour should be. Even if no one contributes such a comment to the discussion, it is important for the teacher to take a suitable opportunity of analyzing the pros and cons of a youthful life of pleasure and so help his pupils to form a healthy view of it.

In dealing with these questions, it is essential for the teacher to draw a clear picture of the disastrous influence of drink in producing uncontrolled sexual desire, blunted judgement, recklessness, and false self-confidence.

It may well be asked what teachers can say in detail about the undesirable influence which modern dance *can* have. Because dancing is so common in social life, the result will almost certainly be to arouse direct opposition. For youth, dancing is a spontaneous expression of the joy of living. Remarks should therefore be confined to pointing out the risks involved in *dancing in conjunction with drinking*. Young people should get a very definite declaration from the school on this point, and suitable opportunities should be taken of repeating this declaration to parents, guardians, and youth festival organizers as well.

It should be emphasized that, apart from actual lessons on sex, the school and all its teachers can carry out another educational function which is also very important for sexual education: that of helping young people to organize their leisure activities suitably and so letting their various interests develop. The school's attention should be particularly concentrated on those pupils who lack healthy interests and appear lax and listless. The more the school can stimulate such pupils to take up games and hobbies and live an open-air life the better it will be for them. One must consider what an artificial life a great part of the youth of our cities are obliged to lead. Overcrowding and other circumstances often drive children out of the home. This makes it all the more imperative for the school to try and direct such pupils' interests into fields which will help them to develop. To do so involves exceptional difficulties for the school, of course; but it is essential to state here as an indisputable fact that this is one of the greatest tasks of education.

When it is necessary to express disapproval of certain sexual conduct, it should be made clear that this does not imply that due consideration and sympathetic understanding are not called for with regard to the special difficulties which some people have. It is essential to avoid assiduously any appearance of passing judgement on those who because of their nature or because of the pressure of their environment have been unable to follow the lines indicated here. The school should stop at giving rules for socially responsible conduct and be on its guard against fostering a pharisaic attitude in young people.

It should be explained that unmarried people, especially if they have children, have special difficulties and problems which do not exist for complete families with husband, wife, and children. This problem is dealt with in detail, but exaggerated attention should not be given to divorced people, widows, widowers, or unmarried mothers. It is well to remark, however, that an unmarried father or mother who does everything possible to overcome these difficulties shows a worthy public spirit, as also do those who give their help to such parents and children.

The subject of sexual knowledge should be thoroughly treated in local geography and nature study in the lower school, and in biology, history, and civics in the upper school. Certain parts can also be taken up in religious knowledge and in child care.

A division according to subject has been advocated in the upper school, so that the medical and biological aspects are covered exclusively in biology, the moral and ethical ones in religious knowledge, and the social and economic ones in history. However, a strict division of tasks in this way is neither possible nor appropriate. Every teacher with experience of giving lessons on sex knows that moral judgements have to be applied in the biology section, and for that matter social and economic considerations as well. There are great difficulties in synchronizing the syllabuses in different subjects, and there is a risk of impairing the effectiveness of moral training if, for example, it has to wait until a suitable occasion presents itself in the course on religious knowledge. For these reasons the biology teacher must deal with moral concepts as well as biological ones in his lessons on sex. Giving pupils a deeper moral appreciation of life in the light of one's own subject does not mean trespassing on religious knowledge. The subject of sex is best served by being viewed objectively in the light of both biology and religious knowledge.

There are, however, certain moral questions which have always been considered as coming under religious knowledge—those, for example, connected with marriage. They are not included in the lesson-examples accompanying this handbook, because it is taken for granted that the scripture teacher will deal thoroughly with them, either by direct information, in class discussion, or by following up a talk from a pupil. It is extremely important that pupils should realize fully that home and family are the groundrock of society, cemented together partly by love between man and woman and between parents and children, partly by law. The latter is a support for the former: without it the bonds of marriage would be easier to dissolve, and this would entail great perils, especially for any children. The changes involved when a marriage is broken up can seriously injure the child's sense of security and make it difficult for him to make adjustments in life. Legal marriage has accordingly a moral value which cannot be dispensed with. This said, it must be pointed out that cases can occur when a marriage cannot and ought not to continue, because its continued existence would cause more harm to husband, wife, and children than its dissolution.

If sex instruction is to enter naturally into general school instruction it should be undertaken by professional teachers. While it has often been maintained that a doctor should undertake it where possible, it is only the teacher who has been specially trained and is accustomed to dealing with children. Only then will sex instruction fuse with other subjects in the frame of which it should be imparted. If, of course, a teacher feels that it involves particular difficulties for him, he should tell his headmaster, so that this part of instruction can be transferred to another member of the staff, to a doctor, or to some other suitable person. Teachers can sometimes turn to the school medical officer for expert advice on some particular feature of instruction. Special lectures by qualified doctors can often play a useful role. The school nurse may be called upon for instruction in menstruation hygiene.

To what extent boys and girls should be taught about sex together depends largely upon who teaches them. For some teachers common instruction in this subject presents difficult or insuperable problems, while others find it easier this way. Common instruction is desirable in principle for several reasons. Sex instruction can then be fitted into the general teaching in the school without any special arrangement, and both boys and girls receive the same information in all parts of the subject. Separate instruction might seem indicated for certain items such as menstruation hygiene so that the subject could be treated more briefly for the boys, who are perhaps less interested in a detailed exposition, but such a procedure would be mistaken. It must not be forgotten that pupils of both sexes must be prepared for the task of being parents one day and teaching their children, both boys and girls. Teaching boys about this should also serve the purpose of stimulating consideration for women's physical and emotional difficulties during menstruation.

If a teacher doubts for one reason or another whether he can give instruction to both sexes together, then the possibility should be considered of separating boys and girls for particular parts of the course, such as those on night emissions, masturbation, menstruation, and contraceptives. But it must be emphasized that both boys and girls should receive identical and adequate knowledge of each topic.

In describing venereal diseases, special care should be taken to avoid frightening children. The description should be put forward briefly, with the main emphasis on the need for living in a manner that excludes the possibility of contracting them.

The fact that there are people with morbid sexual tendencies should also be given—but given in an extremely careful and delicate manner. [. . .] In view of the danger for children from sexually abnormal individuals, it is wise to warn pupils right from the junior school against following strangers.

The discussion of contraceptives in the lesson-example [. . .] starts with brief information on the more important methods and proceeds to a summary of the circumstances in which they are customarily used and the reasons why they are used. It is important to stress that contraceptives afford only partial protection. It must be stated clearly that knowledge of the reduced risk of pregnancy and venereal disease which contraceptives give is not a reason for thinking that there is no harm in entering into sexual relationships during adolescence.

For older pupils sex instruction will pay attention to their future role as builders of families and as parents, and will give them due knowledge about the problems of starting a family, and of pregnancy and childbirth, together with information on social welfare facilities. It is of great importance that full attention should be given to this side of the subject. Nor should the questions of late marriage and choice of marriage partner be overlooked.

It is essential that teachers should find out in advance as much as possible about children's home circumstances, and that they should throughout maintain as close contact as possible with parents. Teachers should bear in mind that, in describing the happy relationship in a proper home with father, mother, and children, they may unwittingly cause pain to children who come from broken homes—to the children of divorced parents, for example, to foster children, and to children who have no father at home. In teaching about sex, teachers should as far as possible work in general agreement with parents, who will appreciate knowing what a *planned* course on sex will include, and how detailed it will be in a given section and for children in different age groups. Attention should be paid to parents' opinions both in the content of the syllabus and in the manner of its presentation. The school should make every effort to keep parents and guardians well informed about the nature and significance of the school's educational activity in this field. A teacher's own efforts will suffice for this, where parent opposition is not too strong. It is, of course, a help and advantage for the teacher as well to be able to hear parents' views on certain questions. The opportunity can also be used to put forward points of view for the direct purpose of enlightening parents as, for example, on the different sides of "having fun", on light reading, parties, drink, etc.—all features of young people's lives which can have repercussions in the field of sex. Parents should be given a chance to express their experiences, worries, and misgivings on these matters. The whole subject is an exceptionally rich one of pressing importance to everyone, and an open discussion in mutual confidence should give many dubious parents clear information and positive viewpoints. Intimate unprejudiced co-operation between home and school is the only way to build afresh and at the same time to help the home in its often difficult task of bringing up children.

If a teacher notices that a pupil shows signs of emotional disturbance or physical disease, he should give a description of the condition to the school medical officer or the school nurse so that as full an investigation as possible can be made; and similarly in the event of disturbances in sexual behaviour, proved cases of homosexuality, pregnancy in a pupil, or venereal disease. [. . .] The living conditions of pupils who live, not at home, but in lodgings, often call for a certain supervision and control. This is an important task for the school nurse.

Society and Sex in Sweden

Birgitta Linnér

FOREWORD

Swedish sex attitudes and practices have aroused considerable interest abroad during recent years. Countless newspaper and magazine articles have dealt with this subject, but more often than not the emphasis has been on sensationalism, with myths presented as facts. In short, there have been far too many "sin in Sweden" stories which seem to serve no other purpose than to sell the periodicals in which they appear.

The aim of this small booklet is to present factual information on various aspects of sexual life in Sweden. First and foremost it is concerned with sex education in the schools, the laws and regulations that deal with sex and marriage, equality of the sexes, and various measures taken by society to support family life.

The different regulations and institutions reflect certain basic principles: that young people should be given information on sexual questions and that this subject can and ought to be discussed objectively and openly; that all children are entitled to the same care, which means that there should be no discrimination against children born out of wedlock; and, lastly, that husband and wife are to be considered equal partners in marriage as well as in other relationships. Maybe it should be added that equality between women and men is accepted in all areas of life as a basic philosophy, but in reality there is a long way to go.

These democratic principles express an attitude toward sexual and family life that officially represents Swedish society. Yet opinion concerning the moral code is far from unanimous. There are people who argue that the official policy is too radical, while other groups maintain that it is too conservative. Values and norms sometimes clash, and from time to time a heated debate flares up.

One can hardly say that at present there exists a generally accepted code for sexual and family life. Indeed, all simplified diagnoses are misleading. Sweden is currently undergoing a process whereby both institutions and evaluations are being transformed. However, it appears quite certain that the principles already established by law and regulations will become part of the new way of life.

331

A good deal of the material presented in this pamphlet is already part of the professional literature on the subject.

SEX EDUCATION IN THE SCHOOLS

Sweden is one of the very few countries in the world where sex education is compulsory in the schools. It was introduced into the school curriculum in the 1940s and became a required course in 1956. This step was taken because of a clear need for the right kind of information on the subject.

There is a widespread belief that the home is the proper place for young people to receive instruction in sex. Parents, in other words, should be the teachers. Far too often, however, they are singularly ill equipped to assume this role.

Dr Gösta Rodhe, Chief Medical Officer of the Swedish National Board of Education, has this to say:

> In my opinion sex education should start as early as possible, that is, as soon as the child can understand what you say. But we all know that many parents are too inhibited to give even small children information about reproduction, and that, when their children are older; they lack the knowledge to give satisfactory sex information. Therefore the responsibility for the information in this field falls on the school.

The basic aim of sex education is to provide knowledge in a subject that is of the greatest importance in the personal development of the students. An urgent task of such instruction, says Dr Rodhe, is to create the necessary conditions for a harmonious sexual life. The ideal thing appears to be cooperation between the home and the school.

The first teachers' manuals on sexual education were published by the National Board of Education some twenty years ago, followed by an illustrated handbook entitled "Handbook on Sex Instruction in the Schools".* The latter was issued in 1956 when the subject became compulsory.

"The purpose of sex instruction in Swedish schools is to present biological information and to impart knowledge in a manner that will help not only in molding ideals but also in building character", it is stated in the preface to this handbook. "Instruction on these lines is intended to have a pronounced ethical basis." These ideas are very much debated right now.

The need for sex education in schools is explained in the manual, as

---

*See pp. 319-330 of *Sex, Schools, and Society.*

well as what kind of sex instruction should be given to pupils in different age groups. There are also suggested lesson outlines.

The manual begins with an examination of the sexual problems of the pre-school child. Instruction starts in the first grade when the children are seven, and it is not conducted on a "birds-and-bees" level. A direct approach is considered the best way of handling the subject.

The initial discussion is limited to how the sexes differ, where children come from, including the role of the father, how they develop before birth, how they are born, and in what ways they are dependent on their mothers, fathers and homes. These fundamental facts are reviewed in the following two classes.

Between the ages of eleven and thirteen (fourth, fifth and sixth grades) instruction continues with the structure and function of the sexual organs, puberty, menstruation, night pollution (wet dreams), masturbation, conception, pregnancy and "traumatic experiences" during pregnancy, development of the fetus, labor, determination of sex, twins, etc.

It's interesting to note that earlier only girls were given information about menstruation and menstrual hygiene, and boys night pollution and masturbation. A step in the right direction was taken in 1956 when instruction in these matters was started for classes of boys and girls together. And at this stage class discussion is encouraged, with questions and answers instead of straight lectures. Visual aids are also used.

The subject matter covered in these grades is as follows: (1) A review of previous items as required. (2) Structure and function of the sexual organs. (3) Development of the fetus and pregnancy. (4) Labor. (5) Sex and youth—moral considerations—abstention from sexual relations during adolescence. (6) Children born out of wedlock. (7) Spontaneous and induced abortions. (8) Venereal diseases. (9) Contraceptives. (10) Sterilization. (11) The climacteric or menopause. (12) Sexual abnormalities. (13) Moral and social aspects of sex. (14) Welfare measures to help in setting up a family. (15) Welfare measures during pregnancy, confinement and nursing. (16) Welfare measures for the care and training of children and adolescents.

Compulsory education ends in Sweden with the ninth school year. Those students who continue with their education—usually between the ages of seventeen and twenty—are given a review of what has already been covered, followed by more comprehensive information on various sexual questions. According to an amendment of 1965 from the National Board of Education contraceptive techniques and venereal diseases should have a special emphasis. This now also holds true for economic and technical schools, which previously had no sex education programs, as well as for various vocational schools. Thus sex education is a part of the school curriculum for all age groups.

Although sex education from the sixth grade up is given chiefly in biology classes, the Board of Education recommends that it also be touched upon in lessons on religion, social studies, and other subjects in which questions of sex come up naturally. Since 1967 there is also a teachers' manual for sex education for psychologically and physically disturbed children in special schools. Earlier very little concern was shown for their needs in this area. On an experimental and limited scale teaching machines and programmed learning are used. Since 1954 the Swedish Broadcasting Corporation has broadcast sex education programs, and later television programs were initiated for both students and adults. Films and slides are among other audio-visual aids used.

Speaking of teaching aids, one should mention a set of color photographs about childbirth by the Swedish photographer Lennart Nilsson, who gained fame on both sides of the Atlantic for his book, *A Child Is Born*. These unusual and excellent photographs, which include pictures of the fetus, are used in schools as well as in medical schools. "A Birth of a Baby", based on the book *A Child Is Born,* is part of a film program, which is used in many schools.

While sex education in the schools has made unmistakable progress it has by no means remained immune from criticism. The teachers' handbook on sex instruction, for instance, has drawn fire from both conservative and radical circles. The former favor a strong moral approach and want strict and clear ethical norms to be taught. The latter group, on the other hand, charges that sex instruction in the schools perpetuates many of the old prejudices. They feel that only factual information should be supplied, leaving the question of norms to the individual.

A heated debate has been going on about how much or how little the school should commit itself to the teaching of modern contraceptive techniques. This involves different and often irreconcilable attitudes to the moral question of premarital sex relations.

The debate flared up when some youngsters suggested that contraceptives should be supplied by the schools. Many citizens wanted teaching about birth control to be excluded; other groups, liberals and youth organizations, were very strongly opposed to that point of view.

One hundred and forty medical doctors in Sweden wanted what they labeled "firmer sexual norms" to be taught. Several women's religious groups got 200,000 names on a petition supporting the doctors' stand. On the other hand, a nationwide organization of students in secondary schools and junior colleges maintained that in this field only facts, and not evaluations, should be taught to the youth.

In 1964 a Royal Commission, with members representing different shades of opinion, was appointed to revise and improve the entire sex education program and the teachers' handbook. It is interesting to note that a young student belongs to the group, as the representative of the whole student body. They are still at work. The Commission has released some investigations about sex education in the schools and sexual behavior and attitudes in Sweden. These are intended as a source of reference for the final report of the Commission. But some revisions already made by the National Board of Education show that the official attitude, often at variance with the attitude of experts and public opinion in general, has come around to recognizing the fact that Sweden is a pluralistic society. For example, one of the passages from the original handbook reads as follows:

> The teacher must uphold the view that continence during adolescence is the only course the school can recommend with good conscience. Pupils should be made to understand that it is better to establish a home at an early age, even if under modest circumstances, than to enter without further scruples into an intimate liaison.

In the amended version this has been changed to read:

> It is important for the students to realize that laws and norms vary from time to time, from people to people, and that within one and the same country, different groups may have different views on sex relations; also that the norms of one culture cannot be directly transferred to another culture. However, the fact that norms are relative should not be taken as implying that no norms are required. As a social being, man must respect the demands of society in his sexual behavior as elsewhere.

The amendments in the handbook reflect the Board of Education's gradual acceptance of some of the liberal views on sex behavior and attitudes.

The pluralistic approach in Swedish sex education is underlined in the newest proposals of 1971 by the Governmental Sex Education Commission. Their basic philosophy can be summarized as follows.

The objective of sex education is to inform people about anatomy, physiology, and sexual life so that shortcomings arising from ignorance are counteracted and harmonious relationships between two people are promoted.

The education also teaches that sex life is closely linked with personality, psycho-social relationships and society in general. Such an insight should help to encourage greater consideration, responsibility and concern.

Further the Commission considers it necessary to draw a line between not taking a stand in certain cases and definitely taking a stand in other cases. This stems from the basic set of values which is included in the recommendations and principles of Swedish education which include the following:

1. One must not force oneself sexually on anyone.
2. The moral implications of the sexual behavior of men and women should be judged equally. The argument that women are not equal to men should be totally dismissed.
3. The school must disassociate itself from discrimination in matters dealing with sex life, a question of greater importance now owing to increased immigration of people from other cultures.
4. The school should not pass moral judgement on sexual minority groups.
5. When one does not want to or cannot take care of a child, one is obliged to use contraceptives to prevent conception when having intercourse.
6. The prohibition against intercourse when one has a venereal disease is not merely a legal one, but also an elementary demand for responsibility and consideration.
7. The school should uphold tolerance for groups with more restrictive or less restrictive views and values on sex life and relationships, provided the behavior is one of responsibility and consideration.

But still the sex education program does not work as well as it ought to. Many circumstances contribute to inadequate treatment of the subject, among them the following: the subject is relatively new and difficult; the teachers' training is not good enough; some embarrassed teachers ignore the subject; some teachers put off the teaching until the end of the semester, when there is little time left for this subject which is of such importance to the students.

In order to try to rectify this situation many efforts have been made to improve the training of teachers in sex education. The National Swedish Association for Sex Education (RFSU)* arranges workshops in different parts of the country. There have been, for instance, university seminars, workshops, and a number of extension courses for teachers. Various experts were called in to lecture.

"Sexology—A Seminar in Relationship" was the title of a very fine seminar conducted at Uppsala University Extension Courses in the spring of 1967. Different professional groups that come in contact with sexual problems and sexual relations, such as medical doctors, psychologists, teachers, lawyers, ministers, social workers, and sociologists, were invited.

The aim was to encourage these professional people to look at sex in a broader context, instead of, for example, the minister examining it from a moral point of view, the doctor considering only its medical aspects, the lawyer concerned only with its legal implications, etc.

---

*RFSU (*Riksförbundet för Sexuell Upplysning*)—The National Association for Sex Education. [Author's note.]

Sexuality's healthier aspects were also to get attention. The discussions were frank and very enlightening.

Workshops for teachers, arranged by the National Board of Education and led by its chief medical officer, also feature lecturers from different professions. Among the subjects taken up are conception and pregnancy, puberty and menopause, venereal diseases, contraceptive techniques, abortion, masturbation, and sexual aberrations. Other topics discussed are of a more general nature, such as problems of teenage girls, the youth of today and their sex life, etc.

Valuable information on sex education is now and then exchanged at various international conferences. The Swedish delegates, backed by wide experience at home, have usually had much to offer their colleagues from other countries.

At a conference convened in 1964 at the UNESCO Institute for Education in Hamburg, Germany,* Dr Maj-Briht Bergström-Walan told about the Swedish program for sex education in the schools. Here are some of the points she stressed:

Tactfulness is required on the part of all educators when giving pupils sexual information. The teacher is asked to present and discuss the different possible attitudes towards life. Teachers ought to convey to pupils good and genuine knowledge but also explain to them the importance of knowing how and where to apply their knowledge.

Children are given the opportunity to ask questions which must be answered with the greatest possible objectivity. Special emphasis is put on individual contact which might be desired between pupils who have special problems and the teacher he or she trusts most.

Sex education should not be isolated in time or space; i.e., it should be built up gradually and be adapted to the different degrees of maturity. The aim of sex education goes beyond mere information; it should have a formative character in the first place. We must make young adolescents understand the importance of individual responsibility, tolerance, human dignity, etc.

Let us not forget that although we can use many audio-visual aids, such as, e.g., films, slides, radio, and television, in addition to lectures, these means can never be a substitute for true human contact between educator and class or between educator and the individual pupil.

It is necessary to contact parents and teachers first before starting sex education. I do not think young people today are any worse regarding their moral attitude and behavior than our generation was, but this young generation is more outspoken and unchecked. They ask for guidance and sincerity. Here, as in many other topics and tasks, the teacher has a key position. Education demands not

---

* See pp. 441-446 of *Sex, Schools, and Society.*

only a great deal of knowledge from the teacher but a great deal
from his or her personality.

At the International Planned Parenthood Federation Conference held
in Copenhagen in 1966 Dr Rodhe discussed "The Role of the Teacher
in Sex Education". In commenting on the moral aspects, Dr Rodhe reflected the National Board of Education's new thinking on the subject,
which resulted in the aforementioned revisions in the teachers' handbook.
Here is an excerpt from the paper he presented at the conference:

> It is of great importance that the teacher should not proclaim
> primarily that a certain moral norm has to be accepted. Any such
> commandment is liable to evoke immediate opposition from many
> young people and therefore lead to no results. From a pedagogical
> standpoint it seems better to give a survey of the different opinions
> on a certain topic, such as premarital intercourse, and to let the
> young people think the problem over. To me this seems to be the
> best way of helping them in the situation where they have to make
> a decision themselves.

To many foreign psychologists, sociologists, or educators who would
like to see sex education introduced into their own school systems
Sweden's viewpoint, as spelled out by the Swedish delegates, must seem
very enlightened indeed. But it is not always easy to put theory into
practice. Sex is certainly a complex subject.

Why some teachers become embarrassed at having to explain the
facts of life to youngsters is quite understandable. When they themselves
went to school sex was little discussed, if at all. And now, almost overnight, so to speak, they are expected to explain it and speak openly
about it in the classroom.

The problems they come up against can be surmised from the experience of Mrs Birgitta Hellstrand-Rystad, who teaches in Lund, a university town in southern Sweden. In a letter to the author she listed
some of the questions among many asked by children of about fourteen
years of age in her seventh-grade class. They are as follows:

> Is having intercourse fun? How does it feel? Does it feel the same
> for girls as for boys? Does it hurt very much the first time? (This
> from a girl) Does something come out of the girl too? Does it
> hurt having children? Does it hurt so much that even grown
> women cry? When do you think we should have intercourse for
> the first time? My opening is so small, will I be able to have inter-
> course? How can a boy put his penis into a girl?—it looks so soft.
> (And after the answer to that question) But what if it isn't erect
> just when one wants to have intercourse? Can a woman have chil-
> dren without intercourse? Do old people (she probably meant

forty-year-olds) also like to have intercourse? Do you have to show your naked body to the boy you sleep with?

It should be pointed out at once that Mrs Hellstrand-Rystad, an experienced and knowledgeable teacher, was fully capable of handling such delicate questions in an open, intelligent manner. And this, of course, is of paramount importance. Children need to know—that's what sex education is all about.

Writing about sex relations, sexual morality, and sexual reality for teenagers is quite difficult. But there are books that attempt to provide teenagers with adequate information and education in this field. Lis Asklund and Torsten Wickbom, who have had the sex education programs on the Swedish Radio and TV, have written a popular book called "Way to Maturity" (*Vägen till mognad,* Sveriges Radio, 1966). They try to combine factual information with moral discussions.

An illustrated booklet published by the RFSU for teenagers—"Harmonious Relationship" (*Samspel,* RFSU, 1967)—gives factual information without any moral evaluations. It covers the following topics: the sex drive, intercourse, fertilization mechanism, infertility, personal hygiene, planned parenthood, children of course—but when you want them, contraceptive methods, where to get advice on contraceptives, Are there age barriers for advice on contraception? Which contraceptive the first time? Harmonious relationships: when? Partnership—sex problems.

The RFSU book has been a center of controversy. Its attitude toward the subject is implied in the following discussion about intercourse. "It is not a question of 'giving in' nor of 'getting', nor of merely 'giving' but a mutually joyful and sincere experience." One of the authors, Thorsten Sjövall, says in an article in the newspaper *Dagens Nyheter:* ". . . the whole content and mode of presentation in 'Harmonious Relationship' is marked by the conviction that sexual activity among teenagers is not merely an occurrence but a common rule. That idea is supported not only by RFSU's experience but by investigations which show that merely a dwindling proportion of young people reach the age of twenty without experience of sexual activity in the form of masturbation, petting, or complete intercourse."

The first textbook to follow the new basic philosophy for sex education programs in secondary schools appeared in the spring of 1968, "Sex Life and Living Together" (*Sexualliv och Samlevnad*) by Linnér-Westholm. This sex education brochure consistently applies a pluralistic view to ethical matters. It discusses questions such as different moral views about sexual attitudes and behavior, What decides our moral views? Do we impose different moral norms on men and women? It might be added that knowledge is included about the Masters and Johnson research, showing that the basic sexual response cycle is the same for both men and women. Chapters on different aspects of family planning, contraceptive techniques, and venereal diseases should also be mentioned.

Recently a four-page brochure, "If You Are Pregnant", was distributed by the National Board of Health and Welfare primarily to ninth-graders, about sixteen years of age. In these days of sexual equality it is aimed not only at girls, "but also at boys who need to know about these matters".

The brochure states:

> If you suspect you are pregnant, because you miss your period, do talk with the school nurse. She will be glad to help you to get the facts; that takes about a week. Or visit a private doctor or the Maternal Health Center. You can get the address from the district nurse.

It states further:

> If you become pregnant accidentally and are considering abortion, do contact at once a doctor or a social worker. An abortion is less troublesome at the beginning of a pregnancy. And if you don't get permission for legal abortion, then you need as much help and support as possible.
>
> If you want to give birth to your child, you ought to register for health control at the Maternal Health Center as soon as possible. There you receive advice and treatment, free of charge.

This brochure has been criticized by more traditional groups as well as by the radicals, but it seems that young people like the information they get here.

The newest little pamphlet, "Women and Men. Sex—Things You Ought to Know", is published by the National Immigration and Naturalization Board (*Statens Invandrarverk*), for the information of immigrants to Sweden. It is published in various languages, not with the intention of imposing on readers what happens to be regarded as a natural and positive attitude toward sex, but with the sole aim of giving non-Swedish-speaking people access to information on a subject area where ignorance can lead to personal tragedies.

Often concerted action by various groups—parents, doctors, teachers, student leaders—at the local level can bring about improvements in sex education. This brings to mind a sound pilot project started recently in Malmö, a fairly large Swedish city. A Malmö gynecologist, concerned about the increase in young teenage pregnancies in the area, appealed to the head administrator of the city school system. Couldn't the schools do more to help young people with information about contraceptive techniques and sex education in a broader sense, he wanted to know.

The administrator gathered a small group of people from one of the schools to discuss the problem. These included the school doctor, school nurse, one of the biology teachers, and two student representatives—a seventeen-year-old boy and an eighteen-year-old girl. All wanted better sex education, including information about contraception.

The adults were of the opinion that the sex programs should be widened in the upper classes, while the students thought changes should take place as early as the eighth or ninth grade. The adults finally went along with the students, and an experimental program—with more emphasis on contraceptives—was started in the eighth grade. The gynecologist was invited to give a series of four lectures to the pupils. This marked the beginning of a new, close collaboration between the medical doctors and the school, and it put them in an excellent position to be of help to the young students.

It should be mentioned that medical students as well as other medical personnel receive needed sex knowledge. For example, medical students in obstetrics and gynecology have instruction in sexology, contraception, questions of abortion and sterilization, in psychosomatic disorders connected with pregnancy and childbirth, and in gynecology.

It should also be added that the Parents and Teachers Organizations of the schools mostly have positive and cooperative attitudes toward the school sex education program.

Some twenty years ago those opposed to sex education in general and teaching about birth control in particular said it would encourage license, and that young people would not want to marry, because they could enjoy sex anyhow. The young generation, it was asserted, would not bother to have children.

It seems, however, that none of these negative predictions have been confirmed by reality. As yet there is no evidence that family life is being destroyed in Sweden. People continue to establish permanent and stable relationships as adults, and they want to provide a home and security for the young.

To sum up, there are those who have a superstitious belief that a good sex program will automatically solve all problems; others believe such a program encourages looseness and promiscuity. It seems that the reality lies somewhere between these extremes. There is no doubt that it takes more to build our psychosexual behavioral pattern and our morality than a mere sex program. Nonetheless, and however controversial the subject may be, we have a clear duty to support the young generation with the knowledge they need so desperately: it is not only the responsibility of the home; sex education should be taught as part of the regular school curriculum.

MARRIAGE, DIVORCE AND CHILDREN BORN OUT OF WEDLOCK

It is common knowledge that a very large percentage of young people in Sweden have premarital sexual relations. Although the figure seems to have increased in the last couple of decades, this is certainly not as recent a phenomenon as some people might think. Sexual relations before marriage were accepted to a great extent in the ancient rural society. Today premarital sex is virtually taken for granted, with only a minority of Swedes considering it absolutely wrong.

A comprehensive investigation of the sexual habits of high-school youngsters (average age was slightly under eighteen) in the fairly large industrial city of Örebro was made in 1964 by Drs Hans Linderoth and Bengt Rundberg. They received excellent cooperation from the Children's Psychiatric Clinic, the Örebro School Board, and the local Parents and Teachers Associations.

The study revealed that 57 percent of the boys had experienced intercourse, the median age for first coitus being sixteen. The figure for the girls was 46 percent and the median age seventeen. In the vast majority of the cases first intercourse was between boys and girls who were either "going steady" or knew each other very well.

The investigation contradicted the widely held notion that girls frequently "give in" to boys because they are afraid of being abandoned. Most of them, in fact, had intercourse simply because they wanted to.

Another important study of attitudes toward sex and sex roles was made in 1967 by Professor Gunnar Inghe and Professor Joachim Israel of Stockholm University. Three thousand Stockholm youths between the ages of fifteen and twenty-five were questioned. Of these, 1,700 had sought treatment for venereal disease, while 1,300 were chosen at random as a control group.

This investigation showed that the debut of coitus starts earlier for both boys and girls than was the case shortly after World War II. Fully two-thirds of the Stockholm youths under study had started before the age of twenty, and more girls than boys fell into this category.

Traditional Swedish attitudes of accepting premarital sex relations but expecting sexual fidelity after marriage were confirmed in this research. Two-thirds of the youths said they would condone an occasional infidelity, but four-fifths of the boys and girls considered fidelity in marriage a necessity.

About 80–85 percent of the girls thought that it was all right to go to bed only if one was in love. Roughly half of the boys agreed with this. A common view was that one should know one's partner for quite a while before engaging in sexual intercourse. About one-third of the group had known their partners for more than one year. As in the Örebro research very few girls felt forced to have intercourse because they thought they would lose their boy friends if they didn't.

While most of the youths were quite frank about relating their sexual intercourse experiences, they showed a marked tendency toward guilt feelings and inhibitions when it came to talking about masturbation. Regarding homosexuality, over 50 percent considered it a private matter when it took place between consenting adults. But more than one-third considered homosexuality abnormal and thought something ought to be done about it.

In a study made by Gustaf Jonsson and Anna-Lisa Kälvesten it was found that fathers and mothers in Sweden generally have a rather open-minded attitude toward child sexuality nowadays, especially in the case of masturbation. The majority did not think it harmful for a child to play with his sexual organs. Mothers who did consider it harmful were to a large extent those who had not given their children any sexual information.

The most recent research was done by the Sex Education Committee, already mentioned, "On Sex Life in Sweden", Official Reports 1969:2, the Ministry of Education and Cultural Affairs, Stockholm. This Swedish Kinsey Report aims at giving broad information about sexual attitudes, knowledge, and behavior in a statistically representative sample of the population between eighteen and sixty years of age.

This investigation confirms the trends in earlier research. Ninety-five percent of the total sample had experienced sexual intercourse. The median age at first intercourse for men was 16.6, and for women in the younger generation 17.2. The median age at first intercourse had decreased by one year between 1920 and 1950.

Premarital sex relations for engaged people and couples going steady are supported by more than 90 percent of all men and women. Casual sex relations before marriage are supported by 53 percent of the younger men and 25 percent of the younger women. Older women are almost all against these types of relations.

Thus, most people openly accept premarital sex relations, but in contrast, most people feel that faithfulness in marriage is absolutely essential. Eighty-seven percent of the men and 91 percent of the women held this view. And it might be of interest to note in these days of equality between men and women, that there is no difference in the view of unfaithfulness by a man or by a woman.

A question as to the number of sexual partners one had had within the last month gave the result that 87 percent reported one partner, 6 percent two, 4 percent three to five, and 2 percent more than five partners.

Seventy-one percent of the total sample felt that the use of contraceptive techniques is mandatory at each intercourse not aimed at conception. It might be of interest to note that according to this research the Swedes "make love" 1,100 times to produce one Swedish baby.

The Swedish attitude toward premarital sex is not entirely unrelated to the fact that historically Swedes tend to marry at a relatively late age. And although during the last two decades the trend has been toward earlier marriage, it is still high by international standards. The median age is slightly under twenty-five years for men and around twenty-two for women. The law stipulates that men and women may marry at the age of eighteen. Below this age special dispensation is required.

There is an interesting trend in our society, with more open acceptance of various types of companionship without legal marriage, and more and more possibilities evolving to meet recognized emotional and sexual needs of the individual, male and female alike. Thus many young people live in informal marriage relationships, trial-marriages, conscience marriages, or whatever name is preferred. It might be added that in the social welfare program varied patterns of living together and various family styles—from one-parent families, including unmarried mothers and fathers with minor children, to communal living—are accepted.

Some groups still feel that marriage and a lifelong relationship are the only life style which could be recommended. But certainly marriage should not serve the purpose of merely legitimizing a child or making sexual intercourse legitimate.

The ethical alternatives can be formulated as follows: If, on the one hand, we assume that "sex within marriage" is the only permissible moral, we commit many young people to the possibility of unwanted pregnancies, unwanted marriages with all their complications, illegal abortions, and so on. If, on the other hand, we assume that some young people may have intercourse before they meet the person they want to marry, and that this may happen also with our own children, the best thing we can do is to teach them about birth control. It may turn out that they are able to handle their sex life in a much more mature way and less destructively than if they are unable to channel their emotions and sexual urges. Case histories often show that those girls who get into trouble are those who have not received good sex education and do not know about contraceptive techniques.

An example of the Swedish view on so-called "forced marriages" is found in "Time of Transition", a book about youth and relations between the sexes published in 1962 and used as supplementary reading in many schools. The authors, Lis Asklund and Torsten Wickbom, have this to say:

> Marriage also comes up for discussion when two minors are expecting a child together but are not in love with each other. Often the parents of the expectant mother exert pressure to prevent a scandal among relatives and friends. They want to "legalize" the

child, and not infrequently marriage results. But to marry only for the sake of the child and without real affection for one another involves, as we see it, great risk. Many unhappy marriages began this way: "We were forced to get married". Afterwards, the couple may have more children and their resulting economic situation makes divorce impossible. But they never enjoy a really pleasurable moment together. The question then arises, how well has the emotional and material welfare of the child, for whose sake the marriage originally took place, been provided for? We would like to give you young people who are confronted with a "forced" marriage some advice: wait a while. Think things through. Get to know one another. Perhaps you will discover that you want to deepen your relationship in the future, perhaps not. In any case, neither of you can lose by delaying a decision. Remember, even an unmarried mother has the right to call herself "Mrs".

Such an attitude is prevalent among large groups of Swedes nowadays. The tendency is for the parents not to force a daughter into marriage because she is expecting a child. Instead, the daughter is encouraged to keep her child, finish her schooling or vocational training, and perhaps at some later date get married to a man whom she really loves. About 80 percent of those with a child out of wedlock marry later on, about 50 percent of them with the father of the child.

Nevertheless, it should be noted that in Sweden about 40 percent of all first-born babies are conceived before the wedding takes place. A certain number of these marriages are surely forced, but many of them tie in with an old tradition in Swedish rural society, namely, that of getting married only after a child is on the way. The current housing shortage in Sweden's larger cities is leading to a new custom of getting married when one has acquired an apartment. And a young couple on the municipal housing queue can reduce their waiting time by a whole year or more if they are expecting a child.

Earlier, marriage was looked upon as the only way of life for normal people. Today many other alternatives are accepted by society, also in the case of women. And within marriage it is more and more stressed that the sexual act is a good thing in itself, an important asset in the interrelation between husband and wife. Children should be wanted and, it naturally follows, planned for. Dr Gunnar af Geijerstam, in his "Sexual Coexistence", published by the Swedish Red Cross, has this to say:

Too frequent childbirth is unsuitable both for the mother and the children. A rule which an experienced professor of pediatrics used to teach is both wise and easy to remember. He said that every mother ought to enjoy the sun of two summers between each childbirth. If better reasons are needed to justify the use of contraceptive measures by married couples one can point to the sharp reduction in child mortality that has occurred during the past century. It was once considered quite natural that half of the children a woman gave birth to failed to reach adulthood. One can understand that under such circumstances there was far less need for voluntary birth control than is the case today when the child mortality rate is held to only a few percentage points.

Dr af Geijerstam's booklet also considers planning for the first child, at the same time recognizing the inescapable fact that frequently the child is already on the way when the marriage ceremony is performed. He writes:

> It is usually wise for a husband and wife not to start the first baby immediately after the wedding. Sometimes, of course, there is no choice. But the majority of young married couples benefit greatly from a period in which they can devote themselves solely to each other. Marriage itself presents such enormous changes in the pattern of living that the spouses need time in which to adapt themselves before they are confronted with the additional adjustment required by a child in the family. If the newlyweds are somewhat older, however, or if there is any other strong reason for haste, they should, of course, not wait. In any case, contraceptive measures, whether used for a long or short period, do not decrease fertility in the man or the woman.

Large families are a rarity in Sweden, where the birth rate is one of the lowest in the world. There has been an increase in recent years, however, from 13.7 per 1,000 population in 1960 to 16.0 in 1964. Swedish babies, according to a United Nations report issued some years ago, are the healthiest in the world, and the infant mortality rate is only 1.5 percent.

Swedish affluence, plus a welfare state philosophy, has resulted in a wide range of social benefits available to all segments of society literally from birth to death. Every expectant mother is entitled to free prenatal and delivery care and a cash payment, a maternity benefit, of U.S. $209 when the child is born. Courses in ante-natal exercises are available, free of charge, to teach women how to make childbirth easier. It should be mentioned that many hospitals nowadays allow expectant fathers to be present when their child is born. A nationwide network of municipal maternal and child health centers exists, free of charge. They aim at protecting the physical and mental health of children of pre-school age and their parents. Women—married or unmarried—who have been at the same job for one year cannot be dismissed because of pregnancy, and, moreover, they are entitled to a six-month leave of absence during which they receive cash benefits equal to two-thirds of their normal earnings. A tax-free yearly allowance of U.S. $240, payable in four installments directly to the mother or guardian regardless of marital status, is provided for all children under the age of sixteen. Newlyweds who are short of funds can obtain government loans of up to U.S. $800 to set up house-keeping. Unwed mothers or fathers with minor children also have this possibility, as well as couples in common law marriages. Day care centers are available, but not as many as are needed.

It would be pleasant to be able to report that, because of such factors as late marriage and people not being forced to marry because of un-wanted pregnancies, the divorce rate is low in Sweden. The fact of the matter is that it is rather high with one divorce out of five marriages.

Among the reasons generally cited for the increase in Sweden are the relative ease of obtaining a divorce nowadays, the declining influence of the church, and the emancipation of the Swedish woman. With greater job opportunities the Swedish woman is now in a better eco-nomic position, and she no longer feels compelled to "stick it out" at all costs if the marriage is very unhappy. There is also a rather high per-centage of remarriage for both men and women, a little higher for men but for both groups more than 50 percent.

It is important to bear in mind that the Swedish divorce law is not based on the traditional Christian concept of condemning the termina-tion of marriage. While before 1915 infidelity and desertion were es-sentially the only grounds for divorce, the new code drawn up that year regarded marriage as a contract which could be broken if both partners desired it.

Except in the case of desertion, bigamy, adultery and a few others, in which circumstances immediate divorce may be granted, the law stipulates that the partners must first be legally separated for a period of one year. During this time both the husband and wife are entitled to enjoy roughly the same standard of living as they did when they were together.

Decisions concerning the custody of minors are always based on what is in the best interests of the children. In nine out of ten cases the mother is judged as the most capable of caring for the children. The other partner, usually the father, must then contribute to the support of the children until they reach at least the age of eighteen.

Unless a married couple have drawn up a special contract providing that in the event of divorce "what is mine is mine, and what is yours is yours", all possessions, including property, are divided equally between the husband and wife. Alimony, unlike in the United States, is not some-thing that a woman can take for granted. A clear need must be shown, and a woman who is young enough and able to work will seldom receive payments for any great length of time. It can also happen that the woman may be obliged to support the man. Alimony automatically stops at remarriage, although support for the children continues.

The divorce law calls for compulsory mediation efforts before legal separation is granted, but it is generally conceded that this process is normally carried on in a rather perfunctory manner and yields few positive results. This has aroused criticism in some circles. Hardly anyone in this country believes that people should be forced to continue a marriage against their wishes.

A new governmental family commission has been appointed to overhaul the present family-law legislation and to suggest reforms and renewals. The Minister of Justice, Mr Herman Kling, has said in his directive of 1969: "The function of legislation in this connection is to solve practical problems, not to favor one form of living above others."

It is significant that in Sweden there is no such a thing as an illegitimate child. At one time the laws did use that term, with all of its undesirable connotations, but that was changed some decades ago as part of a program to improve the status of the unmarried mother and her child.

While a small segment of the Swedish population may still look upon the unwed mother in a "special" way, no stigma whatsoever is attached to her child. All children should be welcomed children, as a Swedish government official put it, and all have the same rights and are treated the same.

Swedish legal provisions reflect a cultural attitude more concerned with the protection of the child than with the punishment of the mother. The basic attitude of society is to afford support for unmarried mothers so that they can take care of their children if they so wish.

And statistics show that the majority of the unwed mothers do choose to keep their children instead of putting them up for adoption or having them placed in foster homes. An unmarried mother and child, as well as an unmarried father and child, moreover, are counted as a family unit, even for tax purposes, which results in a lower income tax than for ordinary single people. In school textbooks there are references to one-parent families, and, as stated earlier, an unwed mother has the right to call herself "Mrs".

Every child born out of wedlock is assigned a child welfare guardian who is responsible not only for safeguarding the child's rights and interests but also for ensuring that parentage is established and that the father agrees to financial support of the child. This support is continued until the age of at least eighteen, but if the child is still in school after that time it could go on until the age of twenty. The monthly payment is dependent in part upon the man's income, and if he is unable to pay, the Welfare Board assumes the obligation. And if it is an unmarried father who has custody of his child, he also has to have a child care officer.

At an international UNICEF conference in 1967 the non-Swedish delegates were astounded to learn that in 90 percent of the cases of children born out of wedlock in Sweden the father is found. In many other countries the attitude is that it is the woman's problem and nothing can be demanded of the man.

In addition to the usual government maternity and child allowances, unmarried mothers are helped with housing and finding employment. At the university an unwed mother is encouraged to continue her studies. She is treated like all other students and may also be provided with a two-room student apartment, on equal terms with other student families.

Even at the high-school level the tendency today is to encourage pregnant schoolgirls to remain in school. This contrasts sharply with the official attitude of the Board of Education some years ago when it was suggested that "a girl who is pregnant should be removed from school" because, among other things, the physical symptoms of pregnancy made her "ill suited to schoolwork". Now schools are instructed to offer all possible aid to pregnant pupils and to urge them to continue their studies.

A child born out of wedlock has since 1970 the same paternal inheritance rights as other children. Thus the last trace of economic discrimination exhibited by society against children born out of wedlock has disappeared.

Being an unmarried mother does not necessarily prevent a woman from leading a happy, normal life, and more and more of them are becoming very self-reliant. So much so, in fact, that it soon won't be obligatory by law for the child to have an official guardian in addition to the mother. About 80 percent of the unmarried mothers marry later, 50 percent to the man who fathered the child, 30 percent to another man.

That attitudes have changed toward unmarried mothers is shown in the newest research. The USSU research (USSU is the Sex Education Commission, appointed by the government in 1964) conducted in the 1960s showed that 99 percent of the people interviewed regard the principle of equal chances and rights for all children, whether born inside or outside marriage, as morally correct. Of the people in the investigation 98 percent think that the community should treat unmarried mothers in exactly the same way as married mothers, with the same aids and benefits and so on. But 16 percent were of the opinion that there is good cause to give unmarried mothers extra help in the various social forms, as it is nevertheless often more difficult for them to raise their children alone. Such surveys show that the Swedish law on equal rights and chances for children born inside and outside marriage is by and large in accordance with Swedish public opinion.

The question is sometimes raised whether the Swedish attitude, however humane and enlightened, doesn't tend to encourage the bearing of children out of wedlock. Actually, many fewer children are born out of wedlock now than in the nineteenth century. And during the last decades the proportion has remained virtually unaltered—about 10–15 percent of all births in Sweden.

FAMILY PLANNING AND BIRTH CONTROL

Most countries have steadily growing populations, and far too many have increases which can only be described as alarming. Sweden, on the other hand, has one of the world's lowest birth rates. In 1964 the birth rate was 16 per 1,000 population, the death rate 10, leaving a birth surplus of 6.

One would expect, then, that family planning would be a dead issue in Sweden. Nothing could be further from the truth. Planned parenthood is considered to be of the utmost importance, though obviously for reasons other than avoiding a population increase. Indeed, the economy of the country would actually benefit from an increase in births.

The basic assumption behind family planning in Sweden is that parents should have the right and responsibility for determining that, as far as possible, every child born should be wanted and well taken care of. Society's concern has been for the rights of each of its members, the aim being to increase the health and full development of the individual. Helping infertile couples to have children is also a part of this family planning program.

It's interesting to note that until as recently as 1938 it was punishable by law in Sweden to provide knowledge publicly about contraceptive methods. Now such information is openly supplied to both adults and adolescents. Maternal health clinics provide information regardless of marital status, and make available diaphragms, pills and IUDs to women requesting them. The quality of all contraceptive devices sold is publicly controlled, and pharmacies routinely supply them. Advertising is permitted. Tax money can be used for all purposes in this area.

Official interest in family planning dates from 1935, when the first Royal Population Commission was appointed to scientifically examine the facts and issues preparatory to the drafting of legislation. This involved close cooperation between social scientists and policymakers. Alva Myrdal, one of the Commission members, put forth the following view:

> People should neither be forced nor, through ignorance or otherwise, be lured into marriage or childbearing. Measures to encourage families should take the form of honest education, and of attempts to remodel the social and economic foundations of the family institutions.

Concurrent with governmental activities were those of the privately run and financed Swedish National Association for Sex Education (RFSU), founded in 1933 by Elise Ottesen-Jensen, a pioneer in the field. Like Margaret Sanger, her friend, Dr Ottesen-Jensen was an early, fierce champion of birth control.

As early as 1924 Dr Ottesen-Jensen wrote a booklet, "Unwelcomed Children", in which she described the plight of poor families whose pitiful conditions were made even worse by the arrival of unwanted children. She lashed out at the then conservative-minded official agencies and lawmakers for not recognizing that true morality must be built upon "freedom, education and self-responsibility, not on medieval laws".

Dr Ottesen-Jensen was President of the International Planned Parenthood Federation from 1959 to 1963, and in 1967 was appointed Honorary Chairman of the organization. At the age of eighty-plus she is today Sweden's grand old lady of planned parenthood. Most of the battles she fought, it should be added, have ended in victory.

RFSU (Dr Thorsten Sjövall, President) describes its aims in a widely circulated folder, as follows:

The Swedish National Association for Sex Education is an independent association, with no political or religious affiliations, founded on democratic principles and including private individuals as well as organizations. The association wishes to create prerequisites for:
1. Harmonious sexual relations.
2. Greater candor and knowledge in regard to sexual questions.
3. More open-mindedness and tolerance regarding sexual morals and sexual behavior.
4. More research and broader information on the biological, psychological, social and cultural aspects of sexual life.
5. Planned parenthood.
6. Improved conditions for families.
7. Increased contributions by Sweden toward solving the world's population problem.
The association has:
1. Extensive informational activities.
2. Clinics for planned parenthood which, in a relaxed and friendly atmosphere, offer professional advice on modern contraceptive techniques and sexual matters. Gynecologists, psychiatrists, social workers, and specially trained nurses are ready to help.
3. A maternity home, "Ottargarden".
4. A laboratory for determining pregnancy.
5. A sales organization including about forty small RFSU-owned stores throughout Sweden where prophylactics are sold, a mail order service, automatic coin-operated dispensers, and other authorized retail selling.

RFSU also publishes books and pamphlets dealing with sexual questions, sponsors lectures, and tries to influence government policy on matters pertaining to sex education, the abortion law, homosexuality, etc. The organization's regular education in sexology courses have been attended by doctors, nurses, midwives, hospital and social workers, teachers, and youth leaders. RFSU also arranges international symposiums on sexology for interested foreigners. The first one was held in 1969 and more are planned.

RFSU conducts many nationwide drives to spread sound and factual sexual knowledge and thereby help to mold public opinion. One of its recent birth control campaigns, via posters and newspaper advertisements, depicted a young couple with the following text: "Children? Yes—but when we want them." All of these activities are financed mainly through profits from the sale of contraceptives, since the RFSU receives no government or other grants.

RFSU has a counseling service for people—young and old—with psychological problems connected with sex. More and more of this counseling has been directed toward sexual satisfaction for mature people, since sex is part of the entire life cycle.

It is significant that RFSU does not attempt to dissuade young people from having sexual intercourse. The stress is on preventing unwanted pregnancies. Combining sexual happiness with sexual responsibility is one of the organization's stated goals.

Membership in RFSU can be on both an individual and a collective basis. From the very beginning collective membership has played a large and important part in the development of the organization. Among these are trade unions, political organizations, women's clubs, youth clubs, etc.

Information on family planning is put out by a variety of private and public agencies. In Dr Gunnar af Geijerstam's "Sexual Coexistence" (see page 345) there is a description of the various contraceptive methods. Abortion and sterilization are also discussed in this context, and the various places to which both married and unmarried persons can turn for advice in matters of family planning are described:

> There is a great need for information about the various methods and devices available for child-spacing, how they are to be used, how dependable they are, to what degree they disturb the spontaneity of sexual intercourse and rhythm, whether they imply risk, etc. [Dr Gunnar af Geijerstam writes]. It is helpful if personal counseling in regard to the choice of method can take place. Since individual differences regarding both physical characteristics and emotional attitudes are great, literature and lectures can provide general information but they cannot take the place of counseling. Generally, the adviser should be a medical doctor, preferably a gynecologist since a gynecological examination is necessary when the use of a diaphragm or similar device is deemed suitable for the woman.

The larger hospitals usually offer such examinations by specialists, and gynecologists in private practice are to be found in many cities. In addition, RFSU has established bureaus in many parts of the country. Advice on sexual problems is also supplied by many county and municipal bureaus which receive state grants for their primary activity of helping women in a situation of an unwanted pregnancy. Sometimes they are called "Family Counseling Bureaus". Also, consulting offices under the same title, run either privately or by the community, deal primarily with problems of marital relationships. And, lastly, advice on birth control methods is provided at all of the maternal health clinics throughout Sweden.

It is of paramount importance that the man and woman should have the right to decide if they want a baby together and when they want a baby, and to choose the contraceptive method—or combination of methods—that is most acceptable to and suitable for both of them. The following are the techniques currently and most often in use in Sweden:

Coitus Interruptus, or withdrawal, is an ancient technique which has been very much used and is, to a certain extent, still used. Its advantages are that it requires no devices or chemicals, and consequently can be employed under all circumstances and at no cost. Certain disadvantages.

Rhythm Method, also called "safe periods technique" or temporary abstinence, has never been particularly popular in Sweden except with certain religious groups. Research into various contraceptive techniques has shown this to be an unreliable method.

Condom, a widely used and easily accessible device, and also highly effective. Quality control is checked by the government, ensuring that only reliable brands are sold. Condoms are comparatively expensive, but they have the advantage of affording reasonably good protection against gonorrhea and other infections.

Diaphragm, with jelly or cream, is very safe and effective. But it has never been used as much as one would have expected, not even before the advent of the Pill. It appears that some women feel some kind of psychological resistance to the diaphragm.

Chemical Preparations, to immobilize the sperm, such as creams, jellies, vaginal tablets and aerosol foams, are very seldom used alone in Sweden. They are, naturally, used in combination with other devices.

Intrauterine Devices, IUDS, more commonly called the plastic spiral or the loop, have been permitted in Sweden since the spring of 1966.

Oral Contraceptives for Females, the Pill, quickly gained widespread acceptance. There are now about 400,000 women out of 1.5 million in the fertile age groups using such pills. Some women, however, may experience certain side effects because of the Pill's hormonal involvement with the body. A committee of experts, appointed by the National Board of Health and Welfare, is still studying oral contraceptives. The "day-after pill" and the "once a month pill" are under research.

Oral Contraceptives for Males are not available, but clinical research is being carried on.

It should also be mentioned that sterilization as a contraceptive technique is against the law, oddly enough. This law, however, is expected to be changed quite soon.

Early in 1967 counseling in contraceptive techniques was started at the Student Medical Health Center at Uppsala University. For three hours each week a gynecologist is on hand to give students birth control advice. This was undertaken under the conviction that the proper application of birth control methods is an important and, indeed, essential aspect of preventive medicine.

The gynecologist, Dr Mats Danielsson, informs students about different types of contraceptives which are available today. Then it is up to his patients—the students—to make up their own minds concerning which contraceptives best fill their individual needs.

According to a recent investigation, about 90 percent of married couples apply some method or another of birth control. It was revealed, moreover, that most married women consider two children an ideal number. Less than one-third want three children or more. The results also showed that the use of contraceptives increases in direct proportion to mobility from rural to urban areas, and to progress in education and advancement in social status. Most church leaders seem to accept in practice planned parenthood within marriage.

One would expect that in Sweden, where birth control is openly accepted by the vast majority of the population, where sex education is part of the school curriculum, where contraceptives are publicly advertised and readily available in shops and from coin-operated dispensers, and where the medical profession, on the whole, has cooperated whole-heartedly, all that should have been done has been done. Unfortunately, this is not quite the case.

In smaller towns and rural districts it is still difficult for people to obtain adequate knowledge about different contraceptive techniques. And sex education in the schools has been far from perfect. Most encouraging, however, is the fact that genuine progress continues to be made.

The attitude of grownups toward giving contraceptive advice to young people, for instance, is becoming more and more enlightened. As one youth leader put it: "For us it is a self-evident expression of responsibility among the youth that they use contraceptives. It is much more of a problem with those young people who don't use contraceptives but still have sexual intercourse."

A neurotic fear of getting pregnant has often led to unsatisfactory sexual relationships between married partners. This is still another situation which the use of contraceptives should be able to correct.

The benefits of birth control have been well summarized in an RFSU pamphlet entitled "Secure Together". A sexual relationship can be a rich source of enjoyment and communion, it was stated, when there is greater knowledge of sexual matters. By eliminating the risk of undesired pregnancies and planning and deciding when children are wanted a married couple can feel secure. Then life together can become an expression of mutual consideration, respect and happiness.

INTERNATIONAL FAMILY PLANNING

Until very recently Sweden was the only country in the world to establish a governmental program to assist other nations requesting aid in family planning. Such assistance has been provided in Ceylon since 1958, in Pakistan since 1961, and in Tunisia since 1963. More than twenty countries in Asia, Africa, and Latin America have now received Swedish assistance.

The early programs included the training of local family planning workers (physicians, nurses, midwives, and social workers), and the development of family planning clinics, mainly as part of the regular health services. By providing consultative services in cases of subfertility the aim was to encourage family planning in the true sense of the word. Efforts were also directed toward compiling and disseminating pertinent audio-visual material, e.g., film slides, news releases and various types of manuals. Research projects, on a modest scale, were conducted in the sociological, statistical, and medical spheres. Today the bilateral assistance is given as support to the developing countries' own family planning programs. It mainly consists of equipment and commodities, including contraceptives.

A serious problem has been the inability of intergovernmental organizations, such as the UN, to assist family planning programs. Other governments, too, were reluctant to cooperate. Remarkable changes in the attitudes have occurred during the years 1965 to 1967. All relevant UN bodies now have mandates to work in the population field. In 1967 the Secretary General set up a trust fund for population (now United Nations Fund for Population Activities) which Sweden has supported since its start (1970–71 U.S. $1.5 million). In 1968 the UN declared family planning a human right.

The Swedish government has always shown a keen interest in the International Planned Parenthood Federation (IPPF), backed up by yearly increasing grants (1970–71 U.S. $1 million) to help finance its activities.

Sweden has also taken an active part in the establishment of the Population Unit at the OECD Development Centre. The Swedish experience of sex education was explained at a seminar in 1970 for participants from Latin America. A second seminar will be arranged in 1972.

The increasing resources of the UN and the IPPF as well as the growing number of donor countries in the population field means that Sweden in the future can concentrate its bilateral assistance on a smaller number of countries.

Sweden's family planning assistance to the developing countries is planned and administered by the Swedish International Development Authority (SIDA), with Ernst Michanek as Director General. Of SIDA's total annual budget of about 800 million Swedish crowns in 1970–71, however, only about 40 million is earmarked for family planning programs.

It is significant that, in sharp contrast to local views in many other countries, Swedish public opinion not only supports family planning but demands that greater efforts be made to expand these programs in the developing lands. Seminars on International Family Planning have been held at Swedish universities. The underlying idea behind Swedish interest in family planning abroad is that the population crisis concerns all of us. This attitude has been strengthened by the growing awareness of the threats to the human environment which are caused by a heavy population pressure. Pollution knows no national boundaries.

The Swedish government supports programs aimed at developing better contraceptives and sponsors nutrition studies for better health. And extensive research in human reproduction is being carried on at the Karolinska Institutet in Stockholm with assistance from SIDA. WHO is planning a concerted international research effort in this field. SIDA is also involved in this endeavour.

When the Government Operations Subcommittee on Foreign Aid Expenditures of the United States Senate held a series of meetings in 1965–66 it was natural for Swedes to be asked to testify. This was a clear mark of recognition of the advanced work done in Sweden and also her interest in international family planning.

Sweden has also, as already mentioned, played a key role in the activities of the International Planned Parenthood Federation (IPPF), which has its headquarters in London. Pioneers in this movement were the late Margaret Sanger, IPPF founder, and Elise Ottesen-Jensen, its past President. The official constitution and by-laws of this highly effective organization were drawn up at a conference held in Stockholm in 1953.

The first IPPF conference ever to take place in South America—in San Diego, Chile, in 1967—was supported by Sweden. In 1966 the IPPF for the first time was officially recognized by the World Health Organization (WHO) and also became a consultant to the United Nations Children's Fund (UNICEF) and others of its organizations.

The worldwide campaign by private and governmental organizations to promote responsible parenthood is unquestionably making considerable progress. Inroads have been made in countries all over the world. But with an estimated 70 million people added every year to an already overcrowded globe it's quite obvious that much still remains to be done.

ABORTION AND THE LAW

During the 1930s a disturbingly high number of illegal abortions, many of them fatal, were performed in Sweden. This naturally caused considerable alarm among responsible citizens concerned not only with principles of morality but also with the reality of people's lives. It was clear that something had to be done, and there were increasing demands to make abortion legal under certain conditions.

The first law legalizing abortion was adopted in 1938 and amended a number of times, the latest in 1963. There are five main grounds: medical; social-medical; humanitarian (referring to cases of rape, incest, etc.); eugenic; and fetal injury.

In more detail, abortion in Sweden is permissible under the following conditions:

1. If childbirth would seriously endanger a woman's life or health due to illness, a physical defect, or weakness.
2. If there is reason to assume that childbirth and child care would seriously reduce a woman's physical or psychic well-being because of her living conditions and other circumstances.
3. If a woman becomes pregnant as a result of rape, other criminal coercion, or incestuous sexual intercourse, or if she has a mental deficiency, or is under fifteen years of age at the time of impregnation.
4. If there is reason to assume that the woman or the father of the expected child would transmit to the offspring either hereditary mental disease, mental deficiency, a serious disease, or physical handicap. An abortion granted for any such hereditary defect in the mother is contingent on simultaneous sterilization unless this is judged risky or unnecessary.
5. If there is reason to assume that the expected child will suffer from severe disease or deformity due to injury during the fetal life.

Authorization for interruption of pregnancy is in most cases decided by a specially appointed committee of the National Board of Health and Welfare after an investigation. In some circumstances abortion may be authorized by two doctors or, in the case of an emergency, by the licensed physician performing the operation.

An abortion for reasons other than disease or physical defect in the woman is not permitted after the twentieth week of pregnancy. The Board may make exceptions, however, and authorize performance of the operation before the end of the twenty-fourth week of pregnancy.

In 1945 the Swedish Parliament made available government grants to counties and cities to help them provide aid and advice (free of charge) to women involved in unwanted pregnancies. By 1964 such counseling took place at twenty bureaus scattered across the country. Psychiatrists, gynecologists and social workers consult with the woman regarding her situation. She herself must sign an application, on which members of the staff then make their recommendations. The application is submitted to a committee of the National Board of Health and Welfare, consisting of both medical and lay members, with a gynecologist as chairman. There should be at least one woman on the committee.

The committee decides whether or not there are grounds for abortion, or whether the investigation should be supplemented by having the applicant undergo clinical observation or further medical examinations. Obviously time is of the essence during this period of investigation. It should be mentioned that irrespective of whether or not the abortion is granted the bureau tries to help the woman in every way possible. This can include not only advice to help solve personal problems but also economic aid. The agency receives annual grants from both the community and the government for use in cases where financial support may be required temporarily.

When permission for an abortion is granted the operation must be performed by a staff surgeon in a public hospital. The Board may permit the operation in a private hospital if a surgeon asks for that. All documents pertaining to legal abortions are strictly confidential.

The Mental Health Agency of Stockholm, which was started in 1942, deals with three areas that are interlocking: advice on abortion, advice about contraceptives, counseling and psychotherapy. The number of cases handled in 1963 in these three fields was, respectively, about 1,200, 1,000 and 500.

The staff consists of a director who is a gynecologist, three psychiatrists trained in psychoanalysis, one consulting psychologist, ten full-time and four half-time social workers, one nurse and about twenty consulting gynecologists and psychiatrists.

The annual number of legal abortions in Sweden at the beginning of the 1950s was approximately 6,000 as compared with about 100,000 live births. There was a gradual decline during the second half of the decade, and by 1960 a level of around 3,000 per 100,000 live births was reached. Thereafter the figures again increased, and by 1965 there were an estimated 6,000 legal abortions compared with 120,000 live births. The applicants were about 6,700. In 1967 the corresponding figures were over 10,000 applicants, of which 90 percent were granted. There are still illegal abortions in Sweden, but the number has declined substantially since the 1930s, when about seventy women died every year as a result of operations performed by quacks. The decrease can be attributed not only to the legalization of abortion but also to better contraceptive techniques and expanded social welfare measures. Certainly there are fewer illegal abortions per capita in Sweden than in most other countries. It might be of interest to mention that Sweden has one of the lowest rates of abortion in the world.

As might be expected there is no general unanimity of opinion in Sweden on the question of legal abortion. In a heated debate which has been going on recently certain groups have maintained that a woman should be allowed to choose whether she wants to give birth to her child or not. Rather many groups have expressed the opinion that free abortions should be granted for all applications made before the twelfth week of pregnancy. At the same time good counseling possibilities have to be available. They believe, furthermore, that if women were given abortions on demand, criminal abortions would eventually disappear completely.

It is also argued in other quarters that the present procedure is far too cumbersome, the result being that many pregnancies proceed beyond the cut-off twentieth week stage before a decision is made by the National Board of Health and Welfare.

Many Swedes, however, view the present system of compromise as on the whole the best possible. Even the Lutheran State Church, for instance, accepts legal abortion for medical and humanitarian reasons. And there are very few people who advocate turning the clock back and making all abortions criminal, thus exposing women to abortionists again.

In 1965 the Swedish government set up a special parliamentary committee to review the entire system of legal abortion. Reforms will undoubtedly be forthcoming, including the possibility that a woman seeking an abortion will have more say in the matter. The interpretation of the law has already been liberalized due to the influence of the public debate and the women's emancipation movement which stated that it is a human right for a woman to make decisions concerning her own body. More and more consideration is given to the woman's own needs and her own feelings for a responsible solution in a difficult situation. Women are encouraged to seek abortions as early as possible.

During recent years there has been a virtual invasion of foreign women coming to Sweden in the mistaken belief that it is easy to get an abortion here. In 1965–66, for example, no fewer than 700 women, half of them American, came for this purpose. Out of this number less than twenty were successful.

While in theory the abortion law does not discriminate against non-Swedes, in actual practice the process makes it extremely difficult for a foreign woman to get the operation performed here. A woman from abroad can count on permission for abortion in Sweden only when a severe disease or physical defect indicates that a continued pregnancy may seriously endanger her life or health. In other words, for strictly medical reasons.

When medical or socio-medical reasons, such as "weakness", are the primary grounds for a desired abortion the application, in most cases, must be rejected since the necessary investigation cannot be performed satisfactorily. Such an investigation has to be made in conformity with Sweden's legal regulations, which means following the procedures outlined on official forms. The National Board of Health and Welfare cannot cooperate in arranging the required contacts with Swedish doctors, hospitals, and abortion authorities to carry out these investigations. And a written petition with a certificate from a foreign physician is not acceptable.

Under certain circumstances a special procedure must be followed. In the case of rape, for example, the abortion law states that the crime is to be reported to the police for investigation and prosecution. Again the question of time is involved, together with the necessity of contacting the law-enforcement agencies of a foreign country.

Swedish authorities have done their best to try to counteract the false information about abortion and thus discourage foreign women from coming to Sweden for this purpose. In a National Board of Health and Welfare memorandum distributed by the Swedish Embassy in Washington, D.C., the conclusion was that the procedure required by Swedish law would "consequently rule out cases where foreign women travel to Sweden with the sole purpose of applying for a legal abortion".

FAMILY COUNSELING

In 1960 the Swedish Parliament decided that government funds should be allocated for support of family counseling work.

A Family Counseling Bureau offers professional help in questions and problems concerning marriage and the family, such as, preparation for marriage, conflicts within marriage, and problems of the single person in relation to a partner. Psychosocial, psychiatric, psychological, and gynecological professional guidance is provided by the bureau, and assistance is given primarily through personal consultations.

Since 1960 such bureaus have been more widely established, but this kind of work is still in the beginning stages. Moreover, the setting up of family counseling bureaus should be seen in a larger social-political perspective. Earlier the chief aim in social work was to provide material and economic assistance. But during recent decades community support of family life has also increasingly focused on the psychological sphere.

This includes psychiatric care for children and adolescents, individual consultation within the area of social welfare, and preventive mental hygiene in general.

Tax-supported family counseling bureaus are found all over the country. There are also some bureaus affiliated with the Church and Ecumenical Boards.

The Municipal Family Counseling Bureau of Stockholm, started in 1951, has remained the largest and most versatile of Sweden's family counseling bureaus. It employs fifteen family counselors, most of them social workers with additional psychiatric training. Associated with the bureau as consultants are psychiatrists, a gynecologist, a child psychologist, a psychoanalyst and a lawyer. Conferences involving the entire staff are regularly held. All Stockholm residents may use the services of the bureau, and there is no charge.

Treatment, then, consists of social casework and psychotherapy, which might include individual talks, joint interviews with couples, and family therapy. There are possibilities for gynecological examination, including advice about contraceptive techniques. A certain amount of group counseling is also available at the bureau. The length of counseling varies according to need. Family pedagogical work is also conducted.

Family problems, among both married and unmarried couples, with which the bureau counselors have to deal fall into the following categories (some of the problems mentioned are symptoms of deeper disrupted relationships):

    Alcoholic problems
    Lack of responsibility in young marriages
    Problems with children
    Bad housing
    Economic problems
    In-law problems
    Cultural and norm differences
    Abuse of drugs and narcotics
    Adultery
    Jealousy problems
    Sexual problems
    Family planning and contraceptive techniques
    Broken emotional involvement. Diminishing or disturbed emotional
        commitment
    Should the wife have a job outside of home or not?
    Problems in roles as housewife and "househusband"
    Premarital counseling and other problem groups

The bureau's marriage courses for engaged couples and newlyweds are very popular. It is preferable that the young people come as couples, since the course is intended not only to impart knowledge but, equally important, to stimulate discussion between them. Lectures are given on legal and economic questions, and sexual relations including family planning, the psychological relationship, and parenthood. A discussion period follows.

Radio and, to a lesser extent, television have played an important role in personal counseling. Author and social worker Lis Asklund conducts a weekly radio program called "Letter Box" in which people are invited to turn to her for help in relationship questions. Mrs Asklund reads selected letters, together with her replies, on this program, which has a very large following—an estimated 700,000 listeners.

It is to the credit of the Swedish Broadcasting Corporation that frank subjects which would not be permitted on the air in many other countries are here openly discussed. The following letter, written by a woman under the signature "Indignant", is a good example:

> I hope you will answer my letter because I think my question is of interest to a great many people. I have an eighteen-year-old daughter who has been going steady with a very nice boy of twenty-one. They have been going together for almost two and a half years now and are very much in love. They plan to marry when they finish their studies, but that means waiting for at least three years. This is why I told my daughter that she ought to visit the county medical officer and be fitted with a diaphragm. The pills seem to be quite expensive for young people still in school and without an income.
>
> When my daughter visited the doctor and he learned that she wasn't married he began to abuse her, calling it shameless to ask for a diaphragm when she was still a schoolgirl. Instead, she should think of her studies, he said, and not concern herself with things that belonged to married life. After a long sermon on morals she was finally fitted with a diaphragm. She arrived home in tears, completely broken down.
>
> I was naturally upset and indignant since I was the one who had urged her to take this step because I understood that she and her boy friend were having sexual relations. And under the present circumstances they don't have any possibility of marrying and taking care of a child.
>
> Now I would like to ask you: Has a medical doctor the right to behave like this? It's no wonder that so many unwanted babies are born into this world. Isn't it better for young people to protect themselves until they are able to take care of a child without having to disrupt their education and damage their future careers?

After reading this letter on her radio program Mrs Asklund answered it as follows:

> I thoroughly agree with your viewpoint and think that both you and your daughter acted very sensibly. I was also sorry to learn that there are still medical doctors in our country who are as short-

sighted as this one. Nowadays in the upper grades of the public schools students receive complete information about contraceptive techniques as part of the sex education programs. It is always emphasized that young people who have sexual relations have a responsibility to protect themselves when they know that they can't take care of a child. But the big problem is that in many parts of the country it is still difficult to get contraceptives, especially in the case of very young girls.

The pills, which are 100 percent safe against conception if one carefully follows the doctor's instructions, have produced a virtual revolution in this sphere. But doctors consider that from a medical point of view it is not advisable to prescribe oral contraceptives for girls who are not physically grown up. Furthermore, contraceptives cost money and girls run the risk of receiving moral lectures instead of help. Unfortunately, there are not many girls who can talk with their mothers confidentially and receive helpful advice as in the case of your daughter.

Therefore, last spring in the school-radio program on sex education for ninth-graders (ages fifteen to sixteen) Lars Engström, a gynecologist, recommended that the boys use condoms. Condoms are an effective contraceptive measure and are easy to buy. But one can only hope that things will soon change so that young people can really get the help they need. The medical doctor who refuses to help young people who contact him in order to receive contraceptive advice is certainly taking on a great responsibility.

And lastly, a few more words about the pill. You say that pills are expensive for young people still in school and without any income. I don't know if I agree with you on this point. If the pills are bought in bulk, twice a year, the costs runs to about six crowns ($1.20) a month. That just about corresponds to the price of a movie ticket. If your daughter would like to use oral contraceptives the best thing to do is to contact a gynecologist, who will give his opinion as to whether or not the pill is suitable for her. The pills are, as I guess you already know, on the prescription list.

VENEREAL DISEASE, PROSTITUTION, AND PORNOGRAPHY

Venereal disease is on the increase all over the world, and Sweden has by no means remained immune from this trend. It is something much on the minds of the health authorities and for which there appears to be no easy solution. Indeed, it's most discouraging that despite all efforts to combat this problem more and more cases crop up each year.

The law concerning venereal disease dates from 1968 and states that a person who suspects he is infected is obligated to seek medical care. Treatment, as well as medicine prescribed by the officially appointed doctor, is entirely free of charge.

Patients are urged to inform their doctors about the source of their infection, so that their partners may also receive treatment before they infect anyone else. It is actually punishable by law to expose another person to venereal infection, but this statute is seldom enforced. In 1964 only twenty-eight persons were convicted under this law.

VD patients, for obvious reasons, are treated with the utmost discretion. However, physicians are compelled to report all cases, without names, to the Public Health Service. This also holds true for private doctors, which is not the case in most other countries.

In cities of more than 20,000 inhabitants there are special clinics for those seeking medical care. Besides medical doctors, these clinics are staffed by social workers with socio-medical training, whose function is to provide factual information and advice to those who seek it. A certain amount of follow-up work by health authorities is also carried out.

During 1966 no fewer than 25,092 cases of gonorrhea and 476 cases of infectious syphilis were registered in Sweden. This was the highest annual incidence since the 1919 legislation dealing with VD went into effect. About 60 percent of those infected with gonorrhea and 69 percent with syphilis were men. Particularly disturbing has been the sharp rise of venereal disease among young people of both sexes, especially those between fifteen and nineteen years of age.

There is no doubt that VD constitutes a public health problem of very serious proportions. The Swedish Medical Society has unmistakably shown its concern by having twice within the postwar period chosen venereal disease as the main topic for general discussion at its annual convention. The Board of Health and Welfare's Dr Malcolm Tottie emphasizes that combating VD is a global necessity in which all nations must use every means at their disposal to prevent themselves from becoming "reservoirs of venereal infection".

Knowledge about VD is included in the school sex education program for children fourteen years of age and over. Among facts stressed in a brochure distributed in Sweden's schools by the National Board of Health and Welfare are the following:

It is every person's duty to protect himself and others against VD.
Even a hasty contact with an infected person can have serious consequences.
The only *sure* way to protect yourself against VD is not to enter into casual sexual relationships.
If you have been infected with VD, seek a doctor's care at once. Don't treat yourself.
The sooner you come under treatment, the better are your chances of being cured.
There is no *sure* preventive measure against VD, but use of a condom affords reasonably good defense if it is used throughout the entire sexual act.

Don't let a sense of shame prevent you from seeking medical attention.

Brochures are also put out by other organizations, such as the Swedish National Association for Sex Education (RFSU). In addition, venereal disease has been discussed on radio and television. One educational TV program presented a hypothetical case history of a schoolboy who had contracted VD, showing how he went to the doctor, etc.

Dr Tottie lists "a blind faith in penicillin" as one of the reasons for the increase in venereal disease. Because they think they can be easily cured many people are not afraid of gonorrhea as they once were. Also, the use of contraceptive pills, which of course provide no protection against venereal infection, instead of condoms, is likely to affect the VD rate and probably already has.

While VD is a problem in Sweden, as elsewhere, there has been a steady decline in prostitution. And what little activity there is in this "oldest of professions" has only a slight influence on the prevalence of venereal disease.

There are no "red-light" districts in Swedish cities and no regular houses of prostitution. Streetwalkers are few and far between. Prostitution, in short, is hardly a problem at all.

An important factor to bear in mind when considering prostitution in Sweden is that it is not considered a crime in itself. The police can and do intervene, however, when minors are involved, and in other special cases.

Among the reasons cited for the decline of prostitution in Sweden the following are probably the most valid: the absence of poverty, which often drives women to prostitution; higher educational standards; the widespread acceptance of premarital sex; and equality between the sexes, which has raised the status of the Swedish woman.

Sex offenses in general are relatively low in Sweden. In 1963 they amounted to no more than one percent of total offenses against the Penal Code.

A word about the attitudes toward pornography. On February 12, 1971, Sweden passed a law openly accepting pornography for private use, but not permitting it to be exposed in show-windows. No one who doesn't want to look at hard-pornography should be forced to do so.

A commission is still working on revising the laws about censorship for films.

A SHORT HISTORY OF CHANGING SEX ROLES AND MARRIAGE

In a country's laws and regulations one can easily trace the history of women and, to some extent, sex roles and marriage as well. Included here are facts about education, political rights, employment, and religious views—all of which show how the woman's role in Swedish society is continually evolving. The trend is clearly toward more and more equality in various fields of endeavor, slowly but surely aiming at new roles for women and men, both inside and outside the family. The historical data presented on these pages have been taken, in part, from a pamphlet put out by the Swedish Federation of Business and Professional Women.

Tenth–Seventeenth Centuries

800–900   As early as the Dark Ages the free-born woman in Northern Europe was held in high esteem. As a wife, she retained a good deal of authority, marrying as she did into "a state of honor and wifehood, bed and board, and a third share of the household goods". Her dowry and morning gift became her own personal property.

c. 1200   The old Swedish patriarchal laws were distinctly unfavorable to the daughter of the house. In one province it was stipulated that the daughter should inherit only if there was no son. If there was a son, the father's entire property went to the male member, completely disregarding the female.

c. 1260   Earl Birger, the most powerful nobleman of his day, can perhaps be considered the Swedish woman's first real champion. He issued a decree prohibiting the taking of any wife by force, and also stipulating that the daughter should inherit a half share as compared with her brother. The law was in force until 1845.

1477   Uppsala University was founded. But it wasn't until almost 400 years later, in 1873, that women were allowed to take degrees there.

1632   Johannes Rudbeckius founded the first formal school for girls in the town of Västerås, where, he stated, "children of the female sex would be well trained and taught the catechism, reading and writing and other subjects proper to their sex which might later be of use to them".

Eighteenth–Nineteenth Centuries

1734   The prevailing concepts concerning the roles of the sexes, with a subordinate role for women, were legalized in family laws that remained valid for more than a century. A married woman was under the guardianship of her husband, who managed all her property, and an unmarried woman, throughout her entire life, could acquire, dispose of or give away property only by consent of her guardian.

A woman was entitled to choose her future husband, but the consent of her guardian—usually her father—was still required.

The law of 1734 established the death penalty for grave cases of adultery. Under the influence of the Age of Reason this law was repealed in 1779, but it wasn't until 1937 that punishment for adultery was completely abolished.

1750 Women were employed in mines and stone quarries as far back as the Middle Ages. In the eighteenth century they also began working in textile factories. In 1750 between 70 and 80 percent of the 15,000 textile workers in Sweden were women, which is about the same proportion as today.

1793 The cause of Women's Emancipation found a champion in the poet Thomas Thorild, who published his essay, "The Natural Dignity of the Female Sex", which upheld a woman's right to be regarded first as a human being and secondly as a female.

1828 Fredrika Bremer, the first real pioneer in women's fight for emancipation, published a number of short sketches and articles setting forth her views on the unfavorable position in society which the female sex had hitherto held. The main themes running through all her writings were the relationship between parents and children, and the rights of women to be regarded as human beings and receive a higher education.

1842 A Royal Statute ordaining each parish to have at least one school staffed by state-approved teachers was issued. Attendance for all children became compulsory.

1845 A law was passed giving men and women equal rights of inheritance.

1856 The Bishop of Karlstad, C. A. Agardh, published a book, "Attempt at a National Economic Analysis of Sweden", in which he pointed out the human, social and economic difficulties faced by women, and the fact that most professions were reserved for men. He also drew attention to the hardships surrounding the lives of unmarried mothers and widows, and considered that the time was ripe for new legislation to improve women's status generally.

1873 Women were allowed to sit for all academic examinations, with the exception of theological and advanced law degrees.

A group called "The Society for Married Women's Rights" was founded, aiming at reform of the Marriage Laws with a view to safeguarding the wife against complete dependence on her husband. The following year a law was passed giving married women the right to dispose of their own property and of any money they might earn by working.

1884   Unmarried women were declared of age at twenty-one.

1896   Ellen Key published her book, "The Abuse of Women's Energy", attacking the ultrafeminine concept of women and singling out their own special gifts and qualities. Her propaganda for "free love" was of course the subject of much shocked debate.

Twentieth Century

1914   An investigating committee to propose alterations in the Marriage Laws included a woman for the first time.

1915   According to a law going back to 1686 a woman who engaged in sexual intercourse before marriage was required to pay a penalty of two silver dollars (*riksdaler*). The money went to the church for the maintenance of its property. This law stood on the books until 1915, though it had long since ceased to be applied.

Before 1915 infidelity and desertion were essentially the only grounds for divorce. Marriage was regarded as a unity, the breaking of which implied guilt by definition. The new law regarded marriage as a contract between two partners. Therefore, a divorce requested by both parties in mutual consent could be granted by the court. An application to the court for legal separation or divorce could be initiated by either the husband or the wife.

1917   The term "illegitimate children" was dropped from the law books. "Children born out of wedlock" was introduced into the language of laws dealing with the family.

1919   Parliament passed a bill amending the Constitution and giving women the right to vote in national elections. They were also eligible for membership in Parliament, thus concluding once and for all the long struggle for political equality.

1920   The "marriage code" of 1920 has probably had a greater effect than anything else on the transition from a patriarchial to a democratic view of the family. The subordinate role of the woman was definitely set aside, replaced by equal and mutual rights and responsibilities for husband and wife. The husband's guardianship over his wife was revoked, and both partners in marriage assumed financial obligations in the support of each other and their children. Married women were also declared of age at twenty-one.

1923   Parliament approved the "Competence Act", which made women eligible for employment in the Civil Service. Certain positions, however, were still reserved exclusively for men.

1927   Girls were admitted to public high schools for the first time.

1933   Mrs Elise Ottesen-Jensen, Norwegian-born pioneer in sex education, founded the Swedish National Association for Sex Education (RFSU), with the object of spreading a wider and basic knowledge about sex. Her work contributed to the introduction of compulsory sex education into the school curriculum.

1935   The first Royal Population Commission was appointed. Gunnar and Alva Myrdal wrote the famous book "Crisis in the Population Question" in 1934.

1938   Until 1938 it was punishable by law to provide knowledge about contraceptive methods. Now all maternal health clinics are required to give information about contraceptives, regardless of marital status.

    Cash maternity benefits were granted by the State.

    Sweden's first therapeutic abortion law went into effect. The grounds for legal abortion have subsequently been amended, most recently in 1963.

1939   A new law forbade the dismissal of an employee because of engagement or marriage. The law was amended in 1945 to prohibit the dismissal of a woman because of pregnancy, regardless of marital status.

1944   Sex education was introduced in the public schools. It became compulsory for all children in 1956.

1949   Under the new "parental code" both parents have legal authority over their minor children. In the case of children born out of wedlock the mother is usually the legal guardian.

1951   Law passed giving a Swedish woman marrying a foreigner the right to retain her Swedish citizenship.

1953   The International Planned Parenthood Federation was founded in Stockholm through the initiative of Elise Ottesen-Jensen and the American Margaret Sanger.

1954   Ulla Lindström, a journalist, was made Minister without

Portfolio. Included among her duties were questions of consumer education and family welfare. In 1967 she was succeeded by Camilla Odhnoff, Ph.D. in Science, wife and mother of four children. The same year Ambassador Alva Myrdal was appointed a member of the Cabinet and she is also the Swedish chief delegate to the Disarmament Conference since 1962.

1958   After years of heated debate women were made eligible to become ministers in the Lutheran State Church.

1962   Parliament approved a new educational system calling for nine years of comprehensive school for all children. The basic philosophy aims at preparing students, both boys and girls, for their future jobs as well as their roles in the family. Thus both boys and girls have compulsory training in home economics and in child care. By the same token, boys and girls are given vocational training. The educational system accepts the implications of the same responsibility and of equal possibilities in society and in education as well as in professional life and in family living.

Eva Moberg wrote a very provocative book, "Women and Human Beings", containing an article about woman's present restricted emancipation ("The Conditional Release of Women", 1961) and advocating dual roles in family and society for both men and women, thus suggesting new ideas about the role of men and their share in the responsibility of the home and for the children.

1964   In the recommendations for a new marriage law adultery was no longer to be considered an unquestioned ground for the dissolution of a marriage. In the past a mother could lose custody of her children if infidelity could be proved. Nowadays, in cases involving custody of the offspring the decision is mostly based on what is considered best for the children.

1965   Equal pay for men and women was in principal realized on the labor market.

1970   Law stipulating the same paternal inheritance rights for children born out of wedlock as for children inside marriage.

1971   Since 1971 the Swedish Parliament consists of one Chamber.

In the spring of 1971 women held 48 of the Chamber's 350 seats. After the 1921 elections there were 3 women in the Second Chamber out of a total of 230 members. Out of the 240 regular members of parliamentary committees 33 are women. The chairmanship of one committee is held by a woman.

Sex Education and the Schools in the United Kingdom

Alan Little

INTRODUCTORY REMARKS

The first thing to make clear is the impossibility of describing British educational practice in the field of either family life education or sex education. Educational administration in the United Kingdom is highly decentralized, and as a result so are the decisions about what is taught and by whom to which pupils. This is not simply the fact that each Education Authority (in England and Wales there are over one hundred and fifty of them) is independent of the Central Government as far as curriculum is concerned, but, equally important, considerable autonomy is given to each school to determine the nature of the teaching programme. Further, within a school the classroom or subject teachers are normally given considerable latitude to decide for themselves the content of any particular course. At best, therefore, I can only highlight the main trends and tendencies—detailed description of actual practice is impossible. Further, I think it best to highlight the innovational part of the general review paper prepared for this meeting.

Perhaps the most important point to be made is that sex, or family life, education has become a matter for formal educational discussion and dispute. Obviously any school system that aims to prepare pupils for life must in some way touch upon the range of problems implied in the title 'family education'. What strikes me about the present situation is that there is growing agreement that these problems should be given a formal place in the school curriculum and are a proper subject for professional thought and discussion. In a sense it is now accepted and acceptable that part of the educational experiences of all pupils should be instruction in these matters. Where disagreement still exists is the age at which this should take place, by whom, using what materials, and covering what topics.

Paradoxically, it is in these controversial areas that exertive innovations in practice have been implemented, and it is these that are of interest to a wider audience. As far as changing or developing course

371

content is concerned, this has been *partly* by national bodies (the Schools Council, the Nuffield Foundation), and also by local authorities in response to various Government reports. It has been mainly the development of materials and approaches for use in any school that is prepared to co-operate. In terms of subject matter the Nuffield science programmes for primary schools, and biology courses for secondary schools, include as part of the curriculum subjects like the physiology of reproduction (human and animal): in a sense they attempt to introduce the subject of sex education as part of a more general course and not as a subject in its own right. The innovation of the Nuffield Programme lies in attempting to introduce science to younger age groups (for example eight- to nine-year-olds), to develop integrated studies of science emphasizing the experimental and project or theme approach to the course. In so far as sex education is part of the programmes, it is a part of a wider curriculum, and is dealt with on a 'factual' basis.

A second innovation relates to the wider area of family life education and the preparation of the individual for human relationships, and this is the Schools Council Humanities Project mentioned in our report. Again, it is not a course on 'human relationships', but an attempt to develop an integrated humanities programme. It touches upon the subject of human relationships as part of a more general educational programme. Where it differs in principle from the science and biology programmes is that it does not emphasize content or factual information, but is concerned with young people's attitudes or 'orientation' towards a certain range of problems. Difficult moral issues are dealt with by a mixture of source material provided by the programme, and group discussions. The role of the teacher is that of a neutral chairman who elicits views from, but does not prescribe solutions to, the pupils.

Out of the two different style programmes certain points might be relevant in other national contexts:

1. The question whether sex education or family education should be a specific course(s) in a school syllabus, or part of the existing educational programmes.

2. The importance of the non-factual side of family life education, concerned with attitudes, opinions, orientation towards other human beings and practices, in a word the morality of life.

3. The extent to which there is no consensus about certain subjects (e.g., pre- or extra-marital sexual relationships) and therefore if the subject is not to be barred from the school curriculum (which would then risk being irrelevant) it must be handled in a different way to other aspects of the school programme. It is neither instilling fact nor imparting attitudes, but giving the pupil-student the skills to arrive at his own responsible decisions.

It is obvious from what I have already said that innovations on several fronts are being made simultaneously. Younger children are being introduced to these subjects (e.g., primary school science) and courses developed that go beyond imparting either fact or conventional wisdom. Because of this there is a danger of crossing public opinion in general or parental opinion in particular. This is a problem common to most communities, and one recent innovation of considerable significance has been the specific attempts to involve parents in this side of the school activities. These attempts are of two broad and overlapping types:

(*a*) An effort of 'public relations' to ensure that parents know what is being done in the schools, how and why. Many schools (especially primary) have special meetings of parents, preparing them for the types of questions children may well ask when such personal matters as sexual relations and reproduction have been touched upon at school. Certain Education Authorities put on specific courses for parents in order both to prepare parents and to enable them to continue and expand the education initiated at school.

(*b*) An alternative approach is to provide parents with the knowledge and equipment that will enable them to meet by themselves their children's needs in this area.

These are not necessarily incompatible programmes, and both have a role in cultures in which there are reservations about the school undertaking the task of sex education or family life education. The first type of programme assumes that this is out of ignorance, the second that the appropriate place for such help and advice for children is in the family.

Given that this last point still has some relevance in contemporary Britain, it is perhaps surprising that the mass media have recently entered this area. Both commercial and public television channels have recently prepared and put out programmes both as 'sex education' in its narrowest sense, and the more general area of 'family life education'. The most striking illustration of this is the recent series of programmes designed for eight- to ten-year-olds in primary schools. This attempts to deal with the sociology, psychology, physiology of human reproduction at a level meaningful to this age group. Various types of techniques are utilised, including diagrams, stills and films of everything from conception to birth of a child. In addition the films do not shirk the 'value issues' involved. It is perhaps indicative of the extent to which the general idea of such programmes has been accepted, that one vocal objection to the programmes concentrated upon the fact that one of the drawings of a couple having intercourse showed a woman not wearing a wedding ring!

It would be incorrect to give the impression that everyone in Britain is agreed about the propriety of the need for instruction in school about these matters. Some people still disagree with the idea in principle, but these are few, now the argument is more about content and method and less about need. More important than this, even when there is agreement in principle, in practice disagreement can arise simply because of uncertainty about what should be taught and how. This is an area not merely of moral conflict but of genuine moral uncertainty. As the burden of a course shifts from sex education, towards family life education, so this uncertainty and doubt increases. When a programme is attempting to influence pupils' attitudes to themselves and each other, then, in an age of personal and inter-personal doubt, that course inevitably reflects that doubt. In a secular society like Britain, agreement about whether certain relationships are 'good' or 'bad' is easier to ask for than achieve. Because of this any educational programme must be placed in a context of moral uncertainty, doubt and conflict. Equally important in a society in which effective contraceptive practice is not merely available but virtually universally used, any programme that concentrates exclusively on the 'facts of life' rather than 'problems of living' is likely to be irrelevant to people's needs.

INTERNATIONAL PLANNED PARENTHOOD FEDERATION: THE REPORT [1]

This report on sex education in Britain outlines some of the most important activities and developments. As in all matters relevant to the attitudes and behaviour of youth and the future of society, it is a field where many agencies, both governmental and non-governmental, have expressed interest and concern, and, in some instances, have been actively involved. Interest in family life and sex education is expressed by educationalists, as well as by medical and welfare personnel, although the former are most frequently in contact with, and are therefore particularly aware of, the variety and complexity of the problems facing all young people today.

Because activities in sex education are concentrated in the educational field, it will be helpful to describe briefly the educational scene in Britain. The structure of the education system is such that specific activities in a particular school are left to the discretion of the head teacher of that school, who is expected to adjust recommendations from Central and Local Government to suit the needs of his own school community. As a result of the autonomous organization of each school, there is wide diversity in sex education activities, as in many other spheres, in different parts of the country. However, each school is answerable to a Local Education Authority, which in some instances attempts to influence the head teachers of the schools of its area by producing reports and circulating recommendations. There are 163 Local Education Authorities in England and Wales. Each of these is responsible to the Central Government, and is expected to promote national education policies at the local level, as well as undertaking general administrative functions in the organization and co-ordination of the educational institutions in a particular area.

The information included in this report is arranged under the following headings:

I Action at the Central Government Level
   Statements and Reports
   Curriculum Development
   Public Examinations
   Schools Broadcasting
II Action at Local Education Authority Level
   Specific Schemes
   Teacher Training
III Surveys
IV Action at a Non-Government Level
   Educational Organizations
   Medical Organizations
   Religious Groups
   Other Groups
V Young People's Attitudes to Sex Education
VI Comment
   Appendices

I. ACTION AT A CENTRAL GOVERNMENT LEVEL

Statements and Reports

A succession of reports and pamphlets have been produced from Central Government agencies indicating an awareness of the urgent need to educate young people in personal relationships including the sexual aspects.

The 1944 Education Act, which reorganized the British education system, contained the following statement, which is generally accepted as including sex education:

> . . . it shall be the duty of the local education authority for every area, so far as their powers extend, to contribute towards the spiritual, moral, mental, and physical development of the community. . . .

Before this, in 1943, the Board of Education, later to become the Ministry of Education, produced a pamphlet entitled *Sex Education in Schools and Youth Organizations*. This drew the attention of Local Education Authorities to the need for special courses in sex education

for teachers and youth leaders. It contained the suggestions that student teachers in training colleges were often in need of personal guidance themselves, and that *ad hoc* courses in sex instruction for mature
teachers and youth leaders would provide the most suitable guidance
'for this difficult and delicate task'.

Since 1956 a number of important Government reports have made
reference to young people's need for adequate sex education, moral
education, education for personal relationships. These include the
Crowther Report (1959), the Newsom Report (1963), the Plowden
Report (1967), among others. In addition to these which were produced by the Ministry of Education and later the Department of Education and Science, other Central Government reports are noted and
summarized in Appendix 1.

In 1956 a Ministry of Education pamphlet entitled *Health Education*
was published which states that there are grounds for believing 'that a
better understanding of the reproductive processes in man, of the nature of sex and sexual behaviour and the basic facts about population'
may help many people to achieve more rational conduct in their sex
lives and in family relations.

The Crowther Report, entitled *15 to 18,* was presented to the Government in 1959. It deals with the needs of fifteen- to eighteen-year-olds
at a time of changing social and industrial conditions. Most of its
recommendations are concerned with the balance and relevance of
school curricula. It emphasizes that changes are needed in the education of adolescent girls, particularly among the less able, to whom
marriage is of great importance, particularly at the present time, when
the age of marriage is getting younger. It points out that 'To preserve
the family in the future a conscious effort is needed by way of the
educational system, on a much greater scale than has yet been envisaged'. At the same time the authors of the report recognize that
sexual problems are not confined to marriage, and suggest that there
should be opportunities to discuss sexual ethics in the school. They also
suggest that these and other needs of the individual could be dealt with
during an extra compulsory year at school, thus raising the leaving
age to sixteen years. New courses of relevance to the demands of the
real world would have to be devised for the extra year.

The education of young people aged thirteen to sixteen years, of
average or less than average ability, is discussed in a report entitled
Half our Future,[2] presented to the Ministry of Education in 1963. It is
important to note that this category of pupils comprises over half of the
school population. Many references to and recommendations on personal and social development of these pupils are made in the report.
Certain specific objectives are stated, which include the need to develop
both a sense of responsibility towards other people, and an internalized
code of moral behaviour. The authors of the report suggest that the

overwhelming influence in the lives of young people of this age is the sexual instinct. One of the main recommendations in the report is that 'Positive and realistic guidance to boys and girls on sexual behaviour is essential', and that such guidance should include biological, moral, social, and personal aspects. Other recommendations include: that sex education schemes in schools should be paralleled by advisory programmes for parents on the physical and emotional problems of their children; that religious instruction has a role in helping boys and girls to find a firm base for sexual morality, based on chastity before marriage, and fidelity within it; that married teachers handle the problems of sex education more easily than others; and that, taking the broadest interpretation of sex education, opportunities should be created for boys and girls to meet members of the opposite sex in a helpful educative environment.

The Plowden Report, *Children and their Primary Schools,* was presented to the Government in 1967. The authors state that sex education is a parental responsibility though often avoided. They suggest that each school should have a definite policy on sex education, made in consultation with the parents; that children should understand the biological nature of reproduction; that any confusion with excretion should be clarified at this early stage; that use of correct scientific terms should be encouraged; that all questions should be answered truthfully; and that ethical aspects of sex education should not be avoided. It is also suggested that the best person in the school to deal with these various matters is the children's usual teacher, but it is recognized that some teachers will not feel comfortable in this situation. The authors of the report request that teacher training colleges should note this point. They also make an interesting comment on children who show 'an unhealthy interest in sex', which, they suggest, is probably not an uncommon phenomenon and should not be dealt with harshly.

An interesting report, known as the Cohen Report but entitled *Health Education,* was produced by the Central and Scottish Health Services Council in 1964. In it several recommendations and comments are made on the content of health education courses in schools, which, it is noted, should include 'more education where it is most necessary', citing sex education as one example. The authors of the report suggest that health education syllabi in schools should aim at giving a child knowledge that will equip him to face the social and health problems he will meet in the future, and should include the social implications of relationships between the sexes, and the social and health problems of adolescence and adulthood. A series of recommendations are made in the report, including a request that the Minister of Health should draw the attention of the Minister of Education to the content of the report. It is also recommended that there should be close co-operation between Local Education Authorities, Public Health Departments, and the Central

Government on the subject of health education; that the Government should foster the training of special health educators, since those teaching the subject require such training in addition to possessing certain personal qualities; that health education should be included in the school syllabus; that the Government should promote training in health education for doctors, nurses, and teachers, although it is pointed out that such people will not be able to use their training unless they have co-operation and support from the Local Education Authority, and the head teacher, the doctor, the health visitor, and the inspector of the school.

In the reports mentioned above, and others noted in Appendix 1, calls are made to Local Education Authorities and to the Central Government to take a greater interest in the field of sex education, in one or more of the following ways: by encouraging increased activity under various sections of the curriculum in schools; by encouraging special training for teachers; by increasing co-operation with parents.

Curriculum Development

In 1964 the Schools Council was set up by the Government to carry out research and development work on curricula, teaching methods, and examinations in schools. One of its main objectives is to maintain the independent responsibility of each school to develop its own curricula and teaching approach, based on the needs of its pupils. With this in mind the Schools Council has produced a number of working papers on a wide range of topics, either as a preliminary to investigating new activities or approaches, or to encourage local developments in the educational field, or to report on existing progressive activities. Some of the papers contain information of relevance to the field of sex education. For example, two papers consider the implications of raising the school leaving age to sixteen years as recommended in the Newsom Report (see page 376). In the initial paper fields of enquiry are outlined, existing work of relevance is noted and reviewed, the Schools Council's programme of work is outlined, and recommendations are made to the schools to develop teaching programmes relevant to the need of young people who will have no education after sixteen years, and who will probably resent having to stay at school for an extra year. The second paper describes some experimental school programmes and curricula in the humanities subjects, and suggests that the main emphasis of the school curriculum should be man and society, commencing with the individual in society and culminating with the function and role of the community. It is suggested that central teams, such as those involved in the Nuffield Foundation Projects (see below), can provide information and take the initiative in specific fields of curriculum development. The information and techniques developed can be passed on to local groups of teachers and others, to be tested and modified in their schools.

As a result, the Nuffield Foundation and the Schools Council have jointly sponsored revision of the content of school courses, particularly in the science field. It is expected that the curriculum recommendations made by the various project groups will gradually be incorporated into future school syllabi.

One of the project groups, the Secondary Science Project, will produce a collection of materials and curriculum suggestions which teachers can use in planning courses for children of average and less than average ability, in a wide variety of schools. This material is at present on trial, and publication is expected in 1971. It includes material for teaching the anatomical, physiological and behavioural aspects of the whole life cycle of man, and will contain suggestions for work on contraception, venereal disease, and population problems. Film loops which can be integrated into this work have been made, covering such topics as human growth, hormones, and world population problems and solutions. Another Schools Council and Nuffield Foundation project is the Resources for Learning Project, which is experimenting with a programmed learning course in sex education. A further project is the Humanities Curriculum Project, which is currently testing teaching methods and materials with fourteen- to sixteen-year-olds of average and less than average ability. The premise behind this project is that work in the humanities will help pupils to develop an understanding of the controversial areas of universal human concern. It is intended to develop a new approach to handling such controversial issues through the technique of discussion, so that pupils are not influenced by the teacher's own views, and to a large extent take responsibility for their own learning. Collections of material have been made which are used to provide evidence during the discussions. Material in these collections ranges from printed extracts of fictional and non-fictional prose, poetry, and drama, to photographs, cartoons, advertisements, and tapes of songs and interviews. Two of the nine subjects selected for experimental study are the family and relations between the sexes. Another curriculum project is the General Certificate of Education Biology Project. As a result of this project a series of five textbooks and five teachers' guides have been produced, to be used during a five-year course for eleven- to sixteen-year-olds. Human sexuality is referred to in years one and five of the course, but no mention is made of venereal diseases or contraception.

In addition to the papers mentioned above, the Schools Council has also prepared a paper called *Counselling in Schools* (Schools Council Working Paper No. 15, published 1967, by Her Majesty's Stationery Office) on counselling and guidance, demonstrating the breadth of the modern concept of curriculum. In it counselling is defined as the guidance of young people in personal, educational and vocational matters. At the time of publication of the working paper five university departments of education and one professional institution were concerned with training school counsellors. It is clearly stated in the paper that, when considering the scope of counselling in schools in Britain, those employed in the field should be prepared to cope with all types of problems experienced by pupils in relationships with home, friends, school and community, as well as with the pupils' employment problems and other difficulties. School counsellors should also influence curriculum content, and should aim towards the adjustment of a school programme to the demands made by the community.

Public Examinations and Regional Examinations Boards

This section reviews the content relevant to sex education of the syllabi of a selection of regional examinations boards. The syllabi used in many schools, particularly for more able pupils, are orientated to the requirements of public examinations. The following short outline, and the contents of Appendix 2, give some indication of the relevance or irrelevance of public examination syllabi, and therefore school syllabi, to pupils' needs.

The Certificate of Secondary Education examination (CSE) can be taken just prior to leaving school at fifteen or sixteen years of age by less academic pupils—a group constituting about three-quarters of the total school population. The CSE is quite a new innovation, and only a proportion of the school leavers take this examination. The CSE syllabi tend to be more oriented to the demands of everyday life than the GCE syllabi (see below). For instance the CSE syllabi of the Metropolitan Examinations Board include: in biology, a simple account of reproduction in the mammal, with particular reference to the human being; in social studies, close relationships, including the family today, changing roles of men and women, relationships with the other sex, marriage, morals, rules of conduct, loyalties and responsibilities; in religious knowledge, a section on Christian obedience mentions, under the heading 'Personal Life', general behaviour and going out, use of leisure, the opposite sex (sex, marriage, divorce), and right choices.

Appendix 2 includes a table indicating the content of the 1969 Ordinary-level General Certificate of Education (GCE) syllabi of eight examining boards throughout the country which might be relevant to sex education in the broadest sense. The GCE examination is taken at sixteen years of age by pupils of above average academic ability. Four out of eight of the biology curricula of these examinations boards include a note that all descriptions of mammalian physiology should make special reference to man. All the syllabi include reproduction in mammals. Therefore it must be assumed that only four of the syllabi are intended to cover human reproduction. Only one religious knowledge syllabus out of eight has any reference to values in the modern world. Only one examinations board offers an examination in sociology at Ordinary level, and the content of this includes aspects of human behaviour, the family, and population (see Appendix 2).

The University of London Examinations Board syllabi for 1970 and 1971 include some relevant content in biology, human biology, and religious knowledge. More details are given in Appendix 2. This appears to be one of the most progressive Boards as regards the relationship of syllabus content to young people's everyday problems and needs, but even this is rather limited.

Schools Broadcasting

The British Broadcasting Corporation plays a recognized role in education and provides both radio and television programmes for schools, and for education of the individual. Its policies for school programmes are laid down by a council consisting of representatives from teachers' associations, Local Education Authorities, and the Department of Education and Science, among others. For a number of years, programme series covering aspects of sex education have been produced. The policy in schools television includes 'the provision of material of clear relevance and interest to a child's needs and interests', presented in such a way as to stimulate further discussion. It is felt that current trends in secondary schools 'towards more active bringing of social and personal problems into discussion make the evidential material which broadcasting can supply especially welcome'. Radio and television programmes for schools are supplemented by teachers' guides and well illustrated pupils' booklets. Recent examples of programmes relevant to sex education include:

1. 'Looking Ahead'—a radio series for school leavers intended as preparation for their lives in the future. About six programmes were devoted to sex education. The topics covered in these programmes included physical and emotional development, personal matters, falling in love, starting a family, birth, parental responsibility, and making choices. In many instances, views of and comments from young people were included.

2. 'Health and Science'—a series of radio programmes on health education. This series included programmes on growing up, put in the context of parental care in animal groups and in different human societies; on changes at puberty related to hormonal changes; on sur-

vival in the context of the welfare state and free health services; and on diet and accident prevention. The final programme in this series was on reproduction, and included heredity, male and female physiology, childbirth, and rearing a family.

3. 'Reproduction and Growth'—a series of broadcasts, lasting for one term, for children aged ten to thirteen years. This series included an elementary explanation of cell types, and asexual and sexual reproduction, culminating in vertebrate, mammalian, and human reproduction. Other programmes dealt with environmental influences and the population explosion.

4. In autumn 1969 a new series of radio-vision programmes on sex education for eight- to eleven-year-olds will be broadcast, which will involve use of filmstrips to the accompaniment of a recorded radio commentary.

The BBC also provide further education programmes for the general public. One series, entitled 'The Science of Man', consisted of eight programmes on reproduction and birth, and four on heredity; each of these topics being dealt with in detail. A similar in-depth series on education is planned for autumn 1969, and some programmes will certainly be devoted to discussing sex education. The series is intended for parents, teachers, and others concerned about or involved in education.

Commercial television companies, under the auspices of the Independent Television Authority, also produce programmes for use in schools. For example, the Granada Television Company has produced a series of television programmes entitled 'Understanding' for fifteen- and sixteen-year-olds. This was designed to encourage responsible discussion on various aspects of sex, marriage, family life, and friendship.

Another series produced by an independent television company, entitled 'What's It All About?', was prepared for young people of over fourteen years of age. Each programme in this series presented a realistic situation relevant to the life of a young person today, and was intended to provide a basis for discussion. In each film a representative of a particular welfare or other agency, or a member of the medical profession, discussed the situation depicted, and suggested some of the sources from which information could be sought. The film topics included unmarried mothers, early marriage, illegitimacy and adoption, housing, family roles, and leisure. Another television company produced a late night documentary for parents called 'What Shall We Tell the Children?', when young mothers discussed their problems and feelings about giving their sons and daughters information about sex, and young people, children, and teachers indicated their opinions or knowledge on the subject.

II. ACTION AT A LOCAL AUTHORITY LEVEL

In an effort to review the policies of Local Education Authorities in the field of sex education, a letter of inquiry was circulated by the IPPF to all Chief Education Officers in England and Wales. This resulted in sufficient responses to make the following generalizations about policies in sex education, which tend to fall into one of three groups:

1. Schools are encouraged to incorporate sex education into the normal curriculum.
2. Schools are encouraged to use the normal curriculum, and to call in agencies such as the local Health Department or the Marriage Guidance Council.
3. The initiative for sex education in schools comes from the Local Authority Health Department, which in some instances employs Health Education Officers for this function.

Since category 2 includes Health Departments, it is apparent that among respondents local Health Departments play an important role in promoting sex education in schools.

Several Authorities also arrange in-service training for teachers responsible for sex education. Examples of such schemes are outlined below (see also page 388). About twelve Local Education Authorities have published documents or reports on sex education, education for personal relationships, or health education in schools. Recommendations and comments from a selection of these publications are outlined below. Summaries from other publications of Local Education Authorities can be found in Appendix 3.

Specific Schemes

At the initiative of the Education Officer, the Gloucestershire Association of Family Life was formed in 1961 to consider whether further steps should be taken to help young people to understand the problems of personal relationships between the sexes, and to obtain a happy relationship in their own lives. The Association consists of representatives from the Local Education Authority, from schools, and from voluntary organizations. The Association has developed a training scheme for teachers and youth leaders from schools and youth groups throughout Gloucestershire. This scheme is run by special staff and is intended to prepare those responsible for educating young people in personal relationships and family life. It is emphasized by the Association that the scheme covers a much broader concept than sex education, and that it includes moral education, and all aspects of personal relationships. The

Association considers that this type of education should be given in three stages in secondary schools (in Britain it is compulsory for children to attend secondary school between the ages of eleven and fifteen years) and that the first stage should be incorporated into the first year at secondary school. This stage should deal with the physiology of human reproduction, laying emphasis on the wonder of life, and the importance of the family. Investigations in schools throughout Gloucestershire indicated that many schools were already giving this information. The Association felt it sufficient to organize annual one-day conferences for teachers responsible for giving this information. It has been suggested that this first stage should take place during the last year at primary school, partly because of the earlier onset of puberty among children today. The Association feels that primary school girls can be advised about menstruation and hygiene by a health visitor, but that education for personal relationships should begin when the child first attends secondary school, as this is often thought of as a first step towards adulthood. The second and third stages of the Association's scheme are concerned with physical and moral aspects of growth to maturity, and are designed to be given to children over fourteen years of age. It is felt that those teachers giving this information require certain personal qualities, so a strict selection procedure has been adopted, which involves teachers attending a twenty-four-hour selection conference when group discussions, open meetings, and private interviews with a psychiatrist and a head teacher take place. At the end of the selection conference candidates may be accepted immediately for this work or may be asked to return to a later selection conference, or may be recommended not to undertake this kind of work. Those selected attend a residential training course for three days, which includes instruction in child development, communication techniques, teacher-pupil relationships, and teaching aids.

Wiltshire Local Education Authority adopted a similar scheme in 1963. In this scheme, before a school embarks on a programme, or as a new group of pupils becomes involved, parents are informed and sometimes are invited to a meeting to hear details of the programme. Head teachers are also encouraged to enlist the help of school doctors and health visitors who have already been involved in this type of work, so that their contribution can be complementary to the scheme and not in conflict with it.

A second part of the Gloucestershire Association of Family Life scheme is aimed at training workers among young adults. This part of the scheme is similar to that conducted for schoolteachers, but it involves the selection and training of group leaders. Candidates come from all walks of life, and those suitable are selected, in the same way as teachers, at one-day selection conferences. Those selected attend a series of training sessions on group discussion, human development and behaviour, family relationships, and community responsibility. The trained group leaders are then available to speak at courses, and give lectures, when requested, to organizations which are usually parent-teacher associations, church organizations, or youth clubs, or at homes for unmarried mothers. Some of the group leaders run a youth advisory service where anonymous help is available to young people requesting it.

Some of the responsibility for sex education in schools in the London Borough of Croydon is taken by members of the Health Education Section of the Public Health Department of the borough. Three or four trained health educators are employed by the Health Department to organize or assist in health education programmes, including sex education, in both primary and secondary schools. In primary schools the health educators' approach is quite formalized, aiming at eight- to eleven-year-olds, and involving co-operation with the children's parents. As part of the primary school programme two evening meetings are held at each primary school in the borough. The first of these meetings is for parents only, and is to present information on the courses which are being given in the school, as well as providing the parents with an opportunity to discuss the problems their children must be prepared to face while growing towards maturity. Films and other teaching aids which are used during the children's lessons are demonstrated during the first meeting. A second evening meeting is held for parents and children together, to provide them with an opportunity to discuss what is being taught at the school, and to encourage a helpful atmosphere for further family discussions. The health education and sex education programmes of a primary school are usually incorporated into nature study classes, and may be given either by one of the professional health educators from the Health Department, or by the usual class teacher. The suggested content of the sex education programme includes information on families, parental care, new babies, and growth and development in all kinds of animals and in man. The introduction of elementary social studies into primary school courses will provide further opportunities for family life and sex education. The health educators of the Croydon Public Health Department will test this possibility during 1970. The secondary school sex education programme of the Croydon Health Department is defined by no set policy. If a secondary school requests assistance, one of the health educators will take a particular class, and show films and slides, in order to stimulate discussion with the pupils. The health educators of the Croydon Public Health Department also prepare and circulate syllabi on community health or a similar subject, which include sessions on venereal diseases, growth and development, the basis of adulthood, and the family.

The City of Oxford Local Education Authority has appointed a health education adviser, who has produced sets of notes to give teachers guidance on education in personal relationships. The notes include suggestions on class discussion topics, and lists of useful films, books, and other teaching material. In addition to these notes, six model lessons for sex education in primary schools have been produced by the health education adviser. Information in the model lesson notes includes simple information on male and female reproductive anatomy, on fertilization and pregnancy, on birth and puberty, and introduces the use of a correct vocabulary at a very early stage. Teachers in the City of Oxford Local Education Authority were circulated with the information and notes mentioned above, through each school in the area.

The Committee of the City of Birmingham Local Education Authority set up a working party of representatives from teachers' organizations, the local Public Health Department, and the local School Health Service. In 1967 the findings of the working party, which were based on a series of surveys and many discussions, were published in a report entitled *Sex Education in Schools*. Copies of this report were sent to every school in the Birmingham area. The report contains suggestions for sex education work programmes for children of different age levels, and for children of different interest groups and abilities (see page 406 Appendix 4). It also includes recommendations on the training of teachers and counsellors, and the suggestion that a counsellor should be appointed to work within a group of secondary schools in the area. A further suggestion from the working party, as noted in the report, is that conferences of head teachers and other representative teachers should be held in every school district in the Birmingham Local Education Authority area, in order to discuss the proposals for a more coordinated and explicit approach to sex education, but it is added that sex education work is not compulsory, and that any teacher who so wishes can opt out of the scheme. As a result of the working group proposals included in the report, in-service training courses in sex education have been organized for teachers at the City of Birmingham College of Education. Participants in the training courses are recommended by the head teacher of the school in which they teach. The course lasts for twelve days, and involves attending a three-day full-time introductory session, and attendance at weekly intervals after this.

The City of Newcastle-on-Tyne Education Committee appointed a curriculum study group to draft a health education syllabus for use in the city's schools. The study group report was presented in 1968. It recommended that at primary school level efforts should be made to encourage parents to take responsibility for informing their children of the 'facts of life', but suggested that, with parents' approval, some supplementary teaching could be provided by the schools. It was suggested that the supplementary teaching should deal with parental care, families and new babies, and the relevant physiological information, including simple explanations of conception and birth, in order to show how life is handed on. It is pointed out in the report that changing morality today necessitates a new approach to sex education in secondary schools, and that the new approach adopted should incorporate time for discussions on human relationships. After considerable discussion it is concluded that the inclusion of contraception in new courses cannot be avoided, particularly with the rising number of illegitimate births and shotgun marriages, and an increasing incidence of venereal disease. However, it is also stated in the report that 'to indulge in premarital sexual intercourse' should be a choice of mature judgement, and that, although teaching should not be indoctrinal, adolescents should be persuaded 'not to jump the gun' in this matter. It is specifically noted in the report that members of the curriculum study group do not support the contention that sex education leads to sexual experimentation. The report includes suggestions for a sex education course in the context of health education (see Appendix 4), with the stated view that no pupil should leave secondary school without having the opportunity to discuss the topics to be covered during the course, which, it is recommended, should be allocated at least one period a week in the school timetable.

An interesting scheme was reported from Lancashire in 1966. In this scheme, the Assistant Medical Officer of Health and a representative from the Lancashire Education Authority, working on the principle that parents are the best people to give children information on sex, approached parents through several different sorts of schools. Initially a series of evening meetings for parents were held at various primary and secondary schools, with the aim of determining reaction to the introduction of sex education programmes into schools in the area. Various films were shown which it was intended to use later in the school programmes. As a result of these meetings it was suggested that the films should be shown again to groups of parents with their children, because it was felt that this would help parents to overcome difficulties with terminology and lack of knowledge. Most parents found these sessions helped them to raise the subject much more freely with their children. An interesting development which emerged out of this scheme was a series of meetings held for parents who accompanied their very young children to a parent craft club. At these meetings films and tape recordings of typical family scenes were used to demonstrate how sex information can be given to children in an easy and natural way. It was reported that this was felt to be the most important programme in the whole scheme.

Teacher Training

In Britain, teachers are trained in one of two ways. Either suitably qualified school leavers, at the age of eighteen years, go directly to a teacher training college, where they specialize in one or two subjects, and also study teaching methods and techniques, and educational theories, over a period of three or four years. Or, university graduates attend a one-year training course, in order to obtain a Certificate of Education. The general tendency is for those trained at teacher training colleges to teach in primary schools, and for those having university degrees to teach in secondary schools. Further training is available for experienced teachers, who, after five years of teaching, may study for a diploma or certificate in educational guidance or counselling. One such course outlines its aims as follows: 'Those trained should be able to recognize and deal with the needs of individual pupils and help each student in his progress through school or college, to help him gain a better understanding of his strengths and limitations, identify his interests and help him plan his vocational goals realistically'. It also adds the point that modern conditions have necessitated a broader and deeper specialist approach to the needs of young people. In addition to the courses mentioned an increasing number of in-service training courses are being organized by Local Education Authorities. Some examples of these have been described previously in this report (pages 383 and 386).

As in the case of schools all establishments concerned with teacher training are to a large extent autonomous, and decisions about curriculum content are left to the teaching staff of the institutions. Some examples of the curriculum content relevant to sex education in a selected sample of the different types of teacher training course available are detailed in Appendix 5.

To give some indication of the amount of training in sex education given to student teachers, a survey produced the following evidence on the situation in 1964.[3] All establishments involved in teacher training were sent a questionnaire, which achieved a 66 per cent response rate. Of those replying to the questionnaire, 38 per cent ran formal courses in sex education, with an increase of twenty such courses since 1958. There appeared to be a preference among the majority of respondents to include sex education in the wider context of other courses. Seventy-one per cent of the courses provided were intended to provide personal help to the students themselves, who are often found to be very ignorant on these matters. Only 32 per cent of the establishments providing relevant courses made any attempt to prepare students to teach sex education, although half of these stressed that the course provided was intended to help the student at a later stage in his or her career. Ninety per cent of the establishments concerned with teacher training felt that the courses they were providing were adequate, but many said that they had difficulty in finding a suitable person to undertake this aspect of training. In twenty-one cases college staff and outside agencies were used, in nineteen cases college staff only were involved, and in eleven cases outside agencies only were used. The National Marriage Guidance Council accounted for half the instances when outside agencies were used, and medical practitioners accounted for most of the remainder.

III. SURVEYS IN THE FIELD OF SEX EDUCATION

To give some indication of the extent of sex education given to young people, the following paragraphs outline some survey findings.

In 1964 a survey into the sexual behaviour of young people was carried out under the auspices of the Health Education Council [4] (see page 397) by its Research Director, Mr Michael Schofield.

The survey findings, which were based on a random sample of 1,873 young people, indicated that there were marked differences in the amount of sex education given to boys and girls. Of the girls 86 per cent said that they had been given some sex education in school, in comparison with 47 per cent of the boys. It is interesting to note that, among the boys, there were marked differences in the information given according to type of school attended. State schools appeared to neglect their duties, and only 43–44 percent of the boys attending these schools had been given any type of sex education, whereas 71 per cent of boys attending private schools were given some instruction in this subject. The figures quoted above give no indication of the quality of the sex education given; however, Mr Schofield did attempt to investigate this. He found that most girls were given biological (excluding man), or physiological (including man) information, but in only 18 per cent of the cases did this information include a description of intercourse. About 20 per cent of the girls were given some form of moral education at school in comparison with 74 per cent of the girls who said that they had been given moral advice by their parents. Boys attending state schools rarely received more than biological or physiological information, although one in three of the boys attending private schools and receiving sex education were given information which included a description of intercourse. It is worth noting that in most cases schools and parents do not appear to have given young people advice on venereal diseases or contraception. Mr Schofield commented that

> The difficulties of providing viable education about sex are immense; much of the moral code is based upon religious thinking which teenagers do not accept, and many of the arguments against premarital intercourse, when unsupported by moral exhortations, sound weak to many young people. . . . But there is also plenty of evidence from this research that teenagers are

anxious to be informed about sex and want sex education providing it is given with an assurance backed by knowledge and with
a proper understanding of their particular problems.

There have been several localized surveys into the amount of sex
education undertaken in schools. One of these was organized by the
City of Birmingham Education Committee in 1965 as a preliminary to
their report *Sex Education in Schools* (see page 386). A questionnaire
was circulated to all primary and secondary schools in the Local
Authority area, which inquired into the extent of sex education provided
in each school, emphasizing that the information should include 'details
of sex education in its truest and deepest sense, based on an education in
human relationships and personal responsibility', and commenting that
instruction in biology and personal hygiene was only a small aspect
of the whole subject. The survey revealed some interesting facts. It was
found that staff of junior schools shrink 'from undertaking much
positive sex education' though they deal with questions which arise.
Only 12 per cent of the schools dealt with menstruation for the girls,
and it seemed to be preferred to leave responsibility for this to the parents, although little effort is made to co-operate or encourage them in this
role. Replies from staff of secondary schools indicated their view that
factual and background information on sexual matters should be given
to the pupils during the last years at junior school. It was also apparent
from replies to the questionnaire that most secondary school staff felt
it to be important to provide young people with advice and guidance on
emotional development, including love, courtship, marriage, home life
and parenthood, and chastity. Most of the surveyed schools stated the
necessity to discuss promiscuity, adultery, illegitimacy, and venereal
diseases, and many believed that information should be given on family
planning and birth control, although 50 per cent of these were not
willing to give details on principles and methods of contraception. About
45 per cent of the schools surveyed encouraged parents to play a role
in sex education, and about 4 per cent of the schools had experienced
difficulties as a result of this.

In 1967 a survey [5] among teachers in 400 primary and secondary
schools throughout the country showed that about 60 per cent of the
teachers thought that periods in the school timetable should be allocated
to moral education other than religious education. Of these teachers
three-quarters thought that moral education should include teaching
about sexual morality. Most of the teachers surveyed thought that moral
education should be taught by teams of teachers and should not be
the responsibility of one individual.

In 1966 the findings of a survey of adults' attitudes to sex education
were published by the Gloucestershire Association of Family Life (see
page 383). Most of those questioned in the survey were women who

were members of Women's Institutes, Mothers' Unions, or Mothers' Clubs. The findings of the survey revealed a very positive attitude among these groups of people indicating that 63.7 per cent feel that sex education is important in encouraging sensible attitudes, while only 13.2 per cent feel that it has little effect. It appeared from answers to questions about sex education that many adults are unaware of what is being attempted in this subject. Many of the respondents in the survey, particularly those from parent-teacher associations, would like more details of the work being done in sex education in schools. Several respondents in the survey expressed concern about the selection of a teacher to undertake this work.

IV. ACTION AT A NON-GOVERNMENTAL LEVEL

There has been no shortage of comments from non-governmental organizations on the need for sex education, although the comments have tended to be confined to educational, medical, or religious groups.

Educational Organizations

In November 1968 the Association of Headmistresses published a report entitled *Sauce for the Goose,* which draws attention to the work being done in girls' schools, in 'an era of intense sexual self consciousness', in response to advances in the effectiveness of birth control, and the weakening of former moral standards. It is suggested that such work should be obligatory in the education of both boys and girls. The authors of the report point out that girls should not have to carry unequal responsibility in sexual matters, which results in overemphasis of their own sexual significance. Reference is also made in the report to the importance of the personality of the teacher responsible for this type of teaching, and it is suggested that the married woman who returns to teaching after rearing a family is an asset in this type of education.

Medical Organizations

At a conference in 1964 the British Medical Association stated that it attached great importance to the role of teachers in framing the attitudes of the young, and that it intended to draw this to the attention of colleges of education.

'Adolescence and its Problems' was the subject discussed at a symposium organized by the Royal College of Practitioners in September

1967. At one of the seminar sessions on 'Adolescents and Family Planning' a speaker, Dr Faith Spicer, suggested some reasons for increases in premarital sexual activity and unmarried pregnancies, and for the general tendency of avoiding the use of contraception and seeking advice. With these being the prevailing conditions among young people she believes that sex education is valuable and important; that it includes, not only anatomical detail, but also learning about the whole conflict of love and sexuality from parents and siblings; that it should contribute to an ability to discuss feelings and behaviour with people who are trained in discussion; and that schools must support any training given by parents, and must help the child to communicate and work out his feelings in discussion, and where necessary should arrange individual counselling sessions.

In 1967, at a Royal College of Midwives symposium on 'Preparation for Parenthood', midwives were informed of some of the approaches to work with young people which could influence them in their roles as prospective parents. In his opening remarks to the conference, Sir John Peel, President of the Royal College of Obstetricians and Gynaecologists, said that education programmes for young people should include information on the pleasure and desirability of parenthood to the individual and the associated responsibilities to the nation. He felt that this information should be soon after puberty.

Religious Groups

In 1963 a group of Quakers published an enlightened essay entitled *Towards a Quaker View of Sex,* in which they put forward the belief that in this era of changing conditions there should be greater understanding of the sexual problems of the individual and a more flexible approach to sexual matters. In the essay they also offered the opinion that the traditional approach of the Christian Church to questions of morality should be replaced by a deeper, more creative and constructive morality. The authors intended that the ideas raised in the essay should help those having personal sexual problems or facing such problems in the lives of others.

In 1964 the Church of England Board of Education produced a pamphlet entitled *Sex Education in Schools.* This was based both on correspondence with 300 schools and on comments received from Local Education Authorities on the contents of a note on sex education. Through the pamphlet, the Church of England Board of Education called on all schools to accept responsibility for some sex education at the present time when so many parents do not feel able to face this responsibility, but it also recommended that schools should establish full co-operation with parents and should encourage parents to educate their own children in sexual matters. The authors of the pamphlet also suggested that physical facts of sex should be related to marriage and family life, and to the pattern of society; that moral education should not be authoritarian, but should be designed to help the child reach its own moral decisions; that the relationship between religious morality and sexual morality should not be overstressed; but that in all sex education the child's need for security should not be ignored. The Church of England Board of Education has no overall policy on sex education, but several of its constituent bodies, including the Youth Council and the Children's Council, have undertaken some work in this field. The Youth Council co-operates in diocesan schemes concerned with sex education, and the Children's Council offers advice on suitable teaching aids and literature for use in sex education.

Another constituent board of the Church of England is the Board of Social Responsibility, which, like the Board of Education, has no definite policy on sex education; however, its Committee of Diocesan Moral and Social Welfare is in touch with sixteen local moral welfare councils, which participate in schemes for education in personal relationships, in co-operation with Health Departments, Marriage Guidance Councils, and social workers.

The British Council of Churches produced a booklet in 1966 entitled *Sex and Morality*. This booklet consisted of a statement, prepared by a joint church working party, which presents the Christian case for abstinence from premarital sexual intercourse. The booklet also contained extensive discussion on the basis of morality in the changing social and cultural scene, and presented the working party's recommendations, which included: that courses on human relationships should be organized for seconded teachers, which could lead to a recognized qualification; that all religious knowledge teachers should take part in such training schemes; that courses in human relationships should be included in the curricula of all schools; and that the local Council of Churches should co-ordinate the activities of all those individuals and organizations having special responsibility for individuals' activities in the local community.

The Catholic Marriage Advisory Council has seventy centres in Britain, and through these provides a marriage counselling service, a medical advisory service, and an educational service. Within the latter, selected educational counsellors work with the staff of a school in the planning and running of courses in family life education for the pupils. At the same time, parallel courses are arranged for parents and teachers. Courses for pupils are aimed at developing an understanding of the implications of manhood and womanhood, and the idea of marriage as a life vocation. However, considerable emphasis is placed on work with parents, which, it is felt, necessitates both good organization and efficient planning. An advice sheet on arranging such occasions has been prepared for schools, together with notes on parents' needs and difficulties. In this it is suggested that two meetings should be held for parents; one before the pupils are given a family life education course, and one as a follow-up at the end of the pupils' course. It is also suggested that programmes for these meetings should be largely based on group discussion, giving the parents, the teachers, and the Catholic Marriage Advisory Council representatives an opportunity to exchange ideas and opinions on such topics as the value of the proposed school course, the parents' role in the total scheme, and the reactions of the children to the course.

Other Groups

The National Childbirth Trust is a voluntary organization aiming to dispel fears associated with childbirth, which believes that it is vitally important to family life to recognize that childbirth can be a satisfying experience. For this reason it believes that a healthy attitude to reproduction must be encouraged through sex education given in schools, and that both boys and girls need education in the understanding of the physical and emotional aspects of childbirth. At the National Childbirth Trust antenatal classes, teaching is based not only on techniques of breathing and relaxing, but also on giving information which provides the woman with a language through which she can accept her own physical experience as part of the normal pattern. Where this occurs, sex education can begin within the family, which, it is generally agreed, is the ideal. The National Childbirth Trust is in contact with the problems facing teachers who are responsible for sex education, through members of the Trust who are already involved with the subject in schools. To assist these teachers, study days are organized, at which teaching aids are demonstrated and discussed, and when information is shared.

One organization which has been closely involved in family life and sex education is the National Marriage Guidance Council. Both the Government and local authorities have recognized and commended its work. The Council undertakes to select marriage guidance counsellors using strict procedures. Selected candidates attend a series of short residential courses over a period of two years, and during the same period are expected to attend practical and case study discussion at least once a fortnight. At present, the work of counsellors is entirely voluntary, and, once qualified, a counsellor is expected to serve a minimum of three hours a week, dealing with both marriage counselling and youth work. Work in schools is co-ordinated from each local marriage council office by an education secretary, who informs the Local Education Authority of the services offered, with the request that all schools in the area be notified of these. Schools then contact the local office when they require assistance. However, before accepting an invitation to visit a school, a counsellor stipulates certain conditions. A counsellor is not prepared to give a single talk on sex to a large group of children, and requests that, if at all possible, a series of discussions be arranged with groups of ten to fifteen pupils at the most. It is also preferred if a series of discussion sessions with pupils' parents can be arranged concurrently. A similar approach is used with other youth groups, and similar conditions are required.

To give some idea of the scope of the Marriage Guidance Council's work among young people, figures for 1968 indicate:

8,318 sessions were held in schools
1,322 sessions were held in youth groups
1,848 sessions were held with parent-teacher associations.

Recently there has been a trend among counsellors from the Marriage Guidance Council towards greater contact with teachers in schools and trainee teachers in colleges. In some cases counsellors have been requested to arrange group discussions with the staff of a school on family life and sex education. In other situations, counsellors have been asked to assist in teacher training colleges. This aspect of the Council's work is increasing in amount, and is considered to be very important.

Other organizations and groups of people have also seen the value of counselling methods to help young people deal with personal problems. In 1963, officials of the Marie Stopes Family Planning Clinic realized that there was a need both to help young people with their sexual problems and to provide birth control advice to the unmarried. A project scheme was organized at the Clinic, consisting of weekly consultation sessions for unmarried clients. This scheme was so much in demand that it was decided to offer a grant for the establishment of a centre exclusively for young unmarried people: thus, the first Brook Advisory Centre was opened in London in 1965. Since then an increasing number of similar youth advisory centres have opened throughout the country, including nine more Brook Centres. The Brook Centres' aims are as follows: to provide birth control advice to the young and unmarried; to provide professional help to those with emotional, sexual and birth control problems; to inculcate a sense of sexual responsibility; and to mitigate the suffering caused by unwanted pregnancy and abortion. The counsellors and other staff working in these centres have found that, although young people come initially for birth control advice, they often require professional help with emotional problems.

Other youth advisory centres have been established by enlightened groups of people, and organizations, in several places, including Southampton and Merseyside. The increasing need for such centres is becoming more widely recognized. This recognition, together with the provisions made under the 1967 Family Planning Act obliging local authorities to reconsider their policies on financing and otherwise supporting local family planning facilities, has encouraged one London borough to open an advice centre with counselling facilities for young people. Young people are referred to the centre from their schools and colleges, or by social workers, or voluntary organizations in contact with young people in difficulties. The staff of the centre aim initially to provide practical advice, on an informal basis, which often results in the provision of counselling facilities in connection with other problems. The policy of the centre also includes the aims of improving sex education programmes in the borough's schools, and of increasing the knowledge of the general public on relevant and related matters. It is envisaged that the centre will, in the future, be part of a network of help-services which will deal with the many different needs of adolescents by providing preventative solutions to many of their problems.

An increasing number of university and college administrations are finding it necessary to provide advice and counselling facilities for the students, although, in some instances, the student body provide and sometimes run their own service. Teachers and other educational administrators are also realizing the need for counselling services in schools. Often, the problems arising during counselling situations are concerned with sexual and emotional problems, although other personality problems may emerge.

Family Planning Association

In the past, the Family Planning Association's activities have been mainly concerned with clinic services. However, a sex education committee has been formed by the Association, which now regards the subject as a priority in its work. All FPA branches organize talks and film shows and participate whenever possible in local sex education activities. In order to launch an integrated, full-scale sex education drive throughout this country, the FPA has initiated an 'Every Child a Wanted Child' campaign. This is a fund-raising campaign which aims to raise the money necessary to provide the trained speakers, audiovisual aids, books and pamphlets which will be needed to suit different audiences and age groups. Teach-ins, brains trusts, lectures, exhibitions, and other events are also planned as part of the FPA's future work.

The FPA 1969 Annual Conference devoted considerable attention to sex education. One of the speakers at the conference was Michael Schofield, who talked about 'Sex and Birth Control in Health Education'. Another speaker was Baroness Birk, Chairman of the Health Education

Council, a Government body which has recently established a sex education advisory panel on which the FPA is represented.

A very interesting development, within the south-west and south-east London branches of the Family Planning Association, has been the establishment of a comprehensive community education project, administered by a full-time salaried education officer, who works with a joint sub-committee from the local branches of the FPA, to the brief that an education programme should be set up to spread knowledge of family planning and elicit motivation towards its use. Since then a programme has been planned which is designed to inform and provide training courses for doctors and other medical personnel, social workers, local authority officials, FPA officials, and others who are, or should be, involved or concerned with family planning. The project will progress using local FPA officials who have already attended a course, to spread relevant information to teachers, parents, students, young couples, and members of youth groups. Finally, it is envisaged that relevant aspects of this information will be included in secondary school courses, and passed on to other specific groups of the general public, by teachers and others who have previously been involved in the first and second parts of the programme. The information given to each group at the different stages in the programme is oriented to the contribution that the group can make to the local community.

V. YOUNG PEOPLE'S ATTITUDES TO SEX EDUCATION

Michael Schofield's survey into the sexual behaviour of young people (see page 389) also investigates young people's attitudes to sex education. The survey findings showed that a quarter of the boys and a third of the girls interviewed thought that they should have been told more about sex by their parents, while it was fairly clear that more boys would prefer to receive this information from a teacher, and that about a third of the girls would also have preferred to be given more information by teachers. There were also indications that both boys and girls would appreciate guidance on sexual problems from teachers. Rather disturbing findings from the survey were that most of the young people interviewed thought that they had learnt more from their friends than they could from adults, and that nearly half of those interviewed thought they knew all that there was to know about sex. Clear indications elsewhere in the survey demonstrated that the information young people thought they possessed included a lot of misinformation about birth control and venereal diseases, and only limited information on other matters.

In a survey among a group of young patients at a venereal diseases clinic,[6]* it was revealed that the majority of the group felt that more sex education should be given in schools by someone who was 'both knowledgeable and unembarrassed'. Most of this group also thought that a doctor or nurse should visit the school in the context of sex education, although, among the control group in the survey, none of the 23 per cent who had any knowledge of venereal disease expressed views on the necessity of such visits.

In 1968 a survey to investigate young people's attitudes [7] which was carried out by the Medical Officer of Health in the City of Leicester showed that 100 per cent of the young males and females interviewed thought that children should be taught the facts about contraception. Among the group interviewed 46 per cent of the males and 40 per cent of the females thought that parents should provide this information, 46 per cent males and 22 per cent females thought that teachers should have this responsibility, and 22 per cent males and 33 per cent females thought that doctors should provide information on contraception.

VI. COMMENT

A final chapter in the report of the investigation *The Sexual Behaviour of Young People* (1965) (see page 389 and above) was headed 'Questions for Public Concern'. The following statement is quoted from this chapter: 'It is an urgent short-term task to make teenage sexual activities less harmful. This may be done by increasing the amount of knowledge and enlightenment on sexual matters, by introducing more and better sex education in the widest sense, and by providing individual counselling . . . above all it is vital that future programmes of advice, help, and restraint should be based more on demonstrable facts, less on substantiated impressions. . . .'

In Britain there is evidence of a noticeable increase in interest and activity in the field of sex education during the last decade and particularly during the last five years. The information in this report, though not comprehensive, illustrates some of the major developments during this period.

APPENDIX 1: OTHER CENTRAL GOVERNMENT REPORTS OF RELEVANCE

In 1956 the Royal Commission on Marriage and Divorce called for a carefully graded system of education for young people as they grow up,

---

* See pp. 415-422 of *Sex, Schools, and Society.*

in order to fit them for marriage and family living, which would also incorporate specific provision for those about to enter marriage. The Commission recommended that public money should be given to voluntary agencies that had already demonstrated their effectiveness in this field, a plea later reiterated in the Latey Report, entitled *The Age of Majority,* which was presented to the Government in 1967.

The Albermarle Report, *The Youth Service in England and Wales,* published in 1960 made the following points. Many factors in society are changing, and these changes necessitate reorganization of the Youth Services to suit the needs of young people today. The factors of change include: earlier age of puberty, increased physical strength, changing pattern of women's lives, increases in delinquency, better housing and schooling standards, improved welfare facilities, increasing affluence, better education, higher expectations, employment problems, together with less measurable factors such as increased social mobility, conflict of values, impact of mass media, and the development of nuclear weapons. The Youth Service must be improved to cope with these, by training more youth leaders for both full and part time work. The training given to youth leaders should provide information on the psychology of adolescence, the physical needs of adolescents, and changing cultural patterns in modern society including the impact of mass media, the effect of modern means of communication, and the values of adolescents at work, at home, in sex and in religion.

The Bessey Report, presented to the Government in 1962, supplemented the Albermarle Report by suggesting that there should be common elements in all youth leaders' training courses, which should include instruction on the value of group work to personal development, and should also provide an opportunity to acquire an understanding of young people's attitudes, beliefs and aspirations, and a knowledge of their physical, emotional, and social development in society.

In 1967 the Department of Education and Science produced a pamphlet entitled *Health in Education.* It draws attention to the features of school life that contribute most to the physical, mental, and social well-being of pupils and makes suggestions on the content of existing health education courses, which should include the necessity to prepare children for puberty. Within the context of sex education emphasis is laid on the children's need for knowledge of the basic facts of reproduction, and the importance of moral education. It suggests that information should be given on venereal diseases and family life and marriage, but that information on birth control should be left to the head teacher's discretion. It states that presentation of the facts on all aspects of intercourse does not seem appropriate. Care should be taken on choice of a suitable teacher to give sex education, but it will usually be the biology teacher.

In 1967, the Latey Report, entitled *The Age of Majority,* was presented to the Government with the following recommendations: that the minimum age for marriage, and for participating in sexual intercourse, should remain at sixteen years; and that the age to consent to marriage without parental permission should be lowered to eighteen years. In a section of the report entitled 'Education for Marriage' it is stated that 'it is absolutely essential that everything possible should be done to educate young people in human relationships while they are still at school', particularly because it is known that more people are marrying younger. It is also stated that boys and girls need a great deal more instruction on the technical, emotional and moral problems of modern family life, and that an extra year at school, as suggested in the Crowther Report, should enable such instruction to be a regular part of the curriculum, and not simply a subject for the visiting specialist. It is also recommended in the Latey Report that high priority should be given to provision of grants from the public sector to such organizations as the Marriage Guidance Council and the Catholic Marriage Advisory Council, to encourage expansion of their important work in this field.

APPENDIX 2: AN EXAMPLE OF TOPICS RELATED TO SEX EDUCATION IN THE GENERAL CERTIFICATE OF EDUCATION SYLLABUS

Excerpts from the syllabus of the University of London Examination Board 1970 to 1971:

In the Biology syllabus 1971 it is noted that 'the relevance of biology to human affairs should be borne in mind'. The syllabus includes:

Reproduction and Development (including growth)
Reproduction in the mammal: sexual rhythm, mating, fertilization, gestation, functions of the placenta, birth, parental care
Man's place in nature: including biological effects of man's activities on the environment.

The Human Biology syllabus 1970 to 1971 includes the following:

In the Anatomy and Physiology section it is noted that anatomy should not be disassociated from any functional implications. This section of the syllabus should include information on the following: the urino-genital system, male and female reproductive organs, functions of gonads, outline of female reproductive cycle, menstruation, an outline of human development, fertilization, implantation, and a brief outline of growth of embryo and foetus, and the functions of placenta.

In the Religious Knowledge syllabus 1970 to 1971 the following topics are noted:

Personal and social relationships and problems, to include such topics as home and family relationships, love, marriage, sex, parents and children.

Excerpts from the Sociology syllabus of the Associated Examinations Board 1970:

The object of the Sociology syllabus is to enable the student to understand better the society of which he is a member. The syllabus includes such topics as the nature, changing role, and function of the family, as well as religion, moral and social behaviour, mass media, and population size and distribution, and contraception.

Table. To indicate content of courses offered by the listed Examinations Boards which could be relevant to sex education

	Subjects which could include information on reproductive anatomy and physiology					Other subjects which could contain relevant information	
	Biology						
Examinations Boards	*Includes reproduction in animals*	*Special reference to man*	*Human biology*	*General science*	*Religious knowledge*	*Sociology*	
University of London	X	X	X	X	X	/	
University of Cambridge	X	—	X	X	—	/	
Joint Matriculation	X	X	X	X	—	/	
Southern University	X	X	X	X	—	/	
Associated Examinations	X	—	X	X	—	X	
Welsh Joint Education	X	X	X	—	—	/	
Oxford and Cambridge	X	—	/	X	—	/	
University of Oxford	X	—	X	X	—	/	

(X) = Some relevant content.
(—) = No relevant content.
(/) = Subject not offered.

APPENDIX 3: OTHER LOCAL EDUCATION AUTHORITY REPORTS AND ACTIVITIES OF RELEVANCE

Aberdeen Education Authority

In 1969 a working party, consisting of head teachers, women advisers, biology, physical education and religious knowledge teachers, primary school teachers, a deputy medical officer of health, and a number of health visitors, produced a report on sex education in schools. The working party recommended that reproduction, as a bodily function, should be included in any health education course, and that schools should help young people to cope with their own development during adolescence. The working party also suggested that in primary schools the class teacher or, if not, a health visitor or another teacher, should aim towards achieving certain objectives in sex education, including adequate preparation for puberty, encouragement of responsible attitudes towards sex, providing information on the factual aspects of reproduction while stressing both the importance of family life and the wonder of creation, and at the same time satisfying the child's natural curiosity. The teacher's approach should be informal until the children are about eight years old, but then the approach should become a formal part of health education in the context of nature study. The working party also recommended that any teachers expected to take responsibility for sex education should be prepared for the task through in-service training or courses at teacher training colleges.

With regard to sex education in secondary schools the working party suggested: that biology should be an essential subject in science during the first two years of the secondary school curriculum; that a course in mothercraft should be given to all third-year girls and an equivalent course on parental responsibility should be considered for boys; that, once a week, all third-year boys and girls should take a course in social studies, designed to include sex education, which would cover the nature and structure of the family and attitudes to sexual behaviour. In addition the working party suggested: that English literature courses can contribute to understanding human rights and motivation, can increase insight into others' feelings, and can be used to evaluate the impact and message of mass media and the 'pop scene'; and that religious education can provide an opportunity for young people to explore the basis of ethics in sexual conduct based on the principle of respect for other persons. It was also suggested that group discussions are a valuable medium for considering sexual behaviour, especially if such discussions are supplemented with personal advice and guidance for both girls and boys.

Cheshire Education Authority

This Education Authority has issued several publications which include suggestions on methods of approach to sex education. A main objective of suggested secondary school courses has been preparation for parenthood and home making. For example, in a book, *The Secondary Modern School,* which the Authority first published in 1958, emphasis is laid on the importance of the parents' role in relation to a child's future family life, choice of partner, and behaviour during adolescence. The book also includes the following suggestions: that problems arising during adolescence are the concern of both the parents and the school, and should if possible be discussed mutually; that the school's function is to establish a moral tone without preaching; that it is helpful to encourage social activities where both sexes are present; that religious education can provide guidance on matters of behaviour; that biology teaching can provide a clear understanding of human reproduction as part of the whole life process, while also supplying the correct scientific terms; that homecraft lessons can include personal hygiene; and that courses in child welfare can cover preparation for motherhood.

In 1965 Cheshire Education Authority published a booklet on health education in schools, in which it is suggested that health education should be included in the timetable of all schools. However, it is noted in the booklet that a child's initial training in health matters is the parents' responsibility, and therefore it is suggested that opportunities should be created in schools for teachers and parents to discuss the varying physical and emotional needs of a child at different stages in its development.

Inner London Education Authority

On commencing work with this Authority all teachers are given a booklet entitled *Some Notes on Sex Education*. This booklet, revised in 1964, was first published in 1949. It contains recommendations that factual information and moral guidance should be available to all children and young people, and suggests that, because parents often neglect this responsibility, the schools must be prepared to assist, but that such assistance needs to be carefully considered because unwise instruction can do more harm than good. It is also suggested in the booklet that sex education does not need to be a separate item in the school syllabus, but that its inclusion should be a conscious and concrete policy in each school, since many parts of the curricula in both primary and secondary schools can provide suitable media for the subject. As an example it is suggested that in secondary schools a comprehensive programme can be carried out with the co-operation of teachers of different subjects, and possibly with the help of outside visitors. It is also suggested that teachers should discuss intended programmes with parents, since understanding and support are required from all concerned, and the teacher can act as an intermediary between parent and child, and can contribute to their mutual understanding. In a section of the booklet devoted to factual content of sex education courses, it is stated that children of eleven to twelve years of age should understand the facts of reproduction in preparation for puberty. It is also suggested: that information on menstruation, nocturnal emissions, masturbation and homosexuality should be given to children before the age of fourteen years; that mothercraft courses for girls should deal with antenatal physiology and hygiene, and attitudes to pregnancy and childbirth; that evening classes could provide courses on preparation for parenthood for mixed groups; that courses on preparation for fatherhood and family life could be organized for boys, either in school, or at evening classes; and that school staff wishing to teach about family planning should consider the depth of information to be given before being faced with the topic in a classroom situation. It is further suggested in the booklet that, although factual information may contribute towards developing responsible and healthy attitudes, more needs to be done, and that group discussion under the leadership of a carefully selected teacher provides one opportunity for achieving this, not by presenting set rules of conduct, but by discussion on generally accepted attitudes, such as 'respect and consideration for members of the opposite sex', the responsibilities of childbearing, present pleasure does not necessarily mean future happiness. Another point which is raised is that schools should provide young people with information on sources of advice and help in an out-of-school situation.

Apart from giving all teachers the booklet, the Inner London Education Authority also provides schools with assistance on sex education through two permanent units. One of the units, which is attached to the Education Department, employs two health educators, who visit as many schools as possible during the school year, giving short talks which in general are either to eleven-year-olds on growing up, or to fourteen- to sixteen-year-olds on personal relationships, including sex, venereal diseases, and birth control if requested. The other Inner London Education Authority unit, which is attached to the Medical Department, also employs two health educators, who provide comprehensive programmes in both primary and secondary schools, although they find it impossible to deal with all the schools requesting their help. The programme they have devised for primary schools is interesting, consisting of a three- to five-day health education programme in each school, which is supported by an exhibition set up in some central place in the school. During the programme, lectures are given on personal hygiene, environmental hygiene, spread of infection, and smoking, and it is terminated with one long session on sex education. One of the aims of this programme is to involve parents as much as possible, and they are welcomed to attend any part of the course, as well as being invited to a special evening meeting. The secondary school programme provided by the unit consists of a series of lectures entitled 'Human Growth and Development'. These include normal growth and development and those factors interfering with this, such as venereal disease, abortion and unwanted pregnancy.

Hampshire Education Authority

In 1964 a working party produced a report called *A New Approach to Health Education in Schools,* which included education for family life. It stated in the report that health education is a proper concern for Education Authorities and that it is important both in individual development and in creating a healthier community. A copy of this report was sent to each head teacher in Hampshire, with the suggestion that its contents and implications should be discussed with the entire teaching staff of the school to encourage the adoption of a forward-looking policy which recognizes the need for primary schools to prepare pupils for adolescence, and for secondary schools to prepare pupils for parenthood. Through the report Hampshire Education Authority offered specialist advice and equipment to assist schools to carry out such policies. The report also contains suggestions on primary and secondary schools' teaching schemes which use the resources of teachers of biology, physical education, domestic science, and religious education, and the support of the school health service.

Luton Education Authority

A teachers' guide for education in human relationships was prepared suggesting how this topic can be dealt with in the religious education syllabus. The suggested religious education syllabus is intended to provide young people with guidance on the practical application of Christianity whether they are non-believers or practising Christians. It is suggested that religious education teachers should deal with aims in life and personal problems from both points of view, including in the course information on consideration of authority, friendship and loyalty, marriage, and boy-girl friendships.

Other Local Education Authority Activities

Several other Local Education Authorities have prepared reports, teachers' notes or syllabi in sex education, and others have appointed working parties to consider or review the policies in the field of sex education. These include:

Glamorgan Education Authority: currently defining its policies on sex education in schools.

London Borough of Waltham Forest Education Authority: have appointed a working group which is studying sex education at present, but has not yet presented a report.

Luton Education Authority: now reviewing the whole question of sex education in schools.

Southampton Education Authority: currently reviewing the place of sex education, and other topics, in the school curriculum.

Sunderland Education Authority: have published a suggested syllabus entitled 'An Approach to Sex Education' (1969).

Surrey Education Authority: have prepared suggestions on topics to be included in sex education at primary and secondary school levels.

APPENDIX 4: SOME SUGGESTED SCHEMES FOR SEX EDUCATION IN THE SCHOOL SYLLABUS

The main part of this report on family life and sex education in Britain includes suggestions for dealing with sex education in schools, which fall into fairly clear categories according to suggested context, and level of approach. Some further examples, in more or less detail, are given below:

1. From the City of Birmingham Education Authority Report, *Sex Education in Schools,* it is suggested that incidental teaching in infant and junior schools should cover health and sex education, and that the last few years at junior schools should have a more detailed and deliberate policy towards this topic. Suggested teaching schemes from this report are outlined below:

Infants

No formal scheme is necessary. Questions should be answered as they arise. Education at this level should be based on discovery and investigation of the environment, and should promote the unconscious formation of those wholesome attitudes to life on which a child's subsequent moral development depends. This can be done through understanding the creative process of life by keeping plants and animals, by going for nature walks, by group and creative activities, children's games, talking about family life, stories, etc.

Juniors

During the latter two years at junior school attention should be given to hygiene, the human body, and plant and animal reproduction, as an introduction to human reproduction and relationships within the family. The suggested scheme in health education includes parental care in nature, body structure and function, hygiene, the lungs, fresh air and smoking, teeth, food and digestion, exercise and rest, cleanliness of the skin, nails, hair, genitals, removal of waste, and aspects of sex education. Topics to be included in sex education in junior schools are given in detail, as a source of guidance to teachers. These are listed below:

(a) Families of living things: distinguishing characteristics of plants, insects, fish.
(b) Mammals—udders, breasts, etc.
(c) A simple but workable vocabulary.
(d) Structure of reproductive organs.
(e) Function of reproductive organs—e.g., womb to protect and nourish baby: baby growing from tiny egg made in ovary.
(f) Egg fertilized by sperm given by male.
(g) The human family and the needs of a baby.
(h) Fertilization—how egg and sperm must be brought together.
(i) Development of baby before and after birth. Getting to know the baby and to recognize its needs and requirements.
(j) Growing up, mentally and physically. Privileges and responsibilities.
(k) The cycle of menstruation—the amount of detail will depend on the readiness of the child or group concerned.
(l) Details of the physical changes arising at puberty in boys, e.g., the body grows faster, the voice breaks and facial and body hair grows.

The Birmingham report on sex education in schools also contains suggestions for a scheme in health education in secondary schools, but these consist only of proposals, and it is suggested that the teachers involved must decide on emphasis given to the suggested topics. However, the report includes an example of a scheme which is taught in three stages. This is described below:

i. Eleven–twelve-plus years. Living for Self

We would hope that adequate preparation for the secondary school course will have been made in primary school.

(a) Revision of human body—structure and functions.
(b) The seven rules of health—fresh air, exercise, food, sleep, clothing, cleanliness and recreation. N.B. smoking, drink.
(c) Growing up—glandular changes in both sexes.
(d) Human reproduction—facts. Fertilization, development of embryo and birth of baby.
(e) The family; thought for others—responsibility and independence. Development of baby and toddler—importance of first five years.

ii. Thirteen–fifteen years. Living for Others

(a) Revision of human reproduction and life with the family.

(b) Making friends; adolescence—physical, mental and emotional changes; becoming adult.

(c) Boy and girl friendships; socially acceptable behaviour, sexual attraction; love.

(d) Sexual relationships—basically for reproduction; children and security; the marriage relationship.

(e) Responsibilities in the home, day-to-day problems, prevention of accidents and illness, home nursing.

(f) Development of social conscience—from the self-regarding baby to self-control. Self-control in children, in adults. Why this is necessary and desirable. Responsibility for those younger and older.

iii. Fifteen years and over. Life in the Community

(a) Attitudes between the sexes; courtship, preparation for marriage; partnership; family, responsibilities. Development of 'whole' personality and marriage relationship; freedom and responsibility.

(b) Home-making—responsibilities, care of young child, preparation for parenthood, budgeting, hire-purchase, etc.

(c) Attitudes at work—transition from school to work. Respect for self and others; evolving a moral code.

(d) Attitudes to others—good manners; good taste; dress; changing standards; social problems, etc.

(e) Leisure—use and misuse; voluntary activities, etc.

(f) Freedom and responsibility.

(g) Prejudices and loyalties; class and racial discrimination, etc.

(h) Mass media and effects—advertising, pop records, TV and cinema, etc.

(i) Public health and social services; community responsibility.

(j) Life in the community. What is an acceptable code of conduct?

2. Newcastle on Tyne Education Committee Report (1969), entitled *Education for Health,* recommends that unit parts of health education should be included within relevant subjects at secondary school. The following examples are cited:

Biology lessons can include information on the body and how it works.

Physical health and fitness including personal hygiene can be taught in physical education.

Home economics lessons can include information on health and the home.

However, it is suggested that the course unit on individual health and community responsibility be allocated one period a week and that such a course could be given in five sections:

Ourselves and our home
Friends and acquaintances
The opposite sex
Personal responsibility
Looking ahead.

It is also suggested that a course of this type should be based on discussions and should aim at helping adolescents to sort out their widely differing problems.

3. Gloucestershire Association for Family Life have produced several reports to which reference has been made previously (see Section II, page 383). The content recommended for each of the three series in a secondary school course, is set out below:

Series 1—for eleven-year-olds

Introduction—Man and the family and home
Reproduction—Male and female organs and their functions
Intercourse
Development of the baby
Birth
Twins
Heredity and development.

Series 2—for fourteen- to fifteen-year-olds

The syllabus should be adapted to the needs of the group and should take from two to ten sessions, which should be based on talks followed by discussions. The following suggested topics should be covered:

(i) *Adolescence—becoming adult*

Growth is a continuous process from birth to death—the process is speeded up during the adolescent period. It must be remembered that, although there is a general pattern of development and decline, each individual is likely to vary from the norm.

An adult should be a person capable of taking decisions, making choices, prepared to accept frustration. Full responsibility can only be achieved by learning about yourself, the effects of your behaviour on those whom you meet, and the wide implications for society in general.

Development from infant dependency to maturity
Physical and psychological changes in adolescence
Relations with parents
Parents' point of view.

(ii) *Making friends—finding out about yourself and other people*

> What do we look for in a friend?
> How do we find out what sort of people we like?
> How do we behave towards people we like?
> How do we behave towards people we don't like?
> Do we have the same sort of relationship with the opposite sex as
> we have with our own sex?

(iii) *Boy-Girl friendships*

Sex roles—socially acceptable behaviour of men and women—why have these roles arisen? Do they remain unchanging? (N.B.) Not all men are completely masculine nor all women completely feminine.

> What is meant by sexual attraction?
> Is sexual attraction different from love?
> Can we be attracted by someone we don't like?
> Can we be attracted by someone we don't know?
> Differences between reactions of men and women.

(iv) *Sexual relationship*

> Basically for reproduction.
> Babies and children need secure home.
> Society concerned with preserving family unit.
> Sexual relationships are also one way among others of expressing
> love, but cannot be separated from the whole personality, and
> should keep pace with whole relationships.
> Sexual intercourse is the most complete way of relating yourself
> physicially, and implies total committal.
> Marriage is a relationship where two people commit themselves
> to each other.

(N.B.) The teacher must expect questions of physiology of reproduction even if Series 1 has already taken place. The members of the group will not necessarily remember all the details, and will need their knowledge extended and re-interpreted, since it will have become more relevant.

> How far can I go with my girl friend?
> Pre-marital intercourse
> Parents' attitude to boy-girl friendships
> Masturbation
> Homosexuality.

(v) *Development of the Moral Sense*

New-born baby self-regarding
Self-control in a child—due to fear or desire to be loved
Self-control in an adult—due to fear?
Knowledge that co-operation necessary to civilized life?—love
your neighbour as yourself?

Series 3—usually for sixteen-year-olds and over

This course is intended for those pupils who will shortly enter the outside world. It should help them to become aware of some of the problems they will have to face in living conditions, working conditions, and social life. It should encourage them to make responsible decisions and live up to the right kind of values. It is suggested that the following topics should be covered:

(i) Revision of Series 1, though more stress to be placed on physiological changes than on physical at this stage. Instincts and heredity should be discussed.
(ii) The World of Work
(a) The value of further education and training including careers and married women.
(b) Attitudes to work, covering popular fallacies.
(iii) Good manners—respect for other people and their ideas.
(iv) Leisure—wasting time, misuse of time, voluntary activity, etc.
(v) Freedom—in relation to responsibilities, choice of career, future happiness.
(vi) Transition into Outside World—life during training, attitude to authority, leaving home, living at home, self-discipline, developing other interests.
(vii) Class and Racial Discrimination: Political and Racial Intolerance.
(viii) Courtship, Marriage and Family. The list below indicates in detail the topics which it is suggested should be included:
(a) Courtship—sexual behaviour; petting; engagements—what should engaged couples be looking for? Liking the same things (perhaps in a different way), looking at things in the same way; behaviour in the same things (morals, religion). People of different religions, morals, interests. Length of time to find out compatibility. Always together—or part of time apart? Risks of engagement—if we break it off—will people talk? Chastity?
(b) Marriage and Family—Functions.
(1) Sexual relationships
(2) Parenthood
(3) Home-making
(4) Government of family affairs
(5) Economic expenditure
(6) Education
(7) Health, particularly mental, in early years of child's life important for subsequent development of adult personality.

(8) Religious functions; beliefs and practices of parents affect children greatly (RC or Jews). Children come to own views later. Family should provide basis for development of well considered views and of satisfactory outlook on life.

(9) Recreation—correlate with leisure.

Discuss:

    (i) mothers at work.

    (ii) divorce.

    (iii) family planning.

    (ix) Why are we here? Who should make society's rules? Personal achievement.

APPENDIX 5: SOME EXAMPLES OF TRAINING SCHEMES FOR TEACHERS AND OTHERS

This appendix includes some further examples of the training in sex education available to teachers and student teachers. The information given is not representative of all courses, but is intended to give some indication of the sort of training that is given in a number of these establishments providing courses for graduate teachers and others. In all cases the information given applies to the course content in 1968 to 1969.

1. School of Education, University of Reading—Post-graduate Certificate of Education.

As part of this certificate course, intending teachers of biology are given some instruction in sex education in a course unit on biology method teaching. This includes discussion on the subject lasting for about two lecture hours out of a total of thirty-nine. The topics covered include:

    (i) Biological teaching of human reproduction

    (ii) Parental responsibility and social organization

    (iii) Child growth, care and development

    (iv) Emotional aspects of sex and its relationship to the life of the individual.

The aim of these lectures is to help the biologists to look beyond their special role to the responsibilities of the parents, schools, and the whole educational system for this aspect of children's education.

2. Institute of Education—University of London

(i) Diploma Course in Health Education.

This is taken by overseas students as well as students from the United Kingdom. Part of the course is aimed at developing a clear understanding of family planning and population control. This is done by means of lectures which cover population problems, social factors, attitudes, methods of contraception, and sex education in different cultures. The British students study sex education in greater depth by reading, seminars and discussion, and lectures from doctors, teachers and psychologists, with the aim of drawing attention to the problems, the need and the possible approaches to sex education in different situations.

(ii) Graduate Certificate Course in Education.

All students taking this course have to attend a series of eight lectures in health education. These include one lecture entitled 'Physical Growth and Development', which provides an outline of these processes from birth to old age, discussion of the concept of developmental age and its implications for the teacher, and information on individual variations and special education. Another lecture in the health education series is entitled 'Family Patterns and Sexual Behaviour', and includes information on different social norms among different groups, discussion of the family as chief role-maker out of school, and discussion of attitudes to marriage, illegitimacy, promiscuity, and changing sex roles. These and other lectures in the course provide an opportunity to discuss sex education in schools, and sex education is an examinable part of the Certificate course.

3. Department of Education, King's College, University of London
Course leading to the Graduate Certificate in Education.

Before any preparation for teaching is undertaken the students are provided with some basic information to answer their own needs, which may include individual counselling. It is considered essential for all students to attend a health education course, which includes three lectures covering heredity and environment, intra-uterine growth, the physical basis of behaviour in adolescence, the history of sex education, and present-day curriculum developments. This health education course is complemented by general sociology, psychology and philosophy lectures. All students are invited to attend the course work on sex education given to biology students, which includes planning a balanced curriculum which incorporates sex education, the therapeutic aspects of sex education, the complementary roles of the science teacher and the school counsellor, and the needs of the school leaver. In 1969–70, it is intended to invite lecturers from the FPA to speak to the students. It is also intended that some lectures on sex education will be organized on an inter-collegiate basis, whereby students from other parts of London University can also attend.

4. City of Birmingham College of Education: This college runs several

courses that include sex education, one of which has been described earlier in this report (see page 386). Relevant aspects of another are described below:

Certificate Course on Health and Social Education for Teachers of at least five years' experience.

The selection procedure for this course is quite stringent, and involves participation in discussion groups, written work, and individual interviews. The course includes study of the biological and social factors which influence the health and well-being of the individual and the community, while also providing information on methods of organizing integrated programmes throughout a school. Specific topics which are covered during the course include the family and its role, personal relationships, role of women, population problems, social problems, moral, ethical and religious issues, and counselling techniques.

NOTES

[1] In collaboration with Dr Alan Little.
[2] The Newsom Report.
[3] 'The Facts of Life for Teachers', by J. Norman Greaves, *New Society*, Vol. 6, No. 157, p. 18.
[4] Then the Central Council for Health Education.
[5] 'Teachers' attitudes to moral education', by P. R. May, *Educational*, Vol. 11, p. 215.
[6] 'Sex Attitudes of Young People', by M. Holmes, C. Nicol, and R. Stubbs, *Educational Research*, November 1968. [See pp. 415-422 of *Sex, Schools, and Society*.]
[7] 'Young Opinions', by Dr R. W. Kind, *Family Planning*, Vol. 18, No. 1, p. 121.

Sex Attitudes of Young People

M. Holmes, C. Nicol, and R. Stubbs

In the general recrudescence of the venereal diseases the increase among teenagers is causing some concern (Ministry of Health, 1965). It seems likely that, among the younger age group, the increase is a symptom of underlying social changes affecting attitudes to sexual relationships. Recent papers on this subject, however, have pointed out that, whatever the cause, education must play a part in meeting the dangers resulting from these changes (Coffari, 1965, Burton, 1965).

It is perhaps pertinent to ask whether simple ignorance plays a part in the incidence of venereal disease, and whether young people are given enough information to recognize symptoms or to go to a clinic if they have put themselves at risk. Schofield (1965) in his survey, *The Sexual Behaviour of Young People,* found that only a very few teenagers are restrained from having sexual intercourse by the fear of venereal infection. Indeed, some adolescents whom he interviewed had never heard of these diseases.

There is some evidence that teachers do not include information or discussion about venereal disease, even when sex education is included in the school curriculum. A small survey carried out among men and women students entering colleges of education at the age of eighteen years showed that 82 per cent of the men and 76 per cent of the women had had no education at all about VD at school, although human reproduction had been taught to 60 per cent of the men and 72 per cent of the women (Holmes, 1965).

The increase in venereal disease may be the inevitable result of increased promiscuity. Burton (1965) suggests in his paper that 'the youngsters most at risk are already emotionally damaged goods', and Ekstrom's study in Copenhagen revealed the importance of social background and showed that 'young persons infected with gonorrhoea do not come from a good social milieu, have left school early and have less vocational training than the average'. As a third possible factor in educational background, Laird (1963) in Manchester found that girls attending the VD clinic usually had a poor educational record and frequently changed their employment.

The chief aim of the exploratory survey reported here was to investigate some aspects of the background of the young people under the age of twenty years who attended the VD clinic at St. Thomas's Hospital, London, between December 1966 and May 1967, in terms of the following: (1) their family background, (2) their educational background, (3) their sex education, (4) their sexual experience and attitudes to pregnancy, and (5) the kind of sex education they would have liked to have had at school.

It will be appreciated how difficult it is to find a suitable control group for a survey of this kind.[1] Part of the questionnaire given to the clinic patients was also given to a group of eighty young people who were members of youth clubs in the area. The questions put to them were concerned only with social and family background and education at school, and they were not asked about their sexual experience, because it was felt that the sexually inexperienced teenager might be made to feel exceptional if asked such questions.

To compensate for the inadequacy of the control, we used the findings of the survey carried out for the Central Council for Health Education by Michael Schofield of the sexual behaviour of cross-sections of ordinary young people for comparison.

RESULTS

The group of 152 young people who attended the Lydia Clinic between December 1966 and May 1967 came from all strata of society, and largely from normal home backgrounds. This differs from Ekstrom's findings in Copenhagen, where 60 per cent of his teenagers with gonorrhoea came from broken homes, but supports Schofield's findings that sexual experience and broken homes were not related. Twenty per cent were regular churchgoers, which is not very different from Schofield's national sample of 23 per cent boys and 29 per cent girls. Sixty-eight per cent thought that they got on well with their parents. Only 8 per cent were foreign born. If they differ at all from a cross-section of ordinary teenagers in this same area, it is that rather more of them live away from home and rather fewer of them have parents who want to know where they are when they go out. It is perhaps worth noting that nearly two-thirds of them were girls, and 4 per cent of the girls, but none of the boys, were under sixteen years of age.

EDUCATIONAL BACKGROUND

Only 5 per cent of the sample had attended grammar schools. Yet in the Inner London Education Authority[2] 23 per cent of this age group are in grammar school, and this latter figure compares quite closely with the national figure quoted by Schofield. Twenty-eight per cent of the control group had attended grammar school. An even more interesting finding is that a high percentage (56 per cent of our sample) came from secondary modern schools: in the ILEA, where comprehensive education is now quite extensive, only 8 per cent of this age group are still in secondary modern schools. However, the number of comprehensive schools in the immediate area is uncertain, and it is possible that patients are drawn from outside the ILEA area. Ponting, in her London survey of patients in a VD clinic in 1963, found that 66 per cent attended secondary modern schools.

On the other hand the public school numbers in the sample were close to the national average. The technical schools contributed 7 per cent, which is also somewhat higher than the 5 per cent in the ILEA or the 3 per cent of the control group. It would appear that the grammar schools and the comprehensive schools have contributed relatively little to the sample from the VD clinic.

A high proportion of the sample from the clinic had left school at the minimum statutory age—43 per cent compared with only 23 per cent for the rest of the Inner London Education Area in 1965. This supports the findings of Ekstrom in Copenhagen and Laird in Manchester. Sixty-three per cent of the sample, compared with only 45 per cent of the control group, had left school without passing any kind of public examination. Only 17 per cent had left with good 'O' level results compared with 33 per cent of the control group. Yet 8 per cent of the clinic sample had stayed on into the sixth form and achieved one or more passes at 'A' level GCE.[3]

Relatively few—16 per cent compared with 35 per cent of the control group—really enjoyed school life.

The jobs they went into were largely unskilled, and they had changed their employment more frequently than the control group. This confirms the findings of Laird, Ponting and Ekstrom, all of whom found a high proportion of VD patients in unskilled or monotonous jobs, which they tended to change frequently. It is worth noting, however, that several of the clinic patients were college students.

SEX EDUCATION AT SCHOOL

The findings seem to show that as far as formal science teaching was concerned, there was little difference between the clinic sample and the control group. But 63 per cent of the boys and 43 per cent of the girls appear to have had no sex education at all at school. This compares with 53 per cent of boys and 14 per cent of girls in Schofield's cross-section of all young people. Seventy-six per cent of the clinic sample had had no education about venereal disease at school, but in the control group only 59 per cent had had no venereal disease education. In the control group 25 per cent appeared to have had adequate sex education, i.e., the physiology of reproduction, sexual intercourse, and childbirth, and some discussions on courtship and marriage, illegitimacy, abortion, venereal disease, and contraception, compared with only 8 per cent in the clinic sample. Of this 25 per cent, 80 per cent had learnt about these topics in more than one school subject, i.e., in biology and also in religious instruction, English, domestic science, or social studies. Only 3 per cent of the clinic sample had learnt about sexual relationships in this way.

In both groups it was found that religious instruction and biology seem equally important as opportunities for sex education. Domestic science, while sometimes dealing with sex education in its widest sense, does not, it seems, provide opportunities to discuss VD. Art, sociology, history, geography, Latin, mothercraft, liberal or general studies were also mentioned as subjects in which education about VD had been received by one or two young people. General studies is often introduced into sixth-form curricula in order to provide for the discussion of current affairs and social problems. However, students who leave at fifteen or sixteen years miss this important opportunity.

There is perhaps some slight indication that the young people who attend the clinic were less well educated about VD than the control group. *But it would appear that it is certainly not the adequacy of the sex education they have had at school that has prevented the majority of young people in the control group from contracting venereal disease.*

SEXUAL EXPERIENCE

In the clinic sample 89 per cent of the men and 54 per cent of the women had had more than one sexual partner, but 57 per cent of the men, compared with only 14 per cent of the women, had had more than five such partners—the partners of the men were far more likely to be casual 'pick-ups'. Thirty-six per cent of the men and 21 per cent of the women had had their first intercourse before the age of sixteen years. The control group was not asked about its sexual experience, but Michael Schofield's study showed that boys tend to have more sexual partners, and girls to develop a more enduring relationship.

A small proportion of patients (11 per cent), even after attending the clinic, were not worried about the possibilities of infection. These included the few who were married and a number who, by their answers, appeared to have a low IQ. It is worth noting that only 2 per cent of the women seemed worried about passing on infections, while a relatively large number (40 per cent) attended the clinic only after being found by a contact tracer.

Although we can assume that the majority of the clinic group were sexually experienced, 53 per cent appeared to have no knowledge of contraception, and 66 per cent usually took no precautions to avoid pregnancy. Illegitimacy is perhaps a greater risk than VD for this age group, and simple ignorance may well be a factor in its incidence.

THE DESIRED SEX EDUCATION

The final question showed that the majority of teenagers in both groups would have liked more sex education at school. Many said that their parents were too embarrassed to discuss sex with them. A number said that sex education should begin in the primary school, i.e., before the age of eleven years. Many stressed that whoever gave this education should be both knowledgeable and unembarrassed. Many of the young people attending the clinic suggested that a doctor or a nurse should visit the school, but it is worth noting that not one of the 23 per cent in the control group who had had education about venereal disease which had been integrated into their school work suggested that a medically qualified person was necessary, though they did stress that the teacher should be unembarrassed and able to allow them to discuss freely and to ask questions. Only 12 per cent of the clinic group and 16 per cent of the control group gave as their reasons for wanting more sex education the need to be warned about the dangers of venereal disease and pregnancy. Thirty per cent of the clinic group and 15 per cent of the control wanted to know more about sex 'as a perfectly normal part of life'. Many felt that simple instruction was not enough and asked for opportunities for discussions and for their questions to be answered.

DISCUSSION

What kind of young people attend the VD Clinic?

There is no evidence that they come from the lower stratum of society and little evidence that they come from broken homes. Many showed responsible attitudes towards their partners and the possibility of an illegitimate child. Some 26 per cent had had only one sexual partner, but it is known, of course, that they were all sexually experienced, and from Schofield's study it seems that these represent less than a quarter of the whole teenage population.

The most outstanding characteristic of the young people who attended the VD clinic was the early age at which many of them had left school. In this and other characteristics, e.g., dislike of school, particularly by the boys, lack of success in school examinations, tendency to change employment frequently, they resembled the group of 'sexually experienced' teenagers delineated by Schofield. Their reasons for leaving school early are not apparent; perhaps certain young people with a particular personality structure who mature early sexually are not easily satisfied with school life. On the other hand, perhaps the schools they attend are in some way inadequate, so that they find no incentive to stay longer in order to pass examinations.

There is no way of telling whether the high incidence of young people from secondary modern schools was related to level of intelligence. It might well be that IQ contributes to school selection, early leaving, and the inability to avoid the venereal infections, and influences the ability to look ahead. It is probable that a number of factors contribute to early leaving, and with undemanding jobs and money in their pockets, these young people spend their leisure time in sexual activities. Few of the boys in our sample were still at school.

What is clear from the survey is that any education about VD which is to prove useful to the group of young people most at risk should be given well before the age of fifteen years. On the other hand, it is now well known that there is a wide variation in the ages at which young people mature. In any group of children under the age of fifteen years, many will be sexually inexperienced and some not even interested in the possibility of sexual intercourse. In Michael Schofield's study 60 per cent of the boys and 83 per cent of the girls had not had sexual intercourse before the age of eighteen years.

Clearly education about venereal disease given before the age of fifteen years should not be in the context of a 'prohibition lecture', nor should it imply that all young people are sexually experienced or likely soon to be so. But information about VD could be introduced without undue stress in the general context of education about the communicable diseases. Quite apart from the danger of venereal infection, education about disease and its control is generally necessary if immunization programmes are to remain effective on a voluntary basis once the fear of the infectious disease recedes. Yet there is evidence that there is little teaching about disease in general, let alone venereal disease in particular, in the schools, and it might be interesting to speculate upon the reasons for this. In the survey of college students (Holmes, 1965), it was found that, although 93 per cent of the women and 80 per cent of the men had learnt biology, less than 15 per cent had learnt anything at all about any of the communicable diseases at school. Only 10 per cent of women and 3 per cent of men had learnt about venereal disease before 'O' level. This may be due not only to social taboos which have affected the attitudes and education of the teachers themselves, but also to sheer factual ignorance about the venereal diseases on the part of the teacher. Until recently there has been no reference book suitable for non-medical students that deals in any way effectively with the venereal diseases.

What kind of education about the venereal diseases is likely to affect their incidence? Can education which does not affect the incidence of casual sexual relationships prevent in any way venereal infection? Can factual knowledge of disease itself have any effect, apart from the development of responsible attitudes to treatment or cure? It is pertinent to ask how these socially important attitudes develop.

There is little evidence that fear is effective in developing responsible attitudes. Indeed, it is believed that the young should be taught to do other potentially dangerous activities, such as climbing and sailing, well and safely. Where the danger extends not only to the individual participant but to other people in the community, as in car driving, some legal restrictions are also imposed.

In the area of sexual relationships the law is becoming increasingly permissive, and the law which prohibits sexual intercourse before sixteen years is not easily enforceable. If fear of the law is no deterrent, is fear of the consequences of VD likely to be so? One would hope that increased understanding of sexual relationships in general and increased knowledge of the consequences of VD may induce, if not greater caution in casual relationships, a willingness to make use of the medical facilities available. Schofield's study showed that there are perhaps some teenagers who suspect they have a venereal infection but do not seek treatment.

If the conquest of disease became an accepted part of the secondary school curriculum, education about the venereal diseases could take its place within it, providing, of course, that the children had already received some sex education. Indeed, the inclusion of VD is specifically suggested in the latest pamphlet, *Health in Education,* published by the Department of Education and Science, 1966. This is not to suggest that education about sexual relationships is not, of course, equally important. There is a great deal to be said for starting sex education in the primary school and continuing it with appropriate emphases throughout the secondary school.

Such teaching now has official support in England. The Newsom Report (1963) states clearly that 'positive guidance to boys and girls on sexual morals is essential with quite specific discussions of the problems they will face'; and in the appendix to the report there is a detailed account of how one school carried out sex education, and indeed introduced discussion of venereal disease, among other social problems, in religious instruction for the fourteen- to fifteen-year-olds.

The Plowden Report (1967) on education in primary schools devotes a section (714) to the possibilities of sex education, and also suggests (605) that human biology is an appropriate study for the primary school child. Yet it is known from Schofield's study and others that many schools find themselves unable to give this kind of education. It would be interesting to find out why this should be so, and what kind of help the teachers need.

Finally, Capinski (1965) has suggested that since patients attending VD clinics are more amenable to education than at any other time, 'they should be considered a "target group" of prime importance', so that they will avoid re-infection and perhaps disseminate the knowledge of venereal disease and the necessity for treatment among their peer group.

NOTES

[1] The authors acknowledge the fact that the results of the survey were to some extent distorted by the limitations of the control group.
[2] The authors gratefully acknowledge the data about schools provided by the ILEA Statistical Department.
[3] 'O' level is the Ordinary level of the General Certificate of Education (GCE), taken at the age of about sixteen. 'A' level is the Advanced level, usually taken two years later (Ed.).

REFERENCES

BURTON, J. (1965). 'VD. The protection of youth through health education', *Proc. XXIVth Gen. Ass. of I.U.V.D.* Lisbon.

CAPINSKI, T. Z. (1965). Evaluation of the present approach to Health Education in prevention and control of VD in Poland.

CENTRAL ADVISORY COUNCIL FOR EDUCATION. (1963). *Half our Future: A Report.* ('The Newsom Report'). London: H.M. Stationery Office.

CENTRAL ADVISORY COUNCIL FOR EDUCATION. (1966). *Children and their Primary Schools.* ('The Plowden Report'). London: H.M. Stationery Office.

COFFARI, V. (1965). 'Le comportement sexuel des jeunes en Italie', *Proc. XXIVth Gen. Ass. of I.U.V.D. Lisbon.*

DEPARTMENT OF EDUCATION AND SCIENCE. (1966). *Health in Education.* London. H.M. Stationery Office.

EKSTROM, K. (1966). 'One hundred teenagers in Copenhagen infected with gonorrhoea', *Brit J. Vener. Dis.,* 42, p. 162.

HOLMES, M. I. (1965). 'Biology teaching and health education', *School Science Review*—July 1965.

LAIRD, S. M. (1963). 'School and employment records of teenage girls with VD in Manchester', *Brit. J. Vener. Dis.,* 39, 280-2.

NICOL, C. S. (1964). 'The recrudescence of venereal disease', *Brit. J. Vener. Dis.,* 40, p. 96-103.

PONTING, L. I. (1963). 'Social aspects of VD in young people in Leeds and Manchester', *Brit. J. Vener. Dis.,* 39, 273-7.

SCHOFIELD, M. (1965). *The Sexual Behaviour of Young People.* London: Longmans.

WILLCOX, B. R. (1966). 'Immigration and venereal disease in Great Britain', *Brit. J. of Vener. Dis.,* 42, pp. 225, 242-4.

MORTON, R. S. (1966). *Venereal Diseases.* Harmondsworth: Pelican.

Sex Instruction in the Home [1]

Aidan Pickering

This is a book on sex instruction, and is written for parents. It is to help you to give your children the information and the training in purity they need.

It must be said at once that the instruction given here is largely spiritual, and utterly different from what non-Catholics call sex instruction. They give detailed information about sex to their children, hoping that knowledge will solve all their difficulties. We give our children what facts are necessary, but we concentrate chiefly on training their will and their character. That is the only real solution to the problem of sex instruction.

DO THEY NEED HELP?

Think back to your own childhood. Some of you, when you remember how you found out the facts of life, may now wish that you had learned them from a better source. Give your children the help which you would like to have had when you were young.

Actually, the whole problem is far more urgent now than when we were young. Then, sex was secret; today, it is advertised. Everywhere, your children are being taught 'Hollywood' morals, at the 'pictures' [movies], on the posters, in the newspapers, everywhere. So, if they are to get a sane, correct, Christian attitude towards sex, it must come from you, in the home.

Too many parents 'leave them to find out for themselves'. That is not right. To prove it, here are some figures from America.[2] Two thousand high-school boys were questioned as to where they got their first knowledge of sex matters, and what effect this knowledge had on them. It was found that if the knowledge came from a good source (parents, priests, nuns, teachers), it had a good effect in ninety-four cases out of a hundred. But where the boys had been left to find out for themselves (from other boys, magazines, the 'pictures'), the effect was harmful in seventy-five cases out of a hundred.

So they need your help. Father Vermeersch, in his world-famous book on Chastity, says: 'We can unhesitatingly affirm that there is occasion for sex instruction, and the only serious question that remains is the best manner and time for giving it.'[3]

WHOSE DUTY IS IT?

It is the parents' duty.

'As regards the parental instruction of children in the matters concerned, we are convinced that herein lies the chief cause and the remedy which is being sought. There is today a lamentable decline in family education, due largely to an ever-increasing tendency on the part of the parents deliberately to shirk their obvious duty' (The English Bishops in their Joint Pastoral).[4]

'The bond established by nature between parent and child is so close that such an intimate and sacred subject as discussion of sex is primarily a matter for parent and child' (The Scottish Bishops).

It is your duty; and I hope to show you that the task is not beyond your powers.

WHAT IS ITS PURPOSE?

What are we aiming to do for our children? Why is sex instruction given?

'Its sole purpose should be to assist the formation of the virtue of purity' (The Scottish Bishops).[5] We must remember this when discussing methods of sex instruction, and, above all, when we are talking to our children. We give them the facts of life only as a means to purity, and because ignorance of the facts of life can endanger purity.

WRONG SEX INSTRUCTION

The sex instruction encouraged by the secular Education Authorities is worse than useless.

It is becoming increasingly popular with non-Catholics, and even with a few Catholics, but it is wrong.

It is far too detailed.[6] You would be appalled to see the anatomy charts of the sexual organs and the growth of the unborn child published for use in schools with boys and girls of twelve and thirteen.[7] All this type of sex instruction misses the point. The problem is not chiefly one of giving information, but of training the will.

Sex instruction is a moral problem. Now God made the Church—

not the secular Education Authorities—our guide in all matters concerning faith and morals; therefore, it is to the Church, to the Bishops and to the Pope, that we must look for the true solution. Unfortunately, the Government may try to force their harmful sex instruction on all our schools. We must resist the attempt. The Bishops in Low Week, 1948, specially declared that sex instruction is part of the religious instruction of the child. Therefore, it does not concern the secular Education Authorities in any way.

THE RIGHT SORT OF SEX INSTRUCTION

First, there is no need for detailed information. 'The history of the world has not yet furnished proof of any need of detailed lessons in sexual physiology', say the Scottish Bishops; and in another place, sex instruction 'must comprise a minimum of factual knowledge'.

But at the same time, we must give them the main facts of life. 'If a youth is to be trained in the virtue of purity, some minimum knowledge of the facts of life is necessary' (Scottish Bishops).

Father Vermeersch gives us this excellent principle to work on: 'Natural ignorance is not necessarily to be dispelled, nor is artificial ignorance necessarily to be fostered; the explanation of sexual matters which we approve of is not that which increases, but that which diminishes worry in these matters.'[8]

So the Church's traditional method of sex instruction is this: to give the facts of life when necessary and as far as necessary, and to give training in modesty and purity from earliest childhood.

TWO STAGES OF KNOWLEDGE

Good Catholic parents do not find much difficulty in the formation of good habits in their children. That is why I used the word 'traditional' just above—they have always done it. It is in the need to give their children information, a need growing very urgent now-a-days, that they find their difficulty. Therefore, we will speak of two stages of knowledge:

1. A knowledge of the mother's part.
2. A knowledge of the father's part.

Let us talk about each separately.

1. A knowledge of the mother's part

By this I mean a knowledge of the facts connected with childbirth.

The proverb 'Well begun is half done' certainly applies to sex instruction. If parents would only begin to answer the questions of their children truthfully, right from the beginning, half the difficulty would disappear. If you do this, your children never lose confidence in you. They will continue to question you as they grow older; therefore, they will provide you with opportunities to give them the further knowledge that they need, all quite gradually and naturally, without the need for 'talks'.

No matter how young they may be when they begin to ask questions, never tell them silly stories about the stork. . . . 'Train the minds of your children. Do not give them wrong ideas or wrong reasons for things; whatever their questions may be, do not answer them with evasions or untrue statements which their minds rarely accept' (Pius XII).[9]

As you put them to bed at night, they will often ask you questions. It will increase their love for you to know that a baby grows inside its mother for nine months; to know how the baby is born; that childbirth hurts you; to know that the baby is fed from the breast after it is born, and that even while inside its mother she feeds it through a tube which is afterwards cut off, leaving a mark called the navel. Even the bodily difference between boy and girl will be quite obvious to them once they know that the baby is born from its mother, and therefore needs a large opening to pass through. It is good that boy and girl should each know how the other is shaped, but this knowledge must come to them very naturally and early on in life.

Make all this explanation spiritual, open, obvious. Make no mystery about it. Take examples from the *Hail Mary,* from the feasts of the Church, just to show how natural it all is to us Catholics. Here is a small practical example: if you are feeding a baby at your breast, you can do it quite modestly, yet without trying to hide it from your other children. Or if you are going to have another baby, you can tell your children a month or so beforehand; let them do small jobs for you to save tiring you and the baby.

Alongside this policy of truthfulness and gradual growth in knowledge, give your child a positive training in modesty right from its earliest days, by gently teaching it not to touch, or show, or speak about these parts except when they have a reason for it. Your help will be especially necessary if they are getting into the habit of rubbing and exciting these parts. But do not be harsh with them, even if they do occasionally embarrass you by their behaviour or questions in the presence of visitors! Correct them, but do it gently.

So much for the knowledge of childbirth which may be given to your youngest children. For the time being, they do not need further knowledge, and I suggest you should not tell them of the father's part just yet: 'unveil the truth as far as it appears necessary' (the Pope.)[10] Often they will seem to be asking for this further information, when really they are not. For instance, if they ask how a baby begins, they are quite satisfied if you tell them that you can feel it begin. Answers of this kind—the truth, yet not the full truth—can be given to similar questions.

2. A knowledge of the father's part

When it becomes necessary, you must also tell them of the father's part; that is, of the marriage act.

This is the advice the Pope gives you:

> . . . you will not fail to watch for and to discern the moment in which certain unspoken questions have occurred to their minds and are troubling their senses. It will then be your duty (mothers) to your daughters, the father's duty to your sons, carefully and delicately to unveil the truth as far as it appears necessary, to give a prudent, true, and Christian answer to those questions, and set their minds at rest. If imparted by the lips of Christian parents at the proper time, in the proper measure, and with the proper precautions, the revelation of the mysterious and marvellous laws of life will be received by them with reverence and gratitude, and will enlighten their minds with far less danger than if they learned them haphazard, from some disturbing encounter, from secret conversations, through information received from over-sophisticated companions, or from clandestine reading, the more dangerous and pernicious as secrecy inflames the imagination and troubles the senses. Your words, if they are wise and discreet, will prove a safeguard and a warning in the midst of the temptations and corruption which surround them.[11]

WHEN TO GIVE IT

It is for you to watch your children carefully. Any time from about ten onwards they may need this extra information. 'The sex-instinct awakes in different children at different ages' (the Scottish Bishops). Even if they are too shy to ask, you should be ready to speak and answer their 'unspoken questions'.

Now supposing your children show no signs of trouble at all. Even so, by the time they are twelve you ought to speak. By then, a boy may already be experiencing the erection about which he needs to be told (p. 437, 5 [I]); by then, a girl is often beginning to feel headachy and miserable monthly; and they begin to wonder what these things mean.

Besides, you will find it far easier to talk to your children at this age than later on when they have already begun to be awkward and self-conscious because of their growing emotions.

Another strong reason for speaking at twelve, rather than later, is this. At twelve, the only temptation and danger that can come from your talk is the temptation to curiosity, to find out more. But if you put it off till later, there is increasing risk of physical temptations to impurity, which are much harder to resist.

Two hints might not be out of place.

First, American statistics show that parents keep putting off this talk, in spite of the best will in the world. Decide definitely that, if you have not had reason to speak before then, you will talk to your child on its twelfth birthday itself. That fixes you down to a definite day, and overcomes the temptation to keep putting it off. If that day passes, and you have to admit to yourself that you are incapable of it, then either read him the talk you will find at the end of this pamphlet, or tear it out and give it to him[12] to read for himself.

Second, you might prefer to talk to your child when you are both out for a walk. It will be less awkward for him to be told in this way than when having to sit facing you while you talk to him at home.

HOW TO GIVE IT

The rest of this pamphlet is taken up with two complete talks, one for a boy of twelve, and the other for a girl of twelve. If you have done your best to answer your child's questions as it grew up, and to train it in modesty, you may find that you can shorten the talk considerably. But each talk has been given in full, just in case. You might prefer to give it all at once, or you might prefer to give it in sections as suitable opportunities arise.

It may be as well to point out how these talks differ from the usual non-Catholic method of sex instruction. We say nothing of internal anatomy; we use no scientific terms; we take no examples from plants or animals. There does not seem need for any of this, and it is only making your task more difficult. Instead, we take our examples from the feasts and prayers of the Church, and keep the whole thing as simple and as spiritual as possible.

Study the talks, but only as examples of how it might be done. Both talks follow the same general pattern. The paragraphs to notice most carefully are those where we wish to indicate the marriage act and the parts used in it, in very delicate and yet very clear language. You must be delicate, yet at the same time you must be easy to understand. These paragraphs may seem indelicate when set out in print, but they will not be when used in conversation between yourself and your child.

Stress the fact that these acts and pleasures are good for married people. 'In marriage sexual pleasure is good, lawful, in fact holy: this principle should be clearly taught to all adolescents' (Scottish Bishops). Even grown-ups are often mistaken on this point.

This duty of sex instruction is certainly a difficult task. But pray about it and think it over beforehand. And remember that when you were married you received the sacrament of Matrimony. This is not a sacrament which is over and done with on your wedding-day; it lasts all your life, and gives you a right to all the graces you need to do your duty as parents, including this particular duty of sex instruction and training in purity. The grace of God is there to help you.

If you do your duty, and help your children, you will always be thankful. By treating sex as a common-sense subject, and purity as a common-sense virtue, and by the very fact that you have talked to your children about them, you will have given them great help. Beyond this, your personal example, your home-life, and the grace they receive in the sacraments, will see them through successfully 'from the unconscious purity of infancy to the triumphant purity of adolescence' (the Pope).

LATER HELP

We have talked all this while of the task of helping your children while they are still young. But even when they are grown up, and begin work, or begin 'going out', or go off to the Army, or become engaged, you can continue to help them. Since they are then almost grown up, they can benefit by reading books for themselves. [. . .]

II. TO GIRLS

Now that you are nearly grown up, there are a few things I'd like to explain to you.

You may have wondered how a baby is born. It is quite natural to want to know, and it is best that you should know.

1. How a baby is born

We all have a body and a soul, as you know from your catechism. God Himself creates the soul of a new baby, but its body comes from the body of its mother, starting to grow from a tiny egg the size of a pinpoint. But before this can begin to grow, it needs to be joined by a special liquid called 'seed' from the father, which is put into the mother when they join their bodies together.

The part the father uses to give the seed is the part from which his water comes; and the part the mother uses to receive the seed is inside the outer opening from which her water comes.

Sometimes, there is no little egg ready in the body of the mother. But if there is, and it meets this seed, God at the same moment creates a soul for the child, and sends down an angel to guard it and help it to get to heaven. We call this first moment the conception of the child. We often talk about Our Lady's Immaculate Conception, don't we?

For nine months, the baby grows inside its mother: here, in her womb. Then, when it is big enough, it is born through the same opening through which she received the seed. The birth of the baby nearly always gives its mother pain, but she puts up with it for love of her baby.

When it is born, the mother begins to feed the baby with milk from her breasts. But even while it was still inside her, she was feeding it through a sort of tube that joined its body to hers. But after the baby is born, the nurse or the doctor cuts off this tube, because it isn't needed any more. And the mark that is left, here, is called the navel.

I want you to see that this act of love between a father and mother, and the conception of a child, is a sacred thing, because God Himself shares in it.

2. It is good to know these things

Some girls have the idea that there is something secret and wrong about these things. You can tell that from the underhand way they sometimes talk among themselves. Really, there is nothing wrong in knowing about them, so long as we treat them reverently.

(a) For example, Our Lady knew these things, so there cannot be anything wrong in knowing. Do you remember when the angel came to ask her to become the Mother of God? Our Lady said: 'How will this be done, since I know not man?' meaning, 'since I have promised God not to receive the seed of any man'. So, you see, Our Lady knew how a baby is conceived and born.

(b) Besides, we often mention these facts in our prayers and in church. For instance:

(i) Every time you say the *Hail Mary,* you say, 'Blessed is the fruit of thy womb, Jesus'. That means, 'Blessed is the baby Jesus you carried in your womb'.

(ii) And every time we say the Angelus, we mention 'conception': 'The angel of the Lord declared unto Mary, and she conceived by the Holy Ghost'.

(iii) When the priest reads out the Epistle at Mass on Sundays, perhaps you have noticed the words 'seed of Abraham'. They mean the children of Abraham who have grown up from the seed he gave to his wife.

(iv) How long does a baby need to grow up inside its mother? Nine months. That's right. Well, the feasts of Our Lord and Our Lady teach us that. When is Our Lord's birthday? Christmas Day, of course—on December 25th. So, if we want to find out when He was conceived, we count back nine months, and we come to the feast of the Annunciation, on March 25th exactly. That was the day when the angel asked Our Lady to be the Mother of God, and she said 'Yes'. It's just the same with Our Lady's feasts. We keep her Immaculate Conception on December 8th. See if you can work this out for yourself—when do we keep Our Lady's birthday? That's right, September 8th. Good.

I have told you that the love between father and mother is holy, and the conception of a child is holy. And just as we don't make fun of holy things or talk about them in a careless way, so we must not talk about love and the birth of a baby disrespectfully. To help us, God puts into us, especially as we grow up, a special virtue called modesty, a shyness and fear which prevents us from leading ourselves or other people into temptation by bad talk or by actions that are dangerous to purity.

3. What purity means

Now I want to explain something else to you: what purity means, and what impurity means.

I'll start this way. God often makes the things that are good for us pleasant for us. For example, eating. We all like eating, don't we? God has made it pleasant for us, to encourage everyone to eat, because eating is good for us. Now, because He gave us free will, we can either use this power of eating properly, and enjoy it, as God meant us to do; or else we can misuse it, out of selfishness, by greediness and gluttony. That would be wrong, and a sin.

In the same way, God has made this act of love between a man and a woman, by which a baby is conceived, a great pleasure, so as to encourage parents to have children. But, God only means this pleasure to be for married people. For them, this act is a good and holy pleasure; but for anyone who is not married, this act is wrong and a very serious sin of impurity. So this means that if ever you were to try to get this pleasure, either by yourself or with someone else, it would be a mortal sin, if you did it deliberately and knowing what you were doing. I want to warn you about that, once and for all.

God has given our bodies these powers and pleasures, and they are good in their proper place, in marriage. Purity is the proper control of these powers. Impurity is giving way to them out of selfishness, just for pleasure, when we have no right to them. So, until you are married, you must control yourself very strictly in your thoughts and words and acts.

4. Thoughts, words and actions

Because girls often get terribly worried and anxious, I'll say something about temptations to impure thoughts and words and deeds.

(*a*) *Thoughts*. Sometimes you will find thoughts in your mind which you suddenly realise are impure thoughts. You cannot be blamed so far, because you didn't bring them into your mind. So far, they are only a temptation; and remember, a temptation is no sin. But as soon as you realise the danger is there, you must do your best to get the thoughts out of your mind. And the best thing to do is just to think of something else (your hobby, for instance), and worry no more about it.

And it is just the same with pictures, either in magazines, or books, or at the 'pictures'. Turn away from them, quietly, without fuss. If you were careless or slow in putting them away, that would be a venial sin; but if you kept them there on purpose to enjoy wrong pleasure, that would be a mortal sin.

(*b*) *Words*. Talking about these things is quite all right if it is necessary. And if there is need to mention them, we call these parts of our body the 'private parts'. If ever there is anything you want to know, I want you to come to me, or your father; or if you want to know whether a thing is right or wrong, ask the priest in confession. You may feel very shy about asking: that's natural. But all the same, if you have a worry or difficulty, get over your shyness and ask.

But don't talk about these things to other girls, especially to joke about them. That would be clearly a sin, and might lead to much more serious sins.

(*c*) *Actions*. This is where you must use your common sense, and not worry where there is no need to worry. For instance, it is obviously all right to touch this part of your body when it is necessary. But to touch yourself or handle these parts through idleness or curiosity would be immodest and sinful, and these actions may lead you into bad habits which seriously offend God. So be strict with yourself.

Use your common sense. Try to please God. If you are doing that, be quite confident, and do not worry.

5. Things you must not worry about

I have spoken straight out about the seriousness of impure thoughts and words and deeds, because you are old enough to understand it.

But here are one or two things that need not worry you.

(1) Soon, within a year or two, you will find that blood will come from this opening of your body, and you may feel headachy and sick for a day or two. It may even happen quite suddenly, and frighten you. But there is nothing to be afraid of, and nothing to worry about. When it happens, come straight to me, and I'll show you what to do. You see, it is quite natural, and only shows that you are grown up and healthy. This blood has in it the tiny egg we talked about. Your body will soon begin to make one every month. But until you get married, you won't need them, so the body gets rid of them this way. You call it your 'monthly period'. Come to me as soon as it happens, won't you? I wanted to tell you about it before it happens, so you won't get frightened.

(2) Another thing. As you get older, you will find yourself more and more attracted to boys. That is quite natural. God makes us like that, or else men and women would never fall in love and get married. God put the attraction in us, and it is good; but, at the same time, we have to control it. Perhaps, at school, you will hear the other girls joking about boys and talking about them in a silly sort of way; don't join in any talk like that.

These feelings and attractions are natural, and shouldn't worry you. But, at the same time, you must be very careful about purity. It is a great virtue, and very pleasing to God and to Our Lady. The best way to keep pure is to be very careful about modesty, which makes us fear to do anything that is a danger to purity. You can easily give serious temptation to others when you are careless about modesty, and if you know what you are doing, God will hold you responsible.

6. Pray to Our Lady

I have tried to help you. In return, there is something I want you to do for me. From now on, each night before you get into bed, I want you to say one *Hail Mary* to Our Lady to ask her to keep you pure. Do that, and do it all your life. Never miss.

Our Lady is the model of purity, and this is the reason why. She is the Mother of God, so God made her perfect in body and in soul, to make her fit to be His Mother.

He made her soul sinless from the first moment of her conception in the womb of St Anne. He made her body perfect and kept her always a virgin. This means that Our Lady conceived Our Lord without receiving the seed of man, and gave birth to Him without any opening of her womb. In the Apostles' Creed, we say that Our Lord 'was conceived by the Holy Ghost, born of the Virgin Mary'; and in the Catechism, we say 'Jesus Christ had no father on earth; St Joseph was only His guardian or foster-father'. It was done by the power of God, by a miracle.

In this way, God has made Our Lady the model of purity for everyone. For married people, because she is the Mother of God: for unmarried people, because she remained a virgin, as you must be until you marry.

God calls most people to marry, and marriage is a real vocation. In fact, it is one of the seven Sacraments. But to some girls He gives the special vocation to live singly and to remain virgins for His sake, as nuns or in ordinary life. You must follow whichever way God calls. That is the best way to heaven for you.

There, I think I have explained everything. But come and talk to me about these things whenever you like. I'll do my best to help you.

III. TO BOYS

You are getting grown up now, so there are one or two things I want to tell you.

Maybe you have wondered, sometimes, just how a baby is born. That's natural, and it is best that you should know, so I'll tell you.

1. How a baby is born

You know from your catechism that you have a body and a soul. The soul of a new baby is made by God Himself, but its body comes from its mother. It begins to grow from a tiny little speck, an egg the size of a pin-point. But before this tiny egg can begin to grow into a baby, it has to be joined by a special liquid called 'seed'. This comes from the father, and is passed into the body of the mother when they join their bodies together. The part the father uses to give her this seed is the part from which his water comes; and the part the mother uses to receive the seed is inside the outer opening from which her water comes.

There may not be an egg ready to grow inside the body of the mother. But if there is, and if it meets some of this seed, the life of the baby begins, because at this same moment God Himself creates a soul for the child, and sends an angel to guard it all its life and to help it to get to heaven. This first moment is called the conception of the baby. We often talk about the Immaculate Conception of Our Lady, don't we?

For nine months after this the baby goes on growing inside its mother, in her womb. Then it is born, and comes out through the same opening through which she received the seed. This birth of a baby nearly always gives the mother a lot of pain, but she puts up with it out of love for her baby.

After it is born, the mother feeds it with the milk from her breasts. But even before it was born she was still feeding it. Its body was joined to hers, inside, by a sort of tube. After it is born, the nurse cuts off this tube; and the mark that everybody has here, just below the belt, marks where it used to be. It is called your navel.

I want you to realise that this act of love by which a child is conceived, is a sacred act. After all, God Himself is taking a share in it. And so we must always treat it and talk about it reverently.

2. It is good to know all this

Some boys don't treat these things reverently. In fact, they have the idea that there is something secret and wrong about it all. You can tell that by the underhand way they sometimes talk among themselves. But there is really nothing to be ashamed of in knowing these things, provided we treat them reverently.

(*a*) For example, Our Lady knew them, so there can't be anything wrong in knowing. Do you remember when the angel came to her to ask her to be the Mother of God? Our Lady said: 'How will this be done, since I know not man?'— meaning, 'since I have promised God not to receive the seed of any man'. So Our Lady knew how a baby is conceived and born.

(*b*) Besides, we actually mention these things in our prayers and in church. For example:

(i) Every time you say the *Hail Mary,* you mention the word 'womb': 'Blessed is the fruit of thy womb, Jesus'. That is, 'Blessed is the child Jesus you carried in your womb'.

(ii) And in the Angelus, we mention 'conception': 'The angel of the Lord declared unto Mary, and she conceived by the Holy Ghost'.

(iii) Perhaps you have heard the priest use the words 'seed of Abraham' sometimes, when he has been reading out the Sunday Epistle. He means the children of Abraham, who grew up from the seed that Abraham gave to his wife.

(iv) How long did we say a baby needed to grow up inside its mother? Nine months. The feasts of Our Lord and Our Lady remind us about that. When is Our Lord's birthday? That's easy.

On Christmas Day—on December 25th. Now, if you wanted to find out the day He was conceived, you would count back nine months. If you did, you would come to March 25th, and that is the very day we keep the Annunciation of Our Lady, when the angel asked her to be the Mother of God, and she said she would. Now you can work the next one out for yourself. If we keep the feast of the Immaculate Conception of Our Lady on December 8th, when is her birthday? That's right: on September 8th.

You must always remember that the love between married people is holy, and that the conception of a child is holy. And just as we don't make fun of holy things or talk about them in a careless way, so you mustn't talk about love, or about the birth of a baby, in a disrespectful way. To help us, God puts into us all, especially as we grow up, a virtue called modesty, a shyness and fear which prevents us from leading ourselves or other people into temptation by bad talk, or by actions that are dangerous to purity.

3. What purity means

I want to tell you quite clearly what we mean by purity, and what we mean by impurity.

Supposing I start with an example. God often makes what is good for us pleasant. For instance, eating. We like eating, because God has made it pleasant, because He wants us to eat. Now, because He gave us free will, we can either use this power of eating properly, and enjoy it, as God meant us to do: or else we can misuse it by greediness and gluttony. That would be wrong, and a sin.

In the same way, He has made this act of love between father and mother, by which a baby is conceived, a great pleasure. But notice this. God only means this pleasure for married people. For them, this act is good, and holy; but for anyone else who is not married, it is very wrong, and a mortal sin of impurity. I think you are old enough to understand all this, and I want to warn you about it. If ever you were to try to get this pleasure, either by yourself or with anyone else, then it would be a serious mortal sin, if you did it deliberately, knowing what you were doing.

God has given our bodies these powers, and they are good. Purity is the proper control of these pleasures; impurity is the selfish attempt to enjoy these pleasures when we have no right to them. So until a person is married he is bound to control himself very strictly in his thoughts, in his words, and in his actions.

4. Thoughts, words and actions

I'll speak about these, because temptations often worry boys.

(*a*) *Thoughts*. Sometimes it might happen that you suddenly realise that there is a wrong thought, an impure thought, in your mind. If you couldn't help it coming into your mind, you are not to be blamed, so far. But as soon as you realise that it is there, you must do your best to put it out. And the best way to do that is just to think of something else (of engines, stamps, football, or whatever your hobby may be) and worry no more about it. And the same goes for pictures you might see in books or at the 'pictures'. Just turn away from them, quite calmly. Remember, there is all the difference in the world between a temptation and a sin. If you try to put the thoughts out of your mind, you have done good. But if you are careless or slow in putting them out, that would be a venial sin; and if you keep them in your mind on purpose to enjoy wrong pleasures, that would be a mortal sin.

(*b*) *Words*. If there is need, of course it is all right to talk about these things; and if ever there is need, you ought to know that we usually call these parts of the body the 'private parts'. So if ever you want to know anything, ask me, or your mother, or if you want to know whether a thing is right or wrong, ask the priest in confession. It will probably happen that as you get older, you will feel shy to ask. But if you have a worry or a difficulty, you should overcome this shyness and get the difficulty cleared up.

But you must not talk of these things to the other boys at school. That would be immodest talk, and sinful, and it might easily lead to much more serious sins.

(*c*) *Actions*. Sometimes boys worry a lot about touching this part of their body. Use your common sense. If there is any need for it, it is all right: that is obvious. But if you were to touch these parts out of curiosity or idleness, that would be immodest and sinful, and these actions may possibly lead you into habits which seriously offend God. So be strict with yourself.

5. Things you must not worry about

I have told you straight out about temptations against purity, because I think you are old enough to understand.

But there are a few things that need not worry you.

(1) First of all, this part of your body sometimes becomes excited. Don't be worried. It is quite natural, but the best thing to do is to take no notice of it or of any slight pleasure you may feel in it. Turn your mind to something else.

(2) Another thing. This might not happen for years yet, but I want you to know beforehand. You may notice that this part of your body has been giving out some thick liquid. Probably it will happen at night while you are asleep. This is the seed that we talked about, and shows

that your body is now fully grown up and healthy. The body begins to make this seed, but it will not be needed until you are married, so your body gets rid of it in the night. You may wake up while this is going on, often with your mind filled with thoughts. If this happens, do your best to take no notice of the pleasure you feel. Say a prayer to Our Lord or Our Lady, turn over at once, and think of something else. But it is all perfectly natural, and needn't cause you trouble. For instance, if you go to Communion each morning, then go next morning just as usual. There is no reason at all why you should miss just because this has happened.

(2) A third thing which need not disturb you is that, as you grow older, you will find yourself attracted to girls. This is natural. God gives us that attraction, or otherwise men and women would never fall in love and get married. The attraction is good, but it has to be controlled. Even if other boys you know talk about girls and carry on with them, you must not.

So God gave our bodies these powers and attractions. They are all good, but must be used properly. Purity is the proper control of these powers; it is a very great virtue, and pleasing to God and to Our Lady. Impurity is the selfish enjoyment of these pleasures when we have no right to them. Be careful about purity, and remember that modesty is meant to protect your purity. If you are careful about modesty—and refuse to do anything dangerous to purity—you will be all right.

6. Pray to Our Lady

There's something I want you to promise me. Each night, from now on, I want you to say one *Hail Mary* to Our Lady for the grace to keep pure. She will help you.

Our Lady is the model of purity, because God made her perfect in body and soul, to make her fit to be His Mother. He made her soul sinless from the first moment of her conception in the womb of St Anne. He made her body perfect, and kept her always a virgin. This means that Our Lady conceived Our Lord without receiving the seed from any man, and gave birth to Him without any opening of her womb. As we say in the Apostles' Creed, Our Lord 'was conceived by the Holy Ghost, born of the Virgin Mary'. And in the Catechism, we say 'Jesus Christ had no father on earth: St Joseph was only His guardian or foster-father'. It was all done by the power of God, by a miracle.

In this way, God made Our Lady the model of purity for everyone: for married people, because she is the Mother of God; for unmarried people, because she remained always a virgin, as unmarried people are bound to do.

Most boys marry when they grow up, and marriage is a real vocation from God. It is one of the seven Sacraments. But to some boys, God gives the special vocation to remain unmarried and pure for His sake, either as a priest, or lay-brother, or in ordinary life. Whichever way you think God is calling you, you must follow. That will be the best way to heaven for you.

Now, I think I have explained everything to you. But come and talk to me about these things whenever you like. I promise to help.

NOTES

[1] Based on an article in *The Clergy Review,* May 1949.
[2] *Lumen Vitae,* 1947, No. 3: 'The American Adolescent and Religion', by Urban Fleege.
[3] A. Vermeersch, S.J., *De Castitate,* Rome, 1919, § 191.
[4] April 1944, published by the Westminster Press.
[5] Memorandum on Sex Education, published with the approval of the Bishops of Scotland. This Memorandum, and the Joint Pastoral of the English Bishops, are given as appendices in *Sex Enlightenment and the Catholic* by J. Leycester King, S.J.
[6] This type of sex instruction has often been condemned. Read Pope Pius XI on *The Christian Education of Youth,* C.T.S. S 99, and the Joint Pastoral of the English Bishops.
[7] It might be mentioned here that, if you have and use any 'Motherhood' books, you should be most careful not to let the children see them or have access to them. These books are good for you, but harmful to the children.
[8] *De Castitate,* § 191.
[9-11] *The Pope Speaks to Mothers.* C.T.S. S I68.
[12] Throughout the rest of this section, 'him' refers to either boy or girl.

Health Education, Sex Education and Education for Home and Family Life Conference Proceedings

UNESCO Institute for Education, Hamburg

SEX EDUCATION [1]

The term *sex education* has caused much misunderstanding. As one of the participants pointed out, this is due to the fact that people seem to emphasize the word *sex* and neglect the word *education*. In the teaching of the subject, *education* is—or ought to be—the main thing. A good way to eliminate this misunderstanding would be to introduce a new term which in a better way emphasizes the psychological facets.

It is most important that sex education should never be allowed to be isolated from other teaching in general, but should be integrated with other subjects, particularly with biology, hygiene, social science, psychology, etc.

It is also important to realize that moral norms are relative concepts which change with time. Another consideration is that within the same country different social groups apply different moral norms. Sex education must naturally follow the values which are valid in that particular society in which they are taught. On the other hand it must be understood that other people have other values, and sex education can contribute to create respect for and understanding of these norms.

An initiation into a healthy sexual life is of the utmost importance for the life and prosperity of the individual and the community. It is the school's duty to deal with this subject which has only rarely appeared in school curricula.

Nevertheless, the group [2] emphasized most strongly that sex education must in the first place be given in the home during the pre-school period. The school can only come in at the second stage; it is recommended, however, that the school should help parents or guardians in this education in the pre-school period.

The schools should at all levels co-operate with the social, educational and religious organizations which are interested in sex education so that various programmes may complement each other.

With the increased speed of communication and mobility in the world, sub-groups of a nation (e.g., rural, religious, working, academic, etc.) which were previously isolated are now becoming integrated to the

441

extent that some have merged with each other and others have even disappeared. This has often resulted in the levelling of different moral values so that in some societies, as one member pointed out, young people feel not only a non-restriction but a positive liberty in sexual relationships. Another phenomenon of certain societies [3] in modern times is that the problem of sexuality has become more central than in former times. One member pointed out that the changed environment contributes to increased eroticism. Again, sex is emphasized commercially in the mass media. One reason suggested for the need for sex education was that of earlier somatic puberty.

There is a rise in the number of divorces. Many families are not so strongly united as formerly. In some countries the age for marriage seems to be dropping and sex education seems to be necessary to prepare young people to fill the roles of husband and wife. In a world where many parents do not take upon themselves the responsibility for the sex education of their children, it is incumbent upon the school to take this education upon itself.

The over-all aim should be to channel each child's natural interest in sex in such a way that the child will achieve an individual equilibrium and at the same time be able to have contact and form wholesome (balanced according to the mores of the particular society) relationships in the home, school and society. Both sexes should learn to respect the dignity of the other, and this education should lay particular emphasis on preparation for unselfish love and marriage. One special aspect of this education is to inculcate healthy attitudes and to correct mistaken and unhealthy attitudes acquired in an "erotic" environment.

Apart from enabling the children to learn the contents laid down in the next paragraph, the school should, if possible, undertake to establish a relationship with the home of each child so that the home participates fully in this sort of education.

A. The Curriculum in Sex Education

Such education should be gradual and questions should be answered as children raise them. It is obvious that there are certain aspects of sex education which should be given at a very early age and that two very important ages for many points of sex education are three to five and ten to twelve years.

Thus, it should be realized that the age of fourteen to sixteen years is too late to begin sex education. The aim here should be to repeat much of what has been taught before. In the fourteen- to sixteen-year group there are many new social and emotional aspects to be considered in sex education. Where possible, boys and girls should be taught together— preferably in small groups for spontaneous discussion according to their social, emotional, physical, and intellectual development and needs. However, it may occur that certain aspects of what is laid down in the contents of the section may be of particular interest to one of the sexes, and, in this case, it would be justified to deal with this separately; at the same time as much as possible of sex education should be covered by both sexes before the end of compulsory education, since in no country can 100 percent of parents be relied upon to give it.

Most subjects can be dealt with in the classroom (either to mixed or separate groups), but for certain children individual talks might be necessary on particular aspects of this education.

It should also not be forgotten that it is possible to integrate the continuation of health education, sex education, and education for home and family life into courses in school or college following the end of compulsory schooling, e.g., "les cours d'apprentissage de l'éducation civique", etc. (in Czechoslovakia 90 percent continue to go to school).

Obviously sex education should preferably be integrated into the whole curriculum. There are many aspects, mental, biological, social, emotional, moral, ethical, etc., which can be dealt with as they come up in various school subjects. It is further desirable that there be close cooperation between members of the school staff and the teacher responsible for sex education in the school (should there be one) or the class teacher; it is most important, where aspects of sex education are touched upon in other subjects, that the specialist or class teacher should be informed of this. This is of paramount importance for the integration of sex education in the school. It should be stressed that what will be taught from the following contents will vary from country to country. The information about sex given to boys and girls should be taught in a way which will support the existing family, social, and educational patterns of individual countries.

Two different versions were presented by the participants as regards the general topics for fourteen- to sixteen-year-olds.

The opinion of the majority of the participants was in favour of version A; some participants were for version B but with fewer details.

Version A

The following general topics are suggested for fourteen- to sixteen-year-olds. These topics should be dealt with not only in a scientific but also in a moral and ethical way.

1. Differences between the sexes
   Anatomical, physiological, emotional, psychological, genetic.
   (Subsumed in the above headings are such topics as: structure and function of the genitals, hormones, menstruation, masturbation.)

2. Boy-girl Relationships
Emotional attraction, responsibility and personal dignity, importance of self-control. Pre-marital relations. Dangers of alcohol and narcotics, stress on moral, ethical, psychological, economic, and social aspects.

3. Childbirth
Conception, development of foetus and pregnancy, confinement and delivery, moral and psychological aspects of pregnancy and delivery, education for childbirth (see also point 11).

4. Incomplete Families

5. Sterility, Impotence and Frigidity

6. Abortion
Spontaneous, legal (in such countries where it exists), warning against illegal abortions.

7. Birth Control

8. Menopause
Age, reasons for (hormones), effects of, e.g., relationships to husband, etc.

9. Venereal Diseases

10. Sexual Deviations

11. Preparation for Further Sex Education
Preparation for parenthood, preparation for childbirth, preparation for role of parent as sex educator (even when this will be available after compulsory schooling).

Version B

The following general topics are suggested for fourteen- to sixteen-year-olds. These points should be dealt with not only from a factual point of view but also from an emotional, social, ethical, etc. point of view.

1. Differences between Sexes
Anatomical, physiological, emotional, psychological, genetic.

2. Boy-Girl Relationships
Emotional attraction, responsibility and personal dignity, dangers of alcohol and narcotics, stress on moral, ethical, psychological, economic, and social aspects.

3. Childbirth
Conception, pregnancy, delivery, post-natal care.

4. Role of the Parents
Respective responsibilities of father and mother.

5. Other Problems
Sex hygiene, family regulation, abortion, venereal diseases, homosexuality, sex and delinquency, etc.

6. Preparation for Marriage in the Future
Importance of self-control.

7. Preparation for Wise Use of Leisure-Time
Literature, films, dances, etc.

In the field of sex education the problem of birth control led to dis-cussions among several participants. One of them stressed the importance of this problem in regard to its repercussions on the religious, social, and economic life. Some participants maintained that the teaching of anti-conceptional methods at school is not advisable, because too early an age constitutes a danger. Other participants did not share these fears. The task of the school mainly consists in creating correct behaviour and healthy attitudes towards sexual problems.

B. Methods of Teaching Sex Education

The schools should aim at the development of sound communication between the parents and the children, especially through establishing a common vocabulary so that parents can assist their children in deepen-ing their knowledge about sex.

Schools may fulfil this function through:

1. group meetings in and out of school
2. individual counselling by teachers
3. informative literature
4. films, filmstrips, and slides
5. newspapers, radio, television broadcasts
6. group meetings with parents and children

The group recommended that specialized services be established whenever possible so that sex problems of children and parents could receive individual attention.

The group recommended that there was a need for continuing inter-national exchange of information and that further research be considered in sex education with regard to the evaluation of contents and methods.

C. The Preparation and the Role of the Teacher in Sex Education

The personal qualities of the educator should include specific knowl-edge, and, like other educators, the individual should be a mature and balanced personality and must be comfortable about providing sex information.

All those who might be required to teach sex information, such as schoolmasters, doctors, nurses, social workers, and other health special-ists, should be taught how to teach this subject in teacher training colleges, graduate schools and universities or through in-service train-ing programmes (training programmes approved by the organization by whom the educator is employed). Ministries of individual countries should establish a separate department concerned with the teaching, co-ordination and the promotion of sex education, in co-operation with existing national organizations or parents and other social, educational, political, and religious associations.

It should be stressed that parents need assistance from the school in teaching their children about sex. The schools have a dual role with respect to sex education: for the children and for the parents.

D. The Role of the Community in Sex Education

Information must be given about sex when this information is required. Thus, it is up to the people or organizations responsible for children and adolescents to give this information. There should be constant communication between these bodies (i.e., the home, the school, industry, and such organizations as the Red Cross, etc.). The school should contact parents before giving sex education and while they are giving it, so as to keep the parents up-to-date with this aspect of their children's education.

One of the participants gave the example of the practice of the administrative authorities in Louisiana. This consists in sending the parents bulletins informing them regularly of the way in which they should educate their child. The parents receive these bulletins from the moment when the wife knows that she is pregnant until the child goes to school.

NOTES

[1] See also contributions of H. Keilson, P. Chambre, M.-B. Bergström-Walan, A. Kelisová, pp. 79-92. [See original report. Ed.]
[2] The group which dealt with sex education was composed of P. Chambre (Chairman), Mrs. Bergström-Walan (rapporteur), J. Bergier, Y. Donnen, H. A. Keilson, Mrs. A. Kelisová, N. W. Paget, T. N. Postlethwaite, T. Wickbom.
[3] The phenomenon is less apparent in Eastern European countries.

On the Regulation of Birth

Encyclical Letter of His Holiness Pope Paul VI

VENERABLE BROTHERS AND BELOVED SONS

The transmission of life

1. The most serious duty of transmitting human life, for which married persons are the free and responsible collaborators of God the Creator, has always been a source of great joys to them, even if sometimes accompanied by not a few difficulties and by distress.

At all times the fulfilment of this duty has posed grave problems to the conscience of married persons, but, with the recent evolution of society, changes have taken place that give rise to new questions which the Church could not ignore, having to do with a matter which so closely touches upon the life and happiness of men.

I. NEW ASPECTS OF THE PROBLEM AND COMPETENCY OF THE MAGISTERIUM

New formulation of the problem

2. The changes which have taken place are in fact noteworthy and of varied kinds. In the first place, there is the rapid demographic development. Fear is shown by many that world population is growing more rapidly than the available resources, with growing distress to many families and developing countries, so that the temptation for Authorities to counter this danger with radical measures is great. Moreover, working and lodging conditions, as well as increased exigencies both in the economic field and in that of education, often make the proper education of an elevated number of children difficult today. A change is also seen both in the manner of considering the person of woman and her place in society, and in the value to be attributed to conjugal love in marriage, and also in the appreciation to be made of the meaning of conjugal acts in relation to that love.

Finally and above all, man has made stupendous progress in the domination and rational organization of the forces of nature, such that he tends to extend this domination to his own total being: to the body, to psychical life, to social life and even to the laws which regulate the transmission of life.

3. This new state of things gives rise to new questions. Granted the conditions of life today, and granted the meaning which conjugal relations have with respect to the harmony between husband and wife and to their mutual fidelity, would not a revision of the ethical norms in force up to now seem to be advisable, especially when it is considered that they cannot be observed without sacrifices, sometimes heroic sacrifices?

And again: by extending to this field the application of the so-called "principle of totality", could it not be admitted that the intention of a less abundant but more rationalized fecundity might transform a materially sterilizing intervention into a licit and wise control of birth? Could it not be admitted, that is, that the finality of procreation pertains to the ensemble of conjugal life, rather than to its single acts? It is also asked whether, in view of the increased sense of responsibility of modern man, the moment has not come for him to entrust to his reason and his will, rather than to the biological rhythms of his organism, the task of regulating birth.

Competency of the Magisterium

4. Such questions required from the teaching authority of the Church a new and deeper reflection upon the principles of the moral teaching on marriage: a teaching founded on the natural law, illuminated and enriched by divine Revelation.

No believer will wish to deny that the teaching authority of the Church is competent to interpret even the natural moral law. It is, in fact, indisputable, as Our Predecessors have many times declared,[1] that Jesus Christ, when communicating to Peter and to the Apostles His divine authority and sending them to teach all nations His commandments,[2] constituted them as guardians and authentic interpreters of all the moral law, not only, that is, of the law of the gospel, but also of the natural law, which is also an expression of the will of God, the faithful fulfilment of which is equally necessary for salvation.[3]

Conformably to this mission of hers, the Church has always provided—and even more amply in recent times—a coherent teaching concerning both the nature of marriage and the correct use of conjugal rights and the duties of husband and wife.[4]

Special studies

5. The consciousness of that same mission induced Us to confirm

and enlarge the Study Commission which Our Predecessor Pope John XXIII of happy memory had instituted in March, 1963. That Commission, which included, besides several experts in the various pertinent disciplines, also married couples, had as its scope the gathering of opinions on the new questions regarding conjugal life, and in particular on the regulation of births, and the furnishing of opportune elements of information so that the Magisterium could give an adequate reply to the expectation not only of the faithful, but also of world opinion.[5]

The work of these experts, as well as the successive judgements and counsels spontaneously forwarded by or expressly requested from a good number of Our Brothers in the Episcopate, have permitted Us to measure more exactly all the aspects of this complex matter. Hence with all Our heart We express to each of them Our lively gratitude.

Reply of the Magisterium

6. The conclusions at which the Commission arrived could not, nevertheless, be considered by Us as definitive, nor dispense Us from a personal examination of this serious question; and this also because, within the Commission itself, no full concordance of judgements concerning the moral norms to be proposed had been reached, and above all because certain criteria of solutions had emerged which departed from the moral teaching on marriage proposed with constant firmness by the teaching authority of the Church.

Therefore, having attentively sifted the documentation laid before Us, after mature reflexion and assidous prayers, We now intend, by virtue of the mandate entrusted to Us by Christ, to give Our reply to these grave questions.

II. DOCTRINAL PRINCIPLES

A total vision of man

7. The problem of birth, like every other problem regarding human life, is to be considered, beyond partial perspectives—whether of the biological or psychological, demographic or sociological orders—in the light of an integral vision of man and of his vocation, not only his natural and earthly, but also his supernatural and eternal vocation. And since, in the attempt to justify artificial methods of birth control, many have appealed to the demands both of conjugal love and of "responsible parenthood", it is good to state very precisely the true concept of these two great realities of married life, referring principally to what was

recently set forth in this regard, and in a highly authoritative form, by the Second Vatican Council in its Pastoral Constitution *Gaudium et Spes*.

Conjugal love

8. Conjugal love reveals its true nature and nobility when it is considered in its supreme origin, God, Who is Love,[6] "the Father, from whom every family in heaven and on earth is named".[7]

Marriage is not, then, the effect of chance or the product of evolution of unconscious natural forces; it is the wise institution of the Creator to realize in mankind His design of love. By means of the reciprocal personal gift of self, proper and exclusive to them, husband and wife tend towards the communion of their beings in view of mutual personal perfection, to collaborate with God in the generation and education of new lives.

For baptized persons, moreover, marriage invests the dignity of a sacramental sign of grace, inasmuch as it represents the union of Christ and the Church.

Its characteristics

9. Under this light, there clearly appear the characteristic marks and demands of conjugal love, and it is of supreme importance to have an exact idea of these.

This love is first of all fully *human,* that is to say, of the senses and of the spirit at the same time. It is not, then, a simple transport of instinct and sentiment, but also, and principally, an act of the free will, intended to endure and to grow by means of the joys and sorrows of daily life, in such a way that husband and wife become one only heart and one only soul, and together attain their human perfection.

Then, this love is *total,* that is to say, it is a very special form of personal friendship, in which husband and wife generously share everything, without undue reservations or selfish calculations. Whoever truly loves his marriage partner loves not only for what he receives, but for the partner's self, rejoicing that he can enrich his partner with the gift of himself.

Again, this love is *faithful* and *exclusive* until death. Thus in fact do bride and groom conceive it to be on the day when they freely and in full awareness assume the duty of the marriage bond. A fidelity, this, which can sometimes be difficult, but is always possible, always noble and meritorious, as no one can deny. The example of so many married persons down through the centuries shows, not only that fidelity is according to the nature of marriage, but also that it is a source of profound and lasting happiness.

And finally, this love is *fecund,* for it is not exhausted by the communion between husband and wife, but is destined to continue, raising up new lives. "Marriage and conjugal love are by their nature ordained toward the begetting and educating of children. Children are really the supreme gift of marriage and contribute very substantially to the welfare of their parents".[8]

Responsible parenthood

10. Hence conjugal love requires in husband and wife an awareness of their mission of "responsible parenthood", which today is rightly much insisted upon, and which also must be exactly understood. Consequently it is to be considered under different aspects which are legitimate and connected with one another.

In relation to the biological processes, responsible parenthood means the knowledge and respect of their functions; human intellect discovers in the power of giving life biological laws which are part of the human person.[9]

In relation to the tendencies of instinct or passion, responsible parenthood means that necessary dominion which reason and will must exercise over them.

In relation to physical, economic, psychological and social conditions, responsible parenthood is exercised, either by the deliberate and generous decision to raise a numerous family, or by the decision, made for grave motives and with due respect for the moral law, to avoid for the time being, or even for an indeterminate period, a new birth.

Responsible parenthood also and above all implies a more profound relationship to the objective moral order established by God, of which a right conscience is the faithful interpreter. The responsible exercise of parenthood implies, therefore, that husband and wife recognize fully their own duties towards God, towards themselves, towards the family and towards society, in a correct hierarchy of values.

In the task of transmitting life, therefore, they are not free to proceed completely at will, as if they could determine in a wholly autonomous way the honest path to follow; but they must conform their activity to the creative intention of God, expressed in the very nature of marriage and of its acts, and manifested by the constant teaching of the Church.[10]

Respect for the nature and purposes of the marriage act

11. These acts, by which husband and wife are united in chaste intimacy, and by means of which human life is transmitted, are, as

the Council recalled, "noble and worthy",[11] and they do not cease to be lawful if, for causes independent of the will of husband and wife, they are foreseen to be infecund, since they always remain ordained towards expressing and consolidating their union. In fact, as experience bears witness, not every conjugal act is followed by a new life. God has wisely disposed natural laws and rhythms of fecundity which, of themselves, cause a separation in the succession of births. Nonetheless the Church, calling men back to the observance of the norms of the natural law, as interpreted by her constant doctrine, teaches that each and every marriage act (*quilibet matrimonii usus*) must remain open to the transmission of life.[12]

Two inseparable aspects: Union and procreation

12. That teaching, often set forth by the Magisterium, is founded upon the inseparable connection, willed by God and unable to be broken by man on his own initiative, between the two meanings of the conjugal act: the unitive meaning and the procreative meaning. Indeed, by its intimate structure, the conjugal act, while most closely uniting husband and wife, capacitates them for the generation of new lives, according to laws inscribed in the very being of man and of woman. By safeguarding both these essential aspects, the unitive and the procreative, the conjugal act preserves in its fulness the sense of true mutual love and its ordination towards man's most high calling to parenthood. We believe that the men of our day are particularly capable of seizing the deeply reasonable and human character of this fundamental principle.

Faithfulness to God's design

13. It is in fact justly observed that a conjugal act imposed upon one's partner without regard for his or her condition and lawful desires is not a true act of love, and therefore denies an exigency of right moral order in the relationships between husband and wife. Hence, one who reflects well must also recognize that a reciprocal act of love which jeopardizes the disponibility to transmit life which God the Creator, according to particular laws, inserted therein is in contradiction with the design constitutive of marriage, and with the will of the Author of life. To use this divine gift destroying, even if only partially, its meaning and its purpose is to contradict the nature both of man and of woman and of their most intimate relationship, and therefore it is to contradict also the plan of God and His will. On the other hand, to make use of the gift of conjugal love while respecting the laws of the generative process means to acknowledge oneself not to be the arbiter of the sources of human life, but rather the minister of the design estab-

lished by the Creator. In fact, just as man does not have unlimited dominion over his body in general, so also, with particular reason, he has no such dominion over his generative faculties as such, because of their intrinsic ordination towards raising up life, of which God is the principle. "Human life is sacred", Pope John XXIII recalled; "from its very inception it reveals the creating hand of God".[13]

Illicit ways of regulating birth

14. In conformity with these landmarks in the human and Christian vision of marriage, We must once again declare that the direct interruption of the generative process already begun, and, above all, directly willed and procured abortion, even if for therapeutic reasons, are to be absolutely excluded as licit means of regulating birth.[14]

Equally to be excluded, as the teaching authority of the Church has frequently declared, is direct sterilization, whether perpetual or temporary, whether of the man or of the woman.[15] Similarly excluded is every action which, either in anticipation of the conjugal act, or in its accomplishment, or in the development of its natural consequences, proposes, whether as an end or as a means, to render procreation impossible.[16]

To justify conjugal acts made intentionally infecund, one cannot invoke as valid reasons the lesser evil, or the fact that such acts would constitute a whole together with the fecund acts already performed or to follow later, and hence would share in one and the same moral goodness. In truth, if it is sometimes licit to tolerate a lesser evil in order to avoid a greater evil or to promote a greater good,[17] it is not licit, even for the gravest reasons, to do evil so that good may follow therefrom;[18] that is, to make into the object of a positive act of the will something which is intrinsically disorder, and hence unworthy of the human person, even when the intention is to safeguard or promote individual, family or social well-being. Consequently it is an error to think that a conjugal act which is deliberately made infecund and so is intrinsically dishonest could be made honest and right by the ensemble of fecund conjugal life.

Licitness of therapeutic means

15. The Church, on the contrary, does not at all consider illicit the use of those therapeutic means truly necessary to cure diseases of the organism, even if an impediment to procreation, which may be foreseen, should result therefrom, provided such impediment is not, for whatever motive, directly willed.[19]

Licitness of recourse to infecund periods

16. To this teaching of the Church on conjugal morals, the objection
is made today, as We observed earlier (No. 3), that it is the prerogative of the human intellect to dominate the energies offered by irrational nature and to orientate them towards an end conformable to the
good of man. Now, some may ask: In the present case, is it not reasonable in many circumstances to have recourse to artificial birth control if,
thereby, we secure the harmony and peace of the family, and better
conditions for the education of the children already born? To this
question it is necessary to reply with clarity: The Church is the first
to praise and recommend the intervention of intelligence in a function
which so closely associates the rational creature with his Creator; but
she affirms that this must be done with respect for the order established by God.

If, then, there are serious motives to space out births, which derive
from the physical or psychological conditions of husband and wife, or
from external conditions, the Church teaches that it is then licit to take
into account the natural rhythms immanent in the generative functions,
for the use of marriage in the infecund periods only, and in this
way to regulate birth without offending the moral principles which
have been recalled earlier.[20]

The Church is coherent with herself when she considers recourse to
the infecund periods to be licit, while at the same time condemning, as
being always illicit, the use of means directly contrary to fecundation,
even if such use is inspired by reasons which may appear honest and
serious. In reality, there are essential differences between the two cases:
in the former, the married couple make legitimate use of a natural
disposition; in the latter, they impede the development of natural processes. It is true that, in the one and the other case, the married couple
are concordant in the positive will of avoiding children for plausible
reasons, seeking the certainty that offspring will not arrive; but it is
also true that only in the former case are they able to renounce the
use of marriage in the fecund periods when, for just motives, procreation is not desirable, while making use of it during infecund periods
to manifest their affection and to safeguard their mutual fidelity. By
so doing, they give proof of a truly and integrally honest love.

Grave consequences of methods of artificial birth control

17. Upright men can even better convince themselves of the solid
grounds on which the teaching of the Church in this field is based,
if they care to reflect upon the consequences of methods of artificial

birth control. Let them consider, first of all, how wide and easy a road would thus be opened up towards conjugal infidelity and the general lowering of morality. Not much experience is needed in order to know human weakness, and to understand that men—especially the young, who are so vulnerable on this point—have need of encouragement to be faithful to the moral law, so that they must not be offered some easy means of eluding its observance. It is also to be feared that the man, growing used to the employment of anti-conceptive practices, may finally lose respect for the woman and, no longer caring for her physical and psychological equilibrium, may come to the point of considering her as a mere instrument of selfish enjoyment, and no longer as his respected and beloved companion.

Let it be considered also that a dangerous weapon would thus be placed in the hands of those public Authorities who take no heed of moral exigencies. Who could blame a Government for applying to the solution of the problems of the community those means acknowledged to be licit for married couples in the solution of a family problem? Who will stop rulers from favouring, from even imposing upon their peoples, if they were to consider it necessary, the method of contraception which they judge to be most efficacious? In such a way men, wishing to avoid individual, family, or social difficulties encountered in the observance of the divine law, would reach the point of placing at the mercy of the intervention of public Authorities the most personal and most reserved sector of conjugal intimacy.

Consequently, if the mission of generating life is not to be exposed to the arbitrary will of men, one must necessarily recognize insurmountable limits to the possibility of man's domination over his own body and its functions; limits which no man, whether a private individual or one invested with authority, may licitly surpass. And such limits cannot be determined otherwise than by the respect due to the integrity of the human organism and its functions, according to the principles recalled earlier, and also according to the correct understanding of the "principle of totality" illustrated by Our Predecessor Pope Pius XII.[21]

The Church guarantor of true human values

18. It can be foreseen that this teaching will perhaps not be easily received by all: too numerous are those voices—amplified by the modern means of propaganda—which are contrary to the voice of the Church. To tell the truth, the Church is not surprised to be made, like her divine Founder, a "sign of contradiction";[22] yet she does not because of this cease to proclaim with humble firmness the entire moral law, both natural and evangelical. Of such laws the Church was not the

author, nor consequently can she be their arbiter; she is only their depositary and their interpreter, without ever being able to declare to be licit that which is not so by reason of its intimate and unchangeable opposition to the true good of man.

In defending conjugal morals in their integral wholeness, the Church knows that she contributes towards the establishment of a truly human civilization; she engages man not to abdicate from his own responsibility in order to rely on technical means; by that very fact she defends the dignity of man and wife. Faithful to both the teaching and the example of the Saviour, she shows herself to be the sincere and disinterested friend of men, whom she wishes to help, even during their earthly sojourn, "to share as sons in the life of the living God, the Father of all men".[23]

III. PASTORAL DIRECTIVES

The Church Mater et Magistra

19. Our words would not be an adequate expression of the thought and solicitude of the Church, Mother and Teacher of all peoples, if, after having recalled men to the observance and respect of the divine law regarding matrimony, We did not strengthen them in the path of honest regulation of birth, even amid the difficult conditions which today afflict families and peoples. The Church, in fact, cannot have a different conduct towards men than that of the Redeemer: she knows their weaknesses, has compassion on the crowd, receives sinners; but she cannot renounce the teaching of the law which is, in reality, that law proper to a human life restored to its original truth and conducted by the Spirit of God.[24] Though We are thinking also of all men of good will, We now address Ourself particularly to Our sons, from whom We expect a prompter and more generous adherence.

Possibility of observing the divine law

20. The teaching of the Church on the regulation of birth, which promulgates the divine law, will easily appear to many to be difficult or even impossible of actuation. And indeed, like all great beneficent realities, it demands serious engagement and much effort, individual, family and social effort. More than that, it would not be practicable without the help of God, Who upholds and strengthens the good will of men. Yet, to anyone who reflects well, it cannot but be clear that such efforts ennoble man and are beneficial to the human community.

Mastery of self

21. The honest practice of regulation of birth demands first of all that husband and wife acquire and possess solid convictions concerning the true values of life and of the family, and that they tend towards securing perfect self-mastery. To dominate instinct by means of one's reason and free will undoubtedly requires ascetical practices, so that the affective manifestations of conjugal life may observe the correct order, in particular with regard to the observance of periodic continence. Yet this discipline which is proper to the purity of married couples, far from harming conjugal love, rather confers on it a higher human value. It demands continual effort yet, thanks to its beneficent influence, husband and wife fully develop their personalities, being enriched with spiritual values. Such discipline bestows upon family life fruits of serenity and peace, and facilitates the solution of other problems; it favours attention for one's partner, helps both parties to drive out selfishness, the enemy of true love; and deepens their sense of responsibility. By its means, parents acquire the capacity of having a deeper and more efficacious influence in the education of their offspring; little children and youths grow up with a just appraisal of human values, and in the serene and harmonious development of their spiritual and sensitive faculties.

Creating an atmosphere favourable to chastity

22. On this occasion, We wish to draw the attention of educators, and of all who perform duties of responsibility in regard to the common good of human society, to the need of creating an atmosphere favourable to education in chastity, that is, to the triumph of healthy liberty over licence by means of respect for the moral order.

Everything in the modern media of social communications which leads to sense excitation and unbridled customs, as well as every form of pornography and licentious performances, must arouse the frank and unanimous reaction of all those who are solicitous for the progress of civilization and the defence of the supreme good of the human spirit. Vainly would one seek to justify such depravation with the pretext of artistic or scientific exigencies,[25] or to deduce an argument from the freedom allowed in this sector by the public Authorities.

Appeal to public Authorities

23. To rulers, who are those principally responsible for the common good, and who can do so much to safeguard moral customs, We say:

Do not allow the morality of your peoples to be degraded; do not permit that by legal means practices contrary to the natural and divine law be introduced into that fundamental cell, the family. Quite other is the way in which public Authorities can and must contribute to the solution of the demographic problem: namely, the way of a provident policy for the family, of a wise education of peoples in respect of the moral law and the liberty of citizens.

We are well aware of the serious difficulties experienced by public Authorities in this regard, especially in the developing countries. To their legitimate preoccupations We devoted Our Encyclical Letter *Populorum Progressio*. But, with Our Predecessor Pope John XXIII, We repeat: No solution to these difficulties is acceptable "which does violence to man's essential dignity" and is based only "on an utterly materialistic conception of man himself and of his life. The only possible solution to this question is one which envisages the social and economic progress both of individuals and of the whole of human society, and which respects and promotes true human values".[26] Neither can one, without grave injustice, consider divine Providence to be responsible for what depends, instead, on a lack of wisdom in government, on an insufficient sense of social justice, on selfish monopolization, or again on blameworthy indolence in confronting the efforts and the sacrifices necessary to ensure the raising of living standards of a people and of all its sons.[27]

May all responsible public Authorities—as some are already doing so laudably—generously revive their efforts. And may mutual aid between all the members of the great human family never cease to grow: this is an almost limitless field which thus opens up to the activity of the great international organizations.

To men of science

24. We wish now to express Our encouragement to men of science, who "can considerably advance the welfare of marriage and the family, along with peace of conscience, if by pooling their efforts they labour to explain more thoroughly the various conditions favouring a proper regulation of births".[28] It is particularly desirable that, according to the wish already expressed by Pope Pius XII, medical science succeed in providing a sufficiently secure basis for a regulation of birth, founded on the observance of natural rhythms.[29] In this way, scientists and especially Catholic scientists will contribute to demonstrate in actual fact that, as the Church teaches, "a true contradiction cannot exist between the divine laws pertaining to the transmission of life and those pertaining to the fostering of authentic conjugal love".[30]

To Christian husbands and wives

25. And now Our words more directly address Our own children, particularly those whom God calls to serve Him in marriage. The Church, while teaching imprescriptible demands of the divine law, announces the tidings of salvation, and by means of the Sacraments opens up the paths of grace, which makes man a new creature, capable of corresponding with love and true freedom to the design of his Creator and Saviour, and of finding the yoke of Christ to be sweet.[31]

Christian married couples, then, docile to her voice, must remember that their Christian vocation, which began at baptism, is further specified and reinforced by the Sacrament of Matrimony. By it husband and wife are strengthened and, as it were, consecrated for the faithful accomplishment of their proper duties, for the carrying out of their proper vocation even to perfection, and the Christian witness which is proper to them before the whole world.[32] To them the Lord entrusts the task of making visible to men the holiness and sweetness of the law which unites the mutual love of husband and wife with their cooperation with the love of God the Author of human life.

We do not at all intend to hide the sometimes serious difficulties inherent in the life of Christian married persons; for them as for everyone else, "the gate is narrow and the way is hard, that leads to life".[33] But the hope of that life must illuminate their way, as with courage they strive to live with wisdom, justice and piety in this present time,[34] knowing that the figure of this world passes away.[35]

Let married couples, then, face up to the efforts needed, supported by the faith and hope which "do not disappoint . . . because God's love has been poured into our hearts through the Holy Spirit, Who has been given to us";[36] let them implore divine assistance by persevering prayer; above all, let them draw from the source of grace and charity in the Eucharist. And if sin should still keep its hold over them, let them not be discouraged, but rather have recourse with humble perseverance to the mercy of God, which is poured forth in the Sacrament of Penance. In this way they will be enabled to achieve the fulness of conjugal life described by the Apostle: "Husbands, love your wives, as Christ loved the Church. . . . Husbands should love their wives as their own bodies. He who loves his wife loves himself. For no man ever hates his own flesh, but nourishes and cherishes it, as Christ does the Church. . . . This is a great mystery, and I mean in reference to Christ and the Church. However, let each one of you love his wife as himself, and let the wife see that she respects her husband".[37]

Apostolate in homes

26. Among the fruits which ripen forth from a generous effort of
fidelity to the divine law, one of the most precious is that married
couples themselves not infrequently feel the desire to communicate
their experience to others. Thus there comes to be included in the vast
pattern of the vocation of the laity a new and most noteworthy form
of the apostolate of like to like: it is married couples themselves who
become apostles and guides to other married couples. This is assuredly,
among so many forms of apostolate, one of those which seem most
opportune today.[38]

To doctors and medical personnel

27. We hold those physicians and medical personnel in the highest
esteem who, in the exercise of their profession, value above every human
interest the superior demands of their Christian vocation. Let them
persevere, therefore, in promoting on every occasion the discovery of
solutions inspired by faith and right reason, let them strive to arouse this
conviction and this respect in their associates. Let them also consider
as their proper professional duty the task of acquiring all the knowledge needed in this delicate sector, so as to be able to give to those
married persons who consult them wise counsel and healthy direction,
such as they have a right to expect.

To priests

28. Beloved priest sons, by vocation you are the counsellors and
spiritual guides of individual persons and of families. We now turn to
you with confidence. Your first task—especially in the case of those who
teach moral theology—is to expound the Church's teaching on marriage
without ambiguity. Be the first to give, in the exercise of your ministry,
the example of loyal internal and external obedience to the teaching
authority of the Church. That obedience, as you know well, obliges
not only because of the reasons adduced, but rather because of the
light of the Holy Spirit, which is given in a particular way to the Pas-
tors of the Church in order that they may illustrate the truth.[39] You
know, too, that it is of the utmost importance, for peace of consciences
and for the unity of the Christian people, that in the field of morals as
well as in that of dogma, all should attend to the Magisterium of the
Church, and all should speak the same language. Hence, with all Our
heart We renew to you the heartfelt plea of the great Apostle Paul:

"I appeal to you, brethren, by the name of Our Lord Jesus Christ, that all of you agree and that there be no dissensions among you, but that you be united in the same mind and the same judgement".[40]

29. To diminish in no way the saving teaching of Christ constitutes an eminent form of charity for souls. But this must ever be accompanied by patience and goodness, such as the Lord Himself gave example of in dealing with men. Having come not to condemn but to save,[41] He was indeed intransigent with evil, but merciful towards individuals.

In their difficulties, may married couples always find, in the words and in the heart of a priest, the echo of the voice and the love of the Redeemer.

To Bishops

Beloved and Venerable Brothers in the Episcopate, with whom We most intimately share the solicitude of the spiritual good of the People of God, at the conclusion of this Encyclical Our reverent and affectionate thoughts turn to you. To all of you we extend an urgent invitation. At the head of the priests, your collaborators, and of your faithful, work ardently and incessantly for the safeguarding and the holiness of marriage, so that it may always be lived in its entire human and Christian fulness. Consider this mission as one of your most urgent responsibilities at the present time. As you know, it implies concerted pastoral action in all the fields of human activity, economic, cultural and social; for, in fact, only a simultaneous improvement in these various sectors will make it possible to render the life of parents and of children within their families not only tolerable, but easier and more joyous, to render the living together in human society more fraternal and peaceful, in faithfulness to God's design for the world.

FINAL APPEAL

31. Venerable Brothers, most beloved sons, and all men of good will, great indeed is the work of education, of progress and of love to which We call you, upon the foundation of the Church's teaching, of which the Successor of Peter is, together with His Brothers in the Episcopate, the depositary and interpreter. Truly a great work, as We are deeply convinced, both for the world and for the Church, since man cannot find true happiness—towards which he aspires with all his being—other than in respect of the laws written by God in his very

nature, laws which he must observe with intelligence and love. Upon this work, and upon all of you, and especially upon married couples, We invoke the abundant graces of the God of holiness and mercy, and in pledge thereof We impart to you all Our Apostolic Blessing.

Given at Rome, from Saint Peter's, this twenty-fifth day of July, Feast of Saint James the Apostle, in the year nineteen hundred and sixty-eight, the sixth of Our Pontificate.

PAULUS PP. VI

NOTES

[1] Cf: Pius IX, Encyclical *Qui Pluribus*, Nov. 9, 1846; in *Pii IX P. M. Acta*, I, pp. 9-10; St Pius X Encyc. *Singulari Quadam*, Sept. 24, 1912; in AAS IV (1912), p. 658; Pius XI, Encyc. *Casti Connubii*, Dec. 31, 1930; in AAS XXII (1930), pp. 579-581; Pius XII, Allocution *Magnificate Dominum* to the Episcopate of the Catholic world, Nov. 2, 1954; in AAS XLVI (1954), pp. 671-672; John XXIII, Encyc. *Mater et Magistra*, May 15, 1961; in AAS LIII (1961), p. 457.

[2] Cf. *Mt.* 28, 18-19.

[3] Cf. *Mt.* 7, 21.

[4] Cf. *Catechismus Romanus Concilii Tridentini*, Part II, Ch. VIII; Leo XIII, Encyc. *Arcanum*, Feb. 10, 1880, in *Acta Leonis XIII*, II (1881), pp. 26-29; Pius XI, Encyc. *Divini Illius Magistri*, Dec. 31, 1929, in AAS XXII (1930), pp. 58-61; Encyc. *Casti Connubii*, in AAS XXII (1930), pp. 545-546; Pius XII, Alloc. to the Italian Medico-Biological Union of Saint Luke, Nov. 12, 1944, in *Discorsi e Radiomessaggi*, VI, pp. 191-192; to the Italian Catholic Union of Midwives, Oct. 29, 1951, in AAS XLIII (1951), pp. 857-859; to the Seventh Congress of the International Society of Haematology, Sept. 12. 1958, in AAS L (1958), pp. 734-735; John XXIII, Encyc. *Mater et Magistra*, in AAS LIII (1961), pp. 446-447; *Codex Iuris Canonici*, Canon 1067; Can. 1968, § 1, Can. 1076 §§ 1-2; Second Vatican Council, Pastoral Constitution *Gaudium et Spes*, Nos. 47-52.

[5] Cf. Paul VI, Allocution to the Sacred College, June 23, 1964, in AAS LVI (1964), p. 588; to the Commission for Study of Problems of Population, Family and Birth, March 27, 1965, in AAS LVII (1965), p. 388; to the National Congress of the Italian Society of Obstetrics and Gynaecology, Oct. 29, 1966, in AAS LVIII (1966), p. 1168.

[6] Cf. *I Jn.*, 4, 8.

[7] Cf. *Eph.*, 3, 15.

[8] Cf. II Vat. Council, Pastoral Const. *Gaudium et Spes*, No. 50.

[9] Cf. St Thomas, *Summa Theologica*, I-II, Q. 94, Art. 2.

[10] Cf. Pastoral Const. *Gaudium et Spes*, Nos. 50, 51.

[11] *Ibid.*, No. 49.

[12] Cf. Pius XI, Encyc. *Casti Connubii*, in AAS XXII (1930), p. 560; Pius XII, in AAS XLIII (1951), p. 843.

[13] Cf. John XXIII, Encyc. *Mater et Magistra,* in AAS LIII (1961), p. 447.

[14] Cf. *Catechismus Romanus Concilii Tridentini,* Part II, Ch. VIII; Pius XI, Encyc. *Casti Connubii,* in AAS XXII (1930), pp. 562-564; Pius XII, *Discorsi e Radiomessaggi,* VI (1944), pp. 191-192; AAS XLIII (1951), pp. 842-843; pp. 857-859; John XXIII, Encyc. *Pacem in Terris,* Apri. 11, 1963, in AAS LV (1963), pp. 259-260; *Gaudium et Spes,* No. 51.

[15] Cf. Pius XI, Encyc. *Casti Connubii,* in AAS XXII (1930), p. 565; Decree of the Holy Office, Feb. 22, 1940, in AAS L (1958), pp. 734-735.

[16] Cf. *Catechismus Romanus Concilii Tridentini,* Part II, Ch. VIII; Pius XI, Encyc. *Casti Connubii,* in AAS XXII (1930), pp. 559-561; Pius XII, AAS XLIII (1951), p. 843; AAS L (1958), pp. 734-735; John XXIII, Encyc. *Mater et Magistra,* in AAS LIII (1961), p. 447.

[17] Cf. Pius XII, Alloc. to the National Congress of the Union of Catholic Jurists, Dec. 6, 1953, in AAS XLV (1953), pp. 798-799.

[18] Cf. *Rom.,* 3, 8.

[19] Cf. Pius XII, Alloc. to Congress of the Italian Association of Urology, Oct. 8, 1953, in AAS XLV (1953), pp. 674-675; AAS L (1958), pp. 734-735.

[20] Cf. Pius XII, AAS XLIII (1951), p. 846.

[21] Cf. AAS XLV (1953), pp. 674-675; AAS XLVIII (1956), pp. 461-462.

[22] Cf. *Lk,* 2, 34.

[23] Cf. Paul VI, Encyc. *Populorum Progressio,* March 26, 1967, No. 21.

[24] Cf. *Rom.,* 8.

[25] Cf. II Vatican Council, Decree *Inter Mirifica* on the media of Social Communication, Nos. 6-7.

[26] Cf. Encyc. *Mater et Magistra,* in AAS LIII (1961), p. 447.

[27] Cf. Encyc. *Populorum Progresso,* Nos. 48-55.

[28] Cf. Pastoral Const. *Gaudium et Spes,* No. 52.

[29] Cf. AAS XLIII (1951), p. 859.

[30] Cf. Pastoral Const. *Gaudium et Spes,* No. 51.

[31] Cf. *Mt.* 11, 30.

[32] Cf. Pastoral Const. *Gaudium et Spes,* No. 48; II Vatican Council, Dogmatic Const. *Lumen Gentium,* No. 35.

[33] *Mt.,* 7, 14; cf. *Hebr.,* 12, 11.

[34] Cf. *Tit.,* 2, 12.

[35] Cf. *I Cor.,* 7, 31.

[36] Cf. *Rom.,* 5, 5.

[37] *Eph.,* 5, 25, 28-29, 32-33.

[38] Cf. Dogmatic Const. *Lumen Gentium,* Nos. 35 and 41; Pastoral Const. *Gaudium et Spes.* Nos. 48-49; II Vatican Council, Decree *Apostolicam Actuositatem,* No. 11.

[39] Cf. Dogmatic Const. *Lumen Gentium,* No. 25.

[40] Cf. *I Cor.,* 1, 10.

[41] Cf. *Jn.,* 3, 17.

Part V
BIBLIOGRAPHY

CONTRIBUTORS

Art Buchwald, "Soda Fountain Guru: Sex Education—A Must!" the *Nashville Tennessean*, 24 April 1969; "Surprise for Youngsters: Sex Education on TV," the *Nashville Tennessean*, 14 October 1969. The author is a well-known humorist whose column is syndicated in newspapers throughout the United States and in many foreign countries.

Robert M. Bjork, "Misconceptions and Conceptions on Sex Education: An International Overview," based on "Towards a Study of Comparative Sex Education: Conceptions and Misconceptions," Chapter IV of *International Education: Understandings and Misunderstandings,* edited by Stewart E. Fraser (Nashville: Peabody International Center, 1969), pp. 53-72. The author is Professor of Economics and Sociology, George Peabody College for Teachers, Nashville, Tennessee.

William Simon and John H. Gagnon, "The Pedagogy of Sex," *Saturday Review,* 18 November 1967, pp. 74-76, 91-92. The authors are members of the Institute for Sex Research, Indiana University, Bloomington, Indiana.

William Barry Furlong, "It's a Long Way from the Birds and Bees," *New York Times Magazine,* 11 July 1967, pp. 24-25, 38, 40, 42, 45, 50, 52, 55, 58, 63. The author is a free-lance journalist whose contributions are to be found in a variety of publications.

Michael Scriven, "Putting the Sex Back into Sex Education," *Phi Delta Kappan,* vol. 49, no. 9 (May 1968), pp. 485-489. The author is Professor of Philosophy, The University of California at Berkeley.

James Elias and Paul Gebhard, "Sexuality and Sexual Learning in Childhood," *Phi Delta Kappan,* vol. 50, no. 7 (March 1969), pp. 401-405. The authors are, respectively, Director and Associate Sociologist, The Institute for Sex Research, Indiana University, Bloomington, Indiana.

A. Gray Thompson and Edward P. DeRoche, "Sex Education: Parent Involvement in Decision Making," *Phi Delta Kappan,* vol. 49, no. 9 (May 1968), pp. 501-503. The authors are Professors of Education, Marquette University, Milwaukee, Wisconsin.

Edward Pohlman, "Premarital Contraception and the School," *Phi Delta Kappan,* vol. 49, no. 9 (May 1968), pp. 495-500. The author is Professor of Counseling Psychology in the School of Education, University of the Pacific, Stockton, California.

Ashley Montagu, "The Pill, the Sexual Revolution, and the Schools," *Phi Delta Kappan,* vol. 49, no. 9 (May 1968), pp. 480-484. The author is a well-known anthropologist and sociologist whose stimulating ideas are to be found in numerous books, articles, and speeches.

Gregory Spencer Hill, "Premarital Sex—Never!: A Teen-ager's Point of View," *Phi Delta Kappan,* vol. 50, no. 1 (September 1968), pp. 48-51. The author, at the time of writing, was a high-school senior and son of a professor of political science at Eastern New Mexico University, Portales, New Mexico.

Ira L. Reiss, "Sex Education in the Public Schools: Problem or Solution?" *Phi Delta Kappan,* vol. 50, no. 1 (September 1968), pp. 52-56. The author, who is Professor of Sociology, The University of Iowa, has undertaken research with the Sex Information and Education Council of the U.S. (SIECUS), and is the author of numerous publications, including *Premarital Sexual Standards in America* and *The Social Context of Premarital Sexual Permissiveness.*

John Kobler, "Sex Invades the Schoolhouse," *Saturday Evening Post,* 29 June 1968, pp. 23-27, 64-66. The author is a free-lance journalist whose contributions are to be found in a variety of publications.

Marjorie F. Iseman, "Sex Education," *McCall's* (January 1968), pp. 37, 115-118. The author is a free-lance journalist and a contributor to *Newsweek* magazine, United Press, and *Life* magazine, and is on the editorial staff of the *Partisan Review.*

W. H. Masters and V. E. Johnson, *"Playboy:* Interview with Masters and Johnson," *Playboy,* May 1968, pp. 199-202. The authors, who are members of the Reproductive Biology Research Foundation in St. Louis, are amongst the most prominent and widely read researchers on sex education and family life studies.

Gordon V. Drake, *Is the Schoolhouse the Proper Place to Teach Raw Sex?* (Tulsa, Oklahoma: Christian Crusade Publications), 1968, 40 pp. The author is an educator, writer, and lecturer who has contributed articles to a variety of journals and has written for Christian Publications of Tulsa, Oklahoma.

Gary Allen, "Sex Study: Problems, Propaganda and Pornography," *American Opinion,* March 1969. Reprinted in John R. Rarick, "Sex and Subversion," 7 February 1968, *Congressional Record,* vol. 114, no. 110 (26 June 1968), [sic] pp. 6-11. The author, a film writer and journalist, has written extensively on civil turmoil and the New Left. His books include *Communist Revolution in the Streets.*

Max Rafferty, "The Dropout Parents: How America Got on a Sex Binge," the *Los Angeles Times,* 15 April 1969. The author was formerly State Superintendent of Public Instruction for California and a columnist for the *Los Angeles Times.*

Tranquilla Rathmines, "Sex and the Single Student: How Not to Be a Mummy," *Farrago* (Melbourne University), 7 March 1966, pp. 4-5. The author, long renowned as a champion of sexual sensibility, has been closely associated with student activities at the University of Melbourne, Victoria, Australia.

Z. N. Kadri, "The Student Health Service and Sex Education," *Malaysian Journal of Education,* vol. 4, no. 2 (December 1967), pp. 185-189. The author is a staff member of the Health Services, University of Singapore, Singapore.

V. N. Kolbanovskii, "The Sex Upbringing of the Rising Generation," *Soviet Education,* vol. 6, no. 11 (Fall 1964), [*Sovetskai Pedagogika,* no. 3, 1964], pp. 3-14. The author is associated with the Scientific Research Institute of Psychology of the RSFSR Academy of Pedagogical Sciences, U.S.S.R.

K'ai Ko and Cheng Lin, "What's to Be Done If One Has Married Young?: A Reader's Letter and Editor's Answer," *Chung-kuo Ch'ing-nien Pao* [China Youth, Peking], 7 July 1962. The authors are, respectively, Correspondent from Han-kiang in Shensi and the Editor of *Chung-kuo Ch'ing-nien Pao.*

Yeh Kung-shao, "For Students and Youths: What Is the Most Suitable Age for Marriage?" *Chung-kuo Ch'ing-nien Pao* [China Youth, Peking], 12 April 1962; "My Views on the Problem of Young People's Marriage, Love and Children," *Chung-kuo Ch'ing-nien Pao* [China Youth, Peking], 21 July 1962. The author is Dean of the Public Health Department, Peking Medical College.

Yang Hsiu, "For Late Marriage: Advice for Students," *Chung-kuo Ch'ing-nien Pao* [China Youth, Peking], 1 June 1962.

Pi-chao Chen, "China's Birth Control Action Programme, 1956-1964," *Population Studies,* vol. 24, no. 2 (July 1970), pp. 141-158. The author is Professor of Political Science, Wayne State University, Detroit, Michigan.

Swedish National Board of Education, *Handbook on Sex Instruction in the Schools* (Stockholm: National Board of Education, 1956), pp. 7-18.

Birgitta Linnér, *Society and Sex in Sweden* (Stockholm: The Swedish Institute for Cultural Relations with Foreign Countries, 1971), pp. 3-53. The author, who has written several textbooks for young people about sex, is a pioneer in the field of sex education. She is an Instructor in Family Life Education at Uppsala University.

Alan Little, "Sex Education and the Schools in the United Kingdom," in *Responsible Parenthood and Sex Education;* Susan Burke (editor), (London: International Planned Parenthood Federation, 1970), pp. 51-78. The author is Head of the Inner London Education Authority Research Group and the United Kingdom consultant at the Directorate of Scientific Affairs, OECD, Paris, France.

M. Holmes, C. Nicol, and R. Stubbs, "Sex Attitudes of Young People," *Educational Research,* vol. 2, no. 1 (November 1968), pp. 38-42.

The authors are, respectively, members of the Institute of Education, University of London, and of St. Thomas's Hospital, London,

Aidan Pickering, *Sex Instruction in the Home* (London: Catholic Truth Society, June, 1965), pp. 3-24. The author is Biology Master at Ushaw College, Durham, England.

UNESCO Institute for Education, *Health Education, Sex Education and Education for Home and Family Life.* Report on an Expert Meeting, February 17-22, 1964, International Studies in Education (Hamburg: UNESCO Institute for Education, 1965), pp. 23-29.

Pope Paul VI, *On the Regulation of Birth* (London: Catholic Truth Society, July, 1968). 36 pp.

SELECTED BIBLIOGRAPHY

Adams, Eleanor. "Sex Education: The Swedish System." *Scholastic Teacher* 90, no. 11 (21 April 1967), pp. 16-17.

Adams, M. F. "Planning for Sex Education: Checklist Boosts Program." *Wisconsin Journal of Education* 101 (November 1968), pp. 16-17.

Allen, Gary. *Sex Education Problems*. Belmont, Mass.: American Opinion, c. 1969. 30 pp.

————. "Sex Study: Problems, Propaganda and Pornography." *American Opinion* (March 1969). Reprinted in John R. Rarick, "Sex and Subversion," 7 February 1968, *Congressional Record* 114, no. 110 (26 June 1968), pp. 6-11.

American Assembly. *The Population Dilemma*. Englewood Cliffs, N.J.: Prentice-Hall, 1963. 188 pp.

Andry, Andrew C. and Schepp, Steven. *How Babies Are Made*. The Netherlands: Time-Life International, 1969. 84 pp.

Arnstein, Helene S. *Your Growing Child and Sex*. Indianapolis: Bobbs-Merrill Co., 1967. 188 pp.

Atarov, T. S. "Sex Education." In *Soviet Educators on Soviet Education*, edited by Helen B. Redl, pp. 53-77. New York: Free Press, 1964.

Australian Catholic Truth Society. *The Daughter of Today; What Can Her Mother Do?* Melbourne: Australian Catholic Truth Society, 1960. 31 pp.

Bach, J. "Health, Sex and Family Education." In UNESCO, *Health Education, Sex Education and Education for Home and Family Life*, pp. 53-54. Hamburg: UNESCO Institute for Education, 1965.

Bachi, Roberto and Matras, Judah. "Contraception and Induced Abortions among Jewish Maternity Cases in Israel." *Milbank Memorial Fund Quarterly* 40, no. 2 (April 1962), pp. 207-229.

Baer, Gabriel. *Population and Society in the Arab East*. Translated by Hanna Szoke. New York: Frederick A. Praeger, 1964. 275 pp.

Baggaley, E. J. "Where We Fail Them." *Learning for Living* 3 (May 1964), p. 156.

Baker, R. T. "New Trouble for Sex Education." *Ohio Schools* 47 (25 April 1969), pp. 13-15.

Barnes, Harry Elmer. "Some Biological, Social, and Educational Aspects of the Sex Problem." Chap. 10 in *Society in Transition*, pp. 381-422. New York: Prentice-Hall, 1946.

Barnes, Kenneth. "Sex and the Teenager." *Learning for Living* 1 (January 1962), pp. 9-12.

Baruch, Dorothy W. *New Ways in Sex Education*. New York: Bantam Books; McGraw-Hill Book Co., 1959. 206 pp.

Bauer, W. W. *Moving into Manhood: A Guide for the Adolescent*. Garden City, N.Y.: Doubleday & Co., 1963. 107 pp.

471

Bauer, W. W. and Florence M. *Way to Womanhood.* Garden City, N.Y.: Doubleday & Co., 1965. 112 pp.

Beauvoir, Simone de. *The Second Sex.* Translated and edited by H. M. Parshley. New York: Bantam Books, 1961. 705 pp.

Beavan, K. A. "Sex Education Plotters—Pitfalls for New Commissioner." *The Times Educational Supplement* (London), no. 2804 (14 February 1969), p. 474.

Bell, A. P. "Adolescent Sexuality and the Schools." *North Central Association Quarterly* 43 (Spring 1969), pp. 342-347.

Bell, R. R. *A Bibliography of American Family Problem Areas.* Philadelphia Temple University, Publications Div., 1964. 99 pp.

Benell, F. B. "Frequency of Misconceptions and Reluctance to Teach Controversial Topics Related to Sex among Teachers." *American Association for Health, Physical Education, and Recreation Research Quarterly* 40 (March 1969), pp. 11-16.

Bennett, Virginia D. C., *et al.* "An Experimental Course in Sex Education for Teachers." *Mental Hygiene* 53 (October 1969), pp. 625-631.

Bensley, Loren, Jr. "Sex Education." *Michigan Education Journal* 46, no. 9 (November 1968), pp. 22, 29.

Berelson, Bernard, *et al. Family Planning and Population Programs: A Review of World Developments.* Chicago: University of Chicago Press, 1966. 848 pp.

Berelson, Bernard and Freedman, Ronald. "A Study in Fertility Control." *Scientific American* 210, no. 4 (May 1964), pp. 29-37.

Bergström-Walan, M.-B. "Sex Education." In UNESCO, *Health Education, Sex Education and Education for Home and Family Life,* pp. 89-90. Hamburg: UNESCO Institute for Education, 1965.

Bibby, Cyril. *Sex Education: A Guide for Parents, Teachers and Youth Leaders.* London: Macmillan & Co., 1962. 291 pp.

Birmingham, William, ed. *What Modern Catholics Think about Birth Control.* New York: New American Library (Signet Books), 1964. 256 pp.

Bjork, Robert M. "International Perspective on Various Issues in Sex Education as an Aspect of Health Education." *Journal of School Health* 39 (October 1969), pp. 525-537.

————. "Towards a Study of Comparative Sex Education: Conceptions and Misconceptions." Chap. IV in *International Education: Understandings and Misunderstandings,* edited by Stewart E. Fraser, pp. 53-72. Nashville: Peabody International Center, 1969.

Blake, Judith. *Family Structure in Jamaica: The Social Context of Reproduction.* New York: Free Press, 1961. 262 pp.

Bloch, Ivan. *Sexual Life in England.* Translated by William H. Forstern. Originally published as *Sexual Life in England, Past and Present.* London: Transworld Publishers, 1958. 542 pp.

Bloom, Jean L. "Sex Education for Handicapped Adolescents." *Journal of School Health* 39 (June 1969), pp. 363-367.

Blos, Peter. *On Adolescence, A Psychoanalytic Interpretation.* New York: Free Press, 1962. 269 pp.

Blyth, W. A. L. *English Primary Education: A Sociological Description.* 2 vols. London: Routledge & Kegan Paul, 1965. 370 pp.

Boll, Eleanor S. *The Man That You Marry*. Philadelphia: Macrae Smith Co., 1963. 191 pp.

Boll, Eleanor S. and Bossard, James H. S. *The Girl That You Marry*. Philadelphia: Macrae Smith Co., 1960. 190 pp.

Booz, C. E. "Sex Education at Whiteface." *Texas Outlook* 52 (November 1968), pp. 22-23.

Boria, Maria Caterina. *The Miracle of Sex*. Sydney: Patrician Publications, n.d. 39 pp.

Bowman, Henry A. *Marriage for Moderns*. New York: McGraw-Hill Book Co., 1965. 709 pp.

Breasted, Mary. *Oh! Sex Education!* New York: Frederick A. Praeger, 1970. 342 pp. New York: New American Library (Signet Books), 1971. 368 pp.

Brecher, Edward and Ruth. *An Analysis of Human Sexual Response*. Boston: Little, Brown & Co.; New York: New American Library, 1966. 318 pp.

Brown, Donald R., ed. *The Role and Status of Women in the Soviet Union*. New York: Teachers College Press, 1968. 137 pp.

Brown, Neville. "Birth Control in Egypt." *New Statesman* 73, no. 1873 (3 February 1967), p. 142.

Brown, Roger L. "Some Reactions to a Schools' Television Programme on Venereal Disease." *Health Education Journal* 26 (September 1967), pp. 108-116.

Brown, T. E. "Sex Education and Life in the Black Ghetto." *Religious Education* 64 (November 1969), pp. 450-458.

Buchwald, Art. "Soda Fountain Guru: Sex Education—A Must!" *Nashville Tennessean*, 24 April 1969.

————. "Surprise for Youngsters: Sex Education on TV." *Nashville Tennessean*, 14 October 1969.

Burke, Susan, ed. *Responsible Parenthood and Sex Education: Proceedings of a Working Group held in Tunisia, November, 1969*. London International Planned Parenthood Federation, 1970. 139 pp.

Byler, Ruth V., ed. *Teach Us What We Want to Know*. Report of Survey on Health Interests, Concerns and Problems of 5,000 Students in Selected Schools from Kindergarten through Grade Twelve. New York: Mental Health Materials Center, 1969. 179 pp.

Cadbury, George W. "Outlook for Government Action in Family Planning in the West Indies." *Research in Family Planning*, edited by Clyde V. Kiser, pp. 317-333. Princeton: Princeton University Press, 1962.

Cain, Arthur H. *Sex for Young People*. London: W. Foulsham & Co., 1967. 111 pp.

————. *Young People and Sex*. New York: John Day Co., 1967. 126 pp.

Calderone, Mary S. "Adolescent Sexual Behavior—Whose Responsibility?" *PTA Magazine* 59, no. 1 (September 1964), pp. 4-7.

————. *Release from Sexual Tensions*. New York: Random House, 1960. 238 pp.

————. "Sex Education for Young People—And for Their Parents and Teachers." In Edward and Ruth Brecher, *An Analysis of Human Sexual Response*, pp. 267-273. New York: New American Library, 1966.

————. "Sexuality and the College Student." *Journal of the American College Health Association* 17 (February 1969), pp. 189-193.

————. "Teenagers and Sex." *PTA Magazine,* October 1965, p. 6.

Calderwood, D. *What Shall I Tell My Children?* New York: Crown Publishers, 1966.

Canadian Education Association. "The Present Status of Sex Education in Canadian Schools." *C.E.A. Research and Information Division Report* no. 2 (September 1964), p. 22.

Canadian Health Education Specialists Society. *Annotated Guide to Health Instruction Materials in Canada.* Ottawa: Canadian Health Education Specialists Society, 1967. 105 pp.

Carrera, M. A. "High School Sex Education: Teaching the Teachers." *Educational Product Report* 3 (March 1970), pp. 15-24.

Carter, Luther J. "Population Control: U.S. Aid Program Leaps Forward." *Science* 159, no. 3815 (9 February 1968), pp. 611-614.

Catholic Marriage Advisory Council. *Sex Education for Your Boys.* London: Catholic Marriage Advisory Council, 1967. 43 pp.

————. *Sex Education for Boys Growing Up.* London: Catholic Marriage Advisory Council, 1968. 27 pp.

————. *Sex Education for Older Boys.* London: Catholic Marriage Advisory Council, c. 1968. 33 pp.

Catholic World. "Sex and Youth; Pastoral Directives of the German Episcopate." *Catholic World* 201 (July 1965), pp. 264-268.

Chanter, Albert G. "Teaching 10-year-olds about Sex." *Where?,* no. 23 (January 1966), pp. 10-11.

————. *Sex Education in the Primary School.* London: Macmillan & Co., 1966. 100 pp.

Chen, Pi-chao. "China's Birth Control Action Programme, 1956-1964." *Population Studies* 24, no. 2 (July 1970), pp. 141-158.

Chigier, E. "A Program of Sex Education in High Schools in Israel." *Journal of School Health* 36, no. 10 (December 1966), pp. 513-515.

Child Study Association of America. *Sex Education and the New Morality.* New York: Columbia University Press, 1967. 90 pp.

————. *What to Tell Your Children about Sex.* New York: Duell, Sloan & Pearce, 1964. 117 pp.

Christensen, Nancy B. and Schlaretzki, Eleanor C. "Incubation and Sex Education." *Science and Children* 6 (April 1969), pp. 9-10.

Clemans, Martyn. "Learning about Sex." *Trends in Education,* no. 5 (January 1967), pp. 9-15.

Cohodes, A. "Sex Education Measures Quality of Communities." *Nation's Schools* 84 (October 1969), p. 30.

Collier, James L. "Sex Education: Blunt Answers for Tough Questions." *Reader's Digest* 92 (June 1968), pp. 80-84.

Comfort, Alexander. *The Anxiety Makers.* London: Thomas Nelson & Sons, 1967. 208 pp.

Corner, George W. *Attaining Manhood; Attaining Womanhood; A Doctor Talks to Boys about Sex.* London: George Allen & Unwin, 1968. 85 pp.

Crawley, Lawrence, *et al. Reproduction, Sex and Preparation for Marriage.* Englewood Cliffs, N.J.: Prentice-Hall, 1964.

Crocker, O. L. "Family Life Education—Some New Findings." *Social Casework* 36 (March 1955), pp. 106-113.

Dalzell-Ward, A. J. "Education in Personal Relationships." *Health Education Journal* 23 (March 1965), pp. 21-27.

———. "New Perspectives in Sex Education." *Health Education Journal* 22 (March 1964), pp. 12-20.

Darden, Joseph S., Jr. "Progress Report of the Health Guidance in Sex Education Committee of the American School Health Association." *Journal of School Health* 38 (September 1968), pp. 462-463.

———. "The Report to the Governing Council of the Study Committee on Health Guidance in Sex Education." *Journal of School Health* 39 (March 1969), pp. 189-190.

Davidson, William. "Sex Education—Yes, Birth Control Education—No." *Michigan Education Journal* 46, no. 1 (September 1968), p. 17.

Davies, Edmund. *Tell Us Now! Open Answers to the Actual Questions of the Young, on Sex and Marriage.* London: Tandem Books, 1966. 155 pp.

Davis, Maxine. *Sex and the Adolescent.* New York: Permabooks, 1960. 239 pp.

Dawkins, Julia. *A Textbook of Sex Education.* Oxford: Basil Blackwell, 1967. 98 pp.

Day, Lincoln and Alice. *Too Many Americans.* Boston: Houghton Mifflin Co., 1964. 298 pp.

Delarge, B. *Girls Growing Up: Parents' Book, The Sexual Education of Preadolescent Girls.* London: Geoffrey Chapman, 1968. 39 pp.

Delarge, B. and Emin, D. *Girls Growing Up.* Translated (from *La vie et l'amour*) by U. Prideaux. London: Geoffrey Chapman, 1968. 88 pp.

De Schweinitz, Karl. *Growing Up.* New York: Macmillan Co., 1965. 54 pp.

Donaldson, J. L. "Innovative Programs in Sex Education." *Education Digest* 35 (April 1970), pp. 46-48.

Dorian, Patrick F. *Instructions for Boys Aged 12-16 Years.* Melbourne: Polding Press, 1968. 16 pp.

———. *The Years Between: A Guide for Catholic Boys.* Brisbane: Polding Press, 1966. 148 pp.

Dorr, R. "Current Attacks on Sex Education." *Illinois Education* 58 (November 1969), pp. 111-114.

Drake, Gordon V. *Blackboard Power; NEA Threat to America.* Tulsa, Okla.: Christian Crusade Publications, 1968. 256 pp.

———. *Is the Schoolhouse the Proper Place to Teach Raw Sex?* Tulsa, Okla.: Christian Crusade Publications, 1968. 39 pp.

———. *Sex Education in the Schools.* Tulsa, Okla.: Christian Crusade Publications, c. 1968. 34 pp.

Dresen-Coenders, H. M. *The Psychology of Sex Instruction: An Educational Study.* Translated by N. D. Smith. London: Sheed & Ward, 1963. 139 pp.

Drinkwater, F. H. *Birth Control and Natural Law.* London: Burns & Oates, 1965. 93 pp.

Dufoyer, Pierre. *Answer Your Child's Questions; A Series of Actual Conversations with Children and Adolescents on the Facts of Life, Conversational Instructions.* Allahabad, India: St. Paul Publications, 1966. N.p.

———. *Answer Your Child's Questions; A Series of Actual Conversations*

with Children and Adolescents on the Facts of Life, General Principles.
Allahabad, India: St. Paul Publications, 1966. 75 pp.

Duvall, Evelyn M. *About Sex and Growing Up.* New York: Association Press, 1968. 96 pp.

————. *Love and the Facts of Life.* New York: Association Press, 1963. 352 pp.

Duvall, Evelyn M. and Sylvanus M. *Sex Ways—In Fact and Faith.* New York: Association Press, 1961. 253 pp.

Duvall, Evelyn M. and Hill, Reuben. *When You Marry.* Boston: D. C. Heath, 1967. 338 pp.

Dykstra, John W. "Imperative: Education for Reproductive Responsibility." *Phi Delta Kappan* 49, no. 9 (May 1968), pp. 503-506.

Edelston, H. *Teenagers Talking.* London: Pitman Medical Publishing Co., 1963. 194 pp.

Elias, J. and Gebhard, P. "Sexuality and Sexual Learning in Childhood." *Phi Delta Kappan* 50, no. 7 (March 1969), pp. 401-405.

Ellis, Albert and Abarbanel, Albert. *The Encyclopedia of Sexual Behavior.* 2 vols. New York: Hawthorn Books, 1963.

Erskine, Hazel Gaudet. "The Polls: The Population Explosion, Birth Control, and Sex Education." *Public Opinion Quarterly* 30, no. 3 (Fall 1966), pp. 490-501.

Feber, Seymour F. and Wilson, Roger H. L., eds. *Teenage Marriage and Divorce.* Berkeley: Diablo Press, 1967. 154 pp.

————. *Sex Education and the Teenager.* Berkeley: Diablo Press, 1967. 151 pp.

Father and Son Movement of Australia. *Children No Longer: A Practical Guide on Understanding the Adolescent.* No. 10. Sydney: Father and Son Movement of Australia, March 1968. 39 pp.

————. *Guide through Boyhood: A Reliable Sex Education Booklet for Boys 8-11 Years.* No. 4. Sydney: Father and Son Movement of Australia, July 1967. 30 pp.

————. *Guide through Girlhood: A Reliable Sex Education Booklet for Girls, 8-11 Years.* No. 1. Sydney: Father and Son Movement of Australia, April 1968. 28 pp.

————. *Guide through Teen Years: A Reliable Sex Education Booklet for Girls 12-14 Years.* No. 2. Sydney: Father and Son Movement of Australia, March 1968. 28 pp.

————. *Guide to Womanhood: A Reliable Sex Education Booklet for Young Women.* No. 3. Sydney: Father and Son Movement of Australia, 1967.

————. *Guide to Youth: A Reliable Sex Education Booklet for Boys 12-14 Years.* No. 5. Sydney: Father and Son Movement of Australia, March 1968. 29 pp.

————. *Guide to Manhood: A Reliable Sex Education Booklet for Young Men 15 Years and Over.* No. 6. Sydney: Father and Son Movement of Australia, June 1968. 31 pp.

————. *Just Friends?: A Reliable and Practical Guide to Boy-Girl Relationships.* No. 7. Sydney: Father and Son Movement of Australia, October 1967. 42 pp.

————. *Tell Your Child the Truth: A Reliable Handbook for Parents on*

Sex Education of Children. No. 9. Sydney: Father and Son Movement of Australia, April 1968. 47 pp.

Fehrie, C. C. "Natural Birth of Sex Education." *Educational Leadership* 27 (March 1970), pp. 573-575.

Ferm, D. W. "Sweden, Sex and the College Student." *Religious Education* 64 (January 1969), pp. 53-60.

Ferrer, H. P. and Hancock, F. R. "Breaking Down the Barriers: An Experiment in Sex Education." *Health Education Journal* 24 (March 1966), pp. 22-27.

————. "Sex and the Parents; Help from Films and Tapes." *The Times Educational Supplement* (London), no. 2705 (24 March 1967), p. 1011.

Finch, Ian J. "Sex and General Studies." *Technical Education* 6 (January 1964), pp. 22-23.

Fishman, Katherine Davis. "Sex Becomes a Brand-New Problem." *New York Times Magazine*, 13 March 1966.

Flanagan, Geraldine Lux. *The First Nine Months of Life.* New York: Simon & Schuster, 1965. 95 pp.

Fletcher, The Rev. F. *Teenage Topics.* Melbourne: Australian Catholic Truth Society Publications, 1968. 27 pp.

————. *Teenage Topics II.* Melbourne: Australian Catholic Truth Society Publications, 1968. 31 pp.

————. *Teenage Topics III.* Melbourne: Australian Catholic Truth Society Publications, 1966. 30 pp.

————. Teenage Topics IV. Melbourne: Australian Catholic Truth Society Publications, 1968. 32 pp.

Force, Elizabeth S. *Teaching Family Life Education—The Toms River Program.* New York: Bureau of Publications, Teachers College, Columbia University, 1962. 38 pp.

Forman, I. "Sex and Family Living: Training Project at Boston University School of Education." *American Education* 5 (October 1969), pp. 11-13.

Fort, J. "How to Teach about Drugs and Sex." *CTA Journal* 65 (January 1969), pp. 22-24.

Frank, Lawrence K. *The Conduct of Sex.* New York: Grove Press, 1963. 160 pp.

Freedman, Mervin B. *The College Experience.* San Francisco: Jossey-Bass, 1967. 202 pp.

Friggens, Paul. "Shameful Neglect of Sex Education." *PTA Magazine* 61, no. 9 (May 1967), pp. 4-7.

Fulton, G. B. "Sex Education: Some Issues and Answers." *Journal of School Health* 40 (May 1970), pp. 263-268.

Furlong, William Barry. "It's a Long Way from the Birds and Bees." *New York Times Magazine*, 11 July 1967, p. 24ff.

Glover, Leland E. *How to Help Your Teen-ager Grow Up.* New York: Collier Books, 1962. 223 pp.

Goldston, Stephen. "Visits to the Kibbutzim." In *Children in Collectives: Child-rearing Aims and Practices in the Kibbutz,* edited by Peter B. Neubauer, pp. 30-32. Springfield: Charles C. Shomas, 1965.

Gordon, Sol. "Anti–Sex Education Crusaders: A New Threat to the Schools." *Changing Education* 4 (Fall 1969), pp. 26-27.

————. *Facts about Sex.* New York: John Day Co., 1970. 48 pp.

Gottlieb, Bernard S. *What a Boy Should Know about Sex.* Indianapolis: Bobbs-Merrill Co., 1960. 192 pp.

————. *What a Girl Should Know about Sex.* Indianapolis: Bobbs-Merrill Co., 1961. 190 pp.

Grams, Armin. *Sex Education: A Guide for Teachers and Parents.* Danville, Ill.: Interstate Printers and Publishers, 1970. 128 pp.

Greaves, Norman J. "Sex Education in Colleges and Departments of Education." *Health Education Journal* 23 (November 1965), pp. 171-177.

Gross, Leonard. "Sex Education Comes of Age." *Look* 30, no. 5 (March 1966), pp. 21-23.

Group for the Advancement of Psychiatry. *Sex and the College Student.* New York: Atheneum Publishers, 1966. 178 pp.

Guerinot, G. T. "Who Makes a Good Instructor in Sex Education?" *Catholic School Journal* 70 (May 1970), pp. 18-19.

Guerrero, Roderige. "Family Planning." *America: National Catholic Weekly Review* 112, no. 19, whole no. 2914 (8 May 1965), pp. 665-666.

Guttmacher, Alan F.; Best, Winfield; and Jaffe, Frederick S. *Planning Your Family: The Complete Guide to Birth Control, Overcoming Infertility, Sterilization with a Special Section on Abortion.* New York: Macmillan Co.; London: Collier-Macmillan, 1964. 329 pp.

Hacker, Andrew. "The Pill and Morality." *New York Times Magazine,* 21 November 1965, pp. 32, 138-140.

Hacker, Rose. *Telling the Teenagers: A Guide for Parents, Teachers, and Youth Leaders.* London: Andre Deutsch, 1966. 254 pp.

Hamburg, M. V. "Sex Education in the Elementary School; Teacher Preparation." *National Elementary Principal* 48 (November 1968), pp. 52-56.

Harris, Alan. *Questions about Sex.* London: Hutchinson Educational, 1968. 64 pp.

Havemann, Ernest (and the Editors of *Life*). *Birth Control.* The Netherlands: Time Inc. International Books, 1967. 118 pp.

Hendryson, E. "Case for Sex Education." *PTA Magazine* 63 (May 1969), pp. 20-21.

Herbst, Winfrid. *Kissing.* Melbourne: Australian Catholic Truth Society Publications, 1968. 32 pp.

Heron, Alastair, ed. *Towards a Quaker View of Sex.* London: Friends Home Service Committee, 1964. 84 pp.

Hettlinger, Richard F. *Living with Sex: The Student's Dilemma.* New York: Seabury Press, 1966. 185 pp.

Hey, Richard N. "What Is the Most Influential Single Factor? It's Sex!" *Minnesota Journal of Education* 47, no. 4 (December 1966), pp. 17-18.

Hill, Gregory Spencer. "Premarital Sex—Never!: A Teen-ager's Point of View." *Phi Delta Kappan* 50, no. 1 (September 1968), pp. 48-51.

Hilu, Virginia, ed. *Sex Education and the Schools.* New York and London: Harper & Row, 1967. 153 pp.

Hoeflin, Ruth M. *Essentials of Family Living.* New York: John Wiley & Sons, 1961. 282 pp.

Holmes, M.; Nicol, C.; and Stubbs, R. "Sex Attitudes of Young People." *Educational Research* 2, no. 1 (November 1968), pp. 38-42.

Hoyman, Howard S. "Impressions of Sex Education in Sweden." *Journal of School Health* 34, no. 5 (May 1964), pp. 209-218.

————. "Our Most Explosive Sex Education Issues: Birth Control." *Journal of School Health* 39 (September 1969), pp. 458-469.

————. "Should We Teach about Birth Control in High School Sex Education?" *Journal of School Health* 38 (November 1968), pp. 545-556. Reply by A. N. Meyerstein, *Journal of School Health* 39 (April 1969), pp. 252-253.

————. "Should We Teach Sexual Ethics in Our Schools?" *Journal of School Health* 40 (September 1970), pp. 339-346.

Hoyt, Robert G., ed. *The Birth Control Debate.* Kansas City, Mo.: National Catholic Reporter, 1968. 224 pp.

Hymes, James L., Jr. *How to Tell Your Child about Sex.* New York: Public Affairs Committee, 1962. 28 pp.

Ingleby, Alan H. B. *Learning to Love: A Wider View of Sex Education.* 3rd edition. London: Robert Hale, 1967. 142 pp.

Interfaith Commission on Marriage and Family Life. "Interfaith Statement on Sex Education." *Catholic School Journal* 68 (December 1968), pp. 43-45.

Irvine, J. J., Jr. "Sex Education for Church Youth." *International Journal of Religious Education* 44 (July 1968), pp. 10-11.

Iseman, Marjorie F. "Sex Education." *McCall's,* January 1968, pp. 37, 115-118.

Jacob, Beryl M. and Wild, David. "Sex Education—A Method." *Health Educational Journal,* November 1963, pp. 230-234.

Jennings, R. E. "Sex Education and Politics." *Educational Forum* 34 (March 1970), pp. 347-352.

Johnson, Warren R. *Human Sex and Sex Education: Perspectives and Problems.* Philadelphia: Lea & Febiger, 1963. 205 pp.

Joint Committee of the National School Boards Association and the American Association of School Administration. "Health Education and Sex/Family Life Education; Statement." *American School Board Journal* 155 (June 1968), pp. 14-15.

Juhasz, Anne M. "Background Factors, Extent of Sex Knowledge and Source of Information." *Journal of School Health* 39 (January 1969), pp. 32-39.

————. "Characteristics Essential to Teachers in Sex Education." *Journal of School Health* 40 (January 1970), pp. 17-19.

Kadri, Z. N. "The Student Health Service and Sex Education." *Malaysian Journal of Education* 4, no. 2 (December 1967), pp. 185-189.

K'ai, Ko and Lin, Cheng. "What's to Be Done If One Has Married Young?: A Reader's Letter and Editor's Answer." *Chung-kuo Ch'ing-nien Pao* [China Youth, Peking], 7 July 1962, and *Survey of China Mainland Press* (Hong Kong), no. 27855 (25 July 1962).

Kans, A. H. "Sex Education and the Health Visitor." *Health Education Journal* 23 (September 1965), pp. 152-156.

Kelly, P. "Sensitive Subject of Sex Needs Honest Handling." *The Times Educational Supplement* (London), no. 2798 (3 January 1969), p. 33.

Kielson, H. F. "Sex Education." In UNESCO, *Health Education, Sex Education and Education for Home and Family Life,* pp. 79-81. Hamburg: UNESCO Institute for Education, 1965.

Kilander, H. Frederick. *Sex Education in the Schools: A Study of Objec-*

tives, Content, Methods, Materials, and Evaluation. London: Macmillan & Co., 1970. 435 pp.

Kind, R. W. and Leedham, John. _Programmed Sex Education._ London: Longmans, Green & Co., 1968. 31 pp.

Kirkendall, Lester A. _A Reading and Study Guide for Students in Marriage and Family Relations._ Dubuque, Iowa: William C. Brown, 1965. 149 pp.

————. "Sex Education." _SIECUS Study Guides._ New York: SIECUS, October 1965. Pp. 1-21.

Kirkendall, Lester A. and Miles, G. T. "Sex Education Research." _Review of Educational Research_ 38 (December 1968), pp. 528-544.

Kirkendall, Lester A. and Levin, Max D. "Sex Education and the Physician: A Comment and a Reply." _Independent School Bulletin_ 28 (May 1969), pp. 7-9.

Kline, L. F. "Social Hygiene Program in a Residential School for Deaf Children." _Volta Review_ 70 (September 1968), pp. 509-512.

Kobler, John. "Sex Invades the Schoolhouse." _Saturday Evening Post,_ 29 June 1968, pp. 23-27; 64-66.

Kolb, Erwin T. _Parents' Guide to Christian Conversation about Sex._ St. Louis, Mo.: Concordia Publishing House, 1967. 127 pp.

Kolbanovskii, V. N. "The Sex Upbringing of the Rising Generation." _Soviet Education_ 6, no. 11 (September 1964), pp. 3-14. (See also _Soviet Review_ 5, no. 3 (Fall 1964), pp. 51-62.)

Korry, Edquard M. "Sex Education in Sweden: They Learn the Facts of Life at School." _Look_ 21, no. 18 (3 September 1957), pp. 34-41.

Krupp, George. "Airing Today's Pairing." _Saturday Review,_ 14 September 1968, pp. 38-39, 112.

Leach, G. V. "Sex Education in a Permissive Society." _Educational Product Report_ 3 (March 1970), pp. 2-4.

Lederer, Esther P. _Ann Landers Talks to Teenagers about Sex._ New York: Prentice-Hall, 1963. 131 pp.

Lee, I. K. and Stith, M. "Opinions about Sex Education Held by Low Income Negro Mothers." _Journal of Home Economics_ 61 (May 1969), pp. 359-362.

Lerrigo, Marion O. _Sex Education Series._ 5 vols. Chicago: American Medical Association; Washington, D.C.: National Education Association, 1961-62.

Lerrigo, Marion O. and Southard, Helen. _Approaching Adulthood._ Chicago: American Medical Association, 1966. 47 pp.

————. _A Story about You._ Chicago: American Medical Association, 1966. 43 pp.

————. _Facts Aren't Enough._ Chicago: American Medical Association, 1962. 70 pp.

————. _Finding Yourself._ Chicago: American Medical Association, 1968. 50 pp.

————. _Parents' Responsibility._ Chicago: American Medical Association, 1967. 47 pp.

Libby, R. W. "Washington State Board Limits Sex Education to the Plumbing." _Phi Delta Kappan_ 51, no. 7 (March 1970), p. 402.

Lin, Cheng. "Editor's Reply to a Reader's Letter, 'What's to Be Done If

One Has Married Young?' " by K'ai Ko, *Chung-kuo Ch'ing-nien Pao,* [China Youth, Peking], 7 July 1962.

Link, W. R. "Teacher's View of Sex Education." *Independent School Bulletin* 29 (December 1969), pp. 10-11. "Discussion," vol. 29 (May 1970), pp. 43-44.

Linnér, Birgitta. *Society and Sex in Sweden.* Stockholm: Swedish Institute for Cultural Relations with Foreign Countries, 1970. 53 pp. Revised edition 1971. 56 pp.

Linnér, Birgitta and Litell, Richard J. *Sex and Society in Sweden.* New York: Pantheon Books, 1967. 204 pp.

Little, Alan. "Sex Education and the Schools in the United Kingdom." In *Responsible Parenthood and Sex Education,* edited by Susan Burke, pp. 51-78. London: International Planned Parenthood Federation, 1970.

Liu, Alfred B. "Population Growth and Educational Development." *Annals of the American Academy of Political and Social Science* 369 (January 1967), pp. 109-120.

Logie, Ray. "Some Thoughts on S** Education." *Monday Morning* 4 (October 1969), p. 21.

Lord, Daniel A. *The Questions They Always Ask.* Melbourne: Australian Catholic Truth Society Publications, 1964. 32 pp.

Luckey, Eleanore B. "Sex Education: Develop an Attitude Before You Develop a Program." *American School Board Journal* 156, no. 10 (April 1969), pp. 20-23.

————. "Sex Education: Stop, Look, and Listen!" *Journal of Home Economics* 61 (January 1969), 31-34.

————. "Sex Education; Why?" *CTA Journal* 65 (January 1969), pp. 9-11.

Macandrew, Rennie. *Approaching Womanhood: Healthy Sex for Girls.* London: Wales Publishing Co., 1961. 92 pp.

Mace, David and Vera. *Marriage: East and West.* Garden City, N.Y.: Doubleday & Co., 1960. 359 pp.

Mah, E. J. "Sex Education Can Start in Kindergarten." *Instructor* 79 (October 1969), pp. 136-137.

Manley, Helen. *A Curriculum Guide in Sex Education.* St. Louis, Mo.: State Publishing Co., 1964. 59 pp.

————. "Sex Education Begins at Birth." *Texas Outlook* 52 (November 1968), pp. 20-21.

Masters, W. H. and Johnson, V. E. *"Playboy:* Interview with Masters and Johnson." *Playboy,* May 1968, pp. 199-202.

Maynard, Fredelle. "The Truth about Sex Myths You Probably Believe." *Ingenue,* September 1968, pp. 56-58; 85-86.

Michigan State Department of Education. *A Broadly Representative Bibliography of Materials on Sex Education.* Lansing, Mich.: Michigan State Department of Education, 1969. 20 pp.

Miller, Derek. "Sexual Development." *New Education* 3, no. 3 (March 1967), pp. 14-15.

Montagu, Ashley. "The Pill, the Sexual Revolution, and the Schools." *Phi Delta Kappan* 49, no. 9 (May 1968), pp. 480-484.

Moore, Donald D. "Sex Education for Blind High School Students." *Education of the Visually Handicapped* 1 (March 1969), pp. 22-25.

Moskin, Robert J. "After 10 Years of Compulsory Sex Education: Sweden's New Battle over Sex." *Look,* 15 November 1966, pp. 37-42.

Müller-Dietz, Waltraud. "Sex Education in the Soviet Union." *Review of Soviet Medical Sciences* 2 (2 November 1965), pp. 1-19.

McCreary, Ann P. "Sex Education in Swedish Schools." *Canadian Education and Research Digest* 4, no. 3 (September 1964), pp. 227-232.

————. "Sex Instruction for B. C. Schools." *The B. C. Teacher* (British Columbia) 43, no. 4 (1964), pp. 163-166.

McGinnis, Tom. *Your First Year of Marriage.* New York: Doubleday & Co., 1967. 202 pp.

McGuigan, Frank B. "Social Revolution and Sex Education." *Clearing House* 43, no. 7 (March 1969), pp. 421-424.

McIntire, W. G. "Attitudes of Connecticut Principals towards Family Life Education." *Journal of School Health* 39 (March 1969), pp. 183-185.

McLaughlin, J. "Education in Sex Education." *Catholic School Journal* 69 (October 1969), pp. 16-18.

Narayanan, P. A. Y. "A Program of Sex Education for Schools: Based on a Course of Sex Education Lectures at Brinkburn County Secondary Modern School, South Shields." *Health Education Journal* 22 (September 1964), pp. 135-140.

Nash, K. B. "Group Guidance and Counseling Programs: A Vehicle for the Introduction of Sex Education for Adolescents in the Public School." *Journal of School Health* 38 (November 1968), pp. 577-583.

National Board of Education in Sweden. *Handbook on Sex Instruction in the Schools.* Board of Education Series no. 28. Stockholm: The National Board of Education, 1956. Revised 1968. 90 pp.

National Marriage Guidance Council. *Sixteen: For All Young Adults.* London: National Marriage Guidance Council, n.d. 23 pp.

————. *Your Teenagers: Help with Parents' Problems.* London: National Marriage Guidance Council, n.d. 23 pp.

National School Public Relations Association. *Sex Education in Schools.* Education U.S.A. Special Report. Washington, D. C.: National School Public Relations Association, 1969. 48 pp.

Nation's Schools. "Opinion Poll: Parents Get Blame for Lack of Sex Education Programs." *Nation's Schools* 77, no. 5 (May 1966), p. 95.

Neff, N. "Sex Education in the Public Schools: An Opinion." *School and Community* 56 (May 1970), p. 20.

New Education. "Facts of Life." *New Education* 3, no. 5 (May 1967), pp. 7-9.

Newland, Mary Reed. *Sex Education in the Family.* Washington, D.C.: Confraternity of Christian Doctrine. Reprinted from *The Living Light* 2, no. 2 (Summer 1965). 16 pp.

New York Times. "Attitudes of Youths toward Sex Are Surveyed by East Germans." *New York Times* 116, no. 39845 (26 February 1967), p. 22:1.

————. "Guide Published on Sex Education: Schools and Parents Advised on Problem Questions." *New York Times,* 21 June 1966, p. 44:1.

————. "Poles Weigh Sex Education." *New York Times* 117, no. 40106 (14 November 1967), p. 5:6.

————. "Sex Advice Given by Czech Panel." *New York Times* 116, no. 39808 (20 January 1967), p. 19:1.

————. "Sex Education Is New." *New York Times* 117, no. 40079 (18 October 1967), p. 26:1.

————. "Students Want Birth Control." *New York Times* 116, no. 40087 (26 October 1967), p. 40:7.

————. "V. D. Rises at British Colleges." *New York Times* 116, no. 39871 (24 March 1967), p. 15:5.

Noebel, David A. *The Beatles: A Study in Drugs, Sex and Revolution.* Tulsa, Okla.: Christian Crusade Publications, 1969. 64 pp.

Nossal, Frederick. "China's Second Experiment." *The Nation* 196, no. 23 (15 June 1963), pp. 503-505.

Oberteuffer, D. "Some Things We Need and Some Things We Do Not Need in Sex Education: 1970." *Journal of School Health* 40 (February 1970), pp. 54-65.

O'Brien, John. *Falling in Love.* Melbourne: Australian Catholic Truth Society, 1963. 23 pp.

Odenwald, Robert P. *How You Were Born.* London: Robert Hale, 1968. 62 pp.

Ogletree, E. "Sex Education for the Masses; By-passing Parents." *The Times Educational Supplement* (London) 2823 (27 June 1969), p. 2100.

Patrick, E. "A Survey of Knowledge of Human Reproduction among University Students." *Malaysian Journal of Education* 4, no. 2 (December 1967), pp. 176-184.

Phillips, L. R. "The Divinity Tutor and Sex Education." *Education for Teaching* 58 (May 1962), pp. 35-37.

Pickering, Aidan. *Sex Education for Your Boys.* London: Catholic Marriage Advisory Council, 1967. 44 pp.

————. *Sex Instruction in the Home.* London: Catholic Truth Society, 1965. 24 pp.

Pitkin, Walter, Jr. "Too Many People: Can Educators Find an Answer?" *Phi Delta Kappan* 49, no. 9 (May 1968), pp. 473-479.

Playboy. "Playboy: Interview with Masters and Johnson." *Playboy,* May 1968, pp. 199-202.

————. "Sex as a Communist Plot," and "Sex as a Capitalist Plot," (2 parts) *Playboy* 16, no. 7 (July 1969), pp. 44-45.

Pohlman, Edward. "Premarital Contraception and the School." *Phi Delta Kappan* 49, no. 9 (May 1968), pp. 495-500.

Pope Paul VI. *On the Regulation of Birth: Encyclical Letter of His Holiness Pope Paul VI.* London: Catholic Truth Society, July 1968. 36 pp.

Porter, D. Lynton. "Facing Up to Questioning." *Health Education Journal* 26 (March 1967), pp. 15-18.

Potter, J. and Libbey, R. W. "Who Should Plan Your District's Sex Education Program?" *American School Board Journal* 157 (December 1969), pp. 19-22.

Powers, G. Pat and Baskin, Wade. *Sex Education: Issues and Directives.* New York: Philosophical Library, 1969. 532 pp.

Rafferty, Max. "The Dropout Parents: How America Got on a Sex Binge." *Los Angeles Times,* 15 April 1969.

————., *et al.* "Is It Desirable for Sex Education to Be Included as Part of the Curriculum in History and Social Studies in Our Public Schools?" *Social Education* 34 (May 1970), pp. 540-541.

Rarick, G. Laurence and Stoedefalke, Karl G. "Health and Safety Education." *Review of Educational Research* 26 (December 1956), pp. 542-558.

Rarick, John R. "Sex Education Fad." *Congressional Record* 114, no. 110 (26 June 1968), pp. E5850-5852.

Rathmines, Tranquilla. "Sex and the Single Student: How Not to Be a Mummy." *Farrago*. Victoria: Melbourne University, 7 March 1966, pp. 4-5.

Rayner, Claire. *A Parent's Guide to Sex Education*. London: Transworld Publishers (Mini-Books ed.), 1968. 123 pp.

———. "Sex Education in Youth Clubs." *New Society*, no. 210 (6 October 1966), pp. 535-536.

Reed, Angela, ed. *Help with Sex Problems in Marriage*. London: National Marriage Guidance Council, 1968. 48 pp.

Reiss, Ira L. *Premarital Sexual Standards in America*. New York: Free Press, 1960. 286 pp.

———. "Sex Education in the Public Schools: Problem or Solution?" *Phi Delta Kappan* 50, no. 1 (September 1968), pp. 52-56.

———. *The Social Context of Premarital Permissiveness*. New York: Holt, Rinehart & Winston, 1967. 256 pp.

———. "The Treatment of Pre-marital Coitus in 'Marriage and the Family' Tests." *Social Problems* 4 (April 1957), pp. 334-338.

RFSU. The Swedish Association for Sex Education. *What the Swedes Teach about Sex*. New York: Grosset & Dunlap, 1970. 79 pp.

Rice, A. H. "Parents Are Entitled to Some Answers about Sex Education." *Nation's Schools* 84 (November 1969), p. 18.

Richards, Barbara. *A Parent Looks at Public School Sex Education*. 10th ed. Santa Anna, Calif.: n.p. (Distributed by Tom Anderson Bookstore, Nashville, May 1969). 40 pp.

Riecken, Klaus. "Sex Education in East Germany." *Review of Soviet Medical Sciences* 2 (2 November 1965), pp. 1-19.

Robinson, J. F. *Family Planning*. 2d ed. Edinburgh and London: E. & S. Livingstone, 1967. 72 pp.

Rosser, D. "Are You Ready to Defend Sex Education?" *School Management* 13 (October 1969), pp. 82-84.

Rowe, Philip. "Birth Control in Britain." *Twentieth Century* 172, no. 1020 (Winter 1963-64), pp. 33-36.

Rubin, Isadore. "Transition in Sex Values—Implications for the Education of Adolescents." *Journal of Marriage and the Family* 26 (May 1965), pp. 185-189.

Rubin, Isadore and Kirkendall, Lester A., eds. *Sex in the Adolescent Years: New Directions in Guiding and Teaching Youth*. London: Fontana Books, 1969. 215 pp.

Ryan, Mary Perkins and John Julian. *Love and Sexuality: A Christian Approach*. Dublin and Sydney: Gill & Son, 1968. 196 pp.

Sacks, S. R. "Pastoral Educators Prepare to Lead Youth: The New Sexuality." *American Journal of Orthopsychiatry* 40 (April 1970), pp. 493-502.

Sagarin, Edward, ed. *Sex and the Contemporary American Scene.* Philadelphia: American Academy of Political and Social Science, 1968. 232 pp.

St. Mary's Training College. *Sex, Marriage and the Family: A Weekend Course for Teachers.* Belfast: St. Mary's Training College, Newry; reprinted by P. Bennett, 1964. 88 pp.

Sakol, Jeanne. *What about Teenage Marriage?* New York: Avon Books, 1961. 190 pp.

Sands, Sidney L. *Growing Up to Love, Sex and Marriage.* Boston: Christopher Publishing House, 1960. 131 pp.

Saxton, Lloyd. *The Individual, Marriage, and the Family.* Belmont, Calif.: Wadsworth Publishing Co., 1968. 515 pp.

Schofield, Michael. *The Sexual Behaviour of Young People.* London: Longmans, Green & Co., 1965. 316 pp.

Schulz, Esther D. *Family Life and Sex Education: Curriculum and Instruction.* New York: Harcourt, Brace & World, 1969. 281 pp.

Scriven, Michael. "Putting the Sex Back into Sex Education." *Phi Delta Kappan* 49, no. 9 (May 1968), pp. 485-489.

Seale, Patrick and Beeson, Irene. "Babies along the Nile." *New Republic* 154, no. 19, issue 2685 (7 May 1966), pp. 10-11.

Shah, Khalida. "Attitudes of Pakistani Students toward Family Life." *Marriage and Family Living* 22, no. 2 (May 1960), pp. 156-161.

Shields, G. "Sex Education: Old Challenge, New Approach." *International Journal of Religious Education* 44 (November 1968), pp. 8-9.

Shuster, George N. *The Problem of Population: Practical Catholic Applications,* vol. 2. South Bend, Ind.: University of Notre Dame Press, 1964. 185 pp.

Simon, William and Gagnon, John H. "The Pedagogy of Sex." *Saturday Review* 50, 18 November 1967, pp. 74-76; 91-92.

Singer-Magdoff, Laura and Baskin, Judith. "Audiovisual Sex Education Materials." *Top News* 26 (November 1969), pp. 43-49.

Sommerville, Rose. "The Relationship between Family Life Education and Sex Education Introduction." *Journal of Marriage and the Family* 29, no. 2 (May 1967), pp. 374-377.

Stafford, Peter. *Sexual Behavior in the Communist World: An Eyewitness Report of Life, Love and the Human Condition behind the Iron Curtain.* New York: Julian Press, 1967. 287 pp.

Stanford Observer. "Colleges and Contraceptives: The Physicians' Dilemma." *Stanford Observer,* January 1967.

Steinmetz, U. G. "Total Approach to Sex Education." *Spectrum* 45 (September 1969), pp. 8-9.

Stephens, William N. *The Family in Cross-cultural Perspective.* New York: Holt, Rinehart & Winston, 1963. 460 pp.

Stewart, Gloria. "Sex Revolution." *New Statesman* 70, no. 1800 (10 September 1965), p. 348.

Strain, Frances B. and Eggart, C. L. "Framework for Family Life Education: A Survey of Present Day Activities in Sex Education." *Bulletin of National Association of Secondary School Principals* 39 (December 1955), pp. 3-117.

Suydam, G. "Sex Education in Kindergarten." *Instructor* 78 (February 1969), p. 43.

Szasz, G. "Sex Education and the Teacher." *Journal of School Health* 40 (March 1970), pp. 150-155.

Thompson, A. Gray and DeRoche, Edward P. "Sex Education: Parent Involvement in Decision Making." *Phi Delta Kappan* 49, no. 9 (May 1968), pp. 501-503..

Thomson, William A. R., ed. *Sex and Its Problems.* London: E & S Livingstone, 1968. 90 pp.

Thornburg, Hershel D. "Administering a Sex Education Program." *Arizona Teacher* 57 (November 1968), pp. 18-19.

———. "Age and First Sources of Sex Information as Reported by 88 College Women." *Journal of School Health* 40 (March 1970), pp. 156-158.

———. "Evaluating the Sex Education Program." *Arizona Teacher* 57 (January 1969), pp. 18-20.

———. "Sex Education: A Teaching Approach." *Arizona Teacher* 56 (May 1968), pp. 12-13.

———. "Sex Education: The Student." Part 1 in series "Sex Education." *Arizona Teacher* 57, no. 1 (September 1968), p. 11.

———. "Sex Education: The Student." Part 2 in series "Sex Education." *Arizona Teacher* 57, no. 1 (September 1968), pp. 11, 27-28.

The Times Educational Supplement (London). "Fallen Women; Sex in a Mixed School." *The Times Educational Supplement,* no. 2589 (1 January 1965), p. 6.

——— "Little Left Unsaid on Sex; Brains Trust in Action." *The Times Educational Supplement,* no. 2797 (27 December 1968), p. 1403.

———. "Most in Favour of Showing Sex Film to Children." *The Times Educational Supplement,* no. 2861 (20 March 1970), p. 11.

———. "Sex and the Single Teacher." *The Times Educational Supplement,* no. 2698 (3 February 1967), p. 378.

———. "Sex Textbook for Youth." *The Times Educational Supplement,* no. 2649 (25 February 1966), p. 549.

———. "Sex When Young." *The Times Educational Supplement,* no. 2654 (1 April 1966).

———. "Storm over Sex Study." *The Times Educational Supplement,* no. 2653 (25 March 1966), p. 909.

Today's Education. "Teen-agers Speak Out about Sex: A Symposium of High School Students and a Reaction by Elizabeth Koontz." *Today's Education* 58 (March 1969), pp. 23-26.

Toohey, J. V. "Sex Education, Water Fluoridation, and Dr. Sigmund Freud." *Journal of School Health* 39, no. 1 (January 1969), pp. 70-73.

UNESCO Institute for Education. *Health Education, Sex Education and Education for Home and Family Life.* Report of a meeting, International Studies in Education, February 17-22, 1964. Hamburg: UNESCO Institute for Education, 1965. 118 pp.

Von Gagern, Frederick. *Difficulties in Sex Education.* Edited and translated by Meyrick Booth. Cork, Ireland: Mercier Press, August 1953. 48 pp.

Wahl, Raymond. *Everybody's Going Steady.* Melbourne: Australian Catholic Truth Society, 1963.

Watson, Frank D. "What Some College Men Wanted to Know about Marriage and the Family." *Social Forces* 11, no. 2 (December 1962), pp. 235-236.

Weinstock, H. R. "Issues in Sex Education." *Educational Forum* 34 (January 1970), pp. 189-196.

Werth, Alexander. "Love among the Russians." *New Statesman* 61, no. 1556 (6 January 1961), pp. 10, 12.

Wessler, Martin F. *Christian View of Sex Education.* St. Louis, Mo.: Concordia Publishing House, 1968. 87 pp.

Westlake, H. G. "Sex Education Controversy." *Illinois Education* 58 (November 1969), pp. 117-119.

Whiteley, Charles H. and Winifred M. *Sex and Morals.* New York: Basic Books, 1967. 135 pp.

Whiting, C. "Sex Education Is Becoming Out-of-Date." *The Times Educational Supplement* (London), vol. 2854 (30 January 1970), p. 19.

Willgoose, C. E. "Sex and Family Living Education." *Instructor* 79 (February 1970), pp. 96-97.

Winefride, Sister Mary. *Instructions for Girls Aged 12-16 Years.* Queensland: Polding Press, 1966. 14 pp.

————. *The Sex Instruction of Children (3-12 years): A Guide for Parents.* Queensland: Polding Press, 1967. 23 pp.

————. *Youth Looks Ahead: A Guide for Catholic Girls.* Brisbane: Polding Press, 1967. 144 pp.

Witt, Elmer N. *Life Can Be Sexual.* St. Louis, Mo.: Concordia Publishing House, 1967. 110 pp.

Wolfram, B. R. "Health Education: Evolution or Revolution?" *Volta Review* 70 (September 1968), pp. 500-507.

Woolston, L. S. "Needed: Better Strategy in Planning for Sex Education in the Schools." *New York State Education* 57 (October 1969), pp. 40-41.

Yang, Hsiu. "For Late Marriage: Advice for Students." *Chung-kuo Ch'ing-nien Pao* [China Youth, Peking], no. 11 (1 June 1962); and *Selections from China Mainland Magazine*, no. 322 (16 July 1962).

Yeh, Kung-shao. "My Views on the Problem of Young People's Marriage, Love and Children." *Chung-kuo Ch'ing-nien Pao* [China Youth, Peking], 21 July 1962, and *Survey of China Mainland Press*, 9 August 1962.

————. "For Students and Youths: What Is the Most Suitable Age for Marriage?" *Chung-kuo Ch'ing-nien Pao* [China Youth, Peking], 12 April 1962.

Young Women's Christian Association. National Board. *Sex Morality Teaching Kit.* New York: National Board, Young Women's Christian Association, 1965.

Young, R. C. "Reactions to a Fifth-Grade Program in Sex Education." *Journal of School Health* 40 (January 1970), pp. 32-34.

Zazzaro, Joanne. "Critics or No Critics, Most Americans Still Firmly Support Sex Education in Schools." *American School Board Journal* 157 (September 1969), pp. 30-32.

————. "War on Sex Education." *American School Board Journal* 157 (August 1969), pp. 7-11; (September 1969), pp. 30-32.

Zetterberg, H. L. "Study of Sex Education Programs." *School and Society* 97 (Summer 1969), p. 271.

Zverev, I. D. "On the Problem of the Sex Education of School Children in Connection with the Study of Human Physiology." *Soviet Education* 10 (June 1968), pp. 47-52.

ACKNOWLEDGMENTS

The editor wishes to acknowledge the courtesy of a number of writers and publishers whose material has been included in this anthology. The *Phi Delta Kappan,* through the interest and encouragement of its Editor, Stanley Elam, has provided a series of articles for specific inclusion in this anthology. Among these are the studies of Michael Scriven, James Elias and Paul Gebhard, A. Gray Thompson and Edward P. DeRoche, Edward Pohlman, Ashley Montagu, Gregory Spencer Hill, and Ira Reiss, which have appeared in various issues of the *Kappan.*

The following publications were of particular assistance, and material which originally appeared in their pages is gratefully acknowledged: the *Saturday Review* for William Simon and John H. Gagnon's "The Pedagogy of Sex"; the *New York Times Magazine* for William Barry Furlong's "It's a Long Way from the Birds and Bees"; the *Saturday Evening Post* for John Kobler's "Sex Invades the Schoolhouse"; *McCall's* magazine for Marjorie F. Iseman's "Sex Education"; *Playboy* magazine for W. H. Masters and V. E. Johnson's *"Playboy* Interview with Masters and Johnson"; Christian Crusade Publications for Gordon V. Drake's *Is the Schoolhouse the Proper Place to Teach Raw Sex?;* the *Los Angeles Times* for Max Rafferty's "Dropout Parents: How America Got on a Sex Binge"; *Farrago* (Melbourne University) for Tranquilla Rathmines' "Sex and the Single Student: How Not to Be a Mummy"; the *Malaysian Journal of Education* for Z. N. Kadri's "The Student Health Service and Sex Education"; *Soviet Education* for V. N. Kolbanovskii's "The Sex Upbringing of the Rising Generation"; the *Chung-kuo Ch'ing-nien Pao* [China Youth, Peking] for the articles of K'ai Ko and Cheng Lin, Yeh Kung-shao, and Yang Hsiu on, respectively, "What's to Be Done If One Has Married Young?" "My Views on the Problem of Young People's Marriage, Love and Children," "For Students and Youths: What Is the Most Suitable Age for Marriage?" and "For Late Marriage: Advice for Students"; *Population Studies* for Pi-chao Chen's "China's Birth Control Action Programme, 1956-64"; the Swedish National Board of Education for *Handbook on Sex Instruction in the Schools; Educational Research* for M. Holmes, C. Nicol, and R. Stubbs' "Sex Attitudes of Young People"; the Catholic Truth Society (London) for Aidan Pickering's *Sex Instruction in the Home,* and for Pope Paul VI, *On the Regulation of Birth;* the UNESCO Institute for Education for *Health Education, Sex Education and Education for Home and Family Life;* the Swedish Institute for Cultural Relations with Foreign Countries for Birgitta Linnér's *Society and Sex in Sweden;* and the International Planned Parenthood Federation for Alan Little's "Sex Education and the Schools in the United Kingdom."

In particular, the editor wishes to acknowledge the inclusion of two lighthearted pieces by Art Buchwald, the distinguished humorist. He was finally stimulated to enter the ranks of the sex educationists when he attended, as guest speaker, an annual meeting of the Tennessee Education Association, arriving as he did in the midst of a highly controversial "sex education in the schools" debate, bitterly contested by diverse local and national factions whose political and intellectual prowess was evidently taxed to the fullest extent.

The editor especially wishes to acknowledge the generous assistance in time and talent of many of his colleagues and students at Peabody College, who so enthusiastically aided in the project to the extent that their motives were continually suspect. In particular, Robert M. Bjork should be eulogized for his temperate and unequivocal contribution to the final assembling of the anthology, for without his assistance the manuscript might have been completed much sooner than was originally anticipated.

Members of the Peabody International Center, especially Gayla Tinnell, Marie Williams, Allan Peterson, Kuang Liang Hsu, and Dorothy Reeves, deserve special acknowledgment for their assistance in a variety of important tasks so necessary to assembling and producing the anthology.

INDEX